Verse by Verse Commentary on

JEREMIAH and LAMENTATIONS

Enduring Word Commentary Series
By David Guzik

The grass withers, the flower fades,
but the word of our God stands forever.
Isaiah 40:8

Commentary on Jeremiah and Lamentations

Copyright ©2021 by David Guzik

Printed in the United States of America or in the United Kingdom

Print Edition ISBN: 978-1-939466-63-1

Enduring Word

5662 Calle Real #184

Goleta, CA 93117

Electronic Mail: ewm@enduringword.com

Internet Home Page: www.enduringword.com

All rights reserved. No portion of this book may be reproduced in any form (except for quotations in reviews) without the written permission of the publisher.

Scripture references, unless noted, are from the New King James Version of the Bible, copyright ©1979, 1980, 1982, Thomas Nelson, Inc., Publisher.

Contents

Jeremiah 1 – The Call of a Reluctant Prophet 7
Jeremiah 2 – Broken Cisterns 16
Jeremiah 3 – A Word to Backsliders 29
Jeremiah 4 – The Terror of Coming Judgment 41
Jeremiah 5 – Searching for a Righteous Man 53
Jeremiah 6 – Full of the Fury of the LORD 63
Jeremiah 7 – Preaching at the Temple Gate 74
Jeremiah 8 – No Cure for Senseless Rejection of God 86
Jeremiah 9 – What to Take Glory In 94
Jeremiah 10 – Yahweh and the Idols of the Nations 103
Jeremiah 11 – A Broken Covenant and a Conspiracy 111
Jeremiah 12 – Running with Footmen and Horses 118
Jeremiah 13 – Two Warning Signs 125
Jeremiah 14 – Judgment Upon False Prophets 135
Jeremiah 15 – The Painful Prayer of the Prophet 143
Jeremiah 16 – Living Signs of Coming Judgment 153
Jeremiah 17 – The Folly of Misplaced Trust 160
Jeremiah 18 – Lessons at the Potter's House 171
Jeremiah 19 – Tophet 178
Jeremiah 20 – Jeremiah in the Stocks 184
Jeremiah 21 – Speaking to King Zedekiah 191
Jeremiah 22 – Speaking to the House of David 197
Jeremiah 23 – The Branch of Righteousness & Unrighteous Prophets 206
Jeremiah 24 – Lessons from Two Baskets of Figs 221
Jeremiah 25 – The Cup of Fury in God's Hand 225
Jeremiah 26 – Jeremiah Spared from Death 236
Jeremiah 27 – Bonds and Yokes 245
Jeremiah 28 – Broken Yokes and Iron Yokes 252
Jeremiah 29 – Letter to the Captives 259

Jeremiah 30 – Saved Out of the Time of Jacob's Trouble 267
Jeremiah 31 – The Glory of the New Covenant 276
Jeremiah 32 – The Property Purchase from Prison 291
Jeremiah 33 – Promises from the Prison 302
Jeremiah 34 – The Emancipation Revocation 311
Jeremiah 35 – The Lesson of the Rechabites 320
Jeremiah 36 – Cutting and Burning God's Word 326
Jeremiah 37 – The King Asks for Prayer & for A Secret Word 338
Jeremiah 38 – The Prophet in the Pit 345
Jeremiah 39 – The Fall of Jerusalem 356
Jeremiah 40 – Jeremiah Among the Remnant in the Land 363
Jeremiah 41 – The Murder of Gedaliah, Governor of the Land 370
Jeremiah 42 – An Insincere Request for Guidance 377
Jeremiah 43 – Jeremiah in Egypt 384
Jeremiah 44 – A Word to God's People in Egypt, Delivered & Rejected 389
Jeremiah 45 – Great Things and Not Seeking Them 400
Jeremiah 46 – A Word of Judgment Against Egypt 405
Jeremiah 47 – A Word of Judgment Against the Philistines 414
Jeremiah 48 – A Word of Judgment Against Moab 418
Jeremiah 49 – Words of Judgment Against the Nations 430
Jeremiah 50 – A Word of Judgment Against Babylon 443
Jeremiah 51 – A Word of Judgment Against Babylon (Continued) 457
Jeremiah 52 – The Fall of Jerusalem and the Captivity of Judah 473

Lamentations 1 - Mourning Over the Fallen City 483
Lamentations 2 – Purpose Proposed, Purpose Fulfilled 493
Lamentations 3 – "Great Is Your Faithfulness" 502
Lamentations 4 – The Woe of the Daughter of Zion 517
Lamentations 5 – From Desolation, Hope for Restoration 525
Bibliography 531

Author's Remarks - 533

Jeremiah 1 – The Call of a Reluctant Prophet

Among all the prophets of the Hebrew people none was more heroic than Jeremiah – G. Campbell Morgan.

A. The life and times of the Prophet Jeremiah.

1. (1) Jeremiah and his background.

The words of Jeremiah the son of Hilkiah, of the priests who *were* in Anathoth in the land of Benjamin,

> a. **The words of Jeremiah**: This begins a remarkable collection of writings revealed through the Prophet Jeremiah. His 40-year ministry was a tremendous display of faithfulness and courage in the face of great discouragement, opposition, and small results.
>
>> i. **Jeremiah**: "The precise meaning of the name is unknown, with suggested interpretations including 'the Lord founds.' 'the Lord exalts' and 'the Lord throws down.'" (Harrison)
>>
>> ii. "The name *Jeremiah* was common in Judah. It occurs several times in the OT. At the time of David there were two, and possibly three Jeremiahs among David's mighty men (1 Chronicles 12:4, 10, 13)." (Thompson)
>
> b. **Who were in Anathoth**: Since Jeremiah was from a priestly family, it made sense that they lived **in Anathoth**, which was a small village about three miles from Jerusalem. It was **in the land of Benjamin** but given over as a priestly city (Joshua 21:18).
>
>> i. "From vantage points in Anathoth one could clearly see the walls of Jerusalem. Jeremiah grew up not *in* the great capital but within sight of it." (Thompson)

2. (2-3) The times of Jeremiah.

To whom the word of the LORD came in the days of Josiah the son of Amon, king of Judah, in the thirteenth year of his reign. It came also in the days of Jehoiakim the son of Josiah, king of Judah, until the end of the eleventh year of Zedekiah the son of Josiah, king of Judah, until the carrying away of Jerusalem captive in the fifth month.

a. **To whom the word of the LORD came**: Though this book contains the *words of Jeremiah*, it also contains **the word of the LORD**. This prophecy, like all inspired Scripture, is both the word of man and the word of God. It is the divinely inspired and infallible word of God but brought through the personality of man.

i. When God uses a person, He does not erase their personality – He wants to *use* that person's sanctified personality. "God wanted a man with a very gentle and tender heart for this unrewarding ministry of condemnation. Jeremiah's subsequent career shows that he had this quality in full measure." (Cundall)

b. **In the days of Josiah**: King Josiah was one of the better kings of Judah, zealous for reform. According to 2 Chronicles 34:3, it was in the eighth year of Josiah's reign that he sought the LORD, and a few years later began an aggressive campaign to purify Israel of idolatry and to return to the LORD.

i. God called these two giants – both Josiah and Jeremiah – to serve Him and His people at the same time. Each supported the other, and though they did not leave behind an enduring transformed Judah, they served God faithfully and removed every excuse Judah might offer for the judgment that eventually came through Babylon.

c. **Josiah…Jehoiakim…Zedekiah**: In this line of succession of the Kings of Judah, some are left out (Jehoahaz in 2 Chronicles 36:1-2 and Jehoiachin in 2 Chronicles 36:8-9).

i. "Jehoahaz and Jehoiachin were probably omitted in this verse because their reigns were so short, comprising only three months each." (Harrison)

d. **Until the carrying away of Jerusalem captive in the fifth month**: In fact, portions of this book address the period after the captivity (Jeremiah 44). Yet that was only as a postscript to the catastrophic fall of Jerusalem.

B. The call and preparation of the Prophet Jeremiah.

1. (4-5) God's call to Jeremiah.

Then the word of the LORD came to me, saying:
"Before I formed you in the womb I knew you;

**Before you were born I sanctified you;
I ordained you a prophet to the nations."**

> a. **Then the word of the LORD came to me**: Jeremiah had a personal encounter with the LORD. He was apparently raised in a godly, priestly home – yet he had to have a *personal* encounter with God and His word.
>
>> i. Because many of his prophecies have echoes and hints of previous prophets of Israel, it seems that Jeremiah grew up knowing God's word. "His future life and thought were moulded to a large extent by an early acquaintance with the utterances of the eight-century BC prophets such as Amos, Hosea, Isaiah and Micah, and probably also by the lives and sayings of Elijah and Elisha." (Harrison)
>
> b. **Before I formed you in the womb I knew you...I ordained you a prophet to the nations**: Jeremiah was already a young man, but God wanted him to know that his call went back even further than his youth. Jeremiah existed in the mind and plan of God before he ever existed in his mother's womb. God told Jeremiah this so that he could walk in God's pre-ordained plan by his own will.
>
>> i. This information wasn't given just to interest Jeremiah or to entertain him. It was given so that he would know God's will, be encouraged by that, and therefore align his will with God's revealed will.
>>
>> ii. "St. Paul speaks of his own call to preach the Gospel to the Gentiles in similar terms (Galatians 1:15-16)." (Clarke)
>>
>> iii. Ancient Jewish legends say that Jeremiah was so called that he was born circumcised and that he came out of the womb prophesying. In fact, as the legend goes, in his out-of-the-womb prophecy he complained of the faithlessness of his mother. When she protested, he had to explain that he meant "mother" as a symbol for Jerusalem.
>
> c. **A prophet to the nations**: Jeremiah's focus was upon Judah in the last decades before the Babylonians conquered it. Yet his work as **a prophet** was not only for Judah, but also for **the nations** – and for us today.
>
>> i. "In this respect Jeremiah was appointed a prophet for a world-wide ministry. This refutes the idea that the work of God's servants was always provincial. God is the Lord of the nations." (Feinberg)

2. (6-10) Jeremiah's objection and God's response to the objection.

**Then said I:
"Ah, Lord GOD!
Behold, I cannot speak, for I *am* a youth."
But the LORD said to me:**

"Do not say, 'I *am* a youth,'
For you shall go to all to whom I send you,
And whatever I command you, you shall speak.
Do not be afraid of their faces,
For I *am* with you to deliver you," says the LORD.

Then the LORD put forth His hand and touched my mouth, and the LORD said to me:
"Behold, I have put My words in your mouth.
See, I have this day set you over the nations and over the kingdoms,
To root out and to pull down,
To destroy and to throw down,
To build and to plant."

> a. **Ah, Lord GOD!** This translates an expression of deep feeling, though the sense is hard to relate in English.
>
> b. **Behold, I cannot speak, for I am a youth**: Jeremiah was probably anywhere from 17 to 20 years old at this time. Apparently, he felt that his **youth** prevented him from being a good or authoritative messenger of God's word.
>
>> i. "Unlike Moses, whose protestations of inadequacy rang a little hollow, Jeremiah really was young, it seems, and inexperienced." (Kidner)
>
> c. **Do not say, "I am a youth"**: Though Jeremiah's protest was *true*, it was *irrelevant* – and God did not want to hear it, nor did He want Jeremiah to say it. God insists on His right to call young people and to use them if they will listen to His call and answer it.
>
>> i. **Do not say, "I am a youth"** – because God used David when he was a young man. As a young man David served his father faithfully in the shepherd's field, killed a lion and a bear protecting the flock, killed Goliath, served King Saul and was a commander in the Israeli army.
>>
>> ii. **Do not say, "I am a youth"** – because God filled John the Baptist with the Holy Spirit *in the womb* (Luke 1:15). You aren't too young to be filled mightily with the Spirit of God.
>>
>> iii. **Do not say, "I am a youth"** – because God used Timothy as a young man, and through the Apostle Paul told him, *Let no one despise your youth, but be an example to the believers in word, in conduct, in love, in spirit, in faith, in purity.* (1 Timothy 4:12)
>>
>> iv. **Do not say, "I am a youth"** – because God used Hudson Taylor as a young man. When he was 17 years old he dared to seek God, and totally surrendered himself to God's will. Almost immediately he felt a

distinct impression that God wanted him to be a missionary to China, and he began to prepare for the mission field by living the kind of life by faith he wanted to live on the mission field and living it right there in England. By the time he was 22, he first arrived in Shanghai.

v. **Do not say, "I am a youth"** – because God used J. Edwin Orr as a young man. Born and raised in Belfast Ireland, at 21 years of age he left a good paying job in the middle of the Great Depression to tour around Great Britain on his bicycle and tell any who would listen about revival. He trusted God to provide for both him and his widowed mother, and God came through gloriously – it was 10,000 miles of miracle through Great Britain. He wrote a popular book about his adventures in faith – so popular that some youth groups banned the book – they were afraid that their youth might take off on their own bikes without really being called by God.

d. **For you shall go to all to whom I send you, and whatever I command you, you shall speak**: God spoke with both encouragement and persuasion to Jeremiah. He protested that he couldn't go because of his youth but God simply said, "**you shall go**."

i. Later, Jeremiah remembered his initial reluctance: *Nor have I desired the woeful day; You know what came out of my lips; it was right there before You.* (Jeremiah 17:16)

ii. Though reluctant, Jeremiah couldn't hold back: *Then I said, "I will not make mention of Him, nor speak anymore in His name." But His word was in my heart like a burning fire shut up in my bones; I was weary of holding it back, and I could not.* (Jeremiah 20:9)

e. **Do not be afraid of their faces, for I am with you to deliver you**: Jeremiah had two reasons to be afraid. First, he was young. Second, his message was hard to hear. But the presence of God with him was greater than those two reasons.

i. "His reluctance may have been based on feelings of personal inadequacy when confronted with the almost hopeless task of recalling apostate Judah to a state of true repentance. To make matters worse, at an early stage in his ministry he was forbidden to marry (16:1-4), and the ominous reasons given made more clear than ever the fact that Judah stood under divine judgment." (Harrison)

ii. "He shrank from his work again and again; he suffered intensely, not merely from the persecution of his foes, but in his own soul, in his fellowship with God and with his nation; he needed very special Divine sustenance." (Morgan)

iii. **I am with you:** "I will not only send thee as other kings do their ambassadors, but I will go with thee." (Poole)

f. **Then the LORD put forth His hand and touched my mouth:** In his vision, Jeremiah saw the LORD touch him in this personal way. As God touched the mouth of Isaiah at his call to the office of prophet, He also touched the mouth of Jeremiah (though in a different way).

g. **See, I have this day set you over the nations and over the kingdoms, to root out and to pull down, to destroy and to throw down, to build and to plant:** As a young man, Jeremiah was an unlikely candidate for such a ministry; yet God knew that Jeremiah had the personality and character to fulfill this call as the years went on.

i. "Jeremiah's commission set the pattern of his calling, with its four verbs of demolition and its two of renewal." (Kidner)

ii. "He did comparatively little of this constructive preaching and a great deal of the destructive kind." (Thompson)

iii. "As Isaiah speaks of the salvation of the Lord, Ezekiel of the glory of the Lord, and Daniel of the kingdom of the Lord, so Jeremiah incessantly proclaims the Lord's judgment." (Feinberg)

h. **See, I have this day set you:** Jeremiah was definitely called, but he did not fulfill his call in his first year – or his first ten years. His 40-year ministry had several different phases, and taken together, they fulfilled God's call.

i. The first period of Jeremiah's ministry took place under the protection of the godly king Josiah, who took advantage of turmoil in the surrounding superpowers (such as Assyria, Egypt, and Babylon) to reform the nation and turn it back to the Lord. During this time, Jeremiah went on a preaching tour through the cities of Judah and the streets of Jerusalem (Jeremiah 11:6). Yet during this time the hearts of the people did not seem changed. He preached for 23 years but no one seemed to listen (Jeremiah 25:3). He even faced many threats against his life (Jeremiah 11:19 and 12:6).

ii. After King Josiah died, things got worse. Jeremiah read a scroll of his collected prophecies to the new king Jehoiakim – and the king took the scroll, cut it in pieces, and threw it in the fire (Jeremiah 36:22-23). In this general period Jeremiah was chained and flogged (Jeremiah 20:2), and survived a close brush with death (Jeremiah 26:10-11).

iii. His most difficult season was under another king, Zedekiah, who was set on the throne by the Babylonians, but didn't continue to obey them. Jeremiah brought a message from God that must have seemed like madness to his generation. The message was that judgment through the Babylonians was inevitable; and they must prepare for it and submit to it. He wrote to those already exiled in Babylon and told them to prepare for a 70-year exile and to have a peaceable attitude towards Babylon (Jeremiah 29:7, 10). He was regarded as a traitor and imprisoned (Jeremiah 37:11-16).

3. (11-12) Jeremiah's first lesson in his training as a prophet.

Moreover the word of the LORD came to me, saying, "Jeremiah, what do you see?" And I said, "I see a branch of an almond tree." Then the LORD said to me, "You have seen well, for I am ready to perform My word."

    a. **Jeremiah, what do you see?** Jeremiah would receive a message to *speak*, but before he could speak he had to **see**.

        i. "Before you can make an impression upon another person's heart, you must have an impression made upon your own soul. You must be able to say, concerning the truth, 'I see it,' before you can speak it so that your hearers also shall see it." (Spurgeon)

    b. **A branch of an almond tree**: Jeremiah saw well. He not only understood that it was a branch but was observant enough to know that it was **a branch of an almond tree**.

        i. "Anathoth remains to this day a center for almond growing. The modern visitor to the area in the very early spring is promised the memorable and unforgettable sight of almond trees in bloom." (Thompson)

        ii. This was young Jeremiah's first lesson in prophetic observance, and the lesson was simple. "We might have thought that, as a preparation for his prophetical work, he would have seen mysterious wheels full of eyes, or flaming seraphs and cherubs, or the wonderful creatures that were caused to appear in the dreams of Ezekiel and the revelation to John. Instead of this, Jeremiah simply sees 'a rod of an almond tree;' and, beloved friends, when you look into the Bible, you will see some very simple things there." (Spurgeon)

        iii. The significance of the **branch of an almond tree** was important in two ways. First, the almond was well known as the first tree to bud in the spring. This indicated that God was ready to quickly fulfill His word, just as the almond tree seems ready to bud.

        iv. Secondly, the Hebrew word for **almond tree** is close to and derived from the Hebrew word for *watchful*, and this word is used in God's response to Jeremiah. "These verses contain a play on words that is lost in English but is vital for the force of the vision. The 'almond tree' is *saqed* and God is 'watching' (*soqed*) over his word to fulfill it." (Feinberg)

4. (13-16) Jeremiah's second lesson in his training as a prophet.

And the word of the LORD **came to me the second time, saying, "What do you see?" And I said, "I see a boiling pot, and it is facing away from the north." Then the L**ORD **said to me:**

**"Out of the north calamity shall break forth
On all the inhabitants of the land.
For behold, I am calling
All the families of the kingdoms of the north," says the L**ORD**;
"They shall come and each one set his throne
At the entrance of the gates of Jerusalem,
Against all its walls all around,
And against all the cities of Judah.
I will utter My judgments
Against them concerning all their wickedness,
Because they have forsaken Me,
Burned incense to other gods,
And worshiped the works of their own hands.**

a. **I see a boiling pot, and it is facing away from the north**: The idea is of a boiling cauldron that will tip over with its opening facing south. This is a vivid picture of destruction and judgment pouring out upon Judah from the north (**out of the north calamity shall break forth on all the inhabitants of the land**).

i. The old Puritan commentator John Trapp showed how wrong the allegorical approach to Scripture can be, describing the interpretation of an ancient writer named Gregory: "Gregory moraliseth the text thus: Man's mind is this pot; that which from the north sets it on fire is the devil, by inflaming it with evil lusts, and then he sets up his throne therein."

b. **They shall come and each one set his throne at the entrance of the gates of Jerusalem**: Jeremiah prophetically saw foreign kings dominating a subservient Jerusalem.

i. "As the gates of the cities were the ordinary places where justice was administered, so the enemies of Jerusalem are here represented as conquering the whole land, assuming the reigns of government, and laying the whole country under their own laws; so that the Jews should no longer possess any *political power*: they should be wholly subjugated by their enemies." (Clarke)

c. **Because they have forsaken Me, burned incense to other gods, and worshiped the works of their own hands**: The main reason for the coming judgment was Judah's chronic idolatry.

5. (17-19) God commands Jeremiah to be steadfast in the face of coming opposition.

Therefore prepare yourself and arise,
And speak to them all that I command you.
Do not be dismayed before their faces,
Lest I dismay you before them.
For behold, I have made you this day
A fortified city and an iron pillar,
And bronze walls against the whole land—
Against the kings of Judah,
Against its princes,
Against its priests,
And against the people of the land.
They will fight against you,
But they shall not prevail against you.
For I *am* with you," says the LORD, "to deliver you."

a. **Therefore prepare yourself and arise**: Jeremiah properly saw and understood the two visions. God felt he was ready to go forth (with additional preparation) and to **speak to them all that I command you**.

b. **Do not be dismayed before their faces, lest I dismay you before them**: God gave Jeremiah the strength he needed – but he had to walk in it. If he did not – if he allowed himself to **be dismayed before their faces** – then God would **dismay** Jeremiah before those whom he feared.

c. **For behold, I have made you this day a fortified city and an iron pillar**: Certainly, Jeremiah didn't *feel* like a **fortified city** or **an iron pillar**. But God's word was true, and Jeremiah needed to believe it and act upon it.

d. **They will fight against you**: This promise of God proved true, but so did the other aspect to the promise. The enemies of Jeremiah did **not prevail against** him, and he served God with distinction through great trials for 40 years.

i. "To this thin-skinned young man, his description of terms of battlements and heavy metal might have seemed a wild exaggeration, but in fact it proved an understatement. He would hold out against all comers for over forty years, outdoing any fortress under siege." (Kidner)

Jeremiah 2 – Broken Cisterns

A. The astonishing nature of Israel's sin.

1. (1-3) The good old days.

Moreover the word of the LORD came to me, saying, "Go and cry in the hearing of Jerusalem, saying, 'Thus says the LORD:

"I remember you,
The kindness of your youth,
The love of your betrothal,
When you went after Me in the wilderness,
In a land not sown.
Israel *was* **holiness to the LORD,**
The firstfruits of His increase.
All that devour him will offend;
Disaster will come upon them," says the LORD.'"

> a. **Go and cry in the hearing of Jerusalem**: This reminds us that the core of Jeremiah's work as a prophet were messages delivered to the southern kingdom of Judah, of which **Jerusalem** was the capital city.
>
> > i. God often refers to Judah and Jerusalem as *Israel* in Jeremiah, though the northern kingdom of Israel (representing the ten northern tribes) fell to the Assyrians some 100 years before Jeremiah's work as a prophet. God refers to Judah and Jerusalem as representing all of Israel because it did.
> >
> > ii. Far back in the days of Jeroboam and his original break with the southern kingdom of Judah, the legitimate priests and Levites who lived in the northern ten tribes did not like Jeroboam's idolatry. They, along with others who *set their hearts to seek the LORD God of Israel*, then moved from the northern kingdom of Israel to the southern kingdom of Judah (2 Chronicles 11:13-16). So actually, the *southern kingdom of Judah* contained Israelites from all of the ten tribes.

b. **I remember you, the kindness of your youth**: Through Jeremiah, God made a heartfelt appeal to Jerusalem, drawing upon the memory of their past relationship. To say, "I remember how wonderful our relationship once was" is a powerful appeal.

i. "God recollects those zealous times, those happy seasons, those enthusiastic hours; and if we have come to an ebb, if we are now cold and almost dead, and have forgotten the better days, God has not forgotten them." (Spurgeon)

c. **When you went after Me in the wilderness**: This has in mind the Exodus, when God led Israel through **the wilderness**. They were not perfect in their relationship with God then, but they had a love for God and a trust in the Lord that was sorely lacking in Jeremiah's days.

d. **Israel was holiness to the LORD**: This is what God commanded of Israel in the wilderness (Leviticus 11:45), and in some measure Israel fulfilled it. They were separated unto God as His own people and had little desire for the idols of Egypt or the Canaanites.

e. **All that devour him will offend; disaster will come upon them**: In this season of special relationship with God, the LORD took special care of Israel. If anyone attempted to **devour** Israel, then **disaster** would **come upon them**. This was a great contrast to the judgment at the hand of Israel's enemies that would eventually come upon an unfaithful Jerusalem.

2. (4-8) The great ingratitude of rebellious Israel.

Hear the word of the LORD, O house of Jacob and all the families of the house of Israel. Thus says the LORD:

"What injustice have your fathers found in Me,
That they have gone far from Me,
Have followed idols,
And have become idolaters?
Neither did they say, 'Where *is* the LORD,
Who brought us up out of the land of Egypt,
Who led us through the wilderness,
Through a land of deserts and pits,
Through a land of drought and the shadow of death,
Through a land that no one crossed
And where no one dwelt?'
I brought you into a bountiful country,
To eat its fruit and its goodness.
But when you entered, you defiled My land
And made My heritage an abomination.

The priests did not say, 'Where *is* the LORD?'
And those who handle the law did not know Me;
The rulers also transgressed against Me;
The prophets prophesied by Baal,
And walked after *things that* do not profit.

a. **What injustice have your fathers found in Me, that they have gone far from Me**: God called the house of Israel to account for their rejection of Him and their pursuit of idols. He asked to know what fault there was in *Him* that caused their idolatry.

i. On **have followed idols and have become idolaters**: "Various attempts have been made to render this in English: 'pursuing empty phantoms and themselves becoming empty' (NEB); they 'went after worthlessness and became worthless' (RSV)." (Thompson)

b. **I brought you into a bountiful country, to eat its fruit and its goodness**: God reminded Israel of how good and kind He had been to them, giving them the **bountiful country** of Canaan.

i. The events of the Exodus had happened some 800 years before Jeremiah's time. It's understandable (though not good) that Israel would come to take the blessing of the land for granted after some 800 years. There is less explanation for why we take the good works of God for granted sometimes only weeks later.

c. **You defiled My land and made My heritage an abomination**: God clearly called the land of Israel *His* **land** and *His* **heritage**. Israel both **defiled** the land and made it **an abomination** through their idolatry.

d. **The priests did not say, "Where is the LORD?" and those who handle the law did not know Me**: The religious leaders of Israel did not serve God or the people well. They did not seek the LORD (asking, **"Where is the LORD?"**) and they did not teach the word of God (**the law**) from a personal relationship with God (**did not know Me**).

i. **Those who handle the law** refers to the priests and the Levites, who were to teach, exposit, interpret, and apply the law for the people. "*They that draw out the law*; they whose office it is to *explain* it, *draw out* its spiritual meanings, and show to what its testimonies refer." (Clarke)

e. **The rulers also transgressed against Me; the prophets prophesied by Baal**: Civic and religious leaders did more harm than good for the people of God and towards the LORD Himself.

3. (9-12) The astonishing nature of Israel's sin.

"Therefore I will yet bring charges against you," says the LORD,
"And against your children's children I will bring charges.
For pass beyond the coasts of Cyprus and see,
Send to Kedar and consider diligently,
And see if there has been such *a thing*.
Has a nation changed *its* gods,
Which *are* not gods?
But My people have changed their Glory
For *what* does not profit.
Be astonished, O heavens, at this,
And be horribly afraid;
Be very desolate," says the LORD.

a. **Therefore I will yet bring charges against you**: God would not allow this great sin on behalf of the leaders and people of Israel to go unaddressed. In formal fashion, God brought a legal complaint against Israel for their sin.

b. **See if there has been such a thing. Has a nation changed its gods, which are not gods?** Since Israel liked to look to surrounding nations in imitation of their idolatry, God asked His rebellious people to look to even distant places (**beyond the coasts of Cyprus** or **Kedar**) and to ask: Do they forsake *their* gods? Strangely, the heathen around Israel were more faithful to their pagan gods than Israel was to the Living God.

i. "Cyprus was the western-most point in Judah's geography, whilst Kedar was a desert tribe in the east, so the appeal is from west to east, i.e. anywhere." (Cundall)

ii. "Think, then, of the rebuke which the obstinate adherence of idolaters to their idols gives to the slack hold which so many professing Christians have on their religion." (Maclaren)

c. **But My people have changed their Glory for what does not profit**: The heathen nations were faithful to their gods, even though their gods did *nothing* for them. Yet Israel had the God of all **Glory** who had blessed them in innumerable ways and they turned from Him.

d. **Be astonished…be horribly afraid…be very desolate**: First this is an *astonishment*, that men can be so foolish, disloyal, and ungrateful. Then it is something *to fear*, because a righteous God must answer such outrageous rebellion. Finally, it is *a desolation*, because the result of judgment upon such rebellious people will leave little behind.

B. The emptiness and shame of Israel's idolatry.

1. (13) Broken cisterns.

"For My people have committed two evils:
They have forsaken Me, the fountain of living waters,
And hewn themselves cisterns—broken cisterns that can hold no water."

>   a. **They have forsaken Me, the fountain of living waters**: This was the first of the evils of God's people – to forsake God. This is evil, not only for disloyalty and ingratitude, but also because it is foolish; God is the **fountain of living waters**, the never-ending supply of the good, pure, essential supplies of life.
>
>   >   i. In the ancient near east a **fountain of living waters** – an artesian spring – was something special. It was a constant supply of good, fresh, life-giving water *that came to you!* In ancient Israel, water was a lot of work, but a **fountain of living waters** brought it right to you.
>
>   b. **And hewn themselves cisterns – broken cisterns that can hold no water**: Having forsaken God's **fountain of living waters**, His people then worked hard (**hewn themselves**) for a greatly inferior supply (**cisterns**). Despite their hard work, all they ended up with were **broken cisterns that can hold no water**.
>
>   >   i. "Directly water is stored in cisterns, it ceases to be living; it is stagnant, and the process of deterioration begins…Moreover, man can never hew cisterns which will hold. They are all broken. We must live by streams, or we perish." (Morgan)
>
>   >   ii. "Leaving God, In whom alone man's thirsty spirit can find satisfaction and thirst-quenching, he hath set himself, with infinite labour, to hew out cisterns of gold and silver, cisterns of splendid houses and reputable characters, and lavish alms deeds, cisterns of wisdom and ancient lore. From any of these the hewer thinks he will obtain sufficient supplies to last him for life. At the best, however, the water is brackish, wanting the sparkle of oxygenated life; hot with the heat of the day." (Meyer)

2. (14-19) God's people look to Egypt and Assyria and forsake the LORD.

"*Is* Israel a servant?
Is he a homeborn *slave?*
Why is he plundered?
The young lions roared at him, *and* growled;
They made his land waste;
His cities are burned, without inhabitant.
Also the people of Noph and Tahpanhes

Have broken the crown of your head.
Have you not brought this on yourself,
In that you have forsaken the LORD your God
When He led you in the way?
And now why take the road to Egypt,
To drink the waters of Sihor?
Or why take the road to Assyria,
To drink the waters of the River?
Your own wickedness will correct you,
And your backslidings will rebuke you.
Know therefore and see that *it is* an evil and bitter *thing*
That you have forsaken the LORD your God,
And the fear of Me *is* not in you,"
Says the Lord GOD of hosts.

> a. **Is Israel a servant? Is he a homeborn slave? Why is he plundered?** Earlier in the chapter (Jeremiah 2:3), God promised that He would defend an obedient Israel. Now through Jeremiah, God asked His people to consider the case of **Israel** in the sense of the conquered northern kingdom, to remember *why* they were now slaves.
>
> b. **The people of Noph and Tahpanhes have broken the crown of your head**: **Noph** and **Tahpanhes** were both Egyptian cities. **Noph** is another name for Memphis, the ancient capital of lower Egypt, near modern Cairo. God here warned Judah not to trust in Egypt, which would (or perhaps had by that time) have **broken the crown of your head** by defeating and killing the good king Josiah in battle (2 Kings 23:29).
>
> c. **Have you not brought this on yourself, in that you have forsaken the LORD your God**: The reason was plain; Israel was captive, her people slaves, her cities burned because they forsook the LORD.
>
> d. **Why take the road to Egypt…why take the road to Assyria**: God cautioned Jerusalem from looking to either Egypt (**the waters of Sihor**, the Nile) or Assyria (**the waters of the River**, the Euphrates) for help. The water of their rivers was nothing compared to the fountains of living water found in the LORD.
>
>> i. "No matter how appealing the prospect of alliance with Egypt might be, Judah will suffer for it if she becomes entangled." (Harrison)
>>
>> ii. "*Sihor*, 'blackness', is a sarcastic reference to the river Nile, one of the most highly venerated of Egyptian gods." (Harrison)
>
> e. **Your own wickedness will correct you, and your backslidings will rebuke you**: If Jerusalem did continue on their destructive course,

there would be more than enough correction and rebuke found in the consequences of their actions. They would certainly **know therefore and see that it is an evil and a bitter thing that you have forsaken the LORD your God.**

f. **"The fear of Me is not in you," says the Lord GOD of hosts**: Jerusalem feared attack from the Babylonians and therefore contemplated alliances with Egypt and Assyria. Yet the real problem was they did not **fear** the LORD, and **the Lord GOD of hosts** – that is, of heavenly armies. God was more than able to protect them if they repented and trusted in Him.

3. (20-25) The unrestrained pursuit of false gods.

"For of old I have broken your yoke *and* burst your bonds;
And you said, 'I will not transgress,'
When on every high hill and under every green tree
You lay down, playing the harlot.
Yet I had planted you a noble vine, a seed of highest quality.
How then have you turned before Me
Into the degenerate plant of an alien vine?
For though you wash yourself with lye, and use much soap,
Yet your iniquity is marked before Me," says the Lord GOD.
"How can you say, 'I am not polluted,
I have not gone after the Baals'?
See your way in the valley;
Know what you have done:
You are a swift dromedary breaking loose in her ways,
A wild donkey used to the wilderness,
That sniffs at the wind in her desire;
In her time of mating, who can turn her away?
All those who seek her will not weary themselves;
In her month they will find her.
Withhold your foot from being unshod, and your throat from thirst.
But you said, 'There is no hope.
No! For I have loved aliens, and after them I will go.'"

a. **You said, "I will not transgress," when on every high hill and under every green tree you lay down playing the harlot**: God symbolically spoke of the idolatry of the conquered northern kingdom as prostitution. In going after idols, Israel was like a wife so unfaithful to her husband that she was a **harlot**, consorting with idols.

i. This is allegorically speaking, but an allegory connected with reality. Many of the pagan and Canaanite idols honored by the Israelites were essentially sex cults, honored with ritual prostitution. Their idolatry was often connected with sexual immorality with the use of male and female prostitutes.

ii. "The many references to abnormal sexual gratification underline one of the most prominent features of the Canaanite religion, where male and female cult-prostitutes were connected with the sanctuaries." (Cundall)

b. **Playing the harlot… the degenerate plant of an alien vine… though you wash yourself with lye**: God used three strong images to describe the sin and shame of Israel. They were like a prostitute, like a weed, and like someone so dirty that no **lye** or **soap** could make them clean.

i. "The *noble* (AV) or *choice* (RSV) vine is literally, 'Sorek vine', a high-quality red grape grown in the Wadi al-Sarar, situated between Jerusalem and the Mediterranean." (Harrison)

ii. "God has planted his people a thoroughly reliable stock hoping to gather a rich harvest of choice grapes. But she became a strange wild vine, a foul-smelling thing." (Thompson)

iii. **Yet your iniquity is marked before Me**: "Sin leaveth behind it a deep stain, so ingrained that it will hardly ever be gotten out, not at all by blanching, extenuating, excusing, etc., or by any legal purifications, hypocritical lotions." (Trapp)

iv. "So ingrained is Judah's foul iniquity that no amount of washing with detergents can remove it. The supreme merit of Christ's work on Calvary is that it removes the dark stain of iniquity (1 John 1:7)." (Harrison)

c. **See your way in the valley; know what you have done**: This refers to the **valley** of Hinnom, the deep gorge that lies to the west and south of Jerusalem. This was a place of idolatry and hideous deeds.

i. "Here all sorts of heathen rites were practiced, including the worship of Baal and the worship of Molech (cf. 7:31-32; 2 Kings 23:10)." (Thompson)

ii. **See your way in the valley; know what you have done**: "How could they claim innocence when they were carrying on their vile worship of Baal in the Valley of Hinnom with their child sacrifices?" (Feinberg)

d. **A wild donkey used to the wilderness, that sniffs at the wind in her desire**: The next images are of a camel (a **swift dromedary**) or a **wild donkey** in heat (**in her time of mating…in her month**) with no control over her desire, allowing any and all to mount her.

i. "Young female camels are altogether unreliable, ungainly, and easily disturbed, so that they dash about in an apparently disorganized fashion." (Thompson)

ii. Apparently (according to Ryken and several others), when in heat, the female donkey goes after the male with abandon. "The female *ass* in heat is almost violent. She sniffs the path in front of her trying to pick up the scent of a male (from his urine). Then she races down the road in search of the male." (Thompson)

e. **Withhold your foot from being unshod, and your throat from thirst**: The bare foot and constant thirst were marks of the exile and slave. This was the fate of the northern kingdom of Israel and would also be the fate of Judah if they did not turn to the LORD. Yet they answered God's heartfelt appeal with a resignation to their idolatry and fate: **There is no hope…I have loved aliens and after them I will go**.

4. (26-28) The shame of Israel.

"As the thief is ashamed when he is found out,
So is the house of Israel ashamed;
They and their kings and their princes, and their priests and their prophets,
Saying to a tree, 'You *are* my father,'
And to a stone, 'You gave birth to me.'
For they have turned *their* back to Me, and not *their* face.
But in the time of their trouble
They will say, 'Arise and save us.'
But where *are* your gods that you have made for yourselves?
Let them arise,
If they can save you in the time of your trouble;
For *according to* the number of your cities
Are your gods, O Judah."

a. **As the thief is ashamed when he is found out, so is the house of Israel ashamed**: The **thief** is only ashamed when he is found out. He regrets getting caught and penalized, not the crime itself. In the same way, Israel under exile was really only sorry they had been caught and had suffered for their sin.

b. **Saying to a tree, "You are my father"**: Jeremiah described their foolish idolatry, worshipping things of wood and **stone**. The **tree** was a wooden idol representing Asherah, the leading female Canaanite deity. The **stone** represented Baal, the leading male Canaanite deity.

i. "These stone pillars have been found in excavations in Palestine. All that remains of the wooden poles is a posthole in which the rotted timber has left a different colored soil. There is enough archaeological evidence for these to indicate a widespread usage." (Thompson)

ii. "At each Canaanite shrine there was an asherah, probably a wooden pillar which was a formal substitute for a sacred tree, representing the female sexual element, and a mazzebah, or stone pillar, indicating the male element." (Cundall)

iii. "There is strong satire here, for it is the female symbol [**tree**] that is called *Father* and the male symbol [**stone**] that is called *You who gave me birth*. Israel was confused about what she was worshipping when she ascribed to the gods of fertility her very existence." (Thompson)

c. **But in the time of their trouble they will say, "Arise and save us"**: God knew that His people would reject useless idolatry when the great crisis came. Yet in that day, God would be justified to ask: "**Where are your gods that you have made for yourselves?**"

d. **Let them arise, if they can save you in the time of trouble**: The idols Israel and Judah loved to worship did them no good in the time of crisis. They worshiped many idols (**for according to the number of your cities are your gods, O Judah**), but either collectively or individually they were of no help in the **time** of **trouble**.

i. **According to the number of your cities are your gods, O Judah**: "Among heathen nations every city had its *tutelary deity*. Judah, far sunk in idolatry, had adopted this custom." (Clarke)

5. (29-32) God will not listen to Israel that has rejected Him.

"Why will you plead with Me?
You all have transgressed against Me," says the LORD.
 "In vain I have chastened your children;
They received no correction.
Your sword has devoured your prophets
Like a destroying lion.
"O generation, see the word of the LORD!
Have I been a wilderness to Israel,
Or a land of darkness?
Why do My people say, 'We are lords;
We will come no more to You'?
Can a virgin forget her ornaments,
Or a bride her attire?
Yet My people have forgotten Me days without number."

a. **Why will you plead with Me? You have all transgressed against Me**: In the previous lines God spoke of how His people would turn to Him in the time of their trouble, yet not out of true repentance; instead out of a mere desire to escape present consequences. Here, God tests the repentance of Israel to see if they will return to Him through difficulty.

b. **Your sword has devoured your prophets**: God's people were guilty of rejecting and murdering the prophets.

c. **Why do My people say, "We are lords; we will come no more to You"**? God's people were guilty of pride, believing they didn't need to come and humble themselves before the living God.

d. **Can a virgin forget her ornaments, or a bride her attire? Yet My people have forgotten Me days without number**: Israel's rejection of God was *unnatural*. It is only natural for a young woman to treasure her **ornaments**, or for a **bride** to value her clothing. When God's people forget their God – who has done so much for them – it is an offence against all that is good and right.

   i. **A bride her attire**: Something like a wedding ring, "The bridal *attire* was a sash or girdle proclaiming her status as a married woman." (Harrison)

6. (33-37) Israel will be disappointed in the false gods they have trusted.

"Why do you beautify your way to seek love?
Therefore you have also taught
The wicked women your ways.
Also on your skirts is found
The blood of the lives of the poor innocents.
I have not found it by secret search,
But plainly on all these things.
Yet you say, 'Because I am innocent,
Surely His anger shall turn from me.'
Behold, I will plead My case against you,
Because you say, 'I have not sinned.'
Why do you gad about so much to change your way?
Also you shall be ashamed of Egypt as you were ashamed of Assyria.
Indeed you will go forth from him
With your hands on your head;
For the LORD has rejected your trusted allies,
And you will not prosper by them."

   a. **Why do you beautify your way to seek love?** Israel felt that the pursuit of love was self-justifying and any pursuit of love could be considered beautiful. In their thinking, the love of idols was just as good as the love of Yahweh, their covenant God. The love expressed in what Yahweh called sexual immorality was just as good as love expressed in what Yahweh called sexual morality. God did not accept their attempt to **beautify** their **way to seek love**.

    i. **Beautify**: "The same word is used of Jezebel's dressing her head (2 Kings 9:30). What need this whorish trick and trimming, if all were right with thee?" (Trapp)

b. **You have also taught the wicked women your ways**: For Israel in Jeremiah's day, it wasn't enough for them to call their sinful pursuit of love beautiful; they also had to teach it to others.

c. **Also on your skirts is found the blood of the lives of the poor innocents**: Their immoral love – which they *called* beautiful – left them stained with the **blood** of the **poor innocents**.

    i. The application of this section of Jeremiah to the modern day is unmistakable.

- Many today justify any pursuit of love as beautiful – such as the supposed pursuit of love in adultery, premarital sex, homosexuality, and in perversions. God does not agree with their justifications.
- Many of these also must teach others their ways, advocating them in the general society, hoping to normalize what was once considered sinful or perverted.
- The **poor innocents** suffer – unborn children are killed, homes are wrecked, perversion imposes itself on innocents.

d. **I have not found it by secret search, but plainly on all these things**: The sin and perversion popularized in Jeremiah's day was evident; only willful blindness kept individuals and society from recognizing it.

e. **Yet you say, "Because I am innocent, surely His anger shall turn from me"**: Despite the plain nature of their sin, Israel could still claim innocence. They felt entitled to Divine mercy.

f. **Behold, I will plead My case against you, because you say, "I have not sinned"**: Their *claim* of innocence did not impress God. He would still bring a **case against** them; their claim to innocence made them *more* guilty, not less.

g. **Why do you gad about to change your way?** To **gad about** is to bounce about on an irregular course. The New Living Translation has this, *First here, then there – you flit from one ally to another asking for help*. There was no reason for them to **gad about** – they should have gone straight away to trusting the LORD.

i. In his sermon titled *Gadding About*, Spurgeon drew two ideas from this text.

- Spurgeon focused on the word **you**: **Why do *you* gad about so much to change your way?** This was Israel, the wife of Yahweh – why should *they* do this?

- Spurgeon focused on the word **why**: ***Why*** **do you gad about so much to change your way?** God requested a reason from Israel to account for their gadding about.

h. **Indeed you will go forth from him with your hands on your head**: God promised to bring their trust in Egypt to nothing, and (without national repentance) they would go forth from Judah as captive slaves, with **your hands on your head**. God would not honor their alliances with Egypt or any other foreign power.

Jeremiah 3 – A Word to Backsliders

A. The unfaithfulness of God's people.

1. (1) God says to His unfaithful people, "**Return to Me.**"

"They say, 'If a man divorces his wife,
And she goes from him
And becomes another man's,
May he return to her again?'
Would not that land be greatly polluted?
But you have played the harlot with many lovers;
Yet return to Me," says the LORD.

> a. **If a man divorces his wife… may he return to her again?** Jeremiah seems to have in mind the command in Deuteronomy 24:1-4, which says that when a man divorces his wife and she becomes the wife of another man, she must not return again to her first husband.
>
> i. This law of Deuteronomy 24:1-4 sounds strange to our modern age where it is not completely uncommon for a wife to return to her first husband after a second or third husband. The sense behind it was that it made the ideas of both marriage and divorce seem of little consequence, as if one might say: "I can divorce her, and remarry her later if I want to." God wanted to speak to that thinking and say, "No you can't treat divorce and remarriage so casually. I won't allow it."
>
> ii. "This law, which forbade a divorced couple to reunite, was aimed against what would amount to virtually *lending* one's partner to another…it would degrade not only her but marriage itself and the society that accepted such a practice." (Kidner)
>
> iii. "The precise reasons for this ancient law may have been various, among them being an attempt to preserve the second marriage." (Thompson)

b. **Would not the land be greatly polluted?** Deuteronomy 24:4 says, *her former husband who divorced her must not take her back to be his wife after she has been defiled; for that is an abomination before the LORD, and you shall not bring sin on the land which the LORD your God is giving you as an inheritance.* God connected disobedience to this law regarding remarriage to a defilement of the land, making it **greatly polluted**.

c. **But you have played the harlot with many lovers; yet return to Me**: God wanted His unfaithful people to know that though returning to the first husband might be wrong on a human level, it was not wrong between God and His people.

i. The line, **"Yet return to Me," says the LORD** is a bit of a mystery to translators. Some (as the NKJV and NLT) translate it as an invitation from God to Israel. Others (such as the NASB and ESV) translate it as an accusation, God accusing Israel of wanting to return to Him lightly or wrongly.

- NASB: *But you are a harlot with many lovers; yet you turn to Me*
- ESV: *And would you return to Me?*
- NLT: *But you have prostituted yourself with many lovers, says the LORD. Yet I am still calling you to come back to me.*

ii. "Scholars are clearly divided on the issue, and the reason is understandable. The verb 'return' (*sob*) in the last line of v.1 is an infinitive that may allow for more than one rendering." (Feinberg)

iii. In the rest of the chapter, since God repeatedly does invite Israel to return to Him, and the thought of this return is presented in a good sense, it is best to take it as rendered in the NKJV – as a plea from God to His people for them to **return to** Him.

2. (2) The depth of their depravity.

"Lift up your eyes to the desolate heights and see:
Where have you not lain *with men?*
By the road you have sat for them
Like an Arabian in the wilderness;
And you have polluted the land
With your harlotries and your wickedness."

a. **Where have you not lain with men?** God asked His people to look up to the **heights** – that is, the high places where altars to pagan gods were often built. According to the picture, upon these **desolate heights** they committed spiritual adultery with pagan gods.

i. "This verse alludes to the worship of Baal and Asherah, which included sex with temple prostitutes at hilltop shrines." (Ryken)

ii. "The word 'ravished' [**lain with men**] is especially powerful. It is an obscene word for sexual violence. Although God's people have been looking for a good time, they have been getting raped. False gods are always abusive." (Ryken) (Deuteronomy 28:30, Isaiah 13:16, where the word is translated *ravished*).

b. **By the road you have sat for them**: Here, God used the picture of a common street prostitute to illustrate the spiritual adultery of Israel. The idea was that they sought out these idols and offered themselves to them.

i. **Like an Arabian in the wilderness**: "Jeremiah likened the national preoccupation with licentiousness to an Arab freebooter waiting in concealment to plunder a passing caravan, or to a wayside prostitute soliciting clients." (Harrison) Sin wasn't searching for them; they were searching for it.

c. **You have polluted the land with your harlotries and your wickedness**: Israel considered their idolatry and sacrifice to pagan gods to be of little consequence. Many of them probably told themselves that they were not forsaking the LORD, only adding the worship of these other gods. God saw their sin for what it was and noted that it **polluted the land**.

3. (3-5) The penalty of their sin and how they *should* have repented.

Therefore the showers have been withheld,
And there has been no latter rain.
You have had a harlot's forehead;
You refuse to be ashamed.
Will you not from this time cry to Me,
'My Father, You *are* the guide of my youth?
Will He remain angry forever?
Will He keep it to the end?'
Behold, you have spoken and done evil things,
As you were able."

a. **Therefore the showers have been withheld and there has been no latter rain**: Spiritually, Israel's idolatry polluted the land – therefore God withheld the rain they needed for crops and food. This had special irony, because many of the pagan gods they went after were associated with weather, rain, and fertility (such as Baal and Ashtoreth).

i. Some of those ancient idol worshippers in ancient Israel went after the idols exactly for the rain and agricultural abundance they hoped their idolatry would bring. They were terribly wrong. Because their pursuit was out of God's will, it left them less satisfied than before.

b. **You have a harlot's forehead; you refuse to be ashamed**: God observed the lack of shame among Israel for their idol worship. Their conscience was dead to its proper workings.

c. **Will you not from this time cry to Me**: God told Israel what they *should* do.

- They should **cry** out unto the Lord with urgency and desperation.
- They should look to Him as their **Father** and their **guide**.
- They should see themselves as those who need guidance and help, as a **youth** needs guidance and help.
- They should hope that God would not **remain angry** with them.

d. **Behold, you have spoken and done evil things, as you were able**: Instead of crying out to the Lord and coming with humble repentance, Israel continued in their evil as they **were able** – hoping to get away with as much as they could.

B. Backsliders called to return.

1. (6-10) God speaks to Jeremiah about backsliding Israel, treacherous Judah.

The LORD said also to me in the days of Josiah the king: "Have you seen what backsliding Israel has done? She has gone up on every high mountain and under every green tree, and there played the harlot. And I said, after she had done all these *things*, 'Return to Me.' But she did not return. And her treacherous sister Judah saw it. Then I saw that for all the causes for which backsliding Israel had committed adultery, I had put her away and given her a certificate of divorce; yet her treacherous sister Judah did not fear, but went and played the harlot also. So it came to pass, through her casual harlotry, that she defiled the land and committed adultery with stones and trees. And yet for all this her treacherous sister Judah has not turned to Me with her whole heart, but in pretense," says the LORD.

a. **In the days of Josiah the king**: Josiah was one of the better kings of Judah, and in his reign there was an aggressive campaign to purify Israel of idolatry and to return to the LORD. God no doubt used these words from Jeremiah as part of this work.

b. **Have you seen what backsliding Israel has done?** God reminded Jeremiah (and those who heard this prophecy) that the northern kingdom of Israel was deeply idolatrous, yet God still called to them saying, "**Return** to Me." Sadly, **she did not return** and perished as a kingdom some 100 years before Jeremiah began his prophetic work.

c. **Her treacherous sister Judah saw it**: The southern kingdom of Judah should have learned from Israel's idolatry, refusal to repent, and fall. Instead, **her treacherous sister Judah did not fear, but went and played the harlot also.**

> i. It's easy for us to think Judah was crazy and ask how they could have missed such obvious lessons. Yet we see the modern world repeating the same mistakes and sins as previous fallen empires and cultures.
>
> ii. **Through her casual harlotry**: "The Hebrew text reads literally 'through the lightness of adultery'; that is, adultery mattered so little to her that she participated in the same evil practices as her sister Israel and polluted the land." (Thompson)

d. **Yet for all this her treacherous sister Judah has not turned to Me with her whole heart, but in pretense**: It seemed that Judah had learned nothing from the sin and consequences that came upon the northern kingdom of Israel. Whatever repentance they did offer was not from the **whole heart**, but only in **pretense**.

> i. On a human level it is difficult and perhaps dangerous to judge the repentance of another person. We should be generous in our assessment of someone's repentance. Nevertheless, repentance only in **pretense** is a real phenomenon, and *God* knows when repentance is insincere and only for show.
>
> ii. "True confession, unfortunately, is a harrowing and humiliating experience, and thus seldom encountered, whether in individuals or nations." (Harrison)
>
> iii. "In his days there had been great reform outwardly. The king had wrought with a true passion for righteousness, but as Huldah, the prophetess, had told him, the reforms, so far as the people were concerned, were unreal, they did not touch the deepest things in life." (Morgan)
>
> iv. "He that repenteth with a contradiction, saith Tertullian, God will pardon him with a contradiction. Thou repentest, and yet continuest in thy sins. God will pardon thee, and yet send thee to hell: there is a pardon with a contradiction." (Trapp)

2. (11-13) God tells Jeremiah to invite Israel to return and find mercy.

Then the LORD said to me, "Backsliding Israel has shown herself more righteous than treacherous Judah. Go and proclaim these words toward the north, and say:

'Return, backsliding Israel,' says the LORD;
'I will not cause My anger to fall on you.
For I *am* merciful,' says the LORD;
'I will not remain angry forever.
Only acknowledge your iniquity,
That you have transgressed against the LORD your God,
And have scattered your charms
To alien deities under every green tree,
And you have not obeyed My voice,' says the LORD."

    a. **Backsliding Israel has shown herself more righteous than treacherous Judah**: This is a startling statement, considering how deeply the northern kingdom of Israel gave themselves to idols. Nevertheless, we can think of several reasons why Judah's sin was even worse.

- Judah had the example of Israel to learn from, an advantage that Israel did not have.
- Judah was closer to the temple and center of true worship.
- Judah had better and more spiritual kings than Israel.
- Judah's problem was treachery and the pretense of repentance; Israel was more honest in their sin.

    b. **Return, backsliding Israel**: God told Jeremiah to invite Israel – though they were scattered in exile throughout the Assyrian empire – to **return** to Him. The key to their return was this: **Only acknowledge your iniquity**. *This* honesty was what Judah lacked and was the key to Israel's restoration to right relationship.

        i. **Return, backsliding Israel**: "The 'backslider' (turn away) is invited to 'come back' (turn back)." (Thompson) The sense is something like, "Slide back to Me, backslider."

        ii. Here, there is no promise that God would restore the northern kingdom to its land and realm. Instead, the promise seems to be of restored relationship with Yahweh, their covenant God.

        iii. The sense seems to be, "Judah has not repented honestly, only in pretense. Perhaps Israel will honestly repent if I invite them."

        iv. "'Alas,' says one, 'I do not know whether I am a backslider, or whether I have been a hypocrite up till now!' Do not argue that question at all. I am constantly asked to decide for people whether they ever were true Christians, or were in error about their condition. It is a difficult enquiry, and of small practical value." (Spurgeon)

3. (14-15) Return and be restored.

"Return, O backsliding children," says the Lord; "for I am married to you. I will take you, one from a city and two from a family, and I will bring you to Zion. And I will give you shepherds according to My heart, who will feed you with knowledge and understanding."

a. **Return, O backsliding children**: Here, God speaks to both "sisters" (Jeremiah 3:7) Israel and Judah and invites them to **return** to Him.

b. **For I am married to you**: Significantly, God said that He gave Israel a certificate of divorce (Jeremiah 3:8). Yet here He says to both Israel and Judah, "**I am married to you**." God was willing to ignore the previous divorce if they would only return to Him.

i. These pleas: "**Return, O backsliding children**" and "**For I am married to you**" have great depth of feeling. This is not a cold, dispassionate God; this is the Lord full of warmth and compassion, pursing His wayward people.

ii. "Oh! it is grace that he should be married to any of us, but it is grace at its highest pitch, it is the ocean of grace at its flood- tide, that he should speak thus of 'backsliding children.'" (Spurgeon)

c. **I will take you, one from a city and two from a family, and I will bring you to Zion**: God promised restoration and repatriation for the remnant that would return to Him.

d. **I will give you shepherds according to My heart, who will feed you with knowledge and understanding**: After the blessing of restoration and repatriation, God promised the blessing of good and godly spiritual leadership, giving an instructive description of what leaders among God's people should be.

- They should be given by God (**I will give you**), not by human ambition or presumed calling.
- They are given *to* the people of God (**I will give you**) for their care and service unto them.
- They should be **shepherds**, caring for the flock of God.
- They should be **according to** God's **heart** in the way they serve and lead God's people.
- They should **feed** God's people with **knowledge**.
- They should **feed** God's people with **understanding**.

4. (16-17) Return and know the presence of the LORD.

"Then it shall come to pass, when you are multiplied and increased in the land in those days," says the LORD, "that they will say no more, 'The ark of the covenant of the LORD.' It shall not come to mind, nor shall they remember it, nor shall they visit *it,* **nor shall it be made anymore. At that time Jerusalem shall be called The Throne of the LORD, and all the nations shall be gathered to it, to the name of the LORD, to Jerusalem. No more shall they follow the dictates of their evil hearts."**

    a. **When you are multiplied and increased in the land in those days… they will say no more, "The ark of the covenant of the LORD"**: Jeremiah looked forward to Israel's ultimate restoration, marked by gathering **in the land** and by the presence of the LORD Himself, not merely the representation of God seen in **the ark of the covenant of the LORD**.

    b. **It shall not come to mind, nor shall they remember it, nor shall they visit it**: Jeremiah looked forward to the day when the reality of God's presence among men surpassed the symbol of it represented by the **ark of the covenant**. It would so far surpass it that when the reality comes, no one would think of the ark of the covenant any longer.

        i. "The ark will not be restored because it will no longer be necessary as a symbol of God's presence. The times of ceremonial emphasis will pass away. The actual glory of God in the presence of his people will be sufficient, and therefore the typical glory will not be missed." (Feinberg)

    c. **At that time Jerusalem shall be called The Throne of the LORD, and all the nations shall be gathered to it**: Jeremiah looked forward to the day when Israel would be the leading nation of the earth, with the LORD Himself enthroned in Jerusalem and the nations coming to give Him honor.

    d. **No more shall they follow the dictates of their evil hearts**: Jeremiah looked forward to the day when the nations would be genuinely transformed as they recognized the LORD and His work from Jerusalem.

        i. Here, without calling it the new covenant, Jeremiah speaks of some of the benefits of the new covenant as will be later developed in Jeremiah 31:31-33.

C. Restoration to the land.

1. (18) A promise of restoration.

"In those days the house of Judah shall walk with the house of Israel, and they shall come together out of the land of the north to the land that I have given as an inheritance to your fathers."

> a. **In those days**: In the previous lines (Jeremiah 3:16-17), God promised many of the features that would later be developed in the promise of the new covenant. Here, we learn of more that will happen **in those days**.
>
> b. **The house of Judah shall walk with the house of Israel**: Long before, the twelve tribes of Israel split into two competing kingdoms. God here looked forward to the day when Judah and Israel would be together again, and no longer separated by their ancient civil conflict.
>
> c. **And they shall come together out of the land of the north to the land that I have given**: The promise of return to the land is again promised to both Judah and Israel. God will gather them to the land again.

2. (19-20) The problem of restoring the treacherous house of Israel.

"But I said:
'How can I put you among the children
And give you a pleasant land, beautiful heritage of the hosts of nations?'"
"And I said:
'You shall call Me, "My Father,"
And not turn away from Me.'
Surely, *as* a wife treacherously departs from her husband,
So have you dealt treacherously with Me,
O house of Israel," says the LORD.

> a. **How can I put you among the children and give you a pleasant land**: Rhetorically, God asked how backsliding Israel and treacherous Judah could receive such a blessing as the restoration to the land.
>
> b. **You shall call Me, "my Father," and not turn away from Me**: Answering His own question, God pointed to an inner transformation that would take place among His people, despite their past treachery. This inner transformation is another feature of the new covenant.
>
> > i. **My Father**: "The term 'father' was sometimes used by a young wife of her husband." (Feinberg)

3. (21-22) The weeping of a repentant Israel.

A voice was heard on the desolate heights,
Weeping *and* supplications of the children of Israel.
For they have perverted their way;
They have forgotten the LORD their God.

"Return, you backsliding children,
And I will heal your backslidings."
"Indeed we do come to You,
For You are the LORD our God."

> a. **Weeping and supplications of the children of Israel**: Jeremiah prophetically saw Israel in true repentance, crying out to God from their desolation. Such deep repentance was necessary because they had **perverted their way** and **forgotten the LORD their God**.
>
>> i. **On the desolate heights**: "Where they were wont to worship idols, now they weep for their sins, and pray for pardon." (Trapp)
>>
>> ii. "Here is the consciousness of sin in its essential character, and that produces godly sorrow. The distinction between mere remorse and repentance is here already, in the 'weeping and supplication.'" (Maclaren)
>
> b. **Return, you backsliding children... Indeed, we do come to You**: Jeremiah spoke of the day when the children of Israel would respond to God's call to return and be healed from their backsliding, recognizing their need and who their God is (**for You are the LORD our God**). This was a contrast to how they had previously **forgotten the LORD their God**.
>
>> i. "He says, 'Return, ye backsliding children.' I notice that he does not say, 'Return, ye penitent children.' He pictures you in your worst colors, yet he says, 'Return, ye backsliding children.' I notice also that he does not say, 'Heal your wounds first, and then come back to me;' but he says, 'Return, ye backsliding children,' with all your backslidings unhealed, – 'and I will heal your backslidings.'" (Spurgeon)
>>
>> ii. The words of Jeremiah 3:21-22 show several things about **backsliding**.
>>
>> - Backsliding brings desolation (**on the desolate heights**).
>> - Backsliding is worthy of great mourning (**weeping and supplication**).
>> - Backsliders may return right from their wayward place (the high places, **the desolate heights**).
>> - Backsliding is shown in a **perverted...way**.
>> - Backsliding is shown in forgetting God (**they have forgotten the LORD their God**).
>> - Backsliding is something only **children** of God can do.
>> - Backsliding is a decision to turn from (**return**).

- Backsliding is disease to be healed from (**I will heal**).
- Backsliding is corrected by the recognition of a wrong way (**we do come to you**).
- Backsliding is corrected by the recognition of having forgotten God (**for You are the LORD our God**).

4. (23-25) The lasting shame of idolatry expressed in a statement of true repentance.

Truly, in vain *is salvation hoped for* **from the hills,**
And from **the multitude of mountains;**
Truly, in the LORD our God
Is **the salvation of Israel.**
For shame has devoured
The labor of our fathers from our youth—
Their flocks and their herds,
Their sons and their daughters.
We lie down in our shame,
And our reproach covers us.
For we have sinned against the LORD our God,
We and our fathers,
From our youth even to this day,
And have not obeyed the voice of the LORD our God."

a. **Truly, in vain is salvation hoped for from the hills**: In their idolatry, Israel often built altars on *high places* – the tops of hills. God reminded them that these **hills**, these high places and the false gods they represented were of no help in their day of need. Instead, **in the LORD our God is the salvation of Israel**.

i. "This is followed by the recitation of an ideal confession for the sinning people. Weeping, they make their supplication. Recognizing the vanity of expecting help from any source other than Jehovah, they turn to Him with confession of sin." (Morgan)

b. **For shame has devoured the labor of our fathers from our youth – their flocks and herds, their sons and daughters**: Upon those altars to pagan gods upon the **hills**, generations of Israelis sacrificed their **flocks and herds** and even **their sons and daughters** (figuratively and sometimes literally). It was all a **shame** that **devoured**.

i. "The 'shameful' thing (v.24, the article is emphatic in the Hebrew) is Baal, the god of shame. In 11:13 Baal and shame are identified." (Feinberg)

ii. "That shameful thing, Baal hath done it (chapter 11:13; Hosea 9:10); he hath even eaten up our cattle and our children, of whom, if any be left, yet there is nothing left for them." (Trapp)

c. **We lie down in our shame, and our reproach covers us**: This shame was constant and could not be done away with until the children of Israel genuinely repented and returned to the LORD.

d. **We have sinned against the LORD our God, we and our fathers…and have not obeyed the voice of the LORD our God**: This is the appropriate expression of broken repentance that should mark God's backsliding children. There is no excuse or explanation given.

Jeremiah 4 – The Terror of Coming Judgment

A. The repentance that brings restoration.

1. (1-2) Blessings to a returning and repentant Israel.

"If you will return, O Israel," says the LORD,
"Return to Me;
And if you will put away your abominations out of My sight,
Then you shall not be moved.
And you shall swear, 'The LORD lives,'
In truth, in judgment, and in righteousness;
The nations shall bless themselves in Him,
And in Him they shall glory."

> a. **Return to Me**: This carries the same theme from Jeremiah 3, where Yahweh pled with Israel to stop their backsliding ways and to **return** to Him. The call went out to **Israel**, with all tribes and both kingdoms in mind (Jeremiah 3).
>
> b. **If you will put away your abominations out of My sight**: For Israel, returning to the LORD meant they had to **put away** their idols (**abominations**). They could not hold on to their idols and still return to Yahweh, even as an adulterous spouse cannot continue to hold on to their illicit lover *and* genuinely return to their marriage partner.
>
>> i. "The term *abominations* was used in Hosea 9:10 and also by both Jeremiah and Ezekiel of pagan deities and their associated cultic rituals." (Harrison)
>
> c. **Then you shall not be moved. And you shall swear, "The LORD lives"**: These were two rewards that would come to a returning, repentant Israel. First, they would have security (**not be moved**). Second, they would be restored to real relationship with Yahweh, able to **swear**, "**The LORD lives**."
>
>> i. **Then you shall not be moved**: "This was spoken before the Babylonish captivity; and here is a promise that if they will return from

their idolatry, they *shall not be led into captivity*. So, even that positively threatened judgment would have been averted had they returned to the Lord." (Clarke)

ii. There are some who at one time claimed to walk with God and experience Him, and then departed from outward profession. Some of those, in their departure, claim that their experience with God was all an illusion and go on to deny the reality of God and His revelation in Jesus Christ. If those would return to the Lord in true repentance, they would be able to once again **swear, "The Lord lives."**

d. **In truth, in judgment, and in righteousness; the nations shall bless themselves in Him, and in Him they shall glory**: This is the understanding of the Lord that belongs to those who return to Him and repent. Once again they see His true, good, righteous character, and His blessing to **the nations**.

2. (3-4) Breaking up the fallow ground.

For thus says the Lord to the men of Judah and Jerusalem:
"Break up your fallow ground,
And do not sow among thorns.
Circumcise yourselves to the Lord,
And take away the foreskins of your hearts,
You men of Judah and inhabitants of Jerusalem,
Lest My fury come forth like fire,
And burn so that no one can quench *it,*
Because of the evil of your doings."

a. **Break up your fallow ground**: God invited Judah and Jerusalem to return to Him from a hardened condition. **Fallow ground** is uncultivated farmland, especially ground that was plowed before but has laid dormant for a year or more. It is hard to plow, but no useful crops can be grown until the **fallow ground** is broken up.

- Fallow ground implies prior fruitfulness.
- Fallow ground needs some hard work to break.
- Fallow ground implies some resistance.

    i. "It would be pointless to sow the seeds of repentance in unsuitable soil." (Harrison)

b. **And do not sow among thorns**: This probably has in mind what *does grow* upon fallow ground – weeds and thorns. It's not as if *nothing* grows upon fallow fields, simply nothing *useful* grows there. Spiritually speaking, returning Judah must put their energy into prepared, repentant hearts.

i. "There must be a deep ploughing, and the eradication of that which hinders growth, both in the realm of the spirit and in nature, before there can be a bountiful harvest." (Cundall)

c. **Circumcise yourselves to the LORD**: Jeremiah switched images, moving away from the idea of an unplowed field to the idea of a baby boy's circumcision, in obedience to the covenant of Abraham. Instead of taking away the literal foreskin, Judah had to remove **the foreskins of your hearts**, cutting away the flesh in covenant dedication to the LORD.

d. **Lest My fury come forth like fire, and burn so that no one can quench it**: God drew His people with kind words, but also told them of the consequences of continued rejection. If they did *not* return, judgment was waiting.

B. A vision of coming judgment.

1. (5-8) A description of coming judgment.

Declare in Judah and proclaim in Jerusalem, and say:
"Blow the trumpet in the land;
Cry, 'Gather together,'
And say, 'Assemble yourselves,
And let us go into the fortified cities.'
Set up the standard toward Zion.
Take refuge! Do not delay!
For I will bring disaster from the north,
And great destruction."
The lion has come up from his thicket,
And the destroyer of nations is on his way.
He has gone forth from his place
To make your land desolate.
Your cities will be laid waste,
Without inhabitant.
For this, clothe yourself with sackcloth,
Lament and wail.
For the fierce anger of the LORD
Has not turned back from us.

a. **Blow the trumpet in the land**: In his prophecy, Jeremiah saw an army come from the north to destroy an unrepentant Judah and Jerusalem. They busily prepared a defense (**assemble yourselves.... go into the fortified cities**), but it would be of no help.

> i. "The blowing of the horn (*sopar*) announced a state of emergency (cf. Amos 3:6). Hearing it citizens would flee for safety behind the walls of their fortified city." (Thompson)
>
> ii. "The description is the more vivid because he uses the prophetic present, which sees the judgment as already in progress, so certain is its fulfillment." (Cundall)

b. **The lion has come up from his thicket, and the destroyer of nations is on his way**: This was prophetically fulfilled when the Babylonians conquered Judah.

> i. There is debate as to if the invasion so vividly described came from the Scythians, the Assyrians, or the Babylonians. The best choice seems to be the Babylonians. "The fact remains that God's word through him not only made no mention of the Scythians, but decisively excluded them at certain points. It was Babylon, a generation later, which would bring all this to pass." (Kidner)
>
> ii. "The *lion* could represent both Assyria and Babylonia here as fierce destroyers of nations." (Harrison)

c. **Clothe yourself with sackcloth, lament and wail**: Jeremiah pictured God's people *finally* repenting, yet when it was too late to prevent the terrible judgment.

2. (9) The effect of the coming judgment.

"And it shall come to pass in that day," says the Lord,
"*That* the heart of the king shall perish,
And the heart of the princes;
The priests shall be astonished,
And the prophets shall wonder."

> a. **The heart of the king shall perish**: When the terrible judgment comes, even the nobility of Judah will lose their courage and hope.
>
> > i. "Even the rumors of impending disaster are a disaster." (Ryken)
>
> b. **The priests shall be astonished, and the prophets shall wonder**: When the terrible judgment comes, the spiritual leaders will not know what to do – because they did not return to the Lord, break up the fallow ground, and circumcise their hearts in answer to God's invitation.

3. (10) In a brief interlude, Jeremiah considers the difficult nature of judgment.

Then I said, "Ah, Lord God!
Surely You have greatly deceived this people and Jerusalem,
Saying, 'You shall have peace,'
Whereas the sword reaches to the heart."

a. **Surely You have greatly deceived this people and Jerusalem**: Jeremiah wondered if God had not **greatly deceived** His people when He promised, "**You shall have peace**." Seemingly, God promised **peace** to His people when an astonishing judgment would come upon them instead (Jeremiah 4:9).

> i. "Here we have an outburst, in which the prophet said what he thought. Many men think things like this who never utter them." (Morgan)
>
> ii. Yet it could be said that it was not the LORD who promised peace, but false prophets who claimed to speak in His name. Another use of the phrase "**You shall have peace**" (in the New King James Bible) is found in Jeremiah 23:16-17, where they are the words in the mouth of *false* prophets who prophesied peace to those who despised the LORD.
>
> iii. It wasn't the Lord GOD who greatly deceived the people and Jerusalem; it was the false prophets who promised peace when judgment was coming instead.

b. **Whereas the sword reaches to the heart**: Instead of peace, judgment would come to an unrepentant Israel, causing the kingdom to die and many with it.

4. (11-12) The sobering announcement of coming judgment.

At that time it will be said
To this people and to Jerusalem,
"A dry wind of the desolate heights *blows* **in the wilderness**
Toward the daughter of My people—
Not to fan or to cleanse—
A wind too strong for these will come for Me;
Now I will also speak judgment against them."

> a. **A dry wind of the desolate heights blows in the wilderness toward the daughter of My people**: Jeremiah announced that judgment would come upon His **people** and upon **Jerusalem**, and it would be like a wind that destroys.
>
> b. **Not to fan or to cleanse – a wind too strong tor these will come**: The judgment that would come like a wind would be so strong that it would not be like a **fan**, cooling the people; nor to **cleanse** with a gentle wind. It would destroy and bring **judgment**, like **a wind too strong**.
>
> > i. "It is the hot breath of divine judgment, consuming good and bad alike." (Harrison)

5. (13) A vision of the coming judgment.

**"Behold, he shall come up like clouds,
And his chariots like a whirlwind.
His horses are swifter than eagles.
Woe to us, for we are plundered!"**

> a. **He shall come up like clouds, and his chariots like a whirlwind**: The instruments of the announced judgment would move quickly. They would come as quickly as **clouds** move through the sky, their **chariots** as fast as **whirlwinds**, and their **horses** faster than **eagles**.
>
> b. **Woe to us, for we are plundered!** The speed of the instruments of the Lord's judgment indicated that they would be unstoppable. They would succeed in conquering and plundering God's people.

C. Appealing to those targeted for judgment.

1. (14-18) An appeal to Jerusalem.

**O Jerusalem, wash your heart from wickedness,
That you may be saved.
How long shall your evil thoughts lodge within you?
For a voice declares from Dan
And proclaims affliction from Mount Ephraim:
"Make mention to the nations,
Yes, proclaim against Jerusalem,
That watchers come from a far country
And raise their voice against the cities of Judah.
Like keepers of a field they are against her all around,
Because she has been rebellious against Me," says the LORD.
"Your ways and your doings
Have procured these *things* for you.
This *is* your wickedness,
Because it is bitter,
Because it reaches to your heart."**

> a. **O Jerusalem, wash your heart from wickedness**: Judah had made a *show* of repentance, but only in pretense (Jeremiah 3:10). Jeremiah begged the people to **wash their heart from wickedness**, not only their outward actions.
>
>> i. "Carnal hearts are stews of unclean thoughts, slaughter-houses of cruel and bloody thoughts, exchanges and shops of vain and vile thoughts, a very forge and mint of false politic undermining, thoughts, yea, oft a little hell of confused and black imaginations." (Trapp)

ii. "The insertion of this call to repentance is quite in keeping with Jeremiah's pleas in chapter 3. Even though judgment was at the doors, it would seem that Jeremiah never thought an appeal to repent was too late." (Thompson)

b. **How long shall your evil thoughts lodge within you?** The wickedness in the heart of the people of Judah brought the threat of God's judgment, but it wasn't just a **heart** problem; it was also a problem with **evil thoughts**. They indulged their evil thoughts and allowed them to **lodge** within their mind.

i. Charles Spurgeon preached a wonderful sermon on this text, titled *Bad Lodgers, and How to Treat Them*. He explained how evil thoughts were like bad renters or lodgers in a property. "Now, the Lord says, 'How long shall thy vain thoughts lodge within thee?' for they are all vain – these delays, these false promises, these self-deceptions. How long shall it be that they shall throng the avenues of your soul and curse your spirit?" (Spurgeon)

ii. Spurgeon described why evil thoughts are like bad lodgers:

- Vain thoughts are bad lodgers because they are deceitful.
- Vain thoughts are bad lodgers because they pay no rent; they bring in nothing good.
- Vain thoughts are bad lodgers because they waste your goods and destroy your property.
- Vain thoughts are bad lodgers because worse than damaging your house, they damage *you*.
- Vain thoughts are bad lodgers because they bring you under condemnation.

iii. Spurgeon then suggested what one should do with these bad lodgers:

- Give them the eviction notice at once.
- If they refuse to leave, then starve them out.
- Sell the house out from under them; put the house under new ownership.

c. **Yes, proclaim against Jerusalem, that watchers come from a far country**: This is the reason why there was an urgent, passionate appeal to truly repent – because judgment was coming in the form of an invading army.

i. "To *declare* the menace is merely to announce it as an item of news; to *proclaim* it is to publish it so forcefully that all must take notice." (Harrison)

ii. The New King James Version (and the King James Version) uses the word **watchers** to describe the invaders. Other translations give a better sense of the invading army coming against Jerusalem:

- NASB, ESV: *besiegers.*
- NIV: *a besieging army.*
- NLT: *the enemy.*

iii. **Like keepers of a field**: "Like men guarding their crops in their fields they settle down to occupy and lay siege to the land. The picture is an apt one since a largely rural population was very familiar with the small shelters or booths erected by sheepherders and farmers to protect their flocks and crops (cr. Isaiah 1:8)." (Thompson)

d. **Your ways and your doing have procured these things for you**: Before the judgment came, God gave Judah and Jerusalem clear warning that the judgment would be their fault and not God's. It would be **bitter** and reach to their **heart**, but it would be because of their **wickedness**, not God's unfaithfulness.

2. (19-21) The anguish of soul on the part of those who face judgment.

O my soul, my soul!
I am pained in my very heart!
My heart makes a noise in me;
I cannot hold my peace,
Because you have heard, O my soul,
The sound of the trumpet,
The alarm of war.
Destruction upon destruction is cried,
For the whole land is plundered.
Suddenly my tents are plundered,
***And* my curtains in a moment.**
How long will I see the standard,
***And* hear the sound of the trumpet?**

a. **O my soul, my soul! I am pained in my very heart!** Jeremiah prophetically spoke in the voice of the one **plundered** by the invading army to come. It was not only an army of material **destruction** with the loss of **land** and **tents** and **curtains**, but a true affliction of the soul.

i. The King James version gives a more literal translation of **O my soul, my soul**: *My bowels, my bowels!*

ii. **Pained**: "Is a word for intestinal discomfort. Literally, Jeremiah was 'sick to his stomach' about what was going to happen to Judah." (Ryken)

b. **How long will I see the standard, and hear the sound of the trumpet?** In the voice of the prophetic future, Jeremiah wondered how long the **destruction** and plunder of the invading army would last.

3. (22) The LORD speaks to the condition of His people.

"For My people *are* foolish,
They have not known Me.
They *are* silly children,
And they have no understanding.
They *are* wise to do evil,
But to do good they have no knowledge."

a. **For My people are foolish, they have not known Me**: God accurately diagnosed their problem when He noted that Judah was **foolish**, and especially so in their lack of true knowledge of God. Yet Yahweh was generous enough to still call them, "**My people**."

b. **They are silly children, and they have no understanding**: It is unlikely that the people of Judah saw themselves as **silly children** and without **understanding**. They probably saw themselves as sophisticated and wise.

c. **They are wise to do evil, but to do good they have no knowledge**: God explained their pretended wisdom. They were indeed wise, but in the ways of **evil**. When it came to doing **good**, they had **no knowledge**.

i. "So perverse were they that their only skills lay in doing evil. Of doing right they knew nothing." (Thompson)

4. (23-26) With prophetic insight, Jeremiah considers the might and power of God.

I beheld the earth, and indeed *it was* without form, and void;
And the heavens, they *had* no light.
I beheld the mountains, and indeed they trembled,
And all the hills moved back and forth.
I beheld, and indeed *there was* no man,
And all the birds of the heavens had fled.
I beheld, and indeed the fruitful land *was* a wilderness,
And all its cities were broken down

At the presence of the LORD,
By His fierce anger.

> a. **I beheld the earth, and indeed it was without form and void**: In turning around the images from Genesis 1, Jeremiah gives a poetic and powerful picture of the utter devastation that would come upon Judah in the coming judgment.
>
>> i. "It was as if the earth had been 'uncreated' and reverted back to its erstwhile primeval chaos. Order seemed to return to confusion." (Thompson)
>
> b. **The heavens, they had no light…the mountains, and indeed they trembled…all the hills moved back and forth…indeed there was no man…all its cities were broken down**: The judgment Jeremiah prophetically saw was complete, and it all happened **at the presence of the LORD, by His fierce anger**.
>
>> i. Similar pictures are used to describe the Day of the LORD, looking forward to the ultimate passing of this world before the new heavens and the new earth (2 Peter 3:12-13, Revelation 21:1, Isaiah 65:17).
>>
>> ii. The point for Jerusalem and Judah was plain: the God who could devastate the entire earth by His **presence** and **fierce anger** could easily bring judgment to them through an invading army. They needed to remember the greatness of the God they had offended.
>>
>> iii. Jeremiah rightly used this poetic imagery to describe the horror that would come upon Judah in the Babylonian invasion. Yet we should consider that the *fullness* of God's judgment – even *worse* than what Judah experienced – came upon Jesus Christ, God the Son, as He was crucified and judged as our substitute.

5. (27-29) The certainty and complete nature of the coming judgment.

For thus says the LORD:
"The whole land shall be desolate;
Yet I will not make a full end.
For this shall the earth mourn,
And the heavens above be black,
Because I have spoken.
I have purposed and will not relent,
Nor will I turn back from it.
The whole city shall flee from the noise of the horsemen and bowmen.
They shall go into thickets and climb up on the rocks.
Every city *shall be* **forsaken,**
And not a man shall dwell in it.

a. **The whole land shall be desolate; yet I will not make a full end**: God promised that judgment would come to Judah and Jerusalem, but the desolation would not be complete. God would not make a **full end** of the place of His people in that **land**.

i. "After this, and after the vision of a deserted landscape in Jeremiah 4:23-26, the saving clause in verse 27, '*yet I will not make a full end*', shines very brightly." (Kidner)

b. **For this shall the earth mourn and the heavens above be black**: In some way, creation itself suffers with the judgment that comes upon God's people. We know that creation groans until the completion of God's plan (Romans 8:20-22). Apparently, creation also sympathized with Israel's humiliation, even as it would rejoice in her restoration (Isaiah 55:12).

c. **Every city shall be forsaken, and not a man shall dwell in it**: God promised that the judgment to come upon Judah was both inevitable (**I have purposed and will not relent**) and would be complete, with no cities successfully holding out against the coming invaders.

6. (30-31) The vanity of hoping to appeal to the invading army of judgment.

"And *when* you *are* plundered,
What will you do?
Though you clothe yourself with crimson,
Though you adorn *yourself* with ornaments of gold,
Though you enlarge your eyes with paint,
In vain you will make yourself fair;
Your lovers will despise you;
They will seek your life.
"For I have heard a voice as of a woman in labor,
The anguish as of her who brings forth her first child,
The voice of the daughter of Zion bewailing herself;
She spreads her hands, *saying*,
'Woe *is* me now, for my soul is weary
Because of murderers!'

a. **When you are plundered, what will you do?** Through Jeremiah the Prophet, God asked Judah this important question. Perhaps they thought they could somehow appeal to the invaders as a woman might adorn and decorate herself to appeal to a man. Yet God warned them, "**In vain you will make yourself fair**."

b. **Your lovers will despise you; they will seek your life**: There was no way to decorate themselves enough to soften the judgment. It was certain. Instead of outward decoration, true repentance was their only hope.

i. "An enemy army was on the march. Yet God's people dressed up like prostitutes, putting on fancy red dresses with spangles and sequins. They took out all their gaudy jewelry and cosmetics." (Ryken)

c. **I have heard a voice as of a woman in labor**: Instead of seductive words from an adorned woman, Jeremiah prophetically heard a woman crying in pain and fear, as if she were giving birth. The screaming came from **the daughter of Zion**, who in the misery of her judgment finally understood her condition.

Jeremiah 5 – Searching for a Righteous Man

A. Looking for a righteous man but finding none.

1. (1-2) Looking for someone who seeks truth.

"Run to and fro through the streets of Jerusalem;
See now and know;
And seek in her open places
If you can find a man,
If there is *anyone* who executes judgment,
Who seeks the truth,
And I will pardon her.
Though they say, '*As* the LORD lives,'
Surely they swear falsely."

> a. **If you can find a man…who seeks the truth, and I will pardon her**: Speaking through Jeremiah, God exposed the corruption of Jerusalem of Jeremiah's day. It was as if there was not even one man who did right and sought after truth.
>
> > i. We think of Jeremiah as a predecessor to the Greek philosopher Diogenes, who reportedly carried a lamp through Athens in the daytime, searching for an honest man. Jeremiah searched for a righteous man (**who executes judgment**) who sought **the truth**. If even one could be found, God would spare His judgment against Jerusalem.
> >
> > ii. We might say that this statement was hyperbole, a literary exaggeration to make a point. After all, we would hope that Jeremiah was such a man, though he was from Anathoth, not Jerusalem (Jeremiah 1:1). Nevertheless, it's possible that this was *literally* true as well as being *poetically* true.
> >
> > iii. One may also say that God today still searches and looks for one man **who executes judgment** and **who seeks the truth** – and finds

only the One Man, Jesus Christ. He is the One Man who can save any city or individual from judgment.

b. **They say, "As the LORD lives," surely they swear falsely**: Jeremiah could find many religious people in Jerusalem – many who would swear by the LORD and say, "**As the LORD lives**." Yet he could not find anyone who sought the LORD in sincerity.

2. (3) Jeremiah's prayer.

O LORD, *are* not Your eyes on the truth?
You have stricken them,
But they have not grieved;
You have consumed them,
But they have refused to receive correction.
They have made their faces harder than rock;
They have refused to return.

a. **O LORD, are not Your eyes on the truth?** Jeremiah appealed to God who saw and cared about truth among men. He prayed with a sense of amazement at the hardness and stubbornness of heart among God's people.

i. "The allusion is not to doctrinal truth, or truth in the abstract, but to practical truth as it should exist in the hearts and lives of men. It might be read 'Lord, are not thine eyes upon truthfulness?' or 'upon faithfulness?'" (Spurgeon)

b. **You have stricken them, but they have not grieved**: Jeremiah mourned over the lack of repentance and brokenness over sin among the people of Jerusalem. They were stricken, yet not grieved; consumed, yet not corrected. Despite all they had and would endure, **they have refused to return**.

i. "There is no surer sign of a carnal Israelite, of a profligate professor, than to be senseless or incorrigible under public judgments." (Trapp)

3. (4-5) Jeremiah's plan to appeal to the great men of Jerusalem.

Therefore I said, "Surely these *are* poor.
They are foolish;
For they do not know the way of the LORD,
The judgment of their God.
I will go to the great men and speak to them,
For they have known the way of the LORD,
The judgment of their God."
But these have altogether broken the yoke
***And* burst the bonds.**

a. **Surely these are poor, they are foolish; for they do not know the way of the LORD**: As he searched for a righteous man, Jeremiah was amazed at the spiritual and moral foolishness of the people of Jerusalem. Then he considered that perhaps it was because they were **poor** and uneducated (**foolish**). *This* explained why **they do not know the way of the LORD**.

b. **I will go to the great men and speak to them**: Jeremiah then turned to the **great men**, the aristocrats of Jerusalem. With all their education and advantages, surely a righteous man could be found among them.

c. **But these have altogether broken the yoke and burst the bonds**: Jeremiah's search among the **great men** of Jerusalem ended in disappointment. They also were rebels; perhaps *educated* rebels, but rebels against God nevertheless.

4. (6-9) The penalty that will come to a rebellious city.

Therefore a lion from the forest shall slay them,
A wolf of the deserts shall destroy them;
A leopard will watch over their cities.
Everyone who goes out from there shall be torn in pieces,
Because their transgressions are many;
Their backslidings have increased.
"How shall I pardon you for this?
Your children have forsaken Me
And sworn by *those that are* **not gods.**
When I had fed them to the full,
Then they committed adultery
And assembled themselves by troops in the harlots' houses.
They were *like* **well-fed lusty stallions;**
Every one neighed after his neighbor's wife.
Shall I not punish *them* **for these** *things?***" says the LORD.**
"And shall I not avenge Myself on such a nation as this?

a. **Therefore a lion from the forest shall slay them**: Most see the **lion** and the **wolf** and the **leopard** described here as pictures of the coming invaders. Yet it is also possible that Jeremiah pictured Jerusalem and the other cities of Judah desolate and given over to wild animals. The coming war of judgment would send Judah back to much more primitive times.

i. "The lion represents strength, the desert wolf ravenousness, and the leopard swiftness – all traits of the Babylonians." (Feinberg) "So Nebuchadnezzar is called [a lion] for his cruelty, a wolf for his voracity, and a leopard for his slyness and swiftness." (Trapp)

ii. "Many towns were destroyed at the beginning of the sixth century BC and never again occupied…Others were destroyed and reoccupied after a long period of abandonment." (William Albright, cited in Ryken, regarding the archaeological evidence of the conquest of Judah).

iii. When in more faithful and obedient times Israel came into the Promised Land, God used nature to fight for them. Deuteronomy 7:20 and Joshua 24:12 speak of how God sent the hornet to chase away Israel's enemies. Now in their rebellion, God sent nature to work against Israel instead of for them.

iv. God promised this to a disobedient Israel in Leviticus 26:22: *I will also send wild beasts among you, which shall rob you of your children, destroy your livestock, and make you few in number.* Jeremiah anticipated the fulfillment of this warning.

b. **Your children have forsaken Me… when I had fed them to the full**: Judah's sin was all the worse when considered as simple *ingratitude*. God had done so much for them, yet spiritually speaking **they committed adultery**.

i. Their spiritual **adultery** – going after pagan gods – was also connected to sexual adultery. The so-called worship of pagan gods often involved ritual prostitutes and sexual immorality. The ideas of spiritual and sexual adultery were connected and combined.

c. **Then they committed adultery and assembled themselves by troops in the harlots' houses**: Jeremiah not only saw multitudes going to the so-called sacred prostitutes, but they were *organized* as if an army (**by troops**). This was a powerful and poetic description of how given over the people were to pagan worship and ritual prostitution.

i. "There was a sexual aspect to religion throughout the Fertile Crescent, although the goddesses of fertility played a much greater role among the Canaanites than among any other ancient people. Sacred prostitution was an almost invariable accompaniment of the cult of the fertility-goddesses in Phoenicia and Syria." (Thompson, referring to Albright's *From the Stone Age to Christianity*, pages 233, 235)

ii. "They preferred to call the temple prostitute a *zona* (profane woman) rather than use the Canaanite term *qedesa* (holy woman)." (Thompson)

d. **Shall I not punish them for these things?** As Jeremiah searched Jerusalem, he found no righteous men or men of truth. He did find spiritual rebels and adulterers. This was a nation due for judgment.

B. Prophets of wind, prophets of fire.

1. (10-13) Destruction without a complete end.

"Go up on her walls and destroy,
But do not make a complete end.
Take away her branches,
For they *are* not the LORD's.
For the house of Israel and the house of Judah
Have dealt very treacherously with Me," says the LORD.
They have lied about the LORD,
And said, "*It is* not He.
Neither will evil come upon us,
Nor shall we see sword or famine.
And the prophets become wind,
For the word *is* not in them.
Thus shall it be done to them."

> a. **Go up on her walls and destroy, but do not make a complete end**: Destroyed walls usually signaled a complete end; but not with the God of Israel. Here is a promise to bring restoration and revival – a promise partially fulfilled in the rebuilding work of Ezra and Nehemiah, and fully fulfilled in the restoration of Israel to their Messiah, Jesus Christ.
>
>> i. **Take away her branches**: "The *branches* of the vine have not borne the fruits of righteousness, and so will be burned up while the stock will be saved. This figure is reflected very closely by Christ in John 15:1-6." (Harrison)
>
> b. **They have lied about the LORD, and said, "It is not He"**: When the false prophets assured the people of Judah and Jerusalem that their present problems were not warnings and corrections from the Lord, they **lied about the LORD**. When they promised, "**Neither will evil come upon us**," they **lied about the LORD**.
>
>> i. Perhaps these false prophets meant well and hoped to encourage Judah and Jerusalem. Perhaps the false prophets actually believed their own message. Nevertheless, they **lied about the LORD** – which is a serious and grievous sin. In our own day, we say to false prophets, even those who mean well and believe their own lies: *stop lying about the LORD*.
>
> c. **And the prophets become wind, for the word is not in them**: The false prophets were nothing more than **wind** – movement without substance. God's **word** was not **in them**, and their so-called prophetic words were from *them*, not from the substance of God's **word**.

i. Several commentators believe the phrase **the prophets have become wind** refers to how the people regarded the true prophets of God – regarding them only as windbags.

2. (14-17) The word of the prophet of fire.

**Therefore thus says the LORD God of hosts:
"Because you speak this word,
Behold, I will make My words in your mouth fire,
And this people wood,
And it shall devour them.
Behold, I will bring a nation against you from afar,
O house of Israel," says the LORD.
"It *is* a mighty nation,
It *is* an ancient nation,
A nation whose language you do not know,
Nor can you understand what they say.
Their quiver *is* like an open tomb;
They *are* all mighty men.
And they shall eat up your harvest and your bread,
Which your sons and daughters should eat.
They shall eat up your flocks and your herds;
They shall eat up your vines and your fig trees;
They shall destroy your fortified cities,
In which you trust, with the sword.**

a. **I will make My words in your mouth fire, and this people wood, and it shall devour them**: In contrast to the prophets of wind mentioned in the previous verse, God would make Jeremiah a prophet of **fire** – whose words would announce the devouring judgment to come. As a true prophet, Jeremiah's words would have substance – but unpleasantly so.

b. **Behold, I will bring a nation against you from afar**: Jeremiah repeated the promise that God would bring a mighty army of judgment against Judah and Jerusalem, later fulfilled by the Babylonians under Nebuchadnezzar.

i. **Their quiver is like an open tomb**: "They would be invincible because their quivers would be filled with death-dealing arrows, always bringing more destruction. Every arrow could be depended on to slay someone." (Feinberg)

3. (18-19) The divine logic behind judgment.

"Nevertheless in those days," says the LORD, "I will not make a complete end of you. And it will be when you say, 'Why does the LORD our God do all these *things* to us?' then you shall answer them, 'Just as you have

forsaken Me and served foreign gods in your land, so you shall serve aliens in a land *that is* not yours.'"

> a. **I will not make a complete end of you**: The gracious promise is again repeated. Though devastating judgment would come to Judah and Jerusalem, God would not forsake His covenant people and would bring restoration.
>
> b. **Just as you have forsaken Me and served foreign gods in your land, so you shall serve aliens in a land that is not yours**: The explanation for God's judgment was basic and sensible. The people of Judah and Jerusalem served foreign gods; now God will send them to serve the people of the gods they worshipped.

C. A foolish people.

1. (20-25) The foolishness of failing to learn from nature.

"Declare this in the house of Jacob
And proclaim it in Judah, saying,
'Hear this now, O foolish people,
Without understanding,
Who have eyes and see not,
And who have ears and hear not:
Do you not fear Me?' says the LORD.
'Will you not tremble at My presence,
Who have placed the sand as the bound of the sea,
By a perpetual decree, that it cannot pass beyond it?
And though its waves toss to and fro,
Yet they cannot prevail;
Though they roar, yet they cannot pass over it.
But this people has a defiant and rebellious heart;
They have revolted and departed.
They do not say in their heart,
"Let us now fear the LORD our God,
Who gives rain, both the former and the latter, in its season.
He reserves for us the appointed weeks of the harvest."
Your iniquities have turned these *things* away,
And your sins have withheld good from you.

> a. **Hear this now, O foolish people**: Through Jeremiah, God spoke to Judah and Jerusalem, exposing their spiritual and moral foolishness in resisting and rejecting Him.
>
> b. **Though its waves toss to and fro, yet they cannot prevail**: Jeremiah used the illustration of the ocean and the sand. The waters of the sea continually

pound upon the sand, yet the sand remains, and the sea remains within its bounds. The analogy is clear: if the ocean cannot prevail against the sand, God's people will never prevail in their rebellion against Him.

> i. "God has chosen to arrest the advance of the mighty billows by a barrier of sand-grains… There are many illustrations of this in the history of the Church. The pride of the persecutor has been arrested by the prayers and tears of men, women, and children, who have had no more strength in themselves than a bank of sand-grains, but have succeeded in arresting the might of their foes." (Meyer)

c. **But this people has a defiant and rebellious heart**: God's people did not learn the lesson that nature clearly teaches – that it is foolish to fight against God.

> i. "God here contrasts the obedience of the strong, the mighty the untamed sea, with the rebellious character of his own people. 'The sea,' saith he, 'obeys me; it never breaks its boundary; it never leapeth from its channel; it obeys me in all its movements. But man, poor puny man, the little creature whom I could crush as the moth, will not be obedient to me.'" (Spurgeon)

d. **Your iniquities have turned these things away, and your sins have withheld good from you**: God described the blessings of rain and harvest and then told Judah why they did not have those blessings in abundance. Their **sins** had **withheld good from** them; it wasn't God's fault.

> i. **Your iniquities**, **your sins**: "The two words used here for Israel's breaches of covenant are common in the OT, but may have some special point here. The first, *awon*, is related to a root which means 'to wander, err,' and the second, *hattat* to a root meaning 'to miss the mark.' Israel had both wandered away from Yahweh and failed to reach the goal set for her." (Thompson)

2. (26-29) The wickedness of those who do not care for their fellow man.

'For among My people are found wicked *men*;
They lie in wait as one who sets snares;
They set a trap;
They catch men.
As a cage is full of birds,
So their houses *are* full of deceit.
Therefore they have become great and grown rich.
They have grown fat, they are sleek;
Yes, they surpass the deeds of the wicked;
They do not plead the cause,

The cause of the fatherless;
Yet they prosper,
And the right of the needy they do not defend.
Shall I not punish *them* for these *things?*' says the LORD.
'Shall I not avenge Myself on such a nation as this?'

> a. **They lie in wait as one who sets snares; they set a trap; they catch men**: In using the picture of a bird-catcher (a fowler), it is possible that Jeremiah had in mind those who steal men unto slavery. It is more likely that he had in mind those who use their positions of power and influence to **become great** and grow **rich**, at the expense of the weak and needy.
>
>> i. "The metaphor of the bird-catcher runs through the passage. As the fowler's basket is filled with birds, so the houses of these wicked men are filled with *treachery* or 'deceit.'" (Thompson)
>
> b. **They do not plead the cause, the cause of the fatherless**: Instead of taking advantage of the weak and needy, these wicked men should have used their positions of power and influence to do good for them.
>
> c. **Yet they prosper**: Their prosperity was not from the blessing of God. It was the result of their own sinful ambition and enterprise – and therefore invited the judgment of God (**Shall I not punish them for these things**).

3. (30-31) The false prophets and the people who love them.

"An astonishing and horrible thing
Has been committed in the land:
The prophets prophesy falsely,
And the priests rule by their *own* power;
And My people love *to have it* so.
But what will you do in the end?"

> a. **An astonishing and horrible thing has been committed in the land**: These were strong words, introducing something that was truly **horrible** in the eyes of God.
>
> b. **The prophets prophesy falsely**: The first **astonishing and horrible thing** was the false words of the pretended prophets. They claimed to speak in the name of the LORD, yet they spoke **falsely**.
>
>> i. "Prophets of God are the nations truest servants and friends. False prophets are the worst enemies of the nation. Their popularity is the last evidence of national decay." (Morgan)
>
> c. **And the priests rule by their own power**: The second **astonishing and horrible thing** was that the leaders among God's people rule not by the love and leadership of God, but **by their own power**. Their authority and

leadership was of man, not of God – like the leadership of the Gentiles later described by Jesus (Matthew 20:25-26).

d. **And My people love to have it so**: The third **astonishing and horrible thing** was that *God's people were perfectly happy to have false prophets and corrupt leadership*. This reminds us that *popularity among God's people* is never to be regarded as a guarantee that one speaks for the Lord or leads in the godly manner.

> i. The people "Are perfectly satisfied with this state of things, because they are permitted to continue in their sins without reproof or restraint. The prophets and the priests united to deceive and ruin the people." (Clarke)

> ii. "Prophets, priests, and people were united in their sin, and there was no alternative other than that of judgment." (Morgan)

e. **But what will you do in the end?** Though the false prophets and corrupt leaders were loved among the people of God, there was no true foundation to their work. There was no substance, and nothing stable to rest upon **in the end**. Disaster would come and the false prophets and corrupt pleaders would be of no help in that day.

> i. "Ah, dear young friends, if I could bring some of the living and some of the dead, and set them to witness here instead of me, they would burn in on you, as my poor words never can do, the insanity of living without a satisfactory and sufficient reply to the question of my text, 'What will ye do in the end?'" (Maclaren)

Jeremiah 6 – Full of the Fury of the LORD

A. Warnings of judgment.

1. (1-5) Disaster from the north.

"O you children of Benjamin,
Gather yourselves to flee from the midst of Jerusalem!
Blow the trumpet in Tekoa,
And set up a signal-fire in Beth Haccerem;
For disaster appears out of the north,
And great destruction.
I have likened the daughter of Zion
To a lovely and delicate woman.
The shepherds with their flocks shall come to her.
They shall pitch *their* tents against her all around.
Each one shall pasture in his own place."
"Prepare war against her;
Arise, and let us go up at noon.
Woe to us, for the day goes away,
For the shadows of the evening are lengthening.
Arise, and let us go by night,
And let us destroy her palaces."

> a. **O you children of Benjamin**: The southern kingdom of Judah began when the two tribes of Judah and Benjamin remained faithful to the line of David in the days of Rehoboam and Jeroboam (1 Kings 12). Because of the place of the tribe of **Benjamin** in the southern kingdom, God sometimes referred to it as **Benjamin**.
>
>> i. "The reason the people of Benjamin are mentioned is that geographically Jerusalem belonged to the territory of Benjamin… Moreover, Jeremiah was a Benjaminite and had strong ties with his own tribesmen." (Feinberg)

b. **Gather yourselves to flee from the midst of Jerusalem**: The idea was that a siege army would come to the capital of the southern kingdom, and those wise enough to see it would **flee** the city before the siege army surrounded and conquered Jerusalem.

> i. The **signal-fire** was specifically mentioned in the Lachish Letters, which documented the eventual Babylonian invasion. "The use of such signals was an ancient Mesopotamian method of military communication." (Harrison)

c. **I have likened the daughter of Zion to a lovely and delicate woman**: Judah liked to think of themselves as beautiful and refined. Yet a **lovely and delicate woman** can't stand before an invading army. They would be terribly mismatched in the coming invasion.

> i. "To the pasture of Zion the *shepherds* (for this description of the invaders see Jeremiah 12:10) drive their flocks of soldiers, eager to feed upon the richness of the area." (Harrison)

> ii. **Prepare war against her**: "The Hebrew verb for *Prepare* (*qaddesu*) may suggest the religious rituals preceding a battle in the ancient institution of the holy war." (Thompson)

d. **Woe to us, for the day goes away, for the shadows of the evening are lengthening**: God reminded Judah that *time was running out*. Even though this judgment would not come for many years, the tipping point that made it certain was much closer than they thought. Soon, the army of Babylon would come to Jerusalem to **destroy her palaces**.

e. **Arise, and let us go by night**: The coming invaders were so urgent they would attack at night, not even waiting for day.

2. (6-8) A siege against Jerusalem.

For thus has the LORD of hosts said:
"Cut down trees,
And build a mound against Jerusalem.
This *is* the city to be punished.
She *is* full of oppression in her midst.
As a fountain wells up with water,
So she wells up with her wickedness.
Violence and plundering are heard in her.
Before Me continually *are* grief and wounds.
Be instructed, O Jerusalem,
Lest My soul depart from you;
Lest I make you desolate,
A land not inhabited."

> a. **For thus has the LORD of hosts said: "Cut down the trees, and build a mound against Jerusalem"**: Jeremiah understood and explained that the coming siege against Jerusalem was *God's* work. Though they were the strange instruments of God's work, one could not simply blame it on the Babylonians as if God had nothing to do it.
>
> b. **She is full of oppression in her midst**: Jerusalem's lack of love for God was demonstrated by a lack of care and concern for their fellow man. Being **full of oppression** was both a horizontal (from man to man) and a vertical (from man to God) phenomenon.
>
>> i. **She wells up with her wickedness**: "Jerusalem is Sin City. There is always a fresh supply of evil welling up like poison within her and overflowing into her streets." (Ryken)
>
> c. **Be instructed, O Jerusalem**: Even within the announcement of judgment is the inherent invitation to *receive* the wisdom of God and avoid the threatened calamity. It was an invitation that Judah would not properly receive.

3. (9-12) The fullness of the fury of the LORD.

> Thus says the LORD of hosts:
> "They shall thoroughly glean as a vine the remnant of Israel;
> As a grape-gatherer, put your hand back into the branches."
> To whom shall I speak and give warning,
> That they may hear?
> Indeed their ear *is* uncircumcised,
> And they cannot give heed.
> Behold, the word of the LORD is a reproach to them;
> They have no delight in it.
> Therefore I am full of the fury of the LORD.
> I am weary of holding *it* in.
> "I will pour it out on the children outside,
> And on the assembly of young men together;
> For even the husband shall be taken with the wife,
> The aged with *him who is* full of days.
> And their houses shall be turned over to others,
> Fields and wives together;
> For I will stretch out My hand
> Against the inhabitants of the land," says the LORD.

> a. **They shall thoroughly glean as a vine the remnant of Israel**: God warned Judah that they would be picked clean by the Babylonians, even as those who gleaned the remaining grapes from a vine took everything they could.

b. **To whom shall I speak and give warning, that they may hear?** We sense the frustration of the prophet; he speaks, but no one listens. Their ears are not spiritual, as if their ears were **uncircumcised** – and they regard God's word as **a reproach**, something to be ashamed of and avoided.

> i. **Indeed their ear is uncircumcised**: The Old Testament speaks many times of uncircumcised hearts and lips, but this is the only mention of the uncircumcised ear. Stephen used this figure of speech in speaking to the Jewish council (Acts 7:51).
>
> ii. **The word of the Lord is a reproach to them**: "It is an object of *derision*; they *despise it*." (Clarke)

c. **They have no delight in it**: Their low regard for the word of the Lord was evident in this. The word of the Lord was of no delight to them; they took no pleasure in it or found no sweetness in it. *This was an indication that the people of God were ripe for judgment.*

d. **Therefore I am full of the fury of the Lord**: Because God's people were full of oppression and wickedness and *would not listen to the word of the Lord*, God was **full** of **fury** against them – and was **weary of holding it in**.

e. **For I will stretch out My hand against the inhabitants of the land**: The judgment to come upon Judah would impact everyone. It would affect the **children**, the **young men**, and the **aged**; both the **husband** and the **wife**, and even the **fields** would feel it.

4. (13-15) The sins of prophets and priests.

> "Because from the least of them even to the greatest of them,
> Everyone *is* given to covetousness;
> And from the prophet even to the priest,
> Everyone deals falsely.
> They have also healed the hurt of My people slightly,
> Saying, 'Peace, peace!'
> When *there is* no peace.
> Were they ashamed when they had committed abomination?
> No! They were not at all ashamed;
> Nor did they know how to blush.
> Therefore they shall fall among those who fall;
> At the time I punish them,
> They shall be cast down," says the Lord.

> a. **Everyone is given to covetousness…everyone deals falsely**: God looked at the culture of the Kingdom of Judah and saw how thoroughly greedy and corrupt it was. Even – or perhaps especially – the **prophet** and the **priest** were part of the greed and corruption.

b. **They have also healed the hurt of My people slightly**: God not only condemned the more obvious sins of **covetousness** and corruption, but also the subtle sins of the prophets who used smooth words to comfort and calm the people when they should be alarmed and provoked to repentance.

i. **Healed the hurt of my people slightly** has the sense, "they dress the wound of my people as though it were not serious." (Feinberg) "As men use to cure the slight hurts of their children by blowing on them only, or stroking them over." (Trapp)

ii. "In our dealings with God let us…ask that He will not spare us, or give us anything less than the best. The process may be painful and protracted, but it will be sure." (Meyer)

c. **Saying, "Peace, peace!" When there is no peace**: These were the smooth words of the false prophets, assuring Judah that everything was fine when in fact it was not.

i. **Peace, peace** is a wonderful message to bring, and one that most people want to hear. The problem is that sometimes it isn't true. Sometimes there is war and conflict that we must deal with, whether we would like to or not. Most significantly, there are times when God's word to His people is not **peace**, but "repent" and "prepare for judgment."

ii. "They may be saying peace, peace, when there is no peace, in many ways. They may do it, by silence, refusing to refer to evil practices. They may do it by speaking of evil as though it were only the underside of good, and inevitable thing. They may even do it in denying that there is any such thing as evil." (Morgan)

iii. In a sermon titled *A Blast of the Trumpet Against False Peace*, Charles Spurgeon suggested a few ways that many people receive a false peace.

- Some have peace because they live for entertainment and excitement, distracting them from higher things.
- Some have peace because they tell themselves there is no God and therefore no accountability before Him.
- Some have peace because they are ignorant of the things of God and need to be told the truth of their responsibility.
- Some have peace because they intend to do better later in life and such future wishes are enough to make them right.

d. **They were not at all ashamed**: For all of Judah's many sins, they were not genuinely **ashamed** at all; **nor did they know how to blush**. It was as if the normal workings of the conscience were damaged or burned over, and they were not ashamed over what they should be.

> i. G. Campbell Morgan considered the work of Jeremiah to be like the work of every faithful preacher: "His business is to create a sense of shame in the souls of men, so to place their corruption before them as to compel the hot blush to their faces."

B. Wisdom available and wisdom rejected.

1. (16-17) The opportunity for wisdom.

Thus says the LORD:
"Stand in the ways and see,
And ask for the old paths, where the good way *is*,
And walk in it;
Then you will find rest for your souls.
But they said, 'We will not walk *in it*.'
Also, I set watchmen over you, *saying*,
'Listen to the sound of the trumpet!'
But they said, 'We will not listen.'

> a. **Stand in the ways and see, and ask for the old paths, where the good way is**: Even though they were in such a bad place, there was wisdom available for Judah. One place they would find wisdom was in **the old paths** – looking to their history and forefathers, to learn from what God had done in and through them before.
>
> > i. "The people have been urged to follow *the ancient paths* of Mosaic tradition, which will be the best because they are tried and true." (Harrison)
> >
> > ii. "The ancient paths and the good way are the same; they are the way of repentance, reconciliation, fear, and love of God. They were the ways of the Mosaic tradition." (Feinberg)
> >
> > iii. Many despise the **old paths**. Perhaps they seem old fashioned or terribly un-cool. Yet there is wisdom – life saving wisdom – in the **old paths** of God's word and work in days gone by.
> >
> > - To benefit from the **old paths**, God told them to position themselves (**stand in the ways**).
> > - To benefit from the **old paths**, God told them to look for them (**see**).
> > - To benefit from the **old paths**, God told them to **ask** for them, to desire them.

- To benefit from the **old paths**, God told them to see them as **the good way**.
- To benefit from the **old paths**, God told them to **walk in it** – to actually *obey* and *follow* God as indicated by His word and work in days gone by.

b. **Then you will find rest for your souls**: This is the rich reward for seeking, seeing, and walking in the **old paths**. This is a reward that can't be matched by anything.

i. "Let us observe the metaphor. A *traveller* is going to a particular city; he comes to a place where the road divides into several paths, he is afraid of going astray; he stops short, endeavours to find out the right path: he cannot fix his choice. At last he sees another traveller; he inquires of him, gets proper directions-proceeds on his journey-arrives at the desired place-and *reposes* after his fatigue." (Clarke)

ii. Jesus likely quoted Jeremiah 6:16 (**rest for your souls**) in Matthew 11:29: *Take My yoke upon you and learn from Me, for I am gentle and lowly in heart, and you will find rest for your souls.*

c. **But they said, "We will not walk in it"**: Despite God's instruction and invitation, Judah rejected the wisdom of the **old paths**. Even though **watchmen** called attention to them, as if blowing **the sound of the trumpet**, yet **they said, "We will not listen."**

i. A phenomenon of the modern age – especially through the internet – there are many who consider themselves **watchmen**, feeling they have a word, instruction, or rebuke for the people of God that can be ignored only at great cost. It may be true that God sends His people **watchmen**; yet there is a great difference between those who are **set** by God and those who are self-appointed. The difference can often be seen in the manner and heart of those who consider themselves watchmen.

2. (18-20) God tells the whole world the result of Judah's rejection of wisdom.

Therefore hear, you nations,
And know, O congregation, what *is* among them.
Hear, O earth!
Behold, I will certainly bring calamity on this people—
The fruit of their thoughts,
Because they have not heeded My words
Nor My law, but rejected it.
For what purpose to Me
Comes frankincense from Sheba,

And sweet cane from a far country?
Your burnt offerings *are* not acceptable,
Nor your sacrifices sweet to Me."

> a. **Hear, O earth!** God spoke to both the **nations**, warning them of the **calamity** to come upon His **people**.
>
>> i. "Ordinarily *edah* ('congregation.' KJV, RSV) refers in the OT to Israel, but here it must mean the Gentiles…The Gentiles are being alerted to what is to happen to Judah." (Feinberg)
>
> b. **I will certainly bring calamity on this people – the fruit of their thoughts, because they have not heeded My words**: This was an important aspect of the guilt of God's people. They did not heed the word of God, and therefore became corrupt in their thinking. The coming **calamity** was **the fruit of their thoughts**.
>
> c. **Your burnt offerings are not acceptable**: The people of God continued bringing offerings and sacrifices to God, even expensive **frankincense from Sheba**. Yet because they did not heed God's words or accept His law, the sacrifices were **not acceptable**. Religious ceremony – even sweet-smelling sacrifices – could not cover over their basic rejection of God's word and ways.

C. The judgment to come again described.

1. (21) The stumbling blocks.

Therefore thus says the LORD:
"Behold, I will lay stumbling blocks before this people,
And the fathers and the sons together shall fall on them.
The neighbor and his friend shall perish."

> a. **I will lay stumbling blocks before this people**: God would deal with His people directly. The coming judgment was not an accident of the expansion of the Babylonian Empire or geopolitics between Babylon and Egypt. The LORD set this stumbling block.
>
>> i. The **stumbling blocks** were the Babylonians, and instruments of God's judgment and correction against Judah.
>>
>> ii. Jeremiah's context is different, but we naturally connect this with the idea that Messiah is the cornerstone and those who reject Him stumble over it (1 Peter 2:7).
>
> b. **The fathers and sons together shall fall on them**: God again tells of the universal character of this judgment coming against Judah. None would escape it; both the **fathers and sons together**, the **neighbor and his friends shall perish**.

2. (22-26) The terror of the coming judgment.

Thus says the LORD**:**
"Behold, a people comes from the north country,
And a great nation will be raised from the farthest parts of the earth.
They will lay hold on bow and spear;
They *are* **cruel and have no mercy;**
Their voice roars like the sea;
And they ride on horses,
As men of war set in array against you, O daughter of Zion."
We have heard the report of it;
Our hands grow feeble.
Anguish has taken hold of us,
Pain as of a woman in labor.
Do not go out into the field,
Nor walk by the way.
Because of the sword of the enemy,
Fear *is* **on every side.**
O daughter of my people,
Dress in sackcloth
And roll about in ashes!
Make mourning *as for* **an only son, most bitter lamentation;**
For the plunderer will suddenly come upon us.

> a. **A people comes from the north country, and a nation will be raised from the farthest parts of the earth**: God again warned Judah that the Babylonians would come to be the messengers of God's judgment against them.
>
> b. **They are cruel and have no mercy**: The coming Babylonian army would bring terrible misery, and Judah would react with **anguish**, **pain**, **fear**, and **mourning**.
>
>> i. "Judah was unequal to the encounter as a weak, defenseless woman in the pangs of childbirth before a powerful, fully equipped soldier." (Thompson)

3. (27-31) God's people judged as metals are tested.

"I have set you *as* **an assayer** *and* **a fortress among My people,**
That you may know and test their way.
They *are* **all stubborn rebels, walking as slanderers.**
They are **bronze and iron,**
They *are* **all corrupters;**
The bellows blow fiercely,
The lead is consumed by the fire;

The smelter refines in vain,
For the wicked are not drawn off.
People will call them rejected silver,
Because the LORD has rejected them."

> a. **I have set you as an assayer and a fortress among My people, that you may know and test their way**: God sent Jeremiah to assess the spiritual condition of God's people and to do it from a position of strength (**a fortress**). Figuratively, the work of the prophet was like metal working – one who tested and refined precious metals.
>
>> i. **Fortress**: "The word *mibsar* (EVV 'fortress') presents difficulties, but if vocalized as *mebasser*, with RSV, it could be rendered 'assessor', thus constituting a gloss on *assayer*." (Harrison)
>>
>> ii. The picture used at the end of Jeremiah 6 works something like this:
>>
>> - Judah was like the metal, claiming to be precious (such as gold or silver).
>> - Like a precious metal, Judah was tested and refined with fire.
>> - Lead was put in to act as flux, to draw the impurities to itself.
>> - The Prophet Jeremiah was like the bellows, used to create an intense heat.
>> - Yet Israel – the supposed precious metal – was so hard and impure that the refining work was useless.
>
> b. **They are bronze and iron, they are all corrupters**: The people of God were not like a soft metal that could be refined and purified (like silver or gold). Instead, they were hard like **bronze and iron**.
>
>> i. **Stubborn rebels**: "Hebrew, Revolters of revolters." (Trapp) "Using a superlative, Jeremiah evaluates them as the rebellious of the rebellious." (Feinberg)
>
> c. **The bellows blow fiercely, the lead is consumed**: The fire was as hot as the bellows could make it and the refining agent (**lead**) was consumed – yet the supposedly precious metal was not refined.
>
> d. **The smelter refines in vain, for the wicked are not drawn off**: Despite the best efforts of the **smelter** – God's prophets such as Jeremiah – the wicked among God's people did not repent and thereby be **drawn off** in the sense of making a purer people of God.
>
>> i. "Jeremiah felt that his task was similar to that of a silver-refiner (*cf.* Malachi 3:3), but it is now clear that his prophetic 'fire' has been unable to remove the impurities from the natural 'silver'." (Harrison)

ii. "Using the picture of a refiner of precious metals, He shows that the normal processes had been completely inefficacious, the dross still remained, contaminating the whole mass of metal. It was, therefore fit only for the scrap-heap." (Cundall)

e. **People will call them rejected silver, because the Lord has rejected them**: At the end of it all, *everyone* knew that Judah was disapproved by God and in the sense of sparing them from judgment, **the Lord has rejected them**.

i. "This picture of the prophet's words as a refiner's fire makes its point not only by its vivid detail but by its tragic outcome. For it emerges that the people of Judah are not, so to speak, precious metal marred by some impurities, but base metal from which nothing of worth can be extracted." (Kidner)

Jeremiah 7 – Preaching at the Temple Gate

A. The sermon at the temple gate.

1. (1-4) Superficial trust in the temple and external religion.

The word that came to Jeremiah from the LORD, saying, "Stand in the gate of the LORD's house, and proclaim there this word, and say, 'Hear the word of the LORD, all *you of* Judah who enter in at these gates to worship the LORD!'" Thus says the LORD of hosts, the God of Israel: "Amend your ways and your doings, and I will cause you to dwell in this place. Do not trust in these lying words, saying, 'The temple of the LORD, the temple of the LORD, the temple of the LORD are these.'

> a. **Stand in the gate of the LORD's house**: God told Jeremiah to publically preach this word from the LORD, and to do it right at the gate of the temple. Jeremiah needed plenty of courage and boldness to do his work.
>
>> i. It's easy to imagine Jeremiah speaking to the busy crowds of people and priests coming in and out of the temple area. Perhaps many stopped to listen, but apparently none truly *heard* his word from the LORD.
>>
>> ii. "Since his message was delivered to all the people, it was most likely preached during one of the great religious festivals, such as Passover or the Feast of Tabernacles, when the whole nation came to Jerusalem to worship." (Ryken)
>>
>> iii. Jeremiah 26 also has Jeremiah preaching at the temple gate in the first year of the reign of Jehoiakim, in a sermon with many of the same themes. Some think this is the same sermon as in Jeremiah 26; others think it is an earlier delivery of a similar sermon, delivered in the same place. Jeremiah 26:8-11 indicates that after that sermon, Jeremiah was attacked and threatened with death.

b. **Amend your ways and your doings, and I will cause you to dwell in this place**: God offered to hold back on promised judgment if Judah would *truly* repent – not only in words, but in their **ways and doings**.

c. **Do not trust in these lying words, saying, "The temple of the LORD, the temple of the LORD"**: The crowds at the temple obviously had some trust in the temple and its service. Jeremiah boldly warned them that their trust was unfounded and dangerous. External religion and rituals would not help them if they failed to **amend** their **ways** and **doings**.

i. "For them, therefore, Temple worship was little better than a charm for averting evil, and they had beguiled the people into trusting in material buildings." (Harrison)

ii. We can imagine how one of the false prophets of Jeremiah's day might twist the Scriptures to "prove" that the temple could never be conquered.

- God promised an everlasting dynasty to David (2 Samuel 7:12-15).
- God chose Zion as His early abode (Psalm 132:13-18).
- Jerusalem and the temple were miraculously saved from destruction from the Assyrian army more than 100 years before (2 Kings 18:13-19:37). Surely this proved God would never allow Jerusalem or the temple to be conquered.

All of this reasoning was faulty, even if scriptures could be twisted to support it. The reasoning forgot that:

- God always holds the inner spiritual reality to be greater than the outward form.
- Any Scriptural reasoning that gives cover for and license to sin and idolatry is wrong and faulty.

iii. We today don't say, **"The temple of the LORD, the temple of the LORD"** as they did in Jeremiah's day. Today some say, "I go to church, I go to church, I go to church"; or "I'm a conservative, I'm a conservative, I'm a conservative"; or "I'm Calvary Chapel, I'm Calvary Chapel, I'm Calvary Chapel." None of these things make one right from God apart from truth faith and true repentance.

iv. "Men may perform the most sacred rites, and yet perpetuate the grossest crimes." (Meyer)

2. (5-7) Real repentance and its reward.

"For if you thoroughly amend your ways and your doings, if you thoroughly execute judgment between a man and his neighbor, *if* you do not oppress the stranger, the fatherless, and the widow, and do not shed innocent blood in this place, or walk after other gods to your hurt, then I will cause you to dwell in this place, in the land that I gave to your fathers forever and ever.

- a. **If you thoroughly amend your ways and your doings**: Through Jeremiah, God explained to the people what real repentance looked like.

  - **If you thoroughly executed judgment between a man and his neighbor**: The courts of ancient Judah had become corrupt and honest judgment could not be found there.

  - **If you do not oppress the stranger, the fatherless, and the widow**: God cared about how His people treated the weak and defenseless in society, and noticed when these weak ones were oppressed instead of helped.

  - **Do not shed innocent blood**: People were murdered, apparently in the name of religion (**in this place**). "Nor could Yahweh tolerate the judicial murders which broke out from time to time in Israel and were evidently perpetrated also during the reign of Jehoiakim (Jeremiah 26:23)." (Thompson)

  - **Or walk after other gods to your hurt**: Idolatry was always a danger, *even for those who came to do business at the temple*. This shared loyalty (to both the LORD and the idols) was always to their **hurt**.

    i. We notice that of these four aspects of demonstrated repentance, only one of them deals with a man's relationship with God; three of the four deal with man's relationship to his fellow man. *God cares about how we treat one another*, and true repentance will extend into the way we treat each other.

- b. **Then I will cause you to dwell in this place**: The previous promises of an army of judgment and exile from the land would be set aside if Judah did truly, deeply repent – not only with words, but with action.

- c. **In the land that I gave to your fathers forever and ever**: Apparently, God considered the promises of the land given to Abraham and his covenant descendants to be an enduring gift all through the history of Israel.

  i. There are some who mistakenly say that the words of Joshua 21:43, 45 say that God completely fulfilled the land promise to Israel, and therefore after that point they had no more claim to the land. Yet a passage like this – written more than 600 years after God's word to Joshua – shows that the land promise to Israel *continued* **forever and ever**.

3. (8-11) Trusting in lying words regarding a temple that is a den of thieves.

"Behold, you trust in lying words that cannot profit. Will you steal, murder, commit adultery, swear falsely, burn incense to Baal, and walk after other gods whom you do not know, and *then* come and stand before Me in this house which is called by My name, and say, 'We are delivered to do all these abominations'? Has this house, which is called by My name, become a den of thieves in your eyes? Behold, I, even I, have seen *it*," says the LORD.

> a. **You trust in lying words that cannot profit**: This was a bold thing to say to the crowds at the temple gates. Yet they needed to know that they could not **steal, murder, commit adultery** and **walk after other gods** thinking the customs and rituals of temple observance could cover it.
>
> b. **And then come and stand before Me in this house which is called by My name and say, "We are delivered to do all these abominations"**: Jeremiah had in mind those who believed that their temple rituals and obligations gave them permission and cover to sin in these ways.
>
>> i. This was not the practice of later Roman Catholic granting of indulgences, but it was the same spirit of that unbliblical practice.
>
> c. **Has this house, which is called by My name, become a den of thieves in your eyes?** Instead of being a place where God was truly sought, where sacrifices were sincerely offered, and where repentance was true, the temple had become a **den** (a gathering and hiding place) **of thieves**.
>
>> i. "The temple is the House of Jehovah in which men may dwell in fellowship with Him, and so in strength and rest, if their ways are in harmony with His will. But the temple is not a refuge for men who are living in rebellion against Him. It gives security and rest to obedient souls. It offers no security to men if they are living in sin." (Morgan)
>>
>> ii. "Robbers and bandits who sally forth for robbery and plunder secure for themselves a hideout in some secluded area, to which they retire for protection and safety." (Thompson)
>>
>> iii. Jesus quoted this "**den of thieves**" line from Jeremiah 7 in Matthew 21:13 (also recorded in Mark 11:17 and Luke 19:46) to speak of the corruption of the temple service in His own day. When the temple should have been a house of prayer for all nations, it had become a **den of thieves**.

d. **Behold, I, even I, have seen it**: Normally a **den of thieves** operates in secret. Through Jeremiah, God wanted His people to know that He *did* see their hidden, secret sins.

4. (12-15) The example of Shiloh.

"But go now to My place which *was* in Shiloh, where I set My name at the first, and see what I did to it because of the wickedness of My people Israel. And now, because you have done all these works," says the LORD, "and I spoke to you, rising up early and speaking, but you did not hear, and I called you, but you did not answer, therefore I will do to the house which is called by My name, in which you trust, and to this place which I gave to you and your fathers, as I have done to Shiloh. And I will cast you out of My sight, as I have cast out all your brethren—the whole posterity of Ephraim.

a. **But go now to My place which was in Shiloh, where I set My name at the first, and see what I did to it because of the wickedness of My people Israel**: Jeremiah spoke to the crowds at the temple gate and asked them to compare Jerusalem and the temple grounds to **Shiloh**.

i. **Shiloh** was the central city of Israel – the religious center – for almost 400 years. It was the place where the tabernacle of meeting and the altar of God stayed for this long period.

ii. **Shiloh** enjoyed all this glory for hundreds of years, but it came to an end abruptly. First, when the Philistines overran Shiloh (1 Samuel 4); finally when the Assyrians conquered the northern kingdom of Israel many years after that (Psalm 78:58-60).

iii. By Jeremiah's day **Shiloh** had been in ruins for a long time, and it showed that hosting the house of God or the ark of the covenant did not mean that judgment was impossible. As it came to Shiloh, it could come to an unrepentant Jerusalem.

iv. "The archaeological evidence shows that Shiloh was destroyed twice over – once by the Philistines and once when the Assyrians carried the northern tribes into captivity. When Jeremiah told the people to go to Shiloh he was telling them to go to the place where God is not." (Ryken)

b. **I spoke to you, rising up early and speaking, but you did not hear, and I called you, but you did not answer**: Judah's greatest sin was ignoring the word of God so plainly and persistently brought to them. This made them without excuse.

c. **Therefore I will do to the house which is called by My name, in which you trust…as I have done to Shiloh**: God promised to bring the same judgment to Jerusalem that came upon Shiloh.

> i. God used Shiloh as a lesson. "Go to Shiloh," He says. "Look what happened to a place of spiritual privilege and glory when they forgot about Me. The same will happen to you if you do not turn again to Me." Many cities are filled with empty and decrepit old churches; these are like Shiloh – places where God was once worshipped and honored, but no more.

> ii. The lesson should be sealed in our hearts: no matter how much spiritual progress, or privilege, or glory one might have, it can all be turned to nothing if we stop listening to God and cultivating our relationship with Him.

B. The price of provoking the LORD God.

1. (16-19) Don't pray for those who provoke the anger of the LORD.

"Therefore do not pray for this people, nor lift up a cry or prayer for them, nor make intercession to Me; for I will not hear you. Do you not see what they do in the cities of Judah and in the streets of Jerusalem? The children gather wood, the fathers kindle the fire, and the women knead dough, to make cakes for the queen of heaven; and *they* pour out drink offerings to other gods, that they may provoke Me to anger. Do they provoke Me to anger?" says the LORD. "*Do they* not *provoke themselves, to the shame of their own faces?*"

a. **Therefore do not pray for this people**: It would seem that the sermon at the temple gates was finished, and now God spoke to Jeremiah about the hardened people. They were past prayer; God simply told Jeremiah, **for I will not hear you**.

> i. It is significant that God had to tell Jeremiah not to pray; the assumption is that he would pray, and that God had to tell him not to. Yet, "Their day of grace is past, their sins are full, the decree is now gone forth, and it is irreversible, therefore pray not for this deplored people." (Trapp)

> ii. There is something along these lines in the New Testament, at 1 John 5:14-16, where John explained that there are some people – at least in theory – who are beyond prayer, and therefore prayer should not be made for them.

> iii. "They have filled up the measure of their iniquity, and they must become examples of my justice. How terrible must the state of that

place be, where God refuses to pour out the spirit of supplication on his ministers and people in its behalf!" (Clarke)

b. **The children gather wood, the fathers kindle the fire, and the women knead dough, to make cakes for the queen of heaven**: The idolatry of Judah and Jerusalem was a family affair. Each member of the family had their own role to play in honoring pagan gods such as **the queen of heaven**.

i. "The 'queen of heaven' was the Babylonian Ishtar, identified with the planet Venus, whose worship, similar to the cults of the Canaanite goddesses, Asherah, Ashtaroth and Anath, was probably introduced into Judah by the apostate king, Manasseh (2 Kings 21:3ff)." (Cundall)

ii. "The word *cakes* (*kawwanim*) is of foreign origin, occurring again only in Jeremiah 44:19, where the same cult is described." (Harrison) "A female deity is foreign to Old Testament theology; so the implication is that this cult was of non-Hebraic origin." (Feinberg)

iii. "There is goddess worship in the Roman Catholic religion, where Mary is sometimes given the title 'The Queen of Heaven.' This title sets off alarm bells for anyone who knows the book of Jeremiah." (Ryken)

iv. "Family worship is a most amiable and becoming thing when performed according to truth. What a pity that so few families show such zeal for the worship of God as those apostate Israelites did for that of their idols!" (Clarke)

c. **Do they not provoke themselves, to the shame of their own faces?** It was true that the sins of Judah provoked the LORD to anger, but it was also true that their sins provoked themselves to open shame.

2. (20) God's answer to the provoking of His anger.

Therefore thus says the Lord GOD: "Behold, My anger and My fury will be poured out on this place—on man and on beast, on the trees of the field and on the fruit of the ground. And it will burn and not be quenched."

a. **Behold, My anger and My fury will be poured out on this place**: Judah provoked the LORD to anger, so it was appropriate that the anger eventually be **poured out**, and poured out upon the land as well as upon the people.

b. **It will burn and not be quenched**: The anger of the LORD would not relent until its full purpose was accomplished.

3. (21-26) Disobedience and sacrifice.

Thus says the LORD of hosts, the God of Israel: "Add your burnt offerings to your sacrifices and eat meat. For I did not speak to your fathers, or

command them in the day that I brought them out of the land of Egypt, concerning burnt offerings or sacrifices. But this is what I commanded them, saying, 'Obey My voice, and I will be your God, and you shall be My people. And walk in all the ways that I have commanded you, that it may be well with you.' Yet they did not obey or incline their ear, but followed the counsels *and* the dictates of their evil hearts, and went backward and not forward. Since the day that your fathers came out of the land of Egypt until this day, I have even sent to you all My servants the prophets, daily rising up early and sending *them.* Yet they did not obey Me or incline their ear, but stiffened their neck. They did worse than their fathers.

a. **Add your burnt offerings to your sacrifices and eat meat**: The **burnt offerings** were to be completely burnt before God. Here God said, "You aren't giving these **burnt offerings** to Me anyway, so you might as well just eat them as you do your other sacrifices."

i. "The essential feature of the whole burnt offering was that it was entirely consumed by fire (Leviticus 1:9, 13), unlike the other offerings, where at least a portion was shared by the priests or the worshippers. God here is virtually saying, 'What does it matter to Me; eat the lot!'" (Cundall)

b. **For I did not speak to your fathers, or command them in the day that I brought them out of the land of Egypt, concerning burnt offerings or sacrifices**: When God gave Israel the Ten Commandments at Mount Sinai, there was nothing about sacrifice or priesthood. That only came later, once Israel had accepted the covenant (Exodus 24:1-8). The point is clear: God's first priority for Israel was obedience – sacrifice and the priesthood were secondary.

i. "Jeremiah was really indicating that the order of revelation was indicative of the relative value of obedience and cultic observances." (Thompson)

ii. "The Hebrew idiom permits denial of one thing in order to emphasize another (cf. for a parallel Luke 14:26). The idiom does not intend to deny the statement but only to set it in a secondary place." (Feinberg)

iii. "It was not wrong for them to sacrifice, but their sacrifices were in vain because they were not pursuing holiness." (Ryken)

c. **This is what I commanded them, saying, "Obey My voice"**: What God had to say about sacrifice in the Old Covenant was rather small compared to what He had to say about simple *obedience*. It was clear at the temple gates that Judah still loved to bring sacrifices to the altar, but what God really wanted was their obedience, that they would **walk in all the ways I have commanded you**.

> i. This is much the same thought as 1 Samuel 15:22: *Then Samuel said: "Has the LORD as great delight in burnt offerings and sacrifices, As in obeying the voice of the LORD? Behold, to obey is better than sacrifice, And to heed than the fat of rams.*

d. **Yet they did not obey or incline their ear, but followed the counsels and the dictates of their evil hearts, and went backward and not forward**: Sacrifice continued, but obedience stopped. Instead of following the LORD, they **followed the counsels and the dictates of their evil hearts**. The heart of man or woman isn't necessarily a good guide to God-pleasing behavior.

> i. This "follow your heart" mentality made the people of Judah feel good, but it did not bring them true blessing and progress. They **went backward and not forward**. It made them **worse than their fathers**. Morally and spiritually they were in a state of regress, not progress.

4. (27) The frustrating work of Jeremiah the prophet.

"Therefore you shall speak all these words to them, but they will not obey you. You shall also call to them, but they will not answer you.

a. **You shall speak all these words to them**: God gave Jeremiah a solemn commission to speak to the people of Jerusalem and Judah. It wasn't Jeremiah's ambition or even his natural desire.

b. **They will not obey you. You shall also call to them, but they will not answer you**: This word to Jeremiah repeats the thought from earlier in the chapter. Jeremiah 7:13 says, *I spoke to you, rising up early and speaking, but you did not hear, and I called you, but you did not answer*. God's word through the prophet was *God's word*, and it was proper to regard it as such.

5. (28-31) The evil of idolatry.

"So you shall say to them, 'This *is* a nation that does not obey the voice of the LORD their God nor receive correction. Truth has perished and has been cut off from their mouth. Cut off your hair and cast *it* away, and take up a lamentation on the desolate heights; for the LORD has rejected and forsaken the generation of His wrath.' For the children of Judah have done evil in My sight," says the LORD. "They have set their abominations in the house which is called by My name, to pollute it. And they have built the high places of Tophet, which *is* in the Valley of the Son of Hinnom, to burn their sons and their daughters in the fire, which I did not command, nor did it come into My heart.

a. **So you shall say to them**: In light of their hardened rejection of Yahweh and His words, Jeremiah was to bring the following message to them.

b. **The LORD has rejected and forsaken the generation of His wrath**: There are several reasons listed *why* God so radically punished Judah.

- **This is a nation that does not obey the voice of the LORD**: They continued with their superficial rituals such as animal sacrifice, but had long abandoned simple obedience.
- **Nor receive correction**: Worse than their disobedience was their inability to be corrected. There was no helping a people who would not **receive correction**.
- **Truth has perished and has been cut off from their mouth**: In rejecting the truth of God, they gave themselves over to lies and falsehood.

c. **Cut off your hair and cast it away, and take up a lamentation on the desolate heights**: The command for Judah to **cut off your hair** was either as an expression of mourning (as in Job 1:20 and Micah 1:16) or of a Nazirite vow ended by defilement.

> i. "The cutting off of the hair was a symbol of grief (Job 1:20; Micah 1:16). The Hebrew text reads literally 'Cut off your crown (*nezer*).' The hair was looked on as, in a sense, a diadem. To cut off the hair was to bring down Israel's pride." (Thompson)

> ii. "The charge stems from the fact that the Nazirite's hair was the mark of his separation to God (Numbers 6:5). When he was ceremonially defiled, he had to shave his head. So Jerusalem because of her corruption must do likewise." (Feinberg)

d. **They have set their abominations in the house which is called by My name, to pollute it**: The people and priests of Judah were so insensitive to the honor of Yahweh that they set up idols in the very house of the LORD, the temple.

> i. Surely they did not put an idol into the holy place or the most holy place, but in some side room of the temple complex. Nevertheless, the idols were **abominations**. "It would be like setting up a Shinto shrine or opening up an adult book shop in your church fellowship hall. Even if everything else in the church remained the same – pews, Bibles, songbooks – the place of worship would still be defiled." (Ryken)

e. **They have built the high places of Tophet, which is in the Valley of the Son of Hinnom, to burn their sons and daughters in the fire**: Worse than the idolatry in the temple was the actual *human sacrifice* carried out right in the region of Jerusalem.

> i. **The high places**: "The 'high places' of Biblical times were not always very high. These particular high places, for example, were down in a valley. It was an inaccessible rocky ravine south and west of the City of Jerusalem. But a 'high place' is a shrine, a raised platform built out of stones for the purpose of worship." (Ryken)
>
> ii. "Topheth probably derives from the Hebrew word for 'fire-place' (cf. Isaiah 30:33)." (Cundall) Kidner also points out that the name **Topheth** rhymes with *bosheth*, the Hebrew word for "shame."
>
> iii. The **Valley of the Son of Hinnom** lies south of the temple mount in Jerusalem. It was used as both a garbage dump (with continually smoldering fires) and a place of child sacrifice.
>
> iv. Some think that child sacrifice in ancient Canaan and Israel was rare, and resorted to only in times of great distress. It's hard to say how common it was, but it was practiced even by kings. "Ahaz, King of Israel, sacrificed his own son in the fire (2 Kings 16:3). The same thing happened in Manasseh's day, when children were sacrificed to the gods of Canaan (2 Kings 21:6)." (Ryken)
>
> v. The Valley of Hinnom gives us the idea of *Gehenna* in the New Testament. *Gehenna* is a Greek word borrowed from the Hebrew language. In Mark 9:43-44, Jesus spoke of *hell* (*gehenna*) referring to this place outside Jerusalem's walls desecrated by Molech worship and human sacrifice (2 Chronicles 28:1-3; Jeremiah 32:35). It was also a garbage dump where rubbish and refuse were burned. The smoldering fires and festering worms of the Valley of Hinnom made it a graphic and effective picture of the fate of the damned. This place is also called the "lake of fire" in Revelation 20:13-15, prepared for the devil and his angels (Matthew 25:41).

f. **Which I did not command, nor did it come into My heart**: Unlike many of the Canaanite deities, Yahweh never commanded human sacrifice. God could say that it never did **come into** His **heart** to ask such a thing; it totally went against His nature.

> i. "Some scholars point out that the priests of Topheth may have used the Torah to justify child sacrifice: 'You must give me the firstborn of your sons…on the eighth day' (Exodus 22:29-30). They were taking that verse out of context; it had nothing to do with child sacrifice." (Ryken)

ii. The incident of Abraham's interrupted sacrifice of Isaac (Genesis 22) was an emphatic way for God to say, "I do not want human sacrifice."

6. (32-34) The dead in the Valley of the Son of Hinnom.

"Therefore behold, the days are coming," says the LORD, "when it will no more be called Tophet, or the Valley of the Son of Hinnom, but the Valley of Slaughter; for they will bury in Tophet until there is no room. The corpses of this people will be food for the birds of the heaven and for the beasts of the earth. And no one will frighten *them away*. Then I will cause to cease from the cities of Judah and from the streets of Jerusalem the voice of mirth and the voice of gladness, the voice of the bridegroom and the voice of the bride. For the land shall be desolate.

a. **It will no more be called Tophet, or the Valley of the Son of Hinnom, but the Valley of Slaughter**: God would answer the idolatry of Judah and the outrageous practice of human sacrifice with devastating judgment. There would be a grotesque slaughter in that valley.

i. The dead corpses in that place would also be disgraced by having no proper burial, and by being food for scavenger birds with **no one to frighten them away**.

ii. "For the body to remain unburied, thereby, providing food for carrion birds and rodents, was a thing of unspeakable horror for the ancient Hebrews. Ironically, their sanctuary would become their cemetery as the treasured homeland was ravaged." (Harrison)

b. **For the land shall be desolate**: When judgment came upon Judah, it would seem that all happiness and hope had departed from the land. No more would there be **the voice of mirth and the voice of gladness**.

Jeremiah 8 – No Cure for Senseless Rejection of God

A. Those fallen, those exiled.

1. (1-2) The disgraced remnants of those fallen in judgment.

"At that time," says the Lord, "they shall bring out the bones of the kings of Judah, and the bones of its princes, and the bones of the priests, and the bones of the prophets, and the bones of the inhabitants of Jerusalem, out of their graves. They shall spread them before the sun and the moon and all the host of heaven, which they have loved and which they have served and after which they have walked, which they have sought and which they have worshiped. They shall not be gathered nor buried; they shall be like refuse on the face of the earth.

> a. **At that time**: This connects with the severe judgment announced in the closing verses of Jeremiah 7. The prophet saw the Valley of Hinnom filled with rotting corpses, food for scavenging birds.
>
> b. **They shall bring out the bones of the kings of Judah...the bones of the priests, and the bones of the prophets**: Jeremiah prophetically saw a final indignity given in judgment to these great transgressors. Even the **bones** of the wicked who died before the Babylonians came would be disgraced; they would **not be gathered nor buried; they shall be like refuse on the face of the earth**.
>
>> i. "This custom of raising the bodies of the dead, and scattering their bones about, seems to have been general. It was the highest expression of hatred and contempt. [The Greek poet] *Horace* refers to it." (Clarke)
>>
>> ii. "There is a gruesome congruity about the bones of the devotees of the heavenly host being openly strewn before their impotent objects of worship." (Cundall)

2. (3) Choosing death rather than life.

Then death shall be chosen rather than life by all the residue of those who remain of this evil family, who remain in all the places where I have driven them," says the LORD of hosts.

> a. **Then death shall be chosen rather than life by all the residue of those who remain**: The misery of the **residue** that survived the Babylonian invasion would be worse than life. Death would look to them like a welcome relief.
>
> b. **Who remain in all the places where I have driven them**: The survivors of the Babylonian invasion would be forced refugees, exiled out of the Promised Land into foreign lands.

B. Judah's stubborn folly.

1. (4-7) Judah's stubborn refusal to return.

"Moreover you shall say to them, 'Thus says the LORD:
"Will they fall and not rise?
Will one turn away and not return?
Why has this people slidden back,
Jerusalem, in a perpetual backsliding?
They hold fast to deceit,
They refuse to return.
I listened and heard,
But they do not speak aright.
No man repented of his wickedness,
Saying, 'What have I done?'
Everyone turned to his own course,
As the horse rushes into the battle.
"Even the stork in the heavens
Knows her appointed times;
And the turtledove, the swift, and the swallow
Observe the time of their coming.
But My people do not know the judgment of the LORD."

> a. **Why has this people slidden back, Jerusalem, in a perpetual backsliding**: Through His prophet, Jeremiah, the LORD expressed amazement that Judah would not return to Him. After all, when one falls, they rise again. When one turns away, they then return. Yet Judah was caught in **a perpetual backsliding**.
>
>> i. **Will they fall and not rise? Will one turn away and not return?** "If men fall it is naturally expected that they will return. In the case of Jerusalem this had not been so, their backsliding had been perpetual. There was no sign of repentance." (Morgan)

b. **Everyone turned to his own course, as the horse rushes into the battle**: Men were determined to go their own way, as determined and as energetic as the horse is as it **rushes into the battle**.

c. **Even the stork in the heavens knows her appointed times**: It is an amazement that birds (**the stork, the turtledove, the swift, and the swallow**) all understand the seasons of the year and how they must respond to them. Yet the people of God were ignorant; **My people do not know the judgment of the LORD**. They were worse off than birds with small brains.

> i. Spurgeon preached a sermon titled, *Migratory Birds*. He began, "We shall mark these migratory birds, and set the wisdom of their instinct in contrast with the folly of mankind." Spurgeon proceeded to make the following four points:
>
> - The migratory birds know *when* to come and go.
> - The migratory birds know *where* to go.
> - The migratory birds, by some strange instinct, also know *the way* to go.
> - The migratory birds show their wisdom by *actually going* to the sunny land.

2. (8-9) The folly of rejecting the word of the LORD.

"How can you say, 'We *are* wise,
And the law of the LORD is with us'?
Look, the false pen of the scribe certainly works falsehood.
The wise men are ashamed,
They are dismayed and taken.
Behold, they have rejected the word of the LORD;
So what wisdom do they have?

> a. **We are wise, and the law of the LORD is with us**: This is what the people of Judah said of themselves. They were so self-deceived that they actually believed they were **wise**, and that they walked according to the **law of the LORD**.
>
> b. **Look, the false pen of the scribe certainly works falsehood**: God reminded Judah that not all who study and teach the word of God do so honestly. There are some who use their **pen** to work **falsehood**, not truth.
>
> c. **They have rejected the word of the LORD; so what wisdom do they have?** Though they claimed to have both wisdom and Biblical truth, they had neither. In rejecting God's **word**, they rejected **wisdom**. They had none.

i. "When men reject the word of Jehovah, 'What manner of wisdom is in them?' The answer is that the manner of such wisdom is, to quote James, 'earthly, sensual, devilish' (James 3:13)." (Morgan)

3. (10-13) The judgment to come upon those who reject the word of the LORD.

Therefore I will give their wives to others,
And* their fields to those who will inherit *them;
Because from the least even to the greatest
Everyone is given to covetousness;
From the prophet even to the priest
Everyone deals falsely.
For they have healed the hurt of the daughter of My people slightly,
Saying, 'Peace, peace!'
When *there is* no peace.
Were they ashamed when they had committed abomination?
No! They were not at all ashamed,
Nor did they know how to blush.
Therefore they shall fall among those who fall;
In the time of their punishment
They shall be cast down," says the LORD.
"I will surely consume them," says the LORD.
"No grapes *shall be* on the vine,
Nor figs on the fig tree,
And the leaf shall fade;
And *the things* I have given them shall pass away from them.""

a. **Therefore I will give their wives to others, and their fields to those who will inherit them**: Because they did not hold the word of God dear, God would take what was dear to the people of Judah and give those things to others.

b. **Everyone is given to covetousness; from the prophet even to the priest everyone deals falsely**: Repeating words from Jeremiah 6:13-15, Jeremiah points out that selfish corruption had become so much a part of life in Judah that it could be said that **everyone deals falsely** and yet **they were not at all ashamed**.

i. The repetition in these verses as compared to Jeremiah 6:13-15 was not accidentally. It was done on purpose, because Judah needed to hear this message, and delivering it one time was simply not enough.

c. **Therefore they shall fall among those who fall...they shall be cast down**: Because the moral and cultural rot was so deep among the people of Judah, God promised to bring a thorough judgment. Like a grape vine or a fig tree picked clean, God promised, **I will surely consume them**.

4. (14) Fleeing to the fortified cities under the judgment of God.

"Why do we sit still?
Assemble yourselves,
And let us enter the fortified cities,
And let us be silent there.
For the L<small>ORD</small> **our God has put us to silence**
And given us water of gall to drink,
Because we have sinned against the L<small>ORD</small>**.**

> a. **Let us enter the fortified cities, and let us be silent there**: The prophet imagined the people of God fleeing to the fortified cities as the Babylonian invaders entered the land. They could only do so in silence, because they knew they had ignored God's warnings and invitations to repent.
>
> b. **For the** L<small>ORD</small> **our God has put us to silence and given us water of gall to drink, because we have sinned against the** L<small>ORD</small>: When the invading army came, they would understand the greatness of their sin – but by then it would be too late.

5. (15-17) Looking for peace, finding trouble.

"*We* looked for peace, but no good *came*;
And for a time of health, and there was trouble!
The snorting of His horses was heard from Dan.
The whole land trembled at the sound of the neighing of His strong ones;
For they have come and devoured the land and all that is in it,
The city and those who dwell in it."
"For behold, I will send serpents among you,
Vipers which cannot be charmed,
And they shall bite you," says the L<small>ORD</small>**.**

> a. **We looked for peace, but no good came**: Those in Judah who heard and believed the message of the false prophets – the message, *Peace, peace!* (Jeremiah 8:11) – these deceived ones **looked for peace, but no good came**.
>
> b. **They have come and devoured the land and all that is in it**: Instead of peace, the Babylonian invaders came with snorting horses and an army so big that the **whole land trembled**.
>
> c. **I will send serpents among you, vipers which cannot be charmed**: The false prophets and priests had convinced the people of Judah and Jerusalem that they could find a way to maneuver around the coming judgment. They would find, to their great sorrow, that God had sent them serpents **which cannot be charmed**.

C. Judah in exile.

1. (18-19) A vision of Judah in exile.

> I would comfort myself in sorrow;
> My heart *is* faint in me.
> Listen! The voice,
> The cry of the daughter of my people
> From a far country:
> "*Is* not the LORD in Zion?
> *Is* not her King in her?"
> "Why have they provoked Me to anger
> With their carved images—
> With foreign idols?"

a. **I would comfort myself in sorrow; my heart is faint in me**: With desperation, Jeremiah prophetically saw the tragedy that followed upon the devastating Babylonian invasion.

b. **The cry of the daughter of my people from a far country**: This was the cause of Jeremiah's desperation. The **daughter of** his **people** no longer lived in the land God promised them. Instead, their cry was heard **from a far country**.

c. **Is not the LORD in Zion? Is not her King in her?** In amazement, Jeremiah wondered how his people ended up in exile. He wondered if God had left His own land; if He no longer reigned as a **King** in Zion.

d. **Why have they provoked Me to anger with their carved images – with foreign idols?** God answered Jeremiah's question with questions of His own. The problem was not that God had abandoned the land of Israel; the problem was Israel had abandoned God.

2. (20) The despair of conquered Judah.

> "The harvest is past,
> The summer is ended,
> And we are not saved!"

a. **The harvest is past, the summer is ended**: In a mostly agricultural society, everyone understood that **summer** was the season of growing, ending with **harvest**. It should be a time of abundance and fulfillment.

> i. "'Harvest' refers to the main cereal harvest, whilst 'summer' refers to the vintage harvest (grapes, etc.) in early autumn. If one failed, it was possible that the other would see the people through the winter, but if both failed, starvation confronted them." (Cundall)

b. **And we are not saved!** This was the sad lament of conquered Judah, even into the exile. Season had come that there should be abundance in the land, yet there was not. They had to face the sad fact: **we are not saved!**

> i. "It was a proverbial saying meaning that people had lost every opportunity given them by God, and now were entirely without hope." (Feinberg)

> ii. "Jeremiah 8:20's analogy is that of a double failure, first of the field-crops, then of the summer fruit, heralding a winter that hardly bears thinking about." (Kidner)

> iii. "We thought that God would help us in the days of harvest; but the harvest is past. We dreamed that he would chase away our enemies when the summer months had come; but the summer is ended, and still Chaldea has her foot upon Judea's neck, still we drink the wormwood and the gall, and our enemies open their mouths at us. The harvest is past, and the summer is ended, and we are not saved." (Spurgeon)

3. (21-22) Jeremiah's pain-filled question.

For the hurt of the daughter of my people I am hurt.
I am mourning;
Astonishment has taken hold of me.
***Is there* no balm in Gilead,**
***Is there* no physician there?**
Why then is there no recovery
For the health of the daughter of my people?

a. **For the hurt of the daughter of my people I am hurt**: Prophetically looking into the future, Jeremiah ached with the hurt of his people. He was in **mourning** and full of **astonishment**.

> i. "Jeremiah could mourn over the sufferings of his people because of his sympathy and love for them; yet his very message spoke doom to them." (Thompson)

> ii. "A preacher whom God sends will often feel more care for the souls of men than men feel for themselves or their own salvation." (Spurgeon)

b. **Is there no balm in Gilead, is there no physician there?** Jeremiah not only saw the hurt of his people in exile, but he also could see no help for them. There was no medicine, there was no physician; all was sadness and mourning.

> i. "Gilead was the land just east of the Jordan River. It was known for its healing balsams… Scholars have been unable to determine how

the balm of Gilead was made, but it seems to have been a soothing, aromatic resin made from a tree or a plant. It might be compared to aloe vera." (Ryken)

Jeremiah 9 – What to Take Glory In

A. The continued lament over Judah in exile.

1. (1-2) Not enough tears.

Oh, that my head were waters,
And my eyes a fountain of tears,
That I might weep day and night
For the slain of the daughter of my people!
Oh, that I had in the wilderness
A lodging place for travelers;
That I might leave my people,
And go from them!
For they *are* all adulterers,
An assembly of treacherous men.

> a. **Oh, that my head were waters**: In the close of the previous chapter, Jeremiah lamented Judah, as he prophetically saw them conquered and exiled. Continuing that thought, he poetically expressed the idea that he didn't have enough tears or time to adequately express his grief over **the slain of the daughter of my people.**
>
>> i. Because there was something tender and sympathetic about Jeremiah's tears, they were *good*. "Such waters will be turned into wine, at the wedding-day of the Lamb; for which purpose also they are kept safe in God's bottle (Psalm 56:8)." (Trapp)
>
> b. **Oh, that I had in the wilderness a lodging place for travelers; that I might leave my people, and go from them!** Jeremiah was filled with sorrow over the coming judgment upon Judah, but he was also filled with a sense of disgust over their sin. He wanted to **leave** his **people** and get away from the corruptions of Jerusalem and Judah.
>
>> i. "From the image of continuous weeping like a perennial spring, Jeremiah passes to that of a person anxious to escape the corruption.

For him the wilderness is preferable to the degradation of city life." (Harrison)

ii. "Even a lonely lodging in the desert was preferable to the soul anguish he experienced in the midst of his people." (Feinberg)

iii. **An assembly of treacherous men**: This was something like saying, *a congregation of treacherous men*. "The Hebrew word *seret* ('crowd') is used for solemn assemblies on pilgrimage feasts." (Feinberg)

2. (3-6) Judah given over to deception and lies.

"And *like* their bow they have bent their tongues *for* lies.
They are not valiant for the truth on the earth.
For they proceed from evil to evil,
And they do not know Me," says the LORD.
"Everyone take heed to his neighbor,
And do not trust any brother;
For every brother will utterly supplant,
And every neighbor will walk with slanderers.
Everyone will deceive his neighbor,
And will not speak the truth;
They have taught their tongue to speak lies;
They weary themselves to commit iniquity.
Your dwelling place *is* in the midst of deceit;
Through deceit they refuse to know Me," says the LORD.

a. **Like their bow they have bent their tongues for lies**: Jeremiah vividly described how given to deception the leaders and people of Judah were. They lied with forethought, with skill, with power, with intent. Their **bent** tongues sent for arrows of lies.

i. It is significant to remember that this comes at the conclusion of a section where Jeremiah desperately lamented the fall and exile of Judah (Jeremiah 8:18-9:6). In the depth of his grief, he still could not forget *they deserved this calamity*. Their rejection of God and devotion to the lie made all that came upon them deserved.

b. **For they proceed from evil to evil, and they do not know Me**: This explains *why* Judah's leaders and people could lie so easily. They were mired in **evil** and far from real relationship with God. They did not **know** Him in a true, relational, honoring way.

i. **They do not know Me**: "The verb *yada*, 'know,' denotes much more than intellectual knowledge but rather that deep intimate knowledge that follows the personal commitment of one life to another." (Thompson)

ii. **For every brother will utterly supplant**: "Judah's treachery and unfaithfulness towards God made Jeremiah realize that everyone was a Jacob or *supplanter*...a pun on the name of Jacob." (Harrison)

iii. **They weary themselves to commit iniquity**: "O, what a drudgery is sin! And how much labour must a man take in order to get to hell!" (Clarke)

c. **Everyone will deceive his neighbor, and will not speak the truth**: Jeremiah observed how *deep* and how *wide* the sin of lying and deception was among the leaders and people of Judah. It was a culture given over to deception, far from truth in either daily matters or in broader concepts.

i. Jeremiah's dark description of Judah also describes today's culture. We live in an age when the very idea of absolute or objective truth is commonly rejected. When truth is not valued, societies crumble.

ii. Many intractable problems in today's world are actually problems of *truth*. In the Arab-Israeli conflict, horrific lies about the Jews are officially promoted and widely believed in the Arab world. If the Arab world only heard and believed the *truth* about Israel and the Jews, their supposed reasons for hatred would largely vanish.

d. **Through deceit they refuse to know Me, says the LORD**: This is the greatest cost of embracing and promoting deception. Since God is a God of truth, those who love the lie have a fundamental distance from Him.

B. The coming judgment, and how to prepare for it.

1. (7-11) The fact, reason, and result of coming judgment.

Therefore thus says the LORD of hosts:
"Behold, I will refine them and try them;
For how shall I deal with the daughter of My people?
Their tongue *is* an arrow shot out;
It speaks deceit;
***One* speaks peaceably to his neighbor with his mouth,**
But in his heart he lies in wait.
Shall I not punish them for these *things*?" says the LORD.
"Shall I not avenge Myself on such a nation as this?"
I will take up a weeping and wailing for the mountains,
And for the dwelling places of the wilderness a lamentation,
Because they are burned up,
So that no one can pass through;
Nor can *men* hear the voice of the cattle.
Both the birds of the heavens and the beasts have fled;
They are gone.

"I will make Jerusalem a heap of ruins, a den of jackals.
I will make the cities of Judah desolate, without an inhabitant."

> a. **I will refine and try them**: Remembering the picture of the metal refiner (Jeremiah 6:27-30), God again told Judah that He would **refine** them. The heat and melting to come were certain. Yet the *purpose* was also certain – not to destroy, but to **refine** and ultimately to purify.
>
>> i. This statement – "**I will refine and try them**" – comes as the answer to God's question, "**how shall I deal with the daughter of My people?**" "In order that we may understand something of the workings of the divine mind, he represents himself as brought to a non-plus, and saying, in the words of our text, 'How shall I do for the daughter of my people?'" (Spurgeon)
>>
>> ii. **I will refine and try them**: "The Lord is so resolved to save his people, that he will use the sternest possible means rather than lose any of those whom he loves." (Spurgeon)
>
> b. **Their tongue is an arrow shot out; it speaks deceit**: Using images from the previous verse, God explained one reason why Judah was a certain target of His judgment. The ingrained and institutionalized deception among the leaders and people of Judah invited His strong correction.
>
>> i. **Such a nation as this**: "The use of the term *goy* for Israel may represent the transfer to Israel of a term which was regularly used of non-Israelite peoples. Its use here suggests that Jeremiah had come to regard the people as no different in their behavior from the *goyim*, the peoples outside the covenant." (Thomspon)
>
> c. **They are burned up, so that no one can pass through**: With a prophet's vision of the future, Jeremiah saw the destroyed and **burned** cities and villages of Judah. There was no civilization, only **a heap of ruins**. There were no more livestock and farm animals, only **a den of jackals**. All this would be the result of the coming Babylonian invasion.
>
>> i. Divine justice sets the fire of indignation burning. Nothing excites God's wrath more than continued falsehood and deceit, unkindness, unbrotherly conduct, and unholiness of life. Put all these evils together, and you have more than enough God-provoking sins calling for an avenging visitation." (Spurgeon)

2. (12-16) The cause and result of judgment summarized.

Who *is* the wise man who may understand this? And *who is he* to whom the mouth of the LORD has spoken, that he may declare it? Why does the land perish *and* burn up like a wilderness, so that no one can pass through? And the LORD said, "Because they have forsaken My law

which I set before them, and have not obeyed My voice, nor walked according to it, but they have walked according to the dictates of their own hearts and after the Baals, which their fathers taught them," therefore thus says the LORD of hosts, the God of Israel: "Behold, I will feed them, this people, with wormwood, and give them water of gall to drink. I will scatter them also among the Gentiles, whom neither they nor their fathers have known. And I will send a sword after them until I have consumed them."

> a. **Because they have forsaken My law…have not obeyed My voice, nor walked according to it**: God *told* Israel in His word what they should believe and how they should live. Yet the leaders and people of Judah rejected His word and disregarded God's law.
>
> b. **But they have walked according to the dictates of their own hearts and after the Baals**: In rejecting the word and guidance of God, Judah did not *stop* believing and serving something. Instead they lifted their **own hearts** to the place of God in their life, and they served the pagan gods of the surrounding culture (**the Baals**).
>
>> i. It could be said that God designed us to be worshipful, obedient beings. If those instincts for worship and obedience are not directed toward the living God and His word, they will be directed somewhere else. In Judah's case, they were directed toward self and cultural gods.
>>
>> ii. Harrison on Baal worship: "This lewd, orgiastic cult had proved attractive to many generations of Israelites."
>>
>> iii. "It is clear from a reading of the religious and legendary texts of Ugarit that many of the cultic practices associated with Baal and the fertility cult were heavily orientated toward sexual activity." (Thompson)
>
> c. **I will feed them, this people, with wormwood, and give them water of gall to drink. I will scatter them also among the Gentiles**: God would not ignore the disobedience and idolatry of Judah. He promised to answer it with bitter judgment and exile.

3. (17-21) Calling for the mourning women.

Thus says the LORD of hosts:
"Consider and call for the mourning women,
That they may come;
And send for skillful wailing women,
That they may come.
Let them make haste
And take up a wailing for us,

That our eyes may run with tears,
And our eyelids gush with water.
For a voice of wailing is heard from Zion:
'How we are plundered!
We are greatly ashamed,
Because we have forsaken the land,
Because we have been cast out of our dwellings.'"
Yet hear the word of the LORD, O women,
And let your ear receive the word of His mouth;
Teach your daughters wailing,
And everyone her neighbor a lamentation.
For death has come through our windows,
Has entered our palaces,
To kill off the children—*no longer to be* outside!
And the young men—*no longer* on the streets!

> a. **Consider and call for the mourning women**: As he thought about the great calamity that was to come upon disobedient and idolatrous Judah, Jeremiah prophetically did something logical. He called for **the mourning women** to be ready to do their job, because there would be a lot of **mourning** to do.
>
>> i. "The 'wailing women' were professionals employed to arouse relatives and others at funerals to outward display of their grief. They used plaintive cries, baring their breasts, flailing their arms, throwing dust on their heads, and disheveling their hair (2 Chronicles 35:25; Ecclesiasts 12:5; Amos 5:16; Matthew 9:23)." (Feinberg)
>>
>> ii. "But it is not merely that the professional mourners are called upon to sing their dirge and their lament. They are to teach their tragic refrain to their daughters and their friends, for the days will be tragic enough to demand a multitude of mourners." (Thompson)
>
> b. **We are greatly ashamed, because we have forsaken the land, because we have been cast out of our dwellings**: This was the mournful complaint of those fortunate enough to survive the terrors of the Babylonian invasion. They would lose everything and be taken as forced refugees to another land.
>
> c. **For death has come through our windows, has entered our palaces**: Not all would be so "fortunate" as to face exile. Many would die as the Babylonians invaded, including **children** and **young men**.
>
>> i. Jeremiah somewhat personified **death** in these verses.

4. (22) A vivid description of judgment.

Speak, "Thus says the Lord:
'Even the carcasses of men shall fall as refuse on the open field,
Like cuttings after the harvester,
And no one shall gather *them*.'"

> a. **Even the carcasses of the men shall fall as refuse on the open field, like cuttings after the harvester**: Jeremiah thought of those slain by the invading Babylonians, and how their dead bodies lay in the fields of battle and destruction **like cuttings after the harvester**.
>
>> i. "The custom was for a reaper to hold in his arm what a few strokes of his sickle had cut. Then he put it down, and behind him another laborer then gathered it into bundles and bound it into a sheaf. So death was to cover the ground with corpses, but the carcasses would lie there unburied because of the paucity of survivors and the great number of dead." (Feinberg)
>
> b. **And no one shall gather them**: This was a double disgrace. To the mind of the ancient Hebrew, death was bad; but the desecration of the dead body through failing to care for and bury the corpse was a kind of double death.

5. (23-24) How to prepare for the coming calamity: a true knowledge of God.

Thus says the Lord:
"Let not the wise *man* glory in his wisdom,
Let not the mighty *man* glory in his might,
Nor let the rich *man* glory in his riches;
But let him who glories glory in this,
That he understands and knows Me,
That I *am* the Lord, exercising lovingkindness, judgment, and righteousness in the earth.
For in these I delight," says the Lord.

> a. **Let not the wise man glory in his wisdom**: Speaking on behalf of Yahweh, Jeremiah described the things that men normally **glory** in – **wisdom, might, riches**. Perhaps for a modern age, Jeremiah would have added *fame* as a fourth thing that men take **glory in** by nature.
>
>> i. To **glory** in something is to celebrate it, and to proclaim it as the source of one's happiness and satisfaction. We think of a champion athlete glorying in the trophy just won. As they hold the trophy high, they proclaim – through their actions, words, facial expressions, everything – *this was my goal, this is my satisfaction, my happiness, and I celebrate it now.*

b. **But let him who glories glory in this**: God did not rebuke man's instinct to look for glory; instead, God *guided* that instinct to its proper destination. The problem with man is not that he longs to **glory** in something; the problem is that he generally **glories** in the wrong things, leading to his own hurt, the hurt of others, and most seriously, to offend his Creator.

> i. "There is a contrast between the three fading glories of verse 23 and the three unfading ones of verse 24: the faithful love, justice, and righteousness which are God's gifts to us before ever they are his expectations from us." (Kidner)

c. **Let him who glories glory in this, that he understands and knows Me**: God says, "Direct your desire to **glory** in something in the right place – toward Me." We can take true glory, even the *greatest* glory in the understanding and knowledge of God.

> i. Kidner on **understands and knows**: "There is a nuance of practical good sense in the Hebrew here for *understand*, while to 'know' God means life itself, even to eternity."
>
> ii. The false things men take glory in – wisdom, might, riches, fame – are not only misguided, they are *lower*. The greatest glory, the highest aspirations, the greatest exultation are fulfilled in God and our true understanding and knowledge of Him.
>
> iii. One way to state the problem of humanity is that it constantly allows itself to be satisfied with these lower and lesser glories. In the understanding and knowledge of God are greater **wisdom**, **might**, and **riches** than can be known merely among men.

d. **That I am the LORD, exercising lovingkindness, judgment, and righteousness in the earth**: This understanding and knowledge of God has specific characteristics. It isn't an unspeakable mystical experience; it is:

- An encounter with His **lovingkindness**, the *hesed* or covenant-love of God to His people.

- An encounter with His **judgment**, His discerning between what is right and wrong.

- An encounter with His **righteousness**, His absolute goodness and purity of moral character.

> i. "Under such conditions of crisis the only rest which the wise can know is in the *mercy* (*hesed*) and the *righteousness* of God.... *Hesed* is commonly used in the Old Testament of covenant love, hence God is emphasizing His own moral consistency as against the infidelity of His people." (Harrison)

e. **For in these I delight**: God *delights* in the display of His nature, His character; and when it is known and understood by humanity. It makes Him happy when people know Him as He really is.

6. (25-26) A warning to those who reject the knowledge of the LORD.

"Behold, the days are coming," says the LORD, "that I will punish all *who are* circumcised with the uncircumcised— Egypt, Judah, Edom, the people of Ammon, Moab, and all *who are* in the farthest corners, who dwell in the wilderness. For all *these* nations *are* uncircumcised, and all the house of Israel *are* uncircumcised in the heart."

a. **I will punish all who are circumcised with the uncircumcised**: In the day of God's judgment, the religious ritual of circumcision will not matter. God will judge on the basis of those who truly understand and know Him, as reflected in their lives.

i. The phrase **all who are in the farthest corners** is translated differently by some. The ESV has, *who cut the corners of their hair*, and the NASB has *who clip the hair on their temples*. The two different senses come from slight variations in the text.

ii. "Trimming the hair away from the temples (*cf.* Jeremiah 49:32) was forbidden in the Law (Leviticus 19:27), and the reference here may be to certain Arab tribes who did this to honour Bacchus (Herodotus iii. 18)." (Harrison)

iii. "The first renderings (so all the ancient versions) see here a reference to a certain style of hair. The Hebrew may be rendered 'corner-clipped' (cf. Jeremiah 25:23, 49:32). Certain Arab tribes practiced this cutting of the hair of their temples in honor of Bacchus, the god of wine." (Feinberg)

b. **For as all these nations are uncircumcised, and all the house of Israel are uncircumcised in the heart**: The covenant people of God may have performed the ritual of circumcision, but spiritually speaking they were just as the **uncircumcised** nations.

i. "You see that Judah is sandwiched in between Egypt and Edom. Those who were the people of God are put in the same category with the accursed nation, because they had forsaken him, and mixed up with them." (Spurgeon)

Jeremiah 10 – Yahweh and the Idols of the Nations

A. The greatness of Yahweh over all the idols.

1. (1-5) The custom of the decorated tree made an idol.

Hear the word which the LORD speaks to you, O house of Israel.
Thus says the LORD:
"Do not learn the way of the Gentiles;
Do not be dismayed at the signs of heaven,
For the Gentiles are dismayed at them.
For the customs of the peoples *are* futile;
For *one* cuts a tree from the forest,
The work of the hands of the workman, with the ax.
They decorate it with silver and gold;
They fasten it with nails and hammers
So that it will not topple.
They *are* upright, like a palm tree,
And they cannot speak;
They must be carried,
Because they cannot go *by themselves*.
Do not be afraid of them,
For they cannot do evil,
Nor can they do any good."

    a. **Do not learn the way of the Gentiles**: At the end of Jeremiah 9, God pointed out that His people were like the uncircumcised nations in their lack of knowing God and their wicked conduct. Here is a plea to separate themselves from the foolish customs of the nations that do not know God.

        i. **Do not learn the way of the Gentiles**: "The verb *learn* (Hebrew *tilmadu*) may have overtones of 'becoming a disciple.' Hence one translation is, 'Do not be disciples of the religion of the nations.'" (Thompson)

ii. "Why did so easy a target as idolatry need so many attacks in the Old Testament? Jeremiah 10:9 suggests one reason: the appeal of the visually impressive; but perhaps verse 2 goes deeper, in pointing to the temptation to fall into step with the majority." (Kidner)

b. **Do not be dismayed at the signs of heaven**: Through the use of astrology, ancient people often discerned signs and warnings from the sky, seeing fearful things in **the signs of heaven**.

i. "The signs of the heavens referred to are not the sun, moon, and stars, or signs of the zodiac, meant by God to be signs (Genesis 1:14), but unusual phenomenon like eclipses, comets, and meteors, which were supposed to portend extraordinary events." (Feinberg)

c. **For the customs of the people are futile; for one cuts a tree from the forest… they decorate it with silver and gold; they fasten it with nails and hammers so that it will not topple**: Jeremiah described the pagan custom of cutting a tree, setting it in a special place, decorating it, and worshipping it. The worship of the tree is indicated by the warning, **Do not be afraid of them**, in the sense that one would give reverence to a pagan idol.

i. Jeremiah mocked the idolatry of Judah, especially as it imitated the idolatry of the surrounding nations. Similar passages mocking the idolatry of the heathen are found in Isaiah 40:18-20 and 44:9-20. Yet, it's difficult to read this description and condemnation of an ancient pagan custom and *not* immediately think of the custom of the Christmas tree as practiced in the modern Christian world.

ii. If, based on a passage like this, a Christian would be convinced that they should *not* have a Christmas tree or even celebrate Christmas, then they should stand in that conviction. It is good to remember what Paul wrote: *whatever is not from faith is sin* (Romans 14:23).

iii. Nevertheless, there are many reasons to believe that despite some similarities, the differences are even greater and do not prohibit the modern custom of the Christmas tree.

- Jeremiah spoke regarding the customs of the Gentiles, and in the modern world the appropriate celebration of Christmas is an expression of belief in God and His Son, not a custom of unbelievers.

- Jeremiah spoke of believers borrowing customs of unbelievers; in the modern world, when an unbeliever has a Christmas tree, it is a case of unbelievers borrowing the customs of believers.

- Jeremiah spoke of a tree regarded as an idol, and (properly understood) the modern Christmas tree is not an idol. If for a family it is or becomes an idol, it should be discarded with.
- Jeremiah spoke to a time in history when trees were often directly connected with idolatry, either literal trees or their representations (Jeremiah 2:27).

d. **Do not be afraid of them, for they cannot do evil, nor can they do any good**: Jeremiah gently mocked the idolatrous worship of inanimate objects such as decorated trees. No particular reverence should be given to them; they are powerless to do anything, either **good** or **evil**.

i. The line in Jeremiah 10:5, **They are upright, like a palm tree** is also translated *like a scarecrow in a cucumber field* (NASB, ESV). The idol is worthless; "It is like an immobile and speechless scarecrow in a patch of cucumbers." (Thompson)

2. (6-10) The greatness of God over all idols.

Inasmuch as *there is* none like You, O Lord
(You *are* great, and Your name *is* great in might),
Who would not fear You, O King of the nations?
For this is Your rightful due.
For among all the wise *men* of the nations,
And in all their kingdoms,
***There is* none like You.**
But they are altogether dull-hearted and foolish;
A wooden idol *is* a worthless doctrine.
Silver is beaten into plates;
It is brought from Tarshish,
And gold from Uphaz,
The work of the craftsman
And of the hands of the metalsmith;
Blue and purple *are* their clothing;
They *are* all the work of skillful *men*.
But the Lord is the true God;
He *is* the living God and the everlasting King.
At His wrath the earth will tremble,
And the nations will not be able to endure His indignation.

a. **Inasmuch as there is none like You, O Lord**: Yahweh, the covenant God of Israel, is different than the inanimate idols men worship. The pagan gods **are altogether dull-hearted and foolish**.

i. **A wooden idol is a worthless doctrine**: "Rendered literally as *an instruction of vanities is the tree itself*. The meaning is that the instruction received from idols is of no more value than the idol itself." (Harrison)

ii. "*Tarshish* was the westward limit of the ancient world, perhaps Tartessus in Spain....*Uphaz* is unknown as a location, and may instead be a metallurgical term for 'refined gold.'" (Harrison)

b. **They are all the work of skillful men. But the LORD is the true God**: The inescapable contrast between Yahweh and the idols of the nations is that *they* are the work of men's hands; *He* is the Creator of those very hands.

i. "Men make idols. Jehovah makes men." (Morgan)

ii. As for the idols, they spared no expense in decorating them; **blue and purple are their clothing**: "These were the most precious dyes; very rare, and of high price." (Clarke)

c. **At His wrath the earth will tremble, and the nations will not be able to endure His indignation**: The gods of the nations were nothing; the projections of the corrupt imaginations of men. Yahweh, the covenant God of Israel, is the God who exists, intervenes, and brings judgment.

3. (11-16) The glory of the Creator God.

Thus you shall say to them: "The gods that have not made the heavens and the earth shall perish from the earth and from under these heavens."
He has made the earth by His power,
He has established the world by His wisdom,
And has stretched out the heavens at His discretion.
When He utters His voice,
***There is* a multitude of waters in the heavens:**
"And He causes the vapors to ascend from the ends of the earth.
He makes lightning for the rain,
He brings the wind out of His treasuries."
Everyone is dull-hearted, without knowledge;
Every metalsmith is put to shame by an image;
For his molded image *is* falsehood,
And *there is* no breath in them.
They *are* futile, a work of errors;
In the time of their punishment they shall perish.
The Portion of Jacob *is* not like them,
For He *is* the Maker of all *things*,
And Israel *is* the tribe of His inheritance;
The LORD of hosts *is* His name.

a. **The gods that have not made the heavens and the earth shall perish from the earth**: In the contrast between Yahweh and the idols, Yahweh pronounced the doom of the pagan **gods**.

  i. Jeremiah 10:11 may have been a popular anti-idolatry proverb or saying of that time, quoted in Aramaic. It is the only verse in Jeremiah in Aramaic, a language quite similar to Hebrew. "Because this verse is in Aramaic, a number of expositors reject it as a gloss. But all the versions have it. Furthermore, it fits the context splendidly. No one has ever explained why an interpolator would introduce it here. It was a proverbial saying; so it was given in the language of the people." (Feinberg)

b. **He has made the earth by His power**: In contrast to the pagan gods, Yahweh is a living, active God who **made the earth** and **established the world**, and who **stretched out the heavens**.

  i. "The test between idols and Jehovah he declared to be the test of creation." (Morgan)

  ii. "The prophet's final word on idols is that they are not only worthless, but also a work of mockery, worthy only of being ridiculed." (Feinberg)

c. **Everyone is dull-hearted, without knowledge**: Jeremiah spoke to the foolish conduct of those who make and worship idols. Many of the idols recovered by archaeology are not even beautiful; surely **they are futile, a work of errors**.

d. **The Portion of Jacob is not like them**: Yahweh is different than the idols worshipped among the Gentiles. He is **the Maker**, He has chosen Israel as **the tribe of His inheritance**, and He is the God of heavenly armies (**The LORD of hosts is His name**).

  i. **The Portion of Jacob**: The idea is that in some sense, Yahweh *belonged* to the people of Israel. "A man's 'portion' referred to some possession that belonged to him." (Thompson)

4. (17-18) A warning to hurriedly flee from the invaders.

Gather up your wares from the land,
O inhabitant of the fortress!
For thus says the LORD:
"Behold, I will throw out at this time
The inhabitants of the land,
And will distress them,
That they may find *it so.***"**

a. **Gather up your wares from the land**: Jeremiah prophetically saw the invading army of the Babylonians, coming as an instrument of God's judgment. He warned the people of the land to quickly prepare.

b. **I will throw out at this time the inhabitants of the land**: Despite whatever hurried preparations they might make, none would be able to stand before the judgment of God against Judah. They would be cast out **of the land**.

> i. **I will throw out** is a vivid phrase; it literally means *to slingshot out*. God will cast Judah out of the land that fast, that hard, and that far. "I will easily and speedily sling them, and sling them into Babylon; so God will one day hurl into hell all the wicked of the earth." (Trapp)
>
> ii. "There is a vividness in the first verb in this verse, which is used of hurling with a sling. It is Yahweh himself who is pictured as casting out the inhabitants of Judah." (Thompson)
>
> iii. "As it turned out, following Nebuchadnezzar's second invasion in 587 BC destruction was widespread. Modern archaeological investing has shown a uniform picture. Many towns were destroyed at the beginning of the sixth century BC and never again occupied...There is no known case of a town in Judah proper which was continuously occupied through the exilic period." (Thompson)

B. Jeremiah's prayer.

1. (19-20) A prayer in the voice of those under the Babylonian invasion.

> **Woe is me for my hurt!**
> **My wound is severe.**
> **But I say, "Truly this *is* an infirmity,**
> **And I must bear it."**
> **My tent is plundered,**
> **And all my cords are broken;**
> **My children have gone from me,**
> **And they *are* no more.**
> ***There is* no one to pitch my tent anymore,**
> **Or set up my curtains.**

a. **Woe is me for my hurt! My wound is severe**: Jeremiah prayed in the voice of someone enduring the Babylonian invasion to come. The prayer is filled with pain and distress.

b. **My tent is plundered...my cords are broken...My children have gone from me, and they are no more**: Jeremiah captures the despair, shock, and loneliness of those who would endure the severe season of judgment.

i. "Jerusalem is personified as a tent-dwelling mother, bereft of her children." (Cundall)

2. (21-22) The trouble that comes from dull-hearted shepherds.

For the shepherds have become dull-hearted,
And have not sought the LORD;
Therefore they shall not prosper,
And all their flocks shall be scattered.
Behold, the noise of the report has come,
And a great commotion out of the north country,
To make the cities of Judah desolate, a den of jackals.

a. **For the shepherds have become dull-hearted, and have not sought the LORD**: In thinking of the despair of Judah under the Babylonian invasion, Jeremiah also considered a significant part of the *cause*. The leaders of Judah – both spiritual and political – did not seek the LORD.

i. "The corrupt prophets and priests, who seduced the people from the truth, were persons that made no conscience of prayer; hence all went to wrack and ruin." (Trapp)

b. **Therefore they shall not prosper, and their flocks shall be scattered**: The unfaithfulness of the **shepherds** meant trouble for them, and for the people they were supposed to faithfully lead. No one would benefit from their **dull-hearted**, detachment from the LORD's leadership.

i. "We must avoid generalizing too widely, but on the whole, it is incontestable that a dwindling flock and waning cause point to prayerlessness perhaps on the part of the members, but almost certainly on the part of the shepherd himself." (Meyer)

3. (23-25) A humble plea to God for recompense to the invading army.

O LORD, I know the way of man *is* not in himself;
***It is* not in man who walks to direct his own steps.**
O LORD, correct me, but with justice;
Not in Your anger, lest You bring me to nothing.
Pour out Your fury on the Gentiles, who do not know You,
And on the families who do not call on Your name;
For they have eaten up Jacob,
Devoured him and consumed him,
And made his dwelling place desolate.

a. **O LORD, I know the way of man in not is himself; it is not in man who walks to direct his own steps**: As Jeremiah considered the great judgment to come upon Judah through the Babylonian army, he also considered that

God sent them. The Babylonians did not think of this apart from God; He would direct their steps.

> i. Morgan also connects this with the prior discussion of idolatry. "The idols which men make are always man's attempts to project, from their own inner consciousness, gods to whom they can yield obedience; or in other words, the making of idols is an attempt on the part of man to direct his own steps." (Morgan)
>
> ii. "Man seems to control his own progress, but the fact is that man, vitiated by sin, is incapable of achieving his own true destiny. He desperately needs God, as the wise man realized." (Cundall)
>
> iii. "This was Jeremiah's consolation, 'I do not know what Nebuchadnezzer may do; but I do know that "the way of man is not in himself: it is not in man that walketh to direct his steps." I know that, in God's eternal purposes, every step of Judah's way is mapped out, and he will make it all work for his own glory and the good of his chosen people in the end.'" (Spurgeon)

b. **O Lord, correct me, but with justice; not in Your anger, lest You bring me to nothing**: Know that the great judgment to come was directed by God, Jeremiah appealed to God for mercy. He knew that Judah must be corrected, but asked for God to show mercy and to not destroy His people.

c. **Pour out Your fury on the Gentiles, who do not know You**: When Jeremiah considered that God would use the Babylonians as the instrument of His correction against Judah, he asked God to also judge them.

> i. "So he asks God, instead of smiting his own children, to smite his enemies, and knowing what we do about the Babylonians, we do not wonder that Jeremiah put up such a prayer as that." (Spurgeon)
>
> ii. "This was fulfilled in the *Chaldeans*. Nebuchadnezzar was punished with madness, his son was slain in his revels, and the city was taken and sacked by Cyrus; and the Babylonish empire was finally destroyed!" (Clarke)

Jeremiah 11 – A Broken Covenant and a Conspiracy

A. A curse to the covenant breakers.

1. (1-5) The covenant and the curse.

The word that came to Jeremiah from the LORD, saying, "Hear the words of this covenant, and speak to the men of Judah and to the inhabitants of Jerusalem; and say to them, 'Thus says the LORD God of Israel: "Cursed *is* the man who does not obey the words of this covenant which I commanded your fathers in the day I brought them out of the land of Egypt, from the iron furnace, saying, 'Obey My voice, and do according to all that I command you; so shall you be My people, and I will be your God,' that I may establish the oath which I have sworn to your fathers, to give them 'a land flowing with milk and honey,' as *it is* this day."'" And I answered and said, "So be it, LORD."

> a. **Hear the words of this covenant, and speak to the men of Judah**: God spoke to Judah about their failure to keep the ancient covenant Israel made with God at Mount Sinai in the days of Moses (Exodus 24:1-8).
>
> > i. In that Sinai (or Mosaic) covenant, "God promised to supply all the material and spiritual needs of the infant nation in return for undivided worship and obedience." (Harrison)
>
> b. **Cursed is the man who does not obey the words of this covenant**: When Israel made the covenant with God at Mount Sinai, there were specific curses pronounced against those who violated the covenant (Deuteronomy 27:15-26). Here, God simply promised that He would enforce the terms of the covenant made **in the day I brought them out of the land of Egypt**.
>
> > i. **Of this covenant**: "It is probable that Jeremiah, when he said this, held the book in his hand, viz., the book of Deuteronomy." (Trapp)

c. **From the iron furnace**: This is the third place in the Scriptures where Israel's agony in Egypt is described as an **iron furnace** (also at Deuteronomy 4:20 and 1 Kings 8:51). Some think that a part of Israel's slave labor in Egypt was to work as slaves in literal iron furnaces.

d. **To give them "a land flowing with milk and honey"**: God fulfilled all His obligations of the covenant, even blessing Israel with an abundant land. It was the children of Israel who did not obey their obligations of the covenant.

> i. **And I answered and said, "So be it, Lord"**: "When God recapitulated his promises in the heart of Jeremiah, even though they involved a curse on those who neutralized his words, there arose from it a deep response. He answered and said, Amen, O Lord. What a remarkable example for us all!" (Meyer)
>
> ii. "There is a vast difference between the liturgical 'Amen' which is merely conventional, and which in the saying means nothing; and the Amen which comes out of the deep inner agreement of mind and heart and will with the purposes and methods of God." (Morgan)

2. (6-8) The command to preach the message of the broken covenant.

Then the Lord said to me, "Proclaim all these words in the cities of Judah and in the streets of Jerusalem, saying: 'Hear the words of this covenant and do them. For I earnestly exhorted your fathers in the day I brought them up out of the land of Egypt, until this day, rising early and exhorting, saying, "Obey My voice." Yet they did not obey or incline their ear, but everyone followed the dictates of his evil heart; therefore I will bring upon them all the words of this covenant, which I commanded *them* to do, but *which* they have not done.'"

a. **Proclaim all these words in the cities of Judah and in the streets of Jerusalem**: Jeremiah's assignment was to preach this message of the broken covenant and its consequences in Jerusalem and the other cities of Judah.

b. **For I earnestly exhorted your fathers**: God gave the people of Israel many warnings and encouragements to do what was right under the covenant. He wanted their obedience and did all He could to cultivate and encourage it, God even **rising early and exhorting** them (to use an understandible figure of speech).

c. **Yet they did not obey or incline their ear, but everyone followed the dictates of his evil heart**: Instead of following God's instructions and warnings, they went their own way, followed their own **heart**. Therefore God said, **I will bring upon them all the words of this covenant**.

3. (9-10) The conspiracy of disobedience.

And the LORD said to me, "A conspiracy has been found among the men of Judah and among the inhabitants of Jerusalem. They have turned back to the iniquities of their forefathers who refused to hear My words, and they have gone after other gods to serve them; the house of Israel and the house of Judah have broken My covenant which I made with their fathers."

> a. **A conspiracy has been found**: God told Jeremiah that the men of Judah and Jerusalem were organized in a conspiracy. Perhaps on a human level they were unaware of the coordination of the **conspiracy**, and perhaps spiritual forces of wickedness in high places organized it. Yet it existed and mattered just the same.
>
>> i. "The term is a metaphor. There was no deep-laid plot, no secrecy behind the apostasy that Jeremiah witnessed, although religiously Judah displayed all that a carefully organized plot would achieve." (Thompson)
>>
>> ii. "So attractive were the depraved Canaanite fertility rites, and so widespread the resultant idolatry in Israel, that it appeared as though the people had deliberately plotted to renounce their covenantal obligations and espouse apostasy." (Harrison)
>
> b. **They have turned their back to the iniquities of their forefathers who refused to hear My words**: The conspiracy was a work of both breaking the commandments of God, and refusing to hear the warnings of God. It ended up being a conspiracy to break their covenant with God.

4. (11-14) The curse to come upon the covenant breakers.

Therefore thus says the LORD: "Behold, I will surely bring calamity on them which they will not be able to escape; and though they cry out to Me, I will not listen to them. Then the cities of Judah and the inhabitants of Jerusalem will go and cry out to the gods to whom they offer incense, but they will not save them at all in the time of their trouble. For *according to* the number of your cities were your gods, O Judah; and *according to* the number of the streets of Jerusalem you have set up altars to *that* shameful thing, altars to burn incense to Baal. So do not pray for this people, or lift up a cry or prayer for them; for I will not hear *them* in the time that they cry out to Me because of their trouble."

> a. **I will surely bring calamity on them which they will not be able to escape**: This was simply the promised consequence of disobedience under the Mosaic Covenant (Deuteronomy 27:15-26).

b. **The inhabitants of Jerusalem will go and cry out to the gods to whom they offer incense, but they will not save them at all in their time of trouble**: One way the people of Judah broke the Mosaic Covenant was by their worship of the false and pagan gods of the surrounding nations. When Yahweh cursed them under the terms of that covenant, they would find no help from those gods.

c. **For I will not hear them in the time that they cry out to Me**: The false gods would be silent because they were nothing. The LORD God of Israel would be silent as an expression of His judgment against His people.

i. Of all the curses that might come upon a people, surely one of the most terrible is the *silence of God* in our time of trouble or need.

5. (15-17) The disappointment of rejected love.

"**What has My beloved to do in My house,**
Having done lewd deeds with many?
And the holy flesh has passed from you.
When you do evil, then you rejoice.
The LORD called your name,
Green Olive Tree, Lovely *and* **of Good Fruit.**
With the noise of a great tumult
He has kindled fire on it,
And its branches are broken.

"**For the LORD of hosts, who planted you, has pronounced doom against you for the evil of the house of Israel and of the house of Judah, which they have done against themselves to provoke Me to anger in offering incense to Baal.**"

a. **What has My beloved to do in My house, having done lewd deeds with many?** God regarded Israel as His **beloved**; yet they played the part of the unfaithful spouse, being unfaithful with false gods. Therefore, God appropriately asked why they were still in His **house**.

i. "As if a husband should say to his adulterous wife, What maketh this strumpet in my bed, since she hath so many paramours?" (Trapp)

ii. **The holy flesh has passed from you**: "The sacrifice sanctified by the altar shall be wholly taken away from you, together with the temple." (Trapp)

b. **When you do evil, then you rejoice**: This is the description of a sin-sick society. Not only do they sin; they openly **rejoice** in their evil.

c. **The LORD called your name, Green Olive Tree, Lovely, and of Good Fruit**: This describes the expressions of love and endearment God gave to

Israel. He loved them tenderly and deeply; yet they returned His love with unfaithfulness. They rejected God's endearment and love.

d. **He has kindled fire on it, and its branches are broken**: Though God once held His people in such dear regard, that would not stop His appropriate judgment against them. Though He had **planted** them, He still **pronounced doom against** them for their stubborn sin and idolatry.

B. The conspiracy and threat against Jeremiah.

1. (18-19) Jeremiah's knowledge of the threat against him.

Now the LORD gave me knowledge *of it*, and I know *it*; for You showed me their doings. But I *was* like a docile lamb brought to the slaughter; and I did not know that they had devised schemes against me, *saying*, "Let us destroy the tree with its fruit, and let us cut him off from the land of the living, that his name may be remembered no more."

a. **Now the LORD gave me knowledge of it, and I know it**: God showed Jeremiah the **doings** of his enemies. By what follows (Jeremiah 11:21), we understand that these **enemies** were the men of Anathoth, which was Jeremiah's home village (Jeremiah 1:1, 29:27, 32:7-9).

i. This was an example of divine protection over the prophet. The day might come when God would allow Jeremiah to lay down his life in faithfulness to the LORD; but that day was not yet.

b. **But I was like a docile lamb brought to the slaughter**: This was Jeremiah's state before God warned him (**I did not know that they had devised schemes against me**). He was defenseless before God showed him that his enemies wanted to cut him down like a tree.

i. The phrase **like a docile lamb brought to the slaughter** reminds us of Jesus, who was also rejected by His own people (John 1:11). In Isaiah's great prophecy of the Suffering Servant, he described the Messiah as *a lamb to the slaughter* (Isaiah 53:7, Acts 8:32). Jeremiah's faithfulness to God built in him a growing likeness to the Messiah who perfectly represented God (John 1:18, John 14:9).

ii. "As another Lamb of God observed, a man's foes shall be those of his own household (Matthew 10:36)." (Harrison)

2. (20) Jeremiah's prayer and confidence.

But, O LORD of hosts,
You who judge righteously,
Testing the mind and the heart,
Let me see Your vengeance on them,
For to You I have revealed my cause.

a. **But, O Lord of hosts**: Knowing the threat against his life, Jeremiah did the right thing – he prayed. He began his prayer addressing God as the **Lord of hosts**, a title recalling that God is the commander of heavenly armies.

b. **You who judge righteously, testing the mind and heart**: Jeremiah prayed for protection, but not to be shielded as an evildoer. He looked for God's protection to be given according to His righteousness and perfect wisdom.

c. **Let me see Your vengeance on them, for to You I have revealed my cause**: Properly, Jeremiah understood that **vengeance** belonged to the Lord (as in Deuteronomy 32:35 and Romans 12:19). He **revealed his cause** to God and would trust Him to deal with it.

> i. "His fierce reaction to the plot will shock us, but God upheld it, for it asked no more than justice." (Kidner)

3. (21-23) God's promise to punish the ones who threatened to kill Jeremiah.

"Therefore thus says the Lord concerning the men of Anathoth who seek your life, saying, 'Do not prophesy in the name of the Lord, lest you die by our hand'— therefore thus says the Lord of hosts: 'Behold, I will punish them. The young men shall die by the sword, their sons and their daughters shall die by famine; and there shall be no remnant of them, for I will bring catastrophe on the men of Anathoth, even the year of their punishment.'"

a. **Thus says the Lord concerning the men of Anathoth who seek your life**: The village of **Anathoth** was Jeremiah's home (Jeremiah 1:1). It was the people of his own village who wanted to kill him.

> i. Much of Jeremiah's work was done during the days of the reforming King Josiah. One thing Josiah did was to shut down the disobedient and unauthorized sacrifices on the high places, outside the altar at the temple in Jerusalem. The local priests at **Anathoth** may have resented that their shrine was shut down and may have hated Jeremiah because he supported Josiah.

> ii. "There would have been some strong reason why Jeremiah's fellow citizens took such strong action against him, although such actions are not unknown even today in the Middle East. Sometimes members of a family will set out to kill a kinsman who has brought disgrace on the family." (Thompson)

b. **Do not prophesy in the name of the Lord, lest you die by our hand**: This was the threat they made against Jeremiah. It was clear that what they hated was the message from God that he brought.

c. **Behold, I will punish them**: God promised to bring particular judgment against the men of Anathoth. Jeremiah must have had mixed feelings about this; he was happy that God defended him and would recompense his enemies, but no doubt grieved at the judgment to come upon the men of his own village.

> i. "And the punishment is, *Their young men shall die by the sword* of the Chaldeans; and *their sons and daughters shall die by the famine* that shall come on the land through the desolations occasioned by the Chaldean army." (Clarke)

Jeremiah 12 – Running with Footmen and Horses

A. Jeremiah's question and God's answer.

1. (1-4) Jeremiah's question to God.

> **Righteous** *are* **You, O L**ORD**, when I plead with You;**
> **Yet let me talk with You about** *Your* **judgments.**
> **Why does the way of the wicked prosper?**
> *Why* **are those happy who deal so treacherously?**
> **You have planted them, yes, they have taken root;**
> **They grow, yes, they bear fruit.**
> **You** *are* **near in their mouth**
> **But far from their mind.**
> **But You, O L**ORD**, know me;**
> **You have seen me,**
> **And You have tested my heart toward You.**
> **Pull them out like sheep for the slaughter,**
> **And prepare them for the day of slaughter.**
> **How long will the land mourn,**
> **And the herbs of every field wither?**
> **The beasts and birds are consumed,**
> **For the wickedness of those who dwell there,**
> **Because they said, "He will not see our final end."**

> a. **Righteous are You, O L**ORD**, when I plead with You; yet let me talk with You about Your judgments**: Jeremiah wanted to ask God a question, and he did so in an appropriate way – first recognizing and submitting to God's righteousness.

> b. **Why does the way of the wicked prosper**: Jeremiah asked a question that Asaph also asked (Psalm 73). Hopefully without pride, Jeremiah understood that he was righteous and most of those in Judah and Jerusalem were wicked. Yet they seemed to **prosper**, while Jeremiah often suffered.

i. "This is that noble question which hath exercised the wits and molested the minds of many wise men, both within and without the Church." (Trapp)

ii. "The *whole book* of Jeremiah shows that there is a moral law operating in the world, but the prophet, smarting at this time under the attack on his life (Jeremiah 11:21), impatiently clamoured for God to hasten up His process of judgment." (Cundall)

c. **You have planted them**: Jeremiah considered that the wicked could not enjoy any prosperity or pleasure unless God allowed it. The **fruit** they enjoyed ultimately came from God in one way or another.

d. **You are near in their mouth but far from their mind**: The people Jeremiah had in mind were those who made an outward profession of religion but did not really care about God and the things of God.

e. **But You, O Lord, know me; You have seen me, and You have tested my heart toward You**: Jeremiah contrasted his life with the life of the wicked – perhaps those who threatened him (Jeremiah 11:18-19). He knew that his life and heart were **tested** before God in a way that their lives did not seem to be.

f. **Pull them out like sheep for the slaughter, and prepare them for the day of slaughter**: In the previous chapter, Jeremiah felt that *he* was like a **sheep for the slaughter** (Jeremiah 11:19). He prayed that the wicked would now be put in that same place.

i. "In asking him to 'set them apart [i.e., "sanctify them"] for the day of slaughter,' Jeremiah is comparing the wicked to animal sacrifices." (Feinberg)

g. **How long will the land mourn**: Jeremiah felt that because God did not answer the wicked with judgment, it brought mourning even to the **land**. Their careless attitude (**He will not see our final end**) had an effect even upon the natural world.

2. (5-6) God's answer to Jeremiah.

"If you have run with the footmen, and they have wearied you,
Then how can you contend with horses?
And *if* in the land of peace,
In which you trusted, *they wearied you*,
Then how will you do in the floodplain of the Jordan?
For even your brothers, the house of your father,
Even they have dealt treacherously with you;
Yes, they have called a multitude after you.

Do not believe them,
Even though they speak smooth words to you."

- a. **If you have run with the footmen and they have wearied you, then how can you contend with horses**: God's answer to Jeremiah was both powerful and profound. Without directly answering the question (a more complete answer is given in Psalm 73), God encouraged Jeremiah to regard his present challenge as a preparation for greater challenges to come.

    i. Jeremiah was certainly in a challenge – like a hard-fought race **with the footmen**. There was a sense of spiritual and mental and emotional exertion involved with the persecution from his fellow villagers from Anathoth and his question regarding the prosperity of the wicked and why God did not seem to deliver justice to them.

    ii. Yet even with the appreciation of that challenge, *there were greater challenges to come.* By analogy, Jeremiah could expect to run against **horses** in the future. He needed to learn how to trust God and to draw on His strength in his present challenge, in order to prepare him for the greater challenges in the future.

    iii. If he found it difficult in Anathoth, how would he fare in Jerusalem? Later on, Jeremiah would have to spend a night in the stocks (Jeremiah 20:1-3), confinement in a cistern (Jeremiah 38:6), and imprisonment in the court of the guard (Jeremiah 28:13). "The troubles he was having in Anathoth were nothing compared to the troubles he would have later in Jerusalem, Babylon, or Egypt." (Ryken)

- b. **And if in the land of peace, in which you trust, they wearied you, then how will you do in the floodplain of the Jordan**: This analogy supplies the same lesson as the analogy of the footmen and the horses. The present circumstance is a challenge, yet a greater one waits.

    i. "If you complain about the simple things God has already asked you to do, then you lack the spiritual strength to do what he wants you to do next." (Ryken)

    ii. "The effect of the questions must have been that of emphasizing the prophet's sense of his own weakness, and thus driving him to yet completer dependence upon God." (Morgan)

    iii. "God never calls us to content with horsemen, until He has trained us by the lesser strain of contending with footmen." (Morgan)

    iv. "He seems to have been a little afraid of the people among whom he dwelt. They had evidently persecuted him very much, mocked at him, and laughed him to scorn; but God tells him to make his face like flint, and not to care for them, for, says he, If thou art afraid of them, 'How wilt thou do in the swelling of Jordan?' This ought to be a rebuke to every Christian who is subject to the fear of man." (Spurgeon)

v. **Floodplain of the Jordan**: "The region surrounding the Jordan was a place of jungle growth, the lair of lions (cf. Jeremiah 49:19; 50:44)." (Thompson)

c. **For even your brothers, the house of your father, even they have dealt treacherously with you**: For Jeremiah, the smaller challenge was the adversity and hatred he faced from the men of Anathoth (Jeremiah 11:21), men of his own village and family. The greater challenge was the **multitude** they had called against him.

d. **Do not believe them, even though they speak smooth words to you**: The open adversity was another example of the smaller challenge; the bigger challenge would be the **smooth words** and flattery others would use against Jeremiah.

B. Judah and her enemies.

1. (7-8) God abandons His people to their enemies.

"I have forsaken My house, I have left My heritage;
I have given the dearly beloved of My soul into the hand of her enemies.
My heritage is to Me like a lion in the forest;
It cries out against Me;
Therefore I have hated it.
My heritage *is* to Me *like* a speckled vulture;
The vultures all around *are* against her.
Come, assemble all the beasts of the field,
Bring them to devour!"

a. **I have forsaken My house, I have left My heritage**: Jeremiah spoke to the future when God will give His **dearly beloved** people **into the hand of her enemies**.

i. "The reference to *house* is not to the temple but to the people. *My house* is parallel to *my heritage* (inheritance), a familiar designation for the people of Israel in the Old Testament." (Thompson)

b. **My heritage to Me is like a lion in the forest; it cries out against Me; therefore I have hated it**: According to Jacob's prophecy in Genesis 49:9, Judah was supposed to be God's lion. They fulfilled the **lion**-like role, but they roared *against* God instead of *for* Him — it was a roar of rebellion.

i. "The people are *enraged* against me; they *roar like a furious lion* against their God. They have proceeded to the most open acts of the most flagrant iniquity." (Clarke)

ii. "Jeremiah does not mean 'hate' in the sense of a violent, angry emotion. What it means is that God intended to perform an act of rejecting his people, at least for a time. He was going to disinherit them." (Ryken)

c. **My heritage is to Me like a speckled vulture**: The idea is of a bird that looks different and is therefore troubled by the other birds. Judah would be set upon by the surrounding nations.

i. "Rebellious Judah will now be as conspicuous as *a speckled bird*, whose unusual plumage provokes the enmity of other predators." (Harrison)

2. (10-13) The mournful harvest of the land.

"Many rulers have destroyed My vineyard,
They have trodden My portion underfoot;
They have made My pleasant portion a desolate wilderness.
They have made it desolate;
Desolate, it mourns to Me;
The whole land is made desolate,
Because no one takes *it* **to heart.**
The plunderers have come
On all the desolate heights in the wilderness,
For the sword of the LORD **shall devour**
From *one* **end of the land to the** *other* **end of the land;**
No flesh shall have peace.
They have sown wheat but reaped thorns;
They have put themselves to pain *but* **do not profit.**
But be ashamed of your harvest
Because of the fierce anger of the LORD**."**

a. **They have made it desolate; desolate, it mourns to Me**: When the judgment comes upon the land of Judah, it will make the land **desolate** – because there will be no one to care for it (**no one takes it to heart**).

i. The KJV has Jeremiah 12:10 as *Many pastors have destroyed my vineyard*. The Hebrew uses the familiar figure of a shepherd (pastor) as a leader of people, not necessarily spiritually. Trapp notes, "Those who before were called beasts (Jeremiah 12:9), are here called pastors – viz., Nebuchadnezzar's captains."

ii. "The Hebrew text plays strong on the word *waste* [desolate] in verses 10 and 11. It is impossible to catch the strong assonance in English, but the effect in Hebrew is striking. There is a sense of completeness and finality about the words." (Thompson)

b. **But be ashamed of your harvest because of the fierce anger of the LORD**: God spoke to the invading Babylonians, warning them that they should take no pleasure or satisfaction in their **harvest** upon the cities and land of Judah. They would have to reckon with **the fierce anger of the LORD**.

i. "All their projects shall fail: none of their enterprises shall succeed. They are enemies to God, and therefore cannot have his blessing." (Clarke)

3. (14-15) A promise of retribution and a promise of restoration.

Thus says the LORD: "Against all My evil neighbors who touch the inheritance which I have caused My people Israel to inherit—behold, I will pluck them out of their land and pluck out the house of Judah from among them. Then it shall be, after I have plucked them out, that I will return and have compassion on them and bring them back, everyone to his heritage and everyone to his land.

a. **I will pluck them out of their land**: God warned those would attack and exile Israel, that *He* would also dispossess them of **their land**. Even though God used them as an instrument of His judgment, He would nevertheless judge them for their evil and brutality against Judah.

i. God called these nations **My evil neighbors** – yet He would use them to chastise His people. "God often uses one wicked nation to scourge another; and afterwards scourges the scourger by some other scourge. In some places a felon who was condemned to be hanged is made the common hangman for the county; he himself being still under the sentence of death." (Clarke)

b. **And pluck out the house of Judah from among them**: God would deal with the invaders (the Babylonian Empire); but He would also take care of His people, and bring them back (**pluck out**) a remnant to return to the land and the promise once again.

c. **I will return and have compassion on them and bring them back, everyone to his heritage and everyone to his land**: The promise of exile and judgment was sure; but so was the promise of **compassion** and return. Jeremiah need not despair at the seeming prosperity of the wicked and trouble of the righteous; God would move all things according to His perfect plan.

4. (16-17) A merciful promise to the nations.

And it shall be, if they will learn carefully the ways of My people, to swear by My name, 'As the LORD lives,' as they taught My people to swear by Baal, then they shall be established in the midst of My people. But if they do not obey, I will utterly pluck up and destroy that nation," says the LORD.

a. **If they will learn carefully the ways of My people**: God made a remarkable offer to Babylonians and to any who opposed His people. If they would turn to Him and **swear by** His name, then they could be **established in the midst of My people**. They could share in the blessing and goodness of God among His people.

i. "He also holds out to pagan peoples the blessings of the covenant relationship if only they will repudiate the Baal deities and swear by the living God." (Harrison)

ii. This reminds us that God's regard for Israel was never based on race or ethnicity. It was based on love and faithfulness to Yahweh. *Any* nation who would honor the LORD in this way would gain the same benefits as belonged to ethnic Israel.

iii. "It is remarkable to observe that these 'evil neighbours' (Jeremiah 12:14) are promised a share in a glorious future, following a chastisement similar to that inflicted upon His covenant-people, providing they accept the testimony of Judah to her Saviour-God." (Cundall)

b. **But if they do not obey, I will utterly pluck up and destroy that nation**: The blessing for turning to the LORD was great; but the price for rejecting God was also great. They could expect the judgment of God, no matter their present prosperity or superiority.

i. "The tartness of the threatening maketh us best taste the sweetness of the promise." (Trapp)

Jeremiah 13 – Two Warning Signs

This chapter seems to be a compilation of several signs and prophetic words given to Jeremiah at different times.

A. The Sign of the Linen Sash.

1. (1-5) Hiding the linen sash.

Thus the Lord said to me: "Go and get yourself a linen sash, and put it around your waist, but do not put it in water." So I got a sash according to the word of the Lord, and put *it* around my waist. And the word of the Lord came to me the second time, saying, "Take the sash that you acquired, which *is* around your waist, and arise, go to the Euphrates, and hide it there in a hole in the rock." So I went and hid it by the Euphrates, as the Lord commanded me.

> a. **Go and get yourself a linen sash**: Yahweh, the covenant God of Israel, told Jeremiah to take a **sash** and tie around himself as an object lesson. The **sash** was associated with the priestly garments both for the High Priest (Exodus 28:4) and the regular priest (Leviticus 16:4). Such a linen belt was a sign of dignity and nobility.
>
>> i. Some such as Harrison believe this **sash** was more properly a waistcloth or loincloth, but it seems to be best understood as a decorative belt, something like a cumberbund.
>>
>> ii. "If Jeremiah wore the traditional prophetic garb he would have been clothed in a fairly tight tunic of coarse material with a hair cloak over it. A linen girdle around his waist, such as was worn by priests and the rich nobility, would have made him something of a spectacle." (Thompson)
>
> b. **Arise, go to the Euphrates, and hide it there in a hole in the rock**: God commanded Jeremiah to make a long journey, all the way north (and somewhat east) to the **Euphrates** River. This was in the direction from

which the future conquerors of Judah would come. Once there, he was to bury the sash, presumably by the river.

> i. Some think that Jeremiah didn't go all the way to the Euphrates, but to a much closer water source with a similar name. Others think this was merely a prophetic vision. Yet there is no good reason to believe that Jeremiah did not take this long journey as an acted-out parable. "Personally, I believe that it is history, that Jeremiah actually travelled to Babylon and back twice." (Morgan)
>
> ii. "A three months' disappearance by the prophet would have caused a stir in Anathoth, and his return without the girdle would have been cause for much comment." (Thompson)
>
> iii. "The prophet's journey therefore thither seemeth to have been but visional, as was Isaiah's going barefoot, Hosea's marriage with a whore, Ezekiel's lying on one side three hundred and ninety days together." (Trapp)

2. (6-7) Finding the decayed, useless sash.

Now it came to pass after many days that the LORD said to me, "Arise, go to the Euphrates, and take from there the sash which I commanded you to hide there." Then I went to the Euphrates and dug, and I took the sash from the place where I had hidden it; and there was the sash, ruined. It was profitable for nothing.

a. **Arise, go to the Euphrates, and take from there the sash**: Some **many days** later, God commanded Jeremiah to take the long journey once again, this time to take the sash from the place he buried it.

b. **There was the sash, ruined. It was profitable for nothing**: Jeremiah found what he might have expected. The sash had deteriorated in the dirt and the moisture. It still existed, but it was **ruined** and good for **nothing**. It had nothing of the previous nobility and prominence that it once displayed.

> i. "Whereas plain words might not have been noticed, this little piece of acting commanded the attention and excited the curiosity of the people. Blame us not if we sometimes dramatize the truth: we must win men's hearts, and to do so we dare even run the risk of being called theatrical." (Spurgeon)

3. (8-12) Ruining the pride of the people.

Then the word of the LORD came to me, saying, "Thus says the LORD: 'In this manner I will ruin the pride of Judah and the great pride of Jerusalem. This evil people, who refuse to hear My words, who follow

the dictates of their hearts, and walk after other gods to serve them and worship them, shall be just like this sash which is profitable for nothing. For as the sash clings to the waist of a man, so I have caused the whole house of Israel and the whole house of Judah to cling to Me,' says the LORD, 'that they may become My people, for renown, for praise, and for glory; but they would not hear.'

a. **In this manner I will ruin the pride of Judah and the great pride of Jerusalem**: The noble sash was taken to the Euphrates and ruined. So also would Judah and Jerusalem be taken to the Euphrates (and beyond) in their coming captivity, and thus God would **ruin the pride** of His people.

i. "Just as the girdle had been spoiled, so also would the gross pride of Judah and the gross pride of Jerusalem be destroyed." (Thompson)

b. **Shall be just like this sash which is profitable for nothing**: At one time God had great use for His people Israel in the world, but they had so rejected God, that at that point they were **profitable for nothing**. This was through their three main sins.

- **Who refuse to hear My words**: The people of God had become hard and cold towards the word of God to them.

- **Who follow the dictates of their hearts**: The people of God instead trusted in their own **hearts**, and looked to self instead of the LORD.

- **And walk after other gods to serve them**: When they stopped listening to God and started following their own hearts, it led them to the corruption of idolatry.

c. **As the sash clings to the waist of a man, so I have caused the whole house of Israel and the whole house of Judah to cling to Me**: Just as a fine sash expressed beauty and nobility, so God wanted His people to be ornaments of His greatness to all the world. If they would **cling to** Him, they would be **My people, for renown, for praise, and for glory**.

i. "The chief purpose and ultimate goal of human beings is to be wrapped around God's waist like a fashion accessory. When we are at our very best, we adorn God with glory." (Ryken)

d. **But they would not hear**: Because of their stubborn and persistent sins against the LORD, Judah did not fulfill the noble and beautiful destiny God planned for them. They became useless and ruined like the buried sash.

i. What was true for ancient Judah is true among God's people today. God's plan is to make His people a noble ornament, a decoration of His own presence and work. If we reject this noble calling, we become useless for His highest and best purpose – and our own.

B. The Sign of the Wine Bottle.

1. (12) Every bottle filled with wine.

"Therefore you shall speak to them this word: 'Thus says the LORD God of Israel: "Every bottle shall be filled with wine."' And they will say to you, 'Do we not certainly know that every bottle will be filled with wine?'"

> a. **Every bottle shall be filled with wine**: This proverbial phrase had the sense, "Everything will fulfill its purpose." A bottle (actually a clay jar to hold wine, not a glass bottle) was meant to contain wine, so to say "**every bottle shall be filled with wine**" was another way to say, "everything shall fulfill its purpose" or "it will all be right in the end."
>
>> i. "Here the tag evidently meant something optimistic, such as, 'The more you expect, the more you'll get,' or perhaps, 'It'll all come right in the end.'" (Kidner)
>>
>> ii. **Bottle**: "The *nebel* was the largest earthenware container used for storing wine (*cf.* Isaiah 22:24; 30:14; Lamentations 4:2)." (Harrison)
>
> b. **Do we not certainly know that every bottle will be filled with wine?** The people's response showed their confidence in the principle of the proverb. If God had planned a noble and high purpose for Israel, surely it would be fulfilled – and good times would follow.

2. (13-14) The people of Judah drunk and destroyed.

"Then you shall say to them, 'Thus says the LORD: "Behold, I will fill all the inhabitants of this land -- even the kings who sit on David's throne, the priests, the prophets, and all the inhabitants of Jerusalem -- with drunkenness! And I will dash them one against another, even the fathers and the sons together," says the LORD. "I will not pity nor spare nor have mercy, but will destroy them."'"

> a. **I will fill all the inhabitants of this land.... with drunkenness**: Instead of fulfilling their purpose before God in a high and noble way, God's rebellious people would be filled with *stupor* and *stupidity*. If they had a fatalistic confidence in their destiny as the people of God, the LORD wanted to break it.
>
>> i. "Their heads (not altogether unlike bottles for roundness and emptiness of all good) shall be filled with a dry drunkenness, even with errors and terrors, a spirit of giddiness." (Trapp)
>
> b. **I will dash them one against another**: Bottles not only have destiny to be filled; they also have a destiny to be broken. God promised His

rebellious people that they would face *this* destiny if they continued in their sin against Him.

i. "Jeremiah announced that God would fill the people with the *wine* of his wrath, and just as wine jars about which the people joked were smashed by dashing them one against the other, so God would destroy his people." (Thompson)

C. How to respond to God's warnings.

1. (15-16) Humble yourself and give glory to the LORD.

Hear and give ear:
Do not be proud,
For the LORD has spoken.
Give glory to the LORD your God
Before He causes darkness,
And before your feet stumble
On the dark mountains,
And while you are looking for light,
He turns it into the shadow of death
And **makes** *it* **dense darkness.**

a. **Do not be proud, for the LORD has spoken**: Every time God speaks to us, we have the choice to respond in pride or humility. We have the choice to reject or resist the word of the LORD, or to humble ourselves before His authority. God warned Judah to take the humble path.

i. "Refusing to hear what Jehovah has spoken, thou wilt follow other voices, which shall allure thee into an Egyptian night of confusion. Thou wilt go on meditating and excogitating, or criticizing and trifling, till thou art enveloped in a cloud of doubts, wrapped as in a dense smoke of speculation, and well nigh smothered in exhalations of unbelief. Thou shalt not know what to do, nor what to think, nor what to say, nor whither to betake thyself, for thou wilt have renounced thy guide and quenched thy torch." (Spurgeon)

b. **Give glory to the LORD your God before He causes darkness**: The promised judgment was not far away. There was urgency for Judah to turn to the LORD **before** the **darkness** came, **before your feet stumble**. In rejecting God, they would become like mountain travelers trying to make their way through dangerous paths **in dense darkness**.

i. Specifically, Judah could **give glory to the LORD** by recognizing His superior place and their proper place beneath Him. They could humbly confess their sin and reject their idols, which robbed God of His glory.

ii. **Give glory to God**: "Confess your sins and turn to him, that these sore evils may be averted." (Clarke)

2. (17-20) The price to be paid for not heeding God's warnings.

But if you will not hear it,
My soul will weep in secret for *your* pride;
My eyes will weep bitterly
And run down with tears,
Because the LORD'S flock has been taken captive.
Say to the king and to the queen mother,
"Humble yourselves;
Sit down,
For your rule shall collapse, the crown of your glory."
The cities of the South shall be shut up,
And no one shall open *them;*
Judah shall be carried away captive, all of it;
It shall be wholly carried away captive.
Lift up your eyes and see
Those who come from the north.
Where *is* the flock *that* was given to you,
Your beautiful sheep?

a. **If you will not hear it, my soul will weep**: This was Jeremiah's painful lament. He wasn't a dispassionate observer, throwing the thunderbolts of God's judgment against Judah. His eyes ran **down with tears** because of their sin and pride, and because soon, **the LORD's flock has been taken captive**.

i. "Good ministers should be full of compassionate tears, weeping in secret for their people's unprofitableness, and their danger thereby." (Trapp)

b. **Say to the king and to the queen mother, "Humble yourselves"**: If Judah's royalty would submit and surrender to God, surely the people of the kingdom would follow. In this spiritual work, the leaders had to take the lead.

i. This word applied to the young King Jehoiachin and his mother Nehushta (2 Kings 24:8-16). They were perhaps already in Babylonia by this time, yet could still benefit if they humbled themselves before Yahweh.

ii. "The address is an exhortation to humility in view of their impending loss of sovereignty. Pride was characteristic of the royal house." (Feinberg)

c. **For your rule shall collapse, the crown of your glory**: If the king and queen mother of Judah had a special *responsibility* to lead in repentance, they also had a special *reason* to do so. Because of their heights, the coming fall would affect them the worst.

i. **The cities of the South shall be shut up**: "Not only the cities of the *north*, the quarter at which the Chaldeans entered, but the cities of the *south* also; for he shall proceed from one extremity of the land to the other, spreading devastation every where, and carrying off the inhabitants." (Clarke)

ii. **Judah shall be carried away captive, all of it**: "The statement that 'all Judah' will be exiled is rhetorical exaggeration, since only some leaders and skilled workmen were taken to Babylon at that time (597 BC). Yet they represented the whole nation." (Feinberg)

d. **Where is the flock that was given to you, your beautiful sheep**: The invaders **from the north** would take the people of Judah captive. Since a king was often thought of as a shepherd of his people, the picture of the invaders stealing the **beautiful sheep** of the king of Judah was especially appropriate.

i. **Lift up your eyes**: "The imperatives are feminine and would appear therefore to be addressed to the city of Jerusalem." (Thompson)

3. (21-23) The guilt of those whom the LORD punishes.

What will you say when He punishes you?
For you have taught them
To be **chieftains, to be head over you.**
Will not pangs seize you,
Like a woman in labor?
And if you say in your heart,
"Why have these things come upon me?"
For the greatness of your iniquity
Your skirts have been uncovered,
Your heels made bare.
Can the Ethiopian change his skin or the leopard its spots?
Then **may you also do good who are accustomed to do evil.**

a. **What will you say when He punishes you?** When the promised calamity came upon Judah, they would have no excuse. Though they did not listen to Jeremiah, he clearly warned them as the messenger of the LORD.

i. "Like nominal believers in all ages, the people were incredulous that such calamities could overtake them." (Harrison)

ii. **You have taught them to be chieftains, to be head over you**: "This is said of their enemies, whether Assyrians or Chaldeans…Their enemies were thus taught to be their lords and masters." (Clarke)

b. **For the greatness of your iniquity your skirts have been uncovered, your heels made bare**: With strong images, God warned Judah that their iniquity was so great that the judgment coming against them would be as a severe violation.

i. The idea here is that unfaithful Judah would be terribly and tragically violated by their conquerors, or that they would be humiliated and exposed as prostitutes for their continual spiritual adulteries (as in Isaiah 47:2-3; Hosea 2:3). Either image fits this context.

ii. "Exposure of the secret parts (here euphemistically described as tearing off the skirt and mistreating the body) was the public disgrace heaped on prostitutes." (Feinberg)

iii. "The expression 'lift up the skirt' is a euphemism for sexual attack both here and elsewhere in the OT (Leviticus 18:6-19; Deuteronomy 23:1 [English 22:30]; 27:20; Isaiah 47:3; Nahum 3:5, etc.)." (Thompson)

iv. "The *heels* of AV is another euphemism, more literally rendered 'body ravished' (RSV *suffer violence*; NEB *limbs uncovered*)." (Harrison)

v. "Under the savage metaphors the lesson is that a people that parts with its virtue – its morals, its integrity, its faith – will find itself not liberated, only cheapened: stripped of everything that gave it value and respect." (Kidner)

c. **Can the Ethiopian change his skin or the leopard its spots? Then may you also do good who are accustomed to do evil**: Jeremiah quoted this proverb to warn the people that they were stuck in their sinful nature, and *unable to change themselves*. The answer was not first in national reform, but in national repentance and reliance upon the God who *can* change the nature of man.

i. "Evil, not only fitting them like a glove, not only deep-dyed, was by now something they could not more change or wish to change than the colour of their skin." (Kidner)

ii. Evil may be so ingrained in men that they find it impossible to change. Yet, especially from a broader Biblical perspective, we see the transforming work of Jesus Christ. *Therefore, if anyone is in Christ, he is a new creation; old things have passed away; behold, all things have become new* (2 Corinthians 5:17). The changes don't come all at once and they are not complete until we are resurrected in glory, but the transformation is nevertheless real. The Ethiopian cannot change his skin nor the leopard his spots; but the LORD God can transform men and women.

iii. "The question of the text is, *'Can* the Ethiopian change his skin?' The answer is, -- No, no, no, no, no, no. Here is the other question, -- *Can the Ethiopian's skin be changed? The* answer to that is, -- Yes, yes, yes, as emphatically as we have just now said no, no, no. Can the Ethiopian's skin be changed? Can the sinner's nature be renewed? Yes, for *God can do everything.*" (Spurgeon)

4. (24-25) The determination of the LORD to scatter His people.

"Therefore I will scatter them like stubble
That passes away by the wind of the wilderness.
This is your lot,
The portion of your measures from Me," says the LORD,
"Because you have forgotten Me
And trusted in falsehood."

a. **I will scatter them like stubble**: Judah would not be conquered and exiled, but scattered across the Babylonian Empire and succeeding empires. This was their **lot**, the **portion of your measures from** the LORD.

i. **This is your lot**: "Look for no better, since thou, by going after lying vanities, forsakes thine own mercies, being miserable by thine own election." (Trapp)

b. **Because you have forgotten Me and trusted in falsehood**: Even in this severe warning, God gave His people a roadmap back to His favor and blessing. Where they had **forgotten** God they must remember Him again, and where they had **trusted in** the **falsehood** of self and idols, they must turn away from them.

i. **Trusted in falsehood**: "The attachment of Judah to *The Lie* was in itself a great shame, an act of adultery." (Thompson)

ii. "The irony of it all is that this will be inflicted by the very people whom Judah once courted. Because of her indulgence in the unfruitful works of darkness Judah would be exposed publicly as the corrupt wanton that she was by the One who had first espoused her in covenant love." (Harrison)

5. (26-27) The exposed shame of God's people.

**"Therefore I will uncover your skirts over your face,
That your shame may appear.
I have seen your adulteries
And your *lustful* neighings,
The lewdness of your harlotry,
Your abominations on the hills in the fields.
Woe to you, O Jerusalem!
Will you still not be made clean?"**

> a. **Therefore I will uncover your skirts over your face, that your shame may appear**: God's people chronically refused to humble themselves before the Lord (as in the plea of Jeremiah 13:18). Therefore they would face a far greater **shame**, one appropriate for their literal and spiritual **harlotry**.
>
>> i. **Your lustful neighings**: "The 'neighings' are a bestial figure for illicit love." (Feinberg)
>
> b. **Woe to you, O Jerusalem! Will you still not be made clean?** It was not only the Prophet Jeremiah who ached over the destiny of this stubborn, self-willed, idolatrous people. Yahweh Himself joined in the **woe** and the plea.
>
>> i. "He closeth with this emphatical and most affectionate contestation, pressing them to hearty and speedy repentance, as he had done oft before, but with little good success." (Trapp)

Jeremiah 14 – Judgment Upon False Prophets

A. A model of repentance never fulfilled.

1. (1-6) The droughts upon Judah.

The word of the LORD that came to Jeremiah concerning the droughts.

"Judah mourns,
And her gates languish;
They mourn for the land,
And the cry of Jerusalem has gone up.
Their nobles have sent their lads for water;
They went to the cisterns *and* found no water.
They returned with their vessels empty;
They were ashamed and confounded
And covered their heads.
Because the ground is parched,
For there was no rain in the land,
The plowmen were ashamed;
They covered their heads.
Yes, the deer also gave birth in the field,
But left because there was no grass.
And the wild donkeys stood in the desolate heights;
They sniffed at the wind like jackals;
Their eyes failed because *there was* no grass."

a. **The word of the LORD that came to Jeremiah concerning the droughts**: Apparently this section of Jeremiah's prophecy came during a season when Judah was afflicted by **droughts**. Sustained or multiple droughts were always a life-or-death issue in ancient societies where most made their living farming.

i. Drought was also a special issue for ancient Israel and Judah, because the often-worshipped Canaanite idol Baal was thought to be the god of weather and rain. Many ancient Israelites were drawn to Baal worship because they wanted rain.

ii. "Drought had been threatened for disobedience (Deuteronomy 28:23-24) and was part of the covenant curses. The Lord's purpose in sending the drought was to bring the nation to repentance." (Feinberg)

iii. "The word *drought* is plural here, indicating a series of such disasters, each one leaving the survivors less able to face the next." (Kidner)

b. **Their nobles have sent their lads for water, they went to the cisterns and found no water**: With both prophecy and poetry, Jeremiah described the great calamity of successive droughts in Judah. The people were brought low because of the lack of life-giving water (**they were ashamed and confounded**).

i. "On the back of that confusion came despair; 'they covered their heads.' The Orientals cover their heads when in the deepest grief, as David did, when he went over the brook Kedron. It means, 'I cannot face it. Do not look on me in my sorrow, nor expect me to look on you. I cover my head, for it is all over with me.'" (Spurgeon)

c. **The deer also gave birth in the field, but left because there was no grass**: When God brought discipline or judgment to Judah through drought, it also affected animals and nature around them. Their sincere and sustained repentance would not only benefit themselves, but also the natural world.

i. "Jeremiah's acquaintance with country-life is shown in the aptness of his illustrations: the hind [**deer**] is a creature renowned for the care of her young; the wild asses [**donkeys**] are amongst the hardest of animals, well able to endure drought." (Cundall)

2. (7-9) A model of godly repentance in the time of drought.

O Lord, though our iniquities testify against us,
Do it for Your name's sake;
For our backslidings are many,
We have sinned against You.
O the Hope of Israel, his Savior in time of trouble,
Why should You be like a stranger in the land,
And like a traveler *who* turns aside to tarry for a night?
Why should You be like a man astonished,
Like a mighty one *who* cannot save?
Yet You, O Lord, *are* in our midst,
And we are called by Your name;
Do not leave us!

a. **O Lord, though our iniquities testify against us, do it for Your name's sake**: Using his prophetic imagination, Jeremiah thought of what true repentance would look like from Judah in response to the droughts. It began with an utter confession of guilt and an appeal to pure mercy, not what they deserved.

b. **O the Hope of Israel, his Savior in time of trouble, why should You be like a stranger in the land**: Having come to God with humility and repentance, now the appeal sought to remind God that He was Israel's **Hope** and **Savior**, and asked Him not to be a **stranger** to them in their great need.

c. **Why should You be like a man astonished, like a mighty one who cannot save**: With great confidence in God's power and ability to save, Jeremiah imagined the repentant one appealing to God's honor in the rescue of His people – that God would show Himself as one who *can* save.

d. **Yet You, O Lord, are in our midst, and we are called by Your name; do not leave us!** The repentant one reminded God that He *was* near to Israel, and that they did belong to Him. He called upon God to act upon that nearness and identification.

   i. "If only the nation had taken up this cry from the heart, and made it its own, then God could have shown forgiveness." (Cundall)

3. (10) God's response to the actual, shallow response of His people.

Thus says the Lord to this people:

"Thus they have loved to wander;
They have not restrained their feet.
Therefore the Lord does not accept them;
He will remember their iniquity now,
And punish their sins."

a. **Thus they have loved to wander; they have not restrained their feet**: God responded to the imagined repentant one – they were just in the imagination. The Judah that actually existed **loved to wander** and did not hold themselves back from sin.

   i. Repentance, confession, humility before God that is only in the mind (or heart) but not in genuine action to Him is of no effect. It must go beyond a feeling. The repentance described in Jeremiah 14:7-9 was wonderful, but not real.

b. **Therefore the Lord does not accept them**: Because the repentant one was only imagined, God would not **accept** an unfaithful people. He would **remember** and **punish their sins**.

B. Exposing the false prophets.

1. (11-12) The futility of the certainty of God's judgment.

Then the LORD said to me, "Do not pray for this people, for *their* good. When they fast, I will not hear their cry; and when they offer burnt offering and grain offering, I will not accept them. But I will consume them by the sword, by the famine, and by the pestilence."

> a. **Do not pray for this people**: God gave a similar command to Jeremiah at Jeremiah 7:16-19. The people of Judah were at this point so hardened that they were past prayer; their course was set. God simply told Jeremiah, **When they fast, I will not hear their cry**.
>
>> i. It is significant that God had to tell Jeremiah not to pray; the assumption is that he would pray and that God had to tell him not to. There is something along these lines in the New Testament, at 1 John 5:14-16, where John explained that there are some people – at least in theory – who are beyond prayer, and therefore prayer should not be made for them.
>>
>> ii. "O, how dreadful is the state of that people in reference to whom the Lord says to his ministers, *Pray not for them*; or, what amounts nearly to a prohibition, withholds from his ministers the spirit of prayer and intercession in behalf of the people!" (Clarke)
>
> b. **I will consume them by the sword, by the famine, and by the pestilence**: The promised judgment would come. The insincere repentance offered would never be enough.
>
>> i. "The three items *sword*, *famine*, and *pestilence* were the regular accompaniment of war and are referred to several times in the OT." (Thompson)

2. (13) Jeremiah reports the words of the false prophets.

Then I said, "Ah, Lord GOD! Behold, the prophets say to them, 'You shall not see the sword, nor shall you have famine, but I will give you assured peace in this place.'"

> a. **Ah, Lord GOD! Behold, the prophets say to them**: Jeremiah had a message in the name of the LORD to deliver to the people of Judah. Yet Jeremiah was not the only one who claimed to bring such a word. Others also claimed to be **prophets**.
>
> b. **You shall not see the sword, nor shall you have famine, but I will give you assured peace in this place**: The message of the other prophets was that there would be deliverance from **sword** and **famine**. God would

rescue. This was a hopeful, positive message that contrasted with what God gave to Jeremiah.

> i. Jeremiah probably hoped to explain or excuse the lack of repentance among the people and leaders of Judah. They didn't truly repent because other **prophets** told them everything would be fine.
>
> ii. "The prophet urged excuses for the people, and cried for mercy upon them, and that persistently. Again and again Jehovah replied, showing His servant the uselessness of all such praying." (Morgan)

3. (14-15) God's assessment of these false prophets.

And the LORD said to me, "The prophets prophesy lies in My name. I have not sent them, commanded them, nor spoken to them; they prophesy to you a false vision, divination, a worthless thing, and the deceit of their heart. Therefore thus says the LORD concerning the prophets who prophesy in My name, whom I did not send, and who say, 'Sword and famine shall not be in this land'—'By sword and famine those prophets shall be consumed!'"

> a. **The prophets prophesy lies in My name**: This was a direct and strong judgment. These pretended **prophets** did not truly speak in the **name** of the LORD; they prophesied **lies**.
>
> b. **I have not sent them, commanded them, nor spoken to them; they prophesy a false vision**: God claimed no responsibility for the words of those supposed prophets. The source of their words was **the deceit of their heart**. Their false prophecies came from themselves, not from the LORD.
>
> c. **By sword and famine those prophets shall be consumed**: The false prophets who spoke words of peace and safety when it was a time to repent and prepare for judgment would themselves be special targets of the **sword and famine** to come.
>
>> i. "The people should have known that the Lord punishes sin, and they should not have believed the false prophets. The judgment of the nation is spoken of here because the people were willing to be deceived." (Feinberg)

4. (16) God's judgment on those who remain under the words of the false prophets.

"And the people to whom they prophesy shall be cast out in the streets of Jerusalem because of the famine and the sword; they will have no one to bury them—them nor their wives, their sons nor their daughters—for I will pour their wickedness on them."

a. **And the people to whom they prophesy**: God did not consider those who received the words of the false prophets as without guilt. They were responsible for rejecting the words of the true prophets (Jeremiah and others like him) and for receiving the smooth but false words of the false prophets.

b. **Shall be cast out into the streets because of the famine and the sword**: Hearing and believing the words of the false prophets did not make it true. They would suffer under the same judgment the false prophets said would never come.

c. **They will have no one to bury them**: This was regarded as a special disgrace, magnifying the dishonor when God would **pour their wickedness on them**.

C. The pain of the prophet.

1. (17-18) Weeping over the judgment to come.

"Therefore you shall say this word to them:
'Let my eyes flow with tears night and day,
And let them not cease;
For the virgin daughter of my people
Has been broken with a mighty stroke, with a very severe blow.
If I go out to the field,
Then behold, those slain with the sword!
And if I enter the city,
Then behold, those sick from famine!
Yes, both prophet and priest go about in a land they do not know.'"

a. **Let my eyes flow with tears night and day**: It wasn't a happy or triumphant thing for Jeremiah to know that he was a true prophet and those who said smooth things were false prophets. His pain at the calamity of coming judgment was far greater than any satisfaction in being right.

b. **The virgin daughter of my people has been broken with a mighty stroke**: Jeremiah looked at the people of God for what they could have been – like a **virgin daughter** unto God – and grieved that there would be no escape from coming judgment, not in **the field** or in **the city**.

   i. "He calls Judah 'the virgin daughter – my people' because she had been jealously kept from the idolatrous nations, as virgins are guarded in Oriental households." (Feinberg)

c. **Both prophet and priest go about in a land they do not know**: Those who should have been a light and a guide to the people of God were themselves blind. This left little hope for the people of God to escape the coming judgment.

2. (19-20) An astonished confession of sin and wickedness.

Have You utterly rejected Judah?
Has Your soul loathed Zion?
Why have You stricken us so that *there is* no healing for us?
We looked for peace, but *there was* no good;
And for the time of healing, and there was trouble.
We acknowledge, O LORD, our wickedness
***And* the iniquity of our fathers,**
For we have sinned against You.

a. **Has Your soul loathed Zion**: Astonished at the calamity to come, Jeremiah was bold enough to wonder if God had cast off His people; if He had **utterly rejected** them, **loathed** them, and **stricken** them beyond **healing**.

i. God told Jeremiah that He would not hear the prayers prayed for the people of Judah (Jeremiah 14:11). Yet Jeremiah could not stop praying. "In spite of it, Jeremiah continued to plead for the people, and that Jehovah permitted him to do so, patiently arguing with him." (Morgan)

ii. "What is Jeremiah to do in such a case as this? He is told that he must not pray for the people, and God seems determined to smite them. What can love do when even the gates of prayer are ordered to be closed? Notice how, after he is told that he must not pray, he edges his way up towards the throne of grace and, at last, he does what he is told not to do." (Spurgeon)

b. **We looked for peace, but there was no good**: Prompted by the smooth words of the false prophets the people of Judah hoped for **peace** and **healing**, but instead came **trouble**.

c. **For we have sinned against you**: This was God's desired result of the **trouble** to come upon them – to bring them to a full knowledge of their **wickedness** and **iniquity**. The hopeful but false words of the self-appointed prophets would not bring this result.

i. "The prophet knows that confession will result in forgiveness, and if the nation will not acknowledge its sin, Jeremiah will do so vicariously." (Harrison)

ii. Adam Clarke saw that the people and leaders of Judah did not confess their sin after Jeremiah's example: "This the prophet did in behalf of the people; but, alas! They did not join him." (Clarke)

3. (21-22) A plea that God would remember them in their misery.

Do not abhor *us*, for Your name's sake;
Do not disgrace the throne of Your glory.
Remember, do not break Your covenant with us.
Are there any among the idols of the nations that can cause rain?
Or can the heavens give showers?
***Are* You not He, O LORD our God?**
Therefore we will wait for You,
Since You have made all these.

a. **Do not abhor us, for Your name's sake; do not disgrace the throne of Your glory**: Seeing nothing good in *them* upon which to appeal to God, Jeremiah prayed with a different approach. He asked on the basis of God's name, on the basis of God's rule and authority (**the throne of Your glory**), and on the basis of His **covenant** with them.

i. "Now he is getting actually to praying; he cannot help himself. He is told that he must not pray, but he feels that he must; he loves the people so much that he must plead for them." (Spurgeon)

ii. This ground of reasoning anticipates the New Covenant. Under the New Covenant we believe God for help and blessing and favor not based upon who we are or what we have done, but upon who God is and what He has done.

b. **Are there any among the idols that can cause rain?** The chapter began with concern over the droughts. Now Jeremiah hopefully speaks for a repentant people who recognize that Baal or any of the other **idols** are powerless to **cause rain**. Not even nature separated from God can do it (**can the heavens give showers**). The judgment of God, severe as it was, separated them from the idolatry and reliance upon the gods of the nations or nature to **cause rain**.

c. **Therefore we will wait for You**: The humbled, surrendered, and submitted heart simply looks to God in patient reliance. The severe work of God's strong correction upon His people has performed a merciful work.

i. "Have you come to a very difficult, place? Are you in very sore trouble, – such trouble as you never knew before? Then wait upon the Lord; and if at first he does not answer you, and it seems as if the very gates of heaven are shut against you, still continue, to wait upon the Lord. Where else can you go if you turn away from him?" (Spurgeon)

Jeremiah 15 – The Painful Prayer of the Prophet

A. The inevitable destiny of Judah: four forms of destruction.

1. (1) The uselessness of intercession for rebellious Judah.

Then the LORD said to me, "*Even* if Moses and Samuel stood before Me, My mind *would* not *be* favorable toward this people. Cast *them* out of My sight, and let them go forth."

> a. **Even if Moses and Samuel stood before Me**: Several times before, God had told Jeremiah to *not* pray for the people, because their fate of judgment and exile was already certain (Jeremiah 7:16, 11:14, and 14:11). Adding to that previous thought, God said that even if two of the giants of the Old Testament – **Moses and Samuel** – were to intercede for Judah, it would not change their fate.
>
>> i. **Moses and Samuel** were both known to be great men of intercession (Psalm 99:6-8). **Moses** seemed to change the destined judgment of Israel through his prayer (Exodus 32). **Samuel** prayed and the people were rescued from what seemed certain destruction (1 Samuel 7).
>>
>> ii. "Those two were famous in their generations for hearty love to, and prayers for, that rebellious people, and did much for them." (Trapp)
>
> b. **My mind would not be favorable toward this people**: By this Jeremiah understood that it wasn't as if he were a greater man of faith or prayer, the catastrophe could be avoided. Even if **Moses and Samuel** were present to pray for Israel, it would not be more effective than the prayers of Jeremiah.
>
> c. **Cast them out of My sight, and let them go forth**: Judah will face its appointed and righteous exile out of the land.

2. (2-4) The four forms of destruction.

"And it shall be, if they say to you, 'Where should we go?' then you shall tell them, 'Thus says the LORD:

"Such as *are* for death, to death;
And such as *are* for the sword, to the sword;
And such as *are* for the famine, to the famine;
And such as *are* for the captivity, to the captivity."'

"And I will appoint over them four forms *of destruction*," says the LORD: "the sword to slay, the dogs to drag, the birds of the heavens and the beasts of the earth to devour and destroy. I will hand them over to trouble, to all kingdoms of the earth, because of Manasseh the son of Hezekiah, king of Judah, for what he did in Jerusalem.

>a. **Where should we go**: God promised in the previous verse that Judah would be cast out of His sight and would be sent forth. Now God anticipated the question, "**Where should we go?**"
>
>b. **Death… sword… famine… captivity**: Some will go to **death** (actually, plague or pestilence), some will die in battle by the **sword**, some will perish through **famine**, and the remaining will go **to the captivity**. There would be no good ways to die.
>
>>i. "Some shall be destroyed by the *pestilence*, here termed *death*. See Jeremiah 18:21." (Clarke)
>
>c. **Four forms of destruction**: Additionally (and poetically speaking), there would be four ways a corpse could be dishonored after death. It could come through the **sword**, through **dogs**, through **the birds of the heavens** or through **the beasts of the earth**. It would seem as if all creation had gathered against judgment-ripe Judah to not only slay them, but to dishonor their dead bodies.
>
>>i. "When slain, the corpses will undergo further humiliation from dogs, carrion birds, and other predators." (Harrison)
>
>>ii. "For the corpse of a man to be dragged on the ground and then become carrion for bird and beast was too horrendous for an Israelite to contemplate. It was the ultimate in desecration of the dead." (Feinberg)
>
>d. **Because of Manasseh the son of Hezekiah**: There were sinful kings in Judah before and after **Manasseh**, and the people themselves did not obey and seek God. Yet there was something so horrific about the sin and rebellion of Manasseh that made judgment inevitable, irreversible.
>
>>i. The history of Judah tells the story of Manasseh's great sin (2 Kings 21:9-17). 2 Kings 21:16 summarized it as so: *Manasseh shed very much innocent blood, till he had filled Jerusalem from one end to another, besides his sin by which he made Judah sin, in doing evil in the sight of the LORD.*

ii. The evil **Manasseh** was the **son of Hezekiah** – generally a good and godly king. "He was therefore the worse, because he should have been better; and yet the worse again, because he was a ringleader of rebellion to others." (Trapp)

iii. Yet, strangely, "The monstrous Manasseh found personal forgiveness (2 Chronicles 33:12-13), but his legacy remained, both in the unrequired crimes of his regime against the innocent, and in the sins he had taught his people to embrace." (Kidner)

iv. **I will hand them over to trouble, to all kingdoms of the earth**: "Never was there a prophecy more literally fulfilled; and it is still a standing monument of Divine truth. Let *infidelity* cast its eyes on the scattered Jews whom it may meet with in every civilized nation of the world; and then let it deny the truth of this prophecy, if it can. The Jews are scattered through every nation, and yet *are not a nation*; nor do they form even *a colony* on any part of the face of the earth. Behold the truth and the justice of God!" (Clarke, 1830)

B. After judgment, mercy on the remnant.

1. (5-9) Woe upon the widows.

"For who will have pity on you, O Jerusalem?
Or who will bemoan you?
Or who will turn aside to ask how you are doing?
You have forsaken Me," says the LORD,
"You have gone backward.
Therefore I will stretch out My hand against you and destroy you;
I am weary of relenting!
And I will winnow them with a winnowing fan in the gates of the land;
I will bereave *them* of children;
I will destroy My people,
Since **they do not return from their ways.**
Their widows will be increased to Me more than the sand of the seas;
I will bring against them,
Against the mother of the young men,
A plunderer at noonday;
I will cause anguish and terror to fall on them suddenly.
"She languishes who has borne seven;
She has breathed her last;
Her sun has gone down
While *it was* **yet day;**
She has been ashamed and confounded.

And the remnant of them I will deliver to the sword
Before their enemies," says the LORD.

> a. **For who will have pity on you, O Jerusalem**: Speaking through the Prophet Jeremiah, Yahweh asked **Jerusalem** to consider if anyone else cared for them and their coming crisis. There was no other who cared, who would **bemoan** their tragedy or take interest in their need.
>
> b. **You have forsaken Me**: Ironically, Judah rejected and rebelled against the only One who cared for them. Instead of progressing, they had **gone backward**. God would answer their rejection of Him with His own kind of rejection of them, giving them over to judgment and destruction.
>
> c. **I am weary of relenting**: Judah was most blind to it, but God had held back His judgment against Judah for a long, long time. They presumed upon God in **relenting** in His own judgment against them, never considering that one day He would become **weary** of it and relent no more.
>
> d. **I will winnow them with a winnowing fan**: The work of **winnowing** used wind to scatter the chaff, separating it from the valuable grain. God would soon scatter Judah and Jerusalem into exile, as if from a **winnowing fan**.
>
> e. **Their widows will be increased to Me more than the sand of the seas**: Considering the destruction and judgment to come upon Judah, God mentioned all the **widows** that would come forth from those slain in battle and exile.
>
> f. **She languishes who has borne seven**: Bearing seven children would normally be considered a sign of great blessing – something of a perfect family. Now even that woman suffers and perishes, **she has been ashamed and confounded** by the great judgment of God to come upon Judah.
>
>> i. "To have seven sons is a Hebrew picture of complete happiness, but the mother in Jeremiah 15:9 has had her happiness pass all too soon." (Feinberg)

2. (10) Jeremiah's personal woe.

**Woe is me, my mother,
That you have borne me,
A man of strife and a man of contention to the whole earth!
I have neither lent for interest,
Nor have men lent to me for interest.
Every one of them curses me.**

a. **Woe is me, my mother, that you have borne me**: In considering the severity of his message, Jeremiah thought of the great **woe** he himself bore. Like Job, he wondered if it would be better if he was never born.

b. **A man of strife and a man of contention to the whole earth**: The **woe** of Jeremiah lay primarily in the fact that he continually battled for the message God gave him to proclaim. His work as a prophet was filled with **strife** and **contention** that seemed to be set against **the whole earth**.

> i. "Generally opposed and quarrelled, for my free and faithful discharge of my duty. This is the world's wages to godly ministers, whom they usually make their butt-mark. But God be thanked, saith he with Jerome, that I am worthy whom the world should hate. Luther said of himself, Luther is fed with reproaches." (Trapp)

c. **Every one of them curses me**: Jeremiah considered it remarkable that he should be so reviled by others when he had not defrauded them by either borrowing or lending to them dishonestly; nevertheless, he felt cursed and not received by all.

> i. "This is one of Jeremiah's most moving confessions. He was complaining of loneliness. His greatness lay in his sensitive nature that felt acute pain for his people and their doom. The hopelessness of the nation's situation and his own difficulties of his position weighed on him." (Feinberg)

> ii. "One of the greatest trials to which the people of God are subject, in trying to serve their Master, is *non-success*. The seven lean kine, as they eat up the seven fat kine, sorely try the believer's faith. Alas! our disappointments seldom come alone, but like Job's messengers, follow close upon each other's heels. When a man succeeds, he continues to succeed, as a rule; he derives encouragement from what God has already done by him, and goes from strength to strength. Probably, however, there is more grace exhibited by the Christian, who, without present success, realises the things not seen as yet, and continues still to work on. To labor is not easy, but to labor *and to wait* is harder far." (Spurgeon)

3. (11-14) Promise of help, promise of exile.

The Lord said:
"Surely it will be well with your remnant;
Surely I will cause the enemy to intercede with you
In the time of adversity and in the time of affliction.
Can anyone break iron,
The northern iron and the bronze?

Your wealth and your treasures
I will give as plunder without price,
Because of all your sins,
Throughout your territories.
And I will make *you* cross over with your enemies
Into a land *which* you do not know;
For a fire is kindled in My anger,
Which shall burn upon you."

> a. **Surely it will be well with your remnant**: God promised Jeremiah – both personally and as a representative of his people – that they would not be utterly forsaken in their exile. God would give him favor among the enemy to come (**I will cause the enemy to intercede with you**).
>
>> i. "Notice that there is no release from his calling: only a renewing of it." (Kidner)
>>
>> ii. "This was literally fulfilled; see Jeremiah 39:11, etc. Nebuchadnezzar had given strict charge to Nebuzar-adan, commander in chief, to look well to Jeremiah, to do him no harm, and to grant him all the privileges he was pleased to ask." (Clarke)
>
> b. **Can anyone break iron, the northern iron and the bronze?** Though God said He would take care of His Prophet Jeremiah in the coming crisis, it did not mean that the fate of Judah generally had changed. The weapons of Babylon – made with strong **northern iron and the bronze** – would surely come against them.
>
>> i. "The finest quality iron (*northern ore*) in the seventh century BC came from the Black Sea region. Clearly the armaments of Judah would be insufficient to repel the Babylonian armies." (Harrison)
>
> c. **I will make you cross over with your enemies into a land which you do not know**: Not only was the judgment and conquest of Judah certain, but they would also be exiled from their land into the unknown land of their enemies.

4. (15-18) The painful prayer of the prophet.

O Lord, You know;
Remember me and visit me,
And take vengeance for me on my persecutors.
In Your enduring patience, do not take me away.
Know that for Your sake I have suffered rebuke.
Your words were found, and I ate them,
And Your word was to me the joy and rejoicing of my heart;
For I am called by Your name,

O Lord God of hosts.
I did not sit in the assembly of the mockers,
Nor did I rejoice;
I sat alone because of Your hand,
For You have filled me with indignation.
Why is my pain perpetual
And my wound incurable,
Which refuses to be healed?
Will You surely be to me like an unreliable stream,
As waters *that* fail?

a. **Remember me and visit me, and take vengeance for me on my persecutors**: Jeremiah did what other godly men in the Bible also did – he looked to God for protection and justice when persecuted for righteousness' sake. Jeremiah could rightly say, "**for Your sake I have suffered rebuke**," so he could also rightly entrust whatever **vengeance** was appropriate unto God's care.

i. **Remember me**: "Israelite 'remembering' was not mere recollection. It was a recapturing of the past in a way that led to action in the present." (Thompson)

ii. "He is alienated from his people because of his witness, yet he has no choice but to proclaim God's word to a recalcitrant nation. He is a lonely, anxious man, yet one who rejoices that God dwells in his heart." (Harrison)

b. **Your words were found, and I ate them, and Your word was to me the joy and rejoicing of my heart**: As Jeremiah continued to plead his case before God, he declared to God his great love for and focus upon God's word.

- Jeremiah first **found** God's word, neither neglecting it nor taking it for granted.
- Jeremiah then **ate** God's word, taking it in as food for the soul and receiving refreshment and nourishment from it.
- Jeremiah then regarded God's word as **the joy and rejoicing of** his **heart**. He delighted upon the word of God and did so in his innermost being.

i. "I have said that Jeremiah lets us into a secret. His outer life, consisting in his perpetual faithful ministry, was to be accounted for by his inward love of the word which he preached." (Spurgeon)

ii. "It is a very different thing from saying, 'Thy word was found, and I did admire it,' or 'Thy word was found, and I did criticise it,' or 'Thy word was found, and I did divide it and make a sermon of it.' That is a minister's temptation." (Spurgeon)

c. **For I am called by Your name**: This interest and value placed upon God's word seemed natural and appropriate for Jeremiah, because he knew that he was **called by** God's own **name**. Jeremiah would think it strange that anyone called by His name would not find interest and nourishment and joy in God's word.

d. **I did not sit in the assembly of the mockers**: Jeremiah pleaded his separation from those who did not value or love God's word. He did so in wording suggestive of Psalm 1, which shows the blessing to attentiveness to God's word.

i. "It was his unhappy duty to denounce the judgments of God upon a people whom he dearly loved, but whom it was impossible to save; for even his deep anguish of heart and melting pathos were powerless with them, and rather excited their ridicule than their attention." (Spurgeon)

e. **I sat alone because of Your hand**: The separation from **the mockers** meant that there were times when the prophet **sat alone**, out of obedience and integrity to God and His word.

i. "The reason why Jeremiah *sat alone* was because of Yahweh's *hand*, that is, he was under divine constraint for his special task." (Thompson)

f. **Why is my pain perpetual… will You surely be to me like an unreliable stream**: Jeremiah had a true trust in God and connection to His Word, yet this did not remove the crisis. There were still times when his pain seemed **perpetual** and he feared God might not be faithful to him – as **an unreliable stream**. This was a genuine challenge to Jeremiah's faith in God's goodness and power.

i. "Time was when Jeremiah thought of Yahweh as a 'fountain of living water (Jeremiah 2:13). But now he seems like *waters that have failed*." (Thompson)

ii. "In his distraught state, Jeremiah charged the Lord with failure to fulfill his promises to strengthen him in his resistance against his enemies." (Feinberg)

iii. "This was a fit of diffidence and discontent, as the best have their outbursts, and the greatest lamps have needed snuffers." (Trapp)

5. (19-21) A promise to protect the prophet.

Therefore thus says the Lord:
"If you return,

Then I will bring you back;
You shall stand before Me;
If you take out the precious from the vile,
You shall be as My mouth.
Let them return to you,
But you must not return to them.
And I will make you to this people a fortified bronze wall;
And they will fight against you,
But they shall not prevail against you;
For I *am* with you to save you
And deliver you," says the Lord.
"I will deliver you from the hand of the wicked,
And I will redeem you from the grip of the terrible."

a. **If you return, then I will bring you back**: God promised Jeremiah that despite the current rejection and the coming crisis, there remained a promise of restoration. If he rejected the temptation to regard God as uncaring or unreliable and continued to **take out the precious from the vile**, he would continue to be a spokesman for God.

i. "In Jeremiah's heart there were unworthy thoughts of God, and these had found expression in his utterances. Let him purge his heart of such alloy (**take out the precious from the vile**), and devote himself only to the true gold of truth concerning God." (Morgan)

ii. "It is ironic that God had to tell Jeremiah to repent. For years Jeremiah had been telling the people of Israel to turn back in repentance. But he had some repenting of his own to do." (Ryken)

b. **Let them return to you, but you must not return to them**: It was important for Jeremiah to remain as an unmovable prophet of God. The people of God could **return** to him, but he must not move from his place to accommodate them.

i. "The end of verse 19 has a play on words; 'turn,' 'not turn.' He must lift his people and not let them drag him down to their level." (Feinberg)

c. **I will make you to this people a fortified bronze wall**: If Jeremiah remained steadfast in his position as God's prophet, God would make him strong and unconquerable. God would fulfill His promise to **deliver from the hand of the wicked** and to **redeem from the grip of the terrible**.

i. "How gracious was God to His overwrought servant in the face of this querulous outburst! He did not write Jeremiah off as a failure, but showing him the worthlessness of such unfounded accusations,

He indicated the way of restoration through repentance and divine strength." (Cundall)

ii. "The promise of deliverance is expressed in three significant Old Testament verbs of deliverance…they are found in such significant passages as the Exodus story, although they have a more general application. The total picture of deliverance is many-sided and each verb provides a different emphasis." (Thompson)

- **Save**: "Its related nouns lay stress on the bringing out of those under restraint into a broad place." (Thompson)
- **Deliver**: "Pictures the activity of one who snatches his prey from the grasp of a powerful possessor." (Thompson)
- **Redeem**: "Normally used in reference to liberation from the possession of another by the giving up of a ransom…it came to refer to acts of deliverance in daily life." (Thompson)

iii. "The heartening promises of verses 20-21 remind Jeremiah of his opening call, almost word for word (*cf.* 1:18-19). They offer nothing easy. But the strength that they speak of, and the undefeated outcome, will be the glory of Jeremiah's ministry." (Kidner)

Jeremiah 16 – Living Signs of Coming Judgment

A. Jeremiah's call to live as a sign of coming judgment.

1. (1-4) Jeremiah commanded to not take a wife or to father children.

The word of the LORD also came to me, saying, "You shall not take a wife, nor shall you have sons or daughters in this place." For thus says the LORD concerning the sons and daughters who are born in this place, and concerning their mothers who bore them and their fathers who begot them in this land: "They shall die gruesome deaths; they shall not be lamented nor shall they be buried, *but* **they shall be like refuse on the face of the earth. They shall be consumed by the sword and by famine, and their corpses shall be meat for the birds of heaven and for the beasts of the earth."**

> a. **You shall not take a wife**: God gave Jeremiah a unique command, one that went against the general will of God for His people and against the strong cultural traditions of the Jewish people. Jeremiah was commanded to neither take a wife nor to **have sons or daughters**.
>
> > i. In ancient Jewish culture (and among many observant Jews today) it was a shame and a dishonor to be single and childless. Marriage and childbearing were expected. Jeremiah's obedience to God's command would attract attention.
> >
> > - "Since marriage was the normal state of life for a healthy adult Hebrew male, abstinence for the reasons given would furnish a powerful object-lesson." (Harrison)
> > - "Celibacy was unusual, not only in Israel, but throughout the Near East." (Feinberg)
> > - "Biblical Hebrew does not even have a word for 'bachelor.'" (Ryken)

ii. We should suppose that like most others, Jeremiah looked for the blessings and benefits of marriage and parenthood. These were legitimate desires for him to have; yet in order to fulfill the call of God upon his life, he may need to deny such things to pursue the higher call. Jesus would later explain that His followers must be willing to deny themselves, take up their cross and follow Him (Luke 9:23). According to the will of God for the individual believer, this may mean giving up otherwise legitimate pursuits.

iii. Under the New Covenant and among Christians, marriage and childbearing are still honored and one might say expected. Nevertheless, the New Testament gives specific honor and status to the unmarried, telling them to regard their state as a calling from God, even as Jeremiah (1 Corinthians 7:7-9; 7:26-35).

b. **They shall die gruesome deaths**: This was God's reason for the unusual command to Jeremiah. The present time was so filled with distress and coming crisis that it was wise for Jeremiah not to marry or have children.

i. This was much the same reasoning Paul used in advising contentment with the unmarried state in 1 Corinthians 7:26-35 – that they could find contentment in light of *the present distress* (1 Corinthians 7:26).

ii. "His being denied a wife and children would be a warning that the family life of the nation was to be disrupted." (Feinberg)

2. (5-7) Jeremiah commanded not to mourn with others.

For thus says the LORD: "Do not enter the house of mourning, nor go to lament or bemoan them; for I have taken away My peace from this people," says the LORD, "lovingkindness and mercies. Both the great and the small shall die in this land. They shall not be buried; neither shall men lament for them, cut themselves, nor make themselves bald for them. Nor shall *men* **break** *bread* **in mourning for them, to comfort them for the dead; nor shall** *men* **give them the cup of consolation to drink for their father or their mother.**

a. **Do not enter the house of mourning, nor go to lament**: It was and is normal to mourn and lament with others in the time of death. Yet because God had **taken away** His **peace from this people**, Jeremiah was not to join with others in their formal expressions of mourning.

i. "Not to show grief was abnormal and was cause for criticism. The rituals for the bereaved – even for those who lost a father or mother – would not be permitted. So Jeremiah would be denied the blessing of serving the sorrowing." (Feinberg)

b. **Both the great and the small shall die in this land**: Jeremiah was to stay away from occasions of mourning with others as a sign of the great calamity to come upon Judah, when death would be so widespread that the dead **shall not be buried; neither shall men lament for them**.

c. **Cut themselves, nor make themselves bald for them**: When the coming judgment struck Judah, none of the mourning practices would be observed. Not those that were culturally accepted (**break bread in mourning for them**) nor those that were disobedient imitations of pagan rituals for the dead (**cut themselves**).

i. **Cut themselves**: "These are rites of self-mutilation, in which the mourners cut or gashed themselves and shaved the head and the beard. They seem to have been widely practiced in Israel (Jeremiah 41:45; 47:5; 48:37; Isaiah 15:2-3; 22:12; Ezekiel 7:18; Micah 1:16, etc.) even though they were forbidden." (Thompson)

3. (8-9) Jeremiah commanded not to feast with others.

"Also you shall not go into the house of feasting to sit with them, to eat and drink." For thus says the Lord of hosts, the God of Israel: "Behold, I will cause to cease from this place, before your eyes and in your days, the voice of mirth and the voice of gladness, the voice of the bridegroom and the voice of the bride."

a. **Also you shall not go into the house of feasting to sit with them**: Just as Jeremiah was commanded to detach himself from normal family relationships and expressions of public mourning, so he was also to detach himself from public celebrations. All these were done as signs of the coming judgment.

i. "What this meant to a heart as exquisitely tender as Jeremiah's can only be imagined. In the tight-knit community of Judah it was tantamount to a self-imposed excommunication." (Cundall)

b. **I will cause to cease from this place…the voice of mirth and the voice of gladness**: When the crisis of judgment came upon Judah there would be no gladness or wedding celebrations. As a sign, Jeremiah was to live in his present day as if that judgment had already come.

B. Alternating words of judgment and restoration.

1. (10-13) Explaining God's judgment to the people of Judah.

"And it shall be, when you show this people all these words, and they say to you, 'Why has the Lord pronounced all this great disaster against us? Or what *is* our iniquity? Or what *is* our sin that we have committed against the Lord our God?' then you shall say to them, 'Because your

fathers have forsaken Me,' says the LORD; 'they have walked after other gods and have served them and worshiped them, and have forsaken Me and not kept My law. And you have done worse than your fathers, for behold, each one follows the dictates of his own evil heart, so that no one listens to Me. Therefore I will cast you out of this land into a land that you do not know, neither you nor your fathers; and there you shall serve other gods day and night, where I will not show you favor.'"

> a. **Why has the LORD pronounced all this great disaster against us**: Several times in the Book of Jeremiah, the LORD anticipated this question from the people and leaders of Judah and was concerned to answer it. It was important to God that they did not regard the calamity as misfortune or bad luck; they needed to see that it was a just response to their sin and rebellion.
>
> b. **Because your fathers have forsaken Me**: This coming conquest and exile of Judah was not due to the sin of only one generation. It was hardened rebellion over several generations that brought Judah to their soon-to-come judgment.
>
> c. **And you have done worse than your fathers, for behold, each one follows the dictates of his own evil heart**: The sins of their fathers were enough to make them liable for judgment, but beyond that they added their own guilt. To the sins of their fathers (idolatry and rejection of the LORD's ways), they also worshipped *self* in a significant way.
>
> d. **I will cast you out of this land into a land you do not know**: Because of the collective guilt of their fathers and their own generation, conquest and exile were sure to come.
>
>> i. **There you shall serve other gods day and night**: "There Jeremiah ironically assures them that they will have the opportunity of indulging their desire for pagan worship day and night." (Feinberg)

2. (14-15) The wonderful promise of restoration from exile.

"Therefore behold, the days are coming," says the LORD, "that it shall no more be said, 'The LORD lives who brought up the children of Israel from the land of Egypt,' but, 'The LORD lives who brought up the children of Israel from the land of the north and from all the lands where He had driven them.' For I will bring them back into their land which I gave to their fathers."

> a. **Therefore behold the days are coming**: The previous word from Jeremiah was about as dark as could be, with God promising *I will not show you favor* in the land of their coming exile. Yet as if God could not

help Himself, that word of despair is immediately followed by a wonderful and gracious promise.

b. **No more shall it be said, "The LORD lives who brought up the children of Israel from the land of Egypt"**: God's deliverance of His people from Egypt was the central act of redemption in the Old Testament. Through the Passover celebration and in many other ways, God constantly reminded Israel of this great work.

c. **But, "The LORD lives who brought up the children of Israel from the land of the north and from all the lands where He had driven them"**: God made a remarkable promise – that there would be a new measure of His greatness and redemptive power. The new measure would be the return from captivity when God would **bring them back into their land**.

i. "The reference to 'all the countries' shows that the prophet was predicting a restoration from a general dispersion after the Exile." (Feinberg)

ii. There is a valuable spiritual analogy here. The initial work of redemption in the life of a believer is great; but the restoring work of the believer – when God brings a chastened child of His out of a metaphorical exile and back into His favor and promise – this work may sometimes be regarded as even greater. This is the principle God revealed to Jeremiah.

3. (16-18) The zeal of God in pursing the people ripe for judgment.

"Behold, I will send for many fishermen," says the LORD, "and they shall fish them; and afterward I will send for many hunters, and they shall hunt them from every mountain and every hill, and out of the holes of the rocks. For My eyes *are* on all their ways; they are not hidden from My face, nor is their iniquity hidden from My eyes. And first I will repay double for their iniquity and their sin, because they have defiled My land; they have filled My inheritance with the carcasses of their detestable and abominable idols."

a. **I will send for many fishermen**: These were fishers of men, but in a negative sense. God would send metaphorical **fishermen** and **hunters** upon His rebellious people to capture them for the promised judgment and exile. They could not hide from the God whose **eyes** were **on all their ways**.

i. "Howbeit, some by fishers understand the Egyptians, who lived much by fishing, and by hunters the Chaldeans (as Genesis 10:8,9)." (Trapp)

ii. "The 'fishers' would first net the big haul, presumably a reference to deportation, to be followed by 'hunters', who would ferret out the individual survivors." (Cundall)

iii. **I will repay double**: "Perhaps a better translation goes like this: 'I will repay them exactly what they deserve for their wickedness and their sin.' Their punishment was not so much double as it was proportional. The punishment fit the crime." (Ryken)

b. **Because they have defiled My land**: This explained one reason why exile was an appropriate answer to Judah's deeply sinful condition. Because they **defiled** the Lord's land, they would be cast out of that land for a season.

i. **The carcasses of their detestable and abominable idols**: "Either meaning the *idols* themselves, which were only *carcasses* without life; or the *sacrifices* which were made to them." (Clarke)

ii. "But to be amazed at her tolerance of other gods is to be no less amazed at a generation – our own – which prides itself on religious pluralism and is embarrassed at the exclusive claims of Christianity." (Kidner)

4. (19-21) Yahweh glorified among the Gentiles.

O Lord, my strength and my fortress,
My refuge in the day of affliction,
The Gentiles shall come to You
From the ends of the earth and say,
"Surely our fathers have inherited lies,
Worthlessness and unprofitable *things*.**"**
Will a man make gods for himself,
Which *are* **not gods?**
"Therefore behold, I will this once cause them to know,
I will cause them to know
My hand and My might;
And they shall know that My name *is* **the Lord.**

a. **O Lord, my strength and my fortress, my refuge in the day of affliction**: Despite the gloom of Judah's condition and their impending judgment, Jeremiah still found **strength** and **refuge** in the Lord.

b. **The Gentiles shall come to You**: Not only would God fulfill the promise to restore His own people from their exile, but He would also do an even greater work. God promised to draw **the Gentiles** unto Himself, drawing them **from the ends of the earth**.

c. **Surely our fathers have inherited lies, worthless and unprofitable things**: This would be the repentant testimony of the Gentiles drawn to the LORD. They would see the vanity of their idols and **unprofitable things**.

> i. "The thought of God's proven reality, over against the phantom gods of heathenism, opens Jeremiah's eyes to foresee the day when far-flung peoples will realize the hollowness of their religions and turn to the Lord." (Kidner)

> ii. **Will a man make gods for himself, which are not gods?** "Can any be so silly, and so preposterously absurd? Yes, fallen man is capable of any thing that is base, mean, vile, and wicked, till influenced and converted by the grace of Christ." (Clarke)

d. **I will cause them to know My hand and My might**: God promised a mighty revelation of His power and greatness to the Gentiles. This promise was fulfilled in the display of God's power and love through the work of Jesus and the ongoing presentation of that message.

> i. **They shall know that My name is the LORD**: "In that way the nations would come to know that his name was Yahweh. But a name denoted one's character, and the very name Yahweh denoted a wide range of attributes not least of which as his power to save." (Thompson)

> ii. "Expositors are divided as to whether the Jews or the Gentiles are meant here. Actually, what is said will apply to both; there is no need to exclude either one (cf. Ezekiel 36:23; 37:14)." (Feinberg)

Jeremiah 17 – The Folly of Misplaced Trust

A. The depth of Judah's sin.

1. (1-4) Pen and paper for Judah's sin.

"The sin of Judah *is* written with a pen of iron;
With the point of a diamond *it is* engraved
On the tablet of their heart,
And on the horns of your altars,
While their children remember
Their altars and their wooden images
By the green trees on the high hills.
O My mountain in the field,
I will give as plunder your wealth, all your treasures,
And your high places of sin within all your borders.
And you, even yourself,
Shall let go of your heritage which I gave you;
And I will cause you to serve your enemies
In the land which you do not know;
For you have kindled a fire in My anger *which* shall burn forever."

> a. **The sin of Judah is written with a pen of iron**: As prophet the begins to describe the character and extent of Judah's sin, he starts with a figure that emphasizes the hardness and strength of Judah's rebellion against God. Their sins were engraved deeply upon them, as if written with an **iron** pen, and with **the point of a diamond**. There was nothing superficial about their sinful state.
>
> > i. "A 'pen of iron' was used for cutting inscriptions in rock or stone. The point of the metaphors is not the hardness of the materials used, but the indelible nature of what is written." (Cundall)

b. **On the tablet of their heart, and on the horns of your altars**: Both the heart and the religious works of the people were deeply etched with sin. These bore the indelible marks of Judah's determined rebellion.

> i. "The people's heart has guilt not only written all over it but etched into it, engraved beyond erasure." (Kidner)
>
> ii. "Only when God wrote his law on his people's heart could obedience replace rebellion." (Thompson)
>
> iii. "The reference to 'the horns of their altars' may be to the altars of Baal." (Feinberg)

c. **While their children remember**: Engraving upon a stone tablet lasts for generations, and so would the etching of sin upon the heart and the altars set a sinful course for coming generations. Their sin was written so deep and in such places that it would be read for generations.

d. **I will cause you to serve your enemies**: For all this deeply ingrained sin – especially idolatry with **wooden images** upon the **high hills** – God promised to bring His judgment upon Judah.

2. (5-8) The folly of trusting in man.

Thus says the LORD:
"Cursed *is* the man who trusts in man
And makes flesh his strength,
Whose heart departs from the LORD.
For he shall be like a shrub in the desert,
And shall not see when good comes,
But shall inhabit the parched places in the wilderness,
***In* a salt land *which is* not inhabited.**
"Blessed *is* the man who trusts in the LORD,
And whose hope is the LORD.
For he shall be like a tree planted by the waters,
Which spreads out its roots by the river,
And will not fear when heat comes;
But its leaf will be green,
And will not be anxious in the year of drought,
Nor will cease from yielding fruit.

a. **Cursed is the man who trusts in man**: One might say that this curse does not require the special activity of God; this curse is simply associated with trust placed on failing and fallible **man**. This is especially true because one cannot make **flesh his strength** without also the **heart** departing **from the LORD**.

b. **He shall be like a shrub in the desert**: Jeremiah pictured a weak, dry **shrub in the desert** about to die from drought. *This* is the picture of the one (believer or not) who trusts in man instead of the LORD; they are dry and unsustainable.

> i. "The 'shrub' of Jeremiah 17:6 could be the dwarf juniper, stunted and barely alive in an area of low rainfall and poor soil." (Cundall)
>
> ii. **Like a shrub in the desert**: "According to Nogah Hareuveni, an expert on plants of the Bible, in Hebrew the name of this tree is called the Arar, which sounds similar to the word for cursed (*arur*) and is part of a wordplay which is central to this poem." (Tverberg)
>
> iii. "The Bedouin call this tree the 'Cursed Lemon' or 'Sodom Apple' because it grows in the desert salt lands that surround the Dead Sea where Sodom and Gomorrah once were. According to their legends, when God destroyed Sodom, he cursed the fruit of this tree also…. When opened, the fruit makes a 'pssst' sound, and is hollow and filled with webs and dust and a dry pit." (Tverberg)
>
> iv. "Interestingly, the cursed tree looks very healthy and abundant, as if it has survived even in hard times and still has done well in life." (Tverberg)

c. **Blessed is the man who trusts in the LORD**: In contrast, the one who **trusts in the LORD** will be **like a tree planted by the waters**, whose **leaf will be green**. Jeremiah drew on the images of Psalm 1, where the **blessed** man is the one who delights in God's word (Psalm 1:1-3). In some sense, Jeremiah thought trusting in the LORD to be the same as delighting in His word.

> i. "Since Jeremiah offers two variations on the theme of Psalm 1, here in 17:5-8 and also in 12:1-2, it seems possible that Psalm 1 was available to the prophet." (Thompson)

3. (9-10) The folly of trusting one's own heart.

"The heart *is* deceitful above all *things*,
And desperately wicked;
Who can know it?
I, the LORD, search the heart,
***I* test the mind,**
Even to give every man according to his ways,
According to the fruit of his doings.

a. **The heart is deceitful above all things**: Trusting the heart is just another way of trusting in man. To this point, the Prophet Jeremiah has given some reason to be cautious about the inclinations and direction of the **heart**. He noted how the evil heart of the people of Judah had led them astray.

- *Yet they did not obey or incline their ear, but everyone followed the dictates of his evil heart.* (Jeremiah 11:8)
- *They prophesy to you a false vision, divination, a worthless thing, and the deceit of their heart.* (Jeremiah 14:14)
- *Each one follows the dictates of his own evil heart, so that no one listens to Me.* (Jeremiah 16:12)

b. **The heart is deceitful above all things**: Our hearts often *deceive* us, presenting heart-fulfillment as the key to happiness. What we desire is often not what we need. The advice "be true to your heart" fails when **the heart is deceitful above all things.**

i. "In the OT usage the heart signifies the total inner being and includes reason. From the heart come action and will." (Feinberg)

ii. "The pravity and perversity of the man's heart, full of harlotry and creature confidence, deceiving and being deceived, is here plainly and plentifully described; and oh that it were duly and deeply considered." (Trapp)

c. **And desperately wicked**: The heart is not only deceitful, but also **wicked** – and **desperately** so. Many have been led to rebellion, disobedience, and great sorrow by following their heart, without challenging their heart and judging it by the measure of God's truth. "Follow your heart" is poor advice when the heart is **desperately wicked**.

i. The sense of the Hebrew for **desperately wicked** seems to have *sickness* more than *depravity* in mind. "Unregenerate human nature is in a desperate condition without divine grace, described by the term *gravely ill* in verse 9 (RSV *desperately corrupt*, NEB *desperately sick*)." (Harrison)

ii. For the believer under the New Covenant, we have a new heart (Ezekiel 36:26), are a new creation (2 Corinthians 5:17), and a new man patterned after Jesus (Ephesians 4:24, Colossians 3:10). Still, there is an element of sin and flesh that remains in the believer. Since Jeremiah used the term **heart** in a general sense, we can say that our identity is not **deceitful** and **desperately wicked**; yet we still have to deal with an element of inward deceit and wickedness.

d. **Who can know it**: The heart's deceit and wickedness are advanced enough that even the individual may not know or understand their own heart, and outsiders have even more difficulty in discerning the heart of others.

e. **I, the LORD, search the heart, I test the mind**: Though knowing the heart of one's self or others is difficult and sometimes impossible, *God* searches, tests, and knows the heart and mind. It is wise to trust what God says about us more than what we think or feel about ourselves.

i. **I test the mind**: "A second word is here set in parallel to *heart*, literally, 'kidneys', *hidden depths*. These, Yahweh assays or 'tests'…the two terms 'heart' and 'kidneys' cover the range of hidden elements in man's character and personality. Nothing is hidden from Yahweh." (Thomspon)

ii. "The Lord is called by his apostles, Acts 1:24, καρδιογνωστης, *the Knower of the heart*. To him alone can this epithet be applied; and it is from him alone that we can derive that *instruction* by which we can in any measure *know ourselves*." (Clarke)

f. **Even to give to every man according to his ways**: Because God perfectly knows the heart and mind of man, His judgment is true. God knows to what extent the heart either justifies or condemns the **doings** of a man or woman.

4. (11) The folly of trusting in riches.

"As **a partridge that broods but does not hatch,**
So is **he who gets riches, but not by right;**
It will leave him in the midst of his days,
And at his end he will be a fool."

a. **As a partridge that broods but does not hatch, so is he who gets riches, but not by right**: Jeremiah just spoke to the folly of trusting one's heart. Now, he states a proverb meant to show the foolishness of trusting in riches. Not all riches are condemned; only those gained **not by right**.

i. "Thus many a rich wretch spinneth a fair thread to strangle himself, both temporally and eternally." (Trapp)

b. **It will leave him in the midst of his days**: According to the ancient proverb, a **partridge** sits upon the eggs of other birds. When they do hatch, the chicks leave the partridge because they don't really belong to that bird. Even so, riches will **leave** a man when he stands before God in judgment. In the **end**, he will be shown to be a **fool** for trusting in his ill-gotten gains.

i. "Ill-gotten gain is, like a bird with young she has not hatched, soon lost." (Feinberg)

ii. "The reference to *the partridge* is to the popular belief that it would hatch the eggs of other birds. Just as the fledglings soon realize the false nature of the mother and depart from the nest, so riches unjustly acquired all disappear just when the owner is counting on them for security." (Harrison)

5. (12-13) The folly of failing to trust in the God of all glory.

A glorious high throne from the beginning
***Is* the place of our sanctuary.**
O LORD, the hope of Israel,
All who forsake You shall be ashamed.
"Those who depart from Me
Shall be written in the earth,
Because they have forsaken the LORD,
The fountain of living waters."

a. **A glorious high throne from the beginning is the place of our sanctuary**: Jeremiah has shown the folly of trusting in anything other than the Lord; now he will show by contrast the greatness of trusting God, who was symbolically enthroned at the temple in Jerusalem (**the place of our sanctuary**).

i. "The phrase *throne of glory* (or glorious throne) is a reference to the temple where Yahweh's presence was known among his people." (Thompson)

ii. **A glorious high throne**: "This may be described as one of the greatest words of the Old Testament. It expresses the deepest secret of life; the discovery of which gives the soul perpetual peace and poise and power, whatever may be the circumstances of the passing hour." (Morgan)

iii. "The throne is sanctuary; in the authority, the executive action, the government of that throne, man finds the place of safety and refuge from all the forces which are against him." (Morgan)

iv. "As he is *cursed* who trusts in man, so he is *blessed* who trusts in GOD. He is here represented as on a throne in his temple; to him in the *means of grace* all should resort. He is the support, and a *glorious support*, of all them that trust in him." (Clarke)

b. **O LORD, the hope of Israel**: Yahweh was the true and confident hope of Israel, even if many turned away from Him. Those who did turn from Him would be noted and recorded (**shall be written in the earth**) and would come to shame for foolishly rejecting Him.

B. Jeremiah's prayer for deliverance.

1. (14-17) A prayer for deliverance and defense.

> Heal me, O Lord, and I shall be healed;
> Save me, and I shall be saved,
> For You *are* my praise.
> Indeed they say to me,
> "Where *is* the word of the Lord?
> Let it come now!"
> As for me, I have not hurried away from *being* a shepherd *who* follows You,
> Nor have I desired the woeful day;
> You know what came out of my lips;
> It was right there before You.
> Do not be a terror to me;
> You *are* my hope in the day of doom.

a. **Heal me, O Lord, and I shall be healed; save me, and I shall be saved**: In contrast to the foolish people of Judah who trusted in man, in their own heart, or in riches, Jeremiah looked to Yahweh, the covenant God of Israel. Jeremiah was confident that healing or salvation from the Lord would be true healing, true rescue.

i. It's hard to say if the healing Jeremiah cried out for was literal or spiritual in nature, and in the bigger picture it doesn't really matter. Either need is real, and God's ability to heal both our physical and spiritual need is true and proven.

b. **You are my praise**: Even in his need of healing and salvation, Jeremiah could praise God, even making God Himself his praise. Though in pride others demanded an immediate revelation of God and His power, Jeremiah was willing to wait and trust in the Lord.

c. **As for me**: In a series of brief statements, Jeremiah defended and justified his ministry before God. He did this to contrast himself with those who demanded God bring immediate revelation and resolution.

- **I have not hurried away from being a shepherd that follows You**: Jeremiah was confident in his pursuit of God's call on his life.

- **Nor have I desired the woeful day**: Jeremiah spoke much of the judgment to come, but he did not desire it. It was a painful message for him to deliver.

- **You know what came out of my lips**: Jeremiah could appeal to God as the One who heard and judged his message, seeing that it really was faithful to the voice and the heart of God.

- **You are my hope in the day of doom**: Jeremiah proclaimed his trust and hope in God alone, not in the folly of most of the people of Judah.

    i. "The word 'shepherd' usually refers to a king, but here it refers to Jeremiah as a leader of the people." (Feinberg)

2. (18) A prayer for the justification of God's prophet.

Let them be ashamed who persecute me,
But do not let me be put to shame;
Let them be dismayed,
But do not let me be dismayed.
Bring on them the day of doom,
And destroy them with double destruction!

   a. **Let them be ashamed who persecute me**: Jeremiah was part of a long tradition of prophets and men of God in Israel who cried out to God for defense. This was a prayer of vengeance, but a prayer that left vengeance in the hands of God.

   b. **But do not let me be put to shame**: Because he could defend and justify his work before God, Jeremiah confidently prayed that God would defend and justify him and bring his enemies and persecutors to shame, dismay, doom, and destruction.

C. An example of Judah's disobedience: breaking the Sabbath.

1. (19-23) Jeremiah delivers a message to the people: obey God's command of the Sabbath.

Thus the Lord said to me: "Go and stand in the gate of the children of the people, by which the kings of Judah come in and by which they go out, and in all the gates of Jerusalem; and say to them, 'Hear the word of the Lord, you kings of Judah, and all Judah, and all the inhabitants of Jerusalem, who enter by these gates. Thus says the Lord: "Take heed to yourselves, and bear no burden on the Sabbath day, nor bring *it* in by the gates of Jerusalem; nor carry a burden out of your houses on the Sabbath day, nor do any work, but hallow the Sabbath day, as I commanded your fathers. But they did not obey nor incline their ear, but made their neck stiff, that they might not hear nor receive instruction."

   a. **Hear the word of the Lord, you kings of Judah, and all Judah, and all the inhabitants of Jerusalem**: At God's direction, Jeremiah brought a strong and public word to all of Judah and Jerusalem, kings and commoners. Their response to this word would measure their surrender or rebellion to God.

i. **The gate of the children of the people**: "*The Benjamin Gate* or the Gate of the Laity (MT *sons of my people*) is of uncertain location, but was apparently used by persons other than priests and Levites." (Harrison)

b. **Bear no burden on the Sabbath day**: Jeremiah simply repeated the Sabbath commands Israel originally agreed to as part of the Sinai Covenant (Exodus 20:8-11). He reminded them that this was **as I commanded your fathers**.

i. "Several of the phrases in these verses are strongly reminiscent of phrases in the Decalog where the Sabbath law is formulated." (Thompson)

c. **But they did not obey nor incline their ear, but made their neck stiff, that they might not hear nor receive instruction**: Jeremiah delivered a clear message, rooted in prior revelation. Yet the kings and commoners rejected the word of the LORD and continued to treat the Sabbath as if it were any other day.

2. (24-27) A promised blessing for obedience and curse for disobedience.

"And it shall be, if you heed Me carefully," says the LORD, "to bring no burden through the gates of this city on the Sabbath day, but hallow the Sabbath day, to do no work in it, then shall enter the gates of this city kings and princes sitting on the throne of David, riding in chariots and on horses, they and their princes, accompanied by the men of Judah and the inhabitants of Jerusalem; and this city shall remain forever. And they shall come from the cities of Judah and from the places around Jerusalem, from the land of Benjamin and from the lowland, from the mountains and from the South, bringing burnt offerings and sacrifices, grain offerings and incense, bringing sacrifices of praise to the house of the LORD. But if you will not heed Me to hallow the Sabbath day, such as not carrying a burden when entering the gates of Jerusalem on the Sabbath day, then I will kindle a fire in its gates, and it shall devour the palaces of Jerusalem, and it shall not be quenched."

a. **If you heed Me carefully**: Jeremiah spoke for the LORD and promised the people of Jerusalem and Judah that if they radically obeyed even this one command, God would preserve their city and their kingdom (**kings and princes sitting on the throne of David**).

i. It wasn't as if the Sabbath was the only command important to God; this offer to Jerusalem and Judah was simply a testing point. If they were willing to radically obey God in this one point, it would indicate a true repentance and submission to God that would extend to all points. This one point of obedience or disobedience would stand for all others, just as the eating of forbidden fruit would stand for all obedience or disobedience for Adam in the Garden of Eden.

ii. "The several regions of Judah are mentioned (v. 26); these were still possessed by Judah and Benjamin. The land of Benjamin was north of Judah. The lowland or Shephelah (NIV, 'western foothills') was the low hills stretching toward the Philistine maritime plain, west and southwest of Judah, and was the center of agriculture. The hill country was the central region, with the wilderness of Judah stretching down to the Dead Sea. The Negev was the arid South (cf. Joshua 15:21-32)." (Feinberg)

b. But if you will not heed Me to hallow the Sabbath.... then I will kindle a fire in its gates, and it shall devour the palaces of Jerusalem: The promise for obedience was great; the promise for disobedience was also significant. God would allow their obedience or disobedience on this one point to stand for all.

i. Obviously – and tragically – Judah and Jerusalem did not return to the Sabbath at Jeremiah's word, and they faced the severe judgment of God.

ii. When God told them to **hallow the Sabbath**, He told them to *hallow the rest*. "The term 'Sabbath' is derived from the Hebrew verb 'to rest or cease from work.'" (Kaiser) The most important purpose of the Sabbath was to serve as a preview picture of the rest we have in Jesus.

iii. Like everything in the Bible, we understand this with the perspective of the whole Bible, not this single passage. With this understanding, we see that there is a real sense in which Jesus fulfilled the purpose and plan of the Sabbath *for* us and *in* us (Hebrews 4:9-11). He is our rest; when we remember His finished work we **hallow the Sabbath**, we *hallow the rest*.

iv. Therefore, the whole of Scripture makes it clear that under the New Covenant, no one is under obligation to observe a Sabbath day (Colossians 2:16-17 and Galatians 4:9-11). Galatians 4:10 tells us that Christians are not bound to observe *days and months and seasons and years*. The rest we enter into as Christians is something to experience every day, not just one day a week – the rest of knowing we don't have to work to save ourselves, but our salvation is accomplished in Jesus (Hebrews 4:9-10).

v. The Sabbath commanded here and observed by Israel was a *shadow of things to come, but the substance is of Christ* (Colossians 2:16-17).

In the New Covenant, the idea isn't that there is *no* Sabbath, but that *every day* is a day of Sabbath rest in the finished work of God. Since the shadow of the Sabbath is fulfilled in Jesus, we are free to keep any particular day – or no day – as a Sabbath after the custom of ancient Israel.

vi. Yet we dare not ignore the importance of a day of rest – God has built us so that we *need* one. Like a car that needs regular maintenance, we need regular rest – or we will not wear well. Some people are like high-mileage cars that haven't been maintained well, and it shows.

vii. Some Christians are also dogmatic about observing Saturday as the Sabbath as opposed to Sunday, but because we are free to regard all days as given by God, it makes no difference. But in some ways, Sunday is more appropriate; being the day Jesus rose from the dead (Mark 16:9), and first met with His disciples (John 20:19), and a day when Christians gathered for fellowship (Acts 20:7 and 1 Corinthians 16:2). Under Law, men worked towards God's rest; but after Jesus' finished work on the cross, the believer enters into rest and goes from that rest out to work.

Jeremiah 18 – Lessons at the Potter's House

A. The lesson at the potter's house and the response to it.

1. (1-4) Jeremiah visits the potter's house.

The word which came to Jeremiah from the LORD, saying: "Arise and go down to the potter's house, and there I will cause you to hear My words." Then I went down to the potter's house, and there he was, making something at the wheel. And the vessel that he made of clay was marred in the hand of the potter; so he made it again into another vessel, as it seemed good to the potter to make.

> a. **Arise and go down to the potter's house**: As God sometimes did with His prophets, He instructed Jeremiah to learn a lesson through a living lesson, something from daily life.
>
> b. **The vessel that he made of clay was marred in the hand of the potter, so he made it again into another vessel**: Watching the potter at work, Jeremiah noticed a lump of clay that seemed uncooperative. The potter decided to start again, making something that **seemed good to the potter to make**.
>
>> i. "Power was manifested in his manipulation of the clay, and pity in his remaking of the marred vessel... The clay was suddenly marred, twisted; it failed to express the potter's thought... He saw that the potter did not abandon it." (Morgan)

2. (5-10) God's right to deal with His people as He pleases.

Then the word of the LORD came to me, saying: "O house of Israel, can I not do with you as this potter?" says the LORD. "Look, as the clay *is* in the potter's hand, so *are* you in My hand, O house of Israel! The instant I speak concerning a nation and concerning a kingdom, to pluck up, to pull down, and to destroy *it*, if that nation against whom I have spoken turns from its evil, I will relent of the disaster that I thought to bring upon it. And the instant I speak concerning a nation and concerning a

kingdom, to build and to plant *it*, if it does evil in My sight so that it does not obey My voice, then I will relent concerning the good with which I said I would benefit it.

> a. **O house of Israel, can I not do with you as this potter**: Through the visit to the potter's house, God spoke to Jeremiah and to all of Israel, reminding them of His sovereign right to do what He pleased with a marred or seemingly uncooperative vessel.
>
>> i. Like any analogy, this figure cannot be applied at every point. In this illustration the clay has no moral choice or dimension, whereas Israel's disobedience was chosen again and again. The vessel at the potter's house was *marred* (Jeremiah 18:4); Israel marred themselves morally and spiritually before God.
>>
>> ii. **O house of Israel**: Notably, God called the southern kingdom – which technically was not the kingdom of all 12 tribes – the **house of Israel**. One reason was because there were truly representatives from all 12 tribes among the people of Judah from the migration of the godly from the tribes of the northern kingdom of Israel to Judah in the days of Jeroboam (2 Chronicles 11:13-16).
>
> b. **If that nation against whom I have spoken turns from its evil, I will relent**: The illustration at the potter's did not only demonstrate God's right to display judgment, but also His right to display mercy. He was free to work with a previously marred vessel if He chose to do so. Yet He was also free to take back good He had done to a nation if they did evil in His sight.
>
>> i. Some translations render **relent** as *repent*. That is fine, if properly understood. "With God repentance is not a change of mind but is his consistent response according to his changeless nature to the change in the nation's conduct." (Feinberg)
>>
>> ii. The lesson of the potter's house was not primarily, "God can do whatever He wants." The main lesson is that God is free to respond to His people according to their own moral conduct and choices, and previous promises do not restrict the exercise of His correction or justice. "Man is never at the mercy of an unfeeling deity; it is in his power to repent and align himself with God's beneficent purposes." (Cundall)
>>
>> iii. "The lesson is all about *re*making, for better or worse." (Kidner)
>>
>> iv. The potter's house showed Jeremiah that "there was a mind, capable of adapting method to meet failure, and in such wise to realize purpose in spite of failure." (Morgan)

v. "He does not cast us utterly away; but puts us afresh upon the wheel, and 'makes us again'…Yield yourself afresh to God. Confess that you have marred his work. Humbly ask that He should make you again." (Meyer)

3. (11) Devising a plan of judgment.

"Now therefore, speak to the men of Judah and to the inhabitants of Jerusalem, saying, 'Thus says the LORD: "Behold, I am fashioning a disaster and devising a plan against you. Return now every one from his evil way, and make your ways and your doings good."'"

a. **Speak to the men of Judah**: The lesson of the potter's house was meant to rebuke the false confidence of **the men of Judah** and **Jerusalem**. They believed that since they were God's covenant people that no harm could come to them. It made it easy for them to believe the positive words of the false prophets.

b. **Behold, I am fashioning a disaster and devising a plan against you**: God wanted the potter's house lesson to awaken them to the danger of impending judgment. Just as a potter fashions the clay, God fashioned **disaster** against His unrepentant people.

i. **Fashioning a disaster**: "In verse 11 the Hebrew verb *yoser* (RSV *shaping*) has the same root as 'potter'. The choice is so deliberate as to reinforce the connection. The nation is to be moulded by means of the Exile." (Harrison)

c. **Return now every one from his way, and make your ways and your doings good**: The lesson of the potter's house could also be taken as an encouragement, reminding them that repentance and surrender to God was not meaningless. God was free to relent from judgment if they did in fact repent in a meaningful way.

i. "Note carefully the cardinal rule of prophecy which is enunciated here, that both the promises and threats of God are not absolute but conditional." (Cundall)

ii. Note the urgency: **return now every one**. "Men are quite willing to promise to return when they have gone a little further; when, perhaps, they will have gone past all possibility of returning; but 'now,' is always an ugly word to them. 'To-morrow,' they like much better. 'Now,' is a monosyllable which seems to Burn into their bosom like a hot coal, and therefore they pluck it out, and throw it from them." (Spurgeon)

4. (12-17) The response of the people, and God's answer to them.

And they said, "That is hopeless! So we will walk according to our own plans, and we will every one obey the dictates of his evil heart."

Therefore thus says the LORD:
"Ask now among the Gentiles,
Who has heard such things?
The virgin of Israel has done a very horrible thing.
Will *a man* **leave the snow water of Lebanon,**
Which comes **from the rock of the field?**
Will the cold flowing waters be forsaken for strange waters?
"Because My people have forgotten Me,
They have burned incense to worthless idols.
And they have caused themselves to stumble in their ways,
From **the ancient paths,**
To walk in pathways and not on a highway,
To make their land desolate *and* **a perpetual hissing;**
Everyone who passes by it will be astonished
And shake his head.
I will scatter them as with an east wind before the enemy;
I will show them the back and not the face
In the day of their calamity."

> a. **That is hopeless! So we will walk according to our own plans**: Judah was in the tragic place of feeling it was **hopeless** to repent. It did not feel **hopeless** because they feared God would not respond as He promised. It seemed **hopeless** because they simply did not feel it was *worth it* to change **the dictates of** their **evil heart** simply because one prophet told them so.
>
>> i. "Thou mayest save a labour of further exhorting us; for we are as good as we man to be, and shall not stir from our resolution. Keep thy breath to cool thy broth." (Trapp)
>
> b. **Ask now among the Gentiles, who has heard such things**: God responded to their answer with astonishment. Not even among the **Gentiles** was there such foolishness and hardness of heart. It was like leaving pure waters (**snow water of Lebanon**) for **strange waters**, a muddy pool of filth. It was like leaving a safe and paved **highway** for unsafe **pathways** where men trip and fall.
>
>> i. **A perpetual hissing; everyone who passes by it will be astonished and shake his head**: "The hissing will be more in amazement than in ridicule. Men will shake their heads at the nation's uncommon stupidity." (Feinberg)

ii. "The term *seriqot*, 'hissing' or 'whistling,' denotes that the land would become a spectacle so shocking as to cause passers-by to whistle in awe. The verse is remarkable for its striking assonance, with its *s*-sounds conveying the impression of hissing." (Thompson)

iii. **I will scatter them as with an east wind before the enemy**: "The *east wind* is the sirocco, a hot dry wind coming from the eastern deserts." (Harrison)

c. **I will show them the back and not the face in the day of calamity**: God commanded the priests of Israel to bless God's people, and part of that blessing was that the LORD would *make His face shine upon you* (Numbers 6:24-26). Soon Israel would sense the complete withdrawing of God's shining, favorable face upon them. They felt it was not worth it to repent; it would be far worse for them in failing to repent.

i. "When the Lord says he will show them his back and not his face, he means that his face will be hidden from them." (Feinberg)

B. Jeremiah's prayer against his enemies.

1. (18) The plot against Jeremiah.

Then they said, "Come and let us devise plans against Jeremiah; for the law shall not perish from the priest, nor counsel from the wise, nor the word from the prophet. Come and let us attack him with the tongue, and let us not give heed to any of his words."

a. **Come and let us devise plans against Jeremiah**: We often think of Jeremiah as a lonely figure, a prophet standing alone for the cause of God. It's easy to forget that there were many who competed with Jeremiah for the ear of Judah and Jerusalem, hoping to give them comfort and encourage when God's message – the message through Jeremiah – was that of warning and judgment.

b. **The law shall not perish from the priest, nor counsel from the wise, nor the word from the prophet**: This was (in part) the message of the false prophets. If a man held the title of **priest**, he must have the **law**. If he were considered **wise**, he must have good **counsel**. If he were called a **prophet**, he must have a **word** from God. This was a mentality that pretty much denied the existence of corrupt priests, foolish elders, and unfaithful prophets.

i. "Jeremiah had been relentless in his condemnation of the three classes of officials referred to here, priests, wise men, and prophets. It is probably a fair inference that it was these men of the establishment who instigated the plot." (Thompson)

ii. A later prophet would state this in the reverse: *Then they will seek a vision from a prophet; but the law will perish from the priest, and counsel from the elders.* (Ezekiel 7:26)

c. **Come and let us attack him with the tongue, and let us not give heed to any of his words**: Jeremiah's enemies used the strategy of deliberate **attack** and denial against him. The strategy did not die with Jeremiah's enemies.

i. **Attack him with the tongue**: "*ON the tongue*; so it should be rendered. Lying and false testimony are punished in the eastern countries, to the present day, by smiting the person on the mouth with a strong piece of leather like the sole of a shoe." (Clarke)

2. (19-20) Jeremiah pleads for himself.

Give heed to me, O LORD,
And listen to the voice of those who contend with me!
Shall evil be repaid for good?
For they have dug a pit for my life.
Remember that I stood before You
To speak good for them,
To turn away Your wrath from them.

a. **Give heed to me, O LORD, and listen to the voice of those who contend with me!** Jeremiah first asked God to listen to *him*; then he asked God to listen to his enemies. Jeremiah believed that the fair God, the righteous God, would see that they were wrong and he was in the right.

b. **Remember that I stood before You to speak good for them**: Jeremiah asked God to remember that he had prayed for these enemies, and prayed *good* for them – that God would **turn away** His **wrath from them**. This was the good he did for them; they **repaid** that good when they **dug a pit for** His **life**.

i. "His wound would have hurt less had he cared less and, paradoxically, prayed less for his people." (Kidner)

3. (21-23) Jeremiah pleads against his enemies.

Therefore deliver up their children to the famine,
And pour out their *blood*
By the force of the sword;
Let their wives *become* **widows**
And bereaved of their children.
Let their men be put to death,
Their young men *be* **slain**
By the sword in battle.

Let a cry be heard from their houses,
When You bring a troop suddenly upon them;
For they have dug a pit to take me,
And hidden snares for my feet.
Yet, LORD, You know all their counsel
Which is against me, to slay *me*.
Provide no atonement for their iniquity,
Nor blot out their sin from Your sight;
But let them be overthrown before You.
Deal *thus* with them
In the time of Your anger.

> a. **Therefore deliver up their children to the famine, and pour out their blood**: Jeremiah prayed a violent prayer against his enemies, asking for all kinds of crises and calamity to be poured out upon them, both in this life (**let their wives become widows**) and in the next (**provide no atonement for their iniquity**).
>
>> i. "Their relentless opposition and willful misunderstanding of his motives drew from him these demands for harsh vengeance." (Cundall)
>>
>> ii. This is in the classic pattern of the imprecatory psalms, such as Psalms 10, 35, 58, and 59 where a strong and violent prayer is offered against an enemy.
>>
>> iii. "While such utterances may constitute a rather shocking revelation of Jeremiah's humanity, they are consistent with other maledictions uttered in the Lord's name (*cf.* Psalm 137:9)." (Harrison)
>
> b. **Deal thus with them in the time of Your anger**: The common link between Jeremiah 18 and these imprecatory psalms is that they bring the longing for vengeance to *God* and surrender it to Him – instead of taking it upon themselves. This is a good and godly impulse when one has been so severely wronged.
>
>> i. "Clearly there was no obligation resting on Yahweh to respond to every utterance of his servant. When he did respond, it was sometimes with a word of encouragement (11:21-23) and sometimes with a word of rebuke (12:5-6; 15:19)." (Thompson)

Jeremiah 19 – Tophet

A. The message at the Potsherd Gate.

1. (1-2) Preparation for the message.

Thus says the Lord: "Go and get a potter's earthen flask, and *take* some of the elders of the people and some of the elders of the priests. And go out to the Valley of the Son of Hinnom, which *is* by the entry of the Potsherd Gate; and proclaim there the words that I will tell you,"

a. **Go and get a potter's earthen flask**: In the previous chapter, God taught Jeremiah at the potter's house. God then told Jeremiah to take a clay bottle (**earthen flask**) to use for a spiritual illustration before **some of the elders of the people and some of the elders of the priests**.

i. The **earthen flask** was probably a small clay bottle with a narrow neck. It was easily broken and could not be repaired if broken. "The Hebrew noun *baqbuq* ('clay jar') is onomatopoeic, sounding like the gurgling of outpouring water. Jars that have been excavated range from four to ten inches in height." (Feinberg)

ii. Centuries later the Apostle Paul wrote, *But we have this treasure in earthen vessels, that the excellence of the power may be of God and not of us* (2 Corinthians 4:7). Paul's point was that the treasure and glory of God is set inside common and ordinary receptacles – His redeemed people.

iii. Jeremiah's point is different. Having come from the potter's house (Jeremiah 18:1-11), God showed him how the potter could mold clay again into a new shape if it should seem resistant. Here, the clay is baked, hardened, and breakable. "If there is nothing so workable as a clay pot in the making, there is nothing so unalterable as the finished article. If it is wrong by then, that is that." (Kidner)

b. **Go out to the Valley of the Son of Hinnom**: Twice previously (Jeremiah 2:23, 7:31) Jeremiah made mention of this terrible place, south of the temple mount in Jerusalem. It was used as both a garbage dump (with continually smoldering fires) and previously as a place of child sacrifice.

> i. "The valley of Ben-hinnom (*cf.* Jeremiah 7:31), south of Jerusalem, as a contemporary locale for Molech worship. Under Josiah the shrine was destroyed and later on the valley was used for burning garbage and cremating the bodies of criminals." (Harrison)

> ii. Presently, there is no archaeological evidence for widespread human sacrifice or child sacrifice in the Valley of Hinnom. This may mean that the practice was rare, perhaps performed only in the most extreme circumstances.

> iii. The Valley of **Hinnom** gives us the idea of *Gehenna* in the New Testament. *Gehenna* is a Greek word borrowed from the Hebrew language. In Mark 9:43-44, Jesus spoke of *hell* (*gehenna*) referring to this place outside Jerusalem's walls desecrated by Molech worship and human sacrifice (2 Chronicles 28:1-3; Jeremiah 32:35). It was also a garbage dump where rubbish and refuse were burned. The smoldering fires and festering worms of the Valley of Hinnom made it a graphic and effective picture of the fate of the damned. This place is also called the "lake of fire" in Revelation 20:13-15, prepared for the devil and his angels (Matthew 25:41).

> iv. "The name 'Potsherd Gate' probably to be identified with the Dung Gate (Nehemiah 2:13, etc.), may indicate that the valley was being used as a rubbish-tip." (Cundall)

> v. "It may have acquired its name from the fact that potters whose workshops were near the gate dumped their broken vessels beyond the gate." (Thompson)

2. (3) The beginning of the message at the Potsherd Gate.

"And say, 'Hear the word of the Lord, O kings of Judah and inhabitants of Jerusalem. Thus says the Lord of hosts, the God of Israel: "Behold, I will bring such a catastrophe on this place, that whoever hears of it, his ears will tingle."'"

> a. **Hear the word of the Lord, O kings of Judah**: The **kings of Judah** needed to hear of God's coming judgment relevant to the Valley of Hinnom, because even some of the kings of Judah sacrificed their children there.

> > i. "He used the plural 'kings' because the message was not only to the reigning king but to the whole dynasty that was responsible for the apostasy." (Feinberg)

ii. "Ahaz, King of Israel, sacrificed his own son in the fire (2 Kings 16:3). The same thing happened in Manasseh's day, when children were sacrificed to the gods of Canaan (2 Kings 21:6)." (Ryken)

b. **I will bring such catastrophe on this place, that whoever hears of it, his ears will tingle**: As before, God promised great destruction and **catastrophe** to come upon this place associated with idolatry and child sacrifice.

3. (4-5) The reason for the catastrophe to come.

"Because they have forsaken Me and made this an alien place, because they have burned incense in it to other gods whom neither they, their fathers, nor the kings of Judah have known, and have filled this place with the blood of the innocents (they have also built the high places of Baal, to burn their sons with fire *for* burnt offerings to Baal, which I did not command or speak, nor did it come into My mind),"

a. **Because they have forsaken Me and made this an alien place**: The idea of human sacrifice – rare or common – was so offensive to God, He called the place it was practiced **an alien place**. Judah's rebellion led them far, far from Yahweh.

i. "The verb *nicker*, 'make alien,' is a vivid and highly suggestive term. The place had been denationalized, so that it could not be recognized as Israelite." (Thompson)

b. **They have filled this place with the blood of innocents**: Either the practice of child sacrifice was more widespread than yet confirmed by archaeologists, or God regarded even a *little* of this horrendous sin to be monstrous in its guilt.

c. **To burn their sons with fire for burnt offerings to Baal**: Child sacrifice was associated with a Canaanite deity known as Molech (Leviticus 20:2-5, Jeremiah 32:35). At least on some occasions, such **offerings** were also made to **Baal**.

i. "The destruction of the sanctuary in the valley of Ben-hinnom in the days of Josiah is referred to specifically in 2 Kings 23:10. Evidently the practice was revived under Jehoiakim, and it was to this that Jeremiah addressed himself." (Thompson)

ii. "The offering of children to Baal, under his title of King, has sometimes been represented as a mere dedication rite, passing the child harmlessly over a flame toward the idol….our verse Jeremiah 19:5 and 7:31 leave no doubt that these were actual burnt-offerings, although not burnt alive." (Kidner)

d. **Which I did not command or speak, nor did it come into My mind**: Unlike many of the Canaanite deities, Yahweh never commanded human sacrifice. God could say that it never did **come into** His **mind** to ask such a thing; it totally went against His nature.

i. The incident of Abraham's interrupted sacrifice of Isaac (Genesis 22) was an emphatic way for God to say, "I do not want human sacrifice."

4. (6-9) The description of the catastrophe to come.

"**Therefore behold, the days are coming," says the LORD, "that this place shall no more be called Tophet or the Valley of the Son of Hinnom, but the Valley of Slaughter. And I will make void the counsel of Judah and Jerusalem in this place, and I will cause them to fall by the sword before their enemies and by the hands of those who seek their lives; their corpses I will give as meat for the birds of the heaven and for the beasts of the earth. I will make this city desolate and a hissing; everyone who passes by it will be astonished and hiss because of all its plagues. And I will cause them to eat the flesh of their sons and the flesh of their daughters, and everyone shall eat the flesh of his friend in the siege and in the desperation with which their enemies and those who seek their lives shall drive them to despair."**

a. **It will no more be called Tophet**: **Tophet** (or in some translations, *Topheth*) was another name for the Valley of **Hinnom**. It was a name that associated it with pagan practices and child sacrifice.

i. "Topheth probably derives from the Hebrew word for 'fire-place' (cf. Isaiah 30:33)." (Cundall) According to Roni Simon, an Israeli tour guide, in modern Hebrew the word still has the association with *fire*. If someone comes under gunfire, they might say "I'm under *tophet*." Kidner also points out that the name **Tophet** rhymes with *bosheth*, the Hebrew word for "shame."

b. **This place shall no more be called Tophet, or the Valley of the Son of Hinnom, but the Valley of Slaughter**: God here repeated a promise first recorded in Jeremiah 7:32 – that He would answer the idolatry of Judah and the outrageous practice of human sacrifice with devastating judgment. There would be a grotesque **slaughter** in that valley.

i. The dead corpses in that place would also be disgraced by having no proper burial, and by being food for scavenger **birds** and the **beasts of the earth**.

ii. "For the body to remain unburied, thereby, providing food for carrion birds and rodents, was a thing of unspeakable horror for the ancient Hebrews. Ironically, their sanctuary would become their cemetery as the treasured homeland was ravaged." (Harrison)

c. **I will make void the counsel**: Because this phrase in the original sounds something like the word used to describe the earthen flask, some think that Jeremiah symbolically emptied the bottle as he said this.

i. " The MT *baqqot, I will make void* (7) contains a play on 'bottle' (*baqbuq*). The prophet may have emptied the flask symbolically as he spoke these words." (Harrison)

d. **I will make this city desolate and a hissing; everyone who passes by it will be astonished and hiss because of all its plagues**: The catastrophe would be seen both in terms of the death of the people and the destruction of the city.

e. **I will cause them to eat the flesh of their sons and the flesh of their daughters**: The city would be reduced to cannibalism, even as Samaria (the former capital of Israel) under siege from the Assyrians (2 Kings 6:26-29) and promised as a curse upon disobedient Israel (Deuteronomy 28:53-57). All this would drive the people of Jerusalem **to despair**.

B. Sign of the broken flask.

1. (10-11) The breaking of the flask.

"**Then you shall break the flask in the sight of the men who go with you, and say to them, 'Thus says the LORD of hosts: "Even so I will break this people and this city, as *one* breaks a potter's vessel, which cannot be made whole again; and they shall bury *them* in Tophet till *there is* no place to bury."**

a. **Even so I will break this people and this city**: God told Jeremiah to break the clay bottle as an illustration of the destruction to come. The clay bottle would break quickly and completely, and that is how God would bring judgment to Judah and Jerusalem.

i. "If a man or nation in spite of all the patient grace of God, persist in courses of evil and rebellion, then He will break in pieces. To find in the redeeming purpose of Jehovah a tolerance of sin, is of all evils the most terrible." (Morgan)

b. **They shall bury them in Tophet till there is no place to bury**: God wanted the demonstration done in the Valley of Hinnom (**Tophet**) because this is where the corpses of the slaughtered would be thrown into mass pits.

2. (12-13) The meaning of the broken flask.

Thus I will do to this place," says the Lord, "and to its inhabitants, and make this city like Tophet. And the houses of Jerusalem and the houses of the kings of Judah shall be defiled like the place of Tophet, because of all the houses on whose roofs they have burned incense to all the host of heaven, and poured out drink offerings to other gods.""

> a. **And make the city like Tophet**: The Valley of Hinnom was a disgusting garbage dump and place of burning; all Jerusalem would see that kind of destruction. They would be destroyed like the broken flask.
>
> b. **Because of all the houses on whose roofs they have burned incense to all the host of heaven**: Because the idolatry was spread throughout the city, God would bring this destruction throughout the city.

3. (14-15) After the message of the broken flask.

Then Jeremiah came from Tophet, where the Lord had sent him to prophesy; and he stood in the court of the Lord's house and said to all the people, "Thus says the Lord of hosts, the God of Israel: 'Behold, I will bring on this city and on all her towns all the doom that I have pronounced against it, because they have stiffened their necks that they might not hear My words.'"

> a. **He stood in the court of the Lord's house**: Jeremiah called the kings and rulers to hear him and see him enact the prophecy of the broken flask. Probably few of them took the trouble. For those who did not come to hear and see him, he brought the message to them, to the **Lord's house**.
>
> b. **Because they have stiffened their necks that they might not hear My words**: The greatest sin of Judah and Jerusalem was not their particular sins themselves, it was their rebellion and refusal to hear God and receive His word and correction.
>
>> i. "Their hand on their ear, their ear in their neck, their neck in the heart, and their heart in obstinancy." (Trapp)

Jeremiah 20 – Jeremiah in the Stocks

A. Jeremiah struck and in the stocks.

1. (1-2) Jeremiah – God's spokesman in the stocks.

Now Pashhur the son of Immer, the priest who *was* also chief governor in the house of the LORD, heard that Jeremiah prophesied these things. Then Pashhur struck Jeremiah the prophet, and put him in the stocks that *were* in the high gate of Benjamin, which *was* by the house of the LORD.

> a. **Pashhur the son of Immer**: This leading priest apparently did not attend Jeremiah's dramatic sermon of the broken flask at the Valley of Hinnom. He **heard** about it, and did not receive it.
>
>> i. **The chief governor** "was apparently the immediate subordinate of the High Priest and maintained order in the area of the Temple." (Harrison)
>>
>> ii. "Pashhur in this chapter was a fairly common name; so we cannot be certain that the Pashhur in this chapter was the father of Gedaliah (Jeremiah 38:1)." (Feinberg)
>>
>> iii. There were descendants of a Pashhur the priest who came back from the Babylonian exile with in the first return under Zerubbabel (Ezra 2:38).
>
> b. **Pashhur struck Jeremiah the prophet, and put him in the stocks**: Jeremiah was beaten and had to endure painful public disgrace. He wasn't only regarded as a false prophet, but surely also as a traitor, discouraging the people who still trusted in help from God or Egypt against Babylon.
>
>> i. "The expression 'smote Jeremiah' is a technical one, and in all likelihood means that the official scourging of 'forty stripes save one' was administered." (Morgan)

ii. "The *stocks* (MT *mahpeket*, from a root 'to distort') were a form of scaffold in which prisoners were detained in a crooked or confined position which produced cramped muscles." (Harrison)

iii. "The Hebrew word is formed from the verb to twist, implying that this 'twist-frame' clamped the victim in a position that would become increasingly distressing." (Kidner)

c. **Which was by the house of the LORD**: Ironically, all this was done near the temple – the center of Pashhur's power, and a very public place.

i. "Jeremiah was put in the stocks at the Upper Benjamin Gate – the northern gate of the upper temple court. It was one of the most conspicuous places in the city." (Feinberg)

2. (3-6) Jeremiah's message to Pashhur upon his release.

And it happened on the next day that Pashhur brought Jeremiah out of the stocks. Then Jeremiah said to him, "The LORD has not called your name Pashhur, but Magor-Missabib. For thus says the LORD: 'Behold, I will make you a terror to yourself and to all your friends; and they shall fall by the sword of their enemies, and your eyes shall see *it*. I will give all Judah into the hand of the king of Babylon, and he shall carry them captive to Babylon and slay them with the sword. Moreover I will deliver all the wealth of this city, all its produce, and all its precious things; all the treasures of the kings of Judah I will give into the hand of their enemies, who will plunder them, seize them, and carry them to Babylon. And you, Pashhur, and all who dwell in your house, shall go into captivity. You shall go to Babylon, and there you shall die, and be buried there, you and all your friends, to whom you have prophesied lies.'"

a. **The next day that Pashhur brought Jeremiah out of the stocks**: Pashhur, the priest and chief governor, likely thought this to be a kind and humanitarian act. He didn't want to be overly cruel to Jeremiah and thought that he had likely learned his lesson.

b. **The LORD has not called your name Pashhur, but Magor-Missabib**: The meaning of the name **Pashhur** is sometimes given as *freedom*, sometimes as *ease* or *peacefulness*. The name **Magor-Missabib** means *terror on every side*. There was a startling contrast between the two names.

i. "The translation most often given for 'Pashhur' is 'ease,' 'tranquility.'" (Feinberg)

c. **I will make you a terror to yourself and to all your friends**: Jeremiah showed that he did not intend to moderate his message. He boldly and plainly told the priest and chief governor that destruction *was* sure to come, and he would in some sense be in the center of it.

d. I will give all Judah into the hand of the king of Babylon: Jeremiah's message was unchanged. Yahweh or Egypt or anyone else would not deliver Judah. The Babylonians would completely conquer them.

e. And you, Pashhur... You shall go to Babylon, and there you shall die: Pashhur's position as priest and chief governor would not help him. He was one of those who **prophesied lies**, and he and his friends who heard him would all die in Babylon.

B. The burden of the persecuted prophet.

1. (7-8) Jeremiah speaks to God of his own faithfulness.

> O LORD, You induced me, and I was persuaded;
> You are stronger than I, and have prevailed.
> I am in derision daily;
> Everyone mocks me.
> For when I spoke, I cried out;
> I shouted, "Violence and plunder!"
> Because the word of the LORD was made to me
> A reproach and a derision daily.

a. You are stronger than I, and have prevailed: Jeremiah explained to God that he was *compelled* to his prophetic work. He had not desired it or pursued it, yet God **prevailed** upon him to take on this prophetic work.

i. **You induced me**: "The verb *seduce* (*pata*) occurs in Exodus 22:16 (cf. Judges 16:5) in a law regarding sexual seduction. Jeremiah seems to be saying that he had understood his relationship to Yahweh to be something like a marriage bond but it was now claimed that he had been deceived, enticed by Yahweh, who had used him and tossed him aside." (Thompson)

b. I am in derision daily; everyone mocks me: Perhaps Jeremiah spoke in light of his recent experience of being set in the public stocks (Jeremiah 20:1-2). Stuck in the stocks, he was the object of mockery and derision, even as Jesus would later endure similar humiliation.

c. The word of the LORD was made to me a reproach and a derision daily: As a faithful messenger of the Lord, it was difficult for Jeremiah to endure the **reproach** and **derision** that came to the one who prophesied coming judgment and catastrophe for Judah.

i. "Because Jeremiah's words remained unfulfilled for so long, people just ridiculed him whenever he spoke about the future." (Harrison)

2. (9-10) Jeremiah resolves to stop his prophetic work.

Then I said, "I will not make mention of Him,
Nor speak anymore in His name."
But *His word* was in my heart like a burning fire
Shut up in my bones;
I was weary of holding *it* back,
And I could not.
For I heard many mocking:
"Fear on every side!"
"Report," *they say,* **"and we will report it!"**
All my acquaintances watched for my stumbling, *saying,*
"Perhaps he can be induced;
Then we will prevail against him,
And we will take our revenge on him."

    a. **I will not make mention of Him, nor speak anymore in His name**: Jeremiah had to bear a painful price to remain a faithful messenger of God. On many occasions, he contemplated either giving up or changing the message.

        i. "This, said Latimer in a like case, was a naughty, a very naughty, resolution." (Trapp)

        ii. "It has often been observed that Jeremiah's doubts were never expressed in public. Outwardly he was the firm, unyielding prophet of the Lord, conveying faithfully the divine will to his people. But when alone with God, the tensions of his position were revealed." (Cundall)

    b. **But His word was in my heart like a burning fire shut up in my bones**: Many times Jeremiah *wanted* to give up, but he couldn't.

- He couldn't because he dealt with God's **word**.
- He couldn't because that **word** lived in his **heart**.
- He couldn't because that **word** *burned* in his heart like **fire**.
- He couldn't because that **word** pressed against his very being, as if it were **shut up in** his **bones**, requiring great energy to hold in (**I was weary of holding it back**).

        i. "He found out the impossibility of denying his call. He learned that it was irreversible and that God's word was irrepressible." (Feinberg)

        ii. "Under the stress and strain of his sufferings, he was tempted to abandon the work, to refuse to speak any more in the name of Jehovah. But when he attempted thus to find release from suffering in silence, it was impossible; for such silence became more intolerable than suffering." (Morgan)

c. **I could not**: Though it cost him much pain and humiliation, Jeremiah **could not** *not* preach God's word, *and preach it faithfully*. It wasn't only that Jeremiah was compelled to preach – there were many unfaithful preachers and prophets in his time. Jeremiah was compelled to preach a message faithful to God.

i. "We have sometimes been weary in God's service; but oh, it would be a greater weariness if we were dismissed from it. To speak is an awful responsibility and weight; but not to speak would be impossible." (Meyer)

ii. "This is the burden of the Word of Jehovah. Perhaps only those who have experienced it can understand it. To publish that word at times brings suffering; but to refrain brings far more terrible suffering. Paul understood this when he said, 'Woe is unto me if I preach not the Gospel.'" (Morgan)

d. **For I heard many mocking**: They mocked Jeremiah's message of fear and coming catastrophe. They waited for his **stumbling**, hoping an unfaithful life would invalidate the message, and then they could **take** their **revenge on him**.

i. **Fear on every side!** "The whisperings were either plots against his life or the sarcastic use of *magor missabib* as a nickname for Jeremiah." (Harrison)

ii. "They called Jeremiah Magor-Missabib, 'terror on every side.' In other words, they took his rebuke of Pashhur and used it against him." (Ryken)

3. (11-12) Jeremiah's confidence in God.

But the Lord is with me as a mighty, awesome One.
Therefore my persecutors will stumble, and will not prevail.
They will be greatly ashamed, for they will not prosper.
***Their* everlasting confusion will never be forgotten.**
But, O Lord of hosts,
You who test the righteous,
***And* see the mind and heart,**
Let me see Your vengeance on them;
For I have pleaded my cause before You.

a. **But the Lord is with me as a mighty, awesome One**: Despite the pain and difficulty of his work and his many enemies, Jeremiah found confidence in Yahweh as **a mighty, awesome One**. God's might and awe was a greater fact than his pain, humiliation, rejection, and beatings. God became bigger and his misery became smaller.

b. **Therefore my persecutors will stumble, and will not prevail**: The mighty God would work for and protect His faithful messenger. Jeremiah would realize that God was his shield and his great reward (Genesis 15:1).

c. **O LORD of hosts, You who test the righteous, and see the mind and heart**: Jeremiah was content to leave the matter to God and His wisdom and strength. The Judge of all the earth would do right.

4. (13) Praising the Mighty God.

Sing to the LORD! Praise the LORD!
For He has delivered the life of the poor
From the hand of evildoers.

a. **Sing to the LORD! Praise the LORD**: The prophet's heart overflowed with praise. He received the sweet strength found in true fellowship with God.

b. **He has delivered the life of the poor from the hand of the evildoers**: It wasn't as if Jeremiah's pain or problems were over. There was still much to come. Yet still, he was confident in the victory and deliverance of the LORD.

5. (14-18) Grief and depression again.

Cursed *be* the day in which I was born!
Let the day not be blessed in which my mother bore me!
Let the man *be* cursed
Who brought news to my father, saying,
"A male child has been born to you!"
Making him very glad.
And let that man be like the cities
Which the LORD overthrew, and did not relent;
Let him hear the cry in the morning
And the shouting at noon,
Because he did not kill me from the womb,
That my mother might have been my grave,
And her womb always enlarged *with me*.
Why did I come forth from the womb to see labor and sorrow,
That my days should be consumed with shame?

a. **Cursed be the day in which I was born**: With startling suddenness, Jeremiah slipped back into grief and depression, wishing that he had never been born.

i. "The whole poem in its final setting comes strangely from the lips of one who had taken his divine call so seriously. Rarely has the question 'Why was I ever born?' been asked so tellingly. To his cry of distress and poignant question Yahweh gave no answer. But what answer could he give?" (Thompson)

ii. "These verses do belong together. They may not belong together by logic, but who says the life of the soul is always logical? Jeremiah's curses follow his praises because that is the way it was during his dark night of the soul." (Ryken)

iii. **Let that man be like the cities which the LORD overthrew**: "*The cities* are Sodom, Gomorrah, and the other cities of the plain (*cf.* Genesis 19:24-28)." (Harrison)

b. **Why did I come forth from the womb to see labor and sorrow**: There was a purpose of God in setting this section of grief immediately after the section of faith and triumph – to show that trusting God did not make it all easy or triumphant for Jeremiah. The battle remained and reliance upon God had to be constant.

i. Jeremiah thought his problems would be over if he was never born. The problem was that God called him *before* he was born or even conceived: *Before I formed you in the womb I knew you; Before you were born I sanctified you; I ordained you a prophet to the nations* (Jeremiah 1:5). "Jeremiah traced his troubles back to the womb. But he did not go back far enough! God could trace his promises back *before* the womb." (Ryken)

ii. **Consumed with shame**: "The shame he refers to is that of his inability to avert the catastrophe threatening his people." (Feinberg)

iii. "This section depicts a man loudly complaining about his lot in life, yet showing that he is still in submission, loyal and obedient to God's will." (Harrison)

iv. "If ever one's morale as a servant of God touches rock-bottom, we may reflect that Jeremiah has been there before, and has survived." (Kidner)

Jeremiah 21 – Speaking to King Zedekiah

A. Message to Zedekiah: Coming judgment.

1. (1-2) The messenger from King Zedekiah.

The word which came to Jeremiah from the LORD when King Zedekiah sent to him Pashhur the son of Melchiah, and Zephaniah the son of Maaseiah, the priest, saying, "Please inquire of the LORD for us, for Nebuchadnezzar king of Babylon makes war against us. Perhaps the LORD will deal with us according to all His wonderful works, that *the king* may go away from us."

a. **The word which came to Jeremiah from the LORD**: The Book of Jeremiah is not arranged chronologically. There is a substantial jump from the end of Jeremiah 20 to the start of Jeremiah 21. Jeremiah 20 ended in the reign of Jehoiakim, the son of Josiah, who reigned for 11 years. Jeremiah 21 fast-forwards about 20 years, to the time when Babylonian armies are in Judah and Jerusalem is besieged.

i. "The episode, *c.* 588, transports us suddenly to the final siege of Jerusalem, some 20 years after the events of chapter 20." (Kidner) In this period, Judah and Jerusalem did not fall in one decisive battle; it happened in stages.

- About 17 years before this, Nebuchadnezzar first came to Jerusalem in the reign of King Jehoiakim and subjugated the city and took captives from the best and the brightest of Judah, such as Daniel (about 605 BC).

- About 10 years before this, Nebuchadnezzar came again in the reign of King Jehoiachin and carried away the treasures of Jerusalem taking more captives (such as Ezekiel), and he deposed King Jehoiachin (about 598 BC). He then put Zedekiah on the throne as a puppet king.

- By the time of Jeremiah 21, King Zedekiah's reign was almost over; Nebuchadnezzar returned a third time to destroy the city of Jerusalem and carry away the remaining people of Judah (about 586 BC).

ii. Zedekiah was the third son of King Josiah. His older brothers Jehoahaz and Jehoiakim (and his nephew Jehoiachin) reigned before him.

b. **When King Zedekiah sent to him Pashhur the son of Melchiah**: This was not the same *Pashhur son of Immer* who struck Jeremiah and put him in the stocks (Jeremiah 20:1-2) 20 years before.

c. **Perhaps the LORD will deal with us according to all His wonderful works, that the king may go away from us**: King Zedekiah sent Pashhur to ask Jeremiah for a favorable word from the Lord. It was as if they never heard what Jeremiah preached before.

i. "It was during the last extremity of the siege that Zedekiah sent this message to Jeremiah. His people and he had postponed their compliance with the warnings and invitations of God's love until the last possible hour, and now they were more eager for immunity from the consequences of their sins than to repent and return to God." (Meyer)

ii. **According to all His wonderful works**: King Zedekiah probably remembered the miracle of deliverance for Jerusalem in the days of Hezekiah, when the Assyrian armies, led by Sennacherib, surrounded the city (2 Kings 18-19). He hoped God might send a miracle again.

iii. **According to all His wonderful works**: "Jehovah will deal with men according to His wondrous works; but that, not in order to deliver rebellious souls from the just punishment of their iniquity, but rather to hand them over to that punishment in spite of all the cleverness of their policies." (Morgan)

2. (3-6) The message to Zedekiah about Jerusalem's coming conquest.

Then Jeremiah said to them, "Thus you shall say to Zedekiah, 'Thus says the LORD God of Israel: "Behold, I will turn back the weapons of war that *are* in your hands, with which you fight against the king of Babylon and the Chaldeans who besiege you outside the walls; and I will assemble them in the midst of this city. I Myself will fight against you with an outstretched hand and with a strong arm, even in anger and fury and great wrath. I will strike the inhabitants of this city, both man and beast; they shall die of a great pestilence."

> a. **Thus you shall say to Zedekiah**: We admire the boldness of Jeremiah, speaking so plainly and boldly to a king who had reigned ten years already.
>
>> i. "He answereth them modestly, and without insultation; but freely and boldly, as a man of a heroic spirit, and the messenger of the King of kings." (Trapp)
>
> b. **Behold, I will turn back the weapons of war that are in your hands**: The prophecy of Jeremiah was right to the point. God would not do a "wonderful work" (Jeremiah 21:2) to rescue them from the coming Babylonian invasion. Their effort at defense would be unsuccessful.
>
> c. **I will assemble them in the midst of this city**: The Babylonians would not only **besiege** Jerusalem, they would breach the walls and be **in the midst of the city**.
>
> d. **I Myself will fight against you with an outstretched hand and with a strong arm**: Judah would not only have to fight against the Babylonians, they would also have to fight against Yahweh Himself. He would **fight against** them, **even in anger and fury and great wrath**.
>
> e. **I will strike the inhabitants of this city, both man and beast; they shall die of a great pestilence**: War would not be the only cause of death in the devastation to come. Many would also die under disease and **pestilence**.

3. (7) The message to Zedekiah about his own terrible fate.

> "And afterward," says the LORD, "I will deliver Zedekiah king of Judah, his servants and the people, and such as are left in this city from the pestilence and the sword and the famine, into the hand of Nebuchadnezzar king of Babylon, into the hand of their enemies, and into the hand of those who seek their life; and he shall strike them with the edge of the sword. He shall not spare them, or have pity or mercy."'
>
> a. **Into the hand of Nebuchadnezzar king of Babylon**: Those fortunate enough to survive the **pestilence and the sword and the famine** would not find deliverance. They would be taken as exiles out of Jerusalem and Judah and to the land of Babylon.
>
>> i. Soon after this prophecy, the Babylonians captured **Zedekiah**. *Then they killed the sons of Zedekiah before his eyes, put out the eyes of Zedekiah, bound him with bronze fetters, and took him to Babylon* (2 Kings 25:7) He died there in misery and grief.
>
> b. **He shall not spare them, or have pity or mercy**: They could expect no mercy from Nebuchadnezzar in the coming war and exile.

i. **Strike them with the edge of the sword**: "The idiom 'put them to the sword' means to slay ruthlessly, mercilessly, without quarter." (Feinberg)

ii. The Puritan commentator John Trapp noticed this about Jeremiah 21:7: "This is noted by the Hebrew critics for a very long verse – as having in it two-and-forty words, which consists of one hundred and threescore letters – and it sounds very heavily all along." (Trapp)

4. (8-10) The message to Jerusalem in light of the coming conquest.

"**Now you shall say to this people, 'Thus says the LORD: "Behold, I set before you the way of life and the way of death. He who remains in this city shall die by the sword, by famine, and by pestilence; but he who goes out and defects to the Chaldeans who besiege you, he shall live, and his life shall be as a prize to him. For I have set My face against this city for adversity and not for good," says the LORD. "It shall be given into the hand of the king of Babylon, and he shall burn it with fire."'**

a. **Behold, I set before you the way of life and the way of death**: Jeremiah spoke now to the people of Jerusalem, calling them to decision. Several times in Israel's history God set this choice before them.

- *See, I have set before you today life and good, death and evil.* (Deuteronomy 30:15)

- *And if it seems evil to you to serve the LORD, choose for yourselves this day whom you will serve, whether the gods which your fathers served that were on the other side of the River, or the gods of the Amorites, in whose land you dwell. But as for me and my house, we will serve the LORD.* (Joshua 24:15)

- *How long will you falter between two opinions? If the LORD is God, follow Him; but if Baal, follow him.* (1 Kings 18:21)

b. **He who remains in this city shall die... but he who goes out and defects to the Chaldeans who besiege you, he shall live**: Jeremiah told them that their only hope was in *surrender*. The leaders of Judah hoped to inspire the people to defend with courage and tenacity; Jeremiah told them that since *God* was against them, their only hope was surrender.

i. Jeremiah did not say this because he was pro-Babylonian, though he was accused of being a traitor. He said this because he was pro-Yahweh. "When Jeremiah counseled surrender he called the nation to accept God's judgment, which was the first step toward future renewal." (Thompson)

ii. This is a paradox of spiritual life with God, much more clearly expressed in the New Testament: we gain life by surrendering it. "This surely is the exact counterpoint of the words which our Lord is recorded as having spoken on four different occasions: 'He that loveth his life shall lose it; and he that loseth his life for my sake, the same shall save it.'" (Meyer)

iii. If the battle was *only* against the Chaldeans, perhaps Jeremiah would urge the people on to courage and sacrifice, but that was not the case. God said, **I have set My face against this city for adversity and not for good**. With God opposing them, continuing the battle was foolish.

iv. This is an enduring spiritual principle: *When we struggle against God, our only hope of success is in surrender.*

B. God's word to the House of David.

1. (11-12) A call to repent.

"**And concerning the house of the king of Judah,** *say,* **'Hear the word of the** LORD**, O house of David! Thus says the** LORD**:**
"**Execute judgment in the morning;**
And deliver *him who is* **plundered**
Out of the hand of the oppressor,
Lest My fury go forth like fire
And burn so that no one can quench *it,*
Because of the evil of your doings."

a. **O house of David**: God established the house of David as an enduring royal line until it was fulfilled in the Messiah (2 Samuel 7:12-16). God had a special interest in this royal line, and here He spoke to them through Jeremiah.

i. Because this section (Jeremiah 21:11-14) holds some hope for restoration if there is repentance, some think that it is from a previous time – before the crisis point of Zedekiah's reign. There was also a sense of confidence (Jeremiah 21:13) that likely did not exist once Nebuchadnezzar started to attack Jerusalem.

ii. "This message, directed to the royal house, relates to a time when there was still a possibility of escape through repentance and righteous living." (Feinberg)

b. **Execute judgment in the morning; and deliver him who is plundered**: God called the **house of David** – the king and royal family of Judah – to faithfully do their job in leading the kingdom. One of the basic responsibilities God has appointed to civil government is the application and execution of justice (Romans 13:1-7). God commanded them to fulfill their responsibility – with the strong implication that they had not done so.

> i. **Execute judgment in the morning**: "Probably the time for dispensing judgment was *the morning*, when the people were going to their work; but the words may mean, Do justice *promptly*, do not *delay*. Let justice be administered *as soon* as required." (Clarke)

c. **Lest My fury go forth like fire and burn so that no one can quench it**: If they did not radically repent, judgment was certain – and would come **like fire**.

> i. "Jeremiah still held out hope – fruitlessly, as events later proved – that swift reformation of public and private life in accordance with the covenant ideals would avert imminent disaster." (Harrison)

2. (13-14) The devouring fire.

> "Behold, I *am* against you, O inhabitant of the valley,
> *And* rock of the plain," says the LORD,
> "Who say, 'Who shall come down against us?
> Or who shall enter our dwellings?'
> But I will punish you according to the fruit of your doings," says the LORD;
> "I will kindle a fire in its forest,
> And it shall devour all things around it.""

a. **Who shall come down against us**: God said He was **against** those who felt safe and secure despite the coming judgment. Though they felt safe and secure as a **rock of the plain**, judgment was coming.

> i. **O inhabitant of the valley**: "The *inhabitant* of the valley was Jerusalem, which had valleys on three sides." (Harrison)

> ii. "The addressee here is undoubtedly Jerusalem, since the feminine gender is used." (Feinberg)

b. **But I will punish you according to the fruit of your doings**: Despite their sense of safety, judgment like fire would come upon them – *unless* they radically repented.

> i. **A fire in its forest**: "Some commentators have proposed that the reference is to the royal palace, which is called in 1 Kings 7:2 the 'House of the Forest of Lebanon' because of the considerable quantity of cedar used in its construction." (Thompson)

Jeremiah 22 – Speaking to the House of David

A. The Message to the House of David.

1. (1-5) An urgent call to repent.

Thus says the LORD: "Go down to the house of the king of Judah, and there speak this word, and say, 'Hear the word of the LORD, O king of Judah, you who sit on the throne of David, you and your servants and your people who enter these gates! Thus says the LORD: "Execute judgment and righteousness, and deliver the plundered out of the hand of the oppressor. Do no wrong and do no violence to the stranger, the fatherless, or the widow, nor shed innocent blood in this place. For if you indeed do this thing, then shall enter the gates of this house, riding on horses and in chariots, accompanied by servants and people, kings who sit on the throne of David. But if you will not hear these words, I swear by Myself," says the LORD, "that this house shall become a desolation."'"

> a. **Hear the word of the LORD, O king of Judah, you who sit on the throne of David**: Jeremiah continued the prophecy from the previous chapter, directed to the house of David. This was a word specifically for the **king**. He should take sober care to listen because he sat **on the throne of David**.
>
> b. **Execute judgment and righteousness**: Jeremiah's first message to the king was very much like the message began in the previous chapter (Jeremiah 21:11-12). Speaking for God, he called upon him to perform his responsibilities as king in a godly and righteous way. This command assumes there was great corruption and injustice at the highest levels of the kingdom.
>
> c. **If you indeed do this thing.... But if you will not hear these words**: Jeremiah warned the king that repentance and the doing of justice would

be rewarded; rejection would be punished. The choice was again set before Judah and her rulers.

> i. "We are close enough to the message sent back to King Zedekiah to suggest at first sight that we are still dealing with the same man. But it seems more likely that this paragraph was a much earlier message, to another king, since there was still time for the house of David to recover strongly." (Kidner)

2. (6-7) The coming judgment.

For thus says the LORD to the house of the king of Judah:
"You *are* Gilead to Me,
The head of Lebanon;
***Yet* I surely will make you a wilderness,**
Cities *which* are not inhabited.
I will prepare destroyers against you,
Everyone with his weapons;
They shall cut down your choice cedars
And cast *them* into the fire.

> a. **You are Gilead to Me, the head of Lebanon**: These were choice regions in or near the Promised Land. God used these valued places to show how valued the house of David was to Him.
>
>> i. "High and happy, as those fruitful mountains, famous for spicery and other things desirable." (Trapp)
>
> b. **I will prepare destroyers against you**: God emphasized the point that He would not fight *for* them against the Babylonians. Instead, He would fight *against* them, preparing the soldiers Himself.

3. (8-9) The nations ask why.

And many nations will pass by this city; and everyone will say to his neighbor, 'Why has the LORD done so to this great city?' Then they will answer, 'Because they have forsaken the covenant of the LORD their God, and worshiped other gods and served them.'"

> a. **Why has the LORD done so to this great city?** Jeremiah pictured the people of the nations seeing the destruction of Jerusalem and wondering why. Were these not the people of God? Was the God of Israel weaker than the god of the Babylonians?
>
> b. **Because they have forsaken the covenant of the LORD their God, and worshiped other gods and served them**: The answer to the question of the nations was simple. It was because Judah departed from the LORD, forsaking their covenant with Him. Their idolatry led to this destruction.

B. The Message about the Sons of Josiah.

1. (10-12) The message about Shallum (also called Jehoahaz).

Weep not for the dead, nor bemoan him;
Weep bitterly for him who goes away,
For he shall return no more,
Nor see his native country.

For thus says the LORD concerning Shallum the son of Josiah, king of Judah, who reigned instead of Josiah his father, who went from this place: "He shall not return here anymore, but he shall die in the place where they have led him captive, and shall see this land no more."

    a. **Weep not for the dead, nor bemoan him**: These poetic words were spoken regarding the death of King Josiah and the exile of his son Shallum (also known as Jehoahaz).

- **The dead** refers to King Josiah, killed in battle at Megiddo.
- **Him who goes away** refers to Jehoahaz (Shallum) who succeeded Josiah but was almost immediately deposed by Pharaoh Necho (2 Kings 23:31-35). He was the brother of Jehoiakim.

        i. "Jeremiah tells the nation at large that they need not mourn the death of the godly king Josiah (22:10), who had been slain at the Battle of Megiddo in 609 BC" (Feinberg)

    b. **Concerning Shallum the son of Josiah, king of Judah**: Jeremiah said that the fate of **Shallum** in exile was worse than the more heroic death of his father Josiah in battle.

        i. "One of Josiah's sons, succeeding after 609 BC when Josiah was killed at Megiddo. He reigned for three months before being deposed by Necho, was taken to Riblah and then to Egypt where he eventually died (*cf.* 2 Kings 23:33f.; 2 Chronicles 36:4)." (Harrison)

2. (13-17) The Message to Jehoiakim.

"Woe to him who builds his house by unrighteousness
And his chambers by injustice,
Who **uses his neighbor's service without wages**
And gives him nothing for his work,
Who says, 'I will build myself a wide house with spacious chambers,
And cut out windows for it,
Paneling *it* **with cedar**
And painting *it* **with vermilion.'**
"Shall you reign because you enclose *yourself* **in cedar?**
Did not your father eat and drink,

And do justice and righteousness?
Then *it was* well with him.
He judged the cause of the poor and needy;
Then *it was* well.
Was not this knowing Me?" says the LORD.
"Yet your eyes and your heart *are* for nothing but your covetousness,
For shedding innocent blood,
And practicing oppression and violence."

a. **Woe to him who builds his house by unrighteousness**: In the custom of Israel's prophets, Jeremiah confronted Jehoiakim for his greed and injustice. He said that he and others of the house of David were guilty of:

- **Unrighteousness** and **injustice**.
- Cheating working men (**gives him nothing for his work**).
- Selfish and indulgent luxury (**I will build myself a wide house with spacious chambers**).
- Presumption (**Shall you reign because you enclose yourself in cedar**).
- Not following the good examples of their forefathers (**Did not your father eat and drink, and do justice and righteousness**).

i. "Faced with a crippling tax imposed by the Egyptians, he extracted this from his subjects by heavy taxation (2 Kings 23:33 ff.) and then embarked on a lavish palace-building scheme, forcing his subjects to work for nothing." (Cundall)

ii. **Who uses his neighbor's service**: "There is a strong democratic note here in that the king is called the *fellow* [**neighbor**] of his builder." (Thompson)

iii. **I will build myself a wide house with spacious chambers**: "Its width of space could not obliterate the memory of the forced and unpaid labour by which it had been reared. And God would plead and avenge the cause of those oppressed labourers." (Meyer)

iv. **Shall you reign because you enclose yourself in cedar?** "Scathingly, Jeremiah asks Jehoiakim (22:15a), 'Does building palaces of cedar make you a king?'" (Feinberg)

b. **Was not this knowing Me**: Jeremiah called upon Jehoiakim to remember his father Josiah, who enjoyed a modest life as a king and did **justice and righteousness**. *This* was evidence of **knowing** God, not fancy palaces.

i. **Did not your father eat and drink**: "He lived well…and yet attended to the important kingly duties of justice and right." (Thompson)

ii. Jeremiah spoke of a principle mentioned several other places in the Bible, especially in 1 John. The idea is that our love and knowledge of God can be accurately measured by how we treat other people, especially others in God's family. The rulers of Judah did not know God at all because they did not live out His love and justice towards others.

- *We know that we have passed from death to life, because we love the brethren. He who does not love his brother abides in death.* (1 John 3:14)

- *But whoever has this world's goods, and sees his brother in need, and shuts up his heart from him, how does the love of God abide in him?* (1 John 3:17)

c. **Yet your eyes and your heart are for nothing but your covetousness**: Instead of knowing God they knew greed, violence, and injustice. They were indeed ripe for judgment.

3. (18-19) The judgment to come upon Jehoiakim.

Therefore thus says the Lord concerning Jehoiakim the son of Josiah, king of Judah:
"They shall not lament for him,
Saying, **'Alas, my brother!' or 'Alas, my sister!'**
They shall not lament for him,
Saying, **'Alas, master!' or 'Alas, his glory!'**
He shall be buried with the burial of a donkey,
Dragged and cast out beyond the gates of Jerusalem."

a. **They shall not lament for him**: Jehoiakim was a cruel and greedy ruler over Judah. When his 11-year reign ended, no one was sorry.

b. **He shall be buried with the burial of a donkey**: Jeremiah spoke of a terrible judgment upon Jehoiakim – a king who died with no **lament**, no sorrow, and no dignified burial.

i. "2 Kings 24:6 gives no hint of this, but Jehoiakim's death occurred whilst Jerusalem was besieged by the Babylonians because of his rebellion. There is plausible support for the view that there was a palace revolt, when the king was assassinated and his body cast over the wall, indicating to the Babylonians that Jerusalem disassociated itself from his rebellious policy. Certain it is that Jerusalem escaped relatively lightly when it eventually surrendered." (Cundall)

4. (20-23) A prophecy against Jerusalem and her rulers.

"Go up to Lebanon, and cry out,
And lift up your voice in Bashan;
Cry from Abarim,
For all your lovers are destroyed.
I spoke to you in your prosperity,
But you said, 'I will not hear.'
This *has been* your manner from your youth,
That you did not obey My voice.
The wind shall eat up all your rulers,
And your lovers shall go into captivity;
Surely then you will be ashamed and humiliated
For all your wickedness.
O inhabitant of Lebanon,
Making your nest in the cedars,
How gracious will you be when pangs come upon you,
Like the pain of a woman in labor?

a. **Go up to Lebanon, and cry out**: The prophecy turns to Jerusalem and to her rulers, who were destined for judgment because of their foolish idolatry and alliances. Looking to distant places – **Lebanon**, **Bashan**, **Abarim** – was foolish and destructive. Spiritually speaking, these were like adulterous **lovers** to Judah and now they were **destroyed**.

i. "Lebanon with its glorious forests was the very picture of beauty and prosperity, as was Bashan (22:20) with its rich pastures. As for Abarim (22:20) this was the mountain range in the south-east from which Moses had viewed the promised land." (Kidner)

ii. "The 'lovers' are her political allies, who have been *broken*... Jerusalem was deserted, isolated, and alone." (Thompson)

iii. "Jeremiah is calling on his contemporaries (included in Jerusalem, for the verbs are in the feminine gender) to mourn the disastrous results brought on the land by the foolish international policy of Jehoiakim." (Feinberg)

b. **I spoke to you in your prosperity, but you said, "I will not hear"**: God's people had much blessing and **prosperity** in the land of Israel. In many of those years of **prosperity**, God spoke to them but they refused to listen.

i. This is one of the great weaknesses and tragedies of the human condition. In **prosperity** we often refuse to listen to God and He only has our attention in seasons of woe. Nevertheless, better to hear God in our woe than to never hear and respond to Him at all.

ii. "Happy if we can yet add the postscript from Psalm 119:67, *Before I was afflicted I went astray; but now I keep thy word.*" (Kidner)

c. **Surely then you will be ashamed and humiliated**: Perhaps this would provide the environment where the people and rulers of Jerusalem would again listen to their God and reject the idols of the nations.

i. **O inhabitant of Lebanon**: " 'You who live in Lebanon' refers to the king and his nobles in their cedar palaces." (Feinberg) Their houses used so much cedar wood that they made their **nest in the cedars**.

C. The Message to Coniah.

1. (24-27) Coming exile for Coniah (also known as Jeconiah and Jehoiachin).

"*As* I live," says the LORD, "though Coniah the son of Jehoiakim, king of Judah, were the signet on My right hand, yet I would pluck you off; and I will give you into the hand of those who seek your life, and into the hand *of those* whose face you fear—the hand of Nebuchadnezzar king of Babylon and the hand of the Chaldeans. So I will cast you out, and your mother who bore you, into another country where you were not born; and there you shall die. But to the land to which they desire to return, there they shall not return.

a. **Though Coniah the son of Jehoiakim, king of Judah, were the signet on My right hand, yet I would pluck you off**: Perhaps Judah and the leaders of the house of David believed they were too loved by God to be judged. God here promised that even if they were as valued as **the signet on** God's **right hand**, so judgment could and would come.

i. "Nothing can now prevent Jehoiachin's exile, for in plucking off the *signet* God has rejected his leadership." (Harrison)

b. **There you shall die**: God pictured His people being as precious to Him as the **signet** ring mentioned. Yet He would (so to speak) take the signet ring off and give it to **Nebuchadnezzar, king of Babylon**. They would be **cast out** of the land and die among the Babylonians – **they shall not return** to the Promised Land.

i. This was precisely fulfilled for **Coniah** (again, also known as Jeconiah and Jehoiachin). After a brief reign, he and other members of the royal family were taken to Babylon as captives (2 Kings 24:8-15).

2. (28-30) The curse on the line of Coniah.

"Is this man Coniah a despised, broken idol—
A vessel in which *is* no pleasure?
Why are they cast out, he and his descendants,
And cast into a land which they do not know?
O earth, earth, earth,
Hear the word of the LORD!
Thus says the LORD:
'Write this man down as childless,
A man *who* shall not prosper in his days;
For none of his descendants shall prosper,
Sitting on the throne of David,
And ruling anymore in Judah.'"

a. **Is this man Coniah a despised, broken idol**: Jeremiah asked this rhetorical question. The answer was, "Yes." **Coniah** was worthless and associated with idolatry and would be associated with misery (**a vessel in which is no pleasure**) and his own exile (**cast into land which they do not know**).

i. **A vessel in which is no pleasure**: "The technical term for *pot* (22:28) describes a vessel of inferior grade, this being a sarcastic reference to the abilities and leadership of the young Jehoiachin." (Harrison)

ii. **A vessel in which is no pleasure**: "That is, by a modest periphrasis [indirect wording], a close-stool [toilet], or piss-pot (so Hosea 8:8)." (Trapp)

iii. **Cast out**: "He was indeed deported (and his name can still be read on a Babylonian list of foreign prisoners and their rations of oil and barley)." (Kidner)

b. **O earth, earth, earth, hear the word of the LORD**: This was a unique and solemn introduction to a vow or promise of God.

i. "The repetition implies strongest emphasis, solemnity, and intensity." (Feinberg)

ii. The Hebrew word here can also be translated *land*. Kidner suggests that in some ways **earth** is a better translation. "The old translation of verse 29 (AV) is uniquely impressive – 'O earth, earth, earth, hear the word of the Lord' – and while the first hearers were doubtless meant to take this word to heart chiefly in its narrower sense (*O land…*), we do well to give it its full scope." (Kidner)

c. **Write this man down as childless… for none of his descendants shall prosper**: 1 Chronicles 3:17-18 lists the sons of Coniah. It wasn't that he had no children, but that he should be *considered* as **childless**, because his descendants would be cursed.

i. **Write this man down**: "The command to 'record' relates to a register of citizens (cf. Isaiah 4:3); the figure is that of a census list." (Feinberg)

d. **For none of his descendants shall prosper, sitting on the throne of David, and ruling anymore in Judah**: This was a unique and powerful curse upon the bloodline of Coniah. God promised that no blood descendant of Jeconiah would reign over Israel.

i. This is similar to the promise – perhaps even an extension of it – recorded later in Jeremiah 36:30 of Coniah's father, Jehoiakim: *Therefore thus says the LORD concerning Jehoiakim king of Judah: "He shall have no one to sit on the throne of David, and his dead body shall be cast out to the heat of the day and the frost of the night."*

ii. These parallel prophecies present a problem. God promised David that his descendant would reign as Messiah over Israel and the world (2 Samuel 7:16). By the time of Jehoiakim and Coniah that descendant had not yet come, and here God seems to promise that it would be impossible for the descendant to come. If someone was a blood descendant of David through Jehoiakim, he could not sit on the throne of Israel and be the king and the Messiah because of this curse recorded in Jeremiah 22:30 and 36:30. But if the conqueror was not descended through David, he could not be the legal heir of the throne because of the promise made to David and the nature of the royal line.

iii. This is where we come to the differences in the genealogies of Matthew and Luke. Matthew recorded the genealogy of *Joseph, the husband of Mary, of whom was born Jesus who is called Christ* (Matthew 1:16). He began at Abraham and followed the line down to Jesus, *through Joseph*. Luke recorded the genealogy of Mary: *being (as was supposed) the son of Joseph* (Luke 3:23). He began with Jesus and followed the line back up, all the way to Adam, *starting from the unmentioned Mary*.

iv. "Matthew's genealogy includes Jehoiachin but shows only who Jesus' legal father was, not his natural one. Luke traces Jesus' parental line through Nathan, a son of David, not through Solomon." (Feinberg)

Jeremiah 23 – The Branch of Righteousness and the Unrighteous Prophets

A. The Branch of Righteousness.

1. (1-2) Woe to the shepherds who destroy.

"Woe to the shepherds who destroy and scatter the sheep of My pasture!" says the Lord. Therefore thus says the Lord God of Israel against the shepherds who feed My people: "You have scattered My flock, driven them away, and not attended to them. Behold, I will attend to you for the evil of your doings," says the Lord.

> a. **Woe to the shepherds**: In the previous chapter, God pronounced His judgment and doom against several kings of Judah. Now, in a general sense, He condemned such unfaithful shepherds. In those days, kings and other leaders were often called **shepherds**; the term didn't necessarily have a spiritual context.
>
>> i. Though Jeremiah spoke to leaders in a general sense (political leaders, business leaders, military leaders, education leaders, and spiritual leaders) we might place first emphasis in our day upon the **shepherds** as being spiritual leaders.
>
> b. **Who destroy and scatter the sheep of My pasture**: These leaders were worthy of special **woe** because they did not benefit (**destroy**) or keep together (**scatter**) the people of God.
>
>> i. The flock of Jeremiah's day was indeed scattered. Some were carried away to Babylon and the nations as captives, and others went as refugees to Egypt. This could all be traced back to ungodly and poor leaders for the people of God.
>
> c. **Against the shepherds who feed My people**: This speaks mostly to the spiritual aspect of leadership, which the kings of Judah were expected to fulfill. It could be said that none of the last kings of Judah (since Josiah:

Jehoahaz, Jehoakim, Jeconiah, and Zedekiah) had *any* spiritual concern for God's people (**My people**).

   i. In the modern setting, this speaks to the great need for spiritual leaders among God's people to **feed** God's **people**. Jesus emphasized this in the restoration of Peter (John 21), twice telling him to *feed His sheep*.

d. **Behold, I will attend to you for the evil of your doings**: God would address the evil work of the unfaithful shepherds. He would hold them accountable.

2. (3-4) The promise to restore the wounded and scattered flock.

"But I will gather the remnant of My flock out of all countries where I have driven them, and bring them back to their folds; and they shall be fruitful and increase. I will set up shepherds over them who will feed them; and they shall fear no more, nor be dismayed, nor shall they be lacking," says the LORD.

a. **I will gather the remnant of My flock out of all countries where I have driven them**: One reason God scattered His people in exile was because of their unspiritual and ineffective leadership. Yet God promised that one day He would **gather** His sheep from **all countries** of their exile.

   i. This is an aspect of the New Covenant God promised to Israel. The promises to **gather** Israel back into the Promised Land are found in many prophecies of the New Covenant (Jeremiah 32:37-41, Ezekiel 11:16-20, Ezekiel 36:16-28, Ezekiel 37:21-28).

   ii. The modern-day miracle of Israel becoming an independent nation once again, after some 2500 years, is an initial fulfillment of these great promises. We say *initial*, because Israel is definitely gathered back to the land, but presently in unbelief.

b. **They shall be fruitful and increase**: Not only would God bring them back into His Promised Land, they would also be blessed there. Their population would grow rapidly.

c. **I will set up shepherds over them who will feed them**: One of the blessings God promised to a gathered Israel was godly leadership. The godly leaders (especially in a spiritual sense) would **feed them**, bring them security, and prosperity (**nor shall they be lacking**).

   i. This was a promise to bring things to a better place than they were before exile, when Israel was in the land but suffered under ungodly leaders. "The promise of restoration to the same state of affairs that obtained before the Exile was hardly adequate. There was a better hope." (Thompson)

ii. In an immediate sense, this was fulfilled in the good and godly leaders Israel had after the exile; men such as Zerubbabel; Ezra; Nehemiah; Joshua the high priest; Haggai; Zechariah and Malachi.

iii. We can see an initial, partial fulfillment of this in modern-day Israel. We can expect a complete fulfillment when they turn to Jesus as their Messiah.

3. (5-6) The King to come.

"Behold, *the* days are coming," says the LORD,
"That I will raise to David a Branch of righteousness;
A King shall reign and prosper,
And execute judgment and righteousness in the earth.
In His days Judah will be saved,
And Israel will dwell safely;
Now this *is* His name by which He will be called:
THE LORD OUR RIGHTEOUSNESS.

a. **I will raise to David a Branch of righteousness**: Long before this, God promised that the Messiah would come from the line of David (2 Samuel 7:5-16). This is a confirmation of that prior prophecy. The **Branch of righteousness** would come from the line of **David**.

i. At the end of the previous chapter, God had promised that none from the royal line of Jeconiah would sit on the throne of David (Jeremiah 22:30). It seemed as if the royal line of David was cut down like a tree and only a stump remained. Yet God would take that stump and bring forth a green shoot, a **Branch**.

ii. "The metaphor is of a shoot bursting forth from the Davidic tree (i.e., the dynasty), which, though cut off, is not dead." (Thomspon)

iii. "The shoot is that which sprouts from the roots of a fallen tree. New life will thus spring forth from the fallen dynasty." (Harrison)

b. **A King shall reign and prosper**: This **Branch of righteousness** will lead God's people as a successful **King**. Prosperity, justice, and righteousness will mark His reign. This reign will extend to **the earth**, not only the boundaries of Israel.

i. **A King shall reign**: "Moreover, he will reign as a true king, not as a puppet like Zedekiah and his immediate predecessors." (Feinberg)

c. **In His days Judah will be saved, and Israel will dwell safely**: Rescue and security would be for all God's people; for **Judah** and **Israel** both. It would be a united monarchy once again.

  i. "*Israel* here refers to the northern kingdom. She too would live in safety." (Thompson)

d. **The LORD Our Righteousness**: Jeremiah announced that **this** would be the **name by which He will be called**. He will be the way that the **righteousness** of Yahweh is given unto His people, so that *He Himself is our righteousness*.

  i. The phrase **The LORD Our Righteousness** is only two words in Hebrew. "Jehovah Tsidkenu. This is a most mellifluous and sweet name of our Lord Jesus Christ, importing his Godhead, as the righteous Branch of David did his manhood." (Trapp)

  ii. *Yahweh Tsidkenu* "is probably a play on the name of Zedekiah [which means], *My righteousness is Yahweh*." (Thompson) "Jeremiah switched Zedekiah's name around to make his pun. Zedekiah was called 'Righteousness is the Lord,' but the Messiah would be called 'the LORD our Righteousness.'" (Ryken)

  iii. As a Messianic reference, *Yahweh Tsidkenu* is strong evidence of the deity of the Messiah – *He is Yahweh*. "The Jews understood the name in v.6b to be that of the Messiah. The Targum reads, 'The Messiah of the righteous,' or 'The Messiah of righteousness'... They acknowledged the two words to be the name of the Messiah." (Feinberg)

  iv. Jesus is **the Lord Our Righteousness**: Righteousness is something *positive*. The work of Jesus in His people is not only to clean the stain of sin. The perfect obedience and righteousness of Jesus is *ours* in Him. "It speaks of one who will not only reflect the righteousness of God but will convey it to his people, making it their own possession." (Kidner)

  v. "Paul may have had this promise in mind when he spoke of 'Christ Jesus....our righteousness...' (1 Corinthians 1:30, *cf.* 2 Corinthians 5:21)." (Kidner)

  vi. Rest in Jesus as **Our Righteousness** is a great strength. "You, Sir Satan, your menaces and terrors trouble me not. For why? There is one whose name is called the Lord our righteousness, on whom I believe. He it is who hath abrogated the law, condemned sin, abolished death, destroyed hell, and is a Satan to thee, O Satan." (Luther, cited in Trapp)

4. (7-8) The greatness of God's work of gathering and restoring.

"Therefore, behold, *the* days are coming," says the LORD, "that they shall no longer say, 'As the LORD lives who brought up the children of Israel from the land of Egypt,' but, 'As the LORD lives who brought up and led the descendants of the house of Israel from the north country and from all the countries where I had driven them.' And they shall dwell in their own land."

> a. **They shall no longer say**: Israel rightly celebrated the deliverance from Egypt. Jeremiah announced that an even more wonderful deliverance would happen in connection with the gathering of Israel presented as an aspect of the New Covenant.
>
>> i. Israel was created in the Exodus out of Egypt and they were restored in the gathering out of Babylon and the nations. God promised that *the restoration of Israel* would be greater than *the creation of Israel*. This connects to the principle that *restored* or *redeemed* man is greater than *created* or *innocent* man.
>
> b. **They shall dwell in their own land**: The emphatic promise is repeated again. God will bring His people back into the Promised Land. Even after the great judgment and exile to come, He would not be finished with them, nor would He be finished with them *in the land*.

B. The pain brought with false prophets.

1. (9-10) Jeremiah's broken heart over false prophets.

My heart within me is broken
Because of the prophets;
All my bones shake.
I am like a drunken man,
And like a man whom wine has overcome,
Because of the LORD,
And because of His holy words.
For the land is full of adulterers;
For because of a curse the land mourns.
The pleasant places of the wilderness are dried up.
Their course of life is evil,
And their might *is* not right.

> a. **My heart within me is broken because of the prophets**: Jeremiah was distressed because of the presence and work of other **prophets** in his day. His heart was not **broken** because he didn't like the competition, but because of the damage they did to the honor of God and the people of God.

i. "*Heart*, as used here, denotes a profoundly disturbed mental rather than emotional state. His mind cannot grasp the way in which these prophets have chose to abuse their professional vocation." (Harrison)

b. **All my bones shake. I am like a drunken man**: This was *not* because he was overcome with a pleasant sense of intoxication because of the work of the Holy Spirit. This was in dread and indignation at the work of the other prophets as he compared their supposed word from God with the **holy words** that Jeremiah brought in God's name.

i. The great contrast between their message and his message made Jeremiah nauseous. His main message was *repent*; their main message was *relax*. They couldn't possibly both be right.

c. **For the land is full of adulterers; for because of a curse the land mourns**: The other prophets promised blessing and abundance, but the evidence was on Jeremiah's side. The heavy presence of sin in the land (*adultery* probably in both its literal and figurative senses) and the **curse** upon the land itself proved that it was time to repent and not to relax.

2. (11-12) Profane prophets and priests.

"For both prophet and priest are profane;
Yes, in My house I have found their wickedness," says the LORD.
"Therefore their way shall be to them
Like slippery *ways;*
In the darkness they shall be driven on
And fall in them;
For I will bring disaster on them,
The year of their punishment," says the LORD.

a. **For both prophet and priest are profane**: Jeremiah could see the fundamental lack of holiness among those who were supposed to be spiritual leaders. To be **profane** is the opposite of holiness. They weren't different from the idol worshipping people surrounding Judah.

i. "Next to the ungodly kings, the false prophets were most responsible for bringing about the nation's ruin." (Feinberg)

b. **In My house I have found their wickedness**: It wasn't just that the personal lives of these prophets and priests lacked holiness. Their **profane** hearts and ways were also evident in the **house** of God. Whatever effort they made to compartmentalize their lack of holiness did not work.

c. **Their way shall be to them like slippery ways**: Their profane ways made them destined to slip and fall. Not everyone falls on a **slippery** path, but most do.

3. (13-15) Judgment promised against the corrupt prophets.

"And I have seen folly in the prophets of Samaria:
They prophesied by Baal
And caused My people Israel to err.
Also I have seen a horrible thing in the prophets of Jerusalem:
They commit adultery and walk in lies;
They also strengthen the hands of evildoers,
So that no one turns back from his wickedness.
All of them are like Sodom to Me,
And her inhabitants like Gomorrah.
"Therefore thus says the LORD of hosts concerning the prophets:
'Behold, I will feed them with wormwood,
And make them drink the water of gall;
For from the prophets of Jerusalem
Profaneness has gone out into all the land.'"

> a. **I have seen folly in the prophets of Samaria...Also I have seen a horrible thing in the prophets of Jerusalem**: God compared the prophets of **Jerusalem** and Judah to be like the **prophets of Samaria** that led the northern kingdom to spiritual and social ruin some 150 years before.
>
> b. **So that no one turns back from his wickedness**: Because their own lives were filled with spiritual compromise (**they commit adultery and walk in lies**), the prophets and priests of Judah had no place or power to turn others **back** from their **wickedness**.
>
>> i. With no one being turned **back from his wickedness**, there was no spiritual or moral restraint upon the people. Everyone did what was right in their own eyes, and the men of God who should have said *stop* did not.
>>
>> ii. With the atmosphere of no restraint, the people of God had become **like Sodom** and **like Gomorrah** to God. "By their worldliness they are secularizing the house of God (23:11), that bastion of holiness; and by their laxity (23:14), whether practiced or preached, they are taking the shame out of sin (especially, it seems, sins of lust, both heterosexual, 23:14a, and homosexual, 23:14b; *cf.* Genesis 19:4-5)." (Kidner)
>
> c. **I will feed them with wormwood, and make them drink the water of gall**: There was a sour, bitter future for these corrupt and compromised prophets.
>
>> i. "Because they had poisoned the nation's spiritual springs, the Lord was to inflict drastic judgment on them – portrayed by 'bitter food'

('wormwood'; i.e., strong smelling and bitter tasting) and 'poisoned water.'" (Feinberg)

d. From the prophets of Jerusalem, profaneness has gone out into all the land: God's desire was that His people would be messengers of His holiness and righteousness. Instead, through these corrupt prophets, they had become messengers of **profaneness**, the opposite of holiness.

4. (16-17) Don't listen to the corrupt prophets.

Thus says the Lord of hosts:
"Do not listen to the words of the prophets who prophesy to you.
They make you worthless;
They speak a vision of their own heart,
Not from the mouth of the Lord.
They continually say to those who despise Me,
'The Lord has said, "You shall have peace"';
And *to* everyone who walks according to the dictates of his own heart, they say,
'No evil shall come upon you.'"

a. **Do not listen to the words of the prophets**: *God Himself* told them this. Normally God wanted His people to pay strict attention to those who brought forth His word. This shows how detached these supposed **prophets** were from the real word of God.

b. **They make you worthless; they speak a vision of their own heart**: These corrupt prophets spoke, but it was **not from the mouth of the Lord**. It was merely a **vision of their own heart**. The effect of these man-made words masquerading as the word of the Lord was to make those who believed them **worthless**.

i. **Not from the mouth of the Lord**: "This was a bold claim from Jeremiah since it implied that his own message came from Yahweh directly." (Thompson)

c. **They continually say to those who despise Me**: The corrupt prophets were afraid to speak a word of rebuke and repentance to those who despised God. Instead they spoke smooth words of **peace**, promising **no evil shall come upon you** to everyone who followed their own heart (**who walks according to the dictates of his own heart**).

i. **You shall have peace**: "The heart of false prophecy was that it always held our false hope." (Feinberg)

ii. They could not or would not rebuke those who lived **according to the dictates of his own heart**. The failure or inability to confront evil is a mark of bad or corrupt leadership.

iii. Our modern culture thinks *follow your heart* is supreme wisdom for living. The Bible says, *there is a way that seems right to a man, but its end is the way of death* (Proverbs 14:12 – repeated for emphasis in Proverbs 16:25).

5. (18-20) The serious nature of God's judgments.

For who has stood in the counsel of the LORD,
And has perceived and heard His word?
Who has marked His word and heard *it?*
Behold, a whirlwind of the LORD has gone forth in fury—
A violent whirlwind!
It will fall violently on the head of the wicked.
The anger of the LORD will not turn back
Until He has executed and performed the thoughts of His heart.
In the latter days you will understand it perfectly.

a. **A whirlwind of the LORD has gone forth in fury**: The corrupt prophets did what they did without fear of punishment. They had forgotten that God's judgments would one day come, and come as **a violent whirlwind**.

i. **Whirlwind**: "The *simoom*: the hot pestilential wind blowing from the south, frequently mentioned or referred to in the sacred writings." (Clarke)

b. **The anger of the LORD will not turn back until He has executed and performed the thoughts of His heart**: God's anger against the corrupt prophets was not just a matter of personal irritation. It was righteous and would be **performed** against them until His justice was accomplished.

i. In the previous verses, God spoke against those who walk *according to the dictate of his own heart* (Jeremiah 23:17). Here, God promised to carry out **the thoughts of His heart** against those who followed their own heart. It would be evident which heart was supreme.

6. (21-22) The corrupt prophets were not sent by God.

"I have not sent these prophets, yet they ran.
I have not spoken to them, yet they prophesied.
But if they had stood in My counsel,
And had caused My people to hear My words,
Then they would have turned them from their evil way
And from the evil of their doings.

a. **I have not sent these prophets, yet they ran**: The corrupt prophets were not called or sent by God, yet they **ran** with great energy to proclaim their self-generated words.

i. "They never received a divine commission; yet they ran, with their false messages, eagerly and energetically trying to accomplish their own objectives." (Feinberg)

b. **If they had stood in My counsel... then they would have turned them from their evil way**: If these *were* true prophets and sent prophets, they would have called people to repent. They did not. Instead of repent, their message was relax.

7. (23-24) The foolishness of resisting or rejecting God.

"Am **I a God near at hand," says the** L`ORD`,
"And not a God afar off?
Can anyone hide himself in secret places,
So I shall not see him?" says the L`ORD`;
"Do I not fill heaven and earth?" says the L`ORD`.

a. **Am I a God near at hand**: Asking rhetorical questions, God reminded Judah that He was near. There was no use in trying to **hide** in **secret places** to avoid the sight of God.

i. "Atheists are apt to think that because they see none, therefore none see them." (Trapp)

b. **Do I not fill heaven and earth**: The same God who fills the universe can also see what we do. This was something that the corrupt prophets and those who went uncorrected because of the corrupt prophets chose to forget.

8. (25-27) Prophetic lies.

"I have heard what the prophets have said who prophesy lies in My name, saying, 'I have dreamed, I have dreamed!' How long will *this* **be in the heart of the prophets who prophesy lies? Indeed** *they are* **prophets of the deceit of their own heart, who try to make My people forget My name by their dreams which everyone tells his neighbor, as their fathers forgot My name for Baal.**

a. **I have heard what the prophets have said who prophesy lies in My name**: This alone should have terrified the corrupt prophets. Even if no *man* would judge and discern their supposed prophetic words, God **heard** them. He would judge.

i. In a New Testament context, God commands that any supposed prophetic word be judged in the congregation.

- *Let two or three prophets speak, and let the others judge.* (1 Corinthians 14:29)

- *Do not despise prophecies. Test all things; hold fast what is good.* (1 Thessalonians 5:20-21)
- *Beloved, do not believe every spirit, but test the spirits, whether they are of God; because many false prophets have gone out into the world.* (1 John 4:1)

ii. It is a great failing among many Christians that any purported prophecy is accepted without any testing or discernment. Yet if they will not judge, God will in some way or another.

b. **I have dreamed, I have dreamed**: The corrupt prophets loved to speak about dreams and great, swelling things. The problem was that these *were lies*. Perhaps the lie was that they even had such a dream, or perhaps they really had a dream but it was not a true message from God. Instead of being from God, these messages were **the deceit of their own heart**.

i. "Man is so constituted that he ever seeks in some form for direction from the spiritual world that lies behind all material manifestations and forms. This quest creates the opportunity of evil men, who having no true light from that world, yet speak as though they had, and so mislead those who hear them." (Morgan)

c. **Who try to make My people forget My name by their dreams**: The corrupt prophets loved to focus on spiritual phenomena such as **dreams**. Though this pretended to be a spiritual focus, it drew attention away from God Himself, from His holy character represented by his **name**.

i. **My people forget My name**: "Once men forgot the character of Yahweh they could be persuaded to accept all kinds of doctrines." (Thompson)

9. (28-29) The low place of spiritual phenomena compared to the word of God.

"The prophet who has a dream, let him tell a dream;
And he who has My word, let him speak My word faithfully.
What *is* the chaff to the wheat?" says the LORD.
"*Is* not My word like a fire?" says the LORD,
"And like a hammer *that* breaks the rock in pieces?

a. **The prophet who has a dream, let him tell a dream**: God invited those obsessed with spiritual phenomena to lay it out. **Tell** the dream. Present your best case.

i. "He clearly regarded dreams as very subjective experiences which had nothing to do with Yahweh's word. There was a difference. Let the dreamer tell his dream if he wished, but it should be made clear that it was a dream and not a word from Yahweh." (Thompson)

b. **And he who has My word, let him speak My word faithfully**: God gave a second invitation; this one to the one who had His **word**. That one was invited to **speak** God's word **faithfully**, to not be silent despite the number and popularity of the corrupt prophets.

i. In Jeremiah's day, there were many more corrupt prophets than those who would **speak** God's **word faithfully**.

c. **What is the chaff to the wheat**: Clearly, the dream of the corrupt prophet was like the **chaff**; something, but of little substance and of no help. God's **word**, **faithfully** presented was like **wheat**; of substance, nourishment, giving life, and having the power of multiplication.

d. **Is not My word like a fire**: God's word has power like **fire**, power to benefit and to judge. **Chaff** has no power against **fire**.

- God's word is **like a fire** that can warm and comfort.
- God's word is **like a fire** that can burn and cause pain.
- God's word is **like a fire** that can melt the hardest materials.
- God's word is **like a fire** that refines and consumes impurity.

e. **And like a hammer that breaks the rocks in pieces**: God's word is as powerful as a **hammer**, with the power to build or break. **Chaff** has no power against a **hammer**.

i. **Like a hammer**: "Whenever a minister has the gospel to use, this simile should teach him how he ought to use it; with his whole might let him strike with it mighty blows for his Lord." (Spurgeon)

ii. "I should think that it does not require any great education to learn how to use a hammer; I do not know, it may do; but it seems that to use a hammer aright, one has nothing to do but to strike with it. Brethren, when you preach, take the gospel hammer, and strike as hard as ever you can with it." (Spurgeon)

iii. Adam Clarke wrote a wise caution against the thought that the word of God can do its work without the Spirit of God. "Let us take heed lest we think, as some have thought and affirmed, that the sacred writings are quite sufficient of themselves to enlighten, convince, and convert the soul, and that there is no need of the Holy Spirit. *Fire itself* must be *applied* by an *agent* in order to produce its effects; and surely the *hammer* cannot *break the rock in pieces*, unless *wielded* by an *able workman*. And it is God's *Spirit* alone that can thus *apply* it; for we find it frequently *read* and frequently *spoken*, without producing any salutary effects." (Clarke)

10. (30-32) God against the corrupt prophets.

"Therefore behold, I *am* against the prophets," says the Lord, "who steal My words every one from his neighbor. Behold, I *am* against the prophets," says the Lord, "who use their tongues and say, 'He says.' Behold, I *am* against those who prophesy false dreams," says the Lord, "and tell them, and cause My people to err by their lies and by their recklessness. Yet I did not send them or command them; therefore they shall not profit this people at all," says the Lord.

> a. **I am against the prophets**: Just because someone claimed to be a prophet did not mean that God was for them or approved them. In Jeremiah's day and our own there were many prophets whom God was **against**.
>
> b. **Who steal My words every one from his neighbor**: When the true word of God was ignored or neglected because people were attracted to the chaff-like spiritual phenomena of the corrupt prophets, God said it was like *stealing* His **words**. God was **against them**.
>
> c. **Who use their tongues and say, "He says"**: God was against those who claimed to speak for God and really only spoke from their own heart.
>
>> i. **Who use their tongues and say, "He says"**: "There is a wordplay here which is difficult to capture in English, literally, 'they take up (use) their (own) tongue and oracle an oracle'... The meaning is that the message of the false prophets originated from themselves and was presented in their own words with something of a flourish as though it were a word from Yahweh." (Thompson)
>
> d. **Those who prophesy false dreams**: God was against those who promoted **dreams** and spiritual phenomena above His word.
>
> e. **Cause My people to err by their lies and by their recklessness**: Deceptive and reckless words spoken in the name of God led God's **people** into error. God was against these reckless ones with little regard for truth.
>
> f. **Yet I did not send them or command them; therefore they shall not profit this people at all**: Because God did not send them, they would do no real good for the people of God, even if they had good intentions. There might be some froth or some excitement, but no true **profit**.

11. (33-40) No longer mention the oracle (burden) of the Lord.

"So when these people or the prophet or the priest ask you, saying, 'What is the oracle of the Lord?' you shall then say to them, 'What oracle? I will even forsake you,' says the Lord. "And *as for* the prophet and the priest and the people who say, 'The oracle of the Lord!' I will even punish that man and his house. Thus every one of you shall say to his neighbor, and every one to his brother, 'What has the LORD answered?' and, 'What has the LORD spoken?' And the oracle of the LORD you shall mention no more. For every man's word will be his oracle, for you have perverted the words of the living God, the LORD of hosts, our God. Thus you shall say to the prophet, 'What has the LORD answered you?' and, 'What has the LORD spoken?' But since you say, 'The oracle of the LORD!' therefore thus says the LORD: 'Because you say this word, "The oracle of the LORD!" and I have sent to you, saying, "Do not say, 'The oracle of the LORD!'" therefore behold, I, even I, will utterly forget you and forsake you, and the city that I gave you and your fathers, and *will cast you* out of My presence. And I will bring an everlasting reproach upon you, and a perpetual shame, which shall not be forgotten.'"

a. **The oracle of the LORD**: This section is somewhat difficult because of a pun and wordplay in Hebrew. The key word is *massa* which meant both *burden* and **oracle** (in the sense of revelation from God). Sometimes one sense of the word is intended, sometimes the other, and sometimes both.

> i. "By usage the word came to mean that which was placed as a burden on the heart of a prophet, having already been such on the heart of God." (Feinberg)

> ii. "The whole argument comes to us as rather complex, probably because the pun is developed in such a sustained manner. The two senses of *massa*, 'prophetic utterance' and 'burden,' and the verb *nasa* occur a number of times. The *massa* of Yahweh is that the people are a *massa*." (Thompson)

b. **What is the oracle of the LORD**: This was probably a mocking question from the corrupt prophets to Jeremiah. Since most of Jeremiah's prophetic work was to announce doom and call for repentance, they jokingly wanted to know what heavy word they had for them today.

> i. "Jeremiah indicates that the people, the priests, and the prophets (Jeremiah 23:33) had begun to use this important word mockingly and derisively. They would ask Jeremiah, 'What is the oracle [burden] now?' 'What is the heavy word from the Lord now?'" (Feinberg)

> ii. "When these people, or a prophet or a priest ask you, 'What burden has the Lord laid on your heart?' say to them, 'You are the burden, and I will cast you off, declares the Lord.'" (Ryken)

c. **You shall say to them, "What oracle"**: God told Jeremiah to respond with this phrase. It either meant that his words should not be thought of as *heavy* as much as *true*; or (perhaps more likely) the idea is that the mocking, corrupt prophets were the burden.

i. **You shall say to them, "What oracle?"** "It is much better to follow LXX, Vulgate, and RSV and translate it 'You are the burden!' This requires no change of consonants in the Hebrew text but only another division of them." (Feinberg)

d. **I will punish that man and his house**: God promised to **punish** those who did presume to speak an oracle and take attention away from God's word. As far as God was concerned, **the oracle of the LORD you shall mention no more**.

e. **For every man's word will be his oracle, for you have perverted the words of the living God**: The institution of prophecy had become so corrupt in Jeremiah's day that anyone who did claim to speak an **oracle of the LORD** could be assumed to be speaking for himself, and speaking words **perverted** from God's true message.

f. **I will bring an everlasting reproach upon you, and a perpetual shame, which shall not be forgotten**: This was the end result of their attraction to oracles, dreams, and other spiritual phenomena.

i. **Cast you out of My presence**: "Finally in verses 39-40 he takes and emphasizes the parent verb of 'burden' in its literal sense, to visualize these men picked up and thrown away in irretrievable disgrace." (Kidner)

ii. "Contempt of the Word is such an engaging sin that God cannot easily satisfy himself in saying what he will do to such as are guilty of it." (Trapp)

Jeremiah 24 – Lessons from Two Baskets of Figs

A. Two baskets of figs.

1. (1) Time and place of the lesson.

The Lord showed me, and there were two baskets of figs set before the temple of the Lord, after Nebuchadnezzar king of Babylon had carried away captive Jeconiah the son of Jehoiakim, king of Judah, and the princes of Judah with the craftsmen and smiths, from Jerusalem, and had brought them to Babylon.

> a. **The Lord showed me and there were two baskets of figs before the temple**: What follows in this short chapter doesn't seem to be a vision or a dream. What Jeremiah described was not so unusual; there were simply **two baskets of figs** somewhere near the temple. Perhaps they were there as some kind of grain offering, or perhaps someone simply left them there from shopping.
>
> > i. Some commentators (such as Thompson and Feinberg) believe the wording points to this being a supernatural vision.
>
> b. **After Nebuchadnezzar, king of Babylon had carried away captive Jeconiah**: King **Jeconiah** of Judah reigned only a few months. He was deposed and exiled (2 Kings 24:8-15) when **Nebuchadnezzar** came a second time to Jerusalem in 597 BC. Since this was **after** his short reign, King Zedekiah reigned. His 11-year reign was the last of the Kings of Judah before a complete Babylonian conquest.
>
> > i. When **Nebuchadnezzar** left Judah with Zedekiah as a puppet king, it was easy for them to think the worst was over and they were fortunate to survive and escape exile. Those who remained thought they were better off than those taken in exile.
> >
> > ii. "After the exile of Jehoiachin and the leading citizens of Judah (2 Kings 24:10-17), those who remained seem to have been full of optimism for the future." (Thompson)

c. **The princes of Judah with the craftsmen and smiths**: King Jeconiah was not the only one **brought** to Babylon in this second invasion of Judah. They also took others of the nobility of Judah and skilled **craftsmen**,

2. (2-3) What Jeremiah saw – the two baskets of figs.

One basket *had* very good figs, like the figs *that are* first ripe; and the other basket *had* very bad figs which could not be eaten, they were so bad. Then the LORD said to me, "What do you see, Jeremiah?" And I said, "Figs, the good figs, very good; and the bad, very bad, which cannot be eaten, they are so bad."

a. **One basket had very good figs… the other basket had very bad figs**: Jeremiah noted that the two baskets of figs were not the same. One had very good figs, and the other had figs that were far past good – they were so spoiled they **could not be eaten**.

b. **What do you see, Jeremiah**: God was about to speak to the prophet through these two different baskets of figs.

B. Learning from the baskets of figs.

1. (4-7) The good basket of figs.

Again the word of the LORD came to me, saying, "Thus says the LORD, the God of Israel: 'Like these good figs, so will I acknowledge those who are carried away captive from Judah, whom I have sent out of this place for *their own* good, into the land of the Chaldeans. For I will set My eyes on them for good, and I will bring them back to this land; I will build them and not pull *them* down, and I will plant them and not pluck *them* up. Then I will give them a heart to know Me, that I *am* the LORD; and they shall be My people, and I will be their God, for they shall return to Me with their whole heart.'"

a. **Like these good figs, so will I acknowledge those who are carried away captive from Judah, whom I have sent out of this place for their own good**: Judgment came (and was to come) upon Judah as a whole; the entire nation would feel the pain of it. Yet that did not mean that everyone in Judah was the same in God's eyes. Some were like the **good figs** – and were essentially **sent out** of Judah to Babylon **for their own good**.

i. Judgment upon a nation or community means that all suffer, even those who may be individually innocent of the sins that brought God's judgment. What God said to Jeremiah through the two baskets of figs means that even when all suffer under a national judgment, God still knows the difference between those caught up in the judgment and those who brought down the judgment.

b. **Those who are carried away captive from Judah**: We might have expected that those first **carried away captive** would be the worst in God's eyes and He allowed them to be first exiled as a demonstration of His displeasure. Jeremiah delivered the surprising message: the first taken were the **good figs**, not the bad figs.

> i. "It was a startling comparison. It is most natural to suppose that those remaining would lay the flattering unction to their souls that those carried away were the more corrupt. This message was in direct contradiction of the false assumption." (Morgan)

c. **I will set My eyes on them for good, and will bring them back to this land**: Those represented by the **good figs** would be blessed even in captivity. God also promised to **bring them back to this land**, and they would be among those who came back to Judah with Ezra and Nehemiah starting around 538 BC.

> i. There *was* a blessing for those first taken in exile and who did not remain in Jerusalem for the catastrophic end. "The captives, augmented by further deportations in 587 and 582 BC (Jeremiah 52:29 f.), turned to the Lord in repentance and under Ezekiel's leadership, a new kind of faith, loyal to the covenant-relationship with God, was forged." (Cundall)

d. **I will build them and not pull them down, and I will plant them and not pluck them up**: When they returned to the land, God would establish them securely again.

e. **Then I will give them a new heart to know Me, that I am the LORD**: This sounds something like the many of the New Covenant promises in Jeremiah and Ezekiel (Jeremiah 23:1-8, Jeremiah 31:31-34, Jeremiah 32:37-41, Ezekiel 11:16-20, Ezekiel 36:16-28, Ezekiel 37:11-14, 37:21-28). Yet it is better to regard it as using the gathering from exile as a prefiguring of the ultimate fulfillment of the promise in the last days.

> i. From a Christian perspective, we know that the New Covenant was not instituted in the return from exile because Jesus Christ specifically instituted it with His work on the cross (Luke 22:20).

> ii. Nevertheless, the return from exile did foreshadow the New Covenant in some important ways. God's people were gathered again into the land, and they were a changed people (**a heart to know Me... they shall be My people... they shall return to Me with their whole heart**). The great change after the exile was that the people of Israel no longer went after the idols of the nations (such as Baal and Ashtoreth)

as they had before. They were separated and devoted to Yahweh in a way they had not been before.

2. (8-10) The basket of bad figs.

"'And as the bad figs which cannot be eaten, they are so bad' -- surely thus says the LORD— 'so will I give up Zedekiah the king of Judah, his princes, the residue of Jerusalem who remain in this land, and those who dwell in the land of Egypt. I will deliver them to trouble into all the kingdoms of the earth, for *their* harm, *to be* a reproach and a byword, a taunt and a curse, in all places where I shall drive them. And I will send the sword, the famine, and the pestilence among them, till they are consumed from the land that I gave to them and their fathers.'"

> a. **As the bad figs which cannot be eaten... so will I give up Zedekiah**: Not all in Judah were good figs. There were also rotten ones, including the king. They were past their expiration date and good for nothing.
>
> > i. Zedekiah and his associates were really the **bad figs**: "Zedekiah and his subjects, who were looked upon as the happier, because at home; and derided, likely, Jeconiah and his concaptives as cowards." (Trapp)
>
> b. **I will deliver them to trouble into all the kingdoms of the earth**: Virtually all of Judah would be taken captive, but God knew how to appoint the **bad figs** among them to particular **trouble**. They would be **a reproach and a byword, a taunt and a curse** in exile. In a sense, God *sent out* the people represented by the good figs (Jeremiah 24:5), but the bad figs He **shall drive out**.
>
> c. **I will send the sword, the famine, and the pestilence among them**: God would complete His judgment against those represented by the **bad figs**.

Jeremiah 25 – The Cup of Fury in God's Hand

A. Seventy years of judgment.

1. (1-2) The word to Judah and Jerusalem.

The word that came to Jeremiah concerning all the people of Judah, in the fourth year of Jehoiakim the son of Josiah, king of Judah (which *was* **the first year of Nebuchadnezzar king of Babylon), which Jeremiah the prophet spoke to all the people of Judah and to all the inhabitants of Jerusalem, saying:**

> a. **In the fourth year of Jehoiakim**: This was 605 BC, an important year in world history and Biblical history. In world history the Egyptians were overwhelmed at Carchemish (Jeremiah 46:2ff.) in modern Turkey, near the Syrian border. The Babylonian armies chased the fleeing Egyptians south. In Biblical history, Nebuchadnezzar came to Jerusalem but had to leave quickly because his father died and it was **the first year** of his reign in Babylon. It's possible that this prophecy came between the two events.
>
>> i. G. Campbell Morgan believed that though this prophecy was first given **in the fourth year of Jehoiakim,** Jeremiah here repeated it as part of the extended prophecy to King Zedekiah (begun in Jeremiah 24). "Thus again Zedekiah, reminded of the prophecy delivered in the fourth year of Jehoiakim, would see how inevitable was the doom now threatening himself and Jerusalem." (Morgan)
>
> b. **Jeremiah the prophet spoke to all the people of Judah and to all the inhabitants of Jerusalem**: Though few received it, this was a message for all.

2. (3-7) The rejected word of the prophets.

"From the thirteenth year of Josiah the son of Amon, king of Judah, even to this day, this *is* **the twenty-third year in which the word of the LORD has come to me; and I have spoken to you, rising early and speaking, but you have not listened. And the LORD has sent to you all His**

servants the prophets, rising early and sending *them*, but you have not listened nor inclined your ear to hear. They said, 'Repent now everyone of his evil way and his evil doings, and dwell in the land that the LORD has given to you and your fathers forever and ever. Do not go after other gods to serve them and worship them, and do not provoke Me to anger with the works of your hands; and I will not harm you.' Yet you have not listened to Me," says the LORD, "that you might provoke Me to anger with the works of your hands to your own hurt.

> a. **This is the twenty-third year in which the word of the LORD has come to me**: Jeremiah was only a little more than halfway through his long work as a prophet. Yet with 23 years of experience, he felt he had something to say to the people of Judah.
>
>> i. Jeremiah had "prophesied for almost twenty years under Josiah, followed by three months under Jehoahaz and three years under Jehoiakim. He was therefore in the middle of his career at this point." (Harrison)
>
> b. **But you have not listened**: Despite his many years of faithful service to God and the people, they did not listen to Jeremiah. They also did not listen to other **servants the prophets** that God sent to them.
>
> c. **They said, "Repent now everyone of his evil way and evil doings"**: This was the message of both Jeremiah and the other faithful prophets. Over his complete ministry there were at times other faithful prophets who spoke a similar message as Jeremiah, warning the people against idolatry and to godly living.
>
>> i. "*The work of your hands* is sometimes taken to mean 'idols your hands have made' (NEB), but it may be a general reference to the actions of the people, that is, what they do." (Thompson)
>
> d. **Yet you have not listened to Me**: When the people of Judah ignored the faithful prophets, they weren't just ignoring the human messengers; they rejected the God who sent the message. This hardened disobedience provoked God **to anger**.

3. (8-11) Seventy years of desolation.

"Therefore thus says the LORD of hosts: 'Because you have not heard My words, behold, I will send and take all the families of the north,' says the LORD, 'and Nebuchadnezzar the king of Babylon, My servant, and will bring them against this land, against its inhabitants, and against these nations all around, and will utterly destroy them, and make them an astonishment, a hissing, and perpetual desolations. Moreover I will take from them the voice of mirth and the voice of gladness, the voice of the bridegroom and the voice of the bride, the sound of the millstones and the light of the lamp. And this whole land shall be a desolation *and* an astonishment, and these nations shall serve the king of Babylon seventy years.

a. **Thus says the LORD of hosts**: When God introduces Himself as the commander of heavenly armies (**hosts**), it is important to listen carefully.

i. **Families of the north**: "These people have been interpreted as being the allies of the king of Babylon, the many nations comprising the Babylonian Empire, subunits or divisions of a tribe, a political unit, or the Babylonians in general. Perhaps the last is the best interpretation because it best suits the context." (Feinberg)

b. **Nebuchadnezzar the king of Babylon, My servant, and will bring them against this land**: The conquering king of Babylon was God's **servant** in accomplishing this work of judgment. God would raise Nebuchadnezzar up not only to conquer Judah, but also **against these nations all around**.

i. When Jeremiah made this prophecy, Babylon had just established itself as the dominant world power by defeating the rival Egyptians at Carchemish. The world waited to see what they would do with their power, and God told them through Jeremiah.

ii. **Nebuchadnezzar My servant**: "*i.e.,* Mine executioner, the rod of my wrath, [Isaiah 10:5] and the scourge of the world, as Attila styled himself." (Trapp)

iii. "It was not so much that God's pleasure was on him but that as the Lord's instrument he was to execute the divine plan for Judah and the nations. He was unconsciously doing God's will by devoting whole populations to destruction." (Feinberg)

iv. The Septuagint – the ancient Greek translation of the Hebrew Scriptures – does not include the words **My servant**. "The omission by LXX of this reference to Nebuchadrezzar may indicate that the translator objected to giving such a title and such a place of honor to a pagan king." (Thompson)

c. **Make them an astonishment, a hissing, and perpetual desolation**: As Jeremiah did many times before, he announced the coming Babylonian conquest of Judah and Jerusalem.

i. **Utterly destroy them**: "They would be devoted *to wholesale destruction* (Hebrew *heherim*). The verb is related to the noun *herem*. It occurs frequently in the early narratives dealing with the holy war especially in Joshua." (Thompson)

ii. **The sound of the millstones and the light of the lamp**: "Where then the *noise of the mill* is not *heard*, nor the *light of the candle seen*, there must be desolation; because these things are heard and seen in every inhabited country." (Clarke)

iii. "Jeremiah graphically highlights the unnatural silence and the frightening darkness of a desolated Judah." (Cundall)

d. **These nations shall serve the king of Babylon seventy years**: Here, God gave Jeremiah an additional revelation. The forced exile of the people of God out of the Promised Land would last for **seventy years**.

i. There are many scholars and commentators (including more conservative ones) who take **seventy years** as an estimation or as a symbol for *many* (Judges 1:7, 8:14; 1 Samuel 6:19; 2 Samuel 24:15; Psalm 90:10; etc.).

ii. Harrison is a good example of this: "The *seventy years* of exile is a round figure, being reckoned from the fourth year of Jehoiakim (605 BC) to the start of the return under Cyrus' regime, about 536 BC (*cf.* Zechariah 1:12; 2 Chronicles 36:20-23)." (Harrison)

iii. However, there is good reason to believe that the **seventy years** spoke of a literal 70 years. "On the other hand, there are many who take the number of years to be precise, namely, from the fourth year of Jehoiakim (the first year of Nebuchadnezzar) to the end of the Babylonian dynasty with the coming of Cyrus (*cf.* 2 Chronicles 36:21-22; Ezra 1:1-3). They hold that the reckoning must be precise because Daniel (*cf.* Daniel 9:1-2) went to Babylon with the first deportation and knew that he had been there seventy years." (Feinberg)

4. (12-14) After the seventy years.

'Then it will come to pass, when seventy years are completed, *that* I will punish the king of Babylon and that nation, the land of the Chaldeans, for their iniquity,' says the LORD; 'and I will make it a perpetual desolation. So I will bring on that land all My words which I have pronounced against it, all that is written in this book, which Jeremiah has prophesied concerning all the nations. (For many nations and great kings shall be served by them also; and I will repay them according to their deeds and according to the works of their own hands.)'"

a. **When the seventy years are complete, that I will punish the king of Babylon and that nation**: 70 years would not only measure the time of exile; it would also measure the time until God brought judgment upon Babylon. Even as they made Judah a desolation (Jeremiah 25:11), so God would make Babylon **a perpetual desolation**.

i. Judah's desolation was appointed for 70 years; Babylon's was to be **perpetual**. The Babylonian Empire never again ruled as such. The nation of Israel was formed again in the ancient world and exists today.

ii. "Babylonia, however, was no pure agent of justice; she was a cruel, avaricious heathen-power, subject herself to the judgment of God." (Cundall)

b. **I will repay them according to their deeds**: Nebuchadnezzar and the Babylonians were God's *servant* (Jeremiah 25:9) in carrying out His judgment against Judah; they would be judged by their evil **deeds** and **works of their own hands**. They served God's purpose, but it did not excuse or justify their actions.

i. **Many nations and great kings**: "The 'many nations' and 'great kings' refer to the Medes and the Persians with their many allies or tributary kings under Cyrus the Great. They would impose forced labor on the once-invincible Babylonians." (Feinberg)

B. Judgment on the nations.

1. (15-16) The cup of God's fury.

For thus says the LORD God of Israel to me: "Take this wine cup of fury from My hand, and cause all the nations, to whom I send you, to drink it. And they will drink and stagger and go mad because of the sword that I will send among them."

a. **Take this wine cup of fury from My hand**: God spoke to Jeremiah with a picture, and in the picture God, as a bartender of judgment, gave the prophet a **cup of fury**, of judgment. "Or, Take this smoking wine cup." (Trapp)

i. Several times in the Old Testament, a **cup** is a powerful picture of the wrath and judgment of God.

- *For in the hand of the Lord there is a cup, and the wine is red; it is fully mixed, and He pours it out; surely its dregs shall all the wicked of the earth drain and drink down.* (Psalm 75:8)

- *Awake, awake! Stand up, O Jerusalem, you who have drunk at the hand of the Lord The cup of His fury; you have drunk the dregs of the cup of trembling, and drained it out.* (Isaiah 51:17)

ii. "The drinking of a potion was also one of the ordeal processes for testing the innocence of a person, and the 'cup of wrath' symbol may have had its origin in such procedures (Numbers 5:11-31)." (Thompson)

iii. Jesus referred to this picture of the **cup of fury** when He asked in Gethsemane if the cup might pass from Him (Luke 22:42). In this sense, the **cup** didn't represent death, but judgment. Jesus became, as it were, an enemy of God, who was judged and forced to drink the **cup of fury** from the Father so we would not have to drink from that cup. Taking this figurative cup was the source of Jesus' greatest agony on the cross.

b. **Cause all the nations, to whom I send you, to drink it**: Jeremiah would announce God's judgment (in the picture of the cup of fury) to the nations surrounding Judah.

i. "It described the processes of the Divine procedure in judgment in enlarging circles. First, there would be the judgment of Judah, Babylon being the instrument. Then would follow the judgment of Babylon by many nations. Then the judgment of the nations shall follow. Finally, the whole earth will be involved." (Morgan)

c. **They will drink and stagger and go mad because of the sword that I will send**: Under the judgment to come, they would act as if they were intoxicated and impaired. They would act as if they were not in their right mind.

i. "The word translated 'stagger' suggests there is something venomous or poisonous in the cup. The cup of God's wrath does not just intoxicate and inebriate; it staggers and stupefies." (Ryken)

ii. "In its familiar reference to the nations and their downfall, its picture of judgment in the form of drunken stupor and collapse is all too recognizable in the collective madness that can take hold of a people to destroy it from within, by godless infatuations and perversions." (Kidner)

2. (17-26) Jerusalem as the cup of staggering.

Then I took the cup from the LORD**'s hand, and made all the nations drink, to whom the L**ORD **had sent me: Jerusalem and the cities of Judah, its kings and its princes, to make them a desolation, an astonishment, a hissing, and a curse, as** *it is* **this day; Pharaoh king of Egypt, his servants, his princes, and all his people; all the mixed multitude, all the kings of the land of Uz, all the kings of the land of the Philistines (namely, Ashkelon, Gaza, Ekron, and the remnant of Ashdod); Edom, Moab, and the people of Ammon; all the kings of Tyre, all the kings of Sidon, and the kings of the coastlands which** *are* **across the sea; Dedan, Tema, Buz, and all** *who are* **in the farthest corners; all the kings of Arabia and all the kings of the mixed multitude who dwell in the desert; all the**

kings of Zimri, all the kings of Elam, and all the kings of the Medes; all the kings of the north, far and near, one with another; and all the kingdoms of the world which *are* on the face of the earth. Also the king of Sheshach shall drink after them.

a. **Then I took the cup from the LORD's hand, and made all the nations to drink**: Jeremiah described either a vision, a dream, or he simply spoke according to the picture described in the previous verses.

b. **Jerusalem and the cities of Judah**: Judgment would begin among the people of God. They would be the first to drink the cup of God's fury. Yet judgment *would* come upon the other nations. This principle was repeated in Proverbs 11:31 and 1 Peter 4:18: *If the righteous one is scarcely saved, where will the ungodly and the sinner appear?*

c. **Pharaoh king of Egypt**: Jeremiah began the list of judgment by mentioning **Egypt**, the other world power of the day. This was followed by a long list of other peoples and nations, with a special focus upon their kings or leaders. Since the list is so complete, there is not likely any particular event or period in which *all* these nations were judged. This list has its ultimate fulfillment at the end of the age in the judgment of the nations.

- **All the mixed multitude.**
- **All the kings of the land of Uz.**
- **All the kings of the land of the Philistines.**
- **Edom, Moab, and the people of Ammon.**
- **All the kings of Tyre, all the kings of Sidon.**
- **The kings of the coastlands.**
- **Dedan, Tema, Buz, and all who are in the farthest corners.**
- **All the kings of Arabia.**
- **All the kings of the mixed multitude who dwell in the desert.**
- **All the kings of Zimri.**
- **All the kings of Elam, and all the kings of the Medes.**
- **All the kings of the north, far and near.**
- **All the kingdoms of the world which are on the face of the earth**, emphasizing the complete character of this judgment.

i. **Pharaoh king of Egypt**: "Of whom Herodotus writeth that he persuaded himself and boasted, that his kingdom was so strong that no god or man could take it from him. He was afterwards hanged by his own subjects." (Trapp)

ii. "*The land of Uz*, the home of Job (Job 1:1) probably lay to the east of Palestine. In Lamentations 4:21 it is connected with Edom." (Thompson)

iii. Adam Clarke identified some of these peoples more specifically.

- **Dedan**: "Was son of Abraham, by Keturah, Genesis 25:3."
- **Tema**: "Was one of the sons of Ishmael, in the north of Arabia, Genesis 36:15."
- **Buz**: "Brother of *Uz*, descendants of Nahor, brother of Abraham, settled in Arabia Deserta, Genesis 22:21."
- **Zimri**: "Descendants of Abraham, by Keturah, Genesis 25:2, 6."

iv. "Since these kingdoms made up virtually the entire world of the Old Testament, the final verses can go on to speak in more and more sweeping terms, to present finally a picture which transcends these limits, to be fulfilled (as I see it) in the truly universal judgment of the end-time." (Kidner)

d. **Also the king of Sheshach shall drink after them**: At the end of this long list, Jeremiah emphasized the judgment to come upon **Sheshach** – a code name for the Babylonians.

i. "Following Jerome, many hold that the name is a cipher (code) that stands for Babylon. The cipher is known as *Atbash*, a system of secret writing that substituted the last letter of the Hebrew alphabet for the first, and next to the last for the second, and so through all the Hebrew consonants." (Feinberg)

ii. "In the text as it stands, where Babylon and Chaldea are named openly and often, it conceals nothing; but it gives a glimpse into the precautions which people evidently had to take at times in conversations or correspondence." (Kidner)

iii. Even though there was a sense in which Nebuchadnezzar was God's servant (Jeremiah 25:9) and God used the Babylonians, judgment still came upon them. "O disobedient and ungodly soul, thou mayest serve God's purpose, yet He will not let thee be unpunished. Your condemnation now for a long time lingereth not." (Meyer)

3. (27-29) The nations *must* drink the cup.

"Therefore you shall say to them, 'Thus says the LORD of hosts, the God of Israel: "Drink, be drunk, and vomit! Fall and rise no more, because of

the sword which I will send among you."' And it shall be, if they refuse to take the cup from your hand to drink, then you shall say to them, 'Thus says the LORD of hosts: "You shall certainly drink! For behold, I begin to bring calamity on the city which is called by My name, and should you be utterly unpunished? You shall not be unpunished, for I will call for a sword on all the inhabitants of the earth," says the LORD of hosts.'"

> a. **Drink, be drunk, and vomit**: As much as they might not want it, there was no escaping this judgment to come. God would judge them with a figurative **cup** but a literal **sword**. If the cup was refused, God would insist: **You shall certainly drink**. Judgment could not simply be avoided by denial or positive thinking.
>
>> i. The King James Version has, *Drink ye, and be drunken, and spue*. Adam Clarke commented: "Why did we not use the word *vomit*, less offensive than the other, and yet of the same signification?" (Clarke)
>
> b. **For behold, I begin to bring calamity on the city which is called by My name, and should you be utterly unpunished**: While judgment would *begin* among God's people (Jeremiah 25:18), it would in no way *finish* there. The judgment of God's people was a certain prophecy of coming judgment upon the nations.
>
> c. **I will call for a sword on all the inhabitants of the earth**: Through history God has dealt with each of the nations listed in the previous verses. Yet the global reach of this judgment points to its ultimate fulfillment at the end of the age. The God of heavenly armies – the **LORD of hosts** – promised it so.

4. (30-33) The LORD's controversy with the nations.

"Therefore prophesy against them all these words, and say to them:
'The LORD will roar from on high,
And utter His voice from His holy habitation;
He will roar mightily against His fold.
He will give a shout, as those who tread *the grapes*,
Against all the inhabitants of the earth.
A noise will come to the ends of the earth—
For the LORD has a controversy with the nations;
He will plead His case with all flesh.
He will give those *who are* wicked to the sword,' says the LORD."

Thus says the LORD of hosts:
"Behold, disaster shall go forth
From nation to nation,

And a great whirlwind shall be raised up
From the farthest parts of the earth.

"And at that day the slain of the LORD shall be from *one* end of the earth even to the *other* end of the earth. They shall not be lamented, or gathered, or buried; they shall become refuse on the ground.

> a. **The LORD will roar from on high, and utter His voice from His holy habitation**: When the judgment comes, God's voice will be heard like the roar from a mighty lion. Those who didn't want to hear God before will be forced to hear Him then. This would be true of His own people (**His fold**) and **all the inhabitants of the earth**.
>
> b. **A shout, as those who tread the grapes**: Treading the grapes at harvest time was a celebration. There will be an element of righteous joy in the judgment of God at the end of the age.
>
> c. **Disaster shall go forth from nation to nation**: Repeatedly, the worldwide nature of the judgment is emphasized.
>
> d. **At that day the slain of the LORD shall be from one end of the earth even to the other end**: This ghastly picture is almost beyond comprehension. Nevertheless, it fits the descriptions of judgment found in the Book of Revelation (Revelation 19:11-18), which may have been inspired by this passage.
>
> > i. **Refuse on the ground**: "As the Judge of all the earth, God reads His *indictment* of mankind: the victims of the coming disaster will lie like so much manure on the surface of the ground." (Harrison)

5. (34-38) The anger of the LORD against the shepherds.

"Wail, shepherds, and cry!
Roll about *in the ashes*,
You leaders of the flock!
For the days of your slaughter and your dispersions are fulfilled;
You shall fall like a precious vessel.
And the shepherds will have no way to flee,
Nor the leaders of the flock to escape.
A voice of the cry of the shepherds,
And a wailing of the leaders to the flock *will be heard*.
For the LORD has plundered their pasture,
And the peaceful dwellings are cut down
Because of the fierce anger of the LORD.
He has left His lair like the lion;
For their land is desolate

Because of the fierceness of the Oppressor,
And because of His fierce anger."

> a. **Wail, shepherds, and cry**: This has reference first to the kings and leaders of the nations, emphasized in the roster of judgment earlier in the chapter (Jeremiah 25:17-26). Kings and other leaders were called **shepherds** in those ancient cultures.
>
>> i. Amos 2:14 describes how the royal and mighty would not be able to escape judgment: *Therefore flight shall perish from the swift, the strong shall not strengthen his power, nor shall the mighty deliver himself.*
>
> b. **For the days of your slaughter and your dispersions are fulfilled**: This has first in mind the judgment against Babylon for their conquest and exile of Judah. Other nations with similar sins would face similar judgment. Using this picture of judgment against shepherds, **the LORD has plundered their pasture**.
>
> c. **He has left His lair like the lion**: The LORD in judgment is pictured as a lion coming against the shepherds and the flocks. They would not be able to resist Him as the shepherd David killed a lion (1 Samuel 17:34-36).
>
> d. **Because of the fierceness of the Oppressor, and because of His fierce anger**: Judgment would certainly come, and it would come with passion, with **fierce anger**.
>
>> i. The translators of the New King James Version see this *oppressor* as the Lord Himself, as if God presents Himself here as **the Oppressor**, the one who would bring His judgment against those nations who rejected Him and performed **slaughter** and **dispersions** against others. Those who refuse to surrender to and embrace God as the *Liberator* will know Him instead as **the Oppressor**.
>>
>> ii. It is also possible that *the oppressor* refers to the agents of God's judgment (such as the Babylonians), and not directly to God Himself. Either way, the promise is sure: judgment is coming.
>>
>> iii. "It is never pleasant to read of destruction, but this is the corollary of the Lord's righteousness. It must also be remembered that it was anticipatory, and thus allowed the nations concerned time to repent." (Cundall)

Jeremiah 26 – Jeremiah Spared from Death

A. Jeremiah in danger of death.

1. (1-3) The command to speak.

In the beginning of the reign of Jehoiakim the son of Josiah, king of Judah, this word came from the LORD, saying, "Thus says the LORD: 'Stand in the court of the LORD's house, and speak to all the cities of Judah, which come to worship *in* the LORD's house, all the words that I command you to speak to them. Do not diminish a word. Perhaps everyone will listen and turn from his evil way, that I may relent concerning the calamity which I purpose to bring on them because of the evil of their doings.'"

  a. **In the beginning of the reign of Jehoiakim**: King **Jehoiakim** came to the throne in 609 BC, about four years before the first Babylonian invasion. This prophecy apparently came before that invasion, when many of the leaders of Judah felt they could avoid the Babylonian conquest.

   i. Jeremiah's message described in chapter 26 seems to be the same message he preached in Jeremiah 7. In Jeremiah 26, the emphasis is on the hostile response to this sermon at the temple.

   ii. "A longer account or a longer version of this sermon, but without the furore that now followed it, appears in chapter 7, undated." (Kidner)

  b. **Do not diminish a word**: God told Jeremiah to stand in the temple court and to preach a message to **all the cities of Judah** and all those who **come to worship in the LORD's house**. It was important that Jeremiah say *everything* God told him to say (**all the words I command you to speak to them**).

   i. John Trapp on **do not diminish a word**: "Here is a mirror for ministers."

c. **Perhaps everyone will listen and turn from his evil way**: God did not wonder if Judah would **listen** and repent or not do so. God knew, but Jeremiah did not. God wanted Jeremiah to preach the message with the hope that they might **listen** and that God might **relent** from the promised judgment.

2. (4-6) The words to speak.

"And you shall say to them, 'Thus says the LORD: "If you will not listen to Me, to walk in My law which I have set before you, to heed the words of My servants the prophets whom I sent to you, both rising up early and sending *them* (but you have not heeded), then I will make this house like Shiloh, and will make this city a curse to all the nations of the earth."'"

a. **If you will not listen to Me, to walk in My law which I have set before you**: God just told Jeremiah to preach as if it were possible that the people of Judah might in fact listen. God then told Jeremiah to warn the people what would happen if they did **not listen** in the sense of not hearing and obeying.

b. **Then I will make this house like Shiloh, and will make this city a curse**: The city of **Shiloh** was the place conquered and destroyed by the Philistines (1 Samuel 4, Psalm 78:56-64). The Philistines killed the priests and captured the ark of the covenant, and Israel felt as if God's glory had departed. God promised to make Jerusalem and the temple like **Shiloh** if Judah continued to **not listen** to Him.

3. (7-9) Opposition from the priests, the prophets, and the people.

So the priests and the prophets and all the people heard Jeremiah speaking these words in the house of the LORD. Now it happened, when Jeremiah had made an end of speaking all that the LORD had commanded *him* to speak to all the people, that the priests and the prophets and all the people seized him, saying, "You will surely die! Why have you prophesied in the name of the LORD, saying, 'This house shall be like Shiloh, and this city shall be desolate, without an inhabitant'?" And all the people were gathered against Jeremiah in the house of the LORD.

a. **The priests and the prophets and all the people**: Jeremiah spoke from the temple court (Jeremiah 26:2), making the message as public as possible. It isn't a surprise that both important people and common people heard him. They were angry at what he said and they **seized him**.

b. **This house shall be like Shiloh**: When Jeremiah prophesied about the coming destruction of the temple and conquest of Jerusalem, most people thought he was disloyal to Judah and all that happened at the temple. Perhaps they thought that he *wanted* these things to happen.

i. "Shiloh was evidently destroyed about 1050 BC by the Philistine incursion into the land referred to in 1 Samuel 4. There is archaeological evidence to support this." (Thompson)

ii. "Shiloh was not far from Jerusalem; the people could see the evidences of its destruction (c. 1050 BC) -- a destruction that overtook it even though it had been the first resting place of the ark of the covenant in the land." (Feinberg)

iii. **The people were gathered against Jeremiah**: "It would seem that the people crowded about Jeremiah. The verb *qahal* normally refers to a gathering for religious purposes but it is also used for war (2 Samuel 20:14), or for hostile intentions (Numbers 16:3). Such a scene in the temple precincts indicates how angry the people were." (Thompson)

4. (10-11) The charge against Jeremiah brought to the princes of Judah.

When the princes of Judah heard these things, they came up from the king's house to the house of the Lord and sat down in the entry of the New Gate of the Lord's *house*. And the priests and the prophets spoke to the princes and all the people, saying, "This man deserves to die! For he has prophesied against this city, as you have heard with your ears."

a. **When the princes of Judah heard these things**: The priests and the prophets and the people had condemned Jeremiah. Now they brought him for judgment to the political leaders of Judah.

b. **This man deserves to die! For he has prophesied against this city**: Jeremiah's message was bad news about Jerusalem – that judgment was on the way. Therefore the priests and the prophets and the people felt he was **against** the city and a traitor to Jerusalem. They believed that Jeremiah dangerously weakened morale and helped the cause of those who threatened Jerusalem.

5. (12-15) Jeremiah defends and explains his message.

Then Jeremiah spoke to all the princes and all the people, saying: "The Lord sent me to prophesy against this house and against this city with all the words that you have heard. Now therefore, amend your ways and your doings, and obey the voice of the Lord your God; then the Lord will relent concerning the doom that He has pronounced against you. As for me, here I am, in your hand; do with me as seems good and proper to you. But know for certain that if you put me to death, you will surely bring innocent blood on yourselves, on this city, and on its inhabitants; for truly the Lord has sent me to you to speak all these words in your hearing."

a. **Then Jeremiah spoke**: Formally accused of treason, **Jeremiah** defended himself before **the princes and all the people**. Obviously, the accusing priests and prophets heard his response, but he did not really direct it toward them.

> i. "Note the admirable courage and quiet dignity of Jeremiah. There was no modification of his message to create a less-prejudicial atmosphere, for he was convinced of the divine source of his message." (Cundall)

> ii. "The prophet defended the message directly, courageously, and appropriately. Nowhere in the book does he appear in a better light than here. He did not trim his message. He did not cower and beg for mercy." (Feinberg)

b. **The LORD sent me to prophesy against this house and against this city**: Jeremiah made it clear that his ministry and his message were not a matter of *choice*. This was God's command and he only did what God **sent** him to do.

> i. "My commission is from him, and my words are his own. I sought not this painful office. I did not run before I was sent." (Clarke)

c. **Therefore, amend your ways and your doings**: Jeremiah was on trial for his life. Yet he still courageously spoke his message and spoke as if *they* were on trial and not he – because there was a real sense in which that was true. Their only hope was that God might **relent** from the promised judgment in response to their repentance.

d. **As for me, here I am, in your hand; do with me as seems good and proper to you**: Jeremiah was determined to speak what God told him to say and to take whatever punishment it might bring. In a remarkable way, Jeremiah put the message God gave him above and before his personal safety.

> i. Jeremiah spoke very much in the same spirit that the apostles would speak centuries later when they stood before a council: *Whether it is right in the sight of God to listen to you more than to God, you judge. For we cannot but speak the things which we have seen and heard* (Acts 4:19-20).

> ii. **Here I am, in your hand**: "See here how God gave his holy prophet a mouth and wisdom, such as his adversaries were not able to resist. The like he did to other of his martyrs and confessors, as were easy to instance. If the queen will give me life, I will thank her; if she will banish me, I will thank her; if she will burn me, I will thank her, said Bradford to Cresswell, offering to intercede for him." (Trapp)

e. **Know for certain that if you put me to death, you will surely bring innocent blood on yourselves**: The choice was left to them, but Jeremiah wanted them to know it was a choice with consequences. Killing God's prophet would only add to the guilt of the leaders and the city.

f. **For truly the LORD has sent me to you to speak all these words in your hearing**: Jeremiah was steadfast before this council of the princes of Judah. He didn't display any doubt about his call or his message.

> i. By nature, Jeremiah seemed to be somewhat shy and hesitant. Here he stood with great courage to give an account for his call and his work, *just as God promised he would* in Jeremiah 1:18-19. "Had John the Baptist spoken thus, or John Knox, we had not been surprised. But for this sensitive, retiring man to speak thus is due to the transforming power of the grace of God." (Meyer)

> ii. John Trapp mentioned an unnamed expositor that noted "five noble virtues" in Jeremiah's brief defense.

- Prudence in proclaiming his divine mission.
- Love in exhorting his enemies to repent.
- Humility in acknowledging their power over him.
- Courage in telling them God would avenge his death.
- Fearlessness before death.

B. Jeremiah spared from death.

1. (16) Jeremiah will not be condemned to death.

So the princes and all the people said to the priests and the prophets, "This man does not deserve to die. For he has spoken to us in the name of the LORD our God."

> a. **This man does not deserve to die**: No doubt moved by the courage of Jeremiah, the ruling of the council of **the princes** and the opinion of **all the people** was that Jeremiah should not die. Though the priests and prophets likely did not agree, Jeremiah would be spared death.

> > i. "The prophet's honesty and conviction by the Spirit gripped the hearts of the civil officials and the people." (Feinberg)

> > ii. The appeal, *Know for certain that if you put me to death, you will surely bring innocent blood on yourselves* (Jeremiah 26:15) seemed to work. Centuries later, another innocent messenger of God was unjustly accused by religious leaders, and in the trial they were warned that an unjust death sentence would bring bloodguilt. Yet Jesus of Nazareth was nevertheless condemned.

b. **For he has spoken to us in the name of the LORD our God**: They didn't *like* Jeremiah's message, but they had to admit that it was God's message. It wasn't right to blame the messenger for faithfully delivering the message.

i. "These princes soon after turned Jeremiah's cruel enemies [Jeremiah 37:15] for his plain dealing. [Jeremiah 34:1-7]." (Trapp)

2. (17-19) Remembering when they used to listen to the prophets.

Then certain of the elders of the land rose up and spoke to all the assembly of the people, saying: "Micah of Moresheth prophesied in the days of Hezekiah king of Judah, and spoke to all the people of Judah, saying, 'Thus says the LORD of hosts:

"Zion shall be plowed *like* a field,
Jerusalem shall become heaps of ruins,
And the mountain of the temple
Like the bare hills of the forest."'

Did Hezekiah king of Judah and all Judah ever put him to death? Did he not fear the LORD and seek the LORD's favor? And the LORD relented concerning the doom which He had pronounced against them. But we are doing great evil against ourselves."

a. **Then certain of the elders of the land rose up**: We don't know exactly who these men were. They don't seem to exactly fit in the previous categories of princes, priests, or prophets. They spoke wisdom to Jeremiah and his situation.

i. There were no elders who spoke up on behalf of Jesus when He was unjustly tried. A pagan ruler proclaimed His innocence but sent Jesus to the cross anyway.

b. **Micah of Moresheth prophesied in the days of Hezekiah king of Judah**: The elders remembered the work of the Prophet Micah, recorded in the Book of Micah (Micah 1:1). They remembered that his message was often not pleasant and remembered what he said that was recorded in Micah 3:12 regarding the destruction of Jerusalem (**Zion shall be plowed like a field**).

i. It is of interest to note what Micah said right before this portion they quoted: *Her prophets divine for money. Yet they lean on the LORD, and say, "Is not the LORD among us? No harm can come upon us"* (Micah 3:11). Micah warned them of judgment specifically in the context of the assurance of false prophets and the sense that *no harm* could come to Jerusalem.

ii. By most chronologies, Micah carried out his prophetic work more than 100 years before the time of Jeremiah. Their exact quotation of his words is significant. "It shows how the words of the great prophets were treasured, and so remembered that they could be readily quoted." (Cundall)

c. **Did Hezekiah king of Judah and all Judah ever put him to death**: The elders wisely remembered that Micah was not punished for bringing a severe message from God. Instead, King Hezekiah responded by fearing the LORD and seeking **the LORD's favor**. God responded favorably when they did this when He **relented concerning the doom which He had pronounced against them**.

d. **We are doing great evil against ourselves**: In a sense of wise self-interest, the elders understood that it was wrong to oppose Jeremiah and to persecute him. Instead they should **fear the LORD and seek the LORD's favor** just as Hezekiah did with Micah's message. If they did not, *they* would suffer from it, not only Jeremiah.

i. "This is really a fine defense, and the argument was perfectly conclusive." (Clarke)

3. (20-23) The faithfulness of the prophet Urijah; his persecution and death.

Now there was also a man who prophesied in the name of the LORD, Urijah the son of Shemaiah of Kirjath Jearim, who prophesied against this city and against this land according to all the words of Jeremiah. And when Jehoiakim the king, with all his mighty men and all the princes, heard his words, the king sought to put him to death; but when Urijah heard *it*, he was afraid and fled, and went to Egypt. Then Jehoiakim the king sent men to Egypt: Elnathan the son of Achbor, and *other* men *who went* with him to Egypt. And they brought Urijah from Egypt and brought him to Jehoiakim the king, who killed him with the sword and cast his dead body into the graves of the common people.

a. **There was also a man who prophesied in the name of the LORD, Urijah the son of Shemaiah**: The elders remembered a second prophet whose name was **Urijah**. We don't know anything of this **Urijah the son of Shemaiah** who also prophesied in the days of **Jehoiakim the king**.

b. **Who prophesied against this city and against this land according to all the words of Jeremiah**: Jeremiah was *not* the only faithful prophet during his years of ministry. There were others who told the truth about the coming judgment, including this **Urijah the son of Shemaiah**.

c. **The king sought to put him to death**: Since the events of this chapter happened in the beginning of the reign of Jehoiakim (Jeremiah 26:1), the king must have tried to kill Urijah even earlier. These things had recently happened.

d. **When Urijah heard it, he was afraid and fled, and went to Egypt**: This faithful prophet did not stay in Jerusalem or Judah. He hoped to find safety in the large Jewish community in **Egypt** but did not. **The king sent men** to find Urijah and bring him back to Jerusalem.

> i. There was no criticism of Urijah's decision to go to Egypt. "Not out of timorousness, but prudence. Tertullian was too rigid in condemning all kinds of flight in times of persecution. God hath not made his people as standing buttmarks to be shot at." (Trapp)

> ii. **They brought Urijah from Egypt**: "International treaties in the ancient Near East called for extradition; it was part of the vassalage terms imposed by Egypt." (Feinberg)

e. **Who killed him with the sword and cast his dead body into the graves of the common people**: The elders remembered that the prophet was brutally executed and disgraced in his death.

> i. The elders did not speak against what Jehoiakim did. This was a not very hidden threat against Jeremiah: *We saved you from death, but if you keep talking you'll end up like Urijah did.*

> ii. "How many more prophets were frightened into silence we do not know." (Cundall)

4. (24) Help for Jeremiah from Ahikam.

Nevertheless the hand of Ahikam the son of Shaphan was with Jeremiah, so that they should not give him into the hand of the people to put him to death.

a. **Nevertheless the hand of Ahikam the son of Shaphan was with Jeremiah**: Perhaps **Ahikam** was one of the elders. Jeremiah had at least one influential friend.

> i. "Ahikam had been a member of the deputation sent by Josiah to the prophetess Huldah (2 Kings 22:12ff.; 2 Chronicles 34:20), and was the father of Gedaliah, the governor of Judah appointed by Nebuchadnezzar (2 Kings 25:22; Jeremiah 39:14)." (Harrison)

> ii. Jesus had no Ahikam to defend Him. Jesus is our Ahikam, defending us from every accusation of the evil one and delivering us from all condemnation.

b. **That they should not give him into the hand of the people to put him to death**: Jeremiah did not only have the threat from the prophets and the priests, but also from the people. The princes would not carry out a formal execution (Jeremiah 26:16), but Jeremiah also needed protection against the mob, from **the hand of the people**.

Jeremiah 27 – Bonds and Yokes

A. The yoke of the king of Babylon.

1. (1-3) The command to make bonds and yokes.

In the beginning of the reign of Jehoiakim the son of Josiah, king of Judah, this word came to Jeremiah from the LORD, saying, "Thus says the LORD to me: 'Make for yourselves bonds and yokes, and put them on your neck, and send them to the king of Edom, the king of Moab, the king of the Ammonites, the king of Tyre, and the king of Sidon, by the hand of the messengers who come to Jerusalem to Zedekiah king of Judah.

a. **In the beginning of the reign of Jehoiakim**: The reference to **Jehoiakim** is a problem, because it isn't in many manuscripts and doesn't match with the rest of the chapter, which seems clearly to speak to the time of *Zedekiah*, not Jehoiakim. This is a likely scribal error.

i. "The first verse is omitted by LXX. Some Hebrew MSS and the Peshitta substituted Zedekiah for Jehoiakim, which is obviously correct chronologically (*cf.* Jeremiah 28:1). The mistake probably arose from a miscopying of 26:1." (Harrison)

ii. "There can be no doubt that the marginal reading of 27:1 must be adopted, and the word 'Zedekiah' substituted for 'Jehoiakim.'" (Morgan)

b. **Make for yourselves bonds and yokes**: God wanted Jeremiah to use visual aids in his prophetic work. He was to make **bonds** – leather straps used to secure **yokes**. A yoke was wood that went under and above the neck of a large animal so the beast could pull a plow.

i. "He made use here of the ox yoke, a wooden bar or bars tied by leather thongs to the animal's neck." (Thompson)

ii. "It is clear that Jeremiah actually wore the yoke in public, because Hananiah broke it (Jeremiah 28:10-11)." (Feinbeg)

iii. The yoke said, "I'm the boss. You work for me. I regard you as a beast of burden."

c. **Send them to the king of Edom, the king of Moab**: Most commentators believe that God told Jeremiah to speak to a gathering of **messengers** from the kings of the surrounding kingdoms (**Edom**, **Moab**, the **Ammonites**, **Tyre**, and **Sidon**). They came to meet with King Zedekiah of Judah to plot a revolt against Nebuchadnezzar's rule over them. Jeremiah probably spoke before them wearing the **bonds and yokes**, giving them a vivid message to take back to their kings.

i. Thompson explains that because of attacks from Elam and a revolt in Syria, "They were troubled times for Nebuchadrezzar, and small states in the west thought they saw an opportunity to revolt and throw off the yoke of Babylon." (Thompson)

ii. "It is clear that the envoys of the nations had assembled in Jerusalem to hatch a scheme for rebellion against Babylon. In Jeremiah 51:59 we discover that Zedekiah was summoned to Babylon in this same year, probably to give an account of his part in this plot which came to nothing." (Cundall)

iii. "Jeremiah required great courage to stand against these envoys as well as his own countrymen, but Jeremiah was exercising his commission as a prophet to the nations (cf. Jeremiah 1:10)." (Feinberg)

iv. "One LXX MS omits the enclitic *mem* ('them'), implying that only one yoke, work by Jeremiah, was actually made, and that news of this was to be sent to those nations plotting revolt. Most probably this is what actually happened." (Harrison)

2. (4-8) The message associated with the bonds and yokes.

And command them to say to their masters, "Thus says the Lord of hosts, the God of Israel—thus you shall say to your masters: 'I have made the earth, the man and the beast that *are* on the ground, by My great power and by My outstretched arm, and have given it to whom it seemed proper to Me. And now I have given all these lands into the hand of Nebuchadnezzar the king of Babylon, My servant; and the beasts of the field I have also given him to serve him. So all nations shall serve him and his son and his son's son, until the time of his land comes; and then many nations and great kings shall make him serve them. And it shall be, *that* the nation and kingdom which will not serve Nebuchadnezzar the king of Babylon, and which will not put its neck

under the yoke of the king of Babylon, that nation I will punish,' says the LORD, 'with the sword, the famine, and the pestilence, until I have consumed them by his hand.

    a. **I have given all these lands into the hand of Nebuchadnezzar**: The messengers were to bring this word from Yahweh, the covenant God of Israel, back to their masters. God wanted them to know that rebellion against Babylon was senseless, because **Nebuchadnezzar** would remain in power over them, and he would do it because God gave it to him.

        i. **My servant**: "It is a most condescending way to speak about the most powerful man on the face of the earth: 'my servant Nebuchadnezzar' (cf. Jeremiah 25:9; 43:10). It is the kind of language an ancient king would use to describe one of his vassals." (Ryken)

        ii. **Shall serve him and his son and his son's son**: "And all nations shall serve him, (Nebuchadnezzar,) *and his son*, (Evil-merodach, Jer 52:31,) *and his son's son*, (Belshazzar, Da 5:11.) All which was literally fulfilled." (Clarke)

    b. **The nation and kingdom which will not serve Nebuchadnezzar the king of Babylon… that nation I will punish**: Through Jeremiah and his messengers, God warned the kings of the region that they should submit to the domination of the King of Babylon. If they did not, God Himself would punish them with **the sword, the famine, and the pestilence** through the **hand** of Nebuchadnezzar.

3. (9-11) Do not believe the lying prophets.

Therefore do not listen to your prophets, your diviners, your dreamers, your soothsayers, or your sorcerers, who speak to you, saying, "You shall not serve the king of Babylon." For they prophesy a lie to you, to remove you far from your land; and I will drive you out, and you will perish. But the nations that bring their necks under the yoke of the king of Babylon and serve him, I will let them remain in their own land,' says the LORD, **'and they shall till it and dwell in it.'**

    a. **Do not listen to your prophets, your diviners, your dreamers, your soothsayers, or your sorcerers**: Just like the kings of Judah, the kings of the surrounding nations had prophets and such who told them that Babylon would be turned back and would not conquer them. God warned the kings, **do not listen** to them, **for they prophesy a lie to you**.

        i. **Diviners**: "To *presage* or *prognosticate*. Persons who *guessed* at futurity by certain signs in the animate or inanimate creation." (Clarke)

        ii. **Dreamers**: "Dream-interpreters, who, from these *broken shreds* patch up a meaning by their own interpolations." (Clarke)

iii. **Soothsayers**: "Cloud-mongers. Diviners by the flight, colour, density, rarity, and shape of clouds." (Clarke)

iv. **Sorcerers**: "The discoverers, the finders out of hidden things, stolen goods, etc. Persons also who use *incantations*, and either by *spells* or *drugs* pretend to find out mysteries, or produce supernatural effects." (Clarke)

v. "In a time of national crisis, religious fakers always flourish because many people want to hear only comforting messages, which may often be untrue." (Feinberg)

b. **The nations that bring their necks under the yoke of the king of Babylon and serve him, I will let them remain in their own land**: God promised that if they did respond to the message of the bonds and the yokes, God would allow them to escape the forced exile that the Babylonians often imposed.

i. It is often best for us to submit to a difficult yoke imposed upon us. "Learn from these striking words that your best attitude is one of humble and reverent submission. Put your neck under the yoke of the king of Babylon…Accept the deserved chastisement, remembering that 'whom the Lord loveth He chasteneth, and scourgeth every son whom He receiveth' Humble yourself under the mighty hand of God." (Meyer)

ii. One aspect of the good news of the New Covenant is that we have a different yoke, a better one: *Come to Me, all you who labor and are heavy laden, and I will give you rest. Take My yoke upon you and learn from Me, for I am gentle and lowly in heart, and you will find rest for your souls. For My yoke is easy and My burden is light* (Matthew 11:28-30).

4. (12-15) The message to King Zedekiah.

I also spoke to Zedekiah king of Judah according to all these words, saying, "Bring your necks under the yoke of the king of Babylon, and serve him and his people, and live! Why will you die, you and your people, by the sword, by the famine, and by the pestilence, as the LORD has spoken against the nation that will not serve the king of Babylon? Therefore do not listen to the words of the prophets who speak to you, saying, 'You shall not serve the king of Babylon,' for they prophesy a lie to you; for I have not sent them," says the LORD, "yet they prophesy a lie in My name, that I may drive you out, and that you may perish, you and the prophets who prophesy to you."

a. **Bring your necks under the yoke of the king of Babylon, and serve him and his people, and live**: God wanted the kings of the surrounding nations to know that this was the same message that He brought to the **king of Judah**. They should **serve the king of Babylon** in order to avoid an even worse fate.

b. **Yet they prophesy a lie in My name, that I may drive you out, and that you may perish, you and the prophets who prophesy to you**: God did not send these false prophets, yet He also did not stop them. He allowed them so that the people and rulers of Judah would have a genuine choice between the false and the true. If they chose the false, God would use it to **drive** them out of the land and to **perish** — both the people and **the prophets**.

B. About the temple vessels.

1. (16-17) What the lying prophets said about the temple vessels.

Also I spoke to the priests and to all this people, saying, "Thus says the LORD: 'Do not listen to the words of your prophets who prophesy to you, saying, "Behold, the vessels of the LORD's house will now shortly be brought back from Babylon"; for they prophesy a lie to you. Do not listen to them; serve the king of Babylon, and live! Why should this city be laid waste?

a. **Behold, the vessels of the LORD's house will now shortly be brought back from Babylon**: This was the falsely optimistic message of the lying prophets of Jeremiah's time. They said that the temple **vessels** that Nebuchadnezzar carried away in earlier invasions would soon **be brought back** to the temple.

i. *Nebuchadnezzar also carried off some of the articles from the house of the LORD to Babylon, and put them in his temple at Babylon.* (2 Chronicles 26:7)

ii. "Normally a conqueror would take the idols of the countries he defeated and place them in the sanctuary of his own god, but as Judah's faith was imageless the Temple vessels had been taken in lieu." (Cundall)

b. **Do not listen to them; serve the king of Babylon, and live**: Their optimism was a **lie**, even if it came as prophecy. Instead of hoping for deliverance from the Babylonians, they would do much better if they simply surrendered to the judgment of God that they brought. Failing to do this would only bring worse judgment on Jerusalem (**why should this city be laid waste**).

2. (18) The test of the prophets regarding the temple vessels.

But if they *are* prophets, and if the word of the Lord is with them, let them now make intercession to the Lord of hosts, that the vessels which are left in the house of the Lord, *in* the house of the king of Judah, and at Jerusalem, do not go to Babylon.'

> a. **But if they are prophets, and if the word of the Lord is with them**: Those who claimed to be prophets could and should be tested. What they said should not be blindly accepted.
>
> b. **Let them now make intercession**: God proposed a simple test for the lying prophets. They should pray asking that the remaining **vessels** stay in Jerusalem and **do not go to Babylon**. This was the same kind of test Elijah brought to the prophets of Baal in 1 Kings 18.
>
>> i. **The vessels which are left in the house of the Lord**: "Some had been left behind in 597 BC and no doubt others had been made to replace important items used in the regular worship of the temple." (Thompson)

3. (19-22) The fate of the temple vessels.

"For thus says the Lord of hosts concerning the pillars, concerning the Sea, concerning the carts, and concerning the remainder of the vessels that remain in this city, which Nebuchadnezzar king of Babylon did not take, when he carried away captive Jeconiah the son of Jehoiakim, king of Judah, from Jerusalem to Babylon, and all the nobles of Judah and Jerusalem— yes, thus says the Lord of hosts, the God of Israel, concerning the vessels that remain in the house of the Lord, and in the house of the king of Judah and of Jerusalem: 'They shall be carried to Babylon, and there they shall be until the day that I visit them,' says the Lord. 'Then I will bring them up and restore them to this place.'"

> a. **Concerning the pillars, concerning the Sea, concerning the carts, and concerning the remainder of the vessels that remain in this city**: These were among the valuables associated with the temple that Nebuchadnezzar had not yet taken. At the time of Jeremiah's prophecy, they still remained in or at the temple.
>
>> i. "According to Jeremiah 52:17 the bronze pillars were damaged and taken to Babylon in 587 BC." (Harrison)
>
>> ii. There is no mention made of the ark of the covenant. Some think that it had already been carried away by Nebuchadnezzar in one of his early invasions of Jerusalem, with other temple treasures (2 Chronicles 26:7). Other Jewish legends say that Jeremiah hid the ark of the covenant before it could be captured by the Babylonians. Others think

that God brought it to heaven because John the Apostle saw the ark there (Revelation 11:19).

b. **When he carried away captive Jeconiah**: This happened in 598 BC, in the second of Nebuchadnezzar's three invasions of Jerusalem. The king of Babylon took **all the nobles of Judah and Jerusalem** but left some of the temple treasures behind.

c. **They shall be carried to Babylon, and there they shall be until the day that I visit them**: God promised that the remaining vessels *would* be carried away from the temple and brought to **Babylon**. In time, God would **restore them to** the temple in Jerusalem (Ezra 1:7-11, 7:19).

Jeremiah 28 – Broken Yokes and Iron Yokes

A. Hananiah and the broken yoke.

1. (1-4) Hananiah contradicts Jeremiah.

And it happened in the same year, at the beginning of the reign of Zedekiah king of Judah, in the fourth year *and* in the fifth month, *that* Hananiah the son of Azur the prophet, who *was* from Gibeon, spoke to me in the house of the LORD in the presence of the priests and of all the people, saying, "Thus speaks the LORD of hosts, the God of Israel, saying: 'I have broken the yoke of the king of Babylon. Within two full years I will bring back to this place all the vessels of the LORD's house, that Nebuchadnezzar king of Babylon took away from this place and carried to Babylon. And I will bring back to this place Jeconiah the son of Jehoiakim, king of Judah, with all the captives of Judah who went to Babylon,' says the LORD, 'for I will break the yoke of the king of Babylon.'"

> a. **At the beginning of the reign of Zedekiah**: Zedekiah was the puppet king put on the throne of Judah by Nebuchadnezzar of Babylon. In this season, Nebuchadnezzar was distracted by problems in other parts of his empire. Judah and some of the surrounding nations thought it was a smart time to rebel against what seemed to be a weakened king of Babylon. In Jeremiah 27, the prophet spoke to a gathering of representatives of those kingdoms, who came to Zedekiah to plot their strategy.
>
> b. **Hananiah**: This prophet and son of a prophet didn't like Jeremiah's gloomy message to the gathered kings (Jeremiah 27:1-11). Jeremiah came to them wearing the yoke an animal would use, to show that they would remain subjected to Nebuchadnezzar and their dreams of successful revolt would be unfulfilled.

i. "Hananiah's name means 'Yahweh has been gracious.' It was an appropriate name for a prophet who believed strongly, if mistakenly, that Judah's fortunes would soon be restored." (Thompson)

ii. **Who was from Gibeon**: Hananiah came from a place with a reputation for deception and violence. "It had a number of important historical associations. The Gibeonites had deceived the Israelites in Joshua's day (Joshua 9:1-15). It was the scene of a contest between Saul's men and David's men (2 Samuel 20:12-17). Here Joab killed Amasa (2 Samuel 20:8-10)." (Thompson)

iii. "He was a native of Gibeon, the modern El-Jib, five miles northwest of Jerusalem. It was one of the priestly cities; so, like Jeremiah, Hananiah may have been a priest (cf. Joshua 21:17)." (Feinberg)

c. **I have broken the yoke of the king of Babylon**: Hananiah spoke in the name of the LORD, contradicting the message of Jeremiah recorded in the previous chapter. Jeremiah said they would be under the yoke of the king of Babylon; Hananiah said the LORD had **broken the yoke**.

d. **I will bring back to this place all the vessels of the LORD's house**: Hananiah's supposed prophecy explained that because the power of Nebuchadnezzar had been broken, the **vessels** of the temple would be returned, King **Jeconiah** would return, along with **all the captives of Judah who went to Babylon**. All this would happen **within two full years**. This was a big, dramatic message – something the frightened people of Judah would *love* to hear.

i. "Hananiah predicted a return of the captives and the temple vessels within two years, emphasizing the time element by putting it first." (Feinberg)

ii. "No doubt Hananiah's message was very popular. It was bold, patriotic, and uplifting. Whose church would you rather go to?" (Ryken)

iii. "Men who follow simply their own thoughts, or are deeply dyed with the spirit of society around, are apt to prophesy smooth things to such as live selfish and worldly lives." (Meyer)

iv. Nevertheless, this was another direct contradiction to Jeremiah's previous prophecy. When Jeremiah prophesied exile and captivity, Hananiah prophesied return and restoration. They *both* spoke in the name of the LORD, and it seemed that they could not *both* be right.

2. (5-6) Jeremiah responds with an amen.

Then the prophet Jeremiah spoke to the prophet Hananiah in the presence of the priests and in the presence of all the people who stood in the house of the LORD, and the prophet Jeremiah said, "Amen! The LORD do so; the LORD perform your words which you have prophesied, to bring back the vessels of the LORD's house and all who were carried away captive, from Babylon to this place."

a. **Then the prophet Jeremiah spoke**: Jeremiah responded publically to Hananiah. Hananiah had publically contradicted him, essentially calling Jeremiah a false prophet; therefore, Jeremiah publically responded.

b. **Amen! The LORD do so**: The words to come would make it clear that Jeremiah did not believe this, but he began by agreeing with Hananiah that it would be nice if it were true. If the **vessels of the LORD's house** and the exiled captives came back, Jeremiah would be happy. He would be glad to be wrong.

i. "Jeremiah's reply to this is an ironic *'Yes indeed! Would that God might do so'*, probably conveying his sense of doubt by his tone of voice." (Harrison)

ii. "When someone tries to minimize the judgment of God, it is appropriate for the Christian to say, 'I hope you're right.'" (Ryken)

3. (7-9) Jeremiah responds by defending his prophetic ministry.

"Nevertheless hear now this word that I speak in your hearing and in the hearing of all the people: The prophets who have been before me and before you of old prophesied against many countries and great kingdoms—of war and disaster and pestilence. As for the prophet who prophesies of peace, when the word of the prophet comes to pass, the prophet will be known *as* one whom the LORD has truly sent."

a. **The prophets who have been before me and before you**: Jeremiah had wished Hananiah's words were true. Then he challenged Hananiah, starting with the word **nevertheless**, and reminding everyone that *most* of the prophets before them had negative, unwelcome messages.

i. "Namely, Joel, Amos, Hosea, Micah, Zephaniah, Nahum, Habakkuk, and others; all of whom denounced similar evils against a corrupt people." (Clarke)

ii. "These verses should not be interpreted to mean that the entire message of all the prophets before Jeremiah was one of judgment. Jeremiah's meaning was that the usual message of the earlier prophets was one of doom, and that when he spoke of judgment he was more in the line of the predecessors than Hananiah." (Thompson)

b. **As for the prophet who prophesies of peace, when the word of the prophet comes to pass**: Jeremiah didn't deny that sometimes God's messengers bring a word of **peace**. He simply said that such a word should be believed when it actually comes to pass, especially when it has a time associated with the prophecy (*within two full years*, 28:3).

4. (10-11) The broken yoke.

Then Hananiah the prophet took the yoke off the prophet Jeremiah's neck and broke it. And Hananiah spoke in the presence of all the people, saying, "Thus says the Lord: 'Even so I will break the yoke of Nebuchadnezzar king of Babylon from the neck of all nations within the space of two full years.'" And the prophet Jeremiah went his way.

a. **Hananiah the prophet took the yoke off the prophet Jeremiah's neck and broke it**: Jeremiah had this yoke when he spoke to King Zedekiah and the messengers from other nations (Jeremiah 27:1-3). Apparently, some days or weeks later (Jeremiah 27:1 and 28:1) he walked the temple courts still wearing the yoke, as a public illustration of his prophecy. Hananiah didn't like the message of the yoke, so he took it from Jeremiah and **broke it**.

i. "A visual prophecy like the yoke made a great impression on the people. So Hananiah took the yoke from Jeremiah's neck and smashed it, to show that Nebuchadnezzar's power would be shattered in two years." (Feinberg)

b. **Even so I will break the yoke of Nebuchadnezzar**: Hananiah said this in the name of the Lord. He illustrated his message that the revolt against Nebuchadnezzar would succeed by breaking the yoke and explaining the meaning of the broken yoke, again giving a time measure for it to happen.

i. It seems plain from the words and actions of Hananiah that he *really believed* his prophetic word was a message from the Lord. He seemed sincere and invested in the message. Yet none of that made it *true*, and in fact it was *not true*.

c. **The prophet Jeremiah went his way**: By all appearances, Hananiah won this public dispute between the prophets. He seemed to overpower Jeremiah, he said the last word, and Jeremiah walked away without a response. In this case, appearances were not true and neither was Hananiah.

B. Yokes of wood, yokes of iron.

1. (12-14) A yoke of iron to replace a yoke of wood.

Now the word of the LORD came to Jeremiah, after Hananiah the prophet had broken the yoke from the neck of the prophet Jeremiah, saying, "Go and tell Hananiah, saying, 'Thus says the LORD: "You have broken the yokes of wood, but you have made in their place yokes of iron." For thus says the LORD of hosts, the God of Israel: "I have put a yoke of iron on the neck of all these nations, that they may serve Nebuchadnezzar king of Babylon; and they shall serve him. I have given him the beasts of the field also."'"

a. **You have broken the yokes of wood, but you have made in their place yokes of iron**: We aren't told how Jeremiah felt when he left the confrontation with Hananiah at the temple. Yet later, God gave him a message to send to Hananiah, who could break the wood yoke Jeremiah wore as a prophetic illustration but could never break the **yokes of iron** God would set upon those who opposed Nebuchadnezzar.

i. Notably, Jeremiah said, **you have made in their place yokes of iron**. The people made their own **yokes**, much stronger than the **yokes of wood** God appointed for them. "The inference is that the people, having rejected the wooden yoke of submission laid upon them for their sins, would find the indestructible iron yoke of servitude infinitely more uncomfortable." (Cundall)

ii. The **yokes of iron** can be understood as God's stricter discipline upon His people. If we resist God's gentler discipline – **yokes of wood** – we may find ourselves under much more unpleasant **yokes of iron**. It is far better to surrender the better yoke of Jesus Christ (Matthew 11:28-30).

iii. The **yokes of iron** may also be expressed in sinful habits that we allow to enslave us. **Yokes** are instruments of servitude. "Do you think it will be easy to serve the base-born parts of your nature, when you set them on the throne and tell them to govern you?" (Maclaren)

iv. "I will ask you a question. You have got rid of the yoke of wood: how about your shoulders now? Your Sundays, are they very pleasant? Your family, is it very happy? Your mind, is it very much at ease? Oh, no!" (Spurgeon)

v. Happily, the power of God can break even an iron yoke – *if* we will only turn to Him and trust Him again.

b. **I have put a yoke of iron on the neck of all these nations**: Their proposed rebellion against Nebuchadnezzar would fail. They would **serve** him, and Nebuchadnezzar's dominion would be so complete that he would rule over **the beasts of the field**.

i. "A symbolic wooden yoke *could* be broken, but the Babylonian overlordship was certain." (Cundall)

2. (15-17) The word to Hananiah.

Then the prophet Jeremiah said to Hananiah the prophet, "Hear now, Hananiah, the LORD has not sent you, but you make this people trust in a lie. Therefore thus says the LORD: 'Behold, I will cast you from the face of the earth. This year you shall die, because you have taught rebellion against the LORD.'" So Hananiah the prophet died the same year in the seventh month.

a. **Hear now, Hananiah, the LORD has not sent you, but you make this people trust a lie**: Jeremiah felt it important to directly and publicly tell Hananiah that whatever his intentions, he was a false prophet. Worse, he harmed the people of Judah, leading them to **trust in a lie** – a **lie** that they *wanted* to believe, because it was a much more positive message than Jeremiah's.

i. "This was a bold speech in the presence of those priests and people who were prejudiced in favour of this false prophet, who prophesied to them smooth things. In such cases men wish to be *deceived*." (Clarke)

ii. "What we might describe as wishful and unorthodox teaching, God more briefly calls *a lie* (Jeremiah 28:15) and *rebellion* (Jeremiah 28:16). He condemns it not only as offending against truth and against his authority, but as doing a fatal disservice to the hearers: *you have made this people* trust *in a lie* (Jeremiah 28:15)." (Kidner)

iii. **You make this people to trust in a lie**: "How much of human prophesying is covered by that word! All those philosophies which attempt to interpret life without the light of revelation -- all so-called theologies, which result from speculations which invalidate the revelation; make men trust in lies, and that because they are the utterances of men not sent by Jehovah." (Morgan)

b. **This year you shall die**: This was *God's* message to Hananiah. He gave a time measure for his prophecy, so God gave him a time measure in return: Hananiah would die within the **year**, and he did.

i. He died in the **seventh month**, only two months after this confrontation (Jeremiah 28:1). Two months is not a long time, but it is plenty of time to repent if one has any inclination to repent.

ii. "God, in mercy, gave him about *two months*, in which he might prepare to meet his Judge. Here, then the *true prophet* was *demonstrated*, and the *false prophet detected*. The death of Hananiah, thus predicted, was God's *seal* to the words of his prophet; and must have gained his other predictions great credit among the people." (Clarke)

c. **Because you have taught rebellion against the Lord:** It is impossible to say what Hananiah's intentions were, but it is not impossible to measure the effect of his lies. Whether he meant to or not, he **taught rebellion against the Lord**, and God would stop him from continuing to do so.

Jeremiah 29 – Letter to the Captives

A. A future and a hope.

1. (1-4) A letter from Jerusalem to the captives in Babylon.

Now these *are* the words of the letter that Jeremiah the prophet sent from Jerusalem to the remainder of the elders who were carried away captive—to the priests, the prophets, and all the people whom Nebuchadnezzar had carried away captive from Jerusalem to Babylon. (This happened after Jeconiah the king, the queen mother, the eunuchs, the princes of Judah and Jerusalem, the craftsmen, and the smiths had departed from Jerusalem.) *The letter was sent* by the hand of Elasah the son of Shaphan, and Gemariah the son of Hilkiah, whom Zedekiah king of Judah sent to Babylon, to Nebuchadnezzar king of Babylon, saying,

Thus says the LORD of hosts, the God of Israel, to all who were carried away captive, whom I have caused to be carried away from Jerusalem to Babylon:

a. **The letter that Jeremiah the prophet sent from Jerusalem**: Jeremiah 29 contains a letter from Jeremiah (writing as the LORD's prophet) to the exiles in Babylon. It was especially directed to the leaders (**the remainder of the elders**) of the Jewish community there.

b. **This happened after Jeconiah**: Jeconiah was taken to Babylon in 598 BC By this time Babylon had already invaded Judah and Jerusalem twice (605 BC and 598 BC) and taken captives each time. There still remained a sizable population in Jerusalem and Judah, but they would also soon be conquered and carried away in forced exile.

   i. **The letter was sent by the hand of Elasah**: "Diplomatic correspondence between overlords and vassals was common in the second millennium BC, as the Amarna letters written from Palestine to the pharaoh indicate." (Thompson)

c. **Thus says the Lord of hosts, the God of Israel, to all who were carried away captive**: This letter was a valid and true expression of Jeremiah's prophetic office, even though it was written and not spoken.

2. (5-9) Make yourself at home and be good citizens in Babylon.

Build houses and dwell *in them;* plant gardens and eat their fruit. Take wives and beget sons and daughters; and take wives for your sons and give your daughters to husbands, so that they may bear sons and daughters—that you may be increased there, and not diminished. And seek the peace of the city where I have caused you to be carried away captive, and pray to the Lord for it; for in its peace you will have peace. For thus says the Lord of hosts, the God of Israel: Do not let your prophets and your diviners who are in your midst deceive you, nor listen to your dreams which you cause to be dreamed. For they prophesy falsely to you in My name; I have not sent them, says the Lord.

a. **Build houses and dwell in them**: The Jewish people were in Babylon by the will of God, in that He was bringing judgment on Judah for their generations of rebellion against Him. In God's plan they would be in Babylon a long time, so it was best for them to settle in and make the best of their lives and families there.

i. "Most likely, in expectation of a brief sojourn in captivity, they were wary of acquiring houses, land, and even children, since these would be encumbrances in the event of a return journey to Jerusalem." (Cundall)

ii. "The freedom allowed them implies they were neither slaves nor prisoners in their new land." (Feinberg)

b. **That you may be increased there, and not diminished**: God wanted the Jewish people to multiply in Babylon, even as they multiplied in Egypt. Exile didn't mean that God forgot about them or wanted to destroy them.

c. **Seek the peace of the city where I have caused you to be carried away captive**: God wanted them to do good in their communities and be a blessing to their Babylonian neighbors. Ultimately, God **caused** them to be in Babylon, and they should be a blessing where they were set.

i. **Pray to the Lord for it**: "Unique in ancient literature was Jeremiah's command for them to pray for their pagan captors." (Feinberg)

ii. Prayer and good works of all sorts are ways to **seek the peace** [*shalom*] **of the city**. Yet, proclaiming the good news of God's rescue in Jesus the Messiah is also part of seeking the peace of the city. "By themselves, random acts of kindness cannot bring enduring peace. The only basis for real and lasting *shalom* is the work of Jesus Christ on the cross." (Ryken)

iii. "Jeremiah had foretold the ultimate overthrow of Babylon with no uncertain sound. Of that issue there could be no doubt. But so long as it remained, and they were held there as captives by the will of God, let them secure peace for themselves, by seeking the peace of the city, and that by prayer." (Morgan)

iv. "Wherever you find yourself, seek the peace and comfort of those about you." (Meyer)

d. **Do not let your prophets and diviners who are in your midst deceive you**: There were false prophets among the Jews in Jerusalem *and* in Babylon. These false **prophets and diviners** likely told the Jews in Babylon that they would soon be allowed back to Judah and they should plan accordingly. God said, "**They prophesy falsely to you in My name; I have not sent them.**"

i. "There was a period of unrest all over the Babylonian empire, and prophets both in Jerusalem and in Babylon were proclaiming the imminent ending of the Exile, evidently believing that Babylon was on the point of collapse. The Babylonian Chronicle hints at internal troubles in Babylon in 595/4 BC in which some of the deported Jews seem to have been involved." (Thompson)

3. (10-14) The promise to bring them back into the land.

For thus says the LORD: After seventy years are completed at Babylon, I will visit you and perform My good word toward you, and cause you to return to this place. For I know the thoughts that I think toward you, says the LORD, thoughts of peace and not of evil, to give you a future and a hope. Then you will call upon Me and go and pray to Me, and I will listen to you. And you will seek Me and find *Me*, when you search for Me with all your heart. I will be found by you, says the LORD, and I will bring you back from your captivity; I will gather you from all the nations and from all the places where I have driven you, says the LORD, and I will bring you to the place from which I cause you to be carried away captive.

a. **After seventy years are completed at Babylon, I will visit you**: As previously promised by Jeremiah, the captivity in Babylon would not go beyond **seventy years**. God had appointed an end to it, but it would be a long season in exile before God would **cause you to return to this place**.

i. The false prophets promised a *quick* return from exile. Through Jeremiah, the LORD told them it would not be a quick return, but there *would be* a return. In time, God would **visit you and perform My good word toward you, and cause you to return to this place**. God had a **good word** for the exiles; it just wasn't the word the false prophets brought.

ii. "The prophet had the double duty of putting down their false hopes, and sustaining their right expectations. He, therefore, plainly warned them against expecting more than God had promised, and he aroused them to look for the fulfillment of what he had promised." (Spurgeon)

iii. "The exile did last seventy years. R.K. Harrison counts seventy years from the Babylonian victory at Carchemish in 605 BC to the return of the first exiles in 536 BC" (Ryken)

b. For I know the thoughts that I think toward you, says the LORD: God knew His own **thoughts** toward these exiled Jews in Babylon. *They* did not know or did not remember His thoughts toward them, so God wanted to state them in writing through Jeremiah's letter.

i. *God thinks about us.* In Psalm 40, David pondered the thoughts of God upon His people: *Your thoughts toward us cannot be recounted to You in order; if I would declare and speak of them, they are more than can be numbered* (Psalm 40:5; see also Psalm 139:17-18).

ii. "God's thoughts run upon his children, the children of affliction especially, as a father's do upon his dear children." (Trapp)

iii. Yet what God told the exiles through Jeremiah was even better. God does not only think *of* His people, His thoughts are **toward** them. "The Lord not only thinks *of* you, but *towards* you. His thoughts are all drifting your way." (Spurgeon)

iv. Furthermore, *we* may not know God's thoughts, but He says, **I know the thoughts that I think toward you**. "Brethren, when we cannot know the thoughts of the Lord because they are too high for our conception, or too deep for our understanding, yet the Lord knows them." (Spurgeon)

c. Thoughts of peace and not of evil, to give you a future and a hope: The exiled Jews lived in the experience of God's judgment upon their nation. It was easy for them to think that God was against them; that He intended **evil** for them. Through Jeremiah, God assured them that His thoughts toward them were **of peace**, and that in His heart and mind He had a **future and a hope** for them.

i. This promise was made to ancient Jews under the Babylonian exile, but they express the unchanging heart of God toward His people. Indeed, these were God's thoughts toward Israel under the Old

Covenant; we should not dare to believe that He is less favorable to those who come to Him in faith, through the Messiah, in the New Covenant.

ii. God has **a future and a hope** for His people even when they suffer in exile, even when they hurt under deserved discipline or judgment. It is the devil's deception to rob God's people of their sense of His **future and a hope** for them.

ii. The **future** and **hope** was not only expressed in a return from exile. "God had a special purpose in allowing the captivity of his people into Babylon. It was to scatter synagogues and the Old Testament, in preparation for the Gospel." (Meyer)

iv. "Jeremiah's words 'hope and a future' are literally 'an end and a hope,' which is a hendiadys (a figure in which a complex idea is expressed in two words linked by a coordinating conjunction) and means 'a hopeful end.'" (Feinberg)

d. **You will call upon Me and go and pray to Me, and I will listen to you**: This helped define the **future and a hope** that God had for His exiled people. Though they were not in Jerusalem and could not perform the appointed temple rituals, God would still **listen** when they prayed. Their prayer and God's answer were part of their **future** and **hope**.

i. Though in exile, they were not without God and those God sent to serve them. "Ezekiel could minister to them, as could other prophets." (Thompson)

e. **You will seek Me and find Me, when you search for Me with all your heart**: God would not hide from His people when they sought Him. They would not suffer under the dark sense that God could not be found. Their seeking and God's revealing were part of their **future** and **hope**.

f. **I will bring you back from your captivity**: This was a further aspect of their **future** and **hope** – that God would not only bless and be with them in Babylon, but allow His people to eventually come back to His and their Promised Land.

4. (15-20) God's displeasure with those who remained in Jerusalem and Judah.

Because you have said, "The LORD has raised up prophets for us in Babylon"— therefore thus says the LORD concerning the king who sits on the throne of David, concerning all the people who dwell in this city, and concerning your brethren who have not gone out with you into captivity— thus says the LORD of hosts: Behold, I will send on them the sword, the famine, and the pestilence, and will make them like rotten figs that cannot be eaten, they are so bad. And I will pursue them with

the sword, with famine, and with pestilence; and I will deliver them to trouble among all the kingdoms of the earth—to be a curse, an astonishment, a hissing, and a reproach among all the nations where I have driven them, because they have not heeded My words, says the Lord, which I sent to them by My servants the prophets, rising up early and sending *them;* neither would you heed, says the Lord. Therefore hear the word of the Lord, all you of the captivity, whom I have sent from Jerusalem to Babylon.

> a. **Concerning your brethren who have not gone out with you into captivity**: Many among the exiles in Babylon believed that those who had not yet been carried **into captivity** were somehow better than those who had been taken away. Perhaps there were prophets who encouraged this thinking. God told the exiles that those who remained would face severe judgment.
>
> b. **Like rotten figs that cannot be eaten**: Jeremiah 24 told of the parable of the baskets of figs, and here the picture is repeated. Those who remained in Jerusalem and Judah were like the **rotten figs**, not the good ones. Their fate was to be **a curse, an astonishment, a hissing, and a reproach among all the nations**.
>
>> i. "Do not envy the state of *Zedekiah* who sits on the throne of David, nor that of the *people* who are now in the land whence ye have been carried captive." (Clarke)
>
> c. **Because they have not heeded my words, says the Lord…neither would you heed**: It wasn't as if those already taken in captivity were righteous and those who remained were far more wicked. It seems what God most objected to was the sense of superiority and favor that those who remained in Jerusalem and Judah held on to.

B. **The message to certain individuals in Babylon.**

1. (21-23) The message to the false prophets Ahab and Zedekiah.

Thus says the Lord of hosts, the God of Israel, concerning Ahab the son of Kolaiah, and Zedekiah the son of Maaseiah, who prophesy a lie to you in My name: Behold, I will deliver them into the hand of Nebuchadnezzar king of Babylon, and he shall slay them before your eyes. And because of them a curse shall be taken up by all the captivity of Judah who *are* in Babylon, saying, "The Lord make you like Zedekiah and Ahab, whom the king of Babylon roasted in the fire"; because they have done disgraceful things in Israel, have committed adultery with their neighbors' wives, and have spoken lying words in My name, which

I have not commanded them. Indeed I know, and *am* a witness, says the LORD.

a. **Concerning Ahab the son of Kolaiah, and Zedekiah the son of Maaseiah**: In God's letter to the exiles through Jeremiah, He addressed some specific individuals. Here, God spoke to **Ahab** and **Zedekiah** – two men considered prophets, and named after a wicked king of Israel and a wicked king of Judah.

b. **I will deliver them into the hand of Nebuchadnezzar king of Babylon, and he shall slay them**: Apparently, Ahab and Zedekiah were among the prophets who lied to the people of God, telling them of Nebuchadnezzar's weakness and the soon restoration of the Jews to Judah. Not only were they wrong generally, they also were wrong regarding themselves personally, and would soon be executed by the king they said was fading in power and influence.

c. **The LORD make you like Zedekiah and Ahab**: This would become a proverb among the Jews in Babylonian exile. These men died such terrible deaths (**roasted in the fire**) that one could curse others by wishing their fate upon them.

i. "Literally, the Bible says Nebuchadnezzar 'roasted' them, which was the proper punishment for treason in Hammurabi's Code." (Ryken)

d. **They have done disgraceful things in Israel, have committed adultery with their neighbors' wives, and have spoken lying words in My name**: These men were unfaithful with their lives and with their words. Though their unfaithfulness was perhaps not public knowledge, God was **a witness** to it all and would hold them to account.

2. (24-28) The message to Shemaiah.

You shall also speak to Shemaiah the Nehelamite, saying, Thus speaks the LORD of hosts, the God of Israel, saying: You have sent letters in your name to all the people who *are* at Jerusalem, to Zephaniah the son of Maaseiah the priest, and to all the priests, saying, "The LORD has made you priest instead of Jehoiada the priest, so that there should be officers *in* the house of the LORD over every man *who* is demented and considers himself a prophet, that you should put him in prison and in the stocks. Now therefore, why have you not rebuked Jeremiah of Anathoth who makes himself a prophet to you? For he has sent to us *in* Babylon, saying, 'This *captivity is* long; build houses and dwell *in them*, and plant gardens and eat their fruit.'"

a. **The LORD has made you priest**: The second message was to **Shemaiah the Nehelamite**, who sent letters to the High Priest **Zephaniah**, telling him to stop and punish **every man who is demented and considers himself a prophet**, meaning Jeremiah (and perhaps others).

i. **Demented**: "*Meshugga, in ecstatic rapture*; such as appeared in the prophets, whether *true* or *false*, when under the influence, the one of God, the other of a demon. See 2 Kings 9:11; Hosea 9:7." (Clarke)

ii. Zephaniah was priest after the good and godly **Jehoiada** (2 Chronicles 23-24).

iii. "He should have known, too, that *the stocks* (or pillory) had not silenced Jeremiah before, nor would the addition of the iron collar." (Kidner)

b. **Why have you not rebuked Jeremiah of Anathoth**: Shemaiah wanted Zephaniah to do everything he could to oppose and discredit Jeremiah, denying his message that they would be in exile for a long time and should make the best of it.

3. (29-32) The judgment to come upon Shemaiah.

Now Zephaniah the priest read this letter in the hearing of Jeremiah the prophet. Then the word of the LORD came to Jeremiah, saying: Send to all those in captivity, saying, Thus says the LORD concerning Shemaiah the Nehelamite: Because Shemaiah has prophesied to you, and I have not sent him, and he has caused you to trust in a lie— therefore thus says the LORD: Behold, I will punish Shemaiah the Nehelamite and his family: he shall not have anyone to dwell among this people, nor shall he see the good that I will do for My people, says the LORD, because he has taught rebellion against the LORD.

a. **Zephaniah the priest read this letter in the hearing of Jeremiah**: When the letter from Shemaiah came to Jerusalem and Zephaniah, Jeremiah heard the letter exalting Shemaiah and criticizing Jeremiah.

b. **Behold, I will punish Shemaiah**: God directed Jeremiah to respond with a prophetic declaration against Shemaiah. God would punish this false prophet and **his family**. They would die out with no descendants and never **see the good that I will do for My people**.

i. One reason to keep faithful to God through the difficulties of life is simply so we can be around when God does remarkable **good** for His people.

Jeremiah 30 – Saved Out of the Time of Jacob's Trouble

"Think no more of Jeremiah as exclusively the weeping prophet; for the flashes of his delight make the night of his sorrow brilliant with an aurora of heavenly brilliance." (Spurgeon)

A. Writing the prophecy down.

1. (1-3) Write the words in a book.

The word that came to Jeremiah from the LORD, saying, "Thus speaks the LORD God of Israel, saying: 'Write in a book for yourself all the words that I have spoken to you. For behold, the days are coming,' says the LORD, 'that I will bring back from captivity My people Israel and Judah,' says the LORD. 'And I will cause them to return to the land that I gave to their fathers, and they shall possess it.'"

> a. **The word that came to Jeremiah from the LORD**: Jeremiah 32:1-2 gives the time of this prophecy and book (covering four chapters, Jeremiah 30 through 33), right before the final fall of Jerusalem. Its general tone of hopefulness and optimism sets it apart from much of the previous in Jeremiah.
>
>> i. Jeremiah 32:1-2 gives the time of this prophecy and book – right before the final fall of Jerusalem. "The historical context is clearly indicated in Jeremiah 32:1 f. (cf. 33:1). Jerusalem was in the final stages of an eighteen-month siege which ended with its destruction by the Babylonians… The situation, humanly speaking, could not have been darker, but at this very point God commands Jeremiah to speak out concerning the future." (Cundall)
>
> b. **Write in a book**: Jeremiah was commanded to write the following prophecy. Previous words from God were obviously written, but there was

special emphasis on the recording of this word. This is likely because its ultimate fulfillment was a long time distant to the days of Jeremiah.

> i. "These are the contents of this precious book; every leaf, nay, line, nay, letter whereof, droppeth myrrh and mercy." (Trapp)

c. **I will bring back from captivity My people Israel and Judah**: This is a promise stated many times before and after in Jeremiah. Yet as this prophecy develops, it seems clear that this return from captivity is later and greater than the relatively soon return from the Babylonian exile.

> i. This is especially indicated by the last words of this chapter, which tell us that *in the latter days you will consider it* (Jeremiah 30:24). Jeremiah here looked beyond his present day and near future to see *the latter days*.

2. (4-7) The time of Jacob's trouble.

Now these *are* the words that the LORD **spoke concerning Israel and Judah.**

"For thus says the LORD**:**
'We have heard a voice of trembling,
Of fear, and not of peace.
Ask now, and see,
Whether a man is ever in labor with child?
So why do I see every man *with* his hands on his loins
Like a woman in labor,
And all faces turned pale?
Alas! For that day *is* great,
So that none *is* like it;
And it *is* the time of Jacob's trouble,
But he shall be saved out of it.

a. **That the L**ORD **spoke concerning Israel and Judah**: The mention of *both* kingdoms is another hint that this written prophecy speaks of something later and greater than the return from Babylonian exile. It is true that the Kingdom of Judah did contain people from all the tribes (2 Chronicles 11:13-16), so these words don't *demand* a greater fulfillment, but they do suggest it.

b. **We have heard a voice of trembling, of fear, and not of peace**: Jeremiah poetically described the terror of the Jewish people (**Israel and Judah**) under a great, incomparable calamity.

> i. "The picture of men clutching their thighs in anguish gives rise to the question *Can a man bear a child?* They behave like women in labor and their faces have turned pale." (Thompson)

c. **That day is great, so that none is like it**: Jeremiah often used similar words to describe the coming judgment upon Judah and Jerusalem in his own day. Yet this describes something beyond that; another time of great terror to come upon the Jewish people and a time worse than ever before (**none is like it**).

i. **That day is great**. The idea of the *great day* is often connected to the calamity that comes upon the earth in the very last days.

- *The great day of the LORD is near; it is near and hastens quickly. The noise of the day of the LORD is bitter; there the mighty men shall cry out* (Zephaniah 1:14).
- *For the great day of His wrath has come, and who is able to stand* (Revelation 6:17).
- *Gather them to the battle of that great day of God Almighty* (Revelation 16:14).

ii. "The phrase *hayyom hahu*, 'that day', is frequently used in the prophetic Scriptures to introduce information concerning the Day of the Lord, a significant eschatological theme." (Feinberg)

iii. **None is like it**: Jesus also said there was coming a day of incomparable tribulation: *Then there will be great tribulation, such as has not been since the beginning of the world until this time, no, nor ever shall be* (Matthew 24:21).

d. **It is the time of Jacob's trouble**: As described in Jeremiah 30, this **time of Jacob's trouble** seems beyond the catastrophe of the Babylonian invasions and exile. This is a coming time of catastrophe appointed for the Jewish people, also described vividly by Jesus in the Olivet Discourse (Matthew 24:15-22), and there connected to what Jesus called *the abomination of desolation*.

i. In connecting Jeremiah 30 with Matthew 24, we note that what we often call the great tribulation is particularly **the time of Jacob's trouble**; it is when a great and terrible world leader and the government he represents will try to destroy the Jewish people. Working through these, Satan himself will hope to devour the Jewish people (Revelation 12:1-6).

ii. This does *not* minimize the persecution that will also be brought against the followers of Jesus, both Jewish and Gentile during that time. Yet in God's plan of the ages, this is noted as **the time of Jacob's trouble**, because God will work in and through this catastrophe to bring salvation to the Jews.

e. **But he shall be saved out of it**: Through this time of incomparable tribulation to come against the Jewish people, God will rescue them and bring them His salvation. He will protect them (as in Revelation 12:6) and bring them to faith in their Messiah, Jesus Christ (Jeremiah 23:6, Romans 11:26).

> i. "Jeremiah is stating that before the just-mentioned promise of restoration can be fulfilled, the nation must be severely disciplined, but not to the extent of final calamity." (Feinberg)

> ii. **But he shall be saved out of it**: "Not from it, but yet out of it; the Lord knoweth how to deliver his." (Trapp) The Jewish people (those not yet trusting in their Messiah) will endure this time of Jacob's trouble and be **saved out of it**. In contrast, Jesus told us to pray to escape these things (Luke 21:36), and Jesus promised His people that they would be kept from the very hour of calamity that comes upon the earth (Revelation 3:10).

3. (8-9) No more slaves.

'For it shall come to pass in that day,'
Says the LORD of hosts,
'*That* I will break his yoke from your neck,
And will burst your bonds;
Foreigners shall no more enslave them.
But they shall serve the LORD their God,
And David their king,
Whom I will raise up for them.

a. **I will break his yoke from your neck**: A false prophet previously used the symbol of the broken yoke to bring false hope (Jeremiah 28:2-4). Here God states the true promise that one day – in the season of the time of Jacob's trouble – there would never again be a **yoke** upon the Jewish people.

b. **Foreigners shall no more enslave them**: This points to something greater than the return from Babylonian captivity, because many times since then have the Jewish people been enslaved to forced labor.

c. **They shall serve the LORD their God**: Instead of being slaves to foreigners, the Jewish people will be faithful servants of Yahweh (and ultimately, His Messiah Jesus Christ).

d. **And David their king**: In that day, God will also **raise up for them** David to reign as king. Most commentators take this as a reference to the Messiah, the Son of David, and not David the Son of Jesse. Yet there are good reasons to believe that this and similar passages speak of David the Son of Jesse.

i. This promise seems impossible, yet is repeated several times in the prophets of the Old Testament (Isaiah 55:3-4, Ezekiel 34:23-24, 37:24-25, Hosea 3:5). This speaks of the reign of the resurrected David, the Son of Jesse, over Israel in the Millennial earth.

ii. We have indications that as God's people rule with Jesus over the millennial earth, people will be entrusted with geographical regions according to their faithfulness (Luke 19:12-19). It seems that David's glorious portion will be to rule over Israel.

4. (10-11) A promise to gather and a promise to correct.

'**Therefore do not fear, O My servant Jacob,**' says the LORD,
'**Nor be dismayed, O Israel;**
For behold, I will save you from afar,
And your seed from the land of their captivity.
Jacob shall return, have rest and be quiet,
And no one shall make *him* **afraid.**
For I *am* **with you,**' says the LORD, '**to save you;**
Though I make a full end of all nations where I have scattered you,
Yet I will not make a complete end of you.
But I will correct you in justice,
And will not let you go altogether unpunished.'

a. **Therefore do not fear, O My servant Jacob**: God foretold a time of terrible catastrophe to come upon the Jewish people, *the time of Jacob's trouble*. Yet God did not want them to fear, but to be confident in His ultimate victory and His promise of salvation: **behold, I will save you from afar**.

b. **Jacob shall return, have rest and be quiet**: In a lesser sense, this was fulfilled in the return from exile under Ezra and Nehemiah, but only in a lesser sense. It could not be said of the return from Babylonian captivity, **no one shall make him afraid**, but it *shall* be said of Israel in the Millennium.

c. **I make a full end of all nations where I have scattered you**: This is another aspect that was fulfilled in a lesser sense in the return from Babylonian exile, but awaits the *latter days* (Jeremiah 30:24) for its full fulfillment.

d. **Yet I will not make a complete end of you**: God's promise to Israel was that they would *not* become extinct as a people, either by death or assimilation. They would endure terrible affliction yet survive.

i. The believer today can draw comfort from this principle of God's character and nature. "Take to heart these tender words: God will not make a full end of you. It may seem as though nothing will be left: the furnace is so hot; the stock is cut down so near to the ground. But God knows just how much you can bear, and will stay his hand. 'I will not make a full end of thee.'" (Meyer)

e. **I will correct you in justice**: God reminded Israel that though they would indeed see the nations that afflicted them judged, God would also **correct** them. As they had sinned, God would not allow them to **go altogether unpunished**.

B. Restoration after incurable affliction.

1. (12-15) Their incurable affliction.

"For thus says the LORD:
'Your affliction *is* incurable,
Your wound *is* severe.
***There is* no one to plead your cause,**
That you may be bound up;
You have no healing medicines.
All your lovers have forgotten you;
They do not seek you;
For I have wounded you with the wound of an enemy,
With the chastisement of a cruel one,
For the multitude of your iniquities,
***Because* your sins have increased.**
Why do you cry about your affliction?
Your sorrow *is* incurable.
Because of the multitude of your iniquities,
***Because* your sins have increased,**
I have done these things to you.

a. **Your affliction is incurable**: God spoke to the Jewish people honestly about their sinful condition, and that among men there was **no one to plead your cause**. Through history there have been few non-Jews willing to stand with Israel and the Jews in the face of deeply ingrained Jew-hatred.

b. **All your lovers have forgotten you**: In Jeremiah's day and beyond, the Jewish people often trusted in and gave themselves to foreign nations hoping they would protect them. They would forget them instead.

i. "The *lovers* were the surrounding nations on whom Judah had relied for help against Babylon." (Harrison)

ii. **Why do you cry about your affliction**: "And not rather for thy sins? Cry not *perii*, I have died, but *peccavi;* I have sinned, not, I am undone; but, I have done very foolishly." (Trapp)

> c. **Because your sins have increased, I have done these things to you**: God reminded them that the catastrophe came upon them from His own hand. They were not accidents or events of bad luck.

2. (16-17) Devouring the devourer.

'Therefore all those who devour you shall be devoured;
And all your adversaries, every one of them, shall go into captivity;
Those who plunder you shall become plunder,
And all who prey upon you I will make a prey.
For I will restore health to you
And heal you of your wounds,' says the LORD,
'Because they called you an outcast *saying*:
"This *is* Zion;
No one seeks her."'

> a. **All those who devour you shall be devoured**: God spoke comfort to His people, assuring their sense of justice that those who had afflicted and **devoured** them would themselves **go into captivity** and **become plunder**.
>
>> i. "Because his people have undergone judgment and have acknowledged their guilt, God pronounces retaliation in kind on their enemies." (Feinberg)
>
> b. **I will restore health to you and heal you of your wounds**: God promised to bring ruin to Israel's enemies, but restoration to Israel. They would both be afflicted, but only one would be restored. God promised to restore them **because** the opposing nations treated Israel as **an outcast**.

3. (18-20) The restoration of Jerusalem and the people of God.

"Thus says the LORD:
'Behold, I will bring back the captivity of Jacob's tents,
And have mercy on his dwelling places;
The city shall be built upon its own mound,
And the palace shall remain according to its own plan.
Then out of them shall proceed thanksgiving
And the voice of those who make merry;
I will multiply them, and they shall not diminish;
I will also glorify them, and they shall not be small.
Their children also shall be as before,
And their congregation shall be established before Me;
And I will punish all who oppress them.

> a. **I will bring back the captivity of Jacob's tents**: For emphasis, God repeated the promise of restoration. Their present captivity in Babylon would not last forever, nor would future captivities.

> i. "By the term *tents* we should understand 'clans,' that is, people who dwell in tents." (Thompson)

b. **The city shall be built upon its own mound**: Jerusalem would never remain a dead or unoccupied city. God would build and restore it again. God promised to bless the *people* in the city, making them **merry** and multiplied.

> i. **I will also glorify them**: "I will put *honour* upon them every where, so that they shall be no longer *contemptible*. This will be a very great *change*, for they are now *despised* all over the earth." (Clarke)

4. (21-22) The One who draws near.

Their nobles shall be from among them,
And their governor shall come from their midst;
Then I will cause him to draw near,
And he shall approach Me;
For who *is* this who pledged his heart to approach Me?' says the LORD.
'You shall be My people,
And I will be your God.'"

a. **Their governor shall come from their midst**: In the context of the ultimate restoration of the Jewish people, Jeremiah prophetically described their **governor**, the One who ultimately rules over them. He comes **from their midst**; He is one of them.

> i. Jeremiah 30:21 in the ESV is perhaps helpful:
>
> *Their prince shall be one of themselves;*
> *Their ruler shall come out from their midst;*
> *I will make him draw near, and he shall approach me,*
> *For who would dare of himself to approach me?*

b. **Then I will cause him to draw near**: The phrasing here indicates that the unique ruler would **draw near** to Yahweh in a special way, as a priest and representative of the people. This refers to the Messiah, who is not only a King but also a Priest according to the order of Melchizedek.

> i. "He will have the privilege of approach to God. Usage in the OT shows that this means priestly position and ministry (cf. Psalm 110:4; Zechariah 6:13)." (Feinberg)

c. **For who is this who pledged his heart to approach Me**: Yahweh did not ask this question because He did not know; He asked the question to draw attention to this One, perfect in obedience and in **heart** and who could **approach** God the Father as priest on behalf of His people.

i. **Who is this**: "Who but my Son Christ durst do it, or was fit to do it? He is a super-excellent person, as is imported by this *Mi-hu-ze*, Who this he?" (Trapp)

ii. **Who pledged his heart**: "Our Lord with all his heart desired to do this: he 'engaged his heart' to perform it. Before all worlds his master purpose was to approach unto God as man's representative…His heart was occupied with love to God and love to man, and he could not rest till he had restored the broken concord between these divided ones." (Spurgeon)

d. **You shall be My people, and I will be your God**: This is the result of the **approach** of the King-Priest. God's people are brought into close and deep relationship with God.

5. (23-24) The whirlwind of the latter days.

Behold, the whirlwind of the LORD
Goes forth with fury,
A continuing whirlwind;
It will fall violently on the head of the wicked.
The fierce anger of the LORD will not return until He has done it,
And until He has performed the intents of His heart.
In the latter days you will consider it.

a. **The whirlwind of the LORD**: The **whirlwind** is here a figure of God's judgment, coming like a tornado that brings destruction and cannot be contained or controlled.

i. "Before there can be blessing, judgment must be meted out to the guilty." (Feinberg)

b. **The fierce anger of the LORD will not return until He has done it, and until He has performed the intents of His heart**: The judgment of God is *certain*. In His mercy He may long delay it, but it will certainly come. The judgment of God also comes *from His heart*. One expression of God's love for the good is His displeasure for what is evil.

c. **In the latter days you will consider it**: God reminds us that much in this chapter waits until **the latter days** for its ultimate and true fulfillment.

i. "In the days of the Messiah, but especially at the end of the world, when all these things shall have their full accomplishment." (Trapp)

Jeremiah 31 – The Glory of the New Covenant

A. The everlasting love of Yahweh for Israel.

1. (1-2) Salvation to Israel in the last days.

"At the same time," says the LORD, "I will be the God of all the families of Israel, and they shall be My people."
Thus says the LORD:
"The people who survived the sword
Found grace in the wilderness—
Israel, when I went to give him rest."

> a. **At the same time**: The last verses of the previous chapter identify this time as *the latter days* (Jeremiah 30:24).
>
> b. **I will be the God of all the families of Israel**: Jeremiah described the great turning to God and His Messiah foretold in the last days. As Paul wrote, *so all Israel will be saved* (Romans 11:26).
>
> c. **The people who survived the sword found grace in the wilderness**: The great persecution of the Jewish people in *the time of Jacob's trouble* (Jeremiah 30:7, Revelation 12) will afflict many and not all will survive. Yet the great majority of those **who survived** will receive God's **grace** and **rest**, finding it in their Messiah Jesus Christ.

2. (3-6) The basis of God's faithfulness to Israel: His everlasting love.

The LORD has appeared of old to me, *saying:*
"Yes, I have loved you with an everlasting love;
Therefore with lovingkindness I have drawn you.
Again I will build you, and you shall be rebuilt,
O virgin of Israel!
You shall again be adorned with your tambourines,
And shall go forth in the dances of those who rejoice.
You shall yet plant vines on the mountains of Samaria;
The planters shall plant and eat *them* as ordinary food.

For there shall be a day
When the watchmen will cry on Mount Ephraim,
'Arise, and let us go up *to* Zion,
To the LORD our God.'"

> a. **The LORD has appeared of old to me**: Jeremiah was careful to set the following words from God in context. They came from a divine appearance, and an appearance anchored in eternity (**of old**).
>
> b. **Yes, I have loved you with an everlasting love**: God's great message to Israel was an assurance of His love. Anchored in eternity past, His love for Israel extended to eternity future. It was **an everlasting love**.
>
>> i. God *assured* Israel of this by starting with **Yes**. Remarkably, some Christians think that God has said *no* to an everlasting love for Israel as Israel; that they should now be regarded as the now unchosen chosen people.
>>
>> ii. "It is not, 'I have pitied thee,' nor 'I have thought about thee,' but 'I have loved thee.' God is in love with you." (Spurgeon)
>>
>> iii. " 'And with the old love I have loved thee.' 'Also, with a love of long standing have I loved thee.'-*Blayney*. 'But I love thee always' --*Dahler*. I still bear to the Jewish people that love which I showed to their fathers in Egypt, in the wilderness, and in the promised land." (Clarke)
>>
>> iv. This statement was spoken to Israel; but the love it describes is God's love for every believer. "You must go back beyond your birth, beyond Calvary and Bethlehem, beyond the fall of man and the Garden of Eden, and as you stand looking out into the immensity of eternity, dare to believe that you were loved and chosen in Christ, the object of God's most tender solicitude and pity." (Meyer)
>
> c. **Therefore with lovingkindness I have drawn you**: Because of God's **everlasting love**, His promise remains to draw Israel with His loyal love, His covenant love, His *hesed* (**lovingkindness**).
>
>> i. The lovingkindness of God *draws* Israel. He does not force or compel them but draws them in love and compassion. In the bigger picture of God's redemptive plan, we can say that God's kindness leads Israel to repentance in the time of Jacob's trouble.
>>
>> ii. "The master-magnet of the gospel is not fear, but love. Penitents are drawn to Christ rather than driven." (Spurgeon)
>>
>> iii. **Lovingkindness**: "The term *hesed*, rendered *faithfulness* (RSV) or *unfailing care* (NEB), is impossible to render by one word, but expresses the divine nature as exemplified in the Sinai covenant." (Harrison)

d. **Again I will build you**: God's loyal love to Israel will mean that He restores and builds them, and this is assured (**you shall be rebuilt**). Israel's restoration will mean joy, dancing, and abundance. The **watchmen** of Israel would not need to warn of approaching enemies, but they would welcome pilgrims on their way **up to Zion, to the LORD our God.**

> i. "The *watchmen* were posted high on vantage points in time of war to warn of an approaching enemy (cf. Jeremiah 6:17). But here the watchman's call is for a nobler purpose, *Up! Let us go up to Zion.*" (Thompson)

3. (7-9) The joyful restoration.

For thus says the LORD:
"Sing with gladness for Jacob,
And shout among the chief of the nations;
Proclaim, give praise, and say,
'O LORD, save Your people,
The remnant of Israel!'
Behold, I will bring them from the north country,
And gather them from the ends of the earth,
***Among* them the blind and the lame,**
The woman with child
And the one who labors with child, together;
A great throng shall return there.
They shall come with weeping,
And with supplications I will lead them.
I will cause them to walk by the rivers of waters,
In a straight way in which they shall not stumble;
For I am a Father to Israel,
And Ephraim *is* My firstborn."

a. **Sing with gladness for Jacob, and shout among the chief of the nations**: This was news so good that it should not be heard in Israel alone. All the earth should hear of God's salvation to Israel and **give praise** for it.

b. **Behold, I will bring them**: God promised to gather the Jewish people from all over the earth, a gathering so complete that even **the blind and the lame** come; **a great throng shall return there**. The **there** is not merely a returning to Yahweh, it is also a returning to *the land*. The promise of *the land* remains for Israel.

> i. A great miracle happened in 1948, when Israel was once again established as a Jewish state in their ancient land. As wonderful and miraculous as that was, it does not yet fulfill the glory of this promise.

Israel is now gathered in unbelief; this will only be completely fulfilled when Israel comes to faith in Yahweh and His Messiah.

c. **They shall come with weeping**: In this great restoration of *the latter days* (Jeremiah 30:24), Israel will return to Yahweh and His Messiah with tears and **supplications**. As one of the other prophets wrote: *And I will pour on the house of David and on the inhabitants of Jerusalem the Spirit of grace and supplication; then they will look on Me whom they pierced. Yes, they will mourn for Him as one mourns for his only son, and grieve for Him as one grieves for a firstborn* (Zechariah 12:10).

i. "I believe in the restoration of the Jews to their own land in the last days. I am a firm believer in the gathering in of the Jews at a future time. Before Jesus Christ shall come upon this earth again, the Jews shall be permitted to go; to their beloved Palestine." (Charles Spurgeon, in an 1855 sermon)

d. **Ephraim is My firstborn**: Ephraim here represents Israel as a whole, as in the previous line. Yet it is significant that **Ephraim** was not the firstborn son of Jacob, yet God regarded him as **firstborn**. This shows that **firstborn** referred to more than birth order, it communicates the concept of preeminence.

i. "Ephraim's condition in blessing will be permanent because Jeroboam's misleading them from the Lord's sanctuary will be a thing of the past, when they return to Zion. The breach of many centuries will at last be healed." (Feinberg)

4. (10-12) Gathering the scattered flock.

"Hear the word of the Lord, O nations,
And declare *it* in the isles afar off, and say,
'He who scattered Israel will gather him,
And keep him as a shepherd *does* his flock.'
For the Lord has redeemed Jacob,
And ransomed him from the hand of one stronger than he.
Therefore they shall come and sing in the height of Zion,
Streaming to the goodness of the Lord—
For wheat and new wine and oil,
For the young of the flock and the herd;
Their souls shall be like a well-watered garden,
And they shall sorrow no more at all."

a. **Declare it in the isles afar off**: Again, God emphasized that the good news of Israel's restoration must be proclaimed to all the **nations**, to the most distant parts of the earth.

i. "Hear and bear witness of the gracious promises that I make to my people; for I would have them noted and noticed." (Trapp)

b. **He who scattered Israel will gather him**: The themes are repeated for emphasis. God will not be finished with Israel as Israel until they are gathered again in the land in the latter days.

c. **Ransomed him from the hand of the one stronger than he**: God promised to rescue the Jewish people from the captivity, held in bondage by those **stronger than he**, both in a natural and spiritual sense.

i. **Redeemed…ransomed**: "The verb 'ransom' in some contexts refers to freedom after paying off a ransom price. Originally it is a term of commercial law….The verb 'redeem' is used often in the context of family obligations. The kinsman was required to redeem the property of a family member, even avenge his death." (Thompson)

d. **They shall come and sing in the height of Zion**: Jeremiah pictured a restored, gathered Israel streaming into Jerusalem. They would be rich with the abundance of God's provision both materially and spiritually (**their souls shall be like a well-watered garden**).

5. (13-14) The joyful response.

"**Then shall the virgin rejoice in the dance,**
And the young men and the old, together;
For I will turn their mourning to joy,
Will comfort them,
And make them rejoice rather than sorrow.
I will satiate the soul of the priests with abundance,
And My people shall be satisfied with My goodness, says the LORD."

a. **I will turn their mourning to joy**: Israel mourned under their exile and captivity, but God promised to turn it to **joy**. With God's **comfort**, all would rejoice together.

b. **I will satiate the soul of the priests with abundance**: The idea is that the priests would have a great **abundance** because the people were so blessed. The people tithed much because they were blessed much.

i. "Abundant offerings to the priests will reflect the productivity of the land." (Harrison)

6. (15-17) Rachel weeping.

Thus says the LORD:
"**A voice was heard in Ramah,**
Lamentation *and* **bitter weeping,**
Rachel weeping for her children,

Refusing to be comforted for her children,
Because they *are* no more."
Thus says the LORD:
"Refrain your voice from weeping,
And your eyes from tears;
For your work shall be rewarded, says the LORD,
And they shall come back from the land of the enemy.
There is hope in your future, says the LORD,
That *your* children shall come back to their own border."

    a. **Rachel weeping for her children**: Here, the LORD spoke through a poetic image, picturing **Rachel** (the mother of Benjamin and Joseph, ancestors of prominent tribes of Israel) **weeping for her children**. She does this from **Ramah**, near where she was buried (1 Samuel 10:2).

        i. "Rachel, the mother of Joseph and Benjamin, is pictured as weeping in despair over the exiled tribes. To her comes the comforting assurance that her children will be miraculously returned to her." (Cundall)

    b. **Because they are no more**: In this poetic picture, Rachel rises from her tomb and sees that her descendants have been taken away in exile and captivity. She is grieved, **refusing to be comforted**.

        i. Matthew the Gospel writer understood this as a type or poetic picture of the horrific slaughter of children in Bethlehem and the surrounding areas because of his fear of the birth of the King of the Jews (Matthew 2:16-18).

        ii. "*Cf.* Matthew 2:18, where the words are cited, not as a prophecy but as a type, in connection with the killing of the infants by king Herod." (Harrison)

    c. **Refrain your voice from weeping, and your eyes from tears**: God gave a remarkable word to poetic Rachel. He commanded comfort to the one who refused to be comforted.

        i. "Sorrow and grief do not have the last word, either in Jeremiah or in Matthew. A mother may refuse to be comforted, but God will comfort her nonetheless." (Ryken)

    d. **For your work shall be rewarded**: God's comfort to poetic Rachel was not empty. She could be comforted because there was a reward and a restoration. Her children would **come back from the land of the enemy**. God's promise of restoration meant that **there is hope in your future**.

7. (18-20) God embraces a repentant Israel.

"I have surely heard Ephraim bemoaning himself:
'You have chastised me, and I was chastised,
Like an untrained bull;
Restore me, and I will return,
For You *are* the LORD my God.
Surely, after my turning, I repented;
And after I was instructed, I struck myself on the thigh;
I was ashamed, yes, even humiliated,
Because I bore the reproach of my youth.'
Is Ephraim My dear son?
Is he a pleasant child?
For though I spoke against him,
I earnestly remember him still;
Therefore My heart yearns for him;
I will surely have mercy on him," says the LORD.

> a. **I have surely heard Ephraim bemoaning himself**: Again, the prominent tribe of **Ephraim** is used as a figure for all of Israel. God says that He heard His people speaking words of humble repentance.
>
>> i. **Surely heard**: "Hebrew, Hearing I have heard; his moans and laments have rung in mine ears." (Trapp)
>>
>> ii. "Rachel can dry her tears, for the excellent reason that (in the prophet's vision) *Ephraim* has at last begun to mourn not for his fate but for his sins." (Kidner)
>
> b. **You have chastised me, and I was chastised**: Israel recognized that their misfortunes were not accidents of blind fate. They were chastisements from the LORD, which they now humbly accepted as if they were **an untrained bull** that needed to be broken in some sense and brought into submission.
>
> c. **Restore me, and I will return**: In total dependence upon God, they realized that they could not **return** to God without His restoring work. They humbly asked God to **restore** them so they could **return**.
>
> d. **After my turning, I repented**: In turning to God, they understood that their behavior had to change. It meant repentance.
>
> e. **I was ashamed, yes, even humiliated**: Having returned to God, they were **ashamed** of their past sin and rebellion, of the sins of their youth. In the manner of a person greatly moved or upset, they **struck** themselves **on the thigh**.
>
>> i. **I struck myself on the thigh**: "My sorrow grew deeper and deeper; I smote upon my thigh through the extremity of my distress. This was a usual sign of deep affliction. See Ezekiel 21:12." (Clarke)

f. **Is Ephraim My dear son**: Jeremiah recorded the wonderful response of God. He received and embraced Israel as His **dear son**, even as the father in the story of the prodigal son embraced his disobedient son (Luke 15:20).

> i. "*My dear son, a child in whom I delight* or 'my darling child.' Yahweh cannot utter his name (speak of him) without remembering him vividly." (Thompson)

> ii. **Is he a pleasant child**: "Ay sure he is; and never more dear and pleasant than when thus beblubbered." (Trapp)

g. **My heart yearns for him**: This is the *everlasting love* and the *lovingkindness* spoken of earlier in the chapter (Jeremiah 31:3).

> i. **My heart yearns for him**: "The Hebrew text in the last line reads literally 'my bowels rumble for him' but has to be rendered *my heart yearns for him*. The very vivid anthropomorphism depicts God's stomach being churned up with longing for his son." (Thompson)

B. Gathering and planting restored Israel to the land.

1. (21-22) The clear path of restoration.

> "Set up signposts,
> Make landmarks;
> Set your heart toward the highway,
> The way in *which* you went.
> Turn back, O virgin of Israel,
> Turn back to these your cities.
> How long will you gad about,
> O you backsliding daughter?
> For the LORD has created a new thing in the earth—
> A woman shall encompass a man."

a. **Set your heart toward the highway**: Jeremiah pictured a clear road with **signposts** and **landmarks** that would guide Israel back to the land and restored relationship with their Covenant God. They would come back to the relationship they once had (**the way in which you went**), to their first love with God.

> i. "Jeremiah now addresses the returning exiles of the northern kingdom. They are to make ample preparation for their homeward journey." (Feinberg)

b. **How long will you gad about, O you backsliding daughter**: In light of the great love and restoration of God, it made no sense for Israel to remain in their backslidden condition a moment longer. If this restoration was promised, they should take it by faith immediately instead of waiting for an undefined time in the future to return.

c. **A woman shall encompass a man**: The best sense of this difficult phrase is that it is a promise that Israel would be so blessed and secure in God's restoration that even the women among them could protect the men and the people as a whole.

> i. "The reference in verse 22, where, in this new situation, 'a woman protects (Hebrew 'compass', as in AV [KJV]) a man', is best interpreted as signifying the absolute security Israel will enjoy. The menfolk will be able to go about their work, for the risk of attack will be so minimal that security can safely be left to the 'weaker sex'!" (Cundall)

> ii. "I think it likely that the Jews in their present distressed circumstances are represented under the similitude of a *weak defenseless female* נקבה *nekebah*; and the *Chaldeans* under that of a *fierce strong man*, גבר *gaber*, who had prevailed over and oppressed this *weak woman*. But, notwithstanding the disparity between them, God would cause the *woman*-the *weak defenseless Jews*, to *compass*-to overcome, the *strong man*-the *powerful Babylonians*. And this the prophet says would be *a new thing in the land*; for in such a case the lame would take the prey." (Clarke)

> iii. Some try to make the words of 31:22 into a prophecy of the Virgin Birth, but this is unsupported by the text.

2. (23-25) The blessing to be pronounced upon Jerusalem.

Thus says the LORD of hosts, the God of Israel: "They shall again use this speech in the land of Judah and in its cities, when I bring back their captivity: 'The LORD bless you, O home of justice, *and* mountain of holiness!' And there shall dwell in Judah itself, and in all its cities together, farmers and those going out with flocks. For I have satiated the weary soul, and I have replenished every sorrowful soul."

a. **The LORD bless you, O home of justice, and mountain of holiness**: The Lord spoke of a coming day when this blessing would be said by the Jewish people as they returned to Zion and came to Jerusalem as pilgrims. This blessing indicates that the government of Israel is transformed and righteously governed by the Messiah, who makes Jerusalem a **home of justice, and mountain of holiness**.

> i. "When the southern kingdom and her cities are restored, the old greeting of those visiting Jerusalem will be heard once more." (Feinberg)

b. **There shall dwell in Judah itself, and in all its cities together, farmers and those going out with flocks**: In that day the Jewish people would not only be blessed spiritually, but also materially. They will be restored in both the city and the country.

c. **For I have satiated the weary soul, and I have replenished every sorrowful soul**: God promised abundance and satisfaction to the empty, tired soul. The soul filled with sorrow would be filled with hope and peace.

3. (26-30) Answering an untrue proverb.

After this I awoke and looked around, and my sleep was sweet to me.

"Behold, the days are coming, says the LORD, that I will sow the house of Israel and the house of Judah with the seed of man and the seed of beast. And it shall come to pass, *that* **as I have watched over them to pluck up, to break down, to throw down, to destroy, and to afflict, so I will watch over them to build and to plant, says the LORD. In those days they shall say no more:**

**'The fathers have eaten sour grapes,
And the children's teeth are set on edge.'**

But every one shall die for his own iniquity; every man who eats the sour grapes, his teeth shall be set on edge."

a. **I awoke and looked around**: Apparently, much of the previous prophecy came to Jeremiah as he slept sweetly, perhaps coming to him in a dream.

b. **I will sow the house of Israel**: God promised to bless and restore the Jewish people, multiplying both their children and their livestock.

c. **I will watch over them to build and to plant**: Earlier in Jeremiah, God gave the prophet the commission *to root out and to pull down, to destroy and to throw down, to build and to plant* (Jeremiah 1:10). Much of the Book of Jeremiah to this point has been a work of plucking up and breaking down; yet God promised to also **build and to plant**.

d. **They shall say no more**: Jeremiah quoted what apparently was a common proverb in his day that promoted the idea that God was punishing Judah for the sins of their forefathers, and they themselves were relatively innocent. God clearly denied this, showing that He will judge individuals for their own sins (Ezekiel 18:1-3).

i. "The proverb quoted here occurs also in Ezekiel 18:2. It seems that the feeling was widespread that the nation was being punished for the sins of past generations and that Yahweh was unjust." (Thompson)

ii. "No child shall suffer Divine punition for the sin of his father; only so far as he acts in the same way can he be said to bear the sins of his parents." (Clarke)

C. The New Covenant.

1. (31-34) The glorious promise of the glorious New Covenant.

"Behold, the days are coming, says the Lord, when I will make a new covenant with the house of Israel and with the house of Judah— not according to the covenant that I made with their fathers in the day *that* I took them by the hand to lead them out of the land of Egypt, My covenant which they broke, 'though I was a husband to them, says the Lord. But this *is* the covenant that I will make with the house of Israel after those days, says the Lord: I will put My law in their minds, and write it on their hearts; and I will be their God, and they shall be My people. No more shall every man teach his neighbor, and every man his brother, saying, 'Know the Lord,' for they all shall know Me, from the least of them to the greatest of them, says the Lord. For I will forgive their iniquity, and their sin I will remember no more."

a. **The days are coming, says the Lord**: What Jeremiah prophesied as God's faithful messenger was not yet present in his day.

b. **I will make a new covenant**: God announced that at a time future to Jeremiah's day, *He* would **make a new covenant**. This **new covenant** would first be with **Israel**, but it would be **not according to the covenant** that God made with Israel in the Sinai desert.

i. Throughout the Bible, God reveals His plan of redemption through a series of covenants. After the extended story of the fall and ruin of humanity in Genesis 1-11, the story of the covenants begins.

- The Abrahamic Covenant promised to Abraham and His covenant descendants a *land*, a *nation*, and a *blessing* to extend to all nations (Genesis 12:1-3).
- The Mosaic or Sinai Covenant gave Israel the *law*, the *sacrifices*, and the *choice* of blessing or curse (Exodus 19).
- The Davidic Covenant that promised an *everlasting dynasty*, a *perfect ruler*, and the *Promised Messiah* (2 Samuel 7).
- God's plan of redemption through the covenants is completed and perfected in the New Covenant. Over the span of Old Testament passages that announce the new covenant (especially Ezekiel 11:16-20, 36:16-28, and 37:21-28), we see the promises of *gathered Israel*, of *cleansing and spiritual transformation*, and the *reign of the Messiah*.

ii. "The promise relates to a 'new covenant' and is a prediction of a radical change in God's economy (i.e., his dealing with humanity)." (Feinberg)

iii. Jesus specifically instituted this new covenant by His death on the cross, and He specifically instituted the recognition and remembrance of it with the bread and cup of communion (Matthew 26:28, Mark 14:24, Luke 22:20). It was future to Jeremiah's day, but it was put into effect by Jesus and specifically by His work of atoning sacrifice at the cross.

iv. The writer to the Hebrews quotes this passage and develops the theme of the new covenant, especially in contrast to the old (Hebrews 8:8, 8:13, 9:15, and 12:14).

c. **My covenant which they broke**: A new covenant was promised and needed because Israel did not and could not keep the covenant God made with them at Sinai. That covenant was not designed to be enough; it was preparation for the new covenant to come.

i. "The old covenant had taken a new lease of life in Jeremiah's early days, when the lost 'book of the covenant' was found and read and reaffirmed, to become the blueprint of Josiah's continuing reformation. Yet everything that we have read in Jeremiah confirms that 'the law made nothing perfect', for the response was skin-deep, and died with the death of Joshua." (Kidner)

d. **I will put My law into their minds, and write it on their hearts**: The new covenant brings *inner transformation*. The law of God was no longer only external; God would change the minds and hearts of those connected to Him by the new covenant.

i. The new covenant does not do away with or renounce the law. It makes the law *closer* and *more* important by setting it in the mind and heart, instead of on a stone tablet or page. "It would no longer be like the external one made with the fathers, but spiritual and internal, and based on an intimate knowledge of Jehovah." (Morgan)

ii. "Obedience to the Law is not a prior condition for entering the New Covenant. Rather, it is one of the promised blessings of the New Covenant." (Ryken)

iii. "Things required by the law are bestowed by the gospel. God demands obedience under the law: God works obedience under the gospel. Holiness is asked of us by the law: holiness is wrought in us by the gospel." (Spurgeon)

iv. Here, the heart is written upon in a good, positive sense. "The heart as a writing material is spoken of in Jeremiah 17:1 in relation to sin." (Thompson)

e. **I will be their God, and they shall be My people**: The new covenant brings *new relationship* with God. Those connected to God by the new covenant have personal, close relationship with God that they did not have before: **they all shall know Me, from the least of them to the greatest of them**.

i. Notably, this relationship with God had a *personal* aspect (**they all show know Me**). "Probably the most significant contribution which Jeremiah made to religious thought was inherent in his insistence that the new covenant involved a one-to-one relationship of the spirit. When the new covenant was inaugurated by the atoning work of Jesus Christ on Calvary, this important development of personal, as opposed to corporate, faith and spirituality was made real for the whole of mankind. Henceforth anyone who submitted himself consciously in faith to the person of Christ as Saviour and Lord could claim and receive membership in the church of God." (Harrison)

f. **I will forgive their iniquity, and their sin I will remember no more**: The new covenant brings *true cleansing from sin*. The sacrificial system under the old covenant could only *cover* sin and its guilt; the new covenant brings forgiveness so complete that it could be said that God no longer remembers the sin of those connected to Him through the new covenant.

i. "The new covenant does not envision sinlessness but forgiveness of sin resulting in restoration of fellowship with God." (Feinberg)

2. (35-37) God's everlasting love for Israel.

Thus says the Lord,
Who gives the sun for a light by day,
The ordinances of the moon and the stars for a light by night,
Who disturbs the sea,
And its waves roar
(The Lord of hosts *is* His name):
"If those ordinances depart
From before Me, says the Lord,
***Then* the seed of Israel shall also cease**
From being a nation before Me forever."
Thus says the Lord:
"If heaven above can be measured,
And the foundations of the earth searched out beneath,

I will also cast off all the seed of Israel
For all that they have done, says the LORD.

- a. **Thus says the LORD**: God introduces Himself with extreme descriptions of His incomparable power. He is the One who gives light, the planets and stars, rules over the storms and seas, and commands heavenly armies (**LORD of hosts**). This statement is clearly given remarkable seriousness.

    - i. **Who gives the sun**: "This regularity is the consequence of sovereign, divine will. These ordinances are not laws of *nature*, but of God." (Maclaren)

- b. **If those ordinances depart from before Me, says the LORD, then the seed of Israel shall also cease from being a nation before Me forever**: The message from God is both powerful and plain. God will stop thinking of and dealing with Israel as a nation when the sun, moon, and stars stop giving light and when the sea stops roaring. As long as those things continue, God will regard Israel as a nation **before** Him **forever**.

- c. **If heaven above can be measured, and the foundations of the earth searched out beneath, I will also cast off all the seed of Israel for all they have done**: For remarkable emphasis, God gave another powerful and plain declaration of the permanence of the Jewish people in His unfolding plan of the ages. Since it is impossible to measure the heavens or search out the foundations of the earth, God will never **cast off the seed of Israel** – *even* taking into account **all they have done**.

    - i. The New Testament later introduces the idea of *spiritual Israel*, an important concept: *For they are not all Israel who are of Israel* (Romans 9:6). The idea of spiritual Israel is significant, *but was not and is not in view* here in Jeremiah's prophecy. To claim that God intended for Jeremiah or anyone else of that day to understand this as regarding spiritual Israel and not genetic Israel does great violence to the text and context.

    - ii. It is impossible to conceive that God could state this principle in any stronger way. The descendants of Abraham, Isaac, and Jacob have an enduring role in God's plan of the ages until the end of the age.

3. (38-40) The restoration of the literal Jerusalem.

"Behold, the days are coming, says the LORD, that the city shall be built for the LORD from the Tower of Hananel to the Corner Gate. The surveyor's line shall again extend straight forward over the hill Gareb; then it shall turn toward Goath. And the whole valley of the dead bodies and of the ashes, and all the fields as far as the Brook Kidron, to the corner of the Horse Gate toward the east, *shall be* holy to the Lord. It shall not be plucked up or thrown down anymore forever."

a. **The city shall be built for the Lord**: God announced that the literal city of Jerusalem would be rebuilt, using specific geographic markers to clearly explain that He intended that literal, material Jerusalem be understood and not symbolic or spiritual Jerusalem. All of it **shall be holy to the Lord**.

> i. "Since a literal nation must have an actual geographical location in which to reside, it is now revealed that the capital, Jerusalem, will be rebuilt and expanded -- yes, the very city that Jeremiah was before long to see destroyed by the Chaldean army." (Feinberg)

> ii. "The Tower of Hananel was the northeast corner of the city....The Corner Gate probably refers to the one at the northwest corner of the city wall" (Feinberg)

> iii. "The sites of *Gareb* and *Goah* are unknown, but the verse seems to indicate an extension of the boundary of Jerusalem on the west side." (Harrison)

> iv. "In the broader context of prophecy, this passage will not permit an interpretation that applies it to a spiritual, heavenly, or symbolic Jerusalem. If that were possible, why is it so full of literal detail?" (Feinberg)

b. **It shall not be plucked up or thrown down anymore forever**: The restoration promised to Israel is *not* only spiritual; it is also material, extending to the city itself and its permanence.

> i. "This cannot mean the city built after the return from Babylon, for two reasons: 1. This is to be much *greater* in *extent*; 2. It is to be *permanent*, never to be *thrown down*, Jeremiah 31:40. It must therefore mean, if taken literally at all, the city that is to be built by them when they are brought in with the fulness of the Gentiles." (Clarke)

Jeremiah 32 – The Property Purchase from Prison

A. Buying a field as a sign for the future.

1. (1-2) Jerusalem under siege.

The word that came to Jeremiah from the LORD in the tenth year of Zedekiah king of Judah, which was the eighteenth year of Nebuchadnezzar. For then the king of Babylon's army besieged Jerusalem, and Jeremiah the prophet was shut up in the court of the prison, which *was in* the king of Judah's house.

a. **In the tenth year of Zedekiah**: Zedekiah was the last king before the final conquest of the Babylonians over Judah, and the final conquest began in his **tenth year**. Jeremiah wrote this even as **Babylon's army besieged Jerusalem**. It was an almost unbelievably stressful crisis for the whole city.

i. "According to Jeremiah 39:1 the siege of Jerusalem began in the ninth year of Zedekiah's reign. It was raised for a short period when Egyptian forces approached Jerusalem (Jeremiah 37:5), but was imposed once more when the Egyptians decided against battle." (Harrison)

b. **Jeremiah the prophet was shut up in the court of the prison**: With Nebuchadnezzar's army outside Jerusalem's walls, Jeremiah was inside the walls of the royal prison (**in the king of Judah's house**).

i. "The courtyard of the guard, probably a stockade (cf. Nehemiah 3:25), was the part of the palace area set apart for prisoners. (Friends could visit them there.) The soldiers who guarded the palace were quartered there." (Feinberg)

2. (3-5) Why Jeremiah was in prison.

For Zedekiah king of Judah had shut him up, saying, "Why do you prophesy and say, 'Thus says the LORD: "Behold, I will give this city into the hand of the king of Babylon, and he shall take it; and Zedekiah king of Judah shall not escape from the hand of the Chaldeans, but

shall surely be delivered into the hand of the king of Babylon, and shall speak with him face to face, and see him eye to eye; then he shall lead Zedekiah to Babylon, and there he shall be until I visit him," says the LORD; "though you fight with the Chaldeans, you shall not succeed"'?"

> a. **I will give this city into the hand of the king of Babylon**: This was the message that got Jeremiah thrown into prison. King **Zedekiah** didn't like that Jeremiah told people that the Babylonians would succeed in conquering the city that Zedekiah and others tried so hard to defend. It was a message of defeat, that **though you fight with the Chaldeans, you shall not succeed**.
>
>> i. "Even though Zedekiah witnessed the fulfillment of Jeremiah's predictions, he was angry enough to imprison him, as if this could alter what was happening. Such is the irrationality of unbelief." (Feinberg)
>
> b. **Zedekiah king of Judah shall not escape from the hand of the Chaldeans**: Jeremiah not only prophesied that Jerusalem would be conquered, but also that the king would be captured. This was obviously displeasing to the king, so he put Jeremiah into prison.
>
>> i. **And shall speak with him face to face, and see him eye to eye**: "This was no small punishment to Zedekiah, that he must look him in the face from whom he had so perfidiously revolted, even against oath; and hear his taunts, before he felt his fingers. How, then, will graceless persons do to stand before the King of kings, whom they have so greatly offended, at that great day?" (Trapp)

3. (6-12) The property deal from prison.

And Jeremiah said, "The word of the LORD came to me, saying, 'Behold, Hanamel the son of Shallum your uncle will come to you, saying, "Buy my field which *is* in Anathoth, for the right of redemption *is* yours to buy *it*."'" Then Hanamel my uncle's son came to me in the court of the prison according to the word of the LORD, and said to me, 'Please buy my field that *is* in Anathoth, which *is* in the country of Benjamin; for the right of inheritance *is* yours, and the redemption yours; buy *it* for yourself.' Then I knew that this was the word of the LORD. So I bought the field from Hanamel, the son of my uncle who *was* in Anathoth, and weighed *out to* him the money—seventeen shekels of silver. And I signed the deed and sealed *it*, took witnesses, and weighed the money on the scales. So I took the purchase deed, *both* that which was sealed *according* to the law and custom, and that which was open; and I gave the purchase deed to Baruch the son of Neriah, son of Mahseiah, in the presence of Hanamel my uncle's *son*, and in the presence of the witnesses who signed the purchase deed, before all the Jews who sat in the court of the prison.

a. **Buy my field which is in Anathoth**: God told Jeremiah that his cousin **Hanamel** would visit him in prison and ask him to buy a field in their hometown of **Anathoth** (Jeremiah 1:1). God told Jeremiah that Hanamel would offer it to him on the basis of **the right of redemption** – that the land was to remain in the family, and must therefore be offered to Jeremiah before anyone else (as in Ruth 4:6).

> i. **Anathoth** was about three miles outside Jerusalem. With Babylonian armies surrounding Jerusalem, the enemy already occupied Anathoth. Jeremiah was offered the purchase of land that was *already* under Babylonian control.
>
> ii. "It has been suggested that Hanamel was short of money due to the siege and that this sale was an obvious solution to this need. But the land itself, at Anathoth, was utterly worthless, since it was already in the hands of the Babylonians, and Jerusalem's days were numbered. Only a fool would buy, or expect another to buy, in such circumstances!" (Cundall)
>
> iii. "Now, this was a strange purchase for a rational man to make. Prudence could not justify it; it was purchasing an estate which was utterly valueless." (Spurgeon)

b. **Then Hanamel my uncle's son came to me in the court of the prison according to the word of the LORD**: It happened just as God told Jeremiah it would happen. His cousin came and offered him the land, because Jeremiah had **the right of inheritance** for this land. From this remarkable fulfillment, Jeremiah knew it **was the word of the LORD**.

> i. "Was there ever a more insensitive prison-visitor?" (Kidner)
>
> ii. **The right of inheritance**: "According to the Law of Moses (Leviticus 25:25-34), the Promised Land was a sacred inheritance. Property was not to leave the family. God did not want his people to go outside their bloodline to get help. If they fell into debt, one of their own kin was supposed to redeem their property." (Ryken)
>
> iii. "This passage reveals that the ancient laws of land tenure were still followed in Judah in spite of its apostasy." (Feinberg)
>
> iv. "It is possible that others closer to Hanamel had refused to redeem the property and that Jeremiah as a more distant kinsman had to be called in (Ruth 3:9-13; 4:1-12). In such disturbed times few relatives would exercise their rights in this respect." (Thompson)
>
> iv. Jeremiah bought the land when no one else would because he **knew that this was the word of the LORD**: "It would seem that the word of Jehovah came to him as an impression, as it so often comes to us. We

often have impressions which seem to be from the Lord. Let us rest assured that what He commands He will make possible. When the call is followed by the open door, we need have no hesitation." (Morgan)

c. So I bought the field from Hanamel: Because God so clearly told him to do it, Jeremiah bought a piece of property that was, in normal terms, an unwise investment. The Babylonian army occupied Anathoth, surrounded the walls of Jerusalem, and was ready to complete their conquest of the area. Jeremiah knew they would succeed, and when they did, his title to the land would be useless because the Babylonians would soon control *everything*. Yet he bought the property anyway.

i. The keepers of the prison and everyone else must have thought Jeremiah was crazy. **Hanamel** must have thought this was the easiest and best **seventeen shekels of silver** he ever made, especially when people needed every bit of money possible to buy food at the much higher prices during a siege.

ii. It may be that cousin Hanamel took advantage of Jeremiah in this situation by challenging him to match his actions to his words. He had prophesied that the land would be restored and blessed; if he really believed it, then he should be happy to buy this land. Hanamel challenged Jeremiah to put his money where his mouth was. One way or another, Jeremiah did what God told him to do – even if he doubted it a short time later (Jeremiah 32:24-25).

iii. "Jeremiah was commanded by God to do this because he was really preaching by what he did. The preacher must believe in what he preaches; and it may be that he will be called to do something which will be to his people the best possible proof that he really does believe it." (Spurgeon)

d. In the presence of witnesses who signed the purchase deed, before all the Jews who sat in the court of the prison: The property purchase itself was strange; it was even stranger in that the deal was conducted from **prison**. Still, Jeremiah completed the deal according to their legal customs.

i. **The purchase deed, both that which was sealed according to the law and custom, and that which was open**: "The proper legal procedures were observed as though the land were at peace. The deed consisted of a sealed copy comprising the contract and the conditions of sale as well as an open copy." (Harrison)

ii. "If the practice was that of the Jewish community at Elephantine in Egypt in the late fifth century BC, the contract was written out on papyrus and was then folded over several times, tied, and sealed. This was the closed official copy. An unsealed copy was attached to it for consultation… Similar 'title deeds' have been discovered in the Judean desert." (Thompson)

4. (13-15) The lesson of the property deal from prison: God will restore.

"Then I charged Baruch before them, saying, 'Thus says the LORD of hosts, the God of Israel: "Take these deeds, both this purchase deed which is sealed and this deed which is open, and put them in an earthen vessel, that they may last many days." For thus says the LORD of hosts, the God of Israel: "Houses and fields and vineyards shall be possessed again in this land."'"

a. **Then I charged Baruch before them**: Jeremiah 32 is the first mention of this **Baruch**, the son of Neriah (Jeremiah 32:12). Baruch was a scribe and an assistant to Jeremiah. Jeremiah spoke to him so that others would hear and be instructed.

b. **Put them in an earthen vessel, that they may last many days**: Jeremiah told Baruch to preserve and hide the title deed and details of the transaction so that they could be read later. This was something of a time capsule, holding items meant to be read in the future.

i. "The form of the transaction is interesting (cf. Leviticus 25:25-28), particularly the storage of the deeds in earthenware jars to ensure their preservation, a feature vividly illustrated in the preservation of the Dead Sea scrolls in similar containers for over 2,000 years." (Cundall)

ii. "To buy land overrun by the world's conqueror, and then to take elaborate care of the title-deeds was a striking affirmation, as solid as the silver that paid for it, that God would bring his people back to their inheritance." (Kidner)

c. **Houses and fields and vineyards shall be possessed again in this land**: This was God's promise, and the purpose for an otherwise foolish property purchase. Through revelation Jeremiah was absolutely sure that the Babylonians would conquer Jerusalem and Judah; yet he was also certain God would restore. The property purchase from prison was an expression of confident trust in God's promise that the land would **be possessed again.**

B. The prophet prays to understand.

1. (16-23) A prayer declaring the greatness of God and the failure of His people.

"Now when I had delivered the purchase deed to Baruch the son of Neriah, I prayed to the LORD, saying: 'Ah, Lord GOD! Behold, You have made the heavens and the earth by Your great power and outstretched

arm. There is nothing too hard for You. *You* show lovingkindness to thousands, and repay the iniquity of the fathers into the bosom of their children after them—the Great, the Mighty God, whose name *is* the LORD of hosts. *You are* great in counsel and mighty in work, for your eyes *are* open to all the ways of the sons of men, to give everyone according to his ways and according to the fruit of his doings. You have set signs and wonders in the land of Egypt, to this day, and in Israel and among *other* men; and You have made Yourself a name, as it is this day. You have brought Your people Israel out of the land of Egypt with signs and wonders, with a strong hand and an outstretched arm, and with great terror; You have given them this land, of which You swore to their fathers to give them—"a land flowing with milk and honey." And they came in and took possession of it, but they have not obeyed Your voice or walked in Your law. They have done nothing of all that You commanded them to do; therefore You have caused all this calamity to come upon them.'"

> a. **I prayed to the LORD**: After the prison property transaction, Jeremiah prayed regarding the matter. He began with a sigh, directed to Yahweh: **Ah, Lord GOD!**
>
>> i. "His heart began to boil with unbelief and carnal reasonings; he therefore setteth himself to pray down those distempers. As a man may sleep out his drunkenness, so he may pray away his perturbations." (Trapp)
>>
>> ii. "And what a prayer! What weight of matter, sublimity of expression, profound veneration, just conception, Divine unction, powerful pleading, and strength of faith! Historical, without flatness; condensed, without obscurity; confessing the greatest of crimes against the most righteous of Beings, without despairing of his mercy, or presuming on his goodness: a confession that, in fact, acknowledges that God's *justice should* smite and destroy, had not his infinite goodness said, I will pardon and spare." (Clarke)
>
> b. **Behold, You have made the heavens and the earth by Your great power**: In his prayer, Jeremiah recognized and praised the great power of God, confessing the truth, **there is nothing too hard for You**.
>
>> i. "Surely if God could make the heavens and the earth by his great power and by his stretched-out arm, He could easily bring it to pass that the Chaldeans should recede from the land, Israel again inhabit it, and the purchase and tenure of property be unhindered." (Meyer)
>
> c. **You show lovingkindness to thousands**: Jeremiah recognized the mercy and love of God.

d. **Your eyes are open to all the ways of the sons of men, to give everyone according to his ways**: Jeremiah recognized the justice and judgment of God.

e. **You have brought Your people Israel out of the land of Egypt**: Jeremiah recognized the particular love, favor, and work of God toward His **people Israel**. They were special objects of His power, mercy, and love.

> i. **You have set signs and wonders in the land of Egypt, to this day**: "Oresius writeth that the tracks of Pharaoh's chariot wheels are yet to be seen at the Red Sea. *Fides sit penes authorem.*" (Trapp)

f. **They have not obeyed Your voice or walked in Your law**: In contrast to the great love and goodness of God – especially as expressed toward Israel – Jeremiah noted the rebellion and disobedience of the same people who were the special object of His favor. This rebellion and disobedience was the reason for the great **calamity to come upon them**.

2. (24-25) Prayer for understanding.

'Look, the siege mounds! They have come to the city to take it; and the city has been given into the hand of the Chaldeans who fight against it, because of the sword and famine and pestilence. What You have spoken has happened; there You see *it!* And You have said to me, O Lord God, "Buy the field for money, and take witnesses"!—yet the city has been given into the hand of the Chaldeans.'"

a. **Look, the siege mounds!** Jeremiah's loving familiarity with God is seen in the way he felt he had to *show* God the **siege** works of the Babylonians surrounding Jerusalem.

b. **Sword and famine and pestilence**: This was life in an ancient city under siege. Some died by the **sword** at the walls of the city. Many others died from **famine** because food supplies were never refreshed. Many also died from **pestilence** as disease worked its way through the closed-up city.

c. **Buy the field for money, and take witnesses**: It was hard for Jeremiah to understand *why* God told him to make the property purchase from prison. The Chaldeans were certainly going to conquer the city and the region. Even if God *could* restore His people to the land, they didn't deserve it. This didn't make much sense to Jeremiah, but he did the right thing: he looked to God and prayed for understanding.

> i. "It was not a sign of Jeremiah's faith, for he was perplexed, while obedient. The sign was in the command; it was God's sign to His servant." (Morgan)

C. Promise of judgment, promise of restoration.

1. (26-35) The promise of judgment.

Then the word of the LORD came to Jeremiah, saying, "Behold, I *am* the LORD, the God of all flesh. Is there anything too hard for Me? Therefore thus says the LORD: 'Behold, I will give this city into the hand of the Chaldeans, into the hand of Nebuchadnezzar king of Babylon, and he shall take it. And the Chaldeans who fight against this city shall come and set fire to this city and burn it, with the houses on whose roofs they have offered incense to Baal and poured out drink offerings to other gods, to provoke Me to anger; because the children of Israel and the children of Judah have done only evil before Me from their youth. For the children of Israel have provoked Me only to anger with the work of their hands,' says the LORD. 'For this city has been to Me *a provocation of* My anger and My fury from the day that they built it, even to this day; so I will remove it from before My face because of all the evil of the children of Israel and the children of Judah, which they have done to provoke Me to anger—they, their kings, their princes, their priests, their prophets, the men of Judah, and the inhabitants of Jerusalem. And they have turned to Me the back, and not the face; though I taught them, rising up early and teaching *them,* yet they have not listened to receive instruction. But they set their abominations in the house which is called by My name, to defile it. And they built the high places of Baal which *are* in the Valley of the Son of Hinnom, to cause their sons and their daughters to pass through *the fire* to Molech, which I did not command them, nor did it come into My mind that they should do this abomination, to cause Judah to sin.'

> a. **I am the LORD, the God of all flesh. Is there anything too hard for Me**: In response to the prayer of Jeremiah, God first affirmed His power and might in the same terms as Jeremiah prayed. Jeremiah said to the Lord, *there is nothing too hard for You* (Jeremiah 32:17). God replied back to His praying servant, **Is there anything too hard for Me?**
>
>> i. "We look upon the church at home in the present day. It is steeped in worldliness, and smothered with false doctrine. Lo! the many have turned aside from the gospel, and given themselves up to a thousand errors: how can the evil be cured? It is to be cured; it must be cured; it shall be cured, for thus saith Jehovah- 'Is anything too hard for me?'" (Spurgeon)
>
> b. **I will give this city into the hand of the Chaldeans**: God affirmed again the promise made many times before. Jerusalem and Judah would

fall to the Babylonians. God did not tell Jeremiah to buy the land because Jerusalem *wouldn't* be conquered.

c. **On whose roofs they have offered incense to Baal and poured out drink offerings to other gods**: God reminded Jeremiah of all the sins of Judah and Jerusalem that invited the punishment of God. All these sins – mainly idolatry of different forms – were **a provocation** of God's **anger**.

> i. **For this city has been to Me a provocation of My anger and My fury from the day that they built it**: "Actually, Solomon completed the building of the city, and he was the first of all Israel's kings to fall into idolatry." (Feinberg)
>
> ii. **I taught them, rising up early and teaching them**: "From the frequent reference to this, we may naturally conclude that *morning preaching* prevailed much in Judea." (Clarke)
>
> iii. **They set their abominations in the house which is called by My name, to defile it**: "The height of the nation's impiety was reached when the people set up their idols in the temple of God himself. Their obscene symbols had been removed during Josiah's reforms. But they were reintroduced in the years of apostasy after Josiah's reign (cf. Jeremiah 7:30; 2 Kings 23:4, 6; Ezekiel 8:3-11)." (Feinberg)

d. **To cause their sons and daughters to pass through the fire to Molech**: Their idolatry went so far that they actually participated in the Canaanite cult of child sacrifice. Even King Ahaz (2 Kings 16:3) and King Manasseh (2 Kings 21:6) took part in this horrific practice.

> i. There is little or none archaeological evidence for child sacrifice among the Israelites of this period. This means that either the practice was very rare or diligently covered up. This may be God's way of saying that even if the practice was rare, it was an abomination to Him.
>
> ii. "The *high places* witnessed the most important rite of Molech cultic worship, namely the offering of human sacrifice (*cf.* Jeremiah 19:5; Leviticus 18:21)." (Harrison)
>
> iii. **Nor did it come into My mind that they should do this abomination**: "So abhorrent was this practice that the Lord by a strong anthropomorphism says that it had never entered his mind that his favored people would stoop so low." (Feinberg)

2. (36-41) The promise of restoration, fulfilled in the new covenant.

"Now therefore, thus says the LORD, the God of Israel, concerning this city of which you say, 'It shall be delivered into the hand of the king of Babylon by the sword, by the famine, and by the pestilence: Behold, I

will gather them out of all countries where I have driven them in My anger, in My fury, and in great wrath; I will bring them back to this place, and I will cause them to dwell safely. They shall be My people, and I will be their God; then I will give them one heart and one way, that they may fear Me forever, for the good of them and their children after them. And I will make an everlasting covenant with them, that I will not turn away from doing them good; but I will put My fear in their hearts so that they will not depart from Me. Yes, I will rejoice over them to do them good, and I will assuredly plant them in this land, with all My heart and with all My soul.'**

a. **Behold, I will gather them out of all the countries where I have driven them**: The same God who promised and fulfilled judgment also promised and would fulfill restoration. One was as sure as the other. Yet these promises, beginning here with the promise to **gather** Israel from the nations back into their own land, looked beyond what was fulfilled in the return under Ezra and Nehemiah some 70 years after the Babylonian exile. These are promises of the new covenant, as previously described in Jeremiah 31:31-34.

i. "*I have driven them* (Jeremiah 32:37) is a prophetic perfect, since the exile has still not taken place." (Harrison)

b. **They shall be My people, and I will be their God**: As with other new covenant passages, God promised a personal and close relationship with His people under the new covenant.

c. **I will give them one heart and one way**: As with other new covenant passages, God promised inner transformation that would bring blessing to successive generations (**for the good of them and their children**).

d. **Yes, I will rejoice over them to do them good**: A further aspect of the new covenant is that the disposition of God towards His people would be changed; instead of judgment, He would rejoice **over them to do them good**. God was so zealous to accomplish this that He promised to perform it **with all My heart and all My soul**.

i. **I will make an everlasting covenant with them**: "Not only will the covenant be new, as promised there, but *everlasting*." (Kidner)

ii. What is unsaid in this passage but detailed in other passages in the Hebrew and Greek Scriptures, is that this change of disposition is due to the atoning work of the Messiah, where His righteousness is granted to His people by faith.

iii. **With all My heart and all My soul**: "See how God puts his whole heart to the work when he is blessing his people. When he forgives sin, it is with his whole heart and soul. May we, with our whole heart and soul, repent of our sin; and then, with all our heart and soul, serve the Lord!" (Spurgeon)

iv. "Our God does not give us his mercies off-hand, as we see a man fling a penny to a beggar. No, no, he blesses us with his whole heart, and with his whole soul." (Spurgeon)

3. (42-46) Connecting the promises to Jeremiah's purchase of land.

"For thus says the LORD: 'Just as I have brought all this great calamity on this people, so I will bring on them all the good that I have promised them. And fields will be bought in this land of which you say, "*It is* desolate, without man or beast; it has been given into the hand of the Chaldeans." Men will buy fields for money, sign deeds and seal *them*, and take witnesses, in the land of Benjamin, in the places around Jerusalem, in the cities of Judah, in the cities of the mountains, in the cities of the lowland, and in the cities of the South; for I will cause their captives to return,' says the LORD."

a. **Just as I have brought all this great calamity on this people, so I will bring on them all the good that I have promised**: The principle is repeated for the sake of emphasis. When Jeremiah spoke this prophecy, the Babylonian armies surrounded Jerusalem and were about to conquer the city – that was sure. It was **just as** sure that God would **bring on them all the good** He had promised.

b. **Men will buy fields for money**: When God brought the restoration – either the near restoration under Ezra and Nehemiah or the ultimate restoration under the new covenant – life would be so safe and secure in Israel that real estate transactions would again happen as normal.

i. **In the land of Benjamin**: "Benjamin may have been mentioned first because of the property of Jeremiah at Anathoth." (Feinberg)

Jeremiah 33 – Promises from the Prison

A. From destruction to restoration.

1. (1-3) Great and mighty things.

Moreover the word of the LORD came to Jeremiah a second time, while he was still shut up in the court of the prison, saying, "Thus says the LORD who made it, the LORD who formed it to establish it (the LORD is His name): 'Call to Me, and I will answer you, and show you great and mighty things, which you do not know.'"

> a. **While he was still shut up in the court of the prison**: As in Jeremiah 32, this word came to Jeremiah during the terrible final siege of the Babylonians against Jerusalem in the last years of King Zedekiah's reign. Zedekiah put Jeremiah in the royal prison for preaching in the name of the LORD that Babylonians would succeed (Jeremiah 32:1-5).

> b. **Thus says the LORD who made it, the LORD who formed it**: In this section there is a strong emphasis on the name Yahweh (**LORD**), the name of God emphasizing His covenant relationship with Israel. God will speak of His faithfulness to the covenant.

> c. **Call to Me, and I will answer you, and show you great and mighty things, which you do not know**: God invited Jeremiah and all who heard to come to Him in faith-filled prayer, confident of His answer. This promise is especially remarkable considering the circumstances: enduring the terror of a siege and the soon fulfillment of promised judgment. As the judgment was even at the door, God spoke a word of hope and invitation and faith to Jeremiah and Jerusalem.

>> i. "He cries to us, Call unto Me, call unto me. Little prayer, little blessing; more prayer, more blessings; much prayer, much blessing." (Meyer)

ii. **Mighty things**: "The MT *besurot* (RSV *hidden things*) usually means 'that which is inaccessible', and here that which is beyond the normal reach of human knowledge." (Harrison)

iii. "The things to be revealed are 'unsearchable' (*basur*, literally, 'inaccessible') because they are beyond the grasp of human knowledge. The principle adjective *basur* is used of the strongly fortified cities of Canaan in Deuteronomy 1:28 ('walled up'); here it refers to matters so far beyond human insight that they require divine revelation." (Feinberg)

2. (4-9) Restoration to a ruined city.

For thus says the LORD, the God of Israel, concerning the houses of this city and the houses of the kings of Judah, which have been pulled down to *fortify* against the siege mounds and the sword: "They come to fight with the Chaldeans, but *only* to fill their places with the dead bodies of men whom I will slay in My anger and My fury, all for whose wickedness I have hidden My face from this city. Behold, I will bring it health and healing; I will heal them and reveal to them the abundance of peace and truth. And I will cause the captives of Judah and the captives of Israel to return, and will rebuild those places as at the first. I will cleanse them from all their iniquity by which they have sinned against Me, and I will pardon all their iniquities by which they have sinned and by which they have transgressed against Me. Then it shall be to Me a name of joy, a praise, and an honor before all nations of the earth, who shall hear all the good that I do to them; they shall fear and tremble for all the goodness and all the prosperity that I provide for it."

a. **Concerning the houses of this city and the houses of the kings of Judah, which have been pulled down to fortify**: God spoke this with an eye to the houses in Jerusalem that were now rubble, having been dismantled to make defensive works against the attacking Babylonians. This was a distressing and depressing sight – but didn't take away the truth of God's promise to restore.

b. **They come to fight with the Chaldeans, but only to fill their places with the dead bodies**: They put a lot of work and people into defending the city, but it would amount to nothing. They should have listened to the previous word of the LORD, announcing the inevitability of God's judgment through the Babylonians.

c. **Behold, I will bring it health and healing**: Jerusalem was filled with destruction and death, and to *this* city God promised to bring **health and healing**, to **reveal to them the abundance of peace and truth**. The promises are stated in ways that include the nearer restoration under Nehemiah and Ezra, but are only truly fulfilled in the new covenant.

- **I will cause the captives of Judah and the captives of Israel to return**: In the new covenant, God will one day gather His scattered people from both the southern and northern kingdoms.
- **I will cleanse them from all their iniquity**: In the new covenant, God will grant a special forgiveness of sin, where sins are not merely covered, but taken away.
- **They shall be to Me a name of joy, a praise, and an honor**: In the new covenant, God will bring such restored relationship that Israel will bring honor to Him instead of defaming His name.

  i. "The great and unsearchable things are now revealed. Yahweh will bring healing, peace, security, restoration, cleansing, and forgiveness." (Thompson)

  ii. **I will cleanse them…I will pardon**: "Cleansing removes guilt, pollution, defilement, morally. Pardon brings the offender back into relationship of favour and fellowship. God never pardons polluted souls; He first cleanses them. Pardon, apart from the communication of purity, would perpetuate pollution, and so violate the moral order beyond remedy." (Morgan)

d. **They shall fear and tremble for all the goodness and all the prosperity that I provide for it**: The contrast is remarkable. At the time Jeremiah delivered this prophecy, God's people were full of fear and trembling because of destruction and death. Here they would **fear and tremble** because of the greatness of God's blessing in restoring His people.

3. (10-11) The voice of gladness.

Thus says the LORD: "Again there shall be heard in this place—of which you say, 'It *is* desolate, without man and without beast'—in the cities of Judah, in the streets of Jerusalem that are desolate, without man and without inhabitant and without beast, the voice of joy and the voice of gladness, the voice of the bridegroom and the voice of the bride, the voice of those who will say:

'Praise the LORD of hosts,
For the LORD is good,
For His mercy *endures* forever'—

***and* of those *who will* bring the sacrifice of praise into the house of the LORD. For I will cause the captives of the land to return as at the first," says the LORD.**

a. **There shall be heard in this place**: In Jerusalem under siege, the sounds of the city were terrible. One can imagine the miserable screams, cries, groans, and the sound of crashing and destruction. Those terrible sounds were eventually replaced by a terrible quiet – of a **desolate** Jerusalem, **without inhabitant and without beast**. God promised better sounds would come.

b. **The voice of joy and the voice of gladness**: Instead of the terrible sounds or more terrible quiet, restored Jerusalem would be filled with the happy sounds of blessed, prosperous people. The sound would be like that heard at the best party ever – a wedding, with **the voice of the bridegroom and the voice of the bride**.

i. "The sounds of joy and gladness and the voice of the bridegroom and of the bride would be heard again, in a reversal of Jeremiah's words of judgment in 7:34; 16:9; 25:10." (Thompson)

c. **Praise the Lord of hosts, for the Lord is good, for His mercy endures forever**: Instead of the anguished cries of a city under judgment, they would hear the sound of people praising God for His goodness and ever-enduring mercy.

i. "Joy and gladness will not only mark the relationships of God's people but will also mark their worship in his temple. The liturgical words were those used by the Levitical singers in the temple service (Psalm 106:1) and showed that the temple would be rebuilt and the ministry restored as in preexilic days." (Feinberg)

4. (12-13) The wonderful extent of the restoration.

Thus says the Lord of hosts: "In this place which is desolate, without man and without beast, and in all its cities, there shall again be a dwelling place of shepherds causing *their* flocks to lie down. In the cities of the mountains, in the cities of the lowland, in the cities of the South, in the land of Benjamin, in the places around Jerusalem, and in the cities of Judah, the flocks shall again pass under the hands of him who counts *them*," says the Lord.

a. **There shall again be a dwelling place of shepherds causing their flocks to lie down**: Instead of a chaos and despair of a city under siege, there would be the peace and goodness of the restored city.

b. **In the cities of the mountains, in the cities of the lowlands**: God described different geographical regions of the land of Israel, explaining that the restoration promised would extend to all of these regions. It wouldn't only be Jerusalem restored, but all the land.

i. **Under the hands of him who counts them**: "Strangely, the Targum has a messianic interpretation here and substitutes the word 'Messiah' for 'the one who counts them.'" (Feinberg)

ii. "He may even have touched each one as it passed through the entrance." (Thompson)

5. (14-17) The certainty of the promise to the house of David.

"Behold, the days are coming," says the LORD, "that I will perform that good thing which I have promised to the house of Israel and to the house of Judah:

In those days and at that time
I will cause to grow up to David
A Branch of righteousness;
He shall execute judgment and righteousness in the earth.
In those days Judah will be saved,
And Jerusalem will dwell safely.
And this *is the name* **by which she will be called:**
THE LORD OUR RIGHTEOUSNESS"

For thus says the LORD: "David shall never lack a man to sit on the throne of the house of Israel; nor shall the priests, the Levites, lack a man to offer burnt offerings before Me, to kindle grain offerings, and to sacrifice continually."

a. **I will perform that good thing which I have promised**: These promises of restoration – fulfilled in part under Ezra and Nehemiah, fulfilled in whole with the completion of the new covenant – these promises were a remarkable contrast to the present state of destruction in Judah and Jerusalem. God repeats them for assurance and emphasis.

i. "This beautiful passage (vv. 14-26) is not in the LXX and has therefore been subject to many commentators." (Feinberg)

b. **In those days and at that time I will cause to grow up to David a Branch of righteousness**: In the context of the new covenant promises, God promised that a descendant of the line of David would be the **Branch of righteousness** (as in Isaiah 4:2 and 11:1; as in Jeremiah 23:5).

i. "Jeremiah does not reveal as much about the coming Messiah as Isaiah does, but nevertheless provides glimpses of Christ as the Fountain of living waters (Jeremiah 2:13), the good Shepherd (Jeremiah 23:4; 31:10), the righteous Branch (Jeremiah 23:5), the Redeemer (Jeremiah 50:34), the Lord our righteousness (Jeremiah 23:6) and David the king (Jeremiah 30:9)." (Harrison)

c. **He shall execute judgment and righteousness in the earth**: The great promises of restoration and blessing under the completion of the new covenant would come about through an appointed Man, the **Branch of righteousness**, who would be a descendant of David. He will reign not only over Jerusalem and Israel, but also over **the earth**, bringing **judgment and righteousness**.

d. **This is the name by which she will be called: The Lord Our Righteousness**: *This* would be the title of restored Jerusalem under her Messiah, the Branch from the line of David. No more would it be a place of idolatry, rebellion, shame, and the destruction that came from all those. It would be a city and a people who truly found their righteousness in the LORD.

i. "Salvation and safety are in store for Judah and Jerusalem because of the presence of justice and righteousness personified. The name given the Messiah in Jeremiah 23:6 is here given to Jerusalem. She can have the same name as the Messiah because she reflects that righteousness the Messiah bestows on her." (Feinberg)

ii. "There is, however, no need to allegorize the name of the city as though it were the NT church. On what grounds could the impartation of such a concept be justified here? Jerusalem will be called by his name because she will partake of his nature, which has been graciously imparted to her." (Feinberg)

B. **The permanent character of God's covenant.**

1. (19-22) The covenant to David is as certain as day and night.

And the word of the LORD came to Jeremiah, saying, "Thus says the LORD: 'If you can break My covenant with the day and My covenant with the night, so that there will not be day and night in their season, then My covenant may also be broken with David My servant, so that he shall not have a son to reign on his throne, and with the Levites, the priests, My ministers. As the host of heaven cannot be numbered, nor the sand of the sea measured, so will I multiply the descendants of David My servant and the Levites who minister to Me.'"

a. **If you can break My covenant with the day and My covenant with the night**: God's covenant with David – the promise to bring the Messiah who will reign from his line (2 Samuel 7:12-16) – was as certain as the reliability of **day** and **night**.

b. **A son to reign on his throne, and with the Levites, the priests, My ministers**: The promised Messiah would reign on David's throne, and with many around Him to reign with Him.

> i. "However prosperous, a people kingless and without a priesthood would consider itself no better than a rabble: so here is the climax of the promise." (Kidner)
>
> ii. "The promised dynasty will be permanent, and will have a succession of levitical priests who will constitute a valid ministry." (Harrison)
>
> iii. These words do not claim a constant reign of David's line and service of Leviticial priests; it claims an *unending* reign and service.

c. **So will I multiply the descendants of David My servant and the Levites who minister to Me**: God promised *innumerable servants* to come alongside of the Messiah to come from David's line. This is fulfilled in the multitudes who reign with Jesus under the new covenant (Revelation 7:9-10).

> i. "As for the pledge that David would *never lack a man to sit on the throne ... of Israel* (Jeremiah 33:17, 21a), we can see how profoundly the fulfillment in the person of Christ transcends the expectation (Revelation 11:15; 22:16). The same is true of the promise to the Levitical priests, since all their atoning work was done to perfection and for eternity by him, and their role in offering 'the sacrifice of praise' has been perpetuated and extended in the royal priesthood of believers." (Kidner)
>
> ii. "In our passage, however, the promise contains no hint of the hidden elements in its fulfillment, but (as A.W. Streane puts it) is 'clothed in a Jewish dress, the only form in which it could present any meaning to those to whom it was delivered'." (Kidner)
>
> iii. "Monarchy and priesthood were the two bases of the OT theocracy. When these appeared to be most in danger of extinction in Jeremiah's day, we find their continuance couched in sure and irrevocable terms." (Feinberg)

2. (23-24) The words of those who despise His people.

Moreover the word of the LORD **came to Jeremiah, saying, "Have you not considered what these people have spoken, saying, 'The two families which the L**ORD **has chosen, He has also cast them off'? Thus they have despised My people, as if they should no more be a nation before them."**

> a. **The two families which the L**ORD **has chosen, He has also cast them off**: The **two families** are those of the northern kingdom of Israel and the

southern kingdom of Judah. There were some (and are some today) who say that though God once chose them, He has now **cast them off**.

b. Thus they have despised My people as if they should no more be a nation before them: God said of those who thought that Israel was cast off from His love or plan that they **despised** His people and therefore sinned. They denied that Israel continued as **a nation**, a collective people with whom God had a special plan and purpose, and a nation **before them** – not only before God, but also before the world.

i. In the new covenant, the purpose of God extends far beyond Israel but never forsakes Israel. Those who say God has **cast them off** and that He is finished with them as a **nation** commit the great sin of despising His people.

3. (25-26) The promise repeated.

"Thus says the LORD: 'If My covenant *is* not with day and night, *and if* I have not appointed the ordinances of heaven and earth, then I will cast away the descendants of Jacob and David My servant, *so* that I will not take *any* of his descendants *to be* rulers over the descendants of Abraham, Isaac, and Jacob. For I will cause their captives to return, and will have mercy on them.'"

a. **If My covenant is not with day and night**: For emphasis, God repeated the same figure used in Jeremiah 33:19-21 to communicate the permanence of the covenant.

i. "God placed the sun and the moon on the bargaining table. He offered the heavenly bodies as a security deposit for his covenant promise. If God ever fails to provide an eternal King or a permanent priest, then the sun and the moon will be yours to keep!" (Ryken)

ii. "Nature will utterly collapse before God will go back on the slightest promise to his people." (Feinberg)

iii. "It should be noted, if only in passing, that these verses form part of the foundation for the modern study of science. They assert that the regularity of day and night is not the product of evolutionary chance. Rather, God has established a covenant with the sun and the moon." (Ryken)

b. **Over the descendants of Abraham, Isaac, and Jacob**: God spoke regarding the *genetic* descendants of Israel, not only spiritual descendants. Again, the new covenant reaches out to the whole world, not only to Israel; but it does not ignore or set aside Israel.

i. "This passage has been a *crux interpretum* for expositors. It is especially difficult for those who hold an amillennial position in eschatology. The only resort for them is in allegorization of the text or the use of a dual hermeneutic." (Feinberg)

Jeremiah 34 – The Emancipation Revocation

A. The word of the LORD against Zedekiah, King of Judah.

1. (1-3) God tells Zedekiah of the soon fall of Jerusalem.

The word which came to Jeremiah from the LORD, when Nebuchadnezzar king of Babylon and all his army, all the kingdoms of the earth under his dominion, and all the people, fought against Jerusalem and all its cities, saying, "Thus says the LORD, the God of Israel: 'Go and speak to Zedekiah king of Judah and tell him, "Thus says the LORD: 'Behold, I will give this city into the hand of the king of Babylon, and he shall burn it with fire. And you shall not escape from his hand, but shall surely be taken and delivered into his hand; your eyes shall see the eyes of the king of Babylon, he shall speak with you face to face, and you shall go to Babylon.'"'

> a. **Fought against Jerusalem and all its cities**: This prophecy against Zedekiah and his kingdom came in his tenth or eleventh year. Nebuchadnezzar and the Babylonian army had come against Jerusalem and circled the city in a siege.
>
>> i. Verses 21 and 22 of this chapter give further information about the time and context. God said regarding the Babylonian army that they had *gone back from* Jerusalem, but that He would *command…and cause them to return to this city* (Jeremiah 34:22). The events of this chapter are in the context of when the Egyptians came against the Babylonians during this siege, and Nebuchadnezzar briefly withdrew from the siege of Jerusalem to fight the Egyptians to the south (Jeremiah 37:5-10). The leaders and people of Jerusalem thought they were delivered, but God and His prophet knew the Babylonians would return.
>>
>> ii. "The strategy of the invaders was to hold the capital under siege and reduce the outlying strongholds one by one during the next year. When only Lachish and Azekah remained (Jeremiah 34:7) it seemed

that some hope of relief had at last appeared, as news of the approach of an Egyptian army under Pharaoh Hophra (Jeremiah 44:30) had reached the capital, probably in the late spring or early summer of 588 BC" (Thompson)

iii. **All the kingdoms of the earth under his dominion**: "Daniel 3:2-4 and 4:1 show the vast extent of the neo-Babylonian empire. Soldiers came from subject countries to join in the siege (cf. 2 Kings 24:2)." (Feinberg)

b. **I will give this city into the hand of the king of Babylon**: Despite the temporarily lifted siege, God wanted Zedekiah to know that the city and the kingdom would be conquered by the will and command of God. It wasn't just the Babylonians who were against Judah.

i. Jerusalem was indeed burned with fire. *He burned the house of the LORD and the king's house; all the houses of Jerusalem, that is, all the houses of the great, he burned with fire* (2 Kings 25:9).

c. **You shall not escape from his hand**: Sometimes when a city or a kingdom falls, the king escapes. God wanted Zedekiah to know this would not be the case. He would be captured by the Babylonian king who set him on the throne of Judah as a vassal king (2 Chronicles 36:10), the same Nebuchadnezzar whom he rebelled against. Nebuchadnezzar would judge him **face to face**.

i. "It was expected that he would suffer severe punishment. The Hebrew idiom is very vivid, 'Your eyes will look at the eyes of the king of Babylon and his mouth will speak with your mouth.' Such confrontations are well known in the extant documents of the ancient Near East." (Thompson)

ii. "The Lord's message to him was that he was not to be led astray by the temporary respite in the siege; the situation was actually hopeless." (Feinberg)

iii. "Remembering the readiness of God to take back a threat (Jeremiah 18:8, 11), and the clemency of Nebuchadrezzar to Jeremiah for his advocacy of surrender (Jeremiah 39:11-12), we may wonder whether even now Zedekiah might have found mercy had he repented." (Kidner)

2. (4-5) The promise that Zedekiah would die a natural death.

Yet hear the word of the LORD, O Zedekiah king of Judah! Thus says the LORD concerning you: 'You shall not die by the sword. You shall die in peace; as in the ceremonies of your fathers, the former kings who

were before you, so they shall burn incense for you and lament for you, *saying, "Alas, lord!" For I have pronounced the word, says the* LORD.'"

a. **You shall not die by the sword**: Zedekiah had a terrible fate in front of him, but he did not **die by the sword**. Soon after this prophecy, the Babylonians captured **Zedekiah**. *Then they killed the sons of Zedekiah before his eyes, put out the eyes of Zedekiah, bound him with bronze fetters, and took him to Babylon* (2 Kings 25:7).

i. **You shall not die by the sword**: "And yet Josiah, his father, a far better man, did; so unsearchable are God's judgments, and his ways past finding out." (Trapp)

b. **So they shall burn incense for you and lament for you**: Zedekiah had the small consolations of a peaceful death and remembrance with lament by his subjects. Some believe this was a *conditional* promise, and because Zedekiah did not turn to God it was never fulfilled.

i. "The Jews have a tradition that Nebuchadnezzar, upon a festival day, caused him to be brought out of prison, and so abused him before his princes to make them sport, that for shame and grief thereof he died soon after; and then Nebuchadnezzar, to make him some recompense, caused him to be honourably buried, suffering his former subjects to burn sweet odours and to bewail his death." (Clarke)

ii. "The 'funeral fire in honor of you fathers' is not to be confused with the funeral pyre so well known in India. Cremation has never been a prevailing custom among the Jews." (Feinberg)

3. (6-7) Jeremiah brings the word to King Zedekiah.

Then Jeremiah the prophet spoke all these words to Zedekiah king of Judah in Jerusalem, when the king of Babylon's army fought against Jerusalem and all the cities of Judah that were left, against Lachish and Azekah; for *only* these fortified cities remained of the cities of Judah.

a. **Jeremiah the prophet spoke all these words to Zedekiah**: Jeremiah remained a courageous prophet. Zedekiah had the power to harm Jeremiah in many ways, but the prophet did not fail to deliver the message from God.

b. **The cities of Judah that were left, against Lachish and Azekah**: The city of **Lachish** was some thirty miles southwest of Jerusalem. Because of the Egyptian threat, Nebuchadnezzar had to secure the strategic points to the south before the complete conquest of Jerusalem.

i. Archaeologists have discovered a pit in Lachish with the remains of about 1,500 casualties of Nebuchadnezzar's attack. The *Lachish Letters* were discovered, urgent writings on bits of pottery, all regarding the Babylonian attack and conquest of cities like **Lachish and Azekah** (which are specifically mentioned in the Lachish Letters).

iii. "A Lachish, twenty-one ostraca (i.e. broken pieces of pottery used for writing lists, letters, etc.) have been discovered dating from the time of the Babylonian invasion. One of them (Ostracon iv) reads, '… we are watching for the signals of Lachish, according to all the indications which my lord hath given, for we cannot see Azekah.' This is usually taken as an allusion that Azekah had just fallen to the Babylonians, and that the smoke-signal or beacon, indicating that the city was still holding out, was no longer made." (Cundall)

iii. "These were two cities of Judah of considerable importance: they had been strongly fortified by Rehoboam, 2 Chronicles 11:9-11; 2 Chronicles 32:9." (Clarke)

B. The sin of setting slaves free and bringing them back into servitude.

1. (8-11) Going back on a covenant to release slaves from their service.

***This is* the word that came to Jeremiah from the LORD, after King Zedekiah had made a covenant with all the people who *were* at Jerusalem to proclaim liberty to them: that every man should set free his male and female slave—a Hebrew man or woman—that no one should keep a Jewish brother in bondage. Now when all the princes and all the people, who had entered into the covenant, heard that everyone should set free his male and female slaves, that no one should keep them in bondage anymore, they obeyed and let *them* go. But afterward they changed their minds and made the male and female slaves return, whom they had set free, and brought them into subjection as male and female slaves.**

a. **King Zedekiah had made a covenant with all the people who were at Jerusalem to proclaim liberty**: At some time in his reign (likely when the Babylonians threatened to conquer Jerusalem), King Zedekiah proclaimed emancipation for the **Hebrew** slaves in Judah.

i. With ancient Israel, as in the *entire* ancient world, there were people who worked for others on the principle of servitude. They were *slaves* in some sense, though not necessarily in the brutal and degraded sense most think of slavery.

ii. Some think that the Bible is *responsible* for slavery. The opposite is true; slavery existed long before Israel or Moses. The Bible is responsible for the *elimination* of slavery, not its establishment.

iii. There were four basic ways a Hebrew might become a slave to another Hebrew.

- In extreme poverty, they might sell their liberty (Leviticus 25:39).
- A father might sell a daughter as a servant into a home with the intention that she would eventually marry into that family (Exodus 21:7).
- In the case of bankruptcy, a man might become servant to his creditors (2 Kings 4:1).
- If a thief had nothing with which to pay proper restitution (Exodus 22:3-4).

iv. "That the people of Israel might be enslaved to their own countrymen was largely a matter of economics. Men in debt might accept a status of servitude till their debt was liquidated." (Thompson)

v. The ideas of *man-stealing* and life-long servitude – the concepts many have of slavery – simply do not apply to the practice of slavery in the Old Testament. Normally, slavery was:

- Chosen or mutually arranged.
- Of limited duration.
- Highly regulated.

vi. **Hebrew**: "The term *Hebrew* (*ibri*) is significant. In the OT it was not normally used by the people of Israel of themselves but appeared in periods in the history when they were in a condition of servitude, as in Egypt in pre-Exodus days, and at the time of the Philistine domination." (Thompson)

b. **They obeyed and let them go**: Because of Zedekiah's command and leadership, they immediately set their slaves free. However, from the words following in this chapter, it seems that they did not let their slaves free before their appointed time. It seems that these were slaves who had been kept past the six years set by the Law of Moses (Exodus 21:2-4).

i. "In their distress they made some shows of remorse, and some overtures of reformation." (Clarke)

ii. It seems that Zedekiah and the people of Israel did not make a generous act; they simply stopped disobeying the command of God in Exodus 21 and Deuteronomy 15:12-15. It seemed that the people of Jerusalem and Judah of that time followed the ancient laws regarding property transfer to the letter (Jeremiah 32:9-15). They didn't obey at all the ancient laws regarding setting Hebrew slaves free in the seventh year.

iii. If we are generous to the people of Judah and Jerusalem, we might say they obeyed the command to set the slaves free because they were desperate and sorry under the Babylonian siege and repented of their prior sin. It is more likely that they did this because under siege the masters did not want to be responsible for feeding their slaves, there was no work in the fields for them to do, and they might be better soldiers against the Babylonians if they were free. This was either panic, piety. or cold self-interest.

iv. "At this point news arrived that an Egyptian army was marching to relieve Jerusalem, and these tidings caused the Babylonians to lift the siege temporarily so as to regroup and attack the advancing Egyptians." (Harrison)

c. **Afterward they changed their minds and made the male and female slaves return, whom they had set free**: They changed their minds when the Babylonian siege was lifted. With the threat gone, there was no more need to radically repent, so they repented of their repentance and forced these slaves back into servitude.

i. "The Chaldeans had drawn off, to go, belike, to fight with the relief that was coming out of Egypt; [Jeremiah 37:7; Jeremiah 37:11] and now these silly Jews thought themselves out of the reach of God's rod perfidiously repealed their vows." (Clarke)

ii. When the siege was lifted, "Now there was no longer a food problem but a servant problem. So the release of the slaves was cancelled, and these unfortunates were back where they had started." (Kidner)

iii. "In this prophecy one of the sins which characterized the times is clearly manifest – oppression of the poor and helpless, against which the indignation of Jehovah is graphically set forth." (Morgan)

iv. By the law of God, by the command of the king, and by the action of their former masters they were free – yet now forced back into servitude. We don't know what power or threat they used to force them. Perhaps they worked hard to persuade them that they really weren't free after all and had to continue to live as slaves. In spiritual analogy, Satan hopes to deceive believers along similar lines. He hopes to persuade them that they are not really free and must come back under his service.

2. (12-16) Reminding them of the law of Moses.

Therefore the word of the LORD came to Jeremiah from the LORD, saying, "Thus says the LORD, the God of Israel: 'I made a covenant with your fathers in the day that I brought them out of the land of Egypt, out of the house of bondage, saying, "At the end of seven years let every man set free his Hebrew brother, who has been sold to him; and when he has served you six years, you shall let him go free from you." But your fathers did not obey Me nor incline their ear. Then you recently turned and did what was right in My sight -- every man proclaiming liberty to his neighbor; and you made a covenant before Me in the house which is called by My name. Then you turned around and profaned My name, and every one of you brought back his male and female slaves, whom he had set at liberty, at their pleasure, and brought them back into subjection, to be your male and female slaves.'"

> a. **I made a covenant with your fathers in the day that I brought them out of the land of Egypt, out of the house of bondage**: God began by reminding them that they *all* came from a slave past. This should have made them more generous and compassionate to their slaves, but it did not.
>
>> i. **Who has been sold to him**: "MT can also be translated literally *who shall have sold himself*, reflecting the long Near Eastern tradition of the voluntary adoption of servitude by individuals for economic reasons." (Harrison)
>
> b. **When he has served you six years, you shall let him go free from you**: This was God's command in Exodus 21:2-4. This was the law that they long disobeyed (**your fathers did not obey Me**) and under Zedekiah's command obeyed (**you recently turned and did what was right**).
>
> c. **Then you turned around and profaned My name**: Their *going back to disobedience* was unholy before God, especially because of the terrible oppression it placed upon others.
>
>> i. "All injustice of man to man creates in the mind of those who suffer, questionings about God. Thus His name is profaned; and His anger is ever stirred against those causing the profanation. The wrong of man to man inflicts on God a deeper wrong." (Morgan)

3. (17) Proclaiming liberty of judgment.

"Therefore thus says the LORD: 'You have not obeyed Me in proclaiming liberty, every one to his brother and every one to his neighbor. Behold, I proclaim liberty to you,' says the LORD -- 'to the sword, to pestilence, and to famine! And I will deliver you to trouble among all the kingdoms of the earth.'"

a. **You have not obeyed Me in proclaiming liberty**: The people of Jerusalem had a great opportunity to obey God and do good to their fellow Hebrews by **proclaiming liberty** to those who were already free by the law of Moses. They did not obey God and missed this great opportunity.

> i. The believer under the new covenant takes great peace in knowing that Jesus is the Liberator who never takes back the liberty He has granted.

b. **Behold, I proclaim liberty to you...to the sword, to pestilence, and to famine**: *This* was the "**liberty**" God proclaimed to these disobedient, cruel slave masters. God would free *them* from His protection; and they would see the **sword**, **pestilence**, and **famine** coming at them with full liberty; and they would see **trouble among all the kingdoms of the earth**.

4. (18-22) The punishment to those who broke the covenant.

"'And I will give the men who have transgressed My covenant, who have not performed the words of the covenant which they made before Me, when they cut the calf in two and passed between the parts of it -- the princes of Judah, the princes of Jerusalem, the eunuchs, the priests, and all the people of the land who passed between the parts of the calf -- I will give them into the hand of their enemies and into the hand of those who seek their life. Their dead bodies shall be for meat for the birds of the heaven and the beasts of the earth. And I will give Zedekiah king of Judah and his princes into the hand of their enemies, into the hand of those who seek their life, and into the hand of the king of Babylon's army which has gone back from you. Behold, I will command,' says the LORD, 'and cause them to return to this city. They will fight against it and take it and burn it with fire; and I will make the cities of Judah a desolation without inhabitant.'"

a. **Who have not performed the words of the covenant which they made before Me**: God had appointed a special judgment for those who went back on their promise to set their slaves free in obedience to the law. This covenant was made formally, by walking through **the parts** of a sacrificed animal (as with Abraham in Genesis 15:9-21). In the phrasing of Biblical Hebrew, you don't *make* a covenant; you *cut* a covenant.

> i. "As in the Assyrian inscriptions, the intention was that, as they passed through the pieces of the divided sacrifice, they invoked on themselves a curse that, if they broke the covenant, they would be cut in pieces like the sacrificial calf." (Feinberg)

b. **I will give them into the hand of their enemies and into the hand of those who seek their life**: God promised that they would not escape judgment. They felt free to determine the destiny of others by acting as master over them; God would show His freedom to destine them for judgment.

c. **I will command...and cause them to return to this city**: Because of the Egyptian threat (Jeremiah 37:5-10), the Babylonian army had **gone back from** Jerusalem. When the people of Jerusalem and Judah went back on their promise to set their slaves free, God would bring the Babylonians back to complete the work of judgment.

i. **Which has gone back from you**: "Nebuchadnezzar, hearing that there was an Egyptian army coming to the relief of Jerusalem, raised the siege, went out, and met and defeated the Egyptians. It was in the interim this prophecy was delivered." (Clarke)

ii. "Many towns were destroyed at the beginning of the sixth century BC and never again occupied; others were destroyed at that time and partly reoccupied at some later date; still others were destroyed and reoccupied after a long period of abandonment...There is not a single known case where a town of Judah proper was continuously occupied through the exilic period." (Albright, cited in Thompson)

Jeremiah 35 – The Lesson of the Rechabites

A. The test of the Rechabites.

1. (1-2) God tells Jeremiah to speak to the Rechabites.

The word which came to Jeremiah from the LORD in the days of Jehoiakim the son of Josiah, king of Judah, saying, "Go to the house of the Rechabites, speak to them, and bring them into the house of the LORD, into one of the chambers, and give them wine to drink."

> a. **In the days of Jehoiakim**: The chronology is difficult to follow and may have been of little concern to Jeremiah. Jehoiakim reigned before Zedekiah. Some (like Morgan) believed this prophecy was delivered during the reign of Zedekiah but recalled events from **the days of Jehoiakim**.
>
>> i. "No precise date is given, but the mention in verse 11 of Chaldean and Aramean forces coming up against the land seems to suit 2 Kings 24:2-4, when bands of Chaldean, Arameans, and other vassal contingents were sent against Jehoiakim." (Thompson)
>
> b. **Go to the house of Rechabites**: We don't know much about the Rechabites, a radically committed sect among the Israelites who emphasized a nomadic life as Israel lived in the wilderness.
>
>> i. Their roots went back to Jethro the Kenite, the father of Moses. Judges 1:16 tells of how the Kenites – the descendants of Jethro, father-in-law of Moses – came from the area of Jericho and lived among in the Wilderness of Judah to the south (Judges 4:17, 1 Samuel 15:6). These nomads were the ancestors of the house of Rechab (1 Chronicles 2:55).
>
>> ii. The inspirational father of the Rechabites was Jonadab (Jehonadab) an associate of Jehu in the violent and radical purge of the House of Ahab in 2 Kings 10:15-28. He taught a life free from idolatry and its associations, and free from the corruptions of city life.

iii. It's possible that the Rechabites were not only connected by family bonds, but also received others into their group who shared their ascetic, simple, nomadic commitment to God. In modern terms, they were something of a combination of back-to-nature hippies and zealously pure in their traditions Amish.

iv. "The Rechabites, these Spartan characters, saw themselves as living witnesses to the pilgrim origins of Israel, shunning the settled life of farms and vineyards for the simplicities of tents and flocks." (Kidner)

v. "Possibly the group transferred itself to the more conservative Judah either before or after the fall of Samaria in 721 BC Most likely they were a voluntary sect rather than the literal descendants of Jonadab, and 'our father' (Jeremiah 25:8) is to be understood in this way." (Cundall)

c. **Give them wine to drink**: Jeremiah was instructed to do this as he brought the Rechabites to the temple in what the following verses describe as a public, formal ceremony.

2. (3-5) Jeremiah does as God instructed him to.

Then I took Jaazaniah the son of Jeremiah, the son of Habazziniah, his brothers and all his sons, and the whole house of the Rechabites, and I brought them into the house of the LORD, into the chamber of the sons of Hanan the son of Igdaliah, a man of God, which *was* by the chamber of the princes, above the chamber of Maaseiah the son of Shallum, the keeper of the door. Then I set before the sons of the house of the Rechabites bowls full of wine, and cups; and I said to them, "Drink wine."

a. **The whole house of the Rechabites**: Jeremiah brought them *all* to the temple for this public ceremony. This would be the focus of attention.

i. "Being an acted parable, the little drama was to be given publicity by being presented in the Temple." (Harrison)

b. **Into the chamber of the sons of Hanan**: Apparently at the time of Jeremiah, certain individuals had some claim to particular chambers or rooms at the temple. **Hanan** seems to have been a supporter of Jeremiah.

i. **Hanan the son of Igdaliah**: "He is here called a *man of God*. In earlier periods 'the man of God' was a title applied to a prophet, not merely the great prophets like Samuel (1 Samuel 10:6-10), Elijah (2 Kings 1:9-13, etc.) and Elisha (2 Kings 4:13), but also to various nameless prophets (1 Samuel 2:27; 9:6, 8, 10; 1 Kings 12:22; 13:1, 11, 12, 21, 26; 17:24; 20:28, etc.)." (Thompson)

ii. "If 'sons' in this verse has the same general force as the expression 'sons of the prophets' had in the tenth and ninth centuries BC, it would appear that Hanan was the head of a group of disciples." (Harrison)

c. **I set before the sons of the house of the Rechabites bowls full of wine and cups**: Jeremiah tested the Rechabites the way God instructed him to. Jeremiah invited them to **drink wine**, but did not command them in the name of the LORD to do it. Since he knew of their commitment to not drink wine, the point of this test was not to persuade them to do it, but to publicly display their obedience to their customs.

i. "Yet if Jeremiah had said, Thus saith the Lord, Drink wine, they ought to have done it; but this he did not." (Trapp)

ii. "We of course understand that it was known that they would refuse, and the offer was made in order to elicit that refusal." (Morgan)

3. (6-11) The Rechabites refuse to drink the wine.

But they said, "We will drink no wine, for Jonadab the son of Rechab, our father, commanded us, saying, 'You shall drink no wine, you nor your sons, forever. You shall not build a house, sow seed, plant a vineyard, nor have *any of these;* but all your days you shall dwell in tents, that you may live many days in the land where you are sojourners.' Thus we have obeyed the voice of Jonadab the son of Rechab, our father, in all that he charged us, to drink no wine all our days, we, our wives, our sons, or our daughters, nor to build ourselves houses to dwell in; nor do we have vineyard, field, or seed. But we have dwelt in tents, and have obeyed and done according to all that Jonadab our father commanded us. But it came to pass, when Nebuchadnezzar king of Babylon came up into the land, that we said, 'Come, let us go to Jerusalem for fear of the army of the Chaldeans and for fear of the army of the Syrians.' So we dwell at Jerusalem."

a. **We will drink no wine**: The sons of Jonadab passed the test and refused the wine. The public nature of the ceremony, the presence of their entire clan, and prominence of the prophet, the proximity of the temple all added pressure to drink the wine. They also had the prior exception of coming into the city and leaving their nomadic life for a period; if that was an exception, it would be easy to make more. Yet they did not and were faithful.

i. The point was not strictly the drinking or not drinking of wine; it was obedience to the teaching of their spiritual father Jonadab. Jeremiah didn't use this to make a point about drinking wine, but about obedience. Nevertheless, *God honored the Rechabites* for their steadfast refusal to drink alcohol, and they were not mocked or criticized for this obedience.

ii. According to Kidner, there was a flourishing temperance movement in nineteenth-century England that took the name *The Rechabites*.

b. **You shall drink no wine, you nor your sons, forever**: Jonadab told his sons not to drink wine as part of a larger pattern of sacrifice and self-denial that also included not building a house and planting fields and vineyards. The sons of Jonadab could say, **we have obeyed and done according to all that Jonadab our father commanded us**.

i. "We find men so eager and devoted to the customs and traditions of their families, and so regardless of the yet higher claims of God." (Meyer)

c. **Let us go to Jerusalem for fear of the army of the Chaldeans**: The Rechabites were committed to life as nomads who avoided houses and cities and instead lived in tents. Yet they were refugees from the **army of the Chaldeans** and therefore reluctantly came to live in Jerusalem.

i. "If at present we appear to be acting contrary in any respect to our institutions, in being found in the city, *necessity* alone has induced us to take this temporary step. We have sought the *shelter of the city* for the *preservation of our lives; so now we dwell at Jerusalem*." (Clarke)

B. The lesson of the Rechabites and the reward to the sons of Jonadab.

1. (12-16) The contrast between the Rechabites and the men of Judah and Jerusalem.

Then came the word of the Lord to Jeremiah, saying, "Thus says the Lord of hosts, the God of Israel: 'Go and tell the men of Judah and the inhabitants of Jerusalem, "Will you not receive instruction to obey My words?" says the Lord. "The words of Jonadab the son of Rechab, which he commanded his sons, not to drink wine, are performed; for to this day they drink none, and obey their father's commandment. But although I have spoken to you, rising early and speaking, you did not obey Me. I have also sent to you all My servants the prophets, rising up early and sending *them*, saying, 'Turn now everyone from his evil way, amend your doings, and do not go after other gods to serve them; then you will dwell in the land which I have given you and your fathers.' But you have not inclined your ear, nor obeyed Me. Surely the sons of Jonadab the son of Rechab have performed the commandment of their father, which he commanded them, but this people has not obeyed Me."'

a. **Will you not receive instruction to obey My words**: God revealed the reason why He instructed Jeremiah to make the unusual offer to the Rechabites. Their remarkable obedience was a strong contrast to the refusal to **receive instruction** among the people of Judah and Jerusalem.

> i. In a sense, God only asks from us what we are willing to give to other people or other things. The Rechabites were willing to obey their ancestral father; it was not wrong for God to simply expect the same heart of obedience from the people of Judah.

b. **This people has not obeyed Me**: A second contrast was evident in the way that the Rechabites obeyed the command of their father, while the people of Judah and Jerusalem disobeyed the commands of God Himself, though He repeatedly brought those commands to them through His prophets.

- The Rechabites obeyed a fallible leader; the people of Judah disobeyed the eternal God.
- The Rechabites received their command only once from their leader and obeyed; the people of Judah received their command from God again and again and still disobeyed.
- The Rechabites obeyed regarding earthly things; the people of Judah disobeyed in regard to eternal things.
- The Rechabites obeyed their leader's commands over about 300 years; the people of Judah continually disobeyed their God.
- The Rechabites would be rewarded; the people of Judah would be judged.

2. (17) Application of the lesson of the Rechabites.

"Therefore thus says the LORD God of hosts, the God of Israel: 'Behold, I will bring on Judah and on all the inhabitants of Jerusalem all the doom that I have pronounced against them; because I have spoken to them but they have not heard, and I have called to them but they have not answered.'"

a. **I will bring on Judah and on all the inhabitants of Jerusalem all the doom that I have pronounced**: The contrast between the Rechabites and the people of Judah and Jerusalem was another indication of their guilt and impending judgment.

b. **I have spoken to them but they have not heard**: Again, the contrast was plain. The Rechabites listened to their father Jonadab; the people of Judah and Jerusalem would not listen to their God.

3. (18-19) The reward of the sons of Jonadab.

And Jeremiah said to the house of the Rechabites, "Thus says the LORD of hosts, the God of Israel: 'Because you have obeyed the commandment of Jonadab your father, and kept all his precepts and done according to all that he commanded you, therefore thus says the LORD of hosts, the God of Israel: "Jonadab the son of Rechab shall not lack a man to stand before Me forever."'"

a. **Because you have obeyed the commandment of Jonadab**: God honored the obedience and the honor of the sons of Jonadab.

b. **Jonadab the son of Rechab shall not lack a man to stand before Me forever**: God promised that the sons of Jonadab would have a special service and standing before Him **forever**.

i. "'To stand before' is a technical expression which includes a sense of privilege in the very act of serving. It is used of prophets (e.g. 1 Kings 17:1), of priests (Numbers 16:9; Deuteronomy 10:8, etc.), and kings (1 Kings 10:8)." (Cundall)

ii. "It is a technical term for the privilege of service…Some scholars think the promise in verse 18 was literally fulfilled in the Rechabites being in some way incorporated into the tribe of Levi." (Feinberg)

iii. "According to the Mishnah 'the children of Jonadab son of Rechab' had a fixed day in the year for bringing wood for the altar of the temple." (Thompson)

iv. "To be beloved by me, and to be in special favour with me, lifting up pure hands in all places of their abode. Captive they were carried among the Jews; but they returned also again with them (as appears 1 Chronicles 2:55)." (Trapp)

v. "True Christians may be considered as the genuine *successors* of these ancient *Rechabites*; and some suppose that the *Essenes*, in our Lord's time, were literally their *descendants*, and that these were they who followed our Lord particularly, and became the *first converts* to the Gospel. If so, the prophecy is *literally* fulfilled: *they shall never want a man to stand before God*, to proclaim his salvation, and minister to the edification and salvation of others, as long as the earth shall endure." (Clarke)

Jeremiah 36 – Cutting and Burning God's Word

A. The making of the scroll.

1. (1-3) The command to compile Jeremiah's prophecies into a single scroll.

Now it came to pass in the fourth year of Jehoiakim the son of Josiah, king of Judah, *that* **this word came to Jeremiah from the LORD, saying: "Take a scroll of a book and write on it all the words that I have spoken to you against Israel, against Judah, and against all the nations, from the day I spoke to you, from the days of Josiah even to this day. It may be that the house of Judah will hear all the adversities which I purpose to bring upon them, that everyone may turn from his evil way, that I may forgive their iniquity and their sin."**

> a. **It came to pass in the fourth year of Jehoiakim**: This was at or near the time of the first Babylonian invasion (605 BC) when Daniel and other captives were taken to Babylon.
>
> b. **Take a scroll of a book and write on it all the words that I have spoken to you**: God commanded Jeremiah not only to *speak* his prophecies, but also to **write** them. This was to include all the prophetic sayings he had given up to that point (**from the day I spoke to you**). Perhaps these were already written in some form and Jeremiah was commanded to compile them.
>
>> i. "If Jeremiah's life were in danger, if he had no sons to carry on his word (Jeremiah 16:2), if the nation and the whole fabric of society were about to collapse, then a scroll would preserve the message. There was a great precedent in the scroll discovered in the temple in 621 BC" (Thompson)
>>
>> ii. "Jeremiah, it seemeth, had either not written his prophecies, or not so legibly, or in loose papers only; now he hath them fair written out into a book, making the same use of Baruch as afterward Paul did of Tertius, [Romans 16:22]." (Trapp)

iii. "The actual contents of the document in question are unknown, though it probably compromised an anthology of material proclaimed between 626 and 605 BC." (Harrison)

iv. "Our word 'volume' -- from the verb 'to roll up' -- goes back to this form of book." (Feinberg)

c. **It may be that the house of Judah will hear**: God commanded Jeremiah to do this so that the message might be more effectively delivered. If the word was present in written form, it could be more easily remembered, consulted, and meditated upon.

i. "This verse helps explain Jeremiah's many terrible prophecies of divine judgment. They were not intended simply to terrify; they were also intended to save." (Ryken)

ii. This was still almost 20 years before the final conquest of Jerusalem, and it was still possible to see God rescue Judah. "It was yet possible to avert the judgments which had been so often denounced against them. But in order to do this they must – 1. *Hear* what God has spoken. 2. Every man *turn* from his evil way. 3. If they do so, God graciously promises to *forgive their iniquity and their sin*." (Clarke)

2. (4-8) Baruch, Jeremiah's scribe, reads the scroll at the temple.

Then Jeremiah called Baruch the son of Neriah; and Baruch wrote on a scroll of a book, at the instruction of Jeremiah, all the words of the LORD which He had spoken to him. And Jeremiah commanded Baruch, saying, "I *am* confined, I cannot go into the house of the LORD. You go, therefore, and read from the scroll which you have written at my instruction, the words of the LORD, in the hearing of the people in the LORD's house on the day of fasting. And you shall also read them in the hearing of all Judah who come from their cities. It may be that they will present their supplication before the LORD, and everyone will turn from his evil way. For great *is* the anger and the fury that the LORD has pronounced against this people." And Baruch the son of Neriah did according to all that Jeremiah the prophet commanded him, reading from the book the words of the LORD in the LORD's house.

a. **Baruch wrote on a scroll**: Baruch was Jeremiah's assistant and secretary. The prophet had Baruch do the actual writing of the words that Yahweh had **spoken to** Jeremiah. The prophet himself didn't need to write the words himself for it to be God's word.

i. There was a long relationship between the scribe and the prophet. "Seventeen years later on the eve of the final fall of Jerusalem Jeremiah entrusted to Baruch the title deed to the field he bought in Anathoth

(Jeremiah 32:13, 16). Baruch finally went with Jeremiah to Egypt (Jeremiah 43:6)." (Thompson)

b. **You go, therefore, and read from the scroll**: Jeremiah was **confined** – not imprisoned, but likely banned from the temple area – he sent Baruch to read the written word of God to the people of Jerusalem at the temple.

> i. **I am confined**: "The Hebrew *asur* describing Jeremiah's debarment (Jeremiah 36:5) occurs in 33:1 and 39:15 in the sense of physical arrest or imprisonment, but that is not the meaning here, since verse 19 shows that Jeremiah was free to escape at will." (Harrison)
>
> ii. "It appears that Jeremiah was excommunicated from the Temple because of his outspoken comment in his Temple Sermon (Jeremiah 5, cf. Jeremiah 7:26). The word 'debarred' ('shut up', AV [KJV]) could indicate ritual defilement, but this was usually for a limited period." (Cundall)
>
> iii. "At a time when Jeremiah was shut up, and unable to go into the house of the Lord, he was commanded to write." This was what Paul did with his prison letters. (Morgan)
>
> iv. The prophet didn't need to present the words himself for the work of the word of God to be effective. The word of God itself had power.

c. **On the day of fasting**: Apparently, even when so many hearts were far from God in Jerusalem and Judah, they still fulfilled particular days **of fasting** as instructed by the Law of Moses. They in some way could fulfill these with their hearts still far from God.

> i. "After the Exile, fast days were specified (cf. Zechariah 7:3, 5; 8:19), but earlier they were called in time of emergency (cf. Joel 2:12, 15)." (Feinberg)

d. **It may be that they will present their supplication before the LORD, and everyone will turn from his evil way**: This was the desired result in bringing God's word to the people. It was hoped that they would hear, pray, and repent – as described before in Jeremiah 36:3.

e. **Baruch the son of Neriah did according to all that Jeremiah the prophet commanded him**: Baruch did as Jeremiah told him, but there was no response from the people mentioned.

B. The reading of the scroll.

1. (9-10) Baruch reads the scroll again the following year.

Now it came to pass in the fifth year of Jehoiakim the son of Josiah, king of Judah, in the ninth month, *that* **they proclaimed a fast before**

the LORD to all the people in Jerusalem, and to all the people who came from the cities of Judah to Jerusalem. Then Baruch read from the book the words of Jeremiah in the house of the LORD, in the chamber of Gemariah the son of Shaphan the scribe, in the upper court at the entry of the New Gate of the LORD's house, in the hearing of all the people.

a. **It came to pass in the fifth year of Jehoiakim**: This was the year following the writing of the scroll described in the first part of Jeremiah 36. It is difficult to know if *this* was the reading of the scroll first described in Jeremiah 36:8 or a second public reading of the scroll some weeks or months later.

b. **They proclaimed a fast before the LORD to all the people in Jerusalem**: With the Babylonians conquering the nations surrounding Judah, the people felt every measure should be taken, so they called a **fast before the LORD**. In the best case, this showed seriousness in seeking God and hearts ready for repentance. There were also people **from the cities of Judah** who gathered for this proclaimed fast.

i. "The ninth month was December, 604 BC, when the Babylonians overthrew Ashkelon in the plain of Philista, an incident which probably provoked the fast." (Harrison)

ii. **They proclaimed a fast**: "Notice it was the people, not the king, who proclaimed the fast." (Feinberg)

c. **Baruch read from the book the words of Jeremiah in the house of the LORD**: Baruch publically read the words of Jeremiah's prophecy, calling the people to repentance and warning them of the judgment to come. He did this **in the hearing of all the people**.

i. **In the chamber of Gemariah**: "*Gemariah* was the son of Shaphan, who had been Secretary of State under Josiah (2 Kings 22:3, 8). If this Shaphan is to be identified with the man mentioned in Jeremiah 26:24, Gemariah would then be the brother of Ahikam who treated Jeremiah kindly." (Harrison)

ii. "Shaphan was a good father as well as a great leader. His sons were among the forgotten heroes of the Bible (Jeremiah 26:24)." (Ryken)

2. (11-15) Baruch brings the scroll to the princes of Judah.

When Michaiah the son of Gemariah, the son of Shaphan, heard all the words of the LORD from the book, he then went down to the king's house, into the scribe's chamber; and there all the princes were sitting—Elishama the scribe, Delaiah the son of Shemaiah, Elnathan the son of Achbor, Gemariah the son of Shaphan, Zedekiah the son of Hananiah, and all the princes. Then Michaiah declared to them all the

words that he had heard when Baruch read the book in the hearing of the people. Therefore all the princes sent Jehudi the son of Nethaniah, the son of Shelemiah, the son of Cushi, to Baruch, saying, "Take in your hand the scroll from which you have read in the hearing of the people, and come." So Baruch the son of Neriah took the scroll in his hand and came to them. And they said to him, "Sit down now, and read it in our hearing." So Baruch read *it* in their hearing.**

a. **Michaiah the son of Gemariah**: This **Michaiah** was a godly man, having been connected with the reforms and revival under King Josiah (2 Kings 22:12-13). He **heard all the words of the LORD from the book**, and knew something of the authority and power of God's word from the work in Josiah's day.

b. **Michaiah declared to them all the words that he had heard when Baruch read the book**: Michaiah brought the message of the book to the **princes** of Judah – sons of nobility and royalty, leaders in the kingdom.

i. **All the words**: They read the whole thing. They didn't just read a verse or two and then come back the next day for another verse or two. They heard the word chapter-by-chapter, verse by verse.

c. **Sit down now, and read it in our hearing**: When the princes of Judah heard the message of Jeremiah's book, they knew others should hear it as well. They wanted it read to others directly from the **scroll in his hand**.

i. "The apparent courtesy with which the state officials treated Baruch indicates their friendly attitude, although it may be too that Baruch was of noble birth." (Thompson)

3. (16-19) The princes of Judah tell Baruch and Jeremiah to hide.

Now it happened, when they had heard all the words, that they looked in fear from one to another, and said to Baruch, "We will surely tell the king of all these words." And they asked Baruch, saying, "Tell us now, how did you write all these words -- at his instruction?" So Baruch answered them, "He proclaimed with his mouth all these words to me, and I wrote *them* with ink in the book." Then the princes said to Baruch, "Go and hide, you and Jeremiah; and let no one know where you are."

a. **They looked in fear from one to another**: The princes of Judah knew Jeremiah's message from God would bring trouble. They thought it best to **tell the king** directly.

i. **We will surely tell the king**: "They durst do no otherwise; for if these things should have come to the king's ear, and they not first tell him, they might come into the danger of his displeasure." (Trapp)

b. **He proclaimed with his mouth all these words to me, and I wrote them**: Baruch explained how he wrote the scroll. Jeremiah said the words, and Baruch **wrote** them down. Baruch made not claim to being a prophet himself, only the scribe of a prophet.

   i. This practice was also carried over with the apostles in New Testament times. Romans 16:22 states how Tertius was the penman for Paul's letter to the Roman Christians.

   ii. "What is also impressive about these men is their careful enquiry into the nature of this document: whether each word of it was authentic or not (Jeremiah 36:17). As soon as they were satisfied of this, they knew what they must do, and did it." (Kidner)

c. **Go and hide, you and Jeremiah; and let no one know where you are**: The princes of Judah knew the king would be displeased and perhaps strike out against the prophet and the scribe for their message.

   i. Jeremiah 26 describes another time in Jehoiakim's reign when Jeremiah was persecuted and perhaps in danger of death, as well as noting the prophet Uriah who *was* in fact murdered for being a faithful prophet (Jeremiah 26:23). The sense is that if Jeremiah and Baruch had not hidden, they too would have been martyred.

   ii. "Jewish tradition has identified the place of concealment with the so-called 'Grotto of Jeremiah', located outside the Damascus Gate, though with what accuracy is uncertain." (Harrison)

4. (20-21) Bringing the scroll to the king.

And they went to the king, into the court; but they stored the scroll in the chamber of Elishama the scribe, and told all the words in the hearing of the king. So the king sent Jehudi to bring the scroll, and he took it from Elishama the scribe's chamber. And Jehudi read it in the hearing of the king and in the hearing of all the princes who stood beside the king.

   a. **They went to the king… but they stored the scroll**: The princes of Judah were sympathetic to Jeremiah, Baruch, and their message on the scroll. They anticipated a bad reception of that message from King Jehoiakim, so for the protection of the scroll **they stored the scroll in the chamber of Elishama**.

   b. **Told all the words in the hearing of the king**: They began by giving Jehoiakim a comprehensive report of what Jeremiah said and Baruch wrote. Then the king commanded that the scroll be brought to him and **read** to him directly and publically.

5. (22-26) King Jehoiakim burns Jeremiah's scroll.

Now the king was sitting in the winter house in the ninth month, with *a fire* burning on the hearth before him. And it happened, when Jehudi had read three or four columns, *that the king* cut it with the scribe's knife and cast *it* into the fire that *was* on the hearth, until all the scroll was consumed in the fire that *was* on the hearth. Yet they were not afraid, nor did they tear their garments, the king nor any of his servants who heard all these words. Nevertheless Elnathan, Delaiah, and Gemariah implored the king not to burn the scroll; but he would not listen to them. And the king commanded Jerahmeel the king's son, Seraiah the son of Azriel, and Shelemiah the son of Abdeel, to seize Baruch the scribe and Jeremiah the prophet, but the LORD hid them.

a. **In the winter house in the ninth month**: This probably refers to a portion or a floor of the palace that was more comfortable in the winter, suited for cooler weather. Jehoiakim sat there with a **fire burning on the hearth before him**.

i. "The king was in the winter house, not a separate dwelling, but a warm apartment in a sheltered part of the palace facing the winter sun (cf. Amos 3:15)." (Feinberg)

ii. "There sat he, in that his stately and sumptuous palace built by iniquity, [Jeremiah 22:13-14]." (Trapp)

b. **The king cut it with the scribe's knife**: Scribes used small, sharp knives to trim their reed pens and to cut the parchments where needed. As Jehudi continued to read each column from the scroll, Jehoiakim cut the part that he just read. His first act against God's word was to *cut it*.

i. The practice of *cutting* God's word continues. Today, some want to decide for themselves what is true and false in the Bible, what actually happened and what is only a fairy-tale story. Some want to decide what moral teaching should be kept for our present age, and which they believe we have "progressed" beyond. Some want to cut the biblical authors and books so completely that they have no connection or harmony between them. Then and now, God's word is **cut** before it is burned.

ii. "We are all tempted to use the penknife to God's Book. There are passages in it which we do not like; those that cross our favourite notions, our cherished sins. Practically, we eliminate them. We never read them, or we explain them away, or profess to doubt their inspiration." (Meyer)

iii. "This was the second time in Jeremiah's lifetime that a portion of God's word had been read to a reigning king, but how different was Josiah's reaction (2 Kings 22:11-20)!" (Cundall)

c. **The king cut it with the scribe's knife and cast it into the fire**: Jehoiakim took the sections he cut and methodically, repeatedly put them into the fire heating the room. This was a deliberate, dramatic way to insult and reject the prophet and the God whom the prophet represented. Jehoiakim hoped to burn and destroy the word of the prophet and his God.

i. Perhaps Jehoiakim thought, *these aren't the words of God; these are the words of Jeremiah. Jeremiah's personality is all over these words.* He was terribly wrong; they were Jeremiah's words, but they were *also* God's words. God was big enough to work through the words of Jeremiah.

ii. At the same time, *King Jehoiakim was afraid of God's word.* He didn't only hold it in contempt and he couldn't bear to simply ignore it. The king hoped to destroy the power of God's word by destroying the scroll.

iii. "The king's slow, methodical destruction of the scroll, keeping pace with the steady progress of the reading, made his rejection a far more emphatic gesture than a swift reaction in hot blood." (Kidner)

iv. This blasphemous and ignorant act failed to see the difference between the living, eternal *word of God* and the media for that word, the ink on the parchment or data on the screen. The ink and parchment can be burned, but God's word can *never* be destroyed. *The grass withers, the flower fades, but the word of our God stands forever* (Isaiah 40:8). If it is the word of God, it can never be destroyed.

v. "The first recorded attempt to obliterate the word of God is something of a foretaste of the attacks on it in days to come: by sceptics, by persecutors, and with whatever good intent, by the rash use of the scholar's knife. On this occasion, as on others to come, God saw to its preservation and completion." (Kidner)

vi. In AD 300, the Roman emperor Diocletian ordered every Bible burned and they destroyed thousands of Bibles, even just portions of Bibles. A Christian could be killed for just having a Bible. Yet it didn't work. The next Roman emperor ordered 50 brand new complete Bibles to be made at government expense.

vii. Early in the 20th century, an Armenian patient in an American hospital in Turkey was given a Bible, which was the first he had ever possessed. When he left the hospital, he proudly took the Bible to his village and showed it to friends. A Moslem teacher snatched the

Bible from him, tore it from its binding, and threw the pieces into the street. A grocer passing down the street picked up the pages and used them for wrapping paper. Soon the pages of the Bible were scattered all over the entire village. Customers read the pages and asked for more. Sometime later, a Bible seller came to the village and was amazed to find a hundred people eager to buy the Holy Bible. Even the torn-up Bible survived and did a great work.

viii. Ravi Zacharias told the story of a Vietnamese Christian named Hien Pham who was his interpreter. Being a Christian and a translator for missionaries and the American forces, Hien was arrested when South Vietnam fell to the Communists. His faith was shaken under the pressure and propaganda of his prison camp and he decided he would no longer pray or think about his faith. The next day he was given the terrible job of cleaning the prison latrines. As he cleaned out a tin can overflowing with toilet paper, his eye caught what seemed to be English printed on a piece of paper. He quickly grabbed it, washed it, and after his roommates went to sleep that night, he brought out the paper and read from Romans 8: *And we know that all things work together for good to those who love God... For I am persuaded...* [that nothing] *shall be able to separate us from the love of God which is in Christ Jesus our Lord.* Hien cried, knowing this was God's word for him, having decided just the previous night to give up on God. The prison official who thought the Bible was only fit for toilet paper actually rescued the faith of a believer. After finding the Scripture, Hien asked the commander if he could clean the latrines regularly. Each day he picked up a portion of Scripture, cleaned it off, and added it to his collection of nightly reading.

ix. "Sin may so deaden spiritual and moral faculties, that men will without fear cast the messages of God to the fire, and commit His messengers to death. But such action never destroys the word of God, nor invalidates its findings." (Morgan)

x. "The captain may destroy the map which indicates the rocks in his course; but that will not rob them of the cruel fangs with which they will pierce the timbers of his ship. Men may deride and destroy the Bible; but this will not empty the future of hell, or hell of its bitter remorse." (Meyer)

xi. "This was not the last attack on the word of God. Kings and governments have set themselves against it; sceptics and liberal scholars have sought to discredit or dismember it; but it remains indestructible. The man who acts as Jehoiakim did will be judged." (Cundall)

d. **Yet they were not afraid, nor did they tear their garments**: Jeremiah noted this strange response. God and His word were both gravely insulted right before their eyes, yet it seemed a small thing to them. They probably didn't approve, thinking something like "Well, I would never do such a thing." Yet they thought it was of little significance that the king over God's covenant people burned the very words of the covenant God.

i. When Josiah heard the Book of the Law read, he tore his clothes in grief and mourning over the sin and rebellion of his people and their leaders (2 Kings 22:11-20). In Jeremiah's time the royal court had a different reaction. "Most of the court officials stood by indifferently. They shared the king's contempt for God's truth." (Feinberg)

ii. "The king and his servants, those court parasites, were not stirred at all at such a Bible bonfire, but jeered when they should have feared." (Trapp)

e. **Nevertheless Elnathan, Delaiah, and Gemariah implored the king not to burn the scroll**: There were some who at least *said* something to the king. Yet Jehoiakim ignored them and commanded that Baruch and Jeremiah be arrested – **but the LORD hid them**.

i. "Three of the princes wished to *save the scroll*, and entreated the king that it might not be burnt. They would have saved it *out of the fire*, but the king would not permit it to be done." (Clarke)

ii. **Nevertheless Elnathan**: "Who had before been active for the king in apprehending and slaughtering the prophet Uriah, [Jeremiah 26:22] but now haply touched with some remorse for having any hand in so bloody an act." (Trapp)

iii. "His further step in ordering the arrest of Baruch and Jeremiah (Jeremiah 36:26) revealed the fury and perhaps the fear beneath the show of cool defiance." (Kidner)

6. (27-31) God's response to the burning of the scroll.

Now after the king had burned the scroll with the words which Baruch had written at the instruction of Jeremiah, the word of the LORD came to Jeremiah, saying: "Take yet another scroll, and write on it all the former words that were in the first scroll which Jehoiakim the king of Judah has burned. And you shall say to Jehoiakim king of Judah, 'Thus says the LORD: "You have burned this scroll, saying, 'Why have you written in it that the king of Babylon will certainly come and destroy this land, and cause man and beast to cease from here?'" Therefore thus says the LORD concerning Jehoiakim king of Judah: "He shall have no one to sit on the throne of David, and his dead body shall be cast out

to the heat of the day and the frost of the night. I will punish him, his family, and his servants for their iniquity; and I will bring on them, on the inhabitants of Jerusalem, and on the men of Judah all the doom that I have pronounced against them; but they did not heed.""**

> a. **Take yet another scroll, and write on it all the former words**: God's response to King Jehoiakim's cutting and burning of the written word was to write it again and publish it again.

>> i. "God's Word cannot be burnt, no more than it can be bound." (Trapp)

> b. **Why have you written in it that the king of Babylon will certainly come and destroy this land, and cause man and beast to cease from here**: This was the aspect of Jeremiah's message that so upset Jehoiakim. He didn't want to hear that Nebuchadnezzar was going to come *again* to Jerusalem and eventually destroy the city.

> c. **He shall have no one to sit on the throne of David**: Jeremiah 22:28-30 records a promise made to Coniah (Jeconiah) the nephew of Jehoiakim – that none of his descendants would *prosper, sitting on the throne of David, and ruling anymore in Judah* (Jeremiah 22:30). What was true of the nephew would also be true of the uncle.

>> i. This prophecy presents something of a problem. God promised David that his descendant would reign as Messiah over Israel and the world (2 Samuel 7:16). By the time of Jehoiakim that descendant had not yet come, and here God seems to promise that it would be impossible for the descendant to come. If someone was a blood descendant of David through Jehoiakim, he could not sit on the throne of Israel and be the king and the Messiah because of this curse recorded in Jeremiah 22:30 and 36:30. But if the conqueror was not descended through David, he could not be the legal heir of the throne because of the promise made to David and the nature of the royal line.

>> ii. This is where we come to the differences in the genealogies of Matthew and Luke. Matthew recorded the genealogy of *Joseph, the husband of Mary, of whom was born Jesus who is called Christ* (Matthew 1:16). He began at Abraham and followed the line down to Jesus, *through Joseph*. Luke recorded the genealogy of Mary: *being, (as was supposed) the son of Joseph* (Luke 3:23). He began with Jesus and followed the line back up, all the way to Adam, *starting from the unmentioned Mary*.

>> iii. "The three-month reign of Jehoiachin (cf. 2 Kings 24:6, 8) does not contradict the prediction of verse 30. Jehoiachin's succession was not a valid one but only a token one because he was immediately

besieged by Nebuchadnezzar, surrendered in three months, and then went into exile, where he died after many years. No other descendant of Jehoiakim ever ascended the throne." (Feinberg)

d. His dead body shall be cast out to the heat of the day and the frost of the night: In the end, it was Jehoiakim who was doomed, not the word of God.

i. "The fulfillment of verse 30 is not recorded in history, and 2 Kings 24:6 says nothing about the circumstances of his burial. Jehoiakim had been just as guilty as his people in rejecting God's word, hence his fate will typify that of the nation." (Harrison)

e. I will punish him, his family, and his servants for their iniquity: God promised to bring upon King Jehoiakim the judgment Jeremiah prophesied, including the disgrace done to his corpse at his death. The catastrophe of judgment would come upon the people of Judah and Jerusalem because they rejected God's word through Jeremiah, just as King Jehoiakim did.

i. **All the doom that I have pronounced against them**: "The dramatic adventures of the scroll should not distract us from what was at stake on this fateful day, when king and people set their course towards the shipwreck of their kingdom, nearly twenty years distant." (Kidner)

7. (32) The second scroll of Jeremiah and Baruch.

Then Jeremiah took another scroll and gave it to Baruch the scribe, the son of Neriah, who wrote on it at the instruction of Jeremiah all the words of the book which Jehoiakim king of Judah had burned in the fire. And besides, there were added to them many similar words.

a. **Jeremiah took another scroll and gave it to Baruch**: Jeremiah and Baruch worked together. The prophet supplied the words and the scribe supplied the ink and the parchment. Together, God's word was published and preserved.

b. **Besides, there were added to them many similar words**: In fact, the opposition of Jehoiakim made his cause worse, not better. Responding to the king's cutting and burning of His word, God was determined to bring more words of judgment, not fewer.

i. "Though he destroyed them, he could not in this way arrest the penalties which they foretold. Indeed, he increased them." (Meyer)

Jeremiah 37 – The King Asks for Prayer and for A Secret Word

A. Despite the release from siege, the Babylonians will conquer Jerusalem.

1. (1-2) The new King Zedekiah fails in the same way as the previous king.

Now King Zedekiah the son of Josiah reigned instead of Coniah the son of Jehoiakim, whom Nebuchadnezzar king of Babylon made king in the land of Judah. But neither he nor his servants nor the people of the land gave heed to the words of the LORD which He spoke by the prophet Jeremiah.

> a. **King Zedekiah the son of Josiah reigned instead of Coniah**: The reign of **Coniah** (also known as *Jehoiachin*) was short, lasting only a few months of 598 BC His reign ended so quickly because Nebuchadnezzar came for a second time to subject Jerusalem under his control.
>
>> i. "Zedekiah was a small man on a great stage, a weakling set to face circumstances that would have taxed the strongest." (Maclaren)
>>
>> ii. In taking the throne, Zedekiah was pledged to obey Nebuchadnezzar. Nevertheless, "Because of Egyptian influence at court, which he could not resist, Zedekiah decided to break his pledge. This was the immediate cause of the final siege of Jerusalem." (Feinberg)
>
> b. **Whom Nebuchadnezzar king of Babylon made king**: When Nebuchadnezzar deposed Coniah, he then put Coniah's uncle **Zedekiah** in power. Yet Zedekiah did not use his position to listen to God or His Prophet Jeremiah.
>
>> i. Specifically, Jeremiah told them that the Babylonians would completely conquer Judah and Jerusalem and resistance was futile. They would be better off surrendering to the Babylonians and submitting to God's correction.

2. (3-5) Zedekiah asks Jeremiah to pray, and Jerusalem seems to be rescued.

And Zedekiah the king sent Jehucal the son of Shelemiah, and Zephaniah the son of Maaseiah, the priest, to the prophet Jeremiah, saying, "Pray now to the LORD our God for us." Now Jeremiah was coming and going among the people, for they had not *yet* put him in prison. Then Pharaoh's army came up from Egypt; and when the Chaldeans who were besieging Jerusalem heard news of them, they departed from Jerusalem.

> a. **Pray now to the LORD our God for us**: When Zedekiah asked this, the Babylonian army threatened Jerusalem. Things were so bad that even the king who would not listen to God asked for prayer and referred to the LORD as **our God**. Desperation drove him to ask for this prayer.
>
>> i. "This king would seem to have some more goodness in him than his brother and predecessor Jehoiakim; but he played the hypocrite exceedingly, as in other things, so in this, that he begged the prophet's prayers, but would not obey his preaching." (Trapp)
>
> b. **They had not yet put him in prison**: Jeremiah's imprisonment in this period is described in Jeremiah 32:1 and following.
>
> c. **Pharaoh's army came up from Egypt**: When the Babylonians left Jerusalem and went south to meet the Egyptian army, it seemed like a miracle and answer to prayer to King Zedekiah. The Babylonian siege was broken, and Jerusalem seemed to be rescued by the Egyptians.
>
>> i. "The pharaoh mentioned in verse 5 was Hophra (*cf.* Jeremiah 44:30), who reigned from 589 to 570 BC, and who rashly marched to support Zedekiah in his revolt against Babylon (Ezekiel 17:11-21). However, he retreated before actually joining battle, leaving Jerusalem to fall to the Babylonians in 587 BC." (Harrison)

3. (6-10) The certainty that the Babylonians will conquer Jerusalem.

Then the word of the LORD came to the prophet Jeremiah, saying, "Thus says the LORD, the God of Israel, 'Thus you shall say to the king of Judah, who sent you to Me to inquire of Me: "Behold, Pharaoh's army which has come up to help you will return to Egypt, to their own land. And the Chaldeans shall come back and fight against this city, and take it and burn it with fire."' Thus says the LORD: 'Do not deceive yourselves, saying, "The Chaldeans will surely depart from us," for they will not depart. For though you had defeated the whole army of the Chaldeans who fight against you, and there remained *only* wounded men among them, they would rise up, every man in his tent, and burn the city with fire.'"

a. **Pharaoh's army which has come up to help you will return to Egypt**: Through the Prophet Jeremiah, God told Zedekiah that the Egyptians would not stand in battle against the Babylonians. Pharaoh's army would return to Egypt before ever engaging the Babylonians. The hope of help from the Egyptians was empty.

b. **The Chaldeans shall come back and fight against this city**: The Egyptians would return to Egypt and the Babylonians would return to Jerusalem. They would conquer it (**take it**) and **burn it with fire**.

c. **There remained only wounded men among them, they would rise up**: God emphasized that there was *no way* the Babylonians would fail to conquer Jerusalem. Even if their army were reduced to **only wounded men**, even they would conquer the city and **burn the city with fire**.

B. Jeremiah arrest and secret message to the king.

1. (11-15) Jeremiah seized and imprisoned as a defector to the Babylonians.

And it happened, when the army of the Chaldeans left *the siege* of Jerusalem for fear of Pharaoh's army, that Jeremiah went out of Jerusalem to go into the land of Benjamin to claim his property there among the people. And when he was in the Gate of Benjamin, a captain of the guard *was* there whose name *was* Irijah the son of Shelemiah, the son of Hananiah; and he seized Jeremiah the prophet, saying, "You are defecting to the Chaldeans!" Then Jeremiah said, "False! I am not defecting to the Chaldeans." But he did not listen to him. So Irijah seized Jeremiah and brought him to the princes. Therefore the princes were angry with Jeremiah, and they struck him and put him in prison in the house of Jonathan the scribe. For they had made that the prison.

a. **Jeremiah went out of Jerusalem to go into the land of Benjamin to claim his property**: Jeremiah 32:6-12 describes the property that Jeremiah purchased as a testimony of God's promise of restoration to Judah. With the siege temporarily broken, Jeremiah could see the property he bought from prison.

i. **To claim his property there among the people**: "The Hebrew expression is obscure and its precise force is not clear -- 'to divide from there among the people'. It may be that the whole question of the patrimony of Jeremiah's family was under discussion because of the Babylonian invasion and a family meeting had been convened to decide about the division. Jeremiah set out to attend this meeting but was arrested." (Thompson)

b. **You are defecting to the Chaldeans**: Because he said that it was futile for the people of Judah to resist the Babylonians, Jeremiah was suspected of being a sympathizer with the Babylonians and maybe even their spy. Here **a captain of the guard** seized the prophet with this accusation.

i. "Jeremiah had urged others to desert (Jeremiah 21:9; 38:2) and in fact a number of Judeans did defect to the enemy (Jeremiah 38:19; 52:15). Further, Jeremiah's message of certain victory for the Babylonians was well known. Hence Irijah's accusation was understandable if mistaken." (Thompson)

c. **They struck him and put him in prison**: Jeremiah was beaten and again imprisoned. He paid a significant price for remaining faithful to God and the message God gave him to deliver.

i. "Without any *proof* of the alleged treachery, without any form of *justice*." (Clarke)

ii. This was some fifteen years after the sympathetic princes of Judah described in Jeremiah 36:11-19. A new generation and new conditions brought forth leaders with no sympathy to Jeremiah or his message.

iii. "Temporary arrangements had been made to incarcerate Jeremiah in the house of the Secretary of State. In situations of this kind cisterns were sometimes used to imprison persons arrested, and such an experience could be extremely unpleasant (Jeremiah 38:6, 13)." (Harrison)

iv. "The home of Jonathan the secretary was made the prophet's prison, perhaps because he was just one of many deserters and political prisoners." (Feinberg)

v. The verses to follow (Jeremiah 37:20-21) show that the conditions of the **prison in the house of Jonathan** were much worse than those in the court of the prison (Jeremiah 32:1-2).

2. (16-17) Delivered from prison, Jeremiah delivers a message to King Zedekiah.

When Jeremiah entered the dungeon and the cells, and Jeremiah had remained there many days, then Zedekiah the king sent and took him out. The king asked him secretly in his house, and said, "Is there *any* word from the LORD?" And Jeremiah said, "There is." Then he said, "You shall be delivered into the hand of the king of Babylon!"

a. **Jeremiah had remained there many days**: This was a further price the prophet had to pay for his faithfulness. There weren't any *false* prophets in that prison, because they gave a message that pleased the rulers and the people.

i. **The dungeon**: "Hebrew, Into a place or house of the pit or hole, where the prophet could neither walk nor handsomely lie down." (Trapp)

ii. **Many days**: "Did the king hope that the ordeal of *many days* would have broken his spirit by the time he sent for him? Certainly Jeremiah was dreading a return to this place of slow death (Jeremiah 37:20), but his prophetic voice was unwavering." (Kidner)

b. **The king asked him secretly**: Zedekiah wanted to know if there was **any word from the LORD** but didn't want to ask the prophet publically. The king did not want it known that he doubted the words of the false prophets that opposed Jeremiah and prophesied only good news.

i. "That the king asked his question secretly goes to show that it was a question of fear; fear growing out of the fact that, in spite of all this man's weakness and wickedness, he knew the power of God." (Morgan)

ii. One commentator pictured Zedekiah, "anxiously watching the lips of the martyr for a favorable word for himself, whispering secretly with the man whom his officials imprisoned for treason, weak, a poor creature but not evil, a king much more bound than the prisoner who stands before him." (Duhm, cited in Thompson)

c. **You shall be delivered into the hand of the king of Babylon**: This was the word of the LORD to Zedekiah. God's message did not change whether it was delivered privately or publically.

i. Zedekiah made the mistake of thinking there was a personal, secret word for him from God *different* from what had already been revealed in God's word, even His written word from Jeremiah. The "secret" word was completely consistent with the written word.

ii. God may bring a personal word to an individual. But a secret word should not be sought. Seek God in His written word.

iii. "A prophet who had faithfully proclaimed the word of God, in the face of intense antagonism, for forty years, was not likely to crack under this kind of pressure. His message was as uncompromising as before." (Cundall)

3. (18-21) Jeremiah appeals to King Zedekiah.

Moreover Jeremiah said to King Zedekiah, "What offense have I committed against you, against your servants, or against this people, that you have put me in prison? Where now *are* your prophets who prophesied to you, saying, 'The king of Babylon will not come against you or against this land'? Therefore please hear now, O my lord the

king. Please, let my petition be accepted before you, and do not make me return to the house of Jonathan the scribe, lest I die there." Then Zedekiah the king commanded that they should commit Jeremiah to the court of the prison, and that they should give him daily a piece of bread from the bakers' street, until all the bread in the city was gone. Thus Jeremiah remained in the court of the prison.

> a. **What offense have I committed against you**: Jeremiah appealed to Zedekiah in consideration of the failure of his favored **prophets** who said, "The king of Babylon will not come against you or against this land." Their failure made it clear that the only supposed **offense** of Jeremiah was to faithfully tell the truth to the king and the people.
>
>> i. "If one really preaches the word of God to a post-Christian world, he must understand that he is likely to end up like Jeremiah." (Schaeffer, cited in Ryken)
>
> b. **Do not make me return to the house of Jonathan the scribe, lest I die there**: Jeremiah made an earnest appeal (**please hear now…Please, let my petition be accepted**) to be spared the terrible conditions of the prison in **the house of Jonathan**.
>
> c. **Zedekiah the king commanded that they should commit Jeremiah to the court of the prison**: Zedekiah didn't seem to like Jeremiah or his message, but he respected the prophet as a man who faithfully told the truth even when it cost him something. He granted the request for Jeremiah to be in the more humane prison and even commanded **daily a piece of bread** be given to the prophet.
>
>> i. Jeremiah asked that his lot, even in persecution, be made better. In a time of persecution, the persecuted one and others can and should do all they can to make their condition better, even if the persecution or imprisonment continues. There is no command to endure and embrace the worst conditions without appeal.
>>
>> ii. "Why did he do so much, and not do more? He knew that Jeremiah was innocent, and that his word was God's; and what he should have done was to have shaken off his masterful 'servants,' followed his conscience, and obeyed God. Why did he not? Because he was a coward, infirm of purpose." (Maclaren)
>>
>> iii. "For whatever reasons in addition to compassion (and Zedekiah's motives will have been as mixed as most of ours), the king did not want the death of this man of God on his hands." (Kidner)

iv. There was a small blessing for Zedekiah in his kindness to Jeremiah. "For this courtesy of his to the prophet, God granted him a natural death, and an honourable burial in Babylon." (Trapp)

Jeremiah 38 – The Prophet in the Pit

A. Jeremiah in the pit.

1. (1-3) Jeremiah preaching in the days of Zedekiah.

Now Shephatiah the son of Mattan, Gedaliah the son of Pashhur, Jucal the son of Shelemiah, and Pashhur the son of Malchiah heard the words that Jeremiah had spoken to all the people, saying, "Thus says the LORD: 'He who remains in this city shall die by the sword, by famine, and by pestilence; but he who goes over to the Chaldeans shall live; his life shall be as a prize to him, and he shall live.' Thus says the LORD: 'This city shall surely be given into the hand of the king of Babylon's army, which shall take it.'"

a. **Shephatiah…Gedaliah…Jucal…Pashur**: These men were princes of Judah, men connected to the royal family in some way. The aristocrats had their own status and interest to protect as the catastrophe of the complete Babylonian conquest of Jerusalem drew near.

i. "Those clamouring princes were unquestionably the politicians who had influenced the king against the word of the prophet; and had advocated resistance to Babylon when Jeremiah had persistently declared its futility." (Morgan)

ii. In 2005 and 2008, Dr. Eilat Mazar discovered in the City of David area of Jerusalem two seal impressions in clay (bulla) with the names **Gedaliah the son of Pashur** and **Jeucal the son of Shelemiah** – two of the names as recorded here and in Jeremiah 37:3. These are some of the most recent of the 52 specific people of the Hebrew Bible to be confirmed by archaeology. (*Biblical Archaeology Review*, 41.5, page 18 – September/October 2015)

b. **He who remains in this city shall die by the sword**: As he had consistently done through his prophetic ministry, Jeremiah told the people to surrender to the Babylonians so that they could live in exile and wait for the promised restoration of God's people.

> i. **He who goes over**: "The verb 'go out to' probably bears the sense 'desert to' or 'give oneself to.' Jeremiah's remarks seemed to be traitorous and to give the officials good grounds to arrest the prophet." (Thompson)

c. **This city shall surely be given into the hand of the king of Babylon's army**: God's message through Jeremiah didn't change. The conquest of Jerusalem was certain.

2. (4-6) For his preaching, Jeremiah is cast into a pit.

Therefore the princes said to the king, "Please, let this man be put to death, for thus he weakens the hands of the men of war who remain in this city, and the hands of all the people, by speaking such words to them. For this man does not seek the welfare of this people, but their harm." Then Zedekiah the king said, "Look, he *is* in your hand. For the king can *do* nothing against you." So they took Jeremiah and cast him into the dungeon of Malchiah the king's son, which *was* in the court of the prison, and they let Jeremiah down with ropes. And in the dungeon *there was* no water, but mire. So Jeremiah sank in the mire.

> a. **Please, let this man be put to death**: The **princes** of Judah mentioned in Jeremiah 38:1 asked King Zedekiah to execute Jeremiah because his message was bad for the morale of those defending Jerusalem.
>
> > i. **He weakens the hands of the men of war**: "A similar expression occurs in the Lachish Letter VI. The military commander there referred to certain elements among the officials in Jerusalem." (Thompson)
> >
> > ii. **The men of war who remain**: "Apparently Judah had lost a few good men. No doubt some had fallen in battle while defending the city walls. Others were slipping out at night by ones and twos and going over to surrender to the Babylonians." (Ryken)
>
> b. **This man does not seek the welfare of this people, but their harm**: This was exactly opposite to the truth. Jeremiah didn't like preaching his message of doom and catastrophe, but in doing it he knew it gave the people of Judah their only chance of survival against the Babylonian threat.
>
> > i. Sometimes God's servants are accused of the exact opposite of the truth. Moses was a remarkably humble man (Numbers 12:3), but was accused of pride (Numbers 16:3). Job was a righteous man (Job 1:1), but was accused of great sin by his friends (Job 4:7-8, 8:20, 11:14-17). Jesus was the spotless Son of God and was accused of being demon possessed (John 7:20, 8:48, 8:52).

ii. "Ahab charged the like crime upon Elijah; the Jews upon Christ, and afterwards upon Paul; the heathen persecutors upon the primitive Christians; the heretics still upon the orthodox, that they were seditious, antimonarchical, etc." (Trapp)

c. **Look, he is in your hand**: Zedekiah could not find the courage to stand up to the princes of Judah and allowed them to do to Jeremiah as they pleased. They lowered him down into a **dungeon**-like pit, where **Jeremiah sank in the mire**.

i. "He was, of course, a puppet king, set up by Nebuchadrezzar after the exile of Jehoiachin and possibly not accepted by everyone in the nation as the true king." (Thompson)

ii. "Poor weak prince! you respect the prophet, you fear the cabal, and you sacrifice an innocent man to your own weakness and their malice!" (Clarke)

iii. "Zedekiah is one more instance of the evil which may come from a weak character, and of evil which may fall on it. He had good impulses, but he could not hold his own against the bad men round him." (Maclaren)

iv. "The intimidation of the princes seem to have paralyzed his will. He was a king with a wish-bone instead of a back-bone." (Cundall)

v. "The king's capitulation to his princes (Jeremiah 38:5) was perhaps the most abject surrender in biblical history until the moment when Pilate washed his hands before the multitude." (Kidner)

vi. "Zedekiah seems to have been an alumnus of the same school of politics that Pontius Pilate later attended." (Ryken)

vii. "If we would judge him, we may be judging ourselves, for his weakness might never have revealed itself had he not been thrust into a position that was far beyond him." (Kidner)

d. **They let Jeremiah down with ropes**: The intention of the princes was clearly to kill Jeremiah (**Please, let this man be put to death**). Yet in the most hypocritical way, they did not want to bear the guilt of *shedding his blood*. So instead of pushing him into the dungeon and allowing him to fall, which would likely open a wound and cause blood to be shed, they carefully lowered the prophet **down with ropes** into the dungeon where he would die a slow death from famine, exposure, or disease – but technically without blood being shed.

i. This **dungeon** at the house of **Malchiah** with no **water** but only mud-like **mire** was certainly a *cistern*. "Most houses in Jerusalem had private cisterns (*cf.* 2 Kings 18:31; Proverbs 5:15) for storing water collected from rainfall or from a spring. They were usually pear-shaped with a small opening at the top, which could be covered over if necessary to prevent accidents or contamination of the water." (Harrison)

ii. "The final intention of the officials was to bring about Jeremiah's death without bloodshed (cf. Genesis 37:18-19). He could well die a slow and painful but bloodless death in a cistern." (Thompson)

iii. "The princes, stopping short of making a violent end to Jeremiah, threw him unceremoniously into a disused water-cistern, with the obvious intention of causing his death either by exposure or starvation." (Cundall)

3. (7-13) Jeremiah rescued from prison pit.

Now Ebed-Melech the Ethiopian, one of the eunuchs, who was in the king's house, heard that they had put Jeremiah in the dungeon. When the king was sitting at the Gate of Benjamin, Ebed-Melech went out of the king's house and spoke to the king, saying: "My lord the king, these men have done evil in all that they have done to Jeremiah the prophet, whom they have cast into the dungeon, and he is likely to die from hunger in the place where he is. For *there is* **no more bread in the city." Then the king commanded Ebed-Melech the Ethiopian, saying, "Take from here thirty men with you, and lift Jeremiah the prophet out of the dungeon before he dies." So Ebed-Melech took the men with him and went into the house of the king under the treasury, and took from there old clothes and old rags, and let them down by ropes into the dungeon to Jeremiah. Then Ebed-Melech the Ethiopian said to Jeremiah, "Please put these old clothes and rags under your armpits, under the ropes." And Jeremiah did so. So they pulled Jeremiah up with ropes and lifted him out of the dungeon. And Jeremiah remained in the court of the prison.**

a. **Ebed-Melech the Ethiopian, one of the eunuchs**: With evil hatred, the princes of Judah put Jeremiah into a dungeon where he would probably soon die. God sent a foreigner, **Ebed-Melech the Ethiopian**, to help Jeremiah and to appeal to the king on the prophet's behalf.

i. It is possible that **Ebed-Melech** was not a literal eunuch. "*Saris* did not always mean a castrated person but had a broader meaning, such as 'officer' or 'court official.'" (Feinberg)

ii. Being a foreigner (and possibly a literal eunuch), Ebed-Melech was excluded from the temple and many Jewish rituals (Leviticus 21:20).

Yet he had a more godly and compassionate heart than most of the ruling class who did participate in those rituals.

iii. "A stranger, but (as that good Samaritan in the Gospel) more merciful than any of the Jewish nation, who gloried in their privileges." (Trapp)

iv. "We may not even know his name, for 'Ebed-Melech' simply means 'servant of the king.' It was not much of a name. Even if it was the man's proper name, it shows that he had no identity of his own." (Ryken)

b. **Lift Jeremiah the prophet out of the dungeon before he dies**: King Zedekiah was a weak man, easily influenced by others. When the princes of Judah demanded Jeremiah be cast into the pit, he agreed. When Ebed-Melech asked he be brought out, he also agreed. Jeremiah was near death, so the king commanded that **thirty men** be called upon to help rescue him.

i. **There is no more bread in the city**: "The suggestion that food supplies were exhausted was somewhat exaggerated in the heat of the moment, since stocks lasted until just before the city fell (Jeremiah 52:6f.)." (Harrison)

ii. "What a brave man was this, to oppose so many princes, and so potent that the king himself dared not displease them! It was God's Holy Spirit that put this mettle into him, and gave him the freedom of speech." (Trapp)

iii. **Thirty men**: So many men were needed not to do the work of pulling, but to be a guard so that none of the influential people who wanted Jeremiah dead could prevent his rescue. "Because the LXX and one Hebrew MS read 'three' for 'thirty,' a number of scholars choose the lesser figure. But such slight evidence is insufficient to overrule the MT." (Feinberg)

c. **Please put these old clothes and rags under your armpits, under the ropes**: Ebed-Melech was not only concerned to rescue Jeremiah, but to do it in the safest and most comfortable way.

i. "It is instructive that Ebed-melech went about his work of deliverance in a thoughtful, compassionate way, knowing how the naked ropes would cut into the limbs of a half-starved Jeremiah." (Cundall)

ii. Psalm 18:16, 35 could be taken out of its context and put into the mouth of a grateful Jeremiah, thanking God and Ebed-Melech:

He sent from above, He took me;
He drew me out of many waters....
Your gentleness has made me great (Psalm 18:16, 35).

iii. Jeremiah 39:15-18 describes how "Ebed-Melech received the same reward as Jeremiah. When Jerusalem fell, both men were rescued, for God delivers all who trust in him. Like all true servants of the King, Ebed-Melech was saved by faith." (Ryken)

d. **Jeremiah remained in the court of the prison**: Jeremiah was rescued from the dungeon pit but remained in custody of the prison.

B. Jeremiah and King Zedekiah.

1. (14-16) The agreement between King Zedekiah and the Prophet Jeremiah.

Then Zedekiah the king sent and had Jeremiah the prophet brought to him at the third entrance of the house of the LORD. And the king said to Jeremiah, "I will ask you something. Hide nothing from me." Jeremiah said to Zedekiah, "If I declare *it* to you, will you not surely put me to death? And if I give you advice, you will not listen to me." So Zedekiah the king swore secretly to Jeremiah, saying, "*As* the LORD lives, who made our very souls, I will not put you to death, nor will I give you into the hand of these men who seek your life."

a. **The king sent and had Jeremiah the prophet brought to him at the third entrance of the house of the LORD**: As in Jeremiah 38:16-17, King Zedekiah wanted a private meeting with Jeremiah.

i. There are several similarities between the events of Jeremiah 37 and Jeremiah 38 and some commentators (such as Thompson) believe the two chapters describe the same event from different perspectives. Nevertheless, the two chapters (Jeremiah 37 and 38) are more different than alike.

- Different charges made against Jeremiah.
- Different places of incarceration.
- Different manners of rescue.
- Different places of meeting with the king.
- Different conversations with the king.

ii. Given this, it is more likely that they are indeed separate though similar events. Jeremiah was true to his character and Zedekiah was true to his character, so the same drama might have been acted out in similar, yet different ways.

b. **If I declare it to you, will you not surely put me to death**: Zedekiah begged Jeremiah to tell him the truth, but Jeremiah feared the king could not handle the truth. Jeremiah feared that at best he would be ignored (**you will not listen to me**); at worst he would be put to death.

c. **I will not put you to death**: Zedekiah swore to Jeremiah in the name of the LORD that he would not kill the prophet nor allow others to do so.

> i. Strangely, a king who did not live as the LORD lived swore an oath, **as the LORD lives**. "But what credit was to be given to his oath, who was notoriously known to be a perjured person, as having broken his oath of fidelity to Nebuchadnezzar?" (Trapp)
>
> ii. "He also knows what poor security a solemn oath (Jeremiah 38:16) from this man amounts to (in inverse ratio, as often happens, to the strength of his language)." (Kidner)

2. (17-18) A final word to Zedekiah, a final offer of mercy.

Then Jeremiah said to Zedekiah, "Thus says the LORD, the God of hosts, the God of Israel: 'If you surely surrender to the king of Babylon's princes, then your soul shall live; this city shall not be burned with fire, and you and your house shall live. But if you do not surrender to the king of Babylon's princes, then this city shall be given into the hand of the Chaldeans; they shall burn it with fire, and you shall not escape from their hand.'"

a. **Thus says the LORD, the God of hosts, the God of Israel**: Jeremiah agreed to take the risk and deliver God's message to King Zedekiah. In speaking through Jeremiah, God began the word by identifying Himself.

- He was **the LORD**, Yahweh, the covenant God of Israel.
- He was **the God of hosts**, the God of heavenly armies and all their power.
- He was **the God of Israel**, the Master and Lord of the covenant descendants of Abraham, Isaac, and Jacob.

b. **If you surely surrender to the king of Babylon's princes, then your soul shall live**: This was not a new word to Zedekiah. Perhaps it had a new urgency, but it was not a new word. The Babylonians were God's instrument of judgment against Judah and therefore resistance against them was foolish and futile. It was better to **surrender** to them and to God's will.

> i. "All was indeed lost, as God announced (Jeremiah 38:3), and Jerusalem's suicidal stand had not even a tactical value, now that the whole country was overrun and the Egyptian thrust had failed. Only

obstinacy, at whatever cost in lives, could prolong the agony; and it was obstinacy not only against the enemy but against the Lord." (Kidner)

ii. This was God's remarkable patience and mercy to a king who rejected God's word many, many times before. Zedekiah could not prevent the conquest of Jerusalem by his repentance, but he could make that conquest much less severe. Even now, at this late hour:

- If he surrendered, his **soul shall live** – he would survive and not be put to death.
- If he surrendered, **this city shall not be burned with fire** – Jerusalem would be spared total destruction.
- If he surrendered, **your house shall live** – his wives, children, and royal family would be largely spared from death.

iii. "All he had to do was trust the prophet, to lift his head high, take up the flag of truce, walk past the princes and out to the Chaldean armies. This simple act of contrition would have saved the city." (Guest, cited in Ryken)

iv. **Surrender to the king of Babylon's princes**: Zedekiah knew what it was to surrender to princes; he shamefully surrendered to the princes of Judah (Jeremiah 38:4). Through Jeremiah, God warned Zedekiah to surrender to the *right* **princes**.

c. **This city shall not be burned with fire**: *The fate of the city rested with one man's repentance and trust in the* LORD. Surrender to the Babylonians would spare the city of Jerusalem. They would be conquered but not destroyed and **burned with fire**.

i. "It was an astounding invitation, all the more so for the previous withholding of all hope for Jerusalem, apart from hope for its rebuilding." (Kidner)

3. (19-23) God's assurance to Zedekiah through Jeremiah.

And Zedekiah the king said to Jeremiah, "I am afraid of the Jews who have defected to the Chaldeans, lest they deliver me into their hand, and they abuse me."

But Jeremiah said, "They shall not deliver *you*. Please, obey the voice of the LORD **which I speak to you. So it shall be well with you, and your soul shall live. But if you refuse to surrender, this *is* the word that the** LORD **has shown me: 'Now behold, all the women who are left in the king of Judah's house *shall be* surrendered to the king of Babylon's princes, and those *women* shall say:**

"Your close friends have set upon you
And prevailed against you;
Your feet have sunk in the mire,
And they have turned away again."

'So they shall surrender all your wives and children to the Chaldeans. You shall not escape from their hand, but shall be taken by the hand of the king of Babylon. And you shall cause this city to be burned with fire.'"

a. **I am afraid of the Jews who have defected to the Chaldeans**: Like all of us, Zedekiah could always think of a reason why obedience to God wasn't such a good idea. He thought that those who had already **defected to the Chaldeans** might **abuse** him in some way.

> i. "Once again Zedekiah's weakness of character shows up. There was a course of action to be followed which he knew to be right, but he lacked the courage to take it." (Thompson)

> ii. It may be that the only **abuse** he had to fear was mocking and contempt from those who surrendered earlier: "We surrendered months ago when you told us to continue to the fight. Look who has surrendered now. Look how wrong you were."

b. **Please, obey the voice of the LORD**: Jeremiah appealed to the king, knowing that always, the safest thing to do is to **obey the voice of the LORD**. There would be a blessing for obedience (**it shall be well with you, and your soul shall live**) and a curse for disobedience (**they shall surrender all your wives and children to the Chaldeans**).

> i. Jeremiah warned the king, "You're worried about what these defectors will say. Don't worry about that. Worry about what the wives of your harem will say when they are **surrendered to the king of Babylon's princes**."

c. **Your close friends have set upon you**: Jeremiah spoke a short piece of poetry voicing the devastation that the **wives and children** of Zedekiah and Jerusalem would feel at the violence and destruction that would come if the king continued his disobedience to God.

> i. "Women and children of the king's household would be led out to the Babylonians officials, chanting as they went what may have been a brief traditional song about being betrayed by friends and being deserted as you sank in the mud (cf. Psalm 69:14)." (Thompson)

> ii. "In the utterance of the prophet hears the female court-members and the royal household singing a bitter taunt-song (Jeremiah 38:22)

expressing the shame of their captivity and degradation by enemy military and diplomatic personnel." (Harrison)

iii. "More cutting than the ridicule of the defectors, whom Zedekiah feared, would be the ridicule the palace women would heap on him for his gullibility in trusting faithless allies." (Feinberg)

d. **They shall surrender all your wives and children to the Chaldeans… you shall cause this city to be burned with fire**: Nothing could change the fact that, as God's instrument, the Babylonians would conquer Judah and Jerusalem. Yet the obedience or disobedience of *one man* could determine the extent of the misery and destruction in that conquest.

i. This was a strong, courageous word Jeremiah brought to Zedekiah. The king had previously shown him mercy and promised him bread (Jeremiah 37:21), but the bread the king put in the mouth of the prophet did not prevent Jeremiah from speaking the truth to Zedekiah.

ii. "Nothing is more marked throughout all this story than the absolute and unswerving loyalty of Jeremiah to the message of judgment which he was called on to deliver." (Morgan)

4. (24-28) Zedekiah, Jeremiah, and the princes of Judah.

Then Zedekiah said to Jeremiah, "Let no one know of these words, and you shall not die. But if the princes hear that I have talked with you, and they come to you and say to you, 'Declare to us now what you have said to the king, and also what the king said to you; do not hide *it* from us, and we will not put you to death,' then you shall say to them, 'I presented my request before the king, that he would not make me return to Jonathan's house to die there.'" Then all the princes came to Jeremiah and asked him. And he told them according to all these words that the king had commanded. So they stopped speaking with him, for the conversation had not been heard. Now Jeremiah remained in the court of the prison until the day that Jerusalem was taken. And he was *there* when Jerusalem was taken.

a. **Let no one know of these words**: Mindful of his own interests, Zedekiah did not want anyone else to know what the Lord told him through Jeremiah. Perhaps he did not want the blame for the catastrophe of misery and destruction that his disobedience would bring.

i. "Even the preview of what he is bringing on his family (Jeremiah 38:23) fails to pull the king together. Like a child, he is only scared for having his secret talk found out. His parting words – virtually, 'Don't tell on me!' – show that God's latest and last call to turn back from the brink (Jeremiah 38:20ff.) has not even registered with him." (Kidner)

b. **He told them according to all the words that the king had commanded**: When the princes of Judah asked Jeremiah about his conversation with the king, Jeremiah did as the king asked. He did not reveal what God said to Zedekiah, apparently believing that it was between the king and God.

i. "This was telling the *truth*, and *nothing* but the truth, but not the *whole* truth. The king did not wish him to defile his conscience, nor did he propose any thing that was not consistent with the truth." (Clarke)

c. **Jeremiah remained in the court of the prison until the day that Jerusalem was taken**: Jeremiah was taken again to the pit dungeon and remained there until Jerusalem was conquered, just as he prophesied.

i. Jeremiah went back to the prison; Zedekiah went to the palace. It would turn out better for the prophet than for the king. "Zedekiah returned to the palace to suffer the anguish of knowing what was right to do but lacking the courage to do it." (Thompson)

Jeremiah 39 – The Fall of Jerusalem

A. The LORD judges King Zedekiah and Jerusalem.

1. (1-3) Jerusalem falls to the Babylonians.

In the ninth year of Zedekiah king of Judah, in the tenth month, Nebuchadnezzar king of Babylon and all his army came against Jerusalem, and besieged it. In the eleventh year of Zedekiah, in the fourth month, on the ninth *day* of the month, the city was penetrated. Then all the princes of the king of Babylon came in and sat in the Middle Gate: Nergal-Sharezer, Samgar-Nebo, Sarsechim, Rabsaris, Nergal-Sarezer, Rabmag, with the rest of the princes of the king of Babylon.

> a. **Nebuchadnezzar king of Babylon and all his army came against Jerusalem, and besieged it**: Nebuchadnezzar used the common method of attack in those days of securely walled cities – a siege. A **besieged** city was surrounded, preventing all business and trade from entering or leaving the city, and eventually starving the population into surrender – or the defenses of the city gave way and the surrounding army poured into the weakened city.
>
>> i. The Book of Lamentations vividly describes some of the agony of Jerusalem under siege.
>>
>> The tongue of the infant clings
>> To the roof of its mouth for thirst;
>> The young children ask for bread,
>> *But* no one breaks *it* for them.
>> Those who ate delicacies
>> Are desolate in the streets;
>> Those who were brought up in scarlet
>> Embrace ash heaps…
>> *Those* slain by the sword are better off
>> Than *those* who die of hunger;

> For these pine away,
> Stricken *for lack* of the fruits of the field.
> The hands of the compassionate women
> Have cooked their own children;
> They became food for them
> In the destruction of the daughter of my people.
> The LORD has fulfilled His fury,
> He has poured out His fierce anger.
> He kindled a fire in Zion,
> And it has devoured its foundations…
> Still our eyes failed us,
> *Watching* vainly for our help; In our watching we watched
> For a nation *that* could not save *us*.
> They tracked our steps
> So that we could not walk in our streets.
> Our end was near;
> Our days were over,
> For our end had come
> (Lamentations 4:4-5, 9-11, 17-18).

b. **The city was penetrated**: It happened just as God said through His Prophet Jeremiah. The Egyptians did not rescue Judah and the LORD did not miraculously deliver them as He did with the Assyrians some 130 years before. The false prophets who promised deliverance and success were wrong, and Jeremiah was proved right.

i. "So the siege lasted for eighteen months, from 10 January 588 to 9 July 587, interrupted briefly by the respite recorded in Jeremiah 37:5ff." (Kidner)

ii. "The battering ram took its last run at the walls. Darts from the enemy siege mounds arched into the midnight sky and struck their mark in flames. Famine had already claimed many lives inside the walls. Five Babylonian princes marched through the streets of Jerusalem, their faces illuminated by the flames of destruction." (Josephus, cited in Ryken)

c. **Then all the princes of the king of Babylon came in and sat in the Middle Gate**: This showed their authority over the conquered city. It belonged to them. The names of the princes listed here is difficult; it isn't easy to tell which is a name and which is a title in this list.

i. In a modern setting, this sitting in the gates of the city was similar to an enemy conquering Washington D.C. and then sitting in the Oval Office.

ii. **Rabmag** is literally, *chief magi* (according to Feinberg).

2. (4-5) The capture of King Zedekiah.

So it was, when Zedekiah the king of Judah and all the men of war saw them, that they fled and went out of the city by night, by way of the king's garden, by the gate between the two walls. And he went out by way of the plain. But the Chaldean army pursued them and overtook Zedekiah in the plains of Jericho. And when they had captured him, they brought him up to Nebuchadnezzar king of Babylon, to Riblah in the land of Hamath, where he pronounced judgment on him.

a. **They fled and went out of the city by night**: They did this not only to escape the Babylonians, but even more so in hope of escaping the promised judgment of God against them.

i. "Zedekiah, who has not dared to let God save him and his city and his family (Jeremiah 38:17-19), now deserts the people he has doomed." (Kidner)

ii. "Probably there was a *private passage under ground*, leading without the walls, by which Zedekiah and his followers might escape unperceived, till they had got some way from the city." (Clarke)

iii. Ezekiel 12:12 is a remarkable prophecy of this event: *And the prince who is among them shall bear his belongings on his shoulder at twilight and go out. They shall dig through the wall to carry them out through it. He shall cover his face, so that he cannot see the ground with his eyes.*

iv. "The king's garden was located near the Pool of Siloam (*cf.* Nehemiah 3:15)." (Harrison)

b. **The Chaldean army pursued them and overtook Zedekiah in the plains of Jericho**: This was a good distance away from Jerusalem. They were not far from the Jordan River and perhaps safety when they were captured. Yet they were captured, and their near success only made their fate more bitter.

i. "Another hour would have seen him safe across the Jordan, but the prospect of escape was only dangled before his eyes to make capture more bitter." (Maclaren)

ii. The Chaldeans captured Zedekiah, but even more so *God* captured him. "There is no escape from God possible. We must have to do with Him." (Morgan)

iii. This fulfilled the prophecy of Ezekiel 12:13: *I will also spread My net over him, and he shall be caught in My snare.*

c. **They brought him up to Nebuchadnezzar king of Babylon**: Several times before Jeremiah prophesied that Zedekiah would meet the king, he rebelled against *face to face* (Jeremiah 32:4, 34:3). Now it was fulfilled.

> i. **Riblah**: "An ancient Syrian town to the south of Kadesh on the river Orontes. It was situated at a strategic point where military highways between Egypt and Mesopotamia met." (Thompson)

3. (6-10) The fate of Zedekiah, Jerusalem, and the people of Judah.

Then the king of Babylon killed the sons of Zedekiah before his eyes in Riblah; the king of Babylon also killed all the nobles of Judah. Moreover he put out Zedekiah's eyes, and bound him with bronze fetters to carry him off to Babylon. And the Chaldeans burned the king's house and the houses of the people with fire, and broke down the walls of Jerusalem. Then Nebuzaradan the captain of the guard carried away captive to Babylon the remnant of the people who remained in the city and those who defected to him, with the rest of the people who remained. But Nebuzaradan the captain of the guard left in the land of Judah the poor people, who had nothing, and gave them vineyards and fields at the same time.

a. **The king of Babylon killed the sons of Zedekiah before his eyes**: God had promised Zedekiah that if he refused to obey Him and surrender to the Babylonians, his wives and children would suffer (Jeremiah 38:23). Here the terrible promise was fulfilled.

b. **The king of Babylon also killed all the nobles of Judah**: The princes of Judah who rebelled against God and hated His Prophet Jeremiah (Jeremiah 38:4) were justly judged.

> i. "The death of Zedekiah's sons, and of the nobles who had scoffed at Jeremiah's warnings, and the binding of Zedekiah, were all measures of precaution as well as of savagery. They diminished the danger of revolt; and a blind, childless prisoner, without counselors or friends, was harmless." (Maclaren)

c. **Moreover he put out Zedekiah's eyes, and bound him with bronze fetters to carry him off to Babylon**: The Babylonians were not known to be as cruel as the Assyrians who conquered the northern kingdom of Israel some 130 years earlier, but they were still experts in cruelty in their own right. They made certain that the last sight King Zedekiah saw was the murder of his own sons, and then spent the rest of his life in darkness.

> i. This fulfilled the mysterious promise God made through Ezekiel regarding Zedekiah shortly before the fall of Jerusalem: *I will bring him*

> to Babylon, to the land of the Chaldeans; yet he shall not see it, though he shall die there. (Ezekiel 12:13)
>
> ii. "The eyes of whose mind had been put out long before; else he might have foreseen and prevented this evil – as prevision is the best means of prevention – had he taken warning by what was foretold." (Trapp)
>
> iii. "But to make the sight of his slaughtered sons the poor wretch's last sight, was a refinement of gratuitous delight in torturing." (Maclaren)
>
> iv. "Assyrian sculptures show how kings delighted to put out, often with their own hands, the eyes of captive rulers." (Feinberg)
>
> v. "He was to die blinded and in exile, as Ezekiel 12:13 predicted, but in peace and with the mourning rites proper to a king." (Kidner)

d. **The Chaldeans burned the king's house and the houses of the people with fire, and broke down the walls of Jerusalem**: Jerusalem was burned and destroyed, just as God promised Zedekiah, the king who was hardened in his disobedience (Jeremiah 38:23).

> i. "The Fall of Jerusalem was so important that Scripture relates it four times – here, in Jeremiah 52, in 2 Kings 25, and in 2 Chronicles 36." (Feinberg)
>
> ii. "The city of Jerusalem has a long and blood-stained history, but possibly only the Roman destruction of A.D. 70 could have been more gruesome than this one in 587 BC" (Cundall)
>
> iii. "Feeble hands can pull down venerable structures built in happier times. It takes a David and a Solomon to rear a temple, but a Zedekiah can overthrow it." (Maclaren)

e. **Nebuzaradan the captain of the guard carried away captive to Babylon the remnant of the people who remained**: All but the poorest of the land were taken as forced refugees and exiles to Babylon.

> i. "Well might the victor think that Nebo had overcome Jehovah, but better did the vanquished know that Jehovah had kept his word." (Maclaren)
>
> ii. It all fulfilled the word of the LORD and vindicated the LORD's prophet, Jeremiah. It happened just as God said.
>
> - God said disaster would come from the north (Jeremiah 1;14, 4:6, 6:22, 13:20).
> - God said a strange, foreign nation would attack (Jeremiah 5:15).

- God said Jerusalem would be surrounded and besieged (Jeremiah 4:17, 6:3, 6:6).
- God said there would be famine in the land (Jeremiah 14:1-6, 14:16-18, 18:21).
- God said the whole land would be laid waste (Jeremiah 25:11).
- God said nations and kingdoms would be torn down (Jeremiah 1:10).
- God said death would enter the city (Jeremiah 9:21, 15:7-9, 18:21).
- God said enemy kings would sit in the gates of Jerusalem (Jeremiah 1:15).
- God said the city would be burned (Jeremiah 21:10, 21:14, 32:29, 34:2, 34:22, 37:8, 38:18, 38:23).
- God said the people would be taken into exile (Jeremiah 10:17-18, 13:17-19, 15:14, 17:4).

B. The LORD cares for His servants.

1. (11-14) Jeremiah protected by the Babylonians.

Now Nebuchadnezzar king of Babylon gave charge concerning Jeremiah to Nebuzaradan the captain of the guard, saying, "Take him and look after him, and do him no harm; but do to him just as he says to you." So Nebuzaradan the captain of the guard sent Nebushasban, Rabsaris, Nergal-Sharezer, Rabmag, and all the king of Babylon's chief officers; then they sent *someone* to take Jeremiah from the court of the prison, and committed him to Gedaliah the son of Ahikam, the son of Shaphan, that he should take him home. So he dwelt among the people.

   a. **Take him and look after him, and do him no harm**: Jeremiah had to wonder what would become of him when the Babylonians eventually conquered Jerusalem. God cared for His faithful servant, keeping him safe and in favor with Nebuchadnezzar and his captains.

   i. "How Jeremiah was known to the Babylonian authorities is not made clear, though very likely it was through the Judean deserters." (Thompson)

   b. **So he dwelt among the people**: Now an old man, Jeremiah was released from prison, protected by the Babylonians, and allowed to live **among the people** once again. This was a demonstration of God's grace, even in the larger context of judgment.

2. (15-18) God's assuring promise to Ebed-Melech.

Meanwhile the word of the LORD had come to Jeremiah while he was shut up in the court of the prison, saying, "Go and speak to Ebed-Melech the Ethiopian, saying, 'Thus says the LORD of hosts, the God of Israel: "Behold, I will bring My words upon this city for adversity and not for good, and they shall be *performed* in that day before you. But I will deliver you in that day," says the LORD, "and you shall not be given into the hand of the men of whom you *are* afraid. For I will surely deliver you, and you shall not fall by the sword; but your life shall be as a prize to you, because you have put your trust in Me," says the LORD.'"

> a. **Go and speak to Ebed-Melech the Ethiopian**: This was the man who rescued Jeremiah when the prophet was near death in the pit-like dungeon described in Jeremiah 38.
>
> b. **I will bring My words upon this city for adversity and not for good**: God assured Ebed-Melech that the catastrophe upon Jerusalem was actually His will and would be completed.
>
> c. **But I will deliver you in that day**: Though the destruction of Jerusalem was certain, so was the deliverance of the man who rescued the prophet of God and who **put** his **trust in** God. It took a lot of courage for Ebed-Melech to oppose the princes of Judah and to appeal the king's decision (Jeremiah 38:7-13), but that risk and courage was rewarded.
>
>> i. This shows that you did not have to be a famous prophet to receive God's grace in the midst of judgment. It was also extended to a Gentile man excluded from the temple who trusted God. This shows us that his compassionate acts were motivated by his trust in the LORD.
>>
>> ii. **Because you have put your trust in Me**: Ebed-Melech could come and find refuge in the God of Israel through trust, through faith. "We can notice that it says nothing of the heroism, the compassion, or the resourcefulness of his rescue-operation, outstanding though these were: only of the faith in God that was the mainspring of them all." (Kidner)
>>
>> iii. "It is prophetic that on the eve of the fall of the nation, a heathen man should be entering into union with God." (Maclaren)
>>
>> iv. "One man, besides Jeremiah, had his confidence in the right place. Was he one of the despised prophet's few 'converts'?" (Cundall)
>>
>> v. **I will surely deliver you**: "Hebrew, *Delivering, deliver thee*. It would be a great stay of mind, if God should say the same to us in particular and by name, as he doth here to this Ethiopian. And yet he saith no less to us in the precious promises, which we are by faith to appropriate." (Trapp)

Jeremiah 40 – Jeremiah Among the Remnant in the Land

A. God cares for faithful Jeremiah.

1. (1) Jeremiah rescued from captivity to Babylon.

The word that came to Jeremiah from the LORD after Nebuzaradan the captain of the guard had let him go from Ramah, when he had taken him bound in chains among all who were carried away captive from Jerusalem and Judah, who were carried away captive to Babylon.

> a. **After Nebuzaradan the captain of the guard had let him go from Ramah**: This word came to Jeremiah after the Babylonians had conquered and destroyed Jerusalem. When Jerusalem was conquered, Jeremiah was briefly collected with the other deportees, the Babylonian **captain of the guard had let him go**.
>
> > i. "The name *Ramah*, meaning a 'height', belonged to several places, but the most likely of these would be a town about six miles north of Jerusalem, two or three miles from Mizpah." (Kidner)
> >
> > ii. "It would appear that there was a staging area at Ramah, the modern Er-Ram some 5 miles north of Jerusalem. From here the deportees would be set off for Babylonia." (Thompson)
>
> b. **Among all who were carried away captive from Jerusalem and Judah**: Apparently, Jeremiah was among those who were being organized for forced relocation to Babylon when Nebuzaradan found him and released him.
>
> > i. "Somehow Jeremiah had been rounded up with the others, and when liberated he had been shackled despite Nebuchadnezzar's orders for considerate treatment." (Harrison)

2. (2-4) Nebuzaradan's word to Jeremiah.

And the captain of the guard took Jeremiah and said to him: "The LORD your God has pronounced this doom on this place. Now the LORD has brought *it*, and has done just as He said. Because you *people* have sinned against the LORD, and not obeyed His voice, therefore this thing has come upon you. And now look, I free you this day from the chains that *were* on your hand. If it seems good to you to come with me to Babylon, come, and I will look after you. But if it seems wrong for you to come with me to Babylon, remain here. See, all the land *is* before you; wherever it seems good and convenient for you to go, go there."

> a. **The LORD your God has pronounced this doom on this place**: Nebuzaradan knew of Jeremiah and his prophecies. He knew that this was the judgment of Yahweh against His people because **they sinned against the LORD**. The Babylonian Nebuzaradan believed the word of God more than Yahweh's covenant people did.
>
>> i. "Unquestionably the words sound like those of Jeremiah himself, and this may show that Nebuzaradan had some acquaintance with the prophet's teaching. The simplest explanation may be that he knew of the content of Jeremiah's main emphasis in preaching and was simply quoting it as appropriate for the occasion." (Feinberg)
>>
>> ii. "A strange speech to come out of such a man's mouth. How could the captives present hear it, and not be affected with it? Thus Balaam's ass sometimes rebuked his master's madness, but to little good effect." (Trapp)
>
> b. **I free you this day from the chains that were on your hand**: Nebuzaradan probably did this out of both respect for Jeremiah's steadfast courage, and what could be interpreted as Jeremiah's favorable message regarding the Babylonians (that Jerusalem should surrender to their invading army).
>
> c. **If it seems good to you to come with me to Babylon, come, and I will look after you**: Jeremiah had a relatively attractive offer from Nebuzaradan. He could go to Babylon with his fellow Jews and know he would have a better life there than many of them, because the captain of the guard would **look after** him.
>
> d. **If it seems wrong for you to come with me to Babylon, remain here**: Nebuzaradan gave Jeremiah a rare choice. Those who went to Babylonia were compelled to go; they did not have a choice to remain. Jeremiah was one of the few Jews who could choose **whatever seems good and convenient** to him.
>
>> i. F.B. Meyer said of Nebuzaradan, "He is a comrade of the centurions of the New Testament."

3. (5-6) Jeremiah chooses to stay in the land.

Now while Jeremiah had not yet gone back, *Nebuzaradan said,* **"Go back to Gedaliah the son of Ahikam, the son of Shaphan, whom the king of Babylon has made governor over the cities of Judah, and dwell with him among the people. Or go wherever it seems convenient for you to go." So the captain of the guard gave him rations and a gift and let him go. Then Jeremiah went to Gedaliah the son of Ahikam, to Mizpah, and dwelt with him among the people who were left in the land.**

> a. **While Jeremiah had not yet gone back**: Perhaps Jeremiah had a difficult time making up his mind, or at least it appeared so to Nebuzaradan.
>
> b. **Go back… dwell with him among the people**: Sensing that Jeremiah really wanted to stay, Nebuzaradan voiced what seemed to be his choice – to stay in the land. The Babylonian captain of the guard made provision that Jeremiah would stay in the care of **Gedaliah**, who was appointed by the king of Babylon as **governor over the cities of Judah**.
>
>> i. Gedaliah was **the son of Ahikam, the son of Shaphan**. "Shaphan the grandfather was Josiah's secretary and carried the newly found scroll to the king (2 Kings 22:3-13). One son, Ahikam, was part of the delegation Josiah sent to the prophetess Huldah (2 Kings 22:12-14). Ahikam offered protection to Jeremiah after he had preached the Temple Sermon (Jeremiah 26:24). It was Ahikam's son Gedaliah who was the new governor of the Babylonian province of Judah." (Thompson)
>>
>> ii. In appointing Gedaliah, it was apparent that Nebuchadnezzar no longer trusted the men of the House of David. He chose a man who had administrative experience, but was not of the royal line. "It is obvious that Nebuchadnezzar had lost all faith in the house of David. His dealings with the last three kings of Judah were disappointing in the extreme." (Feinberg)
>>
>> iii. "A seal dating from this time discovered at Lachish is inscribed with the name of a 'Gedaliah,' who was 'over the House' – i.e. a palace governor (cf. Isaiah 36:22). The man referred to could have been the Gedaliah of Jeremiah's time." (Feinberg)
>
> c. **The captain of the guard gave him rations and a gift and let him go**: This shows God's remarkable care for Jeremiah, even from the hands of a pagan authority. In some ways, Jeremiah received better treatment from Nebuzaradan than from his fellow Jews.

i. "The courteous and humane treatment from the nation's enemy contrasts markedly with what Jeremiah had received from his own countrymen." (Harrison)

ii. "God is able to supply the need of his servants in very remarkable ways; now through ravens, or a widow, and again through a captain of Nebuchadnessar's guard. If we will be all for God, God will be all for us." (Meyer)

d. **Dwelt with him among the people who were left in the land**: Jeremiah lived under the care of the Judean man who was the Babylonian-appointed governor, and he lived **among** the poorest and most wretched of the land, those not sent to Babylon.

i. **The people who were left in the land**: "The great bulk of these Judeans were of the underprivileged classes (Jeremiah 39:10), but there were others including some royal princesses as well as remnants of the Judean army who may have been engaged in guerrilla activity against the Chaldeans." (Thompson)

ii. Jeremiah wanted to live among his people because he loved them. "Jeremiah was not a vindictive man, nor did he feel the slightest elation at the downfall of his adversaries. They were his people, he loved them, and he wept bitterly for them, as the book of *Lamentations* shows." (Cundall)

iii. "It is a revealing fact of the character of Jeremiah, that when, undoubtedly, he might have secured safety and even comfort for himself in Babylon, he elected to remain in his own land and among the weak remnant of his own people." (Morgan)

B. Gedaliah, governor of Judah.

1. (7-10) Gedaliah assures the remaining Jewish military presence.

And when all the captains of the armies who *were* in the fields, they and their men, heard that the king of Babylon had made Gedaliah the son of Ahikam governor in the land, and had committed to him men, women, children, and the poorest of the land who had not been carried away captive to Babylon, then they came to Gedaliah at Mizpah—Ishmael the son of Nethaniah, Johanan and Jonathan the sons of Kareah, Seraiah the son of Tanhumeth, the sons of Ephai the Netopathite, and Jezaniah the son of a Maachathite, they and their men. And Gedaliah the son of Ahikam, the son of Shaphan, took an oath before them and their men, saying, "Do not be afraid to serve the Chaldeans. Dwell in the land and serve the king of Babylon, and it shall be well with you. As for me, I will

indeed dwell at Mizpah and serve the Chaldeans who come to us. But you, gather wine and summer fruit and oil, put *them* in your vessels, and dwell in your cities that you have taken."

> a. **When all the captains of the armies who were in the fields**: When the Babylonians conquered the people of Judah, there were some remaining military **captains** and **their men** who escaped. They had to choose whether they would continue the fight as an underground resistance or submit to Babylonian rule.
>
>> i. "The land had been deprived of its leaders; so chiefs of guerrilla bands, who remained hidden while the Babylonian army was besieging, waited the turn of events after the fall of the capital." (Feinberg)
>
> b. **Heard that the king of Babylon had made Gedaliah the son of Ahikam governor in the land**: These military men wanted to meet with Gedaliah to see if he would support the Babylonians or begin to betray the king of Babylon who put him in power (as King Zedekiah had done) and fight for an independent Judah.
>
> c. **They came to Gedaliah as Mizpah**: The listed military leaders came to Gedaliah at the historic site of **Mizpah** (Genesis 31:45-54, Joshua 11:8, Judges 20:1-3, 1 Samuel 7:5-12, 1 Samuel 10:17).
>
> d. **Do not be afraid to serve the Chaldeans**: Gedaliah said this with **an oath** to assure the officers and their men that truly, their best and wisest action was to surrender to God's judgment through the Babylonians and make the most of the life they had. They had his promise: **Do not be afraid to serve the Chaldeans. Dwell in the land and serve the king of Babylon, and it shall be well with you.**
>
> e. **Gather wine and summer fruit and oil, put them in your vessels, and dwell in your cities**: Gedaliah told them to do what Jeremiah the prophet had told the people to do – submit to God's judgment through the Babylonians and seek to honor God and glorify Him in normal life.
>
>> i. "Gedaliah's responsibility was to help this remnant settle down, work the land and pay tribute to Babylon from the harvests." (Harrison)

3. (11-12) The Jews in neighboring lands come back to Judah.

Likewise, when all the Jews who *were* in Moab, among the Ammonites, in Edom, and who *were* in all the countries, heard that the king of Babylon had left a remnant of Judah, and that he had set over them Gedaliah the son of Ahikam, the son of Shaphan, then all the Jews returned out of all places where they had been driven, and came to the land of Judah, to Gedaliah at Mizpah, and gathered wine and summer fruit in abundance.

a. **All the Jews who were in Moab, among the Ammonites, in Edom, and who were in all the countries**: As the Babylonian threat came closer, many Jews escaped to neighboring nations and peoples.

b. **Then all the Jews returned out of all places where they had been driven, and came to the land of Judah**: Once Judah and Jerusalem were conquered and the land stabilized under Gedaliah, they came back to the land and resumed normal life with a measure of blessing (**gathered wine and summer fruit in abundance**).

4. (13-14) Gedaliah is told of a murder plot.

Moreover Johanan the son of Kareah and all the captains of the forces that *were* in the fields came to Gedaliah at Mizpah, and said to him, "Do you certainly know that Baalis the king of the Ammonites has sent Ishmael the son of Nethaniah to murder you?" But Gedaliah the son of Ahikam did not believe them.

a. **Do you certainly know that Baalis the king of the Ammonites has sent Ishmael the son of Nethaniah to murder you**: Some of the remaining officers of the land brought this warning of an assassination plot to Gedaliah.

i. "Ishmael the son of Nethaniah (Jeremiah 41:1) was of royal heritage (cf. 2 Kings 25:23). An enthusiastic member of the anti-Babylonian party, he was both jealous of and filled with hatred for Gedaliah." (Feinberg)

ii. "Since Ishmael, the would-be executioner, was of the royal house of David, he may have been slighted in being passed over for the responsible office of governor." (Harrison)

iii. "Recently an excavation in Jordan has uncovered the Siran Bottle (dated in the period of 667-580 BC), which bears the name of a King Ba'lay, who has been identified with the Baalis of Jeremiah 40:13-14." (Feinberg)

b. **Gedaliah the son of Ahikam did not believe them**: Gedaliah did not believe this report, though the events of Jeremiah 41 show that it was true. Perhaps Gedaliah was foolish; perhaps **Ishmael the son of Nethaniah** had won his trust in some way.

i. "He seems to have been of a magnanimous disposition and unable to believe evil of one whom he knew personally in the days when he was a state official and Ishmael was a royal prince." (Thompson)

ii. "The next chapter shows that Johanan's information was too true. So noble Gedaliah lost his life by not believing that evil of others of which he himself was incapable." (Clarke)

5. (15-16) Gedaliah rejects an offer of protection against the threat.

Then Johanan the son of Kareah spoke secretly to Gedaliah in Mizpah, saying, "Let me go, please, and I will kill Ishmael the son of Nethaniah, and no one will know *it*. Why should he murder you, so that all the Jews who are gathered to you would be scattered, and the remnant in Judah perish?" But Gedaliah the son of Ahikam said to Johanan the son of Kareah, "You shall not do this thing, for you speak falsely concerning Ishmael."

a. **Let me go, please, and I will kill Ishmael**: One of the leaders who brought the report of a murder plot to Gedaliah pressed him further, speaking to him **secretly**. He offered to eliminate the man accused of plotting the murder.

b. **You shall not do this thing, for you speak falsely concerning Ishmael**: Gedaliah still did not believe the warning, even though **Johanan the son of Kareah** pressed it upon him. Gedaliah continued to trust what he knew of Ishmael and regarded the warning as a false report.

i. "From our vantage-point we can see that Gedliah should have enquired of the Lord, whose Prophet Jeremiah was with him; yet this is easily said." (Kidner)

Jeremiah 41 – The Murder of Gedaliah, Governor of the Land

A. The massacre at Mizpah.

1. (1-3) The murder of Gedaliah.

Now it came to pass in the seventh month *that* Ishmael the son of Nethaniah, the son of Elishama, of the royal family and of the officers of the king, came with ten men to Gedaliah the son of Ahikam, at Mizpah. And there they ate bread together in Mizpah. Then Ishmael the son of Nethaniah, and the ten men who were with him, arose and struck Gedaliah the son of Ahikam, the son of Shaphan, with the sword, and killed him whom the king of Babylon had made governor over the land. Ishmael also struck down all the Jews who were with him, *that is*, with Gedaliah at Mizpah, and the Chaldeans who were found there, the men of war.

> a. **And they ate bread together in Mizpah**: Gathered together at the same place where the remaining officers of Judah's army warned him, Gedaliah the governor of Judah met with **Ishmael the son of Nethaniah** and his associates. The coming treachery was even worse because it violated the hospitality and protection of the shared table (**ate bread together**).
>
>> i. **Ishmael the son of Nethaniah, the son of Elishama**: "Ishmael came from a collateral line of the Davidic family through Elishama, son of David (cf. 2 Samuel 5:16)." (Feinberg)
>>
>> ii. **Ate bread together**: "Since the sharing of a meal was regarded as a covenant of brotherhood (cf. Psalm 41:9; John 13:18, 26-30) the treachery of his act would be the more reprehensible." (Cundall)
>>
>> iii. "The fact that Ishmael was at Gedaliah's table may suggest that the two men knew one another and that Gedaliah was making a gesture of friendship." (Thompson)

iv. "In spite of having been warned of an assassination plot, Gedaliah had taken no precautions." (Feinberg)

v. "They feasted. Much treachery and cruelty hath been exercised at feasts. Absalom slew Amnon at a feast; so did Zimri King Elah; so did Alexander Philotas." (Trapp)

b. **Arose and struck Gedaliah**: Ishmael and his ten men murdered the governor appointed by the king of Babylon, as well as **all the Jews who were with him**, and the Babylonian **men of war** there to protect the governor. Ishmael did this because Baalis, the king of the Ammonites hired him to do it (Jeremiah 40:14).

i. Ishmael was **of the royal family and of the officers of the king**, a descendant of David. He was probably jealous that Gedaliah was appointed governor, making him more willing to do the work of the king of the Ammonites.

ii. "Everything about him disgraced the name of David his forebear, who had resisted every impulse to 'wade through slaughter to a throne' and had awaited God's time and his people's will. This was no David but a Jehu." (Kidner)

iii. Ishmael's crime was all the more startling because he lived through the dramatic display of God's judgment in the fall of Jerusalem and Judah. Nevertheless, it did not make him fear or honor the Lord. "Yet men may hear the word of the Lord, live through the experiences in which it is vindicated, and yet ignore it." (Morgan)

iv. "Gedaliah's death was a tragedy. For years afterward, the Jews held a fast to lament the day of his passing." (Ryken) "In the centuries that followed, the Jews were to observe a fast to commemorate this tragedy (Zechariah 7:5; 8:19)." (Thompson)

v. "The whole shameful incident was bound to encourage stern reprisals by the Babylonians." (Thompson)

2. (4-7) The murder of the men who came to sacrifice.

And it happened, on the second day after he had killed Gedaliah, when as yet no one knew *it*, that certain men came from Shechem, from Shiloh, and from Samaria, eighty men with their beards shaved and their clothes torn, having cut themselves, with offerings and incense in their hand, to bring *them* to the house of the LORD. Now Ishmael the son of Nethaniah went out from Mizpah to meet them, weeping as he went along; and it happened as he met them that he said to them, "Come to Gedaliah the son of Ahikam!" So it was, when they came into the midst

of the city, that Ishmael the son of Nethaniah killed them *and cast them into the midst of a pit, he and the men who were with him.*

a. **On the second day after he had killed Gedaliah, when as yet no one knew it**: Ishmael and his men had so effectively killed the men at the Mizpah settlement that it took some time for the news of the murder to be known.

b. **Certain men came from Shechem, from Shiloh, and from Samaria**: There were worshippers of Yahweh in the lands that were formerly part of the Kingdom of Israel, conquered by the Assyrians more than 100 years before this. Perhaps they were influenced by King Josiah's reforms, or perhaps they came from the southern kingdom of Judah.

i. "These pilgrims may have been descendants of Judeans who had moved north after Samaria fell in 722 BC." (Harrison)

ii. "The cities named, all from the old northern kingdom of Israel, suggest the effects of the reforms of Hezekiah and Josiah in this area (2 Kings 23:15-20; 2 Chronicles 30:1-12)." (Cundall)

iii. "Josiah had destroyed the altar at Bethel (one of the lasting effects of Josiah's reform); so they were bringing offerings to the Jerusalem temple." (Feinberg)

iv. They came with **beards shaved**: "All these were signs of deep mourning, probably on account of the destruction of the city." (Clarke)

v. **Beards shaved…having cut themselves**: "These might be well minded men, though partly through ignorance of the law in those blind times, and partly through excess of passion, they went too far, heathen-like, in their outward expressions of sorrow [Leviticus 19:27 Deuteronomy 14:1] for the public calamity of their country." (Trapp)

c. **With offerings and incense in their hand, to bring them to the house of the LORD**: This large group of men came from the north to bring offerings and sacrifices to the temple. Since the Babylonians destroyed the temple (2 Kings 25:9), they came in respectful mourning to bring grain **offerings** and **incense** to the ruins of the temple.

i. "Their offerings (lit., 'present' or 'tribute') were bloodless sacrifices because no facilities were available for animal sacrifices (cf. Deuteronomy 12:13-14, 17-18)." (Feinberg)

ii. "Their offerings were probably intended for a ceremony in the area of the sacrificial altar." (Harrison)

iii. "In spite of the destruction of the temple itself, they came to the temple site, which was still used for worship by those who survived

d. **Ishmael the son of Nethaniah went out from Mizpah to meet them, weeping as he went along:** The wicked and heartless Ishmael knew how to put on a show and seem harmless to the approaching group of men.

e. **Ishmael the son of Nethaniah killed them and cast them into the midst of a pit:** Ishmael and his gang murdered as many as they could from this group of worshippers, and cruelly threw their bodies into a cistern (**a pit**).

> i. "This hell hound having once, as other hounds, dipped his tongue in blood, can put no period to his unparalleled cruelty." (Trapp)

> ii. "Moreover, since the water supply was so precious in Palestine, the fouling of a cistern was a peculiarly irresponsible act of vandalism." (Cundall)

> iii. "This chapter is full of horrible atrocities. Blow on blow befell the already decimated remnant of Jews." (Meyer)

> iv. "One begins to picture Ishmael as a brutal murderer who enjoyed killing for its own sake." (Thompson)

> v. "Jeremiah inserted a historical notation, showing that King Asa of Judah (913-873 BC) had ordered this cistern to be made to insure ample water for Mizpah when he fortified it against King Baasha of Israel (910-887 BC) (cf. 1 Kings 15:22; 2 Chronicles 16:6)." (Feinberg)

> vi. "Excavations at Tellen-Nasbeh may have brought the cistern to question to light." (Thompson)

3. (8-10) Ishmael takes captive the survivors and returns to the Ammonites.

But ten men were found among them who said to Ishmael, "Do not kill us, for we have treasures of wheat, barley, oil, and honey in the field." So he desisted and did not kill them among their brethren. Now the pit into which Ishmael had cast all the dead bodies of the men whom he had slain, because of Gedaliah, *was* the same one Asa the king had made for fear of Baasha king of Israel. Ishmael the son of Nethaniah filled it with *the* slain. Then Ishmael carried away captive all the rest of the people who *were* in Mizpah, the king's daughters and all the people who remained in Mizpah, whom Nebuzaradan the captain of the guard had committed to Gedaliah the son of Ahikam. And Ishmael the son of Nethaniah carried them away captive and departed to go over to the Ammonites.

a. **Do not kill us, for we have treasures of wheat, barley, oil, and honey in the field**: Among the eighty men who came to Mizpah from the north, ten were able to persuade Ishmael to spare their lives in exchange for all the good things they brought to sacrifice and offer unto the LORD.

> i. "He kept *ten* alive because they told him they had treasures hidden in a field, which they would show him. Whether he kept his word with them is not recorded. He could do nothing good or great; and it is likely that, when he had possessed himself of those treasures, he served them as he had served their companions." (Clarke)

b. **The same one Asa the king had made for fear of Baasha king of Israel**: Asa's reign is described in 1 Kings 15:11-16. Perhaps he made this cistern as a preparation for battle against Baasha king of Israel.

> i. "See 1Kings 15:22. Asa made this cistern as a reservoir for water for the supply of the place; for he built and fortified *Mizpah* at the time that he was at war with Baasha, king of Israel." (Clarke)

c. **Ishmael the son of Nethaniah carried them away captive**: The brutal and cunning Ishmael took the survivors and slaves and servants to the **Ammonites** – likely to sell them as slaves to the foreign king.

> i. **The king's daughers**: "We cannot be certain who they represent, whether Zedekiah's daughters or some other women of royal descent, of whom there may have been quite a number from other branches of the royal family." (Thompson)

> ii. "Ishmael's motive in transporting the remnant may have been threefold: (1) to escape punishment, (2) to find refuge with Baalis who had instigated the assassination of Gedaliah (Jeremiah 40:14), and (3) to sell the remnant as slaves to the Ammonites." (Feinberg)

> iii. "Again we are impressed with the terrible plight of the people." (Morgan)

B. The response of Johanan.

1. (11-13) The rescue of the captives and the escape of Ishmael.

But when Johanan the son of Kareah and all the captains of the forces that *were* with him heard of all the evil that Ishmael the son of Nethaniah had done, they took all the men and went to fight with Ishmael the son of Nethaniah; and they found him by the great pool that *is* in Gibeon. So it was, when all the people who *were* with Ishmael saw Johanan the son of Kareah, and all the captains of the forces who *were* with him, that they were glad. Then all the people whom Ishmael had carried away captive from Mizpah turned around and came back, and went to

Johanan the son of Kareah. But Ishmael the son of Nethaniah escaped from Johanan with eight men and went to the Ammonites.

> a. **When Johanan the son of Kareah and all the captains of the forces that were with him heard of all the evil that Ishmael the son of Nethaniah had done**: This must have been especially tragic news to **Johanan**, because he warned Gedaliah of the murder plot Ishmael had planned against him (Jeremiah 40:15).
>
> b. **They took all the men and went to fight with Ishmael**: Heroically, Johanan would not let this crime go unpunished. He and his men pursued and met Ishmael's party in battle. Apparently both Ishmael's captives and his **captains** were happy to see Johanan, and immediately went to his side. Ishmael was so violent and wicked that he frightened his own men.
>
>> i. "Ishmael finds how delusive is a victory that wins no hearts, as his whole captive company delightedly deserts him." (Kidner)
>>
>> ii. **The great pool that is in Gibeon**: "It has been suggested that 'the great pool' is the same as 'the pool of Gibeon' (cf. 2 Samuel 2:13)." (Feinberg)
>>
>> iii. "Recent excavations at el-Jib some 6 miles northwest of Jerusalem have revealed a large pit hewn out of the rock, some 82 feet deep, which had steps carved around its sides from top to bottom to enable people to reach the water stored there." (Thompson)
>
> c. **Ishmael the son of Nethaniah escaped from Johanan**: Ishmael was able to escape capture when Johanan and his men raided them. He and **eight men** made it to the Ammonites.

2. (16-18) Johanan's leadership.

Then Johanan the son of Kareah, and all the captains of the forces that were with him, took from Mizpah all the rest of the people whom he had recovered from Ishmael the son of Nethaniah after he had murdered Gedaliah the son of Ahikam—the mighty men of war and the women and the children and the eunuchs, whom he had brought back from Gibeon. And they departed and dwelt in the habitation of Chimham, which is near Bethlehem, as they went on their way to Egypt, because of the Chaldeans; for they were afraid of them, because Ishmael the son of Nethaniah had murdered Gedaliah the son of Ahikam, whom the king of Babylon had made governor in the land.

> a. **Then Johanan the son of Kareah**: Johanan and his men took the survivors from the Mizpah massacre and brought them to **Chimham, which is near Bethlehem**, until they eventually went to Egypt.

i. **The habitation of Chimham**: "The estate that David gave Chimham, the son of Barzillai. See 2 Samuel 19:37, etc. He took this merely as a resting-place; as he designed to carry all into Egypt, fearing the *Chaldeans*, who would endeavour to revenge the death of Gedaliah." (Clarke)

b. **For they were afraid of them**: This terrible account is included to show how chaotic and unsafe conditions were in Judah and the region after the fall of the Kingdom of Judah. Many felt they were safer in Egypt than remaining in that lawless land.

i. **As they went on their way to Egypt**: "Johanan now decided to go as quickly as possible to Egypt. He and the army officers with him feared reprisals when the news of Gedaliah's assassination reached Babylon." (Feinberg)

Jeremiah 42 – An Insincere Request for Guidance

A. Guidance requested.

1. (1-3) Johanan and the people ask Jeremiah for guidance.

Now all the captains of the forces, Johanan the son of Kareah, Jezaniah the son of Hoshaiah, and all the people, from the least to the greatest, came near and said to Jeremiah the prophet, "Please, let our petition be acceptable to you, and pray for us to the LORD your God, for all this remnant (since we are left *but* a few of many, as you can see), that the LORD your God may show us the way in which we should walk and the thing we should do."

> a. **Now all the captains of the forces…and all the people, from the least to the greatest, came near**: After the brutal massacre at Mizpah (Jeremiah 41), the leaders and citizens of those left in the land were anxious and asked Jeremiah for a word from the Lord.
>
>> i. "The whole populace came to secure an oracle from him; something which had never happened in the forty years before Jerusalem fell." (Cundall)
>>
>> ii. **The son of Hoshaiah**: "Hoshaiah may be the Hoshaiah whose name appears in the Lachish Letters." (Feinberg)
>
> b. **Please, let our petition be acceptable to you**: When they came to the old and distinguished prophet, they came with great politeness and respect.
>
>> i. "There was some degree of panic among the refugees as to what should be their next move. An oracle from Yahweh would cut short their perplexity." (Thompson)
>
> c. **That the LORD your God may show us the way in which we should walk and the thing we should do**: Rightly concerned over the dangers surrounding them, they asked Jeremiah for guidance from God, with the

idea that if they did what God wanted them to do, they would enjoy His protection. By all appearance this was a humble, wise, and proper request.

> i. On the surface, this was a great prayer to pray. "It is still a prayer worth praying daily. Yet a minute flaw on the surface of it, in the words '*your* God', made an admission that went deeper than they realized." (Kidner)

> ii. Underneath the good words, "Self-interest has predominated once again, and now their concern is merely to know if God will approve of their plan to migrate to Egypt." (Harrison)

> iii. "It is useless to profess our desire to know God's will, whilst in our secret heart we are determined to follow a certain course, come what may. How often do believers ask for prayer that their course may be made clear, when in point of fact they have already decided on it, and are secretly hoping to turn God to their own side!" (Meyer)

> iv. "It is possible to deal deceitfully with our own souls. We do so, as these people did, whenever we ask for Divine guidance, having previously decided as to what our course of action is to be. Such praying is only a superstitious activity. When prayer is conceived of as a means of getting our own desires fulfilled, it is a superstition." (Morgan)

2. (4) Jeremiah promises to answer their request.

Then Jeremiah the prophet said to them, "I have heard. Indeed, I will pray to the Lord your God according to your words, and it shall be, *that* whatever the Lord answers you, I will declare *it* to you. I will keep nothing back from you."

> a. **I will pray to the Lord your God according to your words**: Jeremiah was happy to bring them a word from God, but he had to seek God and **pray** for it.

> > i. "Jeremiah was unwilling to speak until he had received the Lord's explicit word." (Feinberg)

> b. **I will declare it to you. I will keep nothing back from you**: Jeremiah promised to faithfully deliver whatever word God gave him for the leaders and commoners of those remaining in the land after the Babylonian exile.

> > i. "He knew, in all probability by divine revelation, that the prayer they had asked him to offer for them had not been honest." (Morgan)

3. (5-6) Johanan and the people promise to obey the word of the Lord.

So they said to Jeremiah, "Let the Lord be a true and faithful witness between us, if we do not do according to everything which the Lord

your God sends us by you. Whether *it is* pleasing or displeasing, we will obey the voice of the LORD our God to whom we send you, that it may be well with us when we obey the voice of the LORD our God."

> a. **Let the LORD be a true and faithful witness between us, if we do not do according to everything**: With a holy and solemn oath, they promised to do whatever God told them to do through the Prophet Jeremiah, **whether it is pleasing or displeasing**.
>
>> i. "Did these men know what it was so solemnly to swear a thing? Or were they stark atheists, thus to promise that with an oath which they never meant to perform?" (Trapp)
>
> b. **That it may be well with us when we obey**: They properly believed that God would care for them if they obeyed Him. They expected the blessings that would come to God's obedient people under the terms of the Old Covenant (Deuteronomy 28).
>
>> i. "Probably they were sincere, but they were absolutely sure in their own minds concerning the right course, and they could not imagine that the prophet's advice would so flatly contradict the conclusions of their own sound reasoning." (Cundall)

B. Guidance given.

1. (7-12) The blessing to those who remain in the land.

And it happened after ten days that the word of the LORD came to Jeremiah. Then he called Johanan the son of Kareah, all the captains of the forces which *were* with him, and all the people from the least even to the greatest, and said to them, "Thus says the LORD, the God of Israel, to whom you sent me to present your petition before Him: 'If you will still remain in this land, then I will build you and not pull *you* down, and I will plant you and not pluck *you* up. For I relent concerning the disaster that I have brought upon you. Do not be afraid of the king of Babylon, of whom you are afraid; do not be afraid of him,' says the LORD, 'for I *am* with you, to save you and deliver you from his hand. And I will show you mercy, that he may have mercy on you and cause you to return to your own land.'

> a. **After ten days that the word of the LORD came to Jeremiah**: The prophetic word took time to come to Jeremiah. It wasn't an immediate thing to be called upon whenever he pleased. It had to come in God's timing.

i. "The ten days which Jeremiah took before he felt able to pronounce the divine oracle must have seemed interminable to the Jews, living as they were in such apparent danger." (Cundall)

ii. "It is evident the prophets could not prophesy when they pleased, any more than the disciples of our Lord could work miracles when they wished. The gift of prophecy and the gift of miracles were both dependent on the will of the Most High, and each of them was given only for the moment; and when the necessity was over, the influence ceased." (Clarke)

b. **If you will still remain in this land, then I will build you and not pull you down**: Jeremiah delivered God's message to the leaders and common people, that if they stayed in the land God would protect and establish them. Speaking in God's voice, Jeremiah assured them that God would **relent concerning the disaster** God had brought upon them. The days of terrible judgment were over.

i. "As I have punished you only because you continued to be rebellious, I will arrest this punishment as soon as you become obedient to my word. You need not fear the king of Babylon if you have me for your helper; and I will so show mercy to you that he shall see it, and cease from afflicting you, as he shall see that I am on your side." (Clarke)

ii. **For I relent**: "The verb translated 'grieve for' (*niham*) should be translated 'repent' as in AV, RV, and RSV, as though Yahweh realized that he had made a mistake and was sorry for it. LXX translates 'I relent with regard to,' that is, the judgment that had already fallen had satisfied the divine demands resulting from the broken covenant." (Thompson)

c. **I will show you mercy**: God asked the leaders and common people to trust Him that the season of judgment had now been replaced by a season of **mercy**. Before the final Babylonian conquest, the message was, *surrender to exile*. Now in the season of mercy the message was, *trust Me and remain in the land*. If they did, God would bless them with protection and goodness in **your own land**.

i. **I will show you mercy, that he may have mercy on you**: "If Yahweh showed mercy to his people, so would the king of Babylon. He would allow them to return to their homes in peace." (Thompson)

ii. "There is no evidence that Nebuchadnezzar avenged the governor's assassination; he did take more captives in 582 BC (Jeremiah 52:30), but if this was a reprisal it was very much belated one." (Thompson)

2. (13-17) The curse upon those who return to Egypt.

"But if you say, 'We will not dwell in this land,' disobeying the voice of the LORD your God, saying, 'No, but we will go to the land of Egypt where we shall see no war, nor hear the sound of the trumpet, nor be hungry for bread, and there we will dwell'— Then hear now the word of the LORD, O remnant of Judah! Thus says the LORD of hosts, the God of Israel: 'If you wholly set your faces to enter Egypt, and go to dwell there, then it shall be *that* the sword which you feared shall overtake you there in the land of Egypt; the famine of which you were afraid shall follow close after you there *in* Egypt; and there you shall die. So shall it be with all the men who set their faces to go to Egypt to dwell there. They shall die by the sword, by famine, and by pestilence. And none of them shall remain or escape from the disaster that I will bring upon them.'"

   a. **But if you say**: God gave them a great promise if they trusted Him and stayed in the land. If they refused to trust Him and instead went **to the land of Egypt** for security and provision, they would be **disobeying the voice of the LORD your God**.

   i. "Once more Jeremiah had to deliver an unpopular message." (Feinberg)

   b. **Then it shall be that the sword which you feared shall overtake you there in the land of Egypt**: If unbelief drove them to Egypt, what they feared would come upon them in Judea would come upon them in Egypt. The price paid for their unbelief would be to *certainly* **die by the sword, by famine, and by pestilence** in Egypt.

   i. "Disaster would follow the remnant right down to Egypt. Everything that had happened in Jerusalem would happen on the Nile – sword, fear, famine, death, plague, disaster, wrath, cursing, horror, condemnation, and reproach." (Ryken)

   ii. **By the sword**: "Although Egypt had lost the Battle of Carchemish (605 BC), it had not been the scene of military actions. On the other hand, Judah had from the time of the Battle of Megiddo (609 BC) constantly experienced the rigors of war. Thus the remaining Jews could not fail to be impressed by the contrast between peaceful Egypt and war-torn Judah. Actually, however, Judah's trials were past; Egypt's were soon to begin." (Feinberg)

   iii. **By famine**: "Egypt was very fertile, the granary of the world, and yet God could cause a famine there; he hath treasures of plagues for sinners, and can never be exhausted." (Trapp)

3. (18) An oath to punish those to go to Egypt.

"For thus says the LORD of hosts, the God of Israel: 'As My anger and My fury have been poured out on the inhabitants of Jerusalem, so will My fury be poured out on you when you enter Egypt. And you shall be an oath, an astonishment, a curse, and a reproach; and you shall see this place no more.'"

> a. **As My anger and My fury have been poured out on the inhabitants of Jerusalem**: This was a lot of anger and a lot of fury. These survivors of the conquest of Judea and the destruction of Jerusalem saw this **anger** and **fury** with their own eyes.
>
> b. **So will My fury be poured out on you when you enter Egypt**: As much as blessing was promised if they trusted God and remained in the ruined land, so judgment was promised if they looked to Egypt for security and provision.
>
> c. **You shall be an oath, an astonishment, a curse, and a reproach**: Others would see the sad state of those who refused to trust God. Those under this judgment would become an example of those afflicted by God, and they would **see this place no more**, never to return to the Promised Land.
>
>> i. "The risky choice was perfectly safe, while the easy way out was deadly." (Ryken)

4. (19-22) Exposing the hypocrisy of their hearts.

"The LORD has said concerning you, O remnant of Judah, 'Do not go to Egypt!' Know certainly that I have admonished you this day. For you were hypocrites in your hearts when you sent me to the LORD your God, saying, 'Pray for us to the LORD our God, and according to all that the LORD your God says, so declare to us and we will do it.' And I have this day declared it to you, but you have not obeyed the voice of the LORD your God, or anything which He has sent you by me. Now therefore, know certainly that you shall die by the sword, by famine, and by pestilence in the place where you desire to go to dwell."

> a. **You were hypocrites in your hearts when you sent me to the LORD your God**: God clearly told the leaders and common people remaining in the land what His will was – they were to remain in land. Now God spoke to them about their pretended sincerity in seeking a word from Jeremiah the Prophet. When they said, "**so declare to us and we will do it**," they did not speak truthfully.
>
> b. **For you were hypocrites in your hearts**: They acted as if they sought the LORD in sincerity and submission, but it was not true. Many still seek God with pretended sincerity, already determined to do what *they* want to do, and only hoping that God will affirm them in so doing. This teaches

the importance of seeking God with a truly submitted heart that will do *whatever* He tells us to do.

c. Know certainly that you shall die by the sword, by famine, and by pestilence in the place where you desire to go to dwell: Their insincere seeking only added to their guilt. They would go to Egypt as they had already decided to do, and the judgment God promised was certain to come upon them.

> i. "As ye have determined to disobey, God has determined to punish." (Clarke) "In running from death ye shall but run to it." (Trapp)

Jeremiah 43 – Jeremiah in Egypt

A. Jeremiah taken to Egypt against his will.

1. (1-3) Jeremiah accused of prophesying falsely.

Now it happened, when Jeremiah had stopped speaking to all the people all the words of the LORD their God, for which the LORD their God had sent him to them, all these words, that Azariah the son of Hoshaiah, Johanan the son of Kareah, and all the proud men spoke, saying to Jeremiah, "You speak falsely! The LORD our God has not sent you to say, 'Do not go to Egypt to dwell there.' But Baruch the son of Neriah has set you against us, to deliver us into the hand of the Chaldeans, that they may put us to death or carry us away captive to Babylon."

> a. **Azariah… Johanan… and all the proud men spoke**: There were many proud men among the leaders of those remaining in the land. They did not like being confronted with their hypocrisy as Jeremiah had done in Jeremiah 42:20.
>
> b. **You speak falsely! The LORD our God has not sent you to say**: It is remarkable that these men who *lived through* the tragic accuracy of every word of Jeremiah regarding the sin and judgment of Judah would now say he was a false prophet. They said this *despite* the evidence, not because of the evidence.
>
>> i. "They had no other colour for their rebellion than *flatly to deny* that God had spoken what the prophet related." (Clarke)
>>
>> ii. "All along (had they realized it) they had regarded God as a power to enlist, not a lord to obey; and they still cannot believe that his will can be radically different from their own." (Kidner)
>
> c. **Do not go to Egypt to dwell there**: This was the message they plainly *denied* that God gave Jeremiah to deliever.

i. "In their view Yahweh had not forbidden them to go to Egypt. Here is a good example of a man who was so persuaded that his own wrong views were right that his mind was completely closed to any other possibility – an age-old phenomenon." (Thompson)

d. **Baruch the son of Neriah has set you against us, to deliver us into the hand of the Chaldeans**: They accused Jeremiah of not bringing a word from Yahweh, but from the Babylonians. They said it was all planned to bring about either their death or captivity in Babylon.

i. The charge was ridiculous. "The prophet who would not trim his message for the king would never have been manipulated by his secretary." (Feinberg)

ii. "When men do not like the Word of God, they imagine that someone has set the speaker on against them." (Meyer)

iii. "Just what Baruch stood to gain by exerting such influence is not clear." (Cundall)

iv. **Has set you against us**: "How strange it is that ungodly men always think the Word of God is against them, whereas they are set against it!" (Meyer)

2. (4-7) Johanan and the other officers take the remnant to Egypt by force, including Jeremiah.

So Johanan the son of Kareah, all the captains of the forces, and all the people would not obey the voice of the LORD, to remain in the land of Judah. But Johanan the son of Kareah and all the captains of the forces took all the remnant of Judah who had returned to dwell in the land of Judah, from all nations where they had been driven— men, women, children, the king's daughters, and every person whom Nebuzaradan the captain of the guard had left with Gedaliah the son of Ahikam, the son of Shaphan, and Jeremiah the prophet and Baruch the son of Neriah. So they went to the land of Egypt, for they did not obey the voice of the LORD. And they went as far as Tahpanhes.

a. **All the people would not obey the voice of the LORD, to remain in the land of Judah**: They promised to do whatever God told them to do (Jeremiah 42:5-6), and God told them to trust Him and remain in the land. **Johanan**, the other leaders and **all of the people** did not keep their promise and decided to go to Egypt for protection and provision.

i. "Such is the perversity of fallen human nature; when people reach unanimity, too often they are rebels against the will of God (cf. Genesis 11:1-14)." (Feinberg)

ii. "The arm of flesh (Egypt) seemed a greater guarantee of safety than the arm of the Lord." (Cundall)

b. **Took all the remnant of Judah… men, women, children… and Jeremiah the prophet and Baruch**: It wasn't enough for Johanan and the people to disobey God. They also **took** by force everyone else, forcing them to come with them to Egypt.

c. **So they went to the land of Egypt**: There is a sense in which they took **Jeremiah** and his associate **Baruch** as hostages against God. Since the LORD promised judgment against *all* who went to Egypt (Jeremiah 42:17), they virtually dared God to judge His faithful prophet who went to Egypt, even if it was against his will.

i. "It must have been for him one of the most tragic events of his life, since it dashed for ever all hopes he may have had to end his days in his homeland, where Yahweh had promised one day to restore the national life of his people." (Thompson)

ii. "Abraham's descendants returned to Egypt long after their liberation from it. With great suffering they had been delivered from their bondage in Egypt only to return there a defeated and hopeless remnant nearly nine hundred years later." (Feinberg)

iii. **As far as Tahpanhes**: "This city was called *Daphne* by the Greeks, and was situated at the extremity of Lower Egypt, near to Heliopolis. It was called *Daphne Pelusiaca*. They halted at this place, most probably for the purpose of obtaining the king's permission to penetrate farther into Egypt. It was at this place that, according to St. Jerome, tradition says the faithful Jeremiah was stoned to death by these rebellious wretches; for whose welfare he had watched, prayed, gone through many indignities, and suffered every kind of hardship. And now he sealed the truth of his Divine mission with his blood." (Clarke)

B. God's word through Jeremiah in Egypt.

1. (8-9) The sign of the hidden stones.

Then the word of the LORD came to Jeremiah in Tahpanhes, saying, "Take large stones in your hand, and hide them in the sight of the men of Judah, in the clay in the brick courtyard which *is* at the entrance to Pharaoh's house in Tahpanhes;"

a. **The word of the LORD came to Jeremiah in Tahpanhes**: Jeremiah was no longer in the Promised Land, and God commanded His people who remained after the Babylonian exile to remain in that land. By force, Jeremiah was taken to Egypt – yet, **the word of the LORD** still came to him.

He was still God's prophet, and God did not count him as disobedient because of the unique and strange circumstances of his presence in Egypt.

> i. "They ignored the word of Jehovah, and, indeed, openly and willfully refused it, consoling themselves by denying that it was the word of Jehovah. But they had not escaped from God, nor passed beyond the reach of His word." (Morgan)

b. **Take large stones in your hand, and hide them**: God commanded Jeremiah to do the same kind of thing He had commanded him to do in Judah – to do something that would illustrate and memorialize a prophetic word. God commanded Jeremiah to take some **large stones** and hide or bury them at **the entrance to Pharaoh's house**.

> i. "Precisely on that spot, in front of the royal residence, Nebuchadnezzar would assert his sovereignty over Egypt, and would be doing so at God's command." (Kidner)

> ii. "Flinders Petrie, who excavated Tahpanhes in the nineteenth century, cleared a paved area in front of the entrance to the royal dwelling, identifying it with the 'platform' mentioned in this verse." (Harrison)

2. (10-13) The message of the hidden stones.

"And say to them, 'Thus says the LORD of hosts, the God of Israel: "Behold, I will send and bring Nebuchadnezzar the king of Babylon, My servant, and will set his throne above these stones that I have hidden. And he will spread his royal pavilion over them. When he comes, he shall strike the land of Egypt *and deliver* **to death** *those appointed* **for death, and to captivity** *those appointed* **for captivity, and to the sword** *those appointed* **for the sword. I will kindle a fire in the houses of the gods of Egypt, and he shall burn them and carry them away captive. And he shall array himself with the land of Egypt, as a shepherd puts on his garment, and he shall go out from there in peace. He shall also break the sacred pillars of Beth Shemesh that** *are* **in the land of Egypt; and the houses of the gods of the Egyptians he shall burn with fire."'"**

> a. **I will send and bring Nebuchadnezzar the king of Babylon**: God promised that He would bring Nebuchadnezzar to conquer and judge Egypt, just has He had done to Judah. Nebuchadnezzar would **set his throne above these stones**, in the very courtyard of the Pharaoh's palace.

> > i. "Jeremiah must have buried the stones some distance away from the actual building; it seems unlikely that a refugee Judean would be allowed to disturb a laid-out pavement." (Thompson)

ii. "The large stones were symbolic of a pedestal on which Nebuchadnezzar would set up his throne as a sign of his conquest of Egypt." (Thompson)

iii. **Royal pavilion**: This word "is found nowhere else in the OT. Freedman suggests that the term derives from an Assyrian root with the sense of 'to spread out,' hence the variety of meanings offered by scholars." (Feinberg)

b. **I will kindle a fire in the houses of the gods of Egypt**: God promised that the judgment coming to Egypt would be comprehensive. Through the Babylonians would come **death**, **captivity**, and the **sword**. They would also destroy and loot Egyptian temples. The message was clear: If they went to Egypt to escape the wrath and power of the Babylonians, it would follow them there. It was better to stay in Judea and trust God to protect and provide.

i. "A fragmentary inscription records that Nebuchadnezzar actually invaded Egypt in 568/7 BC, when Amasis (570-526 BC) was pharaoh. The attack was more of a punitive expedition than a wholesale reduction of the land." (Harrison)

ii. **As a shepherd puts on his garment**: "With as much ease, and with as little opposition; and with as full a confidence that it is now his own." (Clarke)

iii. The ESV, following some other translations, renders the line in Jeremiah 43:12 as, *he shall clean the land of Egypt as a shepherd cleans his cloak of vermin*. "There is a homely picture here which is well understood by those who have travelled in some parts of the Middle East. The picking of lice from one's clothing is used to describe Nebuchadnezzar's plundering activities when he finally invaded Egypt." (Thompson)

Jeremiah 44 – A Word to God's People in Egypt, Delivered and Rejected

A. The word to God's people in Egypt.

1. (1-6) God speaks to His people regarding their past sins.

The word that came to Jeremiah concerning all the Jews who dwell in the land of Egypt, who dwell at Migdol, at Tahpanhes, at Noph, and in the country of Pathros, saying, "Thus says the LORD of hosts, the God of Israel: 'You have seen all the calamity that I have brought on Jerusalem and on all the cities of Judah; and behold, this day they *are* a desolation, and no one dwells in them, because of their wickedness which they have committed to provoke Me to anger, in that they went to burn incense *and* to serve other gods whom they did not know, they nor you nor your fathers. However I have sent to you all My servants the prophets, rising early and sending *them,* saying, "Oh, do not do this abominable thing that I hate!" But they did not listen or incline their ear to turn from their wickedness, to burn no incense to other gods. So My fury and My anger were poured out and kindled in the cities of Judah and in the streets of Jerusalem; and they are wasted *and* desolate, as it is this day.'"

> a. **The word that came to Jeremiah concerning all the Jews who dwell in the land of Egypt**: Jeremiah 42 described how the captains of those remaining Jews in the land led all they could to Egypt, even against their will and God's command. Jeremiah was among these brought by force to Egypt and he spoke this word to the Jews in Egypt.
>
>> i. This was the word of the LORD, but it was "No word of comfort – how could it be, as long as they lived in open rebellion against the Lord? – but all of reproof and threatening. For what reason? They were obdurate and obstinate." (Trapp)
>
> b. **The LORD of hosts, the God of Israel**: God began this word to these displaced Jews by declaring two names. He remained the **LORD of hosts**,

the God of powerful armies. He remained the **God of Israel**, even though at that time Israel did not even exist as its own kingdom. These things that did not appear to be were nevertheless real before God and in His plan.

c. **You have seen all the calamity that I have brought upon Jerusalem and on all the cities of Judah**: God reminded His people, now in Egypt, why judgment came upon Judah. It came from God Himself, **because of their wickedness which they have committed to provoke Me to anger**, especially their wickedness in idolatry.

> i. "In spite of all that had happened in fulfillment of Jeremiah's warnings of judgment in the fall of Jerusalem, the refugees from Mizpah had learned nothing. Idolatry persisted." (Thompson)

d. **They did not listen or incline their ear to turn from their wickedness**: God sent His prophets to instruct and warn His people, but they did not listen. Their sin (especially idolatry) was bad enough; their refusal to be corrected was fatal. Therefore, **they are wasted and desolate** from God's judgment.

> i. **Oh, do not do this abominable thing that I hate**: "The wrath of God on the impenitent is as unwelcome to him as it is inevitable." (Kidner)
>
> ii. "'Oh!' says someone, 'sin is a sweet thing.' No, no; it is an abominable thing. 'It is a delightful thing,' says another. No, it is an abominable thing. 'Oh, but it is a fashionable thing; you can see it in courts of kings, and princes, and the great men of the earth love it.' Even though they do, it is an abominable thing. Though it should crawl up to a monarch's throne, and spread its slime over crown jewels it would still be an abominable thing." (Spurgeon)
>
> iii. "Beware of bringing pain into the heart of infinite Love; but ask that some of God's hate for sin may be yours." (Meyer)

2. (7-10) God speaks to His people of their present sin.

"Now therefore, thus says the LORD, the God of hosts, the God of Israel: 'Why do you commit *this* great evil against yourselves, to cut off from you man and woman, child and infant, out of Judah, leaving none to remain, in that you provoke Me to wrath with the works of your hands, burning incense to other gods in the land of Egypt where you have gone to dwell, that you may cut yourselves off and be a curse and a reproach among all the nations of the earth? Have you forgotten the wickedness of your fathers, the wickedness of the kings of Judah, the wickedness of their wives, your own wickedness, and the wickedness of your wives, which they committed in the land of Judah and in the

streets of Jerusalem? They have not been humbled, to this day, nor have they feared; they have not walked in My law or in My statutes that I set before you and your fathers.'"

> a. **Why do you commit this great evil against yourselves**: There is a sense of wonder in these words from God, as if God could not believe that His people would be so foolish as to reject His word and rebel against His command with the devastation of recent judgment so near in their memory.
>
>> i. "This is a most pithy and piercing sermon all along, not unlike that preached by Stephen, for the which he was stoned, [Acts 7:54; Acts 7:57-58] and likely enough that this was Jeremiah's last sermon also." (Trapp)
>
> b. **Why do you commit this great evil against yourselves**: There is also a sense of wonder in the *self*-destructive nature of their sin. It was true that they sinned against God, but they also terribly sinned **against** themselves.
>
> c. **To cut off from you man and woman, child and infant, out of Judah, leaving none to remain**: It was bad enough that Nebuchadnezzar took *almost* all the people of God out of the land of Judah in the exile to Babylon. In some ways it was worse that the remaining people of God were all removed from the promised land, either by choice or by force going to Egypt.
>
> d. **Burning incense to other gods in the land of Egypt**: Those who went to Egypt quickly began to worship the gods of Egypt. The same heart of idolatry that led them to sin in Judah with the Canaanite idols now led them to go after the Egyptian idols. This reveals one of the reasons God commanded them not to go to Egypt, but to trust His protection and provision in Judah.
>
> e. **That you may cut yourselves off and be a curse and a reproach among all the nations of the earth**: God promised that He would bless and restore the exiles that went to Babylon. He promised only judgment for those who went by choice to Egypt, promising they would become **a curse and a reproach**.
>
> f. **Have you forgotten the wickedness**: The answer to the question was obvious; they *had* forgotten the wickedness of their fathers, their kings, their wives, and especially their own wickedness. They would suffer greatly for forgetting all this.
>
>> i. "They that will not take example, are worthily made examples." (Trapp)

ii. **They have not been humbled**: "The remnant showed that they were neither repentant nor contrite (*dukkeu*, 'bruised'; cf. Isaiah 53:5)." (Feinberg)

3. (11-14) The promise of judgment upon those who went to Egypt.

"**Therefore thus says the LORD of hosts, the God of Israel: 'Behold, I will set My face against you for catastrophe and for cutting off all Judah. And I will take the remnant of Judah who have set their faces to go into the land of Egypt to dwell there, and they shall all be consumed *and* fall in the land of Egypt. They shall be consumed by the sword *and* by famine. They shall die, from the least to the greatest, by the sword and by famine; and they shall be an oath, an astonishment, a curse and a reproach! For I will punish those who dwell in the land of Egypt, as I have punished Jerusalem, by the sword, by famine, and by pestilence, so that none of the remnant of Judah who have gone into the land of Egypt to dwell there shall escape or survive, lest they return to the land of Judah, to which they desire to return and dwell. For none shall return except those who escape.'"**

a. **Thus says the LORD of hosts, the God of Israel**: God again introduced Himself with titles of authority, power, and ownership.

b. **I will set My face against you for catastrophe and for cutting off all Judah**: Just as God before promised that He would be against Judah and not for them against the invading Babylonians, so He would be **against** those who by choice exiled themselves to Egypt.

i. "If the people had made up their minds to go to Egypt, and also to continue their idolatry, Yahweh had made up his mind to visit them with judgment." (Thompson)

c. **They shall die, from the least to the greatest, by the sword and by famine**: God promised the judgment of an untimely death to those who chose Egypt over trusting God in the Promised Land.

i. **Lest they return to the land of Egypt**: "He makes it clear that he is not referring to any permanent Jewish settlers in Egypt (cf. Jeremiah 44:14) but only to the remnant who had sought refuge there in the hope of returning to the land of Judah at the earliest opportunity. Only casual fugitives will survive. For the remnant the picture is one of unrelieved gloom." (Feinberg)

ii. "Egypt was not in itself forbidden territory; it would become an important centre of learning for the later Dispersion, and would shelter the holy family. The sin of Jeremiah's contemporaries was not geographical; it was a vote of no confidence in God." (Kidner)

d. **For none shall return except those who escape**: God promised that there would be very few who managed to escape the judgment of death coming upon those who chose to find their security in Egypt rather than in the LORD.

i. **Except those who escape**: "Even in punishing the disobedient remnant, God will still allow a few survivors to trickle back to Judea, thereby maintaining the connection between the people and the land." (Harrison)

B. The reaction of God's people in Egypt.

1. (15-16) The general response.

Then all the men who knew that their wives had burned incense to other gods, with all the women who stood by, a great multitude, and all the people who dwelt in the land of Egypt, in Pathros, answered Jeremiah, saying: "*As for* the word that you have spoken to us in the name of the LORD, we will not listen to you!"

a. **A great multitude**: Jeremiah delivered this word from God to a large audience, making up most or all of those who had come to Pathros, Egypt from Judah by choice or force. The group included men **who knew that their wives had burned incense to other gods**.

i. "The inclusive language – 'all the men,' 'all the women,' 'all the people' – is a literary generalization used for emphasis and should not be taken literally." (Feinberg)

b. **We will not listen to you**: The people *knew* that Jeremiah spoke to them **in the name of the LORD**, yet they did not care. They rejected the prophet and they rejected his word and they rejected the God who gave him that word. Their honesty was remarkable, but their sin was great.

i. Once again, it was Jeremiah's sad lot to have his message – Yahweh's message – rejected. "It would appear that, so far as his outward lot was concerned, the Prophet Jeremiah spent a life of more unrelieved sadness than has perhaps fallen to the lot of any other, with the exception of the Divine Lord. This was so apparent to the Jewish commentators on the prophecies of Isaiah that they applied to him the words of the fifty-third chapter." (Meyer, cited in Ryken) Ryken adds: "Jeremiah was not *the* Suffering Servant, but he was *a* suffering servant to the very end."

2. (17-18) The response of the men.

"But we will certainly do whatever has gone out of our own mouth, to burn incense to the queen of heaven and pour out drink offerings to her, as we have done, we and our fathers, our kings and our princes, in the

cities of Judah and in the streets of Jerusalem. For *then* we had plenty of food, were well-off, and saw no trouble. But since we stopped burning incense to the queen of heaven and pouring out drink offerings to her, we have lacked everything and have been consumed by the sword and by famine."

> a. **We will certainly do whatever has gone out of our own mouth**: The men were straightforward and honest. They promised to do **whatever** they wanted to do. They would not let God's command or God's judgment get in the way of what they wanted to say and do.
>
> b. **To burn incense to the queen of heaven and pour out drink offerings to her**: They spoke of the days before the fall of Jerusalem and the conquest of Judah, when they worshipped the Babylonian idol **the queen of heaven** with various rituals. They did this, their **fathers** did this, and their **kings** and **princes** did this, all over Judah and Jerusalem.
>
>> i. "The reference is probably to the Assyro-Babylonian Ishtar. …Ishtar (Canaanite Athtart) was the goddess of war and love. She represented the female principle of fertility. …Ashtoreth is the Hebrew of which Astarte is the Greek. This ancient goddess was called Ishtar in Akkadian, Inanna in Sumerian, and Athtart in Ugaritic. Her counterpart in the NT is Artemis (cf. Acts 19, in Latin, Diana). The worship of this goddess was widespread in the ancient Near East." (Feinberg)
>>
>> ii. For the Babylonians, **the queen of heaven** was a maternal deity connected with the moon, with family, and fertility. It is strange and shocking that Roman Catholics give Mary, the mother of Jesus, this same title and direct to her improper prayer and veneration – sometimes even worship. We have no Biblical permission or encouragement to have any connection with the queen of heaven. Some observe that modern people worship **the queen of heaven** under other names: Mother Nature, Feminism, or Glamor.
>>
>> iii. **As we have done, we and our fathers, our kings and our princes**: "Antiquity is here pleaded, and authority, and plenty and peace. These are now the Popish pleas, and the pillars of that rotten religion. It is the old religion, say they, and hath potent princes for her patrons, and is practised in Rome, the mother Church, and hath plenty and peace where it is professed, and where they have nothing but mass and matins. These are their arguments, but very poor ones." (Trapp)
>
> c. **For then we had plenty of food, were well-off, and saw no trouble**: They remembered the days when they all worshipped the **queen of heaven** as *the good old days*. They claimed that when they **stopped** doing all those

things, they **lacked everything** and were **consumed by the sword and by famine**.

> i. "This is a most revealing glimpse of spiritual perversity – for in blaming all their troubles on the reformation instead of on the evils it had tried to root out, these people were turning the truth exactly upside down." (Kidner)

> ii. "Because Baal worship was eradicated during Josiah's reformation (2 Kings 23:4-20), the rebellious remnant blamed all their misfortunes on this action." (Harrison)

> iii. "The people, by contrast, claimed that things went badly only when they failed to propitiate the Queen of Heaven. Perhaps they had in mind the long and relatively peaceful reign of Manasseh during which the non-Yahwistic cults of all kinds were freely allowed." (Thompson)

> iv. "In short, the remnant claimed that idolatry had done more for them than the Lord whom Jeremiah represented." (Feinberg)

> v. With a clear mind and even the slightest understanding of spiritual things, their analysis was crazy. "Things were great when we rejected and disobeyed God, until the judgment God promised came." Sin is often good until the wages of sin are paid – death (Romans 6:23).

> vi. "At the instinctive level, the fallen mind is always ready to assume that God is the adversary, whom we (like these characters) may blame for our past and distrust for our future." (Kidner)

3. (19) The response of the women.

The women also said, "And when we burned incense to the queen of heaven and poured out drink offerings to her, did we make cakes for her, to worship her, and pour out drink offerings to her without our husbands' *permission?"*

> a. **When we burned incense to the queen of heaven and poured out drink offerings to her**: The women admitted that they played an important part in the worship of the Babylonian **queen of heaven** and other idols.

> b. **Without our husbands' permission**: They tried to make their husbands responsible for their sin, in the sense that they could have stopped them if they wanted to. In the first sin, the man blamed his wife for his sin. Here, the women of Judah in Egypt return the favor.

> > i. "Their husbands well knew that they were making special *crescent cakes* (*kawwan*) which were stamped with the image of the goddess." (Thompson)

ii. Numbers 30:3-12 indicates that a woman's vows were only binding if her husband approved them. "Since their husbands approved, why then should Jeremiah complain about the women's actions?" (Feinberg)

iii. This reminds us that they still sinned, even though their husbands commanded them or permitted them to do it. The women were supposed to submit to their husbands, but not in an absolute sense. If their God-given authority told them to sin, they were to obey God rather than man.

C. Jeremiah answers the people.

1. (20-23) Jeremiah tells them why destruction and judgment came.

Then Jeremiah spoke to all the people—the men, the women, and all the people who had given him *that* answer—saying: "The incense that you burned in the cities of Judah and in the streets of Jerusalem, you and your fathers, your kings and your princes, and the people of the land, did not the LORD remember them, and did it *not* come into His mind? So the LORD could no longer bear *it*, because of the evil of your doings *and* because of the abominations which you committed. Therefore your land is a desolation, an astonishment, a curse, and without an inhabitant, as *it is* this day. Because you have burned incense and because you have sinned against the LORD, and have not obeyed the voice of the LORD or walked in His law, in His statutes or in His testimonies, therefore this calamity has happened to you, as *at* this day."

a. **Did not the LORD remember them**: Jeremiah tried to reason with the people. They had completely left God out of their thinking. They felt that if they ignored God, then He somehow did not matter. Yet the LORD did matter, remaining the God of Israel if they rejected Him or not. He saw and remembered their sins and idolatry.

b. **So the LORD could no longer bear it**: God was very patient with His disobedient people, but they chose to take His patience to mean He didn't care. He did care, and brought judgment against them: **therefore this calamity has happened to you**.

i. "Disaster would not have occurred had Israel obeyed the covenantal stipulations, here described as *law, statutes,* and *testimonies.*" (Harrison)

ii. "His abused mercy turned into fury." (Trapp)

2. (24-29) Jeremiah tells them of the adversity and judgment to come.

Moreover Jeremiah said to all the people and to all the women, "Hear the word of the LORD, all Judah who *are* in the land of Egypt! Thus says the LORD of hosts, the God of Israel, saying: 'You and your wives have

spoken with your mouths and fulfilled with your hands, saying, "We will surely keep our vows that we have made, to burn incense to the queen of heaven and pour out drink offerings to her." You will surely keep your vows and perform your vows!' Therefore hear the word of the LORD, all Judah who dwell in the land of Egypt: 'Behold, I have sworn by My great name,' says the LORD, 'that My name shall no more be named in the mouth of any man of Judah in all the land of Egypt, saying, "The Lord GOD lives." Behold, I will watch over them for adversity and not for good. And all the men of Judah who *are* in the land of Egypt shall be consumed by the sword and by famine, until there is an end to them. Yet a small number who escape the sword shall return from the land of Egypt to the land of Judah; and all the remnant of Judah, who have gone to the land of Egypt to dwell there, shall know whose words will stand, Mine or theirs. And this *shall be* a sign to you,' says the LORD, 'that I will punish you in this place, that you may know that My words will surely stand against you for adversity.'"

    a. **Thus says the LORD of hosts, the God of Israel**: Once again, God spoke to His people with the titles of power, authority, and ownership.

        i. Chronologically speaking, this was probably Jeremiah's last recorded prophecy. He ended as he started: faithful to God, trusting in God's faithfulness. "He had seen his nation decline from a relatively strong independent state to the point of near extinction, and little fruit seemed to have been borne by his ministry. Yet, in these final words, his utter faith in an omnipotent God, and his perception of fundamental truths, are as clear as ever." (Cundall)

    b. **We will surely keep our vows that we have made**: Jeremiah quoted the people in their promise to continue worshipping **the queen of heaven** and other idols. It was a declaration that God heard their defiance clearly.

        i. **You will surely keep your vows and perform your vows**: "In a powerful expression of irony and revulsion, Jeremiah tells the remnant to proceed with fulfilling their godless vows. He may have been pointing to their incense and libations and to the very cakes they were carrying." (Feinberg)

    c. **My name shall no more be named in the mouth of any man of Judah in all the land of Egypt**: God solemnly declared that He rejected those who rejected Him and chose to go to Egypt, those who trusted idols more than Him. He would not allow them to speak His name.

    d. **I will watch over them for adversity and not for good**: God had commanded them to stay in the land of Judah and trust Him that He would watch over them, to protect and provide for them. In rejecting God and His promise, they would still have God **watch over them**, but it would be **for adversity and not for good**. This was a terrifying promise, knowing that God is the best friend but the worst enemy anyone could have.

> i. It's possible that the Jewish community in Egypt heard Jeremiah's warnings and repented. By the time of the New Testament, there was a large and strong Jewish community in Egypt. Perhaps they eventually responded in repentance and were spared this judgment.

e. **A small number who escape the sword shall return from the land of Egypt to the land of Judah**: God promised that if they persisted in these sins, only a remnant would escape the judgment they would face in Egypt. The rest would **be consumed by the sword and by famine**. This would prove true God's terrible promise to watch over them **for adversity**.

> i. "For the apostates in Egypt the future held nothing; but for their compatriots in Babylon who were accepting their punishment there was the hope of freedom." (Kidner)

> ii. "A possible footnote to their story has come to light in the Elephantine papyri, a fifth-century BC collection of letters and documents belonging to a military colony of Jews settled on an island of the Nile at the southern frontier of Egypt. A reference to a temple of theirs which had survived a threat of destruction as far back as 525 BC implies that their colony must have been well established at that date – bringing its origin back, if so, to Jeremiah's time or before. Whether its founders were the men of our chapter or another group, it is interesting to note that their cult is revealed as an unblushing mixture of Israelite and Canaanite religion, such as Jeremiah's opponents would have thoroughly appreciated." (Kidner)

3. (30) Jeremiah tells them of the judgment to come upon Pharaoh and Egypt.

"Thus says the LORD: 'Behold, I will give Pharaoh Hophra king of Egypt into the hand of his enemies and into the hand of those who seek his life, as I gave Zedekiah king of Judah into the hand of Nebuchadnezzar king of Babylon, his enemy who sought his life.'"

> a. **I will give Pharaoh Hophra king of Egypt into the hand of his enemies**: God promised that Nebuchadnezzar and Babylon would come against Egypt (Jeremiah 43:10-13). Here, Jeremiah gave a more specific prophecy of that assured event.

> > i. "Hophra was actually overthrown by Amasis, one of his officers, who revolted against him and then shared rule with him (Herodotus 2:161-163, 169). Amasis rebelled against Nebuchadnezzar in 570 BC and was defeated in 568 BC So sixteen years after the fall of Jerusalem, Hophra

was dethroned and strangled by some of his subjects. Again Jeremiah was vindicated." (Feinberg)

b. As I gave Zedekiah king of Judah into the hand of Nebuchadnezzar: Just as it had happened to Zedekiah, so it would happen to Pharaoh. God's judgments would be proven true.

i. "Jeremiah did not specify that Hophra would fall into the hands of Nebuchadnezzar but merely into the hands of his enemies; just as Zedekiah lost his life so would Pharaoh Hophra." (Thompson)

ii. Chronologically speaking, these were the last prophetic words of Jeremiah recorded. "Scripture is silent on what happened to Jeremiah after the events of this chapter, though tradition has been overly active. There are many legends concerning his death. One states that he was killed at Daphne. Another claims he carried away the tabernacle, hiding it in the mountains where Moses died (2 Maccabees 2:4-8). Yet another indicates he was alive with Enoch and Elijah, expected to return as a forerunner of the Messiah." (Feinberg)

Jeremiah 45 – Great Things and Not Seeking Them

A. What Baruch said.

1. (1) The setting of the word.

The word that Jeremiah the prophet spoke to Baruch the son of Neriah, when he had written these words in a book at the instruction of Jeremiah, in the fourth year of Jehoiakim the son of Josiah, king of Judah, saying,

> a. **The word that Jeremiah the prophet spoke to Baruch**: This was the long-time, trusted associate of Jeremiah. Baruch was the penman to the prophet, having **written these words in a book at the instruction of Jeremiah**. Later, Jeremiah and Baruch were both taken to Egypt against their will (Jeremiah 43:6).
>
>> i. "Baruch happens to be the only man from the Old Testament who has been fingerprinted. In 1975 a group of archaeologists purchased some clay document markers from an Arab antiquities dealer. The archaeologists did not decipher the markers – which were the bookmarks of the ancient world – until 1986. When they did, they discovered that one of them bears the seal of Baruch son of Neriah. Since then, another document marker has been discovered that bears not only Baruch's seal, but also a thumbprint, very probably the thumbprint of the scribe himself." (Ryken)
>
> b. **In the fourth year of Jehoiakim**: Chronological order was not important to the one who arranged the Book of Jeremiah. The previous chapters in this section dealt with the time after the fall of Jerusalem and Judah. This chapter deals with a time many years before that catastrophe, something like a flashback in a film or novel.
>
>> i. "Chronologically this passage is out of order, and should follow 36:8." (Harrison)

2. (2-3) Baruch's grief and sorrow.

"Thus says the LORD, the God of Israel, to you, O Baruch: 'You said, "Woe is me now! For the LORD has added grief to my sorrow. I fainted in my sighing, and I find no rest."'

> a. **Woe is me now! For the LORD has added grief to my sorrow**: As a faithful partner with Jeremiah, Baruch had to endure a lot of opposition and abuse. He certainly suffered much for his faithfulness to God and Jeremiah, and he therefore felt that God could in some way be blamed for his **grief** and **sorrow**.
>
>> i. "Note the self-centeredness of his attitude indicated by the five personal pronouns in verse 3 (the same number in the Pharisee's self congratulatory prayer, Luke 18:11 f.)." (Cundall)
>>
>> ii. "The emphasis in his lamentation is to be placed on the word 'me' – 'Woe is *me* now.'" (Morgan)
>>
>> iii. "He had mourned for the desolations that were coming on his country, and now he mourns for the dangers to which he feels his own life exposed; for we find, from Jeremiah 36:26, that the king had given commandment to take both Baruch and Jeremiah, in order that they might be put to death at the instance of his nobles." (Clarke)
>
> b. **You said**: The fact that God knew what Baruch said and spoke to him about it was somewhat sobering. God heard and responded to Baruch's accusation of unbelief against him.
>
> c. **I fainted in my sighing, and I find no rest**: Baruch was exhausted, probably both physically and spiritually. He felt that God had not blessed or protected him as he had hoped.
>
>> i. This makes sense when we think of what Baruch and Jeremiah had to live through. The world was falling apart around them, and while they had been protected to this point, they still suffered. No golden age had dawned yet. There seemed to be nothing to build on, and the future looked darker rather than brighter. The present and future seemed dark and depressing.
>>
>> ii. "It may be that as he dictated Jeremiah's words of judgment, and knew in his heart that they were true and would certainly come to pass, he became depressed at it all and was filled with foreboding about his own future." (Thompson)

B. What the LORD said.

1. (4) The LORD speaks of His power.

"**Thus you shall say to him, 'Thus says the Lord: "Behold, what I have built I will break down, and what I have planted I will pluck up, that is, this whole land.**

> a. **Thus you shall say to him**: Baruch was used to writing out what God spoke to Jeremiah for *others*, not for himself. God had a word for His discouraged, exhausted servant.
>
> b. **What I have built I will break down, and what I have planted I will pluck up, that is, this whole land**: God spoke to Baruch about His great power, and His great power expressed in judgment. This reminded Baruch of the power and authority of God to do as He pleased, and it also put some of Baruch's perceived problems into perspective. He was discouraged and exhausted; much worse was coming upon the **whole land**.
>
>> i. God reminded Baruch: *I'm not done with My judgment on Jerusalem and Judah. There is more to come until it is complete.*
>>
>> ii. "Jeremiah had to remind Baruch of God's own sorrow at what was to happen. …Yahweh had built something and was about to destroy it. He had planted and was about to uproot it." (Thompson)

2. (5-6) The promise of God's care.

And do you seek great things for yourself? Do not seek *them*; for behold, I will bring adversity on all flesh," says the Lord. "But I will give your life to you as a prize in all places, wherever you go."'"

> a. **Do you seek great things for yourself**: Apparently, some of Baruch's discouragement and exhaustion came from seeking **great things** for himself. He expected to be at a better, different place in his life than where he found himself at the time. The disappointment of **great things** sought and unfulfilled weighed heavily on him.
>
>> i. "He may have had hopes of attaining a high office or even of receiving the gift of prophecy. But such expectations were not to be realized." (Feinberg)
>>
>> ii. "Baruch was an educated man, qualified as a secretary, whose brother (Jeremiah 51:59) was an officer of high rank under Zedekiah. He may have entertained hopes of some distinction in the nation. But whatever 'great things' he sought for himself were forfeited by his loyal support of Jeremiah." (Thompson)
>
> b. **Do not seek them**: God turned Baruch away from the path of self-exaltation. God wanted Baruch to have the right mindset – *not* obsessed or overly-concerned about his own advancement and perceived success.

i. God used this word to Baruch to speak to many throughout the centuries. Dr. J. Oswald Sanders coveted a certain job in a Christian organization, and he almost lobbied some influential friends for it. But walking through downtown Auckland, New Zealand, these words came to him with authority: *"Seekest thou great things for thyself? Seek them not!"* (KJV). Consequently, he didn't seek the position, but it later opened to him on its own in God's timing.

ii. When Charles Spurgeon was eighteen, he applied to Regent's Park College. An interview was set and Spurgeon rose early and set out, but through a misunderstanding he missed his appointment and was not admitted. Bitterly disappointed, Charles walked through the countryside trying to calm down. Suddenly, Jeremiah 45:5 came to mind: *"Seekest thou great things for thyself? Seek them not!"* Spurgeon never made it to college, but he went on to become the most effective preacher in England.

c. **I will bring adversity on all flesh**: God reminded Baruch that one day He would bring judgment on all flesh. Worldly power, popularity, and prestige will be swept away. This should make us less concerned about **great things** like fame and popularity. We have eternity to deal with.

i. To seek a name for yourself, a place of importance and distinction among men, is to look for the wrong thing in the wrong place. To seek social media greatness or internet notoriety shows a lack of appreciation for the God who **will bring adversity on all flesh**.

ii. Philippians twice describes a *bad* kind of ambition, implying that there is a *good* kind of ambition. *The former preach Christ from selfish ambition, not sincerely, supposing to add affliction to my chains* (Philippians 1:16). *Let nothing be done through selfish ambition or conceit, but in lowliness of mind let each esteem others better than himself* (Philippians 2:3).

iii. We could say that Paul was an ambitious man; Peter was an ambitious man; even that *Jesus* was an ambitious man. Yet they were all ambitious for God's glory and fame. We may seek great things, but God's great things, always remembering Luke 14:11: *For whoever exalts himself will be humbled, and he who humbles himself will be exalted.* We should learn from God's word to Baruch and instead of exalting self, we should exalt Jesus. We may long to make a big impact on the world, but be perfectly satisfied if our name remains unknown in doing so.

d. **But I will give your life to you as a prize in all places, wherever you go**: God's assurance to Baruch was strong. He would take care of him. Even when he was later taken to Egypt with Jeremiah, this promise was sure to care for Baruch **wherever** he may go.

i. **Your life to you as a prize**: "The figure is of a soldier barely escaping with his life after a defeat in battle." (Thompson)

ii. "What it had to leave unsaid…was the fact that these two would earn the gratitude of every generation for what they dared to do." (Kidner)

iii. "Ironically, the very suffering through which Baruch passed because of his loyalty to Jeremiah gained him honor beyond anything he could have anticipated." (Thompson)

iv. "The name 'Baruch' means 'Blessed' and is transliterated in the LXX, Vulgate, and Targum." (Feinberg)

v. "Never yet did any one do or suffer aught for God's sake, that complained of a hard bargain." (Trapp)

vi. "It is obvious that when Baruch arranged Jeremiah's scroll he put this prophecy right where it belonged. He treasured the promise God gave him. It reminded him of the way God answered him in his despair. So he put it here at the end of his life to show that God was faithful to his promise." (Ryken)

Jeremiah 46 – A Word of Judgment Against Egypt

A. The defeat at Carchemish.

1. (1-2) Introduction to the prophecy.

The word of the LORD which came to Jeremiah the prophet against the nations. Against Egypt. Concerning the army of Pharaoh Necho, king of Egypt, which was by the River Euphrates in Carchemish, and which Nebuchadnezzar king of Babylon defeated in the fourth year of Jehoiakim the son of Josiah, king of Judah:

a. **The word of the LORD which came to Jeremiah the prophet against the nations**: This begins a section that will continue through Jeremiah 51, where Jeremiah pronounces judgment against the nations surrounding Judah.

i. "In LXX these chapters come after the title in Jeremiah 25:13a and conclude with 25:15-38 (= LXX chapter 32). This suggests that the block of oracles circulated for a time as an independent unit which was woven into the whole book in different ways." (Thompson)

b. **Jeremiah the prophet against the nations**: It is an important reminder that though the Book of Jeremiah deals mostly with the judgment God would bring against Judah, God did not neglect or ignore the Gentile nations. He would also righteously judge them.

i. "God knows who he is. He is not a regional supervisor. He is not a tribal deity. He is the God of all nations. His sovereignty is not limited to a single culture, nation, or ethnic group." (Ryken)

c. **Against Egypt**: Jeremiah 46 describes the judgment that would come upon Egypt, especially at the Battle of **Carchemish** when the Babylonians defeated the Egyptians. When Jeremiah gave this prophecy, the battle was yet future.

i. "Jeremiah commences with Egypt because Palestine had long been a sphere of Egyptian political influence." (Harrison)

ii. "Jeremiah beginneth fitly with the Egyptians, who besides the old enmity, had lately slain good King Josiah, with whom died all the prosperity of the Jewish people." (Trapp)

iii. "Carchemish is not at the junction of the rivers Chebar and Euphrates but further up the Euphrates. The only great city in the region, it was the key to Syria on the east and commanded the passage of the Euphrates." (Feinberg)

iv. "It was on his way there [Carchemish] that Pharaoh Neco had slain King Josiah of Judah in 609 when Josiah tried to turn him back." (Kidner) Pharaoh kept his army in Carchemish four years, dominating the area and waiting for the inevitable confrontation with rising Babylon. When it came, the Egyptians were routed.

d. **In the fourth year of Jehoiakim**: This was 605 BC when the Egyptians were overwhelmed at Carchemish (Jeremiah 46:2ff.) in modern Turkey, near the Syrian border. The Babylonian armies chased the fleeing Egyptians south and came to Jerusalem.

2. (3-5) Soldiers called to battle and quickly routed.

"Order the buckler and shield,
And draw near to battle!
Harness the horses,
And mount up, you horsemen!
Stand forth with *your* helmets,
Polish the spears,
Put on the armor!
Why have I seen them dismayed *and* turned back?
Their mighty ones are beaten down;
They have speedily fled,
And did not look back,
***For* fear *was* all around," says the LORD.**

a. **Draw near to the battle**: In his prophecy, Jeremiah puts the listener and reader right at the scene of battle. The armor is prepared (**order the buckler and shield**), and the mounted soldiers ready themselves (**harness the horses**).

i. Thompson noted of this section, Jeremiah 46:3-12, "The poetry is among the most vivid in all the OT and is certainly unsurpassed in the book of Jeremiah." (Thompson)

ii. "The small shield (*magen*) was generally circular in shape, while the large one (*sinad*) was either oval or rectangular, being designed to protect the entire body." (Harrison)

iii. "An army as well accoutered as the one described here would naturally be victorious. But events take an unexpected turn." (Feinberg)

b. **Why have I seen them dismayed and turned back**: The sense is that the battle is over as soon as it begins. As soon as shields and spears and horses are made ready, **their mighty ones are beaten down, they have speedily fled**.

i. "What! such a numerous, formidable, and well-appointed army panic-struck? So that they have *turned back-fled apace*, and *looked not round*; while their *mighty ones*-their generals and commanders, striving to rally them, are *beaten down*." (Clarke)

ii. "Jeremiah ironically depicts the well-equipped and boastful, highly-skilled forces of Egypt and contrasts them with the sequel of an overwhelming defeat and a shameful flight." (Cundall)

c. **Did not look back, for fear was all around**: Jeremiah described a full retreat of the Egyptian army before the Babylonians.

3. (6-8) The voice of the victorious Babylonian army.

**"Do not let the swift flee away,
Nor the mighty man escape;
They will stumble and fall
Toward the north, by the River Euphrates.
"Who *is* this coming up like a flood,
Whose waters move like the rivers?
Egypt rises up like a flood,
And *its* waters move like the rivers;
And he says, 'I will go up *and* cover the earth,
I will destroy the city and its inhabitants.'"**

a. **Do not let the swift flee away**: In his prophetic vision, Jeremiah could see the captains of the Babylonian army calling out orders, commanding all their soldiers to pursue and utterly defeat the retreating Egyptians.

b. **By the River Euphrates**: The Battle of Carchemish was fought near the Euphrates, in the area that is the border between modern Turkey and Syria.

c. **Egypt rises up like a flood**: When a great river like the Euphrates floods, it brings incredible destruction. Egypt came to battle like an army that would crush its opponent saying, **I will destroy the city and its inhabitants**.

i. **Rises up like a flood, and its waters move like the rivers**: "The *rivers* allude to the Nile and its irrigation canals, hence the plural form. The onrushing Egyptians seem like the Nile when it is inundating the surrounding countryside." (Harrison)

3. (9-10) Proud Egypt destroyed.

Come up, O horses, and rage, O chariots!
And let the mighty men come forth:
The Ethiopians and the Libyans who handle the shield,
And the Lydians who handle *and* **bend the bow.**
For this *is* **the day of the Lord GOD of hosts,**
A day of vengeance,
That He may avenge Himself on His adversaries.
The sword shall devour;
It shall be satiated and made drunk with their blood;
For the Lord GOD of hosts has a sacrifice
In the north country by the River Euphrates.

a. **Come up, O horses, and rage, O chariots**: God called the proud Egyptian army to this battle, bringing them for the purpose of judging them.

b. **The Ethiopians and the Libyans who handle the shield**: Like many armies, the ancient Egyptian army that came to Carchemish had many foreign soldiers, both slaves and mercenaries.

c. **This is the day of the Lord GOD of hosts, a day of vengeance**: God called the arrogant Egyptian army to come to Carchemish so He could show that *He* was the **God of hosts**, that it was *His* **day of vengeance**.

i. The phrase **the day of the LORD** in Jeremiah 46:10 is a good example of the principle that this phrase does not necessarily refer to one single day, but to any time or season when God's might is manifest, especially in judgment against His arrogant opposition, a day when **He may avenge Himself on His adversaries**.

ii. "An army as well accoutered as the one described here would naturally be victorious. But events take an unexpected turn." (Feinberg)

d. **For the Lord GOD of hosts has a sacrifice in the north country by the River Euphrates**: The defeated Egyptian army would please God as a sacrifice pleased Him, bearing the judgment of sin.

i. "The prophet represents this as a *mighty sacrifice*, where innumerable victims were slain." (Clarke)

4. (11-12) Egypt not to be cured from their affliction.

"Go up to Gilead and take balm,
O virgin, the daughter of Egypt;
In vain you will use many medicines;
You shall not be cured.
The nations have heard of your shame,
And your cry has filled the land;
For the mighty man has stumbled against the mighty;
They both have fallen together."

> a. **Go up to Gilead and take balm**: When the Egyptian army suffered such a great defeat at Carchemish, they retreated south towards Egypt but through the Promised Land, including **Gilead**. They would not be brought back to strength there; **in vain you shall use many medicines; you shall not be cured**.
>
>> i. "The reference to *many medicines* is a sarcastic comment on Egypt's inability to heal the wounds of defeat, her final humiliation being that others have now heard this news." (Harrison)
>>
>> ii. "The association of balm with Gilead may be linked to the fact that caravans from the east bearing supplies of balm passed through Gilead." (Thompson)
>
> b. **The nations have heard of your shame**: The defeat of Egypt at Carchemish was famous because it marked the beginning of Babylon as a true superpower in the region and the decline of Egypt.

B. The invasion of Egypt.

1. (13-17) Egypt helpless to defend against Babylon's armies.

The word that the LORD spoke to Jeremiah the prophet, how Nebuchadnezzar king of Babylon would come *and* strike the land of Egypt.

"Declare in Egypt, and proclaim in Migdol;
Proclaim in Noph and in Tahpanhes;
Say, 'Stand fast and prepare yourselves,
For the sword devours all around you.'
Why are your valiant *men* swept away?
They did not stand
Because the LORD drove them away.
He made many fall;
Yes, one fell upon another.
And they said, 'Arise!

Let us go back to our own people
And to the land of our nativity
From the oppressing sword.'
They cried there,
'Pharaoh, king of Egypt, *is but* a noise.
He has passed by the appointed time!'"

> a. **How Nebuchadnezzar king of Babylon would come and strike the land of Egypt**: Many years after his victory at Carchemish, Nebuchadnezzar again sent his army, this time all the way to Egypt itself.
>
>> i. "The place-names in verse 14 are of the frontier towns in the path of an invader from the north-east." (Kidner)
>
> b. **Stand fast and prepare yourselves, for the sword devours all around you**: The people of Egypt could do their best to prepare for this coming Babylonian invasion, but it would be of no help. Their **valiant men** would still be **swept away**.
>
> c. **Because the LORD drove them away**: It wasn't only the power of the Babylonian army at work. God was also determined to drive away the defenders of Egypt to bring a vast judgment upon proud Egypt.
>
> d. **Pharaoh, king of Egypt, is but a noise**: With the Babylonian invasion of Egypt, all could see that Pharaoh was no longer a ruler of great power and authority.
>
>> i. "In verse 16 the speech of the soldiers is overheard, as the mercenary troops decide to return to their own countries. They call Pharaoh 'a noise' (i.e., a braggart), blaming him for ruining his chances for victory." (Feinberg)
>
>> ii. **Pharaoh, king of Egypt, is but a noise**: "NEB has *King Bombast*, while RSV reads *Noisy one*. However, 'Loudmouth' seems to reflect the scorn of MT better, since it depicts the pharaoh as a braggart who has missed his opportunity." (Harrison)
>
>> iii. "Above all there is the devastating summing-up of Pharaoh in verse 17 as *Noisy one who lets the hour go by*." (Kidner)

2. (18-26) The certainty of this judgment upon Egypt.

"*As* I live," says the King,
Whose name *is* the LORD of hosts,
"Surely as Tabor *is* among the mountains
And as Carmel by the sea, *so* he shall come.
O you daughter dwelling in Egypt,
Prepare yourself to go into captivity!

For Noph shall be waste and desolate, without inhabitant.
"Egypt *is* a very pretty heifer,
But destruction comes, it comes from the north.
Also her mercenaries are in her midst like fat bulls,
For they also are turned back,
They have fled away together.
They did not stand,
For the day of their calamity had come upon them,
The time of their punishment.
Her noise shall go like a serpent,
For they shall march with an army
And come against her with axes,
Like those who chop wood.
"They shall cut down her forest," says the LORD,
"Though it cannot be searched,
Because they *are* innumerable,
And more numerous than grasshoppers.
The daughter of Egypt shall be ashamed;
She shall be delivered into the hand
Of the people of the north."

The LORD of hosts, the God of Israel, says: "Behold, I will bring punishment on Amon of No, and Pharaoh and Egypt, with their gods and their kings—Pharaoh and those who trust in him. And I will deliver them into the hand of those who seek their lives, into the hand of Nebuchadnezzar king of Babylon and the hand of his servants. Afterward it shall be inhabited as in the days of old," says the LORD.

> a. **"As I live," says the King**: In the strongest terms, God declared that this would happen. It was so certain that the people of Egypt could be told, **prepare yourself to go into captivity**.
>
>> i. "Both *Tabor* and *Carmel* were conspicuous in relation to the neighboring terrain. Nebuchadnezzar towers in an analogous fashion over other monarchs, even pharaoh must yield to his power and majesty." (Harrison)
>>
>> ii. "Both seemed to Jeremiah to depict Nebuchadnezzar, who towered over Egypt in his might like lofty mountains towering over a plain." (Thompson)
>
> b. **Egypt is a very pretty heifer**: Egypt proudly thought of herself as strong, great, and beautiful. God said they were strong and **pretty** like a young steer, but really just ripe for sacrifice. They would be **cut down** like a forest.

i. "The *mercenaries* (lit. 'hired ones') in her midst were evidently well cared for (*fatted calves*) but useless in the hour of danger, Jeremiah may have had another agricultural picture in mind, that of calves fattened for killing." (Thompson)

  ii. **Her noise shall go like a serpent**: "The reference to Egypt *gliding away* like a snake is a sarcastic comment on the humbling of one of the most vaunted national deities, and one which was prominent in the royal insignia." (Harrison)

c. **Because they are innumerable**: Egypt would be ashamed and delivered into the hand of the people of the north (the Babylonians). When this massive army came against them, God would **bring punishment** on the cities and rulers of Egypt.

  i. **Afterward it shall be inhabited as in the days of old**: "The text suggests that Yahweh was punishing rather than destroying Egypt, so that later she could continue as in the past. This promise of restoration is repeated for other nations (Jeremiah 48:47; 49:6, 39)." (Thompson)

3. (27-28) Comfort to the people of God.

"But do not fear, O My servant Jacob,
And do not be dismayed, O Israel!
For behold, I will save you from afar,
And your offspring from the land of their captivity;
Jacob shall return, have rest and be at ease;
No one shall make *him* afraid.
Do not fear, O Jacob My servant," says the Lord,
"For I *am* with you;
For I will make a complete end of all the nations
To which I have driven you,
But I will not make a complete end of you.
I will rightly correct you,
For I will not leave you wholly unpunished."

a. **Do not fear, O My servant Jacob**: After the Babylonians conquered Jerusalem and Judah, the small remnant remaining in the land was afraid of the continued Babylonian presence and they felt they would be safer in Egypt (Jeremiah 42-43). God wanted them not to **fear** or be **dismayed** and trust Him in the land.

  i. "In the midst of wrath God remembers mercy. Though Judah shall be destroyed, Jerusalem taken, the temple burnt to the ground, and the people carried into captivity, yet the *nation* shall not be destroyed. A seed shall be preserved, out of which the nation shall revive." (Clarke)

b. **I will save you from afar, and your offspring from the land of captivity**: God also promised to end the captivity of His people in Babylon, allowing them to return to their land. It would be fulfilled; **Jacob shall return, and have rest**.

c. **I am with you; for I will make a complete end of all the nations to which I have driven you**: God sent His people to exile in judgment of their great sin against Him. He would also not forget His righteous judgment against the surrounding nations.

> i. "If Egypt's woes were but temporary, those of Israel would be even more so." (Feinberg)

d. **But I will not make a complete end of you**: God's judgment against the nations would be different than the correction of His people. Pagan kingdoms and empires may pass into history, but God would never **make a complete end** of Israel, His covenant people.

> i. "If He has taken us to be his and to give us his best – then, though we suffer chastisement, we shall not be overwhelmed by it: though we are corrected, diminished, and brought low, God will not make a full end of us: though we are pruned, we shall not be cut down to the ground. We may even look out with a quiet mind on the irretrievable disasters which overtake the ungodly." (Meyer)

e. **I will rightly correct you**: Even God's judgment upon His people was evidence of His great love and care for them. Like a faithful Father, He would **correct** them and not leave them **wholly unpunished**.

Jeremiah 47 – A Word of Judgment Against the Philistines

A. The prophecy against the Philistines.

1. (1) Introduction.

The word of the LORD that came to Jeremiah the prophet against the Philistines, before Pharaoh attacked Gaza.

a. **Against the Philistines**: Jeremiah 46 began the section of Jeremiah's prophecies against the nations surrounding Judah. Jeremiah 47 is the record of his prophecy **against the Philistines**, the ancient enemies and rivals of Israel.

b. **Before Pharaoh attacked Gaza**: The prophecy was given **before** the calamity came upon **Gaza**, a significant Philistine city.

   i. **Before Pharaoh attacked Gaza**: "The attack may have occurred when Necho was marching to Harran in 609 BC." (Harrison)

   ii. "In verse 1 the reference is to Pharaoh Neco's campaign of 609 BC, which had a twofold purpose: to prop up a tottering Assyria against a powerful Babylonia, thus maintaining the balance of power; to extend his own empire in a time of international chaos." (Cundall)

   iii. "The Greek historian Herodotus records a tradition that after the battle at Megiddo, Neco overthrew Kadytis, which is usually identified with the Philistine city of Gaza." (Cundall)

2. (2-3) Judgment comes from the north.

Thus says the LORD:
"Behold, waters rise out of the north,
And shall be an overflowing flood;
They shall overflow the land and all that is in it,
The city and those who dwell within;

Then the men shall cry,
And all the inhabitants of the land shall wail.
At the noise of the stamping hooves of his strong horses,
At the rushing of his chariots,
At the rumbling of his wheels,
The fathers will not look back for *their* children,
Lacking courage,"

> a. **Waters rise out of the north**: The Babylonians did not only come to conquer the Kingdom of Judah and the Egyptians, but to rule the entire region as their empire. They would also come from **the north** to overwhelm the Philistines as flood waters overwhelm a land.
>
> b. **All the inhabitants of the land shall wail**: Jeremiah described the vivid sounds of conquest. The people are wailing, the horses with **stamping hooves**, the sound of **rushing chariots** with **rumbling wheels**. These were the sounds of judgment upon the Philistines.
>
> c. **The fathers will not look back for their children, lacking courage**: Jeremiah described the tragedy of the coming Babylonian invasion. It would bring such crisis and fear that natural affection and **courage** would be forgotten.

B. **The sword of the L**ORD **against the cities of the Philistines.**

1. (4-5) The afflicted cities.

"Because of the day that comes to plunder all the Philistines,
To cut off from Tyre and Sidon every helper who remains;
For the LORD shall plunder the Philistines,
The remnant of the country of Caphtor.
Baldness has come upon Gaza,
Ashkelon is cut off
With the remnant of their valley.
How long will you cut yourself?"

> a. **Because of the day that comes to plunder all the Philistines**: The Babylonians would not spare even some of the territory of these coastal people. Acting as agents of the LORD, they **shall plunder** them all.
>
> b. **To cut off from Tyre and Sidon every helper**: Nebuchadnezzar would conquer these great cities, as well as **Caphtor, Gaza**, and **Ashkelon**.
>
> > i. "The obscure clause *to cut off from Tyre and Sidon* seems to mean that any available Phoenician help would be prevented from reaching Philistia." (Harrison) "Tyre and Sidon were Phoenician, not Philistine,

cities, but they were probably in a desperate alliance with the Philistines against the overwhelming might of Babylonia." (Cundall)

ii. Here the Philistines are called, **the remnant of the country of Caphtor**. "*Caphtor* is the Old Testament designation of Crete, the land from which the Philistines came originally." (Harrison)

iii. **Baldness has come upon Gaza**: "They have *cut off their hair* in token of deep sorrow and distress." (Clarke)

iv. **With the remnant of their valley**: "The fate of the 'remnant of the Anakim' (Jeremiah 47:5, RSV) is of peculiar interest, since this aboriginal race of giant-like people was exterminated in Israel and survived only in a few Philistine cities, as noted in Joshua 11:21 f. (cf. Numbers 13:22, 28, 32 f.)." (Cundall)

v. **The remnant of their valley**: "The LXX reading 'Anakim' seeks to link the people of Gaza and Ashkelon with the race of giants that inhabited Canaan before the arrival of the Israelites (Numbers 13:22-23; Deuteronomy 1:28)." (Thompson)

2. (6-7) Speaking to and hearing from the sword of God's judgment.

**"O you sword of the Lord,
How long until you are quiet?
Put yourself up into your scabbard,
Rest and be still!
How can it be quiet,
Seeing the Lord has given it a charge
Against Ashkelon and against the seashore?
There He has appointed it."**

a. **O you sword of the Lord**: Jeremiah spoke, as it were, to the very **sword** of God's judgment that came so heavily upon the Philistines. He wondered **how long** it would continue and asked the sword of judgment to **rest and be still**.

i. "This is a most grand prosopopoeia [a figure of speech in which an abstract thing is personified] – a dialogue between the sword of the Lord and the prophet. Nothing can be imagined more sublime." (Clarke)

b. **Seeing the Lord has given it a charge**: Nevertheless, God's sword of judgment would remain active until the work was complete. Nebuchadnezzar's armies acted as instruments of God.

i. "This is the *answer* of the *Sword*. I am the officer of God's judgments, and he has given me a commission against Ashkelon, and against the sea shore; all the coast where the Philistines have their territories." (Clarke)

ii. The **sword of the Lord** did its work in history. "A Babylonian prism, now in Istanbul, mentions the presence – presumably with little choice in the matter – of the kings of Tyre and Sidon, of Gaza, and of Ashdod, at the court of Nebuchadnezzar, while a prison list now in Berlin records the rations for the king of Ashkelon, among other noted prisoners (including Jehoiachin of Judah)." (Kidner)

iii. There is another sense in which the **sword of the Lord** – in the sense of God's word – has a work to do among God's people today, and will not be stopped until it finishes that work. "O sword of the Lord; thou hast wounded us sore! Like a two-edged sword, the Word of God has pierced to the dividing asunder of soul and spirit, of the joints and marrow. How deeply it has penetrated; how sharply it has cut! And even now it cannot rest." (Meyer)

iv. "How can it be quiet, seeing that this is the only world where pain can reach his saints? And He must do his work quickly, ere we reach the land where the sword is placed in its scabbard, and stilled for ever." (Meyer)

Jeremiah 48 – A Word of Judgment Against Moab

A. Coming judgment against Moab.

1. (1-5) Judgment to come against the cities of Moab.

Against Moab. Thus says the Lord of hosts, the God of Israel:
"Woe to Nebo!
For it is plundered,
Kirjathaim is shamed *and* taken;
The high stronghold is shamed and dismayed—
No more praise of Moab.
In Heshbon they have devised evil against her:
'Come, and let us cut her off as a nation.'
You also shall be cut down, O Madmen!
The sword shall pursue you;
A voice of crying *shall be* from Horonaim:
'Plundering and great destruction!'
"Moab is destroyed;
Her little ones have caused a cry to be heard;
For in the Ascent of Luhith they ascend with continual weeping;
For in the descent of Horonaim the enemies have heard a cry of destruction.

> a. **Against Moab**: In the series of judgments of nations surrounding Judah, Jeremiah now turned his attention to Israel's neighbor to the east, on the other side of the Jordan. The ancestor of **Moab** came from the incestuous pairing of Lot and his daughter (Genesis 19:37).
>
>> i. Moab was something of a cousin to Israel. They feared Israel as they came from Egypt towards Canaan (Numbers 22:3-4) and Balak king of Moab hired Balaam to curse Israel (Numbers 22:5-8). When Israel came into Canaan, sometimes Moab attacked and ruled over them (Judges 3:12-14).

ii. Later, Ruth the Moabite was the great-grandmother of King David, and David sent his parents to Moab for their protection when Saul hunted him (1 Samuel 22:3-4). When he was king, David fought against and defeated Moab (2 Samuel 8:2), and they became a vassal kingdom to Israel, sometimes rebelling (2 Kings 1:1, 2 Kings 3:4-5).

iii. "There was little love lost between the two nations, a fact which is attested by foreign prophecies directed against Moab by Isaiah (chapters 15-16), Amos (2:1-3), Zephaniah (2:9), Jeremiah, and Ezekiel (25:8-11)." (Thompson)

b. **Thus says the LORD of hosts, the God of Israel**: The God of Israel was also God of all the earth and spoke with authority in judgment over Moab. He was also the **LORD of hosts**, the God commanding fearsome heavenly armies.

c. **Woe to Nebo! For it is plundered, Kirjathaim is shamed and taken**: Jeremiah began by listing many of the major cities and places of Moab that would be overwhelmed in judgment including **Nebo**, **Kirjathaim**, **Heshbon**, **Horonaim** and **Luhith**. They would be **plundered**, **shamed**, **cut down**, and **destroyed**.

i. "*Nebo* is not the mountain so named, but the Moabite city of Numbers 32:3, 38, built by the Reubenites." (Harrison)

ii. "Most cities mentioned here had been assigned by Moses to the Reubenites (Numbers 32:33-38; Joshua 13:15-23)." (Harrison)

iii. **No more praise of Moab**: "To us at this distance the very mention of her *renown* is ironic, for we can see how local and how temporary was the fame that meant so much to her." (Kidner)

iv. **A voice of crying shall be from Horonaim**: "They would not cry for their sins: they shall therefore cry for their miseries with desperate and bootless tears, and yet worse one day." (Trapp)

v. **With continual weeping**: "Hebrew, Weeping with weeping shall go up – *i.e.*, they shall weep abundantly." (Trapp)

2. (6-9) The terror of judgment coming upon Moab.

"Flee, save your lives!
And be like the juniper in the wilderness.
For because you have trusted in your works and your treasures,
You also shall be taken.
And Chemosh shall go forth into captivity,
His priests and his princes together.
And the plunderer shall come against every city;

No one shall escape.
The valley also shall perish,
And the plain shall be destroyed,"
As the LORD has spoken.
"Give wings to Moab,
That she may flee and get away;
For her cities shall be desolate,
Without any to dwell in them."

a. **Flee, save your lives**: This was the call that would be heard in Moab when the Babylonian armies advanced upon it.

i. "The picture which this chapter conveys is the shattering of such complacent self-sufficiency in a massive invasion, with its brutal accompaniments: looting, slaughter, captivity, untold misery and bitter lamentation." (Cundall)

b. **Because you have trusted in your works and your treasures**: Moab was wealthy because important trade routes came through their land. Their **treasures** made them proud and self-reliant, ripe for God's judgment.

i. "Geographically, Moab was more isolated than Israel and Judah, which were on the main trade-routs and were also surrounded by other kingdoms. Moab's isolation enabled her to escape many of the international upheavals which weakened her neighbours, and she was often able to strengthen herself at their expense." (Cundall)

c. **Chemosh shall go forth into captivity**: **Chemosh** was the ancient god of the Moabites and sometimes used as a representation of the people. In their conquest, the Babylonians would take the literal idols of **Chemosh** and the people of **Chemosh** into captivity.

i. "Chemosh was the principal Moabite deity (Numbers 21:29) and the sacrificing of children was an important part of his cult (2 Kings 3:27)." (Harrison)

ii. "Solomon erected a high place for Chemosh in Jerusalem (1 Kings 11:7), but it was demolished under Josiah (2 Kings 23:13)." (Harrison)

iii. "Despite his thirst for blood, Chemosh had often been a temptation to Israel. In the days of Balaam, Moabite women seduced the Israelites to worship their gods (Numbers 25). King Solomon later married Moabite women and set up an altar to Chemosh (1 Kings 11:1-13)." (Ryken)

iv. "The carrying off of statues of the gods into exile was common in the ancient Near East (cf. Amos 5:25; Isaiah 46:1,2)." (Thompson)

d. **Give wings to Moab, that she may flee and get away**: The destruction to come would be so complete (**her cities shall be desolate**) that those who could **flee and get away** would be fortunate.

i. **The valley also shall perish**: "The 'valley' is the Jordan Valley, which touched Moab on the west. All the Moabite cities will be involved in the doom. The 'plateau' is the extensive region where most of the Moabite cities were located." (Feinberg)

3. (10-13) Complacent Moab must be emptied.

Cursed *is* he who does the work of the LORD deceitfully,
And cursed *is* he who keeps back his sword from blood.
"Moab has been at ease from his youth;
He has settled on his dregs,
And has not been emptied from vessel to vessel,
Nor has he gone into captivity.
Therefore his taste remained in him,
And his scent has not changed.
"Therefore behold, the days are coming," says the LORD,
"That I shall send him wine-workers
Who will tip him over
And empty his vessels
And break the bottles.
Moab shall be ashamed of Chemosh,
As the house of Israel was ashamed of Bethel, their confidence."

a. **Cursed is he who keeps back his sword from blood**: The armies of Babylon were the unknowing servants of God, executing His judgment upon Judah, Moab, and other nations. They were to do their work without deceit and completely.

i. "Note the fearful twist to what may well have been a proverb or preacher's text in verse 10a (*Cursed is he who does the work of the Lord with slackness*), turning it into a charge to Moab's executioners." (Kidner)

ii. Jeremiah 48:10 was "Described by A.S. Peake as 'This bloodthirsty verse' and regarded by him as an interpolation, is not to be interpreted literally, but as a hyperbolic statement of the completeness of the judgment about to fall. Such an event inevitably involves bloodshed, but the Lord takes no delight in the death of the most rebellious sinner (cf. 2 Peter 3:9)." (Cundall)

b. **Moab has been at ease from his youth**: God spoke through Jeremiah a remarkable picture of Moab's sin and condition. They had **been at ease** for a long time and had **settled on his dregs**.

    i. The picture is from the ancient process of refining wine. After fermentation, the wine would sit in a jar or bottle and the impurities – the **dregs** – would settle on the bottom, something like coffee grounds at the bottom of a cup. It would then be carefully poured into another vessel, leaving the dregs in the first vessel. Doing this a few times made for a wine with fewer impurities to spoil the taste.

    ii. "One secret of the corruption of Moab had been that of its comparative ease." (Morgan)

    iii. "She lay outside the normal route of the invaders of the Middle East and was rarely disturbed." (Thompson)

    iv. "For defence, Moab had towering cliffs, and for wealth, her enormous flocks of sheep, riches that were self-renewing. But the shelter of these things had bred more complacency than character." (Kidner)

c. **Has not been emptied from vessel to vessel**: Moab had not been shaken up in a while and had settled into a comfortable complacency. According to the picture, the remaining **dregs** began to flavor and spoil the wine. Moab – and many people today – would benefit from being **emptied from vessel to vessel**. For them it meant coming **captivity**.

    i. "The simile is particularly apposite because of the esteem in which Moabite vineyards were held (*cf.* Isaiah 16:8-11)." (Harrison)

    ii. "Readers of the missionary classic, *Hudson Taylor in Early Years*, may remember the apt heading, 'Emptied from Vessel to Vessel', to a chapter describing an unsettling but ultimately fruitful few months in the missionary's second year in China." (Kidner)

d. **Therefore his taste remained in him, and his scent has not changed**: The picture remains true. If we are not **emptied** out from time to time we never grow, and our **scent** does not change. God promised to send **wine-workers** to Moab who would **tip him over and empty his vessels** and will faithfully do a similar work in lives of His people today.

    i. For Moab, this was a demonstration of God's judgment and anger. For the believer under the new covenant, it is a demonstration of God's goodness and compassion.

    ii. "Unlike an earthenware jar that is carefully tilted so as not to lose the sediment of the wine, Moab will be roughly dealt with ('pour her out') and emptied like jars and smashed like jugs." (Feinberg)

e. **Moab shall be ashamed of Chemosh**: Through the coming Babylonian conquest and captivity, God promised to break down their confidence in their local deity **Chemosh**, even as He broke the confidence of the northern kingdom of Israel in Bethel, their center of idolatry.

4. (14-17) The calamity to come upon Moab.

"How can you say, 'We *are* mighty
And strong men for the war'?
Moab is plundered and gone up *from* her cities;
Her chosen young men have gone down to the slaughter," says the King,
Whose name *is* the LORD of hosts.
"The calamity of Moab *is* near at hand,
And his affliction comes quickly.
Bemoan him, all you who are around him;
And all you who know his name,
Say, 'How the strong staff is broken,
The beautiful rod!'"

a. **We are mighty and strong men for the war**: This was the attitude of Moab in the face of the Babylonian threat. God showed how this was foolish and vain confidence. They would be **plundered** and exiled (**gone up from her cities**).

i. "Partly because of isolation, Moab had never undergone the experience of exile, even though invaded and occupied periodically." (Harrison)

b. **Says the King, whose name is the LORD of hosts**: It wasn't a local deity who brought this word to Moab. It was the **King** over all, Yahweh, who commanded the armies of heaven (**the LORD of hosts**).

c. **How the strong staff is broken**: This would be the response of surrounding nations. Moab seemed like a **beautiful** and **strong staff**, but would be broken by the Babylonians.

i. **The strong staff**: "The expressions *mighty scepter* and *glorious staff* refer back to the days when Moab was able to exert some influence in the neighboring areas (Jeremiah 27:3; 2 Kings 1:1; 3:4-5; 24:2)." (Thompson)

5. (18-24) The complete nature of the conquest of Moab.

"O daughter inhabiting Dibon,
Come down from *your* glory,
And sit in thirst;
For the plunderer of Moab has come against you,

He has destroyed your strongholds.
O inhabitant of Aroer,
Stand by the way and watch;
Ask him who flees
And her who escapes;
Say, 'What has happened?'
Moab is shamed, for he is broken down.
Wail and cry!
Tell it in Arnon, that Moab is plundered.
"And judgment has come on the plain country:
On Holon and Jahzah and Mephaath,
On Dibon and Nebo and Beth Diblathaim,
On Kirjathaim and Beth Gamul and Beth Meon,
On Kerioth and Bozrah,
On all the cities of the land of Moab,
Far or near."

> a. **O daughter inhabiting Dibon, come down from your glory**: God spoke to Moab in its cities and landmarks, telling them to humble themselves and prepare for the judgment to come as **the plunderer of Moab has come**.
>
>> i. "*Dibon*, the modern Diban, was four miles north of the Arnon and thirteen miles east of the Dead Sea. The Moabite Stone was discovered here in 1868." (Harrison)
>
> b. **All the cities of the land of Moab, far or near**: To give a sense of completeness of the judgment, Jeremiah listed at least 14 specific cities or places in Moab.

B. The reason for judgment: the pride of Moab.

1. (25-28) Proud Moab thought itself better than Israel.

"The horn of Moab is cut off,
And his arm is broken," says the LORD.
"Make him drunk,
Because he exalted *himself* against the LORD.
Moab shall wallow in his vomit,
And he shall also be in derision.
For was not Israel a derision to you?
Was he found among thieves?
For whenever you speak of him,
You shake *your head in scorn.*
You who dwell in Moab,

Leave the cities and dwell in the rock,
And be like the dove *which* makes her nest
In the sides of the cave's mouth."

> a. **The horn of Moab is cut off, and his arm is broken**: The **horn** and the **arm** were representations of strength, one from the world of animals and the other from men. God would show Moab to be empty of all strength.
>
>> i. **The horn of Moab is cut off**: "*i.e.,* His strength, power, glory, kingdoms; his sultans and princes, saith the Chaldee." (Trapp)
>
> b. **Make him drunk, because he exalted himself against the LORD**: Proud Moab believed they were greater than Yahweh, the covenant God of Israel. They also believed they were greater than Israel, holding them in **derision**. They held this sense of superiority when the Assyrians conquered the northern king of Israel and they escaped.
>
>> i. **Moab shall wallow in his vomit**: "*Wallow in his vomit* (EVV) uses the Hebrew verb *sapaq*, which, however, means to clap the hands (Numbers 24:0; Lamentations 2:15) and to clap the thigh (Jeremiah 31:19). Presumably the reference here is to a person holding his abdomen as he vomits." (Harrison)
>
>> ii. "The drunken stupor of Moab is a warning to everyone who mocks God. God suffers himself to be ridiculed by his creatures. …But God will not be mocked forever. There was nothing humorous about Moab wallowing in her own vomit." (Ryken)
>
>> iii. "The picture of a drunken man doubled over by vomiting is both disgusting and likely to provoke derision. Once Moab had laughed at Israel as she drank the cup of Yahweh's wrath, regarding her as a laughingstock." (Thompson)
>
> c. **Leave the cities and dwell in the rock**: The coming judgment would make the people of Moab refugees from their cities, forced to find refuge in the mountains and their rocks.

2. (29-35) Proud Moab brought low.

"We have heard the pride of Moab
(He *is* exceedingly proud),
Of his loftiness and arrogance and pride,
And of the haughtiness of his heart."
"I know his wrath," says the LORD,
"But it *is* not right;
His lies have made nothing right.
Therefore I will wail for Moab,
And I will cry out for all Moab;

I will mourn for the men of Kir Heres.
O vine of Sibmah! I will weep for you with the weeping of Jazer.
Your plants have gone over the sea,
They reach to the sea of Jazer.
The plunderer has fallen on your summer fruit and your vintage.
Joy and gladness are taken
From the plentiful field
And from the land of Moab;
I have caused wine to fail from the winepresses;
No one will tread with joyous shouting—
Not joyous shouting!"
"From the cry of Heshbon to Elealeh and to Jahaz
They have uttered their voice,
From Zoar to Horonaim,
Like a three-year-old heifer;
For the waters of Nimrim also shall be desolate.
"Moreover," says the LORD,
"I will cause to cease in Moab
The one who offers *sacrifices* in the high places
And burns incense to his gods."

> a. **We have heard of the pride of Moab**: There was a lot to say about the pride of Moab. God described it as **exceedingly proud**, as **loftiness and arrogance and pride**, and as **haughtiness of his heart**.
>
> > i. "Jeremiah here piles up a number of synonymous terms designed to emphasize Moab's pride." (Thompson)
>
> b. **I know his wrath**: Moab's pride was also connected to their **wrath** or anger. Believing themselves to be better than others, they found it easy to feel and act in an angry manner. God knew that **it is not right**. Their pride *explained* their anger but did not *justify* it.
>
> c. **Therefore I will wail for Moab**: Even though the judgment was richly deserved, it was not rejoiced in. God and His prophet would **cry out** and **mourn** because of the destruction to come upon Moab and her people.
>
> d. **Joy and gladness are taken from the plentiful field**: Moab's previous prosperity in the **field** and the **winepress** would turn to sorrow and desolation. This would happen all over the land of Moab. Their idol sacrifices on the **high places** would stop.
>
> > i. **No one will tread with joyous shouting**: "Verse 33 is a variant of Isaiah 16:10. The implication is that the shout will not be the glad cry of the vintagers, but the noise of warriors bent on destruction." (Harrison)

ii. **Like a three-year-old heifer**: "Which runs lowing from place to place in search of her calf, which is lost or taken from her." (Clarke)

3. (36-42) Mourning for Moab.

**"Therefore My heart shall wail like flutes for Moab,
And like flutes My heart shall wail
For the men of Kir Heres.
Therefore the riches they have acquired have perished.
"For every head** *shall be* **bald, and every beard clipped;
On all the hands** *shall be* **cuts, and on the loins sackcloth—
A general lamentation
On all the housetops of Moab,
And in its streets;
For I have broken Moab like a vessel in which** *is* **no pleasure," says the LORD.
"They shall wail:
'How she is broken down!
How Moab has turned her back with shame!'
So Moab shall be a derision
And a dismay to all those about her."
For thus says the LORD:
"Behold, one shall fly like an eagle,
And spread his wings over Moab.
Kerioth is taken,
And the strongholds are surprised;
The mighty men's hearts in Moab on that day shall be
Like the heart of a woman in birth pangs.
And Moab shall be destroyed as a people,
Because he exalted** *himself* **against the LORD."**

a. **Therefore My heart shall wail like flutes for Moab**: God and His prophet did not celebrate the coming doom upon Moab. Though they deserved the judgment, it was still painful to see it come upon Israel's cousin and neighbor.

b. **Every head shall be bald, and every beard clipped**: Jeremiah recounted their many demonstrations of mourning, including ritual cutting (**on all the hands shall be cuts**) and the wearing of **sackcloth**.

c. **I have broken Moab like a vessel in which is no pleasure**: Clay pots or vessels were cheaply made in the ancient world. When the use or pleasure of a pot had ended, it was quickly and easily broken. This was a picture of how God's judgment would come upon Moab. It would be so bad that men would show the pain and fear of a woman in the labor of birth.

> i. **One shall fly like an eagle**: "The *eagle*, ready to swoop on its prey, was an apt figure of Nebuchadnezzar (*cf.* Deuteronomy 28:49; Jeremiah 49:22)." (Harrison)

d. **Moab shall be destroyed as a people**: The people of Moab would no longer continue as a separate, defined people. In a sense they would be lost to history, unlike Israel. All this came **because he exalted himself against the LORD**.

> i. "Moab's predicted extinction began with a heavy Nabatean settlement in the first century BC, and culminated under the Arabs in the Byzantine period." (Harrison)

> ii. "The end of Moab as an independent nation seems to have come in 582 BC when Nebuchadnezzar, no doubt because of a rebellion, marched against Moab and Ammon. …Not long after this the small states in Transjordan were overwhelmed by an Arab invasion and ceased to exist as a nation." (Thompson)

4. (43-47) Unrelenting judgment, a glimmer of hope.

Fear and the pit and the snare *shall be* upon you,
O inhabitant of Moab," says the LORD.
"He who flees from the fear shall fall into the pit,
And he who gets out of the pit shall be caught in the snare.
For upon Moab, upon it I will bring
The year of their punishment," says the LORD.
"Those who fled stood under the shadow of Heshbon
Because of exhaustion.
But a fire shall come out of Heshbon,
A flame from the midst of Sihon,
And shall devour the brow of Moab,
The crown of the head of the sons of tumult.
Woe to you, O Moab!
The people of Chemosh perish;
For your sons have been taken captive,
And your daughters captive.
"Yet I will bring back the captives of Moab
In the latter days," says the LORD.
Thus far *is* the judgment of Moab.

> a. **Fear and the pit and the snare shall be upon you**: God promised that the judgment to come upon Moab would be thorough. If someone escaped an aspect of it, another aspect of judgment would catch up with them.

i. Thompson observed on Jeremiah 48:45-46: "It would appear that these verses consist of free quotation from the old song of Heshbon which occurs in Numbers 21:28-29 and also from Numbers 24:17. We may see in these words a claim that Balaam's oracle against Moab was about to be enacted." (Thompson)

b. **Yet I will bring back the captives of Moab**: Despite the complete nature of the judgment to come against them, God promised a measure of mercy to Moab **in the latter days**.

i. "Perhaps the restoration spoken of here, which was to take place in the *latter days*, may mean the conversion of these people, in their existing remnants, to the faith of the Gospel. Several judicious interpreters are of this opinion. The Moabites were partially restored; but never, as far as I have been able to learn, to their national consequence. Their conversion to the Christian faith must be the main end designed by this prophecy." (Clarke)

Jeremiah 49 – Words of Judgment Against the Nations

A. Judgment against Ammon.

1. (1) Ammonites in Israel's inheritance.

Against the Ammonites.
Thus says the LORD:
"Has Israel no sons?
Has he no heir?
Why *then* does Milcom inherit Gad,
And his people dwell in its cities?

a. **Against the Ammonites**: The **Ammonites** lived in the area on the east side of the Jordan River, north of the Moabites. Their lands are included in what is today Jordan, and the capital of Jordan is named *Ammon* because of this connection.

i. "The Ammonites were often in conflict with Israel: they opposed Judah during Johoiakim's reign (cf. 2 Kings 24:2) and helped the downfall of the remnant after the Fall of Jerusalem (cf. Jeremiah 40:11-14). They joined in the invasion of Judah in 602 BC (cf. 2 Kings 24:2)." (Feinberg)

b. **Has Israel no sons? Has he no heir? Why then does Milcom inherit Gad**: Through Jeremiah, God spoke of the fact that the Ammonites occupied land that was apportioned for the tribes of **Gad**, Reuben, and Manasseh. In the name of their god **Milcom** they lived in that land, acting as if Israel's inheritance was invalid.

i. In God's estimation, that land belonged to Israel, not Ammon. "Although the northern tribes had been carried away by Tiglath-Pileser III, their land still belonged to them and was to be inherited by their sons." (Feinberg)

ii. "The Ammonites, it appears, took advantage of the depressed state of Israel, and invaded their territories in the tribe of Gad, hoping to make them their own for ever. But the prophet intimates that God will preserve the descendants of Israel, and will bring them back to their forfeited inheritances." (Clarke)

iii. We could say there is similar wonder today when God's people forsake their inheritance and do not possess it. Under the new covenant, the believer has an inheritance of peace and power and love in Jesus; it is an inheritance to actually possess.

iv. **Milcom**: "Better known to us as Molech, he had been worshipped here with rites of child-sacrifice since before the days of Moses. The mention of this god as the invader at the head of his people (Jeremiah 49:1) puts the matter on a plane above the political." (Kidner)

2. (2-3) The coming days of judgment.

Therefore behold, the days are coming," says the LORD,
"That I will cause to be heard an alarm of war
In Rabbah of the Ammonites;
It shall be a desolate mound,
And her villages shall be burned with fire.
Then Israel shall take possession of his inheritance," says the LORD.
"Wail, O Heshbon, for Ai is plundered!
Cry, you daughters of Rabbah,
Gird yourselves with sackcloth!
Lament and run to and fro by the walls;
For Milcom shall go into captivity
With his priests and his princes together."

a. **I will cause to be heard an alarm of war**: God promised that the same devastation of war that came upon Judah would also come upon the Ammonites. Their great cities like **Rabbah** would be made **a desolate mound**.

i. "Ai is not the Ai captured by Joshua (cf. Joshua 8:1-29) but the Ammonite Ai mentioned only here." (Feinberg)

b. **Then Israel shall take possession of his inheritance**: God promised a day when Israel *would* possess these lands on the eastern side of the Jordan River. It can be argued that this prophecy is yet to be fulfilled.

i. "How Israel would repossess these areas is not clear. Historically this did not take place." (Thompson)

c. **Milcom shall go into captivity**: The Babylonians would not only conquer the land and the peoples of the Ammonites, but also their national deity **Milcom**, together with **his priests and his princes**.

> i. In the ancient world when one nation conquered another, it was seen as the victory of that nation's gods over the conquered nation's gods. There is much in the prophets and the Hebrew Scriptures in general that shows Yahweh, the covenant God of Israel, carefully showed that He was *not* just the national deity of Israel; He was and is King of all the Earth. When Babylon conquered Ammon, one might say the Babylonian idols were superior. When Babylon conquered Judah, it was *at the very direction of Yahweh*, whose purpose the Babylonians served.

3. (4-6) Coming captivity and a promise of mercy.

"Why do you boast in the valleys,
Your flowing valley, O backsliding daughter?
Who trusted in her treasures, *saying,*
'Who will come against me?'
Behold, I will bring fear upon you,"
Says the Lord GOD of hosts,
"From all those who are around you;
You shall be driven out, everyone headlong,
And no one will gather those who wander off.
But afterward I will bring back
The captives of the people of Ammon," says the LORD.

a. **Why do you boast in the valleys**: The Ammonites believed their geography would help defend them against the Babylonians, but it was a poorly placed trust. The same could be said as they **trusted in her treasures**. All would fail them in the days of judgment.

b. **I will bring fear upon you**: Their day of judgment would be marked by fear and captivity (**you shall be driven out**).

> i. "Within a century, the Arabian tribes that overran Moab and Ammon would have driven the Edomites out of their land in to the south of Judah, and these invaders would be replaced in turn by the powerful kingdom of the Nabateans." (Kidner)

c. **But afterwards I will bring back**: In the midst of judgment, God had mercy and some promise of restoration even for the Ammonites.

> i. "The *Ammonites* are supposed to have returned with the Moabites and Israelites, on permission given by the edict of Cyrus." (Clarke)

ii. The promise of some kind of restoration for *other* nations shows God's mercy and plan extends past Israel. "He saw also that the ultimate purpose of the activity of wrath is that of restoration, not in the case of Israel only, but also in that of all the nations. The fact that for some of these nations no such restoration is foretold, reveals the awful possibility of resisting not only the mercy of God, but His judgments also, so completely that there is no possibility of restoration." (Morgan)

B. Judgment against Edom.

1. (7-8) The time of Edom's punishment.

Against Edom.
Thus says the LORD of hosts:
"*Is* wisdom no more in Teman?
Has counsel perished from the prudent?
Has their wisdom vanished?
Flee, turn back, dwell in the depths, O inhabitants of Dedan!
For I will bring the calamity of Esau upon him,
The time *that* I will punish him."

a. **Against Edom**: The Edomites were also a cousin-nation to Israel. Their founder was Esau, the son of Isaac, twin brother of Jacob. They also lived in the lands east of the Jordan River and the Dead Sea, toward the south mountains and deserts.

i. "Edom's cardinal sin was its pride manifested in its unrelenting and violent hatred of Israel and its rejoicing in her misfortune (Obadiah 3, 10-14). There is no prophecy of future restoration for Edom." (Feinberg)

ii "When Judah felt the weight of Nebuchadrezzar in 589-587 BC Edom not only gave assistance but seems to have collaborated with the Babylonians (Ezekiel 25:12-14; Psalm 137:7; Obadiah; Lamentations 4:21)." (Thompson)

b. **Is wisdom no more in Teman**: Part of God's judgment against the Edomites was to bring them foolish and incompetent leadership. To this day, this is one way God may show His displeasure against a nation.

i. "*Teman* (lit. 'south') was either a district or a city of Edom, but here it is a poetic name for Edom." (Thompson)

ii. "The reference to wisdom in Teman may be a satirical literary allusion to the fact that it was the birthplace of Eliphaz, the counselor of Job." (Morgan)

c. **Dwell in the depths**: This has occasionally been a preacher's verse, especially as given in the King James: *Dwell deep*. Preachers have found in this an encouragement for believers to *dwell deep* in God. This is always a good and valid encouragement, but not what Jeremiah had in mind. He told the Edomites to dig in deep, as a soldier does in a foxhole or trench, trying to find some shelter against the judgment to come.

i. "Hide yourselves in holes of the earth, grots in the ground, clefts of the rocks, where you may best secure yourselves from the pursuing enemy." (Trapp)

- This may be taken *sarcastically*, daring Dedan to go deep enough to avoid the judgment of God.
- This may be taken as *instruction*, warning Dedan to escape judgment coming upon Edom.

ii. "As originally spoken, these words summoned the people of Edom to seek the shadows of impenetrable forests, and retire into the secrecy of the caves and the dens of the rocks. The deeper their hiding place, the better it would be when the storm of invasion swept across the land." (Meyer)

iii. F.B. Meyer went on to make spiritual application to the believer:

- Dwell deep in the peace of God.
- Dwell deep in communion with God.
- Dwell deep in stillness of soul.

iv. **O inhabitants of Dedan**: "Dedan (Jeremiah 49:8), a tribe living south of Edom, was known for its commerce (Jeremiah 25:23; Ezekiel 25:13). The people of Dedan are warned to flee from their usual contacts with Edom, lest they be overtaken in its destruction."

d. **I will bring the calamity of Esau upon him**: The **calamity of Esau** refers to Esau's sense that he lost everything when the birthright was given to Jacob. God promised that the Edomites would also feel that they lost everything when judgment came against them.

2. (9-11) A call to trust despite losing everything.

"If grape-gatherers came to you,
Would they not leave *some* gleaning grapes?
If thieves by night,
Would they not destroy until they have enough?
But I have made Esau bare;
I have uncovered his secret places,
And he shall not be able to hide himself.

His descendants are plundered,
His brethren and his neighbors,
And he *is* no more.
Leave your fatherless children,
I will preserve *them* alive;
And let your widows trust in Me."

> a. **Would they not leave some gleaning grapes**: In normal times, it is common for people to leave some things behind and not take *everything*. It was generally true for a grape harvest and even when a house is robbed. Yet when God came against Edom in judgment, He would make **Esau bare**. All would be taken.
>
>> i. "Contrary to the practice of grape gatherers, who left something for the poor, the enemies of Edom will leave nothing but will plunder everything." (Feinberg)
>
> b. **Leave your fatherless children, I will preserve them alive**: Here was a glimmer of hope for Edom, even with the devastation to come. God invited the remnant remaining – made up of **fatherless children** and **widows** – to trust in Him.

3. (12-16) The cup of judgment for proud Edom.

For thus says the Lord: "Behold, those whose judgment *was* not to drink of the cup have assuredly drunk. And *are* you the one who will altogether go unpunished? You shall not go unpunished, but you shall surely drink *of it.* For I have sworn by Myself," says the Lord, "that Bozrah shall become a desolation, a reproach, a waste, and a curse. And all its cities shall be perpetual wastes."

I have heard a message from the Lord,
And an ambassador has been sent to the nations:
"Gather together, come against her,
And rise up to battle!
"For indeed, I will make you small among nations,
Despised among men.
Your fierceness has deceived you,
The pride of your heart,
O you who dwell in the clefts of the rock,
Who hold the height of the hill!
Though you make your nest as high as the eagle,
I will bring you down from there," says the Lord.

> a. **You shall drink of it**: The mountainous and wilderness terrain of Edom gave them many natural advantages, and they proudly thought they would

escape the judgment that came upon Judah and the surrounding nations. God assured them that they would in fact **drink** of His cup of judgment and Edom's **cities shall be a perpetual waste**.

> i. "The Edomites had long enjoyed a reputation for rugged military strength but their trust in the physical prowess would fail them at the critical moment." (Harrison)
>
> ii. **Bozrah shall become a desolation**: "Bozrah is referred to because it was the capital of Edom in Jeremiah's time. It was midway between Petra and the Dead Sea, and here it represents all the Edomite cities (cf. Isaiah 63:1)." (Feinberg)

b. **An ambassador has been sent to the nations**: Jeremiah and other prophets were consciously prophets to **the nations**, not only to God's covenant people in Judah and Israel.

c. **Your fierceness has deceived you…O you who dwell in the clefts of the rock**: Edom's trust in the courage of their soldiers and their defensible territory would be broken. They thought of themselves as high and safe as **the eagle**, yet God promised to **bring you down from there**.

> i. **Your fierceness has deceived you**: "The unusual noun in Jeremiah 49:16, *tipleset*, may be a derogatory substitute for one of Edom's deities." (Thompson)
>
> ii. **The clefts of the rock**: "The 'rock' (*sela*, NIV, 'rocks') referred to was later called Sela (*Petra*, Greek) – the capital city and chief fortress of the Edomites." (Feinberg)

4. (17-22) The astonishing judgment to come upon Edom.

"Edom also shall be an astonishment;
Everyone who goes by it will be astonished
And will hiss at all its plagues.
As in the overthrow of Sodom and Gomorrah
And their neighbors," says the LORD,
"No one shall remain there,
Nor shall a son of man dwell in it.
"Behold, he shall come up like a lion from the floodplain of the Jordan
Against the dwelling place of the strong;
But I will suddenly make him run away from her.
And who *is* a chosen *man that* I may appoint over her?
For who *is* like Me?
Who will arraign Me?
And who *is* that shepherd
Who will withstand Me?"

Therefore hear the counsel of the LORD that He has taken against Edom,
And His purposes that He has proposed against the inhabitants of Teman:
Surely the least of the flock shall draw them out;
Surely He shall make their dwelling places desolate with them.
The earth shakes at the noise of their fall;
At the cry its noise is heard at the Red Sea.
Behold, He shall come up and fly like the eagle,
And spread His wings over Bozrah;
The heart of the mighty men of Edom in that day shall be
Like the heart of a woman in birth pangs.

> a. **Edom also shall be an astonishment**: Other nations noticed the many advantages Edom had in self-defense. They would also be **astonished** by the judgment that came upon those they believed were secure.
>
> b. **As in the overthrow of Sodom and Gomorrah**: These were chosen as warnings, not only for the complete nature of the devastation that came upon them, but also because they were in the region of later Edom.
>
>> i. "The destruction of Sodom and Gomorrah and the neighbouring cities was so terrible, that, when God denounces judgments against incorrigible sinners, he tells them they shall be like Sodom and Gomorrah." (Clarke)
>
> c. **He shall come up like a lion from the floodplain of the Jordan**: This described Nebuchadnezzar, who would come against Edom, **the dwelling place of the strong**. In God's great providence, Nebuchadnezzar was His instrument – so in that sense God could even equate resisting Nebuchadnezzar to be as foolish as resisting God (**who will withstand Me?**).
>
> d. **He shall come up and fly like the eagle**: The people of Edom thought of themselves as secure as an eagle (Jeremiah 49:16). God promised that **He** would conquer over them like a mighty eagle and they would respond in pain and fear, **like the heart of a woman in birth pangs**.

C. Judgment against Damascus.

1. (23-24) Weak Damascus, ready for judgment.

Against Damascus.

"**Hamath and Arpad are shamed,**
For they have heard bad news.
They are fainthearted;

There is **trouble on the sea;**
It cannot be quiet.
Damascus has grown feeble;
She turns to flee,
And fear has seized *her.*
Anguish and sorrows have taken her like a woman in labor."

> a. **Against Damascus**: This is the famous city of Syria, one of Israel's neighbors to the north. **Damascus** is one of the oldest continually occupied cities of the world.
>
>> i. **There is trouble on the sea**: "The reference to the 'sea' (Jeremiah 49:23) must be figurative, because Syria had no seacoast in ancient times. Suggestions as to the meaning are 'restlessness' (so WBC) or 'trouble' (so Freedman)." (Feinberg)
>
> b. **Damascus has grown feeble**: In comparison to the might of the rising Babylonian Empire, Damascus was weak and **feeble**. They could not stand against the coming judgment, and would respond in paid and sorrow.

2. (25-27) Damascus defeated but not depopulated.

"Why is the city of praise not deserted, the city of My joy?
Therefore her young men shall fall in her streets,
And all the men of war shall be cut off in that day," says the LORD **of hosts.**
"I will kindle a fire in the wall of Damascus,
And it shall consume the palaces of Ben-Hadad."

> a. **Why is the city of praise not deserted**: God gave honor to this ancient city, evening calling it the city of His **joy**. He noted that it would not be **deserted** of population like other major cities of surrounding nations.
>
> b. **All the men of war shall be cut off**: They would suffer great defeat and death, and even **the palaces of Ben-Hadad** would be burned – yet they would not be exiled in the same manner as Judah and some of the neighboring nations.
>
>> i. "The *young men* and the *warriors* are identical. They would fall in the city streets and lie silent on the day of judgment." (Thompson)
>>
>> ii. Perhaps the greatest fulfillment of this is still in the future. "Expositors have difficulty fitting this prophecy into any recorded event related to Damascus." (Feinberg)

D. **Judgment against Kedar and Hazor.**

1. (28) A word against Kedar and Hazor.

Against Kedar and against the kingdoms of Hazor, which Nebuchadnezzar king of Babylon shall strike.

Thus says the LORD:
"Arise, go up to Kedar,
And devastate the men of the East!"

>a. **Against Kedar**: Kedar describes a tribe of Arabic peoples, descended from Ishmael (Genesis 25:13). Isaiah prophesied against Kedar as among Arabic peoples (Isaiah 21:13-17).

>>i. "Kedar was an Ishmaelite desert tribe (cf. Genesis 25:13; Isaiah 21:13, 16, Ezekiel 27:21)." (Feinberg)

>>ii. **Kingdoms of Hazor**: "The *kingdoms* of some English versions is better rendered 'village chiefs'." (Harrison)

>b. **And against the kingdoms of Hazor**: This is likely *not* the Canaanite city conquered by Joshua. A more likely connection is with Judges 4, describing how Deborah defeated Sisera, the commander of the armies of Jabin, King of Hazor (Judges 4).

>>i. "Some expositors believe it was an Arab settlement in the south of Palestine (so Cowles); others take it as a collective name for villages in which half-nomadic Arabs lived (cf. Isaiah 42:11)." (Feinberg)

>>ii. "Kedar and Hazor represent the Arab peoples, the former such as were nomadic, the latter those who dwelt in settled centers, and yet not in walled cities." (Morgan)

>>iii. Some regard **the men of the East** as an additional group. "A third group, the *People of the East*, is known in other parts of the OT. These people are associated with Midianites and Amalekites in Judges 6:3, nomadic groups who raided Israelite territory in the days of the Judges." (Thompson)

2. (29-33) Conquest and plunder.

"Their tents and their flocks they shall take away.
They shall take for themselves their curtains,
All their vessels and their camels;
And they shall cry out to them,
'Fear *is* on every side!'
"Flee, get far away! Dwell in the depths,
O inhabitants of Hazor!" says the LORD.
"For Nebuchadnezzar king of Babylon has taken counsel against you,
And has conceived a plan against you.
"Arise, go up to the wealthy nation that dwells securely," says the

LORD,
"Which has neither gates nor bars,
Dwelling alone.
Their camels shall be for booty,
And the multitude of their cattle for plunder.
I will scatter to all winds those in the farthest corners,
And I will bring their calamity from all its sides," says the LORD.
"Hazor shall be a dwelling for jackals, a desolation forever;
No one shall reside there,
Nor son of man dwell in it."

> a. **Their tents and their flocks they shall take away**: In God's plan, Nebuchadnezzar would conquer Kedar. They would take the wealth of their nomadic herdsman lives: **tents and their flocks, their curtains, all their vessels and their camels**.
>
>> i. "This description of *property* shows that they were *Scenite* or *Nomad Arabs*; persons who dwell in *tents*, and whose principal property was *cattle*, especially *camels*, of the whole of which they were plundered by the Chaldeans." (Clarke)
>
> b. **Nebuchadnezzar king of Babylon has taken counsel against you**: God gave a similar warning to Hazor, which was a **wealthy nation**, yet would be conquered, plundered, and left **a desolation forever**.

E. Judgment against Elam.

1. (34-36) Elam conquered and scattered.

The word of the LORD that came to Jeremiah the prophet against Elam, in the beginning of the reign of Zedekiah king of Judah, saying, "Thus says the LORD of hosts:
'Behold, I will break the bow of Elam,
The foremost of their might.
Against Elam I will bring the four winds
From the four quarters of heaven,
And scatter them toward all those winds;
There shall be no nations where the outcasts of Elam will not go.'"

> a. **The prophet against Elam**: **Elam** is the ancient names for some of the peoples of Persia, modern day Iran. The Persians were at first allies to the Babylonians, and later they conquered the Babylonian Empire. This prophecy is spoken of their eventual conquest and fall.

i. "Elam (Jeremiah 49:34-39), a powerful kingdom more than 200 miles *east* of Babylonia, was the most distant nation referred to by Jeremiah." (Cundall)

ii. "The Elamites lived far from Israel, but they did not live outside the sovereignty of God." (Ryken)

iii. "A broken text in the Babylonian Chronicle may indicate a clash between Nebuchadrezzar and Elam in 596/4 BC to prevent an Elamite advance into Babylonia. If the interpretation of the fragmentary text is correct, Jeremiah's date of 597 BC (the accession year of Zedekiah) would predate this event." (Thompson)

b. **I will break the bow of Elam**: Isaiah 22:6 makes reference to the role of Elam's archers in the conquest of Jerusalem, where they served as allies to the Babylonians. God promised a day when He would **break the bow of Elam**.

i. "They were eminent archers; and had acquired their power and eminence by their dexterity in the use of the bow. See Isaiah 22:6. *Strabo, Livy*, and others speak of their eminence in archery." (Clarke)

c. **Scatter them towards all those winds**: God promised to not only conquer Elam, but to scatter their peoples all over the world.

i. "The purpose of this prophecy may have been to show that Elam would not and could not curb the Babylonian power." (Feinberg)

2. (37-39) Elam under disaster and under mercy in the latter days.

"For I will cause Elam to be dismayed before their enemies
And before those who seek their life.
I will bring disaster upon them,
My fierce anger,' says the LORD;
'And I will send the sword after them
Until I have consumed them.
I will set My throne in Elam,
And will destroy from there the king and the princes,' says the LORD.
'But it shall come to pass in the latter days:
I will bring back the captives of Elam,' says the LORD."

a. **I will bring disaster upon them, My fierce anger**: When judgment eventually did come upon the Persians by the armies of Greece, it was a **disaster** to their empire. God would assert His rule, His **throne** over them.

i. The Babylonians never conquered Elam, but Jeremiah never specifically said Nebuchadnezzar would do this. "When compared with other prophecies of Jeremiah against foreign nations, this one against Elam does not mention Nebuchadnezzar but refers only to enemies in general (Jeremiah 49:37)." (Feinberg)

b. **In the latter days: I will bring back the captives of Elam**: God promised mercy to the people of Elam in the latter days. On fulfillment of this was the message of the Gospel and the new covenant coming to and embraced by the people of Elam, who were among Peter's audience on Pentecost (Acts 2:9).

i. "Then grace breaks through for Elam (Jeremiah 49:39), as for others. The movements of peoples over the millennia make their fortunes hard to trace, but the curtain lifts an inch or two on the day of Pentecost, when Elamites were found to be among the multitude who heard 'the wonderful works of God' in their own tongue." (Kidner)

Philip Ryken has a good summary of this chapter and what it teaches us about the judgment of God: "Wealth did not save the Ammonites. They were not able to buy their way out of judgment. Wisdom did not save the Edomites, nor did their military might. Fame did not save the Arameans because God is no respecter of persons. Independence did not save the Bedouin; God found them in the wilderness and destroyed them just the same. Weapons did not save the Elamites."

Jeremiah 50 – A Word of Judgment Against Babylon

"It is to be observed that there is no gleam of hope for Babylon; that power, for some time material, and persistently spiritual, which was conceived in an attempt to make man great by frustrating Divine purpose. Her doom is irremediable in Old and New Testaments." (Morgan)

A. Babylon conquered, Israel and Judah restored.

1. (1-3) The conquest of Babylon and the humiliation of her idols.

The word that the LORD spoke against Babylon *and* against the land of the Chaldeans by Jeremiah the prophet.
"Declare among the nations,
Proclaim, and set up a standard;
Proclaim—do not conceal *it*—
Say, 'Babylon is taken, Bel is shamed.
Merodach is broken in pieces;
Her idols are humiliated,
Her images are broken in pieces.'
For out of the north a nation comes up against her,
Which shall make her land desolate,
And no one shall dwell therein.
They shall move, they shall depart,
Both man and beast."

> a. **Against Babylon and against the land of the Chaldeans**: The larger region was known as *Chaldea* and the great city of the region was **Babylon**. This was a word of judgment against the empire that God used to bring judgment upon Judah in Jeremiah's day.
>
> b. **Declare among the nations**: The Babylonian empire had an impact on all surrounding **nations**, so they needed to hear this word of the LORD through **Jeremiah the prophet**.

c. **Babylon is taken, Bel is shamed**: The city would be conquered and the idols in whom they trusted would be **humiliated** – most notably **Bel** and **Merodach**. They and their city would be **broken in pieces** by the coming judgment of God.

> i. "*Bel* ('lord') was the title of the storm-god Enlil, and when *Marduk* became head of the Babylonian pantheon in the second millennium BC he received the designation of Bel also." (Harrison)

> ii. **Her idols are humiliated**: The word translated **her idols** is an unusual one, "not the usual Hebrew term for idols, ne of which appears earlier in the verse. *Young's Concordance* lists ten different Hebrew words for idols, but even so fails to list the noun under discussion. *Gillal*, used many times in the OT but always in the plural, denotes 'logs,' 'blocks,' that is, shapeless things…Ewald, after the rabbis, renders it 'dungy things.'" (Feinberg)

> iii. "The word *gillulim* is indelicate, meaning 'balls of excrement.' It is applied to pagan idols in Leviticus 26:30; Deuteronomy 29:17; 1 Kings 15:12, 21:25; etc. Ezekiel used the word some thirty-eight times." (Thompson)

d. **For out of the north a nation comes up against her**: God used Babylon to bring judgment against Judah and other nations. When the time was right God would use a nation **out of the north** to judge Chaldea and **make her land desolate**.

> i. **Out of the north**: "The *Medes*, who formed the chief part of the army of Cyrus, lay to the *north* or *north-east* of Babylon." (Clarke)

2. (4-5) The restoration of Israel and Judah.

"In those days and in that time," says the LORD,
"The children of Israel shall come,
They and the children of Judah together;
With continual weeping they shall come,
And seek the LORD their God.
They shall ask the way to Zion,
With their faces toward it, *saying,*
'Come and let us join ourselves to the LORD
In a perpetual covenant
That will not be forgotten.'"

> a. **In those days and in that time**: Jeremiah connected the coming judgment upon Babylon to the restoration of Israel and Judah. They woud return to God with repentance (**continual weeping**) and they would **seek the LORD their God**.

i. The restoration of the people of Israel is clearly an aspect of God's plan for the last days (Matthew 23:39, Romans 11:26). Judgment upon Babylon is also an aspect of the last days (Revelation 17-18). Both the judgment of Babylon and the restoration of Israel here prophesied had a near fulfillment and will have an ultimate fulfillment in the very last days.

ii. The phrase **with continual weeping they shall come** speaks to the *depth* of Israel's repentance in the last days, spoken of also in Zechariah 12:10. "We notice again that the exiles on their return were mourning while marching. Observe the words- 'going and weeping.' We might have thought, perhaps, that when they began to go to their God, so much light would break in upon them that they would cease to weep: but no, it is 'going and weeping.'" (Spurgeon)

b. **They shall ask the way to Zion, with their faces toward it**: Part of the restoration would be the gathering of Israel and Judah back to the land promised to them as the covenant descendants of Abraham, Isaac, and Jacob.

c. **Come and let us join ourselves to the LORD in a perpetual covenant**: They would come back to God on His terms, the terms of His **covenant**. These are promises associated with the new covenant (Jeremiah 31:31-34 and 23:3-8, Ezekiel 11:16-20 and 36:24-28).

i. This reminds the believer that our relationship with God is based on something with great foundation – on **perpetual covenant**. Hebrews 8:7-13 is a powerful description of this great covenant. God's goodness and care is given to us on the basis of **covenant**.

ii. "I rejoice in those old Scotch books about the covenant: covenant truth was so inwrought into the Scotch heart that Scottish peasants as well as divines talked about it perpetually. You remember the good old cottager's grace over her porridge. I cannot repeat it in pure Doric, but it ran like this: 'Lord, I thank thee for the porridge, I thank thee for an appetite for the porridge, but I thank thee most of all that I have a covenant right to the porridge.' Only think of that, a covenant right to the porridge." (Spurgeon)

3. (6-7) The need for restoration.

"My people have been lost sheep.
Their shepherds have led them astray;
They have turned them away *on* the mountains.
They have gone from mountain to hill;
They have forgotten their resting place.

All who found them have devoured them;
And their adversaries said, 'We have not offended,
Because they have sinned against the LORD, the habitation of justice,
The LORD, the hope of their fathers.'"

> a. **My people have been lost sheep**: Speaking through Jeremiah, Yahweh spoke tenderly of His people as **lost sheep** betrayed by **their shepherds**. The poor leadership of these shepherds led to God's people being **turned** away and scattered **from mountain to hill**, with no **resting place**.
>
> b. **We have not offended, because they have sinned against the LORD**: The adversaries of God's people **devoured** them, claiming justification as instruments of God's judgment. Though it was true that Israel and Judah had **sinned** and deserved judgment, it did not justify those God used to bring the judgment.

B. Babylon fallen, Israel pardoned.

1. (8-10) Fleeing from Babylon under attack.

"Move from the midst of Babylon,
Go out of the land of the Chaldeans;
And be like the rams before the flocks.
For behold, I will raise and cause to come up against Babylon
An assembly of great nations from the north country,
And they shall array themselves against her;
From there she shall be captured.
Their arrows *shall be* like *those* of an expert warrior;
None shall return in vain.
And Chaldea shall become plunder;
All who plunder her shall be satisfied," says the LORD.

> a. **Move from the midst of Babylon**: God called upon the doomed **Chaldeans** to flee from their land. God would assemble a great army from **the north country** to come against Babylon and capture it.
>
>> i. **Like the rams before the flocks**: "Once the sheepfold was opened the male goats would rush to leave the enclosure first. So Judah would be in the forefront of captive peoples breaking loose from Babylon to return home." (Thompson)
>>
>> ii. **An assembly of great nations from the north country**: "The army of Cyrus was composed of Medes, Persians, Armenians, Caducians, Sacae, etc. Though all these did not come from the *north*; yet they were arranged under the *Medes*, who did come from the north, in reference to Babylon." (Clarke)

b. **Chaldea shall become plunder**: The great army that would come against Babylon would take its wealth and greatness. This was fulfilled when the Medes and Persians conquered Babylon, and will be even more completely fulfilled in the fall of Babylon in the end times (Revelation 17-18).

2. (11-16) The fall of Babylon is the vengeance of the LORD.

"Because you were glad, because you rejoiced,
You destroyers of My heritage,
Because you have grown fat like a heifer threshing grain,
And you bellow like bulls,
Your mother shall be deeply ashamed;
She who bore you shall be ashamed.
Behold, the least of the nations *shall be* a wilderness,
A dry land and a desert.
Because of the wrath of the LORD
She shall not be inhabited,
But she shall be wholly desolate.
Everyone who goes by Babylon shall be horrified
And hiss at all her plagues.
Put yourselves in array against Babylon all around,
All you who bend the bow;
Shoot at her, spare no arrows,
For she has sinned against the LORD.
Shout against her all around;
She has given her hand,
Her foundations have fallen,
Her walls are thrown down;
For it *is* the vengeance of the LORD.
Take vengeance on her.
As she has done, so do to her.
Cut off the sower from Babylon,
And him who handles the sickle at harvest time.
For fear of the oppressing sword
Everyone shall turn to his own people,
And everyone shall flee to his own land."

a. **Because you rejoiced, you destroyers of My heritage**: God promised this judgment against Babylon because they took undue pleasure in being the instrument of Yahweh's judgment against His people. They were also ripe for judgment because they were proud and self-satisfied (**fat like a heifer threshing grain**).

i. **Shall be a wilderness**: "Its eventual decline into *a heap of ruins* (Jeremiah 51:37), *a wilderness dry and desert* (50:12b), was gradual, due largely to the building of a new capital, Seleucia on the Tigris, in 275 BC; but it still had inhabitants in the first century AD." (Kidner)

b. **Everyone who goes by Babylon shall be horrified**: The coming judgment on Babylon would astonish the nations, who would become agents of God's judgment (**for it is the vengeance of the LORD**). The same devastation the Chaldeans brought to others would come upon them (**as she has done, so do to her**).

i. "Powerful Babylon will be reduced to minor status in the Near East when God punishes her, and once more the passer-by will gasp in astonishment." (Harrison)

c. **Her foundations have fallen, her walls are thrown down**: These phrases (and similar phrases in Jeremiah 50-51) are an interesting challenge in understanding prophetic fulfillment. Not very long after Jeremiah's prophecy, Babylon was *conquered*, but not *destroyed*. The **foundations** did *not* fall and the walls *were not* **thrown down**.

i. "Cyrus, who unified the Medo-Persian Empire and then overwhelmed Babylon, was careful to spare the country; so the references (Jeremiah 50:16) must be to a later attack." (Feinberg)

ii. "According to Herodotus (1.191), Cyrus captured Babylon by diverting the Euphrates River into a trench. The Persians attacked Babylon so unexpectedly that when the outer areas of the city had already been taken those in the center did not realize that they were captured." (Feinberg)

iii. One important factor to take into account is that Nebuchadnezzar, king of Babylon, radically repented before God. It is possible that the worst of what was prophesied did not happen because God mercifully responded to Nebuchadnezzar's repentance. "It is at least possible that the humbling of Nebuchadnezzar, culminating in his testimony in Daniel 4:34-37, opened the door to the mercy of 539 – for it is obvious from God's generous response to even an Ahab, a Manasseh, or the city of Nineveh, that he meets a change of attitude more than halfway." (Kidner)

iv. Another important factor to take into account is that God is not done with His judgment upon Babylon – the city *second* most mentioned in the Scriptures. Babylon was judged not far from Jeremiah's time, but even that judgment pointed towards a greater fulfillment in the last days. The fall of Babylon prophesied by Jeremiah was partially fulfilled when the Medes and Persians conquered ancient Babylon. Yet the connection between this fall of Babylon and Revelation 18:2 (*Babylon the great is fallen, is fallen*) shows that there is an ultimate fall of Babylon to come.

v. "It has troubled some scholars that chapters 50-51 predict the violent destruction of Babylon, whereas its defeat by Cyrus in 539 BC took place without a battle and with no damage to the city. But with other predictive prophecies, if a fulfillment does not occur in one period, it is to be sought for in another and future one." (Feinberg)

vi. In truth, this intereprtive challenge is a strong testimony to the *authenticity* of Jeremiah's prophecy. "Those critical scholars who reject the possibility of such a foretelling of the future, and who would put these chapters after Babylonia's fall in 539 BC, face an insurmountable problem. If these words were written after the event, they would surely correspond more accurately with the events themselves." (Cundall)

3. (17-20) God will pardon and preserve Israel.

"Israel *is* like scattered sheep;
The lions have driven *him* away.
First the king of Assyria devoured him;
Now at last this Nebuchadnezzar king of Babylon has broken his bones."
Therefore thus says the LORD of hosts, the God of Israel:
"Behold, I will punish the king of Babylon and his land,
As I have punished the king of Assyria.
But I will bring back Israel to his home,
And he shall feed on Carmel and Bashan;
His soul shall be satisfied on Mount Ephraim and Gilead.
In those days and in that time," says the LORD,
"The iniquity of Israel shall be sought, but *there shall be* none;
And the sins of Judah, but they shall not be found;
For I will pardon those whom I preserve."

a. **Israel is like scattered sheep; the lions have driven him away**: Earlier in this prophecy, Jeremiah spoke of Israel as *lost sheep* (Jeremiah 50:6). Now he sees them as sheep **scattered** by the mighty lions of Assyria and Babylon.

i. **Now at last this Nebuchadnezzar king of Babylon has broken his bones**: "All the descendants of Jacob have been harassed and spoiled, first by the Assyrians, and afterwards by the Chaldeans. They acted towards them as a lion to a sheep which he has caught; first he devours all the flesh, next he breaks all the bones to extract the marrow." (Clarke)

b. **I will punish the king of Babylon and his land, as I have punished the king of Assyria**: God promised that just as the Assyrian empire was gone, so too would the mighty Babylonian empire one day be **punished**.

c. **But I will bring back Israel to his home**: In contrast to the passing empires of Assyria and Babylon, God would restore Israel to her land. They would once again **feed on Carmel and Bashan** and be **satisfied on Mount Ephraim and Gilead**.

d. **The iniquity of Israel shall be sought, but there shall be none**: This wonderful promise is another in the great promises of the new covenant, an aspect of which is the restoration and salvation of Israel. God promised to both **pardon** and **preserve** Israel.

> i. **I will pardon those whom I preserve**: "One of the important features of the days of restoration is spiritual renewal with its concomitant of forgiveness. …The forgiveness of the remnant will be such that their *guilt* and their *sins* will be completely obliterated." (Thompson)

C. Babylon broken, Israel redeemed.

1. (21-27) Babylon's slaughter.

"Go up against the land of Merathaim, against it,
And against the inhabitants of Pekod.
Waste and utterly destroy them," says the LORD,
"And do according to all that I have commanded you.
A sound of battle *is* in the land,
And of great destruction.
How the hammer of the whole earth has been cut apart and broken!
How Babylon has become a desolation among the nations!
I have laid a snare for you;
You have indeed been trapped, O Babylon,
And you were not aware;
You have been found and also caught,
Because you have contended against the LORD.
The LORD has opened His armory,
And has brought out the weapons of His indignation;
For this *is* the work of the Lord GOD of hosts
In the land of the Chaldeans.
Come against her from the farthest border;
Open her storehouses;
Cast her up as heaps of ruins,

And destroy her utterly;
Let nothing of her be left.
Slay all her bulls,
Let them go down to the slaughter.
Woe to them!
For their day has come, the time of their punishment."

a. **Go up against the land of Merathaim**: God spoke judgment against specific regions of Babylon, **Merathaim** and **Pekod**. The command was clear: **waste and utterly destroy them**. Babylon was like a **hammer against the whole earth**, and she would be **cut apart and broken** because they **contended against the LORD**.

i. "Merathaim and Pekod were real locations in Babylon. Ironically, those place names sounded like the Hebrew words for 'double rebellion' and 'punishment.'" (Ryken)

- **The land of Merathaim**: This was a literal place, but also "There is a play on words here, for the root *mrh* means 'to rebel' and the form of the word is dual, meaning '(land of) double rebellion,' or 'twofold rebel,' that is, 'rebel of rebels.'" (Thompson)
- **The inhabitants of Pekod**: "The root *pqd* means 'to punish.' Hence the land of Pekod is the 'land of doom.'" (Thompson)
- "The prophets were fond of giving a word this kind of twist, adding to the liveliness of the attack and fastening it in the memory." (Kidner)

ii. "He recognized that Babylon had been the instrument in the hand of Jehovah as he referred to her as 'the hammer of the whole earth.' But the hammer is broken, and Babylon become a desolation." (Morgan)

iii. "Babylon was the maul or hammer of many nations, Nimrod began it, and his successors took after him. Charles Martel, King of France, was so called for like cause. Augustine also was worthily styled *Haereticorum malleus,* the hammer of heretics." (Trapp)

iv. **You have indeed been trapped, O Babylon**: "It was not by *storm* that Cyrus took the city. The *Euphrates* ran through it; he dug a channel for the river in another direction, to divert its stream; he waited for that time in which the inhabitants had delivered themselves up to debauchery: in the dead of the night he turned off the stream, and he and his army entered by the *old channel,* now void of its waters. This was the *snare* of which the prophet here speaks. See *Herodotus,* lib. i., c. 191." (Clarke)

b. **The LORD has opened His armory**: In His judgment God **brought out the weapons of His indignation**, coming against Babylon as the **Lord GOD of hosts**, Yahweh of heavenly armies.

c. **Slay all her bulls, let them go down to the slaughter**: The bulls once sacrificed to the idols of Babylon would be destroyed in the coming **slaughter** to come upon Babylon.

2. (28-32) Proud Babylon repaid.

The voice of those who flee and escape from the land of Babylon
Declares in Zion the vengeance of the LORD our God,
The vengeance of His temple.
"Call together the archers against Babylon.
All you who bend the bow, encamp against it all around;
Let none of them escape.
Repay her according to her work;
According to all she has done, do to her;
For she has been proud against the LORD,
Against the Holy One of Israel.
Therefore her young men shall fall in the streets,
And all her men of war shall be cut off in that day," says the LORD.
"Behold, I *am* **against you,**
O most haughty one!" says the Lord GOD of hosts;
"For your day has come,
The time *that* **I will punish you.**
The most proud shall stumble and fall,
And no one will raise him up;
I will kindle a fire in his cities,
And it will devour all around him."

a. **The voice of those who flee and escape from the land of Babylon**: In his prophecy, Jeremiah could hear those who managed to escape speak of **the vengeance of the LORD**. It was even **the vengeance of His temple** – the destroyed temple of Jerusalem visiting destruction upon Babylon. As they destroyed, so they would be destroyed.

b. **For she has been proud against the LORD**: This was the root of Babylon's sin. Her pride led her to arrogantly think that she could measure out destruction to others without having it measured out against her, the **most haughty one**.

i. "He was under no delusion concerning Babylon itself. He knew its wickedness; and he knew that though God so overruled the affairs of men that Babylon was His instrument of chastisement, she herself must be judged." (Morgan)

3. (33-34) Israel's strong Redeemer.

Thus says the LORD of hosts:
"The children of Israel *were* oppressed,
Along with the children of Judah;
All who took them captive have held them fast;
They have refused to let them go.
Their Redeemer *is* strong;
The LORD of hosts *is* His name.
He will thoroughly plead their case,
That He may give rest to the land,
And disquiet the inhabitants of Babylon."

a. **All who took them captive have held them fast**: When the empires of Assyria and Babylon took Israel and Judah **captive**, they did not let them go. It was only under those who conquered Babylon – the Medes and Persians – that the Jewish people were given permission to return to the Promised Land.

b. **Their Redeemer is strong**: Assyria and Babylon held Israel and Judah, but their strong **Redeemer** would **thoroughly plead their case**. Though God would **disquiet the inhabitants of Babylon**, He would **give rest to the land**.

i. "Few nations have ever realized that God is the Kinsman-Redeemer of Israel (Jeremiah 50:34). ...The Kinsman-Redeemer is voluntarily committed to champion Israel's cause. He brings peace to his own but unrest to his oppressors." (Feinberg)

ii. All who dare to trouble Israel should remember, **their Redeemer is strong**. "The Jew has been held in contempt as the afflicted of God, and that has been the excuse urged sometimes even by so-called Christian nations for wrong and injustice done to him. Let it never be forgotten that God has not cast off His people, though He chastise them; and whatever nations persecutes them, sooner or later knows the fire of Divine wrath." (Morgan)

iii. **That He may give rest to the land**: "The place where we lie down to rest is under the shadow of the Cross. Whilst we remain there, we are perfectly safe and blessed." (Meyer)

D. The greatness of the judgment to come against Babylon.

1. (35-38) The sword against Chaldea.

"A sword *is* against the Chaldeans," says the LORD,
"Against the inhabitants of Babylon,

And against her princes and her wise men.
A sword *is* against the soothsayers, and they will be fools.
A sword *is* against her mighty men, and they will be dismayed.
A sword *is* against their horses,
Against their chariots,
And against all the mixed peoples who *are* in her midst;
And they will become like women.
A sword *is* against her treasures, and they will be robbed.
A drought *is* against her waters, and they will be dried up.
For it *is* the land of carved images,
And they are insane with *their* idols."

> a. **A sword is against the Chaldeans**: God promised that His sword of judgment would come against the people of Babylon, as well has **her princes and her wise men**, as well as the **soothsayers**, **mighty men** – even her **horses** and her **chariots**.
>
> b. **It is the land of carved images, and they are insane with their idols**: Everything that Babylon trusted in would feel the **sword** of God's judgment. This included the **mixed peoples** who made up her armies, her **treasures**, and her idols. Idol-mad Chaldea would feel the complete edge of God's sword.

2. (39-40) The complete nature of Babylon's destruction.

"Therefore the wild desert beasts shall dwell *there* with the jackals,
And the ostriches shall dwell in it.
It shall be inhabited no more forever,
Nor shall it be dwelt in from generation to generation.
As God overthrew Sodom and Gomorrah
And their neighbors," says the LORD,
"*So* no one shall reside there,
Nor son of man dwell in it."

> a. **The wild desert beasts shall dwell there with the jackals**: Babylon's devastation would be so complete that the city would become a wasteland inhabited by wild animals – or unclean spirits.
>
> > i. **Wild desert beasts, jackals**: "The terms *siyyim* and *iyyim* are sometimes regarded as animals, but there was something uncanny about creatures who inhabited ruined cities and the terms *demons* and *evil spirits* would seem more appropriate." (Thompson)
>
> b. **As God overthrew Sodom and Gomorrah**: The destruction of Babylon would be so complete that the prophet could liken them to Sodom and Gomorrah.

3. (41-44) Destruction from the north.

"Behold, a people shall come from the north,
And a great nation and many kings
Shall be raised up from the ends of the earth.
They shall hold the bow and the lance;
They *are* cruel and shall not show mercy.
Their voice shall roar like the sea;
They shall ride on horses,
Set in array, like a man for the battle,
Against you, O daughter of Babylon.
The king of Babylon has heard the report about them,
And his hands grow feeble;
Anguish has taken hold of him,
Pangs as of a woman in childbirth.
Behold, he shall come up like a lion from the floodplain of the Jordan
Against the dwelling place of the strong;
But I will make them suddenly run away from her.
And who *is* a chosen *man that* I may appoint over her?
For who *is* like Me?
Who will arraign Me?
And who *is* that shepherd
Who will withstand Me?"

    a. **A people shall come from the north**: Babylon's end would come from the Medes and Persians, roughly from their north. Since much of this prophecy speaks not only of that soon conquest but an ultimate destruction of Babylon (Revelation 17-18), their destruction will also in some way **come from the north**.

    b. **They are cruel and shall not show mercy**: The conquerors of Babylon will be ruthless warriors. Babylon rarely showed mercy; they should expect none from their eventual conquerors.

    c. **Anguish has taken hold of him**: In many places, Jeremiah described this effect of Babylon and her armies upon those they conquered (Jeremiah 13:8, 22:23, 48:41, 49:22). Now, a similar terror would come upon the **king of Babylon**.

        i. "Small wonder that the Babylonian king, used to being the victor, is now petrified with fear as the potential victim." (Thompson)

        ii. **He shall come up like a lion**: "The lion (Jeremiah 50:44) now is Cyrus; in Jeremiah 49:19 it was Nebuchadnezzar." (Feinberg)

d. **Who is that shepherd who will withstand Me**: God spoke the obvious. There was no shepherd, no king, no leader who could stand against Him and His coming judgment.

4. (45-46) The counsel of the Lord against Babylon.

Therefore hear the counsel of the Lord that He has taken against Babylon,
And His purposes that He has proposed against the land of the Chaldeans:
Surely the least of the flock shall draw them out;
Surely He will make their dwelling place desolate with them.
At the noise of the taking of Babylon
The earth trembles,
And the cry is heard among the nations.

a. **Therefore hear the counsel of the Lord that He has taken against Babylon**: God invited not only Israel and Judah, but also Babylon herself and all the nations to **hear the counsel of the Lord**. Judgment was coming against them and God wanted the entire world to know.

b. **At the noise of the taking of Babylon the earth trembles**: God would show His might, His wisdom, His justice, and His unfolding plan of the ages in and through the judgment of Babylon.

Jeremiah 51 – A Word of Judgment Against Babylon (Continued)

A. Babylon winnowed in the wind of God's judgment.

1. (1-5) A destroying wind against Babylon.

Thus says the LORD:
"Behold, I will raise up against Babylon,
Against those who dwell in Leb Kamai,
A destroying wind.
And I will send winnowers to Babylon,
Who shall winnow her and empty her land.
For in the day of doom
They shall be against her all around.
Against *her* let the archer bend his bow,
And lift himself up against *her* in his armor.
Do not spare her young men;
Utterly destroy all her army.
Thus the slain shall fall in the land of the Chaldeans,
And *those* thrust through in her streets.
For Israel is not forsaken, nor Judah,
By his God, the LORD of hosts,
Though their land was filled with sin against the Holy One of Israel."

    a. **I will raise up against Babylon**: The prophecy of Jeremiah continues from the previous chapter. In what was probably a collection of prophecies against Babylon collected together, God announced His coming judgment againt the empire that Yahweh Himself used to bring judgment against Judah.

    b. **Against those who dwell in Leb Kamai**: The phrase **Leb Kamai** is literally translated *The Midst of Those Who Rise Up Against Me*. Most regard this as a poetic reference to Babylon.

i. "*Leb-kami* is an Atbash for Chaldea (so LXX)." (Thompson)

ii. "The use of the Atbash to disguise the identity of the adversary would, in the context of the Exile, and particularly in the early period of the Exile, seem to make historical sense. But one would wonder why a writer would introduce the device at this point when Babylon has been referred to already." (Thompson)

c. **I will send winnowers to Babylon**: God used the picture of **a destroying wind** that would **winnow** Babylon as grain is processed, with a wind blowing away the useless chaff. They would **utterly destroy all her army**.

i. **I will send winnowers**: "When the corn is trodden out with the feet of cattle, or crushed out with a heavy wheel armed with iron, with a shovel they throw it up against the wind, that the chaff and broken straw may be separated from it. This is the image used by the prophet; these people shall be trodden, crushed, and fanned by their enemies." (Clarke)

ii. **Destroying wind**: "It is possible, however, that the reference is to 'the spirit of the destroyer' (cf. Jeremiah 51:11). In either case the result is the same." (Thompson)

iii. As in many of the predictions of Jeremiah 51, we have prophecies that were fulfilled in one sense in the conquest of Babylon not far from Jeremiah's own time. Still, because the Babylon of Jeremiah's day was defeated yet not utterly destroyed, the devastation predicted in these chapters will have a second and ultimate fulfillment in the last days. This is vividly described in Revelation 17 and 18.

d. **For Israel is not forsaken, nor Judah**: God's judgment upon Babylon would be one display of the truth that He had not **forsaken** His people, but would bring judgment against those who conquered them. His people had sinned, but they were not **forsaken** of God.

i. It was true in a *direct* sense that the conquest of Babylon was a blessing for God's people. They had no release from exile under the Babylonians, but under the Persians, the Jews were allowed to return to the Promised Land.

ii. **Israel is not forsaken**: "Sin is mighty; but there is one thing that it cannot do, it cannot make God forsake those whom He has adopted into his family." (Meyer)

2. (6-8) Fleeing from fallen Babylon.

Flee from the midst of Babylon,
And every one save his life!

Do not be cut off in her iniquity,
For this *is* the time of the LORD's vengeance;
He shall recompense her.
Babylon *was* a golden cup in the LORD's hand,
That made all the earth drunk.
The nations drank her wine;
Therefore the nations are deranged.
Babylon has suddenly fallen and been destroyed.
Wail for her!
Take balm for her pain;
Perhaps she may be healed.

> a. **Flee from the midst of Babylon**: It is never good to remain in a place that is a target of God's judgment. Because Babylon's fall was sure, it was best to **flee** to save one's life.
>
>> i. Here, in verses 6-10, is the seminal picture of Babylon as the metropolis of evil and the seducer of mankind which will be elaborated in Revelation 17-18." (Kidner)
>
> b. **Babylon was a golden cup in the LORD's hand**: Drinking a cup of judgment is a familiar picture in the Hebrew prophets. Here, Babylon is represented as God's instrument of judgment against the nations, many of which are described in Jeremiah 46-49.
>
>> i. "The cup is depicted as a *golden cup* because of Babylon's great wealth." (Thompson)
>
> c. **Wail for her**: With sarcasm, the prophet mocked Babylon. The nations would not **wail** over the empire that made them suffer so. They would have no interest in a **balm for her pain** or her healing.

3. (9-14) The vengeance of God against Babylon.

We would have healed Babylon,
But she is not healed.
Forsake her, and let us go everyone to his own country;
For her judgment reaches to heaven and is lifted up to the skies.
The LORD has revealed our righteousness.
Come and let us declare in Zion the work of the LORD our God.
Make the arrows bright!
Gather the shields!
The LORD has raised up the spirit of the kings of the Medes.
For His plan *is* against Babylon to destroy it,
Because it *is* the vengeance of the LORD,
The vengeance for His temple.

Set up the standard on the walls of Babylon;
Make the guard strong,
Set up the watchmen,
Prepare the ambushes.
For the LORD has both devised and done
What He spoke against the inhabitants of Babylon.
O you who dwell by many waters,
Abundant in treasures,
Your end has come,
The measure of your covetousness.
The LORD of hosts has sworn by Himself:
"Surely I will fill you with men, as with locusts,
And they shall lift up a shout against you."

> a. **Forsake her, and let us go**: This is the response of the nations to God's sarcastic invitation to seek Babylon's healing (Jeremiah 51:8). They were happy to **forsake her** and go their own way, leaving her judgment to heaven.
>
>> i. **Her judgment reaches to heaven and is lifted up to the skies**: "Like many such expressions in the OT indicates that the judgment was of vast proportions (cf. Numbers 13:28; Deuteronomy 1:28)." (Thompson)
>
> b. **The LORD has revealed our righteousness**: The right standing of God's people was revealed in the eventual judgment of Babylon. This showed that it was not merely a matter of Babylon's gods being mightier than Yahweh. The eventual judgment of Babylon showed that Yahweh was in control; that He used Babylon as it pleased Him and judged them when it pleased Him. This was a kind of a justification of God's people and a revelation of their **righteousness** and of **the work of the LORD our God**.
>
>> i. "By punishing Babylon God has justified the remnant, so that they can emerge from captivity to new life in the homeland." (Harrison)
>>
>> ii. "She had now received from Yahweh's hand adequate compensation for all her iniquity (Isaiah 4:2). Now she would be reinstated and shown to be what she really was, Yahweh's elect nation." (Thompson)
>
> c. **Make the arrows bright**: Using his characteristic powerful and vivid word pictures, Jeremiah envisions the battle coming against Babylon through **the kings of the Medes**.
>
>> i. "The Medes lived in northwest Iran in the general region of the modern Iranian Kurdistan." (Thompson)

ii. "The Medes were allied with Babylon in the destruction of Nineveh in 612 BC Later they joined the Persians to defeat Babylon in 539 BC (Feinberg)

iii. "It is known that the mother of Cyrus the Persian was a Mede, and the Medes and Persians are linked together several times in the book of Daniel (e.g. Daniel 5:28; 6:8, 12, 15)." (Thompson)

iv. "Of Cyaxares king of Media, called *Darius the Mede* in Scripture; and of Cyrus king of Persia, presumptive heir of the throne of Cyaxares, his uncle. Cambyses, his father, sent him, Cyrus, with 30,000 men to assist his uncle Cyaxares, against Neriglissar king of Babylon, and by these was Babylon overthrown." (Clarke)

d. **The vengeance for His temple**: God's judgment against Babylon was in part because they destroyed the temple Solomon had built unto the LORD. It was a strange process, repeated often through history.

- God appointed a judgment to come.
- God used a human instrument in that judgment.
- The human instrument was not motivated by God, but by their own sinful desires.
- God brought judgment on the instrument He used.

e. **Your end has come, the measure of your covetousness**: Jeremiah revealed another reason for God's judgment against Babylon – their great **covetousness**. God would give them judgment according to the **measure** of their covetousness, and that was a big measure.

i. **O you who dwell by many waters**: "While *many waters* (Jeremiah 51:13) refers primarily to the Euphrates, it also alludes sarcastically to the great subterranean ocean, a theme prominent in ancient Babylonian mythology. The Babylonians had lived by the erroneous beliefs for many centuries, and they would now die by them." (Harrison)

f. **I will fill you with men, as with locusts**: Jeremiah envisioned swarms of invaders and conquerors in the land of Babylon.

i. **Lift up a shout**: "The noun *hedad* occurs in Jeremiah 25:30 and 48:33 for the grape-treader's song. The entry of warriors into Babylon has about it something of the quality of grape-treaders trampling the grapes when the harvest has been taken in." (Thompson)

4. (15-19) The power of Yahweh contrasts with empty idols.

He has made the earth by His power;
He has established the world by His wisdom,

And stretched out the heaven by His understanding.
When He utters *His* voice—
There is a multitude of waters in the heavens:
"He causes the vapors to ascend from the ends of the earth;
He makes lightnings for the rain;
He brings the wind out of His treasuries."
Everyone is dull-hearted, without knowledge;
Every metalsmith is put to shame by the carved image;
For his molded image *is* falsehood,
And *there is* no breath in them.
They *are* futile, a work of errors;
In the time of their punishment they shall perish.
The Portion of Jacob *is* not like them,
For He *is* the Maker of all things;
And *Israel is* the tribe of His inheritance.
The LORD of hosts *is* His name.

> a. **He has made the earth by His power**: Yahweh is not only a God of judgment; His **power**, His **wisdom** and His **understanding** are also evident in creation.
>
> b. **He makes lightnings for the rain**: Yahweh's power in creation is not only a thing of the past. He presently works in and through creation.
>
> c. **Every metalsmith is put to shame by the carved image**: Understanding the greatness of Yahweh makes the idols made by men's hands seem even more ridiculous. Even the one who makes the idol is ashamed of what he has done.
>
> d. **The Portion of Jacob is not like them, for He is the Maker of all things**: The work of the metalsmith is powerless; Yahweh is **Maker of all things**.
>
>> i. "The Creator and little Israel are everything to one another: the Creator as Israel's *portion*, and Israel as his *inheritance*." (Kidner)
>>
>> ii. **The Portion of Jacob**: "In human affairs a man's portion was the inheritance he received from his father. It was his by legal and moral right. So Yahweh was peculiarly the proper inheritance of Israel…Israel had Yahweh as her very own possession, her *Portion*." (Thompson)

5. (20-24) Breaking in pieces the might of Babylon.

"You *are* My battle-ax *and* weapons of war:
For with you I will break the nation in pieces;
With you I will destroy kingdoms;
With you I will break in pieces the horse and its rider;

With you I will break in pieces the chariot and its rider;
With you also I will break in pieces man and woman;
With you I will break in pieces old and young;
With you I will break in pieces the young man and the maiden;
With you also I will break in pieces the shepherd and his flock;
With you I will break in pieces the farmer and his yoke of oxen;
And with you I will break in pieces governors and rulers.
"And I will repay Babylon
And all the inhabitants of Chaldea
For all the evil they have done
In Zion in your sight," says the LORD.

a. **You are My battle-ax and weapons of war**: The God whose power was evident in creation (Jeremiah 51:15-19) also shows His power, wisdom, and understanding in His work of judgment. Using poetic repletion, God called upon the peoples that would come against Babylon to do His work of judgment.

i. "Everything here stresses the indiscriminate ruin that an aggressor spreads around him, whatever his military objectives; yet God is using this cruel instrument before he breaks it." (Kidner)

ii. "Since Jeremiah 50:23 describes Babylon as 'the hammer of the whole earth' it seems best to refer this section to her also. But because of her sin, especially against the Lord's people (Jeremiah 51:24), she would incur His implacable judgment." (Cundall)

iii. "Ten times the phrase 'with you' falls like hammer blows." (Feinberg)

iv. **Break**: "The Hebrew verb *nippes* indicates a violent and intensive shattering." (Feinberg)

b. **I will repay Babylon**: The judgment was to come upon **Chaldea** not only for their general sins, but specifically for **all the evil they have done in Zion**.

6. (25-32) Bringing many kingdoms against Babylon.

"Behold, I *am* against you, O destroying mountain,
Who destroys all the earth," says the LORD.
"And I will stretch out My hand against you,
Roll you down from the rocks,
And make you a burnt mountain.
They shall not take from you a stone for a corner
Nor a stone for a foundation,
But you shall be desolate forever," says the LORD.
Set up a banner in the land,

Blow the trumpet among the nations!
Prepare the nations against her,
Call the kingdoms together against her:
Ararat, Minni, and Ashkenaz.
Appoint a general against her;
Cause the horses to come up like the bristling locusts.
Prepare against her the nations,
With the kings of the Medes,
Its governors and all its rulers,
All the land of his dominion.
And the land will tremble and sorrow;
For every purpose of the LORD shall be performed against Babylon,
To make the land of Babylon a desolation without inhabitant.
The mighty men of Babylon have ceased fighting,
They have remained in their strongholds;
Their might has failed,
They became *like* women;
They have burned her dwelling places,
The bars of her *gate* are broken.
One runner will run to meet another,
And one messenger to meet another,
To show the king of Babylon that his city is taken on *all* sides;
The passages are blocked,
The reeds they have burned with fire,
And the men of war are terrified.

    a. **Behold, I am against you, O destroying mountain**: Here the mighty empire of Babylon is represented as a **mountain**. The Hebrew prophets sometimes used the figure of a mountain to represent a government or kingdom (as in Daniel 2:35). God would make Babylon as **a burnt mountain**.

    b. **Call the kingdoms together against her**: When Babylon fell to the Medes and Persians, it was by a confederation of nations. This will also be true in the ultimate destruction of Babylon as described in Revelation 17 and 18.

        i. **Prepare the nations against her**: "Hebrew, Sanctify, call them together to wage this sacred war against Babylon." (Trapp)

        ii. **Ararat, Minni, and Ashkenaz**: "Three groups are specified, all of which were to be found in the area of present-day Armenia. Each is known in Assyrian cuneiform texts." (Thompson)

iii. "The three kingdoms of verse 27, all within Armenia, were part of the empire of the Medes (Jeremiah 51:28), which spread in a great arc to the north of Babylon's dominions." (Kidner)

iv. "These three are called to aid the Medes against Babylon." (Feinberg)

c. **Their might has failed, they became like women**: The soldiers of Babylon would not be able to stand against their invaders. They would fall in the same terror and confusion of battle they had inflicted upon many others.

i. "The death-throes of the land; the collapse of the soldiers' morale; and the frantic scurrying of messengers bearing the evil news, are graphically depicted." (Cundall)

ii. **One runner will run to meet another**: "In the conduct of warfare in the ancient world specially trained runners brought news from the scene of battle to the king (cf. 2 Samuel 18:19-33). Babylon's runners were renowned, and it was these men who came running from every direction to announce to the king that the city had fallen." (Thompson)

iii. **The reeds they have burned with fire**: "The reedy swamps [surrounding Babylon] were set on fire. The burning of the swamp reeds would deprive refugees of a place to hide and would flush out any who might have escaped there already." (Thompson)

iv. **The reeds**: "Or, Marshes, made by Euphrates overflowing. It is well observed that the Babylonians might by this prophecy have been forewarned and forearmed against Cyrus's stratagem; but they slighted it, and never inquired after it likely." (Trapp)

B. Babylon on the threshing floor.

1. (33-35) Threshing Babylon as they had threshed Zion.

For thus says the LORD of hosts, the God of Israel:
"The daughter of Babylon *is* like a threshing floor
***When it is* time to thresh her;**
Yet a little while
And the time of her harvest will come."
"Nebuchadnezzar the king of Babylon
Has devoured me, he has crushed me;
He has made me an empty vessel,
He has swallowed me up like a monster;
He has filled his stomach with my delicacies,
He has spit me out.
Let the violence *done* to me and my flesh *be* upon Babylon,"

The inhabitant of Zion will say;
"And my blood be upon the inhabitants of Chaldea!"
Jerusalem will say.

> a. **Babylon is like a threshing floor**: Earlier, God likened the work of judgment to winnowing (Jeremiah 51:1-2). The **threshing floor** is another agricultural image – the place where grain is crushed under a stone or the hoofs of an ox. Babylon would be crushed by the coming judgment, and the result would be good like a **harvest** unto God and His people.
>
>> i. "Babylon was a threshing floor to be leveled to the ground. It would be trodden down in preparation for the harvest which was to come." (Thompson)
>
> b. **Nebuchadnezzar the king of Babylon has devoured me, he has crushed me**: Nebuchadnezzar treated **the inhabitant of Zion** as his own threshing floor, bringing a crushing judgment to them. Therefore, **Zion** and **Jerusalem** take satisfaction in the same **violence** done unto Babylon.
>
>> i. "Nebuchadnezzar had devoured Jerusalem with the greedy gulp of a *monster* (NEB *dragon*), and for his excess his land would be punished." (Harrison)
>
>> ii. "Nebuchadnezzar is compared with a gluttonous man devouring Jerusalem and setting her aside as one does an empty vessel whose contents have been quaffed." (Thompson)

2. (36-40) Babylon like lambs to the slaughter.

Therefore thus says the LORD:
"Behold, I will plead your case and take vengeance for you.
I will dry up her sea and make her springs dry.
Babylon shall become a heap,
A dwelling place for jackals,
An astonishment and a hissing,
Without an inhabitant.
They shall roar together like lions,
They shall growl like lions' whelps.
In their excitement I will prepare their feasts;
I will make them drunk,
That they may rejoice,
And sleep a perpetual sleep
And not awake," says the LORD.
"I will bring them down
Like lambs to the slaughter,
Like rams with male goats.

a. **I will plead your case and take vengeance for you**: Yahweh pledged to take up the cause of Judah and Jerusalem, bringing Babylon to judgment and desolation.

i. **I will plead your case**: "The term *rib* points to a legal process and is used in several contexts in Jeremiah. …Here, Yahweh pleads Israel's cause as he conducts his case against Babylon." (Thompson)

b. **I will make them drunk**: The conquest of Babylon came as her rulers enjoyed a drunken feast (Daniel 5).

i. "According to Herodotus, 'owing to the great size of the city the outskirts were captured without the people in the centre knowing anything about it: there was a festival going on, and they continued to dance and enjoy themselves, until they learned the news the hard way'." (Kidner)

ii. **Sleep a perpetual sleep**: "As it was in the *night* the city was taken, many had retired to rest, and *never awoke*; slain in their beds, *they slept a perpetual sleep*." (Clarke)

3. (41-48) Punishing Babylon and her idols.

"Oh, how Sheshach is taken!
Oh, how the praise of the whole earth is seized!
How Babylon has become desolate among the nations!
The sea has come up over Babylon;
She is covered with the multitude of its waves.
Her cities are a desolation,
A dry land and a wilderness,
A land where no one dwells,
Through which no son of man passes.
I will punish Bel in Babylon,
And I will bring out of his mouth what he has swallowed;
And the nations shall not stream to him anymore.
Yes, the wall of Babylon shall fall.
"My people, go out of the midst of her!
And let everyone deliver himself from the fierce anger of the LORD.
And lest your heart faint,
And you fear for the rumor that *will be* heard in the land
(A rumor will come *one* year,
And after that, in *another* year
A rumor *will come*,
And violence in the land,
Ruler against ruler),
Therefore behold, the days are coming

That I will bring judgment on the carved images of Babylon;
Her whole land shall be ashamed,
And all her slain shall fall in her midst.
Then the heavens and the earth and all that *is* in them
Shall sing joyously over Babylon;
For the plunderers shall come to her from the north," says the LORD.

> a. **How Sheshach is taken**: As before in Jeremiah 25:26, Babylon is referred to as **Sheshach** – a code name for the Babylonians.
>
>> i. "Following Jerome, many hold that the name is a cipher (code) that stands for Babylon. The cipher is known as *Atbash*, a system of secret writing that substituted the last letter of the Hebrew alphabet for the first, and next to the last for the second, and so through all the Hebrew consonants." (Feinberg)
>>
>> ii. "Another possibility is that the Babylonians themselves made use of the Atbash and that Sheshak was an alternate name. There is some evidence that this was so." (Thompson)
>
> b. **The sea has come up over Babylon**: Jeremiah used **the sea** as a figure of speech regarding landlocked Babylon. She would be overwhelmed by the coming judgment of God, left **a desolation** and **a land where no one dwells**.
>
> c. **Yes, the wall of Babylon has fallen**: The defenses of Babylon were compromised when she was conquered by the Medes and Persians, so in a symbolic sense **the wall of Babylon** fell. Yet an even more literal fulfillment will come when Babylon the Great is felled (Revelation 17 and 18).
>
> d. **My people, go out of the midst of her**: This was a helpful call to God's people in exile, that they should not put their trust, confidence, and resources into a kingdom that would be judged and conquered. Regarding the ultimate judgment of Babylon, it is a call for believers to heed today and in the future (Revelation 18:4).
>
> e. **Then the heavens and the earth and all that is in them shall sing joyously over Babylon**: The righteous rejoice – even singing with joy – over the justice and judgments of God.
>
>> i. "This is an exaggerated personification. There shall be, as it were, a new face set upon the world, and all the creatures shall appear to be well paid at the downfall of Babylon, under the oppressions whereof they even groaned and laboured." (Trapp)

4. (49-56) Babylon that plundered the LORD's house will be plundered.

As Babylon *has caused* the slain of Israel to fall,
So at Babylon the slain of all the earth shall fall.
You who have escaped the sword,
Get away! Do not stand still!
Remember the LORD afar off,
And let Jerusalem come to your mind.
We are ashamed because we have heard reproach.
Shame has covered our faces,
For strangers have come into the sanctuaries of the LORD's house.
"Therefore behold, the days are coming," says the LORD,
"That I will bring judgment on her carved images,
And throughout all her land the wounded shall groan.
Though Babylon were to mount up to heaven,
And though she were to fortify the height of her strength,
Yet from Me plunderers would come to her," says the LORD.
The sound of a cry *comes* from Babylon,
And great destruction from the land of the Chaldeans,
Because the LORD is plundering Babylon
And silencing her loud voice,
Though her waves roar like great waters,
And the noise of their voice is uttered,
Because the plunderer comes against her, against Babylon,
And her mighty men are taken.
Every one of their bows is broken;
For the LORD is the God of recompense,
He will surely repay.

> a. **As Babylon has caused the slain of Israel to fall**: Jeremiah continues this prominent theme in Jeremiah 50-51. Because of what Babylon did to Judah and Jerusalem, judgment would come upon them.
>
> b. **Remember the LORD afar off**: Knowing the coming judgment upon Babylon, it was right for God's people to take the warning, to **get away** from her, and to **remember the LORD** in humble repentance.
>
>> i. "The term *remember* (*zakar*) generally involves something more than mere mental recall. The act of remembering involves an active indentification of one's whole being with the object of remembering." (Thompson)
>
> c. **Shame has covered our faces**: Jeremiah described the sense of shame felt by God's people when **strangers** invaded and destroyed **the sanctuaries of the LORD's house**. This was part of the pain of judgment that came upon Judah and Jerusalem.

i. "The lament of verse 51 arises from the fact that the desecration of the Temple appeared to involve Yahweh's inferiority, but the desolation of Babylon would reveal the utter impotence of her idols." (Cundall)

d. **Though Babylon were to mount up to heaven**: This is an allusion to the Tower of Babel, constructed as a defense and in defiance against God (Genesis 11:1-9). God came against that tower and would come against **the height of her strength** in Jeremiah's era and beyond.

i. "The towering ziggurats (*cf.* NEB *their high towers*) and palaces of Babylon are neither inaccessible nor impregnable, and soon will collapse in ruins." (Harrison)

e. **For the LORD is the God of recompense, He will surely repay**: Babylon would receive judgment in a pure form. The evil they had done to others would be done to them.

5. (57-58) Babylon's broken walls.

"And I will make drunk
Her princes and wise men,
Her governors, her deputies, and her mighty men.
And they shall sleep a perpetual sleep
And not awake," says the King,
Whose name *is* the LORD of hosts.
Thus says the LORD of hosts:
"The broad walls of Babylon shall be utterly broken,
And her high gates shall be burned with fire;
The people will labor in vain,
And the nations, because of the fire;
And they shall be weary."

a. **I will make drunk her princes and wise men**: This aspect of Babylon's judgment was exactly fulfilled in Jeremiah's era (Daniel 5).

b. **The broad walls of Babylon shall be utterly broken**: This aspect of Babylon's judgment was not literally fulfilled in Jeremiah's era; it waits for a final fulfillment that will certainly come (Revelation 17-18).

i. "Babylon as a spirit was not then destroyed. Like an evil spirit it found other places in which to dwell, and work its designs, and through which to exercise its dark and baleful influence among men. And this because, at the very core of Babylon, is Satan himself." (Morgan)

ii. Babylon did have **broad walls**. "In addition to the two massive walls surrounding the heart of Babylon, an inner one some 21 feet thick and an outer one over 12 feet thick, there were great walls thrown up at intervals beyond the city." (Thompson)

C. The postscript to Jeremiah's prophecy against Babylon.

1. (59-60) Zedekiah's visit to Babylon.

The word which Jeremiah the prophet commanded Seraiah the son of Neriah, the son of Mahseiah, when he went with Zedekiah the king of Judah to Babylon in the fourth year of his reign. And Seraiah *was* the quartermaster. So Jeremiah wrote in a book all the evil that would come upon Babylon, all these words that are written against Babylon.

a. **The word which Jeremiah the prophet commanded**: The prophecy of Jeremiah 50 and 51 was from the LORD, yet came through His servant **Jeremiah**.

b. **In the fourth year of his reign**: This was not a year when Babylon came against Judah. It was a year when Zedekiah and neighboring kings plotted a rebellion against Babylon when she seemed weakened (Jeremiah 27). This journey of King Zedekiah to Babylon is not recorded elsewhere and was likely to make things right with Nebuchadnezzar after the plot.

i. "This was the year of the plot to rebel against Babylon recorded in Jeremiah 27. Zedekiah seems to have been implicated in the plot. Although the plot was abortive, Nebuchadnezzar's 'intelligence' got wind of it and some explanation was needed." (Thompson)

ii. "Zedekiah's summons to Babylon was doubtless to make sure of his loyalty, perhaps in view of reports that envoys of five neighboring states had been conferring with him at Jerusalem." (Kidner)

c. **Seriah the son of Neriah**: Jeremiah sent a copy of these prophesies against Babylon with **Seriah**, who was a Judean **quartermaster** taken to Babylon in exile **with Zedekiah king of Judah**.

i. "Seriah was the grandson of the high priest Hilkiah who had discovered the lost book of the law in Josiah's reign. He was himself the grandfather of Joshua-ben-Jozdak, the high priest at the return from exile. So the family line survived his violent death, and another branch of it would produce the great Ezra, a century hence." (Kidner)

ii. **Quartermaster**: Seriah was "the staff officer who was responsible for looking after the comfort of the king of Judah whenever he stopped for the night." (Feinberg)

iii. "Like his brother Baruch (Jeremiah 32:12; 36:1-10), Seraiah served as Jeremiah's spokesperson. (Also like Baruch, his name has been found on an ancient seal)." (Ryken)

2. (61-64) A graphic illustration of Babylon's coming judgment.

And Jeremiah said to Seraiah, "When you arrive in Babylon and see it, and read all these words, then you shall say, 'O LORD, You have spoken against this place to cut it off, so that none shall remain in it, neither man nor beast, but it shall be desolate forever.' Now it shall be, when you have finished reading this book, *that* you shall tie a stone to it and throw it out into the Euphrates. Then you shall say, 'Thus Babylon shall sink and not rise from the catastrophe that I will bring upon her. And they shall be weary.'" Thus far *are* the words of Jeremiah.

a. **When you arrive in Babylon**: Jeremiah gave a copy of the prophecy to Seriah because he did not go to Babylon himself. Jeremiah ended his days in Egypt.

b. **Read all these words**: Jeremiah instructed Seriah to read this prophecy and then say a certain prayer after the words had been read, announcing the coming judgment upon Babylon.

i. "This visit of Zedekiah was the aftermath of an abortive attempt at rebellion by an alliance of states, including Judah, to which Jeremiah was diametrically opposed. It is significant that at the very time when he was counseling submission to Babylon he could also foretell, in such uncompromising terms, her ultimate overthrow." (Cundall)

c. **Tie a stone to it and throw it out into the Euphrates**: Jeremiah told Seriah to literally take the scroll, weight it with a **stone**, and then throw it into the **Euphrates** as a graphic illustration of the catastrophe of judgment that would soon sink Babylon.

i. "Seriah's symbolic act was a visual enactment of the fall of Babylon. ... It is remarkable that at the very time Jeremiah was advising submission to that city, he was also foretelling her final overthrow." (Feinberg)

ii. "The scroll never surfaced. Like the Babylonian empire, it stayed submerged." (Ryken)

iii. "The symbolic action would be repeated still more impressively in John's vision of the Babylon of the Apocalypse: *Then a mighty angel took up a stone like a great millstone and threw it into the sea, saying, 'So shall Babylon, that great city be thrown down with violence, and shall be found no more.'*" (Kidner)

iv. "Ceremonies are to little purpose unless they have divine expositions annexed unto them." (Trapp)

Jeremiah 52 – The Fall of Jerusalem and the Captivity of Judah

Several commentators believe this final chapter was not authored by Jeremiah, but perhaps by Baruch. It testifies to the truthfulness and integrity of Jeremiah's long, faithful work as a prophet of God.

"It appears that the following chapter is not the work of this prophet: it is not his style. The author of it writes Jehoiachin; *Jeremiah writes him always* Jeconiah, *or* Coniah. *It is merely historical, and is very similar to 2 Kings 24:18-25:30."* (Clarke)

"Nearly every verse of Jeremiah 52 is a fulfilled prophecy. In fact, reading the chapter is a good way to review the entire book of Jeremiah. The facts speak for themselves: Jeremiah spoke the true words of God." (Ryken)

"In its present context the chapter seems to say: the divine word both has been fulfilled – and will be fulfilled!" (Bright, cited in Kidner)

"The Septuagint have set this title upon it: And it came to pass after that Israel was carried captive, and Jerusalem laid waste, the Prophet Jeremiah sat weeping, and wailing, and bitterly lamenting the case of his people. Thus they knit together this chapter and the ensuing Lamentations, which the Jews also are still said to read together in their synagogues on the ninth day of the month Ab, which answereth to our July, because that on that day the city was taken and destroyed by the Chaldeans. [Jeremiah 52:7]." (Trapp)

A. The siege and conquest of Jerusalem.

1. (1-3) The evil reign and rebellion of Zedekiah.

Zedekiah *was* twenty-one years old when he became king, and he reigned eleven years in Jerusalem. His mother's name *was* Hamutal the daughter of Jeremiah of Libnah. He also did evil in the sight of the Lord, according to all that Jehoiakim had done. For because of the anger of the Lord this happened in Jerusalem and Judah, till He finally

cast them out from His presence. Then Zedekiah rebelled against the king of Babylon.

>   a. **Zedekiah was twenty-one years old when he became king**: 2 Kings 25:17 explains that Nebuchadnezzar set young Zedekiah on the throne of Judah as his puppet king after the rebellion of Jehoiachin.
>
>> i. 2 Kings 25:17 also says that Zedekiah's name was originally *Mattaniah*, and that Nebuchadnezzar changed it to **Zedekiah**. The name **Zedekiah** means, *The Lord is Righteous*. The righteous judgment of God would soon be seen against Judah.
>
>   b. **He also did evil in the sight of the LORD**: 2 Chronicles 36:11-20 tells us more of the evil of Zedekiah, specifically that he did not listen to Jeremiah or other messengers of God. Instead, he mocked and disregarded the message.
>
>> i. "Zedekiah's *evil* (v. 19) is fully explained in 2 Chronicles 36:12-14. (i) He was not willing to listen to God's word through Jeremiah; (ii) he broke an oath made in Yahweh's name as a vassal of Babylon; (iii) he was unrepentant and failed to restrain leaders and priests from defiling the temple with the reintroduction of idolatrous practices." (Wiseman)
>
>   c. **He finally cast them out from His presence**: God's patience and longsuffering had finally run its course and He allowed – even prompted – the Babylonian conquest of the Kingdom of Judah.
>
>> i. "The absence of every expression of emotion is most striking. In one sentence the wrath of God is pointed to as the cause of all: and, for the rest, the tragic facts which wrung the writer's heart are told in brief, passionless sentences." (Maclaren)
>>
>> ii. "The Book of Lamentations weeps and sobs with the grief of the devout Jew; but the historian smothers feeling while he tells of God's righteous judgment." (Maclaren)
>
>   d. **Zedekiah rebelled against the king of Babylon**: Jeremiah tells us that there were many false prophets in those days who preached a message of victory and triumph to Zedekiah, and he believed them instead of Jeremiah and other godly prophets like him. Therefore, he **rebelled against the king of Babylon**.
>
>> i. For example, Jeremiah 32:1-5 tells us that Jeremiah clearly told Zedekiah that he would not succeed in his rebellion against Babylon. Zedekiah arrested Jeremiah and imprisoned him for this, but the prophet steadfastly stayed faithful to the message God gave him.

2. (4-6) The final siege of Jerusalem.

Now it came to pass in the ninth year of his reign, in the tenth month, on the tenth *day* of the month, *that* Nebuchadnezzar king of Babylon and all his army came against Jerusalem and encamped against it; and *they* built a siege wall against it all around. So the city was besieged until the eleventh year of King Zedekiah. By the fourth month, on the ninth day of the month, the famine had become so severe in the city that there was no food for the people of the land.

    a. **They built a siege wall against it all around**: Nebuchadnezzar used the common method of attack in those days of securely walled cities – a **siege wall**. A siege was intended to surround a city, prevent all business and trade from entering or leaving the city, and to eventually starve the population into surrender.

        i. "So crucial was this event that the OT records it four times – in 2 Kings 25; 2 Chronicles 36:11-21; Jeremiah 39:1-14; and in this passage." (Feinberg)

    b. **The famine had become so severe in the city**: This was the intended goal of a siege. This indicates that Nebuchadnezzar and the Babylonians were at the point of victory over Jerusalem.

        i. "An eighteen months' agony is condensed into three verses (Jeremiah 52:4-6)." (Maclaren)

3. (7-11) Zedekiah is captured and executed.

Then the city wall was broken through, and all the men of war fled and went out of the city at night by way of the gate between the two walls, which *was* by the king's garden, even though the Chaldeans *were* near the city all around. And they went by way of the plain. But the army of the Chaldeans pursued the king, and they overtook Zedekiah in the plains of Jericho. All his army was scattered from him. So they took the king and brought him up to the king of Babylon at Riblah in the land of Hamath, and he pronounced judgment on him. Then the king of Babylon killed the sons of Zedekiah before his eyes. And he killed all the princes of Judah in Riblah. He also put out the eyes of Zedekiah; and the king of Babylon bound him in bronze fetters, took him to Babylon, and put him in prison till the day of his death.

    a. **Then the city wall was broken through**: At this desperate point for Judah at the siege of Jerusalem, Zedekiah made a last-chance effort to escape the grip of the nearly-completely successful siege. They planned a secret break through the city walls and the siege lines of the Babylonians, using a diversionary tactic.

b. **The army of the Chaldeans pursued the king, and they overtook him in the plains of Jericho**: This was a considerable distance from Jerusalem. Zedekiah probably thought that his strategy was successful, and that he had escaped the judgment that prophets such as Jeremiah had promised. Yet God's word was demonstrated to be true and he was captured **in the plains of Jericho**.

> i. "It seems ironic that here, at the very spot where Israel first set foot on the Promised Land, the last of the Davidic kings was captured and his monarchy shattered. Here, where Israel experienced her first victory as the walls of Jericho fell before unarmed men who trusted God, was the scene of her last defeat." (Dilday)

c. **Then they killed the sons of Zedekiah before his eyes, put out the eyes of Zedekiah**: The Babylonians were not known to be as cruel as the Assyrians who conquered the northern kingdom of Israel some 150 years earlier, but they were still experts in cruelty in their own right. They made certain that the last sight King Zedekiah saw was the murder of his own sons, and then he spent the rest of his life in darkness.

> i. This fulfilled the mysterious promise God made through Ezekiel regarding Zedekiah shortly before the fall of Jerusalem: *I will also spread My net over him, and he shall be caught in My snare. I will bring him to Babylon, to the land of the Chaldeans; yet he shall not see it, though he shall die there.* (Ezekiel 12:13)

> ii. "With his eyes put out, and bound in fetters, he was carried to the court of the conqueror, the symbol of the people who had rebelled against God, and had been broken in pieces." (Morgan)

> iii. "The eyes of whose mind had been put out long before; else he might have foreseen and prevented this evil – as prevision is the best means of prevention, – had he taken warning by what was foretold." (Trapp)

> iv. "Josephus (*Antiquities* x.8.8) says Nebuchadnezzar 'kept Zedekiah in prison until he died; and then buried him magnificently.' This agrees with Jeremiah 34:5." (Knapp)

4. (12-14) The destruction of Jerusalem.

Now in the fifth month, on the tenth *day* **of the month (which** *was* **the nineteenth year of King Nebuchadnezzar king of Babylon), Nebuzaradan, the captain of the guard,** *who* **served the king of Babylon, came to Jerusalem. He burned the house of the L**ORD **and the king's house; all the houses of Jerusalem, that is, all the houses of the great, he**

burned with fire. And all the army of the Chaldeans who *were* with the captain of the guard broke down all the walls of Jerusalem all around.

    a. **He burned the house of the** LORD: Solomon's great temple was now a ruin. It would stay a ruin for many years, until it was humbly rebuilt by the returning exiles in the days of Ezra.

        i. **On the tenth day**: "For the *tenth day* (Jeremiah 52:12), 2 Kings 25:8 has seventh day, the difference perhaps embracing the interval between the arrival of Nebuzaradan and the beginning of the destruction." (Harrison)

        ii. "The Talmud declares that when the Babylonians entered the temple, they held a two-day feast there to desecrate it; then, on the third day, they set fire to the building. The Talmud adds that the fire burned throughout that day and the next." (Dilday)

        iii. **The nineteenth year of King Nebuchadnezzar**: "The apparent contradiction between verses 12 and 29 is readily explained; in the former the accession year of Nebuchadnezzar has been included, in the later it has not." (Cundall)

    b. **Broke down the walls of Jerusalem all around**: The walls of Jerusalem – the physical security of the city – were now destroyed. Jerusalem was no longer a place of safety and security. The walls would remain a ruin until they were rebuilt by the returning exiles in the days of Nehemiah.

        i. On **Nebuzaradan the captain of the guard**: "That title in Hebrew is literally, 'the chief executioner' or 'the slaughterer.' Methodically, he set about to demolish the beautiful city, burning the palace and the chief buildings, breaking down the walls, and wrecking the temple." (Dilday)

B. Judah and Jerusalem under the Babylonians.

1. (15-23) The captives, those left in the land, and the plunder.

Then Nebuzaradan the captain of the guard carried away captive *some* of the poor people, the rest of the people who remained in the city, the defectors who had deserted to the king of Babylon, and the rest of the craftsmen. But Nebuzaradan the captain of the guard left *some* of the poor of the land as vinedressers and farmers. The bronze pillars that *were* in the house of the LORD**, and the carts and the bronze Sea that *were* in the house of the** LORD**, the Chaldeans broke in pieces, and carried all their bronze to Babylon. They also took away the pots, the shovels, the trimmers, the bowls, the spoons, and all the bronze utensils with which the priests ministered. The basins, the firepans, the bowls, the**

pots, the lampstands, the spoons, and the cups, whatever *was* solid gold and whatever *was* solid silver, the captain of the guard took away. The two pillars, one Sea, the twelve bronze bulls which *were* under *it, and* the carts, which King Solomon had made for the house of the LORD— the bronze of all these articles was beyond measure. Now *concerning* the pillars: the height of one pillar *was* eighteen cubits, a measuring line of twelve cubits could measure its circumference, and its thickness *was* four fingers; *it was* hollow. A capital of bronze *was* on it; and the height of one capital *was* five cubits, with a network and pomegranates all around the capital, all of bronze. The second pillar, with pomegranates was the same. There were ninety-six pomegranates on the sides; all the pomegranates, all around on the network, *were* one hundred.

> a. **Carried away captive the rest of the people who remained in the city**: This was the third major wave of captivity taking the remaining people, all except for the **poor of the land**.
>
> b. **And carried their bronze to Babylon.... the things of solid gold and solid silver, the captain of the guard took away**: As the remaining people were taken captive to Babylon, so also the remaining valuables from the temple were taken. Jerusalem was left desolate, completely plundered under the judgment of God.
>
>> i. Jeremiah 52:17-23 is a detailed inventory of all that the Babylonians looted from the temple. "The material in Jeremiah 52 is thus merely a summary, and it is not surprising that it is not always possible to match this account with that in 1 Kings 7. The aim was not to give a detailed technical account but rather to stress two facts, first, that there was a very considerable amount of bronze, and second, that the pillars were very beautiful, which made their destruction all the more tragic." (Thompson)

2. (24-27) The authority of Nebuchadnezzar over Jerusalem and Judah.

The captain of the guard took Seraiah the chief priest, Zephaniah the second priest, and the three doorkeepers. He also took out of the city an officer who had charge of the men of war, seven men of the king's close associates who were found in the city, the principal scribe of the army who mustered the people of the land, and sixty men of the people of the land who were found in the midst of the city. And Nebuzaradan the captain of the guard took these and brought them to the king of Babylon at Riblah. Then the king of Babylon struck them and put them to death at Riblah in the land of Hamath. Thus Judah was carried away captive from its own land.

a. **The king of Babylon struck them and put them to death**: These last leaders of Jerusalem and Judah were also captured and put to death. The **king of Babylon** had what seemed to be complete rule over the former Kingdom of Judah.

   i. **Struck them**: "The root *nkh* is difficult to translate. The Hiphil is often translated 'smite,' but it can mean 'wound, hurt, torture, flog,' etc." (Thompson)

b. **Thus Judah was carried away captive from its own land**: This was the land God gave to His people, the tribes of Israel. They had possessed this land for some 860 years; they took it by faith and obedience, but they lost it through idolatry and sin.

   i. "The reader cannot help but be struck by the passionless tone of the narrative in this chapter. Not once does the author show his feelings, even though he is describing the tragic downfall of his country. We have to turn to the Book of Lamentations for weeping and groaning." (Dilday)

3. (28-30) The register of the final phase of exile.

These *are* the people whom Nebuchadnezzar carried away captive: in the seventh year, three thousand and twenty-three Jews; in the eighteenth year of Nebuchadnezzar he carried away captive from Jerusalem eight hundred and thirty-two persons; in the twenty-third year of Nebuchadnezzar, Nebuzaradan the captain of the guard carried away captive of the Jews seven hundred and forty-five persons. All the persons *were* four thousand six hundred.

   a. **These are the people whom Nebuchadnezzar carried away captive**: This described part of the *final* exile and forced depopulation of the land. The conquest and exile of Judah came in waves, of which this was the last.

   b. **All the persons were four thousand six hundred**: This relatively small number is normally understood as referring to a portion of the exiles, and only the adult males of that portion.

   i. "If only Jews are numbered or only males reckoned in Jeremiah 52:28-30, the ultimate total of exiles was doubtless much higher." (Feinberg)

   ii. "The figures given here vary from those in 2 Kings 24:14, 16. 3,023 may be the actual head count of the deported adult males, while the Kings' figures may comprise the total number of deportees." (Harrison)

4. (31-34) A small ray of hope seen in Jehoiachin improved situation in Babylon.

Now it came to pass in the thirty-seventh year of the captivity of Jehoiachin king of Judah, in the twelfth month, on the twenty-fifth day of the month, *that* **Evil-Merodach king of Babylon, in the first** *year* **of his reign, lifted up the head of Jehoiachin king of Judah and brought him out of prison. And he spoke kindly to him and gave him a more prominent seat than those of the kings who** *were* **with him in Babylon. So Jehoiachin changed from his prison garments, and he ate bread regularly before the king all the days of his life. And as for his provisions, there was a regular ration given him by the king of Babylon, a portion for each day until the day of his death, all the days of his life.**

> a. **In the thirty-seventh year of the captivity of Jehoiachin king of Judah**: This King **Jehoiachin** was not the last king of Judah; Zedekiah came after him. But he was taken away to Babylon in bronze fetters (2 Kings 24:10-12). This happened when Jehoiachin had been a captive for many years.
>
>> i. "Thirty-seven years in prison! And so long a sentence for a reign of three months." (Kidner)
>
> b. **Spoke kindly to him, and gave him a more prominent seat**: This describes small kindness and blessings given in the worst circumstances. Judah was still depopulated; the people of God were still exiled; and the King of Judah was still a prisoner in Babylon. Yet, looking for even small notes of grace and mercy as evidences of the returning favor of God, the divine historian noted that King Jehoiachin began to receive better treatment in Babylon.
>
>> i. **Lifted up the head of Jehoiachin king of Judah**: "This phrase is taken from Genesis 40:13. It is founded on the observation that those who are in sorrow hold down their heads, and when they are comforted, or the cause of their sorrow removed, *they lift up their heads*. The Hebrew phrase, *lift up the head*, signifies to *comfort, cheer, make happy*." (Clarke)
>
>> ii. "Tablets recovered from the ruined Ishtar Gate in Babylon confirm that Jehoiachin was a recipient of the king's bounty." (Harrison)
>
>> iii. "The fact that Jehoiachin lived on long after the exile and that he was finally released from prison may have seemed like the first signs of the fulfillment of Jeremiah's promise of a day of restoration." (Thompson)
>
>> iv. This was small, but evidence nonetheless that God was not done blessing and restoring His people, foreshadowing even greater blessing and restoration to come. "God has finally brought the promised

punishment upon His apostate and idolatrous people, and the chastening discipline of exile has begun. Despite this dreadful calamity there lingers the hope that God will restore His people, bringing a faithful remnant back to repopulate the homeland." (Harrison)

v. "No hosts encamped against the people of God can gain any advantage over them, so long as they remain loyal in heart and mind and will to their One King. But when they are disloyal, and persist in disloyalty, then no force can save them from the opposing hosts." (Morgan)

vi. "If the King of Babylon did this for a captive king, his prisoner, will your heavenly Father do less for you?" (Meyer)

Cundall gives a good postscript to Jeremiah: *"Jeremiah may have failed in his strenuous efforts to turn his people back to the Lord, but in his conception of true religion as a vital, inward relationship with the living God (e.g. Jeremiah 9:24) he was to set the necessary standard, not only for the immediate future, but for all time."*

Lamentations 1 - Mourning Over the Fallen City

The Book of Lamentations is the collection of five poems or songs mourning the conquest of Jerusalem and the Kingdom of Judah.

"Dirge poetry of the kind exemplified by Lamentations was by no means uncommon in Near Eastern antiquity. The author of Lamentations stood therefore in a long and respectable literary tradition when he bewailed the destruction of Jerusalem and the desolation of Judah in 587 BC." (R.K. Harrison)

Lamentations is a remarkable written work, because the first four of the five poems are written as acrostics. The twenty-two letters of the Hebrew alphabet are used in succession to begin the lines and sections of those songs.

"The use of the alphabet symbolizes that the completeness—'the A to Z'—of grief is being expressed." (H.L. Ellison)

Lamentations both reflected and gave words to the deliberate choice of the Jewish people to remember and mourn their fallen city and kingdom. "For as far back as tradition reaches, Lamentations has been read on Tisha b'Av; and it is not unreasonable to assume that it was intended for this purpose from the first." (H.L. Ellison)

"As oft as I read the Lamentations of Jeremiah, saith Gregory Nazianzen, my voice faileth me, and I am overwhelmed with tears. The misery of that poor people cometh under my view, as it were, and my heart is therewith very much affected and afflicted." (John Trapp)

A. Jerusalem afflicted with no comfort.

1. (1-2) Grieving over an empty city.

How lonely sits the city
***That was* full of people!**
***How* like a widow is she,**
Who *was* great among the nations!
The princess among the provinces

Has become a slave!
She weeps bitterly in the night,
Her tears *are* on her cheeks;
Among all her lovers
She has none to comfort *her.*
All her friends have dealt treacherously with her;
They have become her enemies.

> a. **How lonely sits the city**: Writing after the catastrophe of Jerusalem's defeat, Jeremiah thought of the contrast between happy, prosperous Jerusalem and the **lonely**, empty, conquered city after the Babylonian conquest. Once she was **full of people**, now she is empty. Once she was **great among the nations**, now she is like **a slave**.
>
>> i. Jeremiah is never specifically mentioned as the author of Lamentations, but it is a reasonable conclusion from both long-standing tradition and great similarity to the book of Jeremiah. It is likely that he wrote this collection of five poems after the Babylonians conquered Jerusalem but before he was taken to Egypt against his will (Jeremiah 43). Jeremiah is specifically mentioned as the author of other laments (2 Chronicles 35:25).
>>
>> ii. "In all copies of the *Septuagint*, whether of the Roman or Alexandrian editions, the following words are found as a part of the text: 'And it came to pass after Israel had been carried away captive, and Jerusalem was become desolate, that Jeremiah sat weeping: and he lamented with this lamentation over Jerusalem; and he said.'" (Clarke)
>>
>> iii. **How lonely sits the city**: "The coin struck by Vespasian on the capture of Jerusalem, on the obverse of which there is a *palm-tree*, the emblem of Judea, and under it a woman, the emblem of Jerusalem, sitting, leaning as before described, with the legend *Judea capta*, illustrates this expression." (Clarke)
>>
>> iv. **Who was great among the nations**: "So was Athens, once the glory of Greece, for both arts and arms, now a dog hole in comparison. Sparta also, that other eye of Greece, is now a small burrow called Misithra, having nothing to boast of but the fame and thoughts of its former greatness." (Trapp)
>
> b. **She weeps bitterly in the night**: With poetic skill Jeremiah thought of Jerusalem as the widow princess brought low, weeping uncontrollably with **none to comfort her**. Jeremiah's sorrow is deep and plain; even though Jerusalem's conquest vindicated Jeremiah's many prophecies, he has no sense of triumph or "I told you so." Jeremiah deeply sorrows with the sorrow of Jerusalem and Judah.

i. "To heighten the tragedy of destruction the author uses the image of a woman bereaved of her husband and children, bitterly lamenting her present sorry state in anguish and apprehension." (Harrison)

ii. "In this brief Book of Lamentation the spirit of the man is strikingly revealed. There is no exultation over the fulfilment of his predictions, and there is a twofold loyalty manifest throughout, first to God in the confession of sin, and then to his people in the expression of their sorrow." (Morgan)

c. **All her friends have dealt treacherously with her**: In better days, Jerusalem enjoyed loyal alliances. Those one-time friends became **her enemies**.

i. "Israel was always faced with an inescapable choice. She could rely on God for her safety against external aggression, or she could turn to allies great and small." (Ellison)

2. (3-6) Under affliction from the LORD.

Judah has gone into captivity,
Under affliction and hard servitude;
She dwells among the nations,
She finds no rest;
All her persecutors overtake her in dire straits.
The roads to Zion mourn
Because no one comes to the set feasts.
All her gates are desolate;
Her priests sigh,
Her virgins are afflicted,
And she *is* in bitterness.
Her adversaries have become the master,
Her enemies prosper;
For the LORD has afflicted her
Because of the multitude of her transgressions.
Her children have gone into captivity before the enemy.
And from the daughter of Zion
All her splendor has departed.
Her princes have become like deer
***That* find no pasture,**
That flee without strength
Before the pursuer.

a. **Judah has gone into captivity**: After the poetic images of the first few verses, Jeremiah simply reported the fact. Judah was conquered and captive. Once busy entrances to the city seemed empty (**all her gates are** desolate), and all who were connected with Jerusalem are dispirited; they **sigh** and **are afflicted**. Judah's enemies are blessed as they **prosper** and **master** over them.

> i. **No one comes to the set feasts**: "The routes to Jerusalem, once thronged with pilgrims going up to the Temple to participate in festal rites, are now completely deserted." (Harrison)

b. **For the LORD has afflicted her**: Jeremiah understood that this catastrophe was not due to fate, human cruelty, or blind cycles of history. It was because Judah had sinned so long and so deep that it was God's will to afflict her with severe correction. It was **because of the multitude of her transgressions**.

> i. **The multitude of her transgressions**: "Though *pesa* is traditionally rendered 'transgression,' it is essentially a secular word meaning 'rebellion'—a word that brings out more fully its meaning in this type of context." (Ellison)

> ii. **Her children have gone into captivity before the enemy**: "For the multitude of our sins, directly contrary to his promise in case of obedience… Not only our young and old men, but the little children, have been driven like sheep before the enemy into a miserable captivity." (Poole)

c. **All her splendor has departed**: Jeremiah's pain was amplified as he thought of how it *used to be* in Jerusalem. Now, the people and place of Jerusalem were desolate and defeated.

d. **Her princes have become like deer**: Both hope and leadership for the city abandoned Jerusalem. The **princes** ran away **like deer, but also without success (that flee without strength before the pursuer)**.

> i. "The image of pastureless *deer* contrasts sharply with the situation depicted in Psalm 23." (Harrison)

3. (7) Remembering pleasant days.

In the days of her affliction and roaming,
Jerusalem remembers all her pleasant things
That she had in the days of old.
When her people fell into the hand of the enemy,
With no one to help her,
The adversaries saw her
And mocked at her downfall.

> a. **Jerusalem remembers all her pleasant things**: The tragedy of Jerusalem's fall was worse after considering how things were once so much better. The

memory of days of **pleasant things** stung **in the days of her affliction and roaming**.

b. **When her people fell into the hand of the enemy, with no one to help her**: When the enemy came against her, Jerusalem was completely alone; the help many hoped for from Egypt never arrived. Because of this, **the adversaries saw her and mocked at her downfall**.

4. (8-11) The reason Jerusalem is left without comfort.

Jerusalem has sinned gravely,
Therefore she has become vile.
All who honored her despise her
Because they have seen her nakedness;
Yes, she sighs and turns away.
Her uncleanness *is* in her skirts;
She did not consider her destiny;
Therefore her collapse was awesome;
She had no comforter.
"O LORD, behold my affliction,
For *the* enemy is exalted!"
The adversary has spread his hand
Over all her pleasant things;
For she has seen the nations enter her sanctuary,
Those whom You commanded
Not to enter Your assembly.
All her people sigh,
They seek bread;
They have given their valuables for food to restore life.
"See, O LORD, and consider,
For I am scorned."

    a. **Jerusalem has sinned gravely, therefore she has become vile**: As Jeremiah described the tragedy of Jerusalem's fall, one would rightly ask *why*. The answer was simple; it was because of the great sin of the people of the city over many generations.

        i. "The story of her desolation is mingled with confessions of her sin. She asks boldly if any sorrow could be compared to her sorrow, and then confesses that not one pang or stroke had been in excess of her sin." (Meyer)

    b. **They have seen her nakedness**: The once dignified city was humiliated and exposed. Like a queen stripped of her royal robes, **she sighs and turns away**.

i. "Here she is compared to a debased, slatternly harlot, shamelessly exposing her nakedness and indifferent to the marks of menstrual blood." (Ellison)

ii. **Her uncleanness is in her skirts**: "She rather glorieth in her wickedness, than is any whit abashed of it - a metaphor from a menstruous woman that is immodest." (Trapp)

c. **She did not consider her destiny**: Like a foolish woman (or man), Jerusalem never thought about where her path of sin and rebellion would lead her. Her lack of forethought meant **her collapse was awesome**.

d. **O Lord, behold my affliction**: A prayer, as if from the lips of the afflicted city, breaks into the description of misery. With no **comforter** to help when the enemy exalted himself, all Jerusalem could do was cry out to the God she had rejected.

i. **She has seen the nations enter her sanctuary**: "Now those very foreigners who had been prohibited from entering the congregation of the Israelites were polluting the sacred house in the most wanton manner." (Harrison)

e. **See, O Lord, and consider, for I am scorned**: Another prayer rises from Jerusalem, crying out for help from the starving city (**they seek bread**).

5. (12) Incomparable sorrow.

"*Is it* nothing to you, all you who pass by?
Behold and see
If there is any sorrow like my sorrow,
Which has been brought on me,
Which the Lord has inflicted
In the day of His fierce anger.

a. **It is nothing to you, all you who pass by?** An unsympathetic world looked upon Jerusalem's misery and regarded it as **nothing**. She had no comforter at all (Lamentations 1:9). Jerusalem personified wondered at the lack of sympathy.

b. **Is there any sorrow like my sorrow**: Jerusalem felt what many sufferers feel; that her **sorrow** was incomparable to others and incomprehensible to others. There is a sense in which this is true, but it is true for everyone who endures a deep season of suffering. Few if any can truly relate to the depths of their **sorrow**.

i. "The desolations and distress brought upon this city and its inhabitants had scarcely any parallel. Excessive abuse of God's accumulated mercies calls for singular and exemplary punishment." (Clarke)

c. **When the LORD has inflicted**: Jeremiah (and Jerusalem personified) knew the true source of their sorrow. It was not the Babylonians; it was the LORD who had **inflicted** this devastation.

B. God's hand in Jerusalem's tragedy.

1. (13-15) What the LORD did to Jerusalem.

"From above He has sent fire into my bones,
And it overpowered them;
He has spread a net for my feet
And turned me back;
He has made me desolate
And faint all the day.
"The yoke of my transgressions was bound;
They were woven together by His hands,
And thrust upon my neck.
He made my strength fail;
The Lord delivered me into the hands of *those whom* I am not able to withstand.
"The Lord has trampled underfoot all my mighty *men* in my midst;
He has called an assembly against me
To crush my young men;
The Lord trampled *as* in a winepress
The virgin daughter of Judah.

a. **From above He has sent fire into my bones**: In the context, this **fire** was the judgment God sent upon Jerusalem. The judgment came from heaven (**from above**). The context makes it clear that this is Jerusalem personified speaking, yet Jeremiah used the same image of **fire into my bones** that he used of his own prophetic call in Jeremiah 20:9.

i. "Not Jerusalem's enemies, but God himself had entrapped the city, bringing it to an inescapable and ignominious end." (Ellison)

b. **He has made me desolate and faint all the day**: Jerusalem was like a trapped, blocked, empty, and exhausted foe.

c. **The yoke of my transgressions was bound; they were woven together by His hands**: Jeremiah pictured Jerusalem as bound with a **yoke** like a brute ox; yet the **yoke** was fashioned out of their own **transgressions**. It was **bound** to them by cords **woven** by God's own **hands**.

i. **The yoke of my transgressions was bound**: "I am now tied and bound by the chain of my sins; and it is so *wreathed*, so *doubled* and *twisted* round me, that I cannot free myself. A fine representation of the miseries of a penitent soul, which feels that nothing but the pitifulness of God's mercy can loose it." (Clarke)

d. The Lord trampled as in a winepress the virgin daughter of Judah: Jeremiah set forth image after image to describe the ruin of Jerusalem and **Judah**, but each image understood it to come from the hand of God.

i. "God had trodden upon the Jews as men use to stamp grapes in a wine-press, where they use to crush them to pieces to get out the juice, and then they throw the husks, that are good for nothing, upon the dunghills. These are but various expressions to set out the misery into which God had brought this people for their sins." (Poole)

2. (16-17) Weeping without comfort.

"For these *things* I weep;
My eye, my eye overflows with water;
Because the comforter, who should restore my life,
Is far from me.
My children are desolate
Because the enemy prevailed."
Zion spreads out her hands,
But no one comforts her;
The LORD has commanded concerning Jacob
That those around him *become* his adversaries;
Jerusalem has become an unclean thing among them.

a. **For these things I weep**: Sometimes Jeremiah is described as *the weeping prophet*, and he would agree with the description. Lamentations was not written with a dry eye, but with overflowing eyes.

b. **Because the comforter, who should restore my life, is far from me**: The worst aspect of Jerusalem's misery was not the catastrophe of itself. It was that in the catastrophe, they had little or no sense of God's comfort or help. It felt as if He were **far from** them.

c. **Zion spreads out her hands, but no one comforts her**: Jerusalem felt no comfort from God, and received none from man. By God's design (**the LORD has commanded**) all her neighbors had become her **adversaries**, and regarded her as **an unclean thing**.

i. **The LORD has commanded**: "God is here presented as the righteous judge who has finally punished His recalcitrant people for their long-standing rebellion." (Harrison)

ii. **Jerusalem has become an unclean thing**: "Jerusalem is as a menstruous woman, to whom none dared to approach, either to help or comfort, because of the law, Leviticus 15:19-27." (Clarke)

3. (18-19) Confessing God's righteousness and Jerusalem's sin.

"The LORD is righteous,
For I rebelled against His commandment.
Hear now, all peoples,
And behold my sorrow;
My virgins and my young men
Have gone into captivity.
"I called for my lovers,
But they deceived me;
My priests and my elders
Breathed their last in the city,
While they sought food
To restore their life."

>   a. **The LORD is righteous, for I rebelled against His commandment**: Jerusalem personified confessed her sin and proclaimed the righteousness of God. Her **sorrow** and **captivity** were because she was a rebel against God.
>
> > i. "Again there is the confession which admits that God is in the right. This is often a hard admission to make. One can feel the agony of heart that is wrung out even while the people make confession." (Wright)
>
>   b. **I have called for my lovers, but they deceived me**: Jerusalem cried out for her **lovers** – a metaphor for those in whom she placed her love and trust in rather than Yahweh – for help. They **deceived** Jerusalem and were of no help as the city starved to death.

4. (20-22) Out of distress, a call for justice.

"See, O LORD, that I *am* in distress;
My soul is troubled;
My heart is overturned within me,
For I have been very rebellious.
Outside the sword bereaves,
At home *it is* like death.
"They have heard that I sigh,
But no one comforts me.
All my enemies have heard of my trouble;
They are glad that You have done *it*.
Bring on the day You have announced,
That they may become like me.
"Let all their wickedness come before You,
And do to them as You have done to me
For all my transgressions;

For my sighs *are* many,
And my heart *is* faint."

> a. **See, O Lord, that I am in distress**: All Jerusalem could do was cry out to the God whom she had rejected. There was no one else who could or would help. War and destruction brought death both **outside** and **at home**.
>
> b. **They are glad that You have done it**: This was the response of the neighboring nations, Judah's **enemies**. Knowing that, the prophet prayed that their appointed judgment would come soon (**do to them as You have done to me**).
>
>> i. **They are glad**: "It must have been a matter of some gratification to the enemies of the Israelites to know that God, who in earlier days had wrought such havoc on the foes of the Chosen People, had now recoiled in punitive wrath upon His own." (Harrison)
>>
>> ii. **Do to them as You have done to me**: "We may lawfully pray for such evils to the implacable enemies of the church and people of God, as may restrain and weaken their hands, and put them out of a capacity of wasting the Lord's heritage: we are only obliged by it to wish well to their souls, and to desire no evil against them out of private revenge or malice, but only out of love to God, and zeal for his glory." (Poole)
>>
>> iii. "The last two verses are a tentative prayer that God will vindicate His righteousness among the other nations. If Judah has needed to experience judgement to lead her to repentance, then others need the experience of judgement also." (Wright)
>
> c. **For my sighs are many, and my heart is faint**: We see Jerusalem almost gone; all she can manage are a series of **sighs**, and a **faint** heart.

Lamentations 2 – Purpose Proposed, Purpose Fulfilled

A. God as the enemy of Jerusalem.

1. (1-5) The Lord as Jerusalem's enemy.

How the Lord has covered the daughter of Zion
With a cloud in His anger!
He cast down from heaven to the earth
The beauty of Israel,
And did not remember His footstool
In the day of His anger.
The Lord has swallowed up and has not pitied
All the dwelling places of Jacob.
He has thrown down in His wrath
The strongholds of the daughter of Judah;
He has brought *them* down to the ground;
He has profaned the kingdom and its princes.
He has cut off in fierce anger
Every horn of Israel;
He has drawn back His right hand
From before the enemy.
He has blazed against Jacob like a flaming fire
Devouring all around.
Standing like an enemy, He has bent His bow;
With His right hand, like an adversary,
He has slain all *who were* pleasing to His eye;
On the tent of the daughter of Zion,
He has poured out His fury like fire.
The Lord was like an enemy.
He has swallowed up Israel,
He has swallowed up all her palaces;

He has destroyed her strongholds,
And has increased mourning and lamentation
In the daughter of Judah.

> a. **How the Lord has covered the daughter of Zion with a cloud in His anger**: In previous generations, Jerusalem knew the cloud of God's glory (1 Kings 8:10-12). Ezekiel saw the cloud of glory depart the city under judgment (Ezekiel 10). Now Jeremiah laments the presence of a **cloud** – not a cloud of glory, but a cloud of **anger**.
>
>> i. "The women in the eastern countries wear veils, and often very costly ones. Here, Zion is represented as being veiled by the hand of God's judgment. And what is the veil? A *dark cloud*, by which she is entirely obscured." (Clarke)
>>
>> ii. "Neither Jehovah nor the daughter of Zion is conceived of as departed, or destroyed. She is covered in a cloud, and so cut off from the vision of Jehovah, that is, she cannot see Him. Clouds hide God from men; they never hide men from God." (Morgan)
>>
>> iii. **Did not remember His footstool**: "The earth is called the Lord's footstool, Isaiah 66:1 Matthew 5:35 Acts 7:49, but here plainly the *temple* is understood, called God's footstool, 1 Chronicles 28:2; and the whole temple seems rather to be understood than the ark." (Poole)
>
> b. **He has thrown down in His wrath the strongholds of the daughter of Judah**: This begins a long series of **He has** statements. The emphasis is again on the idea that all this destruction comes from God, even if it was through the instrument of the Babylonian army.
>
>> i. **Daughter of Zion** and **daughter of Judah** are privileged titles, yet that privledge carries with it great responsibility. For many generations God's people thought only in terms of the priviledge and not of the responsibility. "The nation had imagined that it occupied a privileged position because it stood in covenant relationship with God, and was seemingly unaware that such a status involved important obligations in the moral and spiritual realm." (Harrison)
>>
>> ii. "In New Testament times, Capernaum was promised a share in the fate of Chorazin and Bethsaida (Matthew 11:21ff.) because she, too, had resisted the challenge of God's redemptive works." (Harrison)
>
> c. **Standing like an enemy, He has bent His bow**: Jeremiah saw that God treated Jerusalem as an **enemy** and **like an adversary**. His skill and strength (**with His right hand**) was *against* them, not *for* him.
>
>> i. "In a strange twist on the Old Testament motif of the divine warrior, God was not fighting *for* his people, but *against* them." (Ryken)

ii. "That is, God (whom by their sins they had provoked and made their enemy) behaved himself as an enemy, bending his bow, and stretching out his right hand, and slew their young men and maidens, who were pleasant to look upon; and had brought judgments upon them like fire, which devours without any discrimination." (Poole)

2. (6-7) The Lord destroys His own tabernacle.

He has done violence to His tabernacle,
As if it were a garden;
He has destroyed His place of assembly;
The LORD has caused
The appointed feasts and Sabbaths to be forgotten in Zion.
In His burning indignation He has spurned the king and the priest.
The Lord has spurned His altar,
He has abandoned His sanctuary;
He has given up the walls of her palaces
Into the hand of the enemy.
They have made a noise in the house of the LORD
As on the day of a set feast.

a. **He has done violence to His tabernacle**: Here the temple was referred to as a **tabernacle**, just as sometimes the tabernacle was referred to as a temple. They were simply various ways of describing the house of God, **His place of assembly**.

b. **The LORD has caused the appointed feasts and Sabbaths to be forgotten in Zion**: When the temple and the city were destroyed, so were all the observances and institutions connected with them.

- **Feasts and Sabbaths** were no longer observed.
- **His altar** was rejected.
- **His sanctuary** was **abandoned**.
- **Her palaces** were given **into the hand of the enemy**.

c. **They have made a noise in the house of the LORD**: The sound of shouting and noise and commotion was common on **the day of a set feast**. Now they heard the sound from enemies who set the city in subjection.

B. A city reacts to the judgment of God.

1. (8-9a) The defenses of the city react.

The LORD has purposed to destroy
The wall of the daughter of Zion.
He has stretched out a line;

He has not withdrawn His hand from destroying;
Therefore He has caused the rampart and wall to lament;
They languished together.
Her gates have sunk into the ground;
He has destroyed and broken her bars.

> a. **The LORD has purposed to destroy the wall of the daughter of Zion**: Jerusalem's wall was its security. Once the wall was destroyed, the city was prey for anyone and everyone. God **purposed to destroy**, and the purpose was declared fulfilled in Lamentations 2:17.
>
> b. **He has stretched out a line**: The idea is that God did His work with careful measuring and precision. There was nothing accidental or haphazard about it.
>
> > i. **A line**: "Of destruction, or a levelling line. See 2 Kings 21:13, Isaiah 34:11. Jerusalem was built by line, and so it was destroyed by him who doeth all things in number, weight, and measure." (Trapp)
> >
> > ii. "Just as a builder measured levels carefully in the process of construction, so God had been equally precise in the work of demolition to ensure that one stone did not stand upon another." (Harrison)
>
> c. **Her gates have sunk into the ground**: The walls were destroyed, the **gates** were **sunk**, and the **bars** protecting the city were **broken**.

2. (9b-10) The people of the city react.

Her king and her princes *are* among the nations;
The Law *is* no *more,*
And her prophets find no vision from the LORD.
The elders of the daughter of Zion
Sit on the ground *and* keep silence;
They throw dust on their heads
And gird themselves with sackcloth.
The virgins of Jerusalem
Bow their heads to the ground.

> a. **Her king and her princes are among the nations**: The royalty and nobles have been taken to Babylon. Government institutions had disappeared and were of no help.
>
> b. **The Law is no more, and her prophets find no vision from the LORD**: The spiritual institutions had also failed, and could give no help. There were no faithful priests to teach the **Law**, and the **prophets** were silent.

i. "Jeremiah was alone, and haply thought, when he saw all ruined, that he should prophesy no more. Ezekiel and Daniel were far remote. This was no small affliction that is here complained of." (Trapp)

c. **The elders of the daughter of Zion sit on the ground and keep silence**: The leaders of the community were stunned into **silence** and of no help. All they could do was mourn (**throw dust on their heads**).

d. **The virgins of Jerusalem bow their heads to the ground**: The younger generation was of no help. All they could do was **bow their heads to the ground** in despair.

i. "The mention of the 'elders' and 'young women' is probably intended to include the whole surviving population." (Ellison)

3. (11-12) The prophet reacts.

My eyes fail with tears,
My heart is troubled;
My bile is poured on the ground
Because of the destruction of the daughter of my people,
Because the children and the infants
Faint in the streets of the city.
They say to their mothers,
"Where *is* grain and wine?"
As they swoon like the wounded
In the streets of the city,
As their life is poured out
In their mothers' bosom.

a. **My eyes fail with tears**: All this made Jeremiah undone. His **eyes** wept, his **heart** broke, his **bile** poured out in nausea. He saw the city's **destruction** – especially the effect on the **children and the infants** and reacted this way.

i. "This whole verse is but expressive of the prophet's great affliction for the miseries come upon the Jews: he wept himself almost blind, his passion had disturbed his bodily humours, that his bowels were troubled; his gall lying under his liver, upon this disturbance was vomited up: they are all no more than expressions of very great affliction and sorrow." (Poole)

ii. **My bile is poured on the ground**: More literally, **bile** is *liver*. In particular the liver (MT *kabed*, 'heavy'), which is actually the weightiest organ of the human body, was held in antiquity to be one of the locales of psychic life, being associated with profound emotional reactions, generally of a depressive nature." (Harrison)

> b. **They swoon like the wounded**: Jeremiah saw children fall to the ground as if they had been shot through with an arrow. They collapsed **as their life is poured out in their mothers' bosom**.
>
>> i. **The children and the infants faint in the streets**: "This pathetic and tragic scene stands in stark contrast to the ideal of happy, carefree children playing in the streets of Jerusalem, a situation which is promised when the nation is restored (Zechariah 8:5)." (Harrison)

C. Longing to comfort a forsaken city.

1. (13-14) False prophets cannot comfort Jerusalem.

How shall I console you?
To what shall I liken you,
O daughter of Jerusalem?
What shall I compare with you, that I may comfort you,
O virgin daughter of Zion?
For your ruin *is* spread wide as the sea;
Who can heal you?
Your prophets have seen for you
False and deceptive visions;
They have not uncovered your iniquity,
To bring back your captives,
But have envisioned for you false prophecies and delusions.

> a. **How shall I console you?** Jeremiah has often spoke of Jerusalem being without comfort. Now he finds himself unable to comfort the devastated city. Jerusalem's **ruin is spread wide as the sea** and could not be helped.
>
>> i. "Divine retribution has burst in on Zion in the same manner as the sea forces its way through a gap in the protective wall." (Harrison)
>
> b. **Your prophets have seen for you false and deceptive visions**: There were many false prophets in the last days of Judah, according to both Jeremiah and Ezekiel. They promised that God would rescue Jerusalem and Judah from the Babylonians and that He would quickly **bring back your captives**. They were all **false prophecies and delusions**.

2. (15-16) Friends and foes cannot comfort Jerusalem.

"The normal order of the Hebrew consonants ayin and pe in the acrostic structure of the poem is reversed in verse 16, as in the two subsequent dirges, for unknown reasons." (Harrison)

All who pass by clap *their* hands at you;
They hiss and shake their heads
At the daughter of Jerusalem:

"*Is* this the city that is called
'The perfection of beauty,
The joy of the whole earth'?"
All your enemies have opened their mouth against you;
They hiss and gnash *their* teeth.
They say, "We have swallowed *her* up!
Surely this *is* the day we have waited for;
We have found *it*, we have seen *it!*"

> a. **All who pass by clap their hands at you**: This was not applause; it was a mournful reaction, fitting to those who **hiss and shake their heads**. All who saw it were astonished at the city that was once marked by **beauty** and **joy**.
>
> b. **We have swallowed her up**: This was the triumphant cry of Jerusalem's enemies. They **waited** long for the day of her conquest and were now happy to have **seen it**.
>
>> i. "Jerusalem was the envy of the surrounding nations: they longed for its destruction, and rejoiced when it took place." (Clarke)

D. God's purpose in the day of the Lord's anger.

1. (17) The judgment of Jerusalem as what God purposed.

The Lord has done what He purposed;
He has fulfilled His word
Which He commanded in days of old.
He has thrown down and has not pitied,
And He has caused an enemy to rejoice over you;
He has exalted the horn of your adversaries.

> a. **The Lord has done what He purposed**: Jeremiah announced God's purpose in Lamentations 2:8 (*The Lord has purposed to destroy the wall of the daughter of Zion*). In the judgment upon Jerusalem and Judah, Yahweh fulfilled **what He purposed** and **has fulfilled His word**.
>
> b. **He has caused an enemy to rejoice over you**: If Jerusalem had remained faithful to Yahweh, no enemy could have conquered them. Yet because of their persistent sin and rebellion, God had **exalted the horn** of their **adversaries**.

2. (18-19) The prayer of Jerusalem's enemies.

Their heart cried out to the Lord,
"O wall of the daughter of Zion,
Let tears run down like a river day and night;
Give yourself no relief;

Give your eyes no rest.
"Arise, cry out in the night,
At the beginning of the watches;
Pour out your heart like water before the face of the Lord.
Lift your hands toward Him
For the life of your young children,
Who faint from hunger at the head of every street."

> a. **O wall of the daughter of Zion, let tears run down like a river day and night**: This was the taunting prayer of the enemies rejoicing over Jerusalem (as in the previous lines). They wanted Jerusalem to weep forever.
>
> b. **Lift your hands toward Him for the life of your young children**: The enemies of Jerusalem were happy by the sight of the people of the city crying out in prayer, pleading for their **young children** perishing from hunger.
>
>> i. **Your young children, who faint from hunger**: "The dying children seem to have crawled from their homes towards the main city streets in a desperate, though vain, service for food. A personified Zion turns away in shock from this horrible scene with a desperate plea to God." (Harrison)

3. (20-22) The agony of the perishing city.

"See, O LORD, and consider!
To whom have You done this?
Should the women eat their offspring,
The children they have cuddled?
Should the priest and prophet be slain
In the sanctuary of the Lord?"
"Young and old lie
On the ground in the streets;
My virgins and my young men
Have fallen by the sword;
You have slain *them* in the day of Your anger,
You have slaughtered *and* not pitied.
"You have invited as to a feast day
The terrors that surround me.
In the day of the LORD's anger
There was no refugee or survivor.
Those whom I have borne and brought up
My enemies have destroyed."

> a. **To whom have You done this?** Jerusalem's agonized cry to God asked Him to consider the city and people He had loved. He asked God to

consider the depths of their agony, including cannibalism (**the women eat their offspring**) and the death of **the priest and prophet**.

i. **The women eat their offspring**: "That they did so in the siege of Jerusalem by the Chaldees, it appeareth by this question. In the famine of Samaria, under Joram, they did likewise; [2 Kings 6:28-29] as also at the last destruction of Jerusalem by the Romans; and at the siege of Sancerra, in France, A.D. 1572." (Trapp)

b. **You have slain them in the day of Your anger**: Jerusalem personified knew it was all the deserved judgment of God. It was Yahweh who **invited** a collection of **terrors** to **surround** Jerusalem. All those sustained by Jerusalem (**those whom I have borne and brought up**) have been **destroyed** by her enemies.

i. **My virgins and my young men have fallen by the sword**: "The slaughter of the young men and women was particularly serious because it precluded the appearing of another generation." (Harrison)

ii. **You have invited as to a feast day**: "Perhaps the figure is the collecting of the people in Jerusalem on one of the solemn annual festivals. God has called terrors together to feast on Jerusalem, similar to the convocation of the people from all parts of the land to one of those annual festivals." (Clarke)

Lamentations 3 – "Great Is Your Faithfulness"

"The third poem is significantly different in structure from the others, being made up of single lines grouped in threes, and commencing with the same consonant of the Hebrew alphabet." (R.K. Harrison)

"In the Hebrew Bible, the first three verses all start with aleph, *the second three verses with* beth, *and so forth." (Philipp Ryken)*

A. Opposed by the Lord.

1. (1-9) The man afflicted by the Lord.

I *am* the man *who* has seen affliction by the rod of His wrath.
He has led me and made *me* walk
In darkness and not *in* light.
Surely He has turned His hand against me
Time and time again throughout the day.
He has aged my flesh and my skin,
And broken my bones.
He has besieged me
And surrounded *me* with bitterness and woe.
He has set me in dark places
Like the dead of long ago.
He has hedged me in so that I cannot get out;
He has made my chain heavy.
Even when I cry and shout,
He shuts out my prayer.
He has blocked my ways with hewn stone;
He has made my paths crooked.

> a. **I am the man who has seen affliction by the rod of His wrath**: In chapters 1 and 2, Jeremiah wrote mainly as Jerusalem personified. Here he began to write as the voice of an individual sufferer. Yes, this was Jeremiah,

but it certainly was not *only* him. He and many others had **seen affliction**, and they knew that it came as God's discipline (**the rod of His wrath**).

i. "The sufferings of the people of Judah are described as though one man had experienced them. It is possible to interpret this chapter as a record of the feelings of Jeremiah himself, or as a personification in an otherwise unknown individual or the nation's tragic sufferings." (Harrison)

ii. "Jeremiah's personal lament is a reminder that suffering is always personal. When nations go through times of tragedy and tribulation, the greatest suffering always takes place at the individual level." (Ryken)

iii. "That which is most impressive in this song is the identification of the prophet with the people and with God. He recognized the necessity of the suffering, but suffered with the sufferers." (Morgan)

iv. **He has led me and made me walk in darkness**: "This seems to be the hardest part of our lot, that God should lead us into darkness: 'He hath led me, and brought me into darkness.' Yet dear brethren, that is, on the other hand, the sweetest thing about our trial; because, if the darkness be in the place where God has led us, it is best for us to be in the dark." (Spurgeon)

b. **Surely He has turned His hand against me**: Jeremiah did not *stay* in this dark and desperate place, but he would not deny being there. Many times through the affliction he felt God to be his adversary, not his friend.

i. **He has turned His hand against me**: "A metaphor from buffeters, who double their blows, beating their adversaries on both sides, as the smith doth his red hot iron upon the anvil till he hath shaped it." (Trapp)

c. **He has besieged me**: Even as Jerusalem was literally **besieged**, so Jeremiah (and countless others) felt themselves **surrounded** by **bitterness and woe** and slowly strangled by God.

i. **He has hedged me in**: "This also may refer to the lines drawn round the city during the siege. But these and similar expressions in the following verses may be merely metaphorical, to point out their *straitened, oppressed*, and *distressed* state." (Clarke)

ii. **He has hedged me in**: Harrison saw this as a picture of cruel imprisonment. "The walling-up of prisoners within confined spaces so that they died very quickly was a form of torture made popular by the Assyrians."

iii. **He has made my chain heavy**: "As the convict sometimes drags about his chain, and has a ball at his foot, so the prophet felt as if God had clogged him with a heavy chain, so that he could not move because of its terrible weight." (Spurgeon)

d. **He shuts out my prayer**: When things are right with our relationship with God, He is our refuge and defense in affliction. In their depths of affliction, this was not the experience of Jeremiah and the people of Judah. They were **surrounded**, **hedged**, and **blocked**.

2. (10-18) God an adversary in many ways.

He *has been* to me a bear lying in wait,
***Like* a lion in ambush.**
He has turned aside my ways and torn me in pieces;
He has made me desolate.
He has bent His bow
And set me up as a target for the arrow.
He has caused the arrows of His quiver
To pierce my loins.
I have become the ridicule of all my people—
Their taunting song all the day.
He has filled me with bitterness,
He has made me drink wormwood.
He has also broken my teeth with gravel,
And covered me with ashes.
You have moved my soul far from peace;
I have forgotten prosperity.
And I said, "My strength and my hope
Have perished from the LORD."

a. **He has been to me like a bear lying in wait**: Using the eloquence that misery sometimes brings, Jeremiah described all the ways that they felt God opposed and even attacked them.

- God was the like the **bear** and the **lion** waiting for a surprise attack.
- God was like the archer who **bent His bow** and was directed at the **target**.
- God was like the mocker who led the **taunting song** against His people.
- God was like the judge, giving a cup of judgment and **wormwood** for the condemned to drink.
- God was the brute, breaking **my teeth with gravel**.

i. **He has bent His bow**: "This figure shows the power of the archer's arm, which transfixed the poet with arrows." (Ellison)

ii. **He has also broken my teeth with gravel**: "What a figure to express *disgust, pain*, and the consequent incapacity of *taking food* for the support of life; a man, instead of bread, being obliged to eat *small pebbles* till all his teeth are *broken to pieces* by endeavouring to grind them. One can scarcely read this description without feeling the *toothache*." (Clarke)

iii. **With gravel**: "It could be argued that it refers to the type of bread made from the sweepings of the granary floor that Jeremiah must have received toward the end of the siege." (Ellison)

iv. **To pierce my loins**: Literally, *kidneys*. "In the sacrificial tariffs of the Pentateuch, animal kidneys were held to be one of the locations of life, this being thought true of human kidneys also. In addition, emotional attributes of joy (Proverbs 23:16) and sorrow (Job 19:27; Psalm 73:21) were credited to them." (Harrison)

b. **My strength and my hope have perished from the LORD**: No wonder Jeremiah and Jerusalem could say this. With God as adversary, what **strength** is there? What **hope** is there of either **peace** or **prosperity**?

i. "The poet's mention of 'the LORD' broke the spell of misery that had bound him." (Ellison)

B. Rising hope in God's help.

1. (19-20) The sinking soul.

Remember my affliction and roaming,
The wormwood and the gall.
My soul still remembers
And sinks within me.

a. **Remember my affliction and roaming**: Jeremiah did not prescribe positive thinking for this deep **affliction**. He actually felt it useful to **remember** it, to understand it for what it was, and to not pretend it wasn't there.

b. **My soul still remembers and sinks within me**: It was good for Jeremiah's soul to sink, to find its bottom point so that he could build on the right foundation.

i. "It is evident that in the preceding verses there is a *bitterness* of *complaint* against the *bitterness* of *adversity*, that is not becoming to *man* when under the chastising hand of God; and, while indulging this feeling, all *hope* fled. Here we find a different feeling; he *humbles* himself under the mighty hand of God, and then his *hope* revives." (Clarke)

2. (21-23) New mercies from a faithful God.

This I recall to my mind,
Therefore I have hope.
Through **the LORD's mercies we are not consumed,**
Because His compassions fail not.
They are **new every morning;**
Great *is* **Your faithfulness.**

> a. **This I recall to mind, therefore I have hope**: For perhaps the first time in the book, **hope** is allowed. Having sunk low in his soul (Lamentations 3:20), Jeremiah now remembered something that started **hope** within.
>
>> i. "In a magnificent expression of faith in the unfailing mercies of God, the writer looks to the distant future with renewed hope." (Harrison)
>>
>> ii. "At the south of Africa the sea was generally so stormy, when the frail barks of the Portuguese went sailing south, that they named it the Cape of Storms; but after that cape had been well rounded by bolder navigators, they named it the Cape of Good Hope. In your experience you had many a Cape of Storms, but you have weathered them all, and now, let them be a Cape of Good Hope to you." (Spurgeon)
>
> b. **Through the LORD's mercies we are not consumed**: This was one of the things Jeremiah remembered. He remembered that as beat down and defeated the people of Jerusalem and Judah were, they were not yet completely **consumed**. There was still a remnant, and remnant with a promise of restoration. Wherever God leaves life, He leaves **hope**.
>
>> i. "The vital word in this verse is *hesed* ('great love' [**mercies**]), the covenant love and loyalty of the Lord that leads to *rahamim* ('compassion,' 'mercy'), derived from *rehem* ('womb')." (Ellison)
>>
>> ii. "See where Jeremiah gets his comfort; he seems to say, 'Bad as my case is, it might have been worse, for I might have been consumed, and I should have been consumed if the Lord's compassions had failed.'" (Spurgeon)
>
> c. **Because His compassions fail not**: Even in the severity of correction God's people endured, there was evidence of **His compassions**. There was rich comfort in realizing that the tender affection of God was not completely spent; these **compassions** were **new every morning**.

i. "The passage is full of beauty, as it deals with that tender compassion of God which had never been absent even in the work of punishment." (Morgan)

d. **They are new every morning**: Each dawning day gives mankind hope in fresh **mercies** and **compassions** from God. We need a constant supply and God has promised to send them without fail. No matter how bad the past day was, God's people can look to the new **morning** with faith and hope.

i. These **mercies** are always **new** because they come from God. "Our treasures, which we lay up on earth, are the stagnant pools; but the treasure which God gives us from heaven, in providence and in grace, is the crystal fount which wells up from the eternal deeps, and is always fresh and always new." (Spurgeon)

- Every morning ends the night.
- Every morning brings a new day.
- Every morning brings new provision for the day.
- Every morning brings new forgiveness for new sins.
- Every morning brings new strength for new temptations, duties, and trials.

e. **Great is Your faithfulness**: All this made Jeremiah consider the great **faithfulness** of God; that He never fails in sending His **mercies** and **compassions**. Even in their catastrophe, God was faithful. He faithfully announced His judgments and performed them, and God would prove to be just as faithful in His promised restoration.

i. "The prophet addressed him personally and directly: 'Great is *your* faithfulness'. In the process of remembering God's attributes, Jeremiah was drawn back into living fellowship and intimate communion with his faithful God." (Ryken)

3. (24-26) God's goodness to the seeking soul.

"The LORD is my portion," says my soul,
"Therefore I hope in Him!"
The LORD is good to those who wait for Him,
To the soul *who* seeks Him.
It is good that *one* should hope and wait quietly
For the salvation of the LORD.

a. **The LORD is my portion**: As in Psalm 119:57, Jeremiah found the key to satisfaction—finding one's **portion** in the LORD. Whatever measure he was to receive, whatever inheritance, whatever future, it would all be found in Yahweh.

>   i. These are the words of a *satisfied soul*. Jeremiah had no other place of satisfaction, so he was settled with the **portion** received, and that portion was the LORD Himself.
>
>   ii. "The poet said in effect, that he has had so little of this world's goods and pleasures because his share has been the Lord." (Ellison)

b. **Therefore I hope in Him**: God couldn't really be his **hope** until he was first his **portion**. This was a pathway to hope for him.

c. **The LORD is good to those who wait for Him, to the soul who seeks Him**: All the misery of God's people had come because they would not truly seek God and **wait for Him**. They rejected and rebelled for generations, then looked to others for rescue. Seeking Him again would bring renewed expressions of His goodness.

>   i. "Do not be in a hurry; do not expect to be delivered out of your trouble the first time you begin to cry unto God. Oh, no: 'the Lord is good unto them that wait for him, to the soul that seeketh him.'" (Spurgeon)
>
>   ii. "There are times when the only thing a sufferer can do is wait for God. But waiting is good because God is worth waiting for." (Ryken)

d. **It is good that he should hope and wait quietly for the salvation of the LORD**: Everything previous in Lamentations was deep in despair, and the misery was by no means over. Yet these flashes of light are welcome and necessary. Against all the despair, Jeremiah proclaimed to himself and all others the goodness of **hope** and patient seeking of God.

>   i. "*Hoping* and *waiting* differ but as the mother and daughter, hope being the mother of patience and waiting; or as the *habit* and *act*, hoping and waiting being ranch the same, flowing from a gracious power and habit given the soul to wait. *Quietness* is necessary to waiting, for all turbulency and impatience of spirit under sad providences is opposed to waiting." (Poole)

4. (27-29) Hope for the silent soul.

It is **good for a man to bear**
The yoke in his youth.
Let him sit alone and keep silent,
Because *God* **has laid** *it* **on him;**
Let him put his mouth in the dust—
There may yet be hope.

a. **It is good for a man to bear the yoke in his youth**: There are seasons of adversity, and sometimes it is better to have those seasons when one is young. If God disciplines us when we are young, it is to train us for a fruitful future.

i. **The yoke in his youth**: "Early *habits*, when good, are invaluable. Early *discipline* is equally so. He who has not got under wholesome restraint in youth will never make a useful man, a good man, nor a happy man." (Clarke)

ii. "Such burdens can best be borne in youth when a man has the requisite vigour, and when his personality needs to be disciplined more than would be the case in his more mature years." (Harrison)

iii. Spurgeon suggested many reasons why it is good to bear the yoke when young:

- It is good because obedience to God is best learned when young.
- It is good because it saves from a thousand snares.
- It is good because it keeps from bearing the devil's yoke.
- It is good because it gives you more years to serve God.
- It is good because it gives one many years of experience.

b. **Let him sit alone and keep silent**: Under adversity, it is best to not try and figure everything out right away. These are good times for reflection (**sit alone**) and listening rather than speaking. In this patient seeking of God, there is reason for **hope**.

i. **Keep silent**: "There came a young man to Demosthenes to learn oratory; he talked away at a great rate, and Demosthenes said, 'I must charge you double fees.' 'Why?' he asked. 'Why,' said the master, 'I have first to teach you to hold your tongue, and afterwards to instruct you how to speak.' The Lord teaches true penitents how to hold their tongues." (Spurgeon)

ii. "Silence implies both an acceptance of God's will and a refusal to complain to men. With this should go the complete submission to God pictured in v.29 by the Oriental obeisance. It leads too to the willingness to be treated like a slave (v.30), for the yoke was a symbol of servitude (but cf. Jeremiah 20:1–2)." (Ellison)

5. (30-36) The goodness of God even in His justice.

Let him give *his* cheek to the one who strikes him,
And be full of reproach.
For the Lord will not cast off forever.

Though He causes grief,
Yet He will show compassion
According to the multitude of His mercies.
For He does not afflict willingly,
Nor grieve the children of men.
To crush under one's feet
All the prisoners of the earth,
To turn aside the justice *due* **a man**
Before the face of the Most High,
Or subvert a man in his cause—
The Lord does not approve.

a. **Let him give his cheek to the one who strikes him**: Jeremiah said this in the context of patiently enduring suffering (Lamentations 3:27-29). His sense is that they should patiently receive the suffering and **reproach** God had appointed for them.

i. "In offering the cheek to the smiter the captive was conveying the idea of absolute surrender." (Harrison)

ii. Jesus gave **his cheek to the one who strikes him** as He patiently received the suffering His Father had appointed (Matthew 26:67-68, Luke 22:64).

b. **For the Lord will not cast off forever**: The suffering endured was not everlasting. In His wise judgments God caused **grief**, but promised to also **show compassion**, and would do so **according to the multitude of His mercies**.

c. **For He does not afflict willingly, nor grieve the children of men**: When God does allow or send His judgments, He does not do it with a happy heart. His discipline is not happy nor is it unfair (**to turn aside the justice due a man**). As Abraham said of God, *shall not the Judge of all the earth do right?* (Genesis 18:25).

i. "It is no pleasure to God to afflict men. He takes no delight in our pain and misery: yet, like a tender and intelligent parent, he uses the rod; not to gratify himself, but to profit and save us." (Clarke)

ii. **To turn aside the justice due a man before the face of the Most High**: "The MT of verse 35 lends force to the concept of natural or inherent human rights when rendered, *to pervert the right which a man has in the very presence of the Most High*. God therefore disapproves heartily of any attempt to deprive an individual of his rights in the law (36), or to condemn him unjustly." (Harrison)

C. Prayers of humble trust in God.

1. (37-39) The God who cannot be opposed.

Who *is* he *who* speaks and it comes to pass,
***When* the Lord has not commanded *it*?**
***Is it* not from the mouth of the Most High**
That woe and well-being proceed?
Why should a living man complain,
A man for the punishment of his sins?

> a. **Who is he who speaks and it comes to pass, when the Lord has not commanded it?** In a season of great suffering or calamity, it may be difficult to remember that God rules over all things – if not directly, then in what He allows. Yet the consideration of God's sovereignty would also become the source of their hope. It was and is *worse* to be at the mercy of blind fate.
>
> b. **Is it not from the mouth of the Most High that woe and well-being proceed?** To give emphasis, Jeremiah asked the same question in different words.
>
> c. **Why should a living man complain**: We may complain against God and His sovereignty, but that is profitless and ungrateful. The **living man** should be grateful he still has life, and recognize there is some justice in the **punishment of his sins**.
>
>> i. "He who has his life still lent to him has small cause of complaint. How great soever his affliction may be, he is still *alive*; therefore, he may seek and find mercy unto eternal life. Of this, *death* would deprive him; therefore let not a *living* man complain." (Clarke)
>>
>> ii. "If he be tempted to murmur, let him remember that he is yet alive, and that is more than his part cometh to, since it is the Lord's mercy that he is not consumed, and sent packing hence to hell. Life in any sense is a sweet mercy, even that which to the afflicted may seem a lifeless life." (Trapp)

2. (40-47) Humbly turning back to God.

Let us search out and examine our ways,
And turn back to the LORD;
Let us lift our hearts and hands
To God in heaven.
We have transgressed and rebelled;
You have not pardoned.
You have covered *Yourself* with anger
And pursued us;
You have slain *and* not pitied.

You have covered Yourself with a cloud,
That prayer should not pass through.
You have made us an offscouring and refuse
In the midst of the peoples.
All our enemies
Have opened their mouths against us.
Fear and a snare have come upon us,
Desolation and destruction.

> a. **Let us search out and examine our ways, and turn back to the LORD**: Even under the great sense that God was their opponent and adversary (Lamentations 3:1-18), Jeremiah recommended the proper and humble approach.
>
> b. **Search out and examine our ways**: Sins must not be casually and superficially confessed and dealt with. We don't live constantly focused on our sins and failings, but there are appropriate times to carefully, deliberately **search out and examine our ways**.
>
> c. **And turn back to the LORD**: All the self-examination in the world does little good if it does not lead us back to this place. We should, we must, turn away from sin and self and **turn back to the LORD**.
>
> d. **You have made us an offscouring and refuse**: In the desire to **turn back to the LORD**, Jeremiah knew that it was important to honestly see their condition. They were under God's severe discipline, and that because of their deep and persistent sin.
>
>> i. "The nation's recognition of itself as *offscouring* (so most evv) employs a descriptive term *sehi*, occurring here only in the Hebrew Bible, and in the context denotes anything rejected as unfit for use. Its New Testament counterpart (1 Corinthians 4:13) is equally rare, depicting the suffering of the apostles." (Harrison)
>>
>> ii. "That is, thou hast made us to all nations extremely contemptible, so as they value us no more than the sweepings of their houses, or the most vile, refuse, and contemptible things imaginable." (Poole)

3. (48-51) Weeping over destruction.

My eyes overflow with rivers of water
For the destruction of the daughter of my people.
My eyes flow and do not cease,
Without interruption,
Till the LORD from heaven
Looks down and sees.

My eyes bring suffering to my soul
Because of all the daughters of my city.

> a. **My eyes overflow with rivers of water**: Earlier in Lamentations 2:18 Jeremiah expressed a prayer in the mouth of Jerusalem's enemies, a prayer that the city and her walls would weep without end. Here Jeremiah fulfills that role with tears that **flow and do not cease, without interruption**.
>
> b. **Till the LORD from heaven looks down and sees**: The intense weeping of Jeremiah and those like him must continue until God **looks** and **sees**, taking notice of and mercy to their misery.

4. (52-56) Praying for help under enemy attack.

**My enemies without cause
Hunted me down like a bird.
They silenced my life in the pit
And threw stones at me.
The waters flowed over my head;
I said, "I am cut off!"
I called on Your name, O LORD,
From the lowest pit.
You have heard my voice:
"Do not hide Your ear
From my sighing, from my cry for help."**

> a. **My enemies without cause hunted me down like a bird**: Jeremiah and those like him felt under constant pressure from capture or killing. They were against him like a fowler is against a bird. He was overwhelmed like a man drowning in a pit (**the waters flowed over my head**).
>
>> i. **Silenced my life in the pit**: "Seemeth not to be here taken literally, for the lowest and nastiest place in prisons, which probably was the portion but of a few of the Jews; but metaphorically, for the lowest and saddest condition of misery. Their enemies had brought them into the deepest miseries." (Poole)
>
> b. **I called on your name, O LORD**: Even from the pit Jeremiah knew he could call upon the LORD, and that God would hear His voice. Even if he could only manage a sigh, it would be his **cry for help** that he longed for God to hear.
>
>> i. **From my sighing, my cry for help**: "He dared not even to *complain*, nor to *cry*, nor to *pray aloud*: he was obliged to *whisper* his prayer to God. It was only a *breathing*." (Clarke)
>>
>> ii. "As breathing is a proof of animal life, so is prayer, though never so weak, of spiritual. If therefore you cannot speak, weep - tears also have

a voice; [Psalms 39:12] if you cannot weep, sigh - a storm of sighs may do as much as a shower of tears; if you cannot sigh, yet breathe, as here. God feels breath; and happy is he that can say, In thee I hope, Lord, and after thee I breathe or pant." (Trapp)

iii. "A mother listens for the breathing of her babe in the dark. It will tell her so much. The soft, measured breath, or the laboring, gasping breath. God never hides His ear from our breathing; or from those inarticulate cries, which express, as words could not do, the deep anguish and yearning of the heart. If you cannot speak, cry, sob, or groan, then be still. God can interpret all." (Meyer)

5. (57-63) Thankful and confident of future help.

You drew near on the day I called on You,
And said, "Do not fear!"
O Lord, You have pleaded the case for my soul;
You have redeemed my life.
O Lord, You have seen *how* **I am wronged;**
Judge my case.
You have seen all their vengeance,
All their schemes against me.
You have heard their reproach, O Lord,
All their schemes against me,
The lips of my enemies
And their whispering against me all the day.
Look at their sitting down and their rising up;
I *am* **their taunting song.**

a. **You drew near on the day I called on You**: Jeremiah knew that God responded when he called upon Him. God's response to this seeking soul was, **"Do not fear!"**

i. **You drew near**: "Jeremiah seems to record this fact with a considerable amount of surprise. He marvels that God should have drawn near to him, for his condition was a very pitiful one. He was so low that life seemed ebbing out, and he groaned." (Spurgeon)

ii. **Do not fear**: "How powerful is this word when spoken by the Spirit of the Lord to a disconsolate heart. To *every mourner* we may say, on the authority of God, *Fear not!* God will plead thy cause, and redeem thy soul." (Clarke)

b. **Lord, You have pleaded the case for my soul**: From formerly feeling forsaken, Jeremiah rested in the confidence that God was his advocate. Like a lawyer pleading for his client, God **pleaded the case** for his life.

i. Earlier in this chapter, Jeremiah felt God was his adversary (Lamentations 3:1-18). Now he prayed to God as his advocate.

  ii. "You perceive there is not a word concerning himself or his own pleadings. He doth not ascribe his deliverance in any measure to any man, much less to his own merit; but it is 'thou'." (Spurgeon)

c. **LORD, You have seen how I am wronged**: Jeremiah rested in the confidence that God was a righteous judge, who would see how he was **wronged** and who would rightly **judge** his **case**.

  i. "If you will turn to the lives of any of the saints of God, you will discover that they were the victims of slanders of the grossest kind. To this very day it is asserted by Romanists that Martin Luther was a drunkard. In his own day he was called the German beast, that for lust must needs marry Catharine. If you turn to the life of Whitfield – our great and mighty Whitfield – in more modern times, what was his character? Why, he was accused of every crime that even Sodom knew; and perjury stood up and swore that all was true. As for Wesley – I have heard that on one occasion he said that he had been charged with every crime in the calendar, except drunkenness; and when a woman stood up in the crowd and accused him of that, he then said, 'Blessed God, I have now had all manner of evil spoken against me falsely, for Christ's name sake.'" (Spurgeon)

d. **You have seen all their vengeance**: Jeremiah brought his case to God, telling him of all the ways that his enemies had attacked him. They did it by despising him (**their reproach**), with **schemes**, with **whispering** lies, and their **taunting song** against him.

  i. **Their taunting song**: "Mocking or taunt-songs were also frequently used to express derision or contempt for an enemy." (Harrison)

6. (64-66) Giving vengeance to God.

Repay them, O LORD,
According to the work of their hands.
Give them a veiled heart;
Your curse *be* upon them!
In Your anger,
Pursue and destroy them
From under the heavens of the LORD.

  a. **Repay them, O LORD, according to the work of their hands**: God had repaid Jerusalem and Judah for all their sin and disobedience. Now Jeremiah prayed that Yahweh would repay their enemies, and **give them a veiled heart** even as Judah was blind.

b. **Your curse be upon them**: According to the terms of the covenant Israel made with God (as in Deuteronomy 27-28), Israel would be terribly cursed if they disobeyed and rejected God. Those curses came upon Jerusalem in Jeremiah's day; now he prayed that those curses come upon their enemies.

c. **In Your anger, pursue and destroy them from under the heavens of the LORD**: Jerusalem and Judah had faced the anger of God and the destruction that came from it. Now he prayed that their enemies would face God's **anger**.

> i. "These past deliverances created his assurance that Jehovah would yet act on behalf of His people and destroy their enemies from under the heavens." (Morgan)

Lamentations 4 – The Woe of the Daughter of Zion

A. The punishment of the Daughter of Zion.

1. (1-2) The dimmed gold of Zion.

How the gold has become dim!
***How* changed the fine gold!**
The stones of the sanctuary are scattered
At the head of every street.
The precious sons of Zion,
Valuable as fine gold,
How they are regarded as clay pots,
The work of the hands of the potter!

> a. **How the gold has become dim!** Jeremiah lamented the loss of the **precious sons of Zion**, who were **valuable as fine gold**. The best and the brightest were all taken from Judah and Jerusalem and only the poorest and least able left behind.
>
>> i. "Although gold does not tarnish, it does lose its shine when it is covered with dust, which is precisely what happened to the golden articles from Jerusalem's temple. They were trampled in the city's dusty streets, for her glory had departed." (Ryken)
>
> b. **How they are regarded as clay pots**: The generation lost to Babylon would never be as valued there as they would be in Jerusalem. They were as cheap and lowly regarded as **clay pots**.

2. (3-5) The cruelty of Zion's depravation.

Even the jackals present their breasts
To nurse their young;
***But* the daughter of my people *is* cruel,**
Like ostriches in the wilderness.
The tongue of the infant clings
To the roof of its mouth for thirst;

The young children ask for bread,
But no one breaks *it* for them.
Those who ate delicacies
Are desolate in the streets;
Those who were brought up in scarlet
Embrace ash heaps.

> a. **The daughter of my people is cruel**: Jeremiah lamented the cruelty of those exiled and those remaining. They seemed worse than **jackals**, and more like **ostriches in the wilderness**, who were thought to be cruel to their young. Even so, **the young children** of Judah **ask for bread, but no one breaks it for them**.
>
>> i. "The pathetic scenes of young children begging in vain for food seems to have etched themselves deeply on the mind of the author, who must have witnessed the events described here and in the first two dirges." (Harrison)
>>
>> ii. "For her carelessness about her *eggs*, and her inattention to her *young*, the ostrich is proverbial." (Clarke)
>
> b. **Those who ate delicacies are desolate in the streets**: No one was safe from the judgment that came upon Jerusalem, and those once high were brought very low.
>
>> i. **Those who were brought up in scarlet embrace ash heaps**: "It is a pity that any child of God, washed in Christ's blood, should bedabble his scarlet robe in the stinking guzzle of the world's dunghill; that anyone who hath heretofore soared as an eagle should now creep on the ground as a beetle, or wallow as a swine in the mire of sensuality." (Trapp)

3. (6) The greatness of Zion's punishment.

The punishment of the iniquity of the daughter of my people
Is greater than the punishment of the sin of Sodom,
Which was overthrown in a moment,
With no hand to help her!

> a. **The punishment of the iniquity of the daughter of my people**: Jeremiah again stated his understanding that the destruction of Jerusalem was due to **the iniquity** of God's people.
>
> b. **Is greater than the punishment of the sin of Sodom**: In Ezekiel 16:48-49, the prophet said that the sin of Jerusalem was worse than that of Sodom. Here we learn that her **punishment** would also be greater. One way was that it would be more prolonged and agonizing, as opposed to Sodom, **which was overthrown in a moment**.

i. "He thinks the punishment of *Jerusalem* far greater than that of *Sodom*. That was destroyed *in a moment*, while all her inhabitants were in *health* and *strength*; Jerusalem fell by the most *lingering* calamities; her men partly destroyed by the sword, and partly by the famine." (Clarke)

4. (7-10) The stricken people of Zion.

Her Nazirites were brighter than snow
And whiter than milk;
They were more ruddy in body than rubies,
Like **sapphire in their appearance.**
Now **their appearance is blacker than soot;**
They go unrecognized in the streets;
Their skin clings to their bones,
It has become as dry as wood.
Those **slain by the sword are better off**
Than *those* **who die of hunger;**
For these pine away,
Stricken *for lack* **of the fruits of the field.**
The hands of the compassionate women
Have cooked their own children;
They became food for them
In the destruction of the daughter of my people.

a. **Her Nazirites were brighter than snow**: At one time, the spiritual devotion of those in Jerusalem was an adornment to the city, **like sapphire in their appearance**. Yet after the calamity that fell upon Jerusalem, **their appearance is blacker than soot**.

i. Most all commentators agree that **Nazirites** is not a reference to those who took the vow of a Nazirite according to Numbers 6:1-21, and instead refers to leaders or notable people.

ii. "Persons that were nobly and ingenuously bred; the word *Nezer* signifying a crown, or ensign of honour, 2 Samuel 1:10 2 Kings 11:12. The name Nazirite was given to persons splendid for their breeding and education, or honour and dignity; it is given to Joseph, Genesis 49:26, we translate it *separate from his brethren*, Deuteronomy 33:16; so Nahum 3:17. *Her Nazirites* in this place signifieth her separated ones, who either in respect of birth, education, estate, places of magistracy, or the like, were distinguished from the rest of the people." (Poole)

iii. **They go unrecognized in the streets**: "The nobility cannot be recognized on the streets because famine has reduced all the citizens of Jerusalem to a common level of physical exhaustion." (Harrison)

b. **Those slain by the sword are better off than those who die of hunger**: Jeremiah explained why Jerusalem's agony was worse than what fell upon Sodom. Zion's destruction came slowly with **hunger** so badly that **the hands of the compassionate women have cooked their own children**.

> i. **These pine away**: "By a lingering death, as Drusus the Roman, to whom food being denied, he had eaten the stuffings of his bed, saith Suetonius; and our Richard II, who was tantalised and starved to death at Pomfret Castle, where his diet being served in and set before him in the wonted princely manner, he was not suffered either to taste or touch thereof." (Trapp)
>
> ii. **Cooked their own children**: "Sodden [boiled] them rather than roasted them, lest they should be discovered by the smell, and so in danger to be despoiled of them, as it happened at the last siege by the Romans." (Trapp)

5. (11-13) The LORD's fury against the sins of His people.

The LORD has fulfilled His fury,
He has poured out His fierce anger.
He kindled a fire in Zion,
And it has devoured its foundations.
The kings of the earth,
And all inhabitants of the world,
Would not have believed
That the adversary and the enemy
Could enter the gates of Jerusalem—
Because of the sins of her prophets
***And* the iniquities of her priests,**
Who shed in her midst
The blood of the just.

> a. **The LORD has fulfilled His fury**: Jeremiah thought of Jerusalem and Judah completely devastated and could see the **fierce anger** of God **fulfilled** upon Zion. It was so great that **the kings of the earth** would **not have believed** that **the enemy could enter the gates of Jerusalem**.
>
> b. **Because of the sins of her prophets and the iniquities of her priests**: The doom of Zion was especially appropriate given the sins of their spiritual leaders. Among other sins, they murdered faithful prophets and people of God (**who shed in her midst the blood of the just**).
>
> > i. "The *prophets* and *priests*, who ought to have been proclaiming the covenant ideals in the nation, were actually the responsible agents for

perpetrating much of the iniquity so characteristic of pre-exilic life." (Harrison)

ii. "These most wretched beings, under the pretense of *zeal for the true religion*, persecuted the *genuine prophets, priests*, and *people of God*, and caused their blood to be shed in the midst of the city, in the most open and public manner; exactly as the murderous priests, and blood-thirsty preachers, under the reign of bloody Queen Mary, did in England." (Clarke)

iii. "Ezekiel 22:1–12 shows that the concept of bloodshed was far wider than murder or homicide, all that cut at the roots of society or that deprived men of their land and livelihood shortened their lives and so was bloodshed. Priest and prophet contributed positively and negatively—positively by advocating or condoning such behavior, negatively by failing to condemn those who wronged their fellow men." (Ellison)

B. The Daughter of Zion and the nations.

1. (14-17) Scattered by the face of the Lord.

They wandered blind in the streets;
They have defiled themselves with blood,
So that no one would touch their garments.
They cried out to them,
"Go away, unclean!
Go away, go away,
Do not touch us!"
When they fled and wandered,
***Those* among the nations said,**
"They shall no longer dwell *here*."
The face of the Lord scattered them;
He no longer regards them.
***The people* do not respect the priests**
Nor show favor to the elders.
Still our eyes failed us,
***Watching* vainly for our help;**
In our watching we watched
For a nation *that* could not save *us*.

a. **They wandered blind in the streets; they have defiled themselves with blood**: Jeremiah pictured the people of Jerusalem wandering blind through the streets, stepping on dead bodies and therefore defiling themselves.

b. **The face of the LORD scattered them**: As God **scattered** His people from Jerusalem, they were not welcome in other places. The nations said to these wandering refugees, "**They shall no longer dwell here**."

c. **The people do not respect the priests nor show favor to the elders**: God did not regard His people with favor because of sins such as these. Yet, as Jeremiah told us in Lamentations 4:13, it was the sins of the priests and the prophets that invited this lack of respect.

d. **We watched for a nation that could not save us**: Judah's false prophets and political leaders put their trust in Egypt to rescue them from the Babylonians. They watched **vainly for help**.

i. "Now we are taken back to memories of the fall of the city. There was a vain and persistent hope that the Egyptians would come to the rescue (17; Jer. 37.5-10; Ezek. 29.6,7)." (Wright)

2. (18-20) Pursued by the enemies of God's people.

They tracked our steps
So that we could not walk in our streets.
Our end was near;
Our days were over,
For our end had come.
Our pursuers were swifter
Than the eagles of the heavens.
They pursued us on the mountains
And lay in wait for us in the wilderness.
The breath of our nostrils, the anointed of the LORD,
Was caught in their pits,
Of whom we said, "Under his shadow
We shall live among the nations."

a. **They tracked our steps so that we could not walk in our streets**: When Jerusalem was finally conquered and occupied by the Babylonians, the Jewish citizens had very little freedom. They were soon prepared for exile to Babylon.

i. **We could not walk in our streets**: "Supposed to refer to the *darts* and other *missiles* cast from the mounds which they had raised on the outside of the walls, by which those who walked in the streets were grievously annoyed, and could not shield themselves." (Clarke)

ii. "The tall Babylonian siege towers made it dangerous for anyone to walk in the streets within range of arrows or stones." (Wright)

b. **Our end was near; our days were over, for our end had come**: Jeremiah had long prophesied that the Babylonians would conquer Jerusalem and Judah. Finally, the time had come and their **days were over**.

c. **Our pursuers were swifter than the eagles of the heavens**: The Babylonians pursued any who tried to escape. This included their king Zedekiah, who tried to escape but was captured (Jeremiah 52:5-11). The people of Jerusalem regarded Zedekiah as **the anointed of the LORD**, and hoped that **under his shadow we shall live among the nations**. The hope was bitterly disappointed.

> i. "Zedekiah was a weak and treacherous individual who condoned the religious corruption and moral degeneracy of the time, and generally ignored the advice proffered by Jeremiah (Jeremiah 37:2), except on occasions of grave crisis." (Harrison)

3. (21-22) The judgment coming to Edom.

Rejoice and be glad, O daughter of Edom,
***You* who dwell in the land of Uz!**
The cup shall also pass over to you
And you shall become drunk and make yourself naked.
***The punishment of* your iniquity is accomplished,**
O daughter of Zion;
He will no longer send you into captivity.
He will punish your iniquity,
O daughter of Edom;
He will uncover your sins!

a. **Rejoice and be glad, O daughter of Edom**: Jeremiah sarcastically spoke to **Edom**, who was happy that their neighbors Jerusalem and Judah were conquered.

> i. **The land of Uz**: "Whether or not this territory is identical with that regarded as the homeland of Job is unknown. Since, however, Uz seems to have been consistently accessible both to Sabaean Bedouin from Arabia and Chaldean invaders from Mesopotamia (Job 1:15, 17), it would appear to have been located in the general area of Edom." (Harrison)

b. **This cup shall also pass over to you**: As Edom found happiness in Zion's misery, so they would drink the **cup** of judgment from the hand of the Babylonians.

> i. "There is little doubt that the Edomites, who knew the routes and crossings, helped the Babylonians here, and this is why vs. 21,22 turn against Edom. Obad. 14 clearly shows what they did. So, when Zion

is restored, Edom will still be kept low, and Mal. 1.2-5 records that this was fulfilled. Ultimately Edom was subdued and absorbed into Israel." (Wright)

c. **The punishment of your iniquity is accomplished**: In this sense, God was finished with His great judgment against Jerusalem. The punishment of Edom was yet to come; God would soon **uncover** their **sins**.

i. "When sin is *pardoned*, it is said to be *covered*: here, God says he will *not cover the sins of Edom* – he will not *pardon them*; they shall drink the cup of wrath." (Clarke)

Lamentations 5 – From Desolation, Hope for Restoration

"Though this chapter consists of exactly twenty-two verses, the number of letters in the Hebrew alphabet, yet the acrostic form is no longer observed. Perhaps any thing so technical was not thought proper when in agony and distress (under a sense of God's displeasure on account of sin) they prostrated themselves before him to ask for mercy." (Adam Clarke)

A. What has come upon Jerusalem.

1. (1-8) Zion's great misery.

Remember, O LORD, what has come upon us;
Look, and behold our reproach!
Our inheritance has been turned over to aliens,
And our houses to foreigners.
We have become orphans and waifs,
Our mothers *are* like widows.
We pay for the water we drink,
And our wood comes at a price.
***They* pursue at our heels;**
We labor *and* have no rest.
We have given our hand *to* the Egyptians
***And* the Assyrians, to be satisfied with bread.**
Our fathers sinned *and are* no more,
But we bear their iniquities.
Servants rule over us;
***There is* none to deliver *us* from their hand.**

a. **Remember, O LORD, what has come upon us**: In his theology, Jeremiah understood that God knew what had **come upon** Jerusalem. Yet he understandably *felt* that God had forgotten them. He prayed that God would **look** upon them and **behold** the scorn and spite directed at them (**reproach**).

b. **Our inheritance has been turned over to aliens**: The land and **houses** God gave to the tribes of Israel as an **inheritance** was now in control of **foreigners**.

c. **We have become orphans and waifs**: The people were devastated by the loss of their families, by economic catastrophe (**we pay for the water we drink**), by **labor** with **no rest**.

> i. **Orphans and waifs**: "2 Kings 24:14; 25:12, and Jeremiah 39:10 make it clear that most of those left in Judah were the very poor, who were expected to keep the fields and vineyards in order." (Ellison)
>
> ii. **We pay for the water we drink**: "I suppose the meaning of this is, that every thing was taxed by the Chaldeans, and that they kept the management in their own hands, so that *wood* and *water* were both sold, the people not being permitted to help themselves. They were now so lowly reduced by servitude, that they were obliged to pay dearly for those things which formerly were *common* and of *no price*." (Clarke)

d. **We have given our hand to the Egyptians**: The leaders of Judah hoped that an alliance with Egypt or the **Assyrians** would rescue them. There was no help from them.

> i. "The reference to Assyria in v. 6 is difficult, since she had long ceased to be an empire, although Egypt was a place to which refugees had gone (Jer. 43}. Perhaps the verse is a condensed allusion to former alliances with Assyria and Egypt that the prophets had denounced (2 Kings16.7-9; Isa.7.1-9; 30.1-7), i.e. once our fathers looked to them for grand military help; now we should be thankful if they would give us enough employment to supply the bare necessities of life." (Wright)

e. **Our fathers sinned and are no more, but we bear our iniquities**: Jeremiah quoted a common proverb and complaint from that time (found also in Ezekiel 18:2 and Jeremiah 31:29-30). This popular proverb both expressed and promoted a popular idea. The idea was that God was unfair; unfair in *not* punishing the **fathers** as they deserved, and unfair in punishing the present generation.

> i. Ezekiel 18 is an eloquent refutation of this proverb. It answers the serious error of believing in communal or family salvation or damnation and teaches the great truth of the individual's responsibility before God.

ii. "*Nations*, as such, cannot be punished in the *other world*; therefore national judgments are to be looked for only in this life. The punishment which the Jewish nation had been meriting for a series of years came now upon them, because they copied and increased the sins of their fathers, and the cup of their iniquity was full." (Clarke)

f. **Servants rule over us**: The catastrophe of Jerusalem's fall meant that all of society's order was upset. Now lowly men ruled and there was **none to deliver us from their hand**.

2. (9-16) More of Zion's misery.

We get our bread *at the risk* of our lives,
Because of the sword in the wilderness.
Our skin is hot as an oven,
Because of the fever of famine.
They ravished the women in Zion,
The maidens in the cities of Judah.
Princes were hung up by their hands,
And elders were not respected.
Young men ground at the millstones;
Boys staggered under *loads of* wood.
The elders have ceased *gathering at* the gate,
And the young men from their music.
The joy of our heart has ceased;
Our dance has turned into mourning.
The crown has fallen *from* our head.

a. **We get our bread at the risk of our lives**: Under Babylonian occupation, everything was rationed and controlled. Getting enough bread was risky, under **the sword in the wilderness**.

i. "They could not go into the wilderness to feed their cattle, or to get the necessaries of life, without being harassed and plundered by marauding parties, and by these were often exposed to the peril of their lives. This was predicted by Moses, Deuteronomy 28:31." (Clarke)

b. **Our skin is hot as an oven**: The people were sick and suffered under sunstroke.

i. **Our skin is hot as an oven**: "'Hot' skin is literally 'scorched' or 'blackened' skin, showing general starvation." (Ellison)

c. **They ravished the women in Zion**: The women of Jerusalem and **in the cities of Judah** were raped and brutalized by the Babylonian soldiers.

i. "The evil mentioned here was predicted by Moses, Deuteronomy 28:30, 32, and by Jeremiah, Jeremiah 6:12." (Clarke)

d. **Princes were hung up by their hands**: All the people suffered. The **women** were **ravished**, the **princes** held in chains, the **young men** and **boys** made slaves. The joys of life – elders **gathering at the gate**, **young men** enjoying their **music**, the **dance** – all had **turned into mourning**.

> i. **Princes were hung up by their hands**: "It is very probable that this was a species of punishment. They were suspended from hooks in the wall by their hands till they died through torture and exhaustion." (Clarke)

> ii. **Young men ground at millstones**: "In happier days they would have been soldiers; now they had to do women's work." (Ellison)

3. (16b-18) The cause of Zion's desolation.

Woe to us, for we have sinned!
Because of this our heart is faint;
Because of these *things* **our eyes grow dim;**
Because of Mount Zion which is desolate,
With foxes walking about on it.

> a. **Woe to us, for we have sinned**: The familiar theme is repeated. Jeremiah understood that all the calamity came upon them because of their sin.

> b. **Because of this our heart is faint**: Their sin brought judgment and faintness of heart, which brought dimming eyes, which brought desolation to **Mount Zion**.

B. A prayer for restoration.

1. (19-20) Praying for the everlasting God to remember His people.

You, O Lord, remain forever;
Your throne from generation to generation.
Why do You forget us forever,
And **forsake us for so long a time?**

> a. **You, O Lord, remain forever**: At the conclusion of the Book of Lamentations, Jeremiah put the focus upon God's eternal and unchanging nature. His reign is eternal, with His **throne** enduring **from generation to generation**.

>> i. As Hebrews 13:8 would later say, *Jesus Christ is the same yesterday, today, and forever.*

>> ii. "THOU sufferest no *change*. Thou didst once *love* us, O let that love be renewed towards us!" (Clarke)

> b. **Why do You forget us forever**: God remains forever; but now it seemed to Jeremiah and the survivors of Jerusalem that He had forgotten them

forever. The theological truth of God's eternal, unchanging nature had yet to be experienced in their present situation.

2. (21-22) Praying for restoration.

Turn us back to You, O LORD, and we will be restored;
Renew our days as of old,
Unless You have utterly rejected us,
And are very angry with us!

> a. **Turn us back to You, O LORD**: Despite feeling forgotten by God, Jeremiah represented the people before God in a proper way. He understood that their only hope was to cry out to God for the gift of repentance. Jeremiah knew they didn't even have the power to properly repent on their own; they needed Yahweh to **turn** them **back to** Himself. If He would, then they **will be restored**.
>
>> i. If God is not the author of our repentance, we will never properly repent. Sometimes the best prayer possible is *not* "I repent" (though that is a good prayer). A better prayer is, *turn me back to You, O LORD. I need you to give me the gift of true repentance.*
>>
>> ii. "In a last brief and yet forceful word, he prayed Jehovah to turn the people unto Himself. This he introduced by a declaration of his confidence in the perpetual enthronement of Jehovah. It was a cry which recognized the last helplessness of man, namely, his inability even to repent." (Morgan)
>>
>> iii. "There is nothing better than to adopt the cry of the prophet, and ask God to turn the soul, and renew its blessed and holy experiences. There will be no doubt of our being turned, if He turns us." (Morgan)
>
> b. **Renew our days as of old**: With God turning us back to Himself, we can trust renewal, a return to our better days as in time past. If we have backslidden or declined, we can pray that God would grant us repentance so that we may **renew our days as of old**.
>
> c. **Unless You have utterly rejected us, and are very angry with us**: Lamentations seems unable to end on a positive hope for the future, even if the *general* trend is positive towards the end. Yet, Jeremiah ended with the fear that perhaps God had **utterly rejected** Israel and that His **anger** would remain forever. The specific words of Scripture and the history of Israel since this prayer confirm beyond question that God had not and did not later **utterly** reject His people, nor did His **anger** last forever. The days of lamentation would not be the final chapter of Israel's history.
>
>> i. "Several Old Testament prophecies conclude on a negative or inauspicious note (*cf.* Ecclesiastes 12:14; Isaiah 66:24; Malachi 4:6),

as does Lamentations. Consequently in synagogue readings it became customary to conclude such compositions with a repetition of the preceding verse, so that under these circumstances verse 21 would be read again after verse 22." (Harrison)

ii. "The book ends the way God intended it to end, with the kind of unresolved anguish we have come to expect from the Weeping Prophet. Yet Lamentations was never intended to have the last word." (Ryken)

Bibliography

Clarke, Adam *The Holy Bible, Containing the Old and New Testaments, with A Commentary and Critical Notes, Volume IV – Isaiah to Malachi* (New York: Eaton and Mains, 1827?)

Cundall, Reverend Arthur E. "Proverbs-Jeremiah" *Daily Bible Commentary, Psalms-Malachi* (London: Scripture Union, 1973)

Dilday, Russell *Mastering the Old Testament Volume 9: 1, 2 Kings* (Dallas: Word Publishing, 1987)

Ellison, H.L. "Lamentations" *The Expositor's Bible Commentary, Volume 6* (Grand Rapids, Michigan: Zondervan, 1986)

Feinberg, Charles Lee "Jeremiah" *The Expositor's Bible Commentary, Volume 6* (Grand Rapids, Michigan: Zondervan, 1986)

Ginzberg, Louis *The Legends of the Jews, Volumes 1-7* (Philadelphia: The Jewish Publication Society of America, 1968)

Harrison, R.K. *Jeremiah and Lamentations, an Introduction and Commentary* (Downers Grove, Illinois: Inter-Varsity Press, 1973)

Kidner, Derek *The Message of Jeremiah* (Leicester, England: Inter-Varsity Press, 1987)

Knapp, Christopher *The Kings of Judah and Israel* (New York: Loizeaux Brothers, 1956)

Maclaren, Alexander *Expositions of Holy Scripture, Volume 5* (Grand Rapids, Michigan: Baker Book House, 1984)

Meyer, F.B. *Our Daily Homily* (Westwood, New Jersey: Revell, 1966)

Morgan, G. Campbell *Searchlights from the Word* (New York: Revell, 1926)

Morgan, G. Campbell *An Exposition of the Whole Bible* (Old Tappan, New Jersey: Revell, 1959)

Ryken, Philip Graham *Jeremiah and Lamentations: From Sorrow to Hope* (Wheaton, Illinois: Crossway, 2001)

Spurgeon, Charles Haddon *The New Park Street Pulpit, Volumes 1-6* and *The Metropolitan Tabernacle Pulpit, Volumes 7-63* (Pasadena, Texas: Pilgrim Publications, 1990)

Thompson, J.A. *The Book of Jeremiah* (Grand Rapids, Michigan: Eerdmans, 1980)

Trapp, John *A Commentary on the Old and New Testaments, Volume 1 – Genesis to Second Chronicles* (Eureka, California: Tanski Publications, 1997)

Trapp, John *A Commentary on the Old and New Testaments, Volume 3 – Proverbs to Daniel* (Eureka, California: Tanski Publications, 1997)

Wiseman, Donald J. *1 and 2 Kings, An Introduction and Commentary* (Leicester, England: Inter-Varsity Press, 1993)

Wright, Reverend J. Stafford "Lamentations" *Daily Bible Commentary, Psalms-Malachi* (London: Scripture Union, 1973)

As the years pass I love the work of studying, learning, and teaching the Bible more than ever. I'm so grateful that God is faithful to meet me in His Word.

Once again I am tremendously grateful to Debbie Pollaccia for her excellent proofreading and editorial suggestions. Debbie has faithfully helped me for some 20 years - Debbie, thank you so much!

Thanks to Brian Procedo for the cover design and the graphics work.

Most especially, thanks to my wife Inga-Lill. She is my loved and valued partner in life and in service to God and His people.

David Guzik

David Guzik's Bible commentary is regularly used and trusted by many thousands who want to know the Bible better. Pastors, teachers, class leaders, and everyday Christians find his commentary helpful for their own understanding and explanation of the Bible. David and his wife Inga-Lill live in Santa Barbara, California.

You can email David at
david@enduringword.com

For more resources by David Guzik,
go to www.enduringword.com

www.ingramcontent.com/pod-product-compliance
Lightning Source LLC
Chambersburg PA
CBHW020727160426
43192CB00006B/137